A Handbook of Neuropsychological Assessment

Edited by

John R. Crawford and Denis M. Parker

University of Aberdeen

William W. McKinlay

*Case Management Services, Edinburgh, and
ScotCare Brain Injury Rehabilitation Unit, Lanarkshire*

 LAWRENCE ERLBAUM ASSOCIATES, PUBLISHERS
Hove (UK)   Hillsdale (USA)

Lawrence Erlbaum Associates Ltd., Publishers
27 Palmeira Mansions
Church Road
Hove
East Sussex, BN3 2FA
U.K.

British Library Cataloguing in Publication Data
A handbook of neuropsychological assessment
    I. Crawford, J.R.   II. Parker, D.M.
    III. McKinlay, W.
    616.80475

    ISBN 0-86377-210-2 (Hbk)
    ISBN 0-86377-274-9 (Pbk)

Cover by Joyce Chester
Author and subject indices by Sue Ramsey

Typeset by Woodfield Publishing Services, Fontwell, West Sussex
Printed and bound by BPCC Wheatons, Exeter

Contents

SECTION C: MAJOR CLINICAL DISORDERS

Anatomy provided

List of Contributors[1]

Marian Annett, Department of Psychology, University of Leicester, Leicester, LE1 7RH.

J. Graham Beaumont, Department of Psychology, University College of Swansea, Singleton Park, Swansea, SA2 8PP.

W.H. Brouwer, Traffic Research Center, State University Groningen, Rijksstraatweg 76, 9752 AH Haren, The Netherlands.

John R. Crawford, Department of Psychology, University of Aberdeen, Kings College, Old Aberdeen, AB9 2UB.

Jules B. Davidoff, Department of Psychology, University College of Swansea, Singleton Park, Swansea, SA2 8PP.

Haydn D. Ellis, School of Psychology, University of Wales College of Cardiff, PO Box 901, Cardiff, CF1 3YG.

John M. Gray, Newcastle Mental Health NHS Trust, Newcastle General Hospital, Newcastle-upon-Tyne.

Peter W. Halligan, The Rivermead Rehabilitation Centre, Abingdon Road, Oxford, OX1 4XD.

Anne Hickox, Principal Clinical Neuropsychologist, Middlesbrough General Hospital, Ayresome Green Lane, Middlesbrough, Cleveland, TS5 5AZ.

Michael D. Kopelman, The Academic Unit of Psychiatry, United Medical and Dental Schools of Guy's and St. Thomas's, St. Thomas's Campus, London, SE1 7EH.

---

[1] This is the list of current (at time of publication) addresses for correspondence with the authors who have contributed to this volume.

Andrew Mayes, Department of Psychology, University of Liverpool, Eleanor Rathbone Building, PO Box 147, Liverpool, L69 3BX.

William W. McKinlay, Case Management Services, Psychological Consultants, 17A Main Street, Balerno, Edinburgh, EH14 7EQ, and ScotCare Brain Injury Rehabilitation Unit, Wishaw, Lanarkshire, Scotland.

T.M. McMillan, Department of Clinical Psychology, Wolfson Medical Rehabilitation Centre, Atkinson Morley's Hospital, Wimbledon, London, SW20 0NE.

Edgar Miller, Department of Health, Room 307, Wellington House, 133-135 Waterloo Road, London, SE1 8UG.

Robin G. Morris, Institute of Psychiatry, Department of Psychology, De Crespigny Park, Denmark Hill, London, SE5 8AF.

Denis M. Parker, Department of Psychology, University of Aberdeen, Kings College, Old Aberdeen, AB9 2UB.

Ian H. Robertson, MRC Applied Psychology Unit, 15 Chaucer Road, Cambridge, CB2 2EF.

Michael D. Rugg, Wellcome Brain Research Group, Psychological Laboratory, University of St. Andrews, St. Andrews, Fife, KY16 9JU.

Philip H.K. Seymour, Department of Psychology, University of Dundee, Dundee, DD1 4HN.

Clive Skilbeck, Newcastle Psychology Agency, Royal Victoria Infirmary, Newcastle-upon-Tyne, NE1 4LP.

Alan Sunderland, Department of Psychology, University of Leicester, Leicester, LE1 7RH.

Sandra Walker, Department of Geriatric Medicine, University of Glasgow, Southern General Hospital, Govan Road, Glasgow, GS1 4TF.

Richard Warburg, Department of Clinical Psychology, North Manchester General Hospital, Manchester, M8 6RB.

K.D. Wiedmann, Department of Psychology, University of Stirling, Stirling, FK9 4LA.

J.T.L. Wilson, Department of Psychology, University of Stirling, Stirling, FK9 4LA.

Sarah L. Wilson, Lecturer in Psychology, University of Surrey, Guildford, Surrey, GU2 5XH.

A.H. van Zomeren, Department of Neurology J-1, University Hospital, 9713 EZ Groningen, The Netherlands.

1 Introduction

John R. Crawford and Denis M. Parker
Department of Psychology, University of Aberdeen,
Kings College, Old Aberdeen AB9 2UB

Clinical neuropsychology is a demanding profession, requiring not only a high level of clinical skills but also a detailed and highly specialised knowledge base. In the U.K., acquisition of this knowledge base is not easy because, with one exception, there are no postclinical/postgraduate courses on offer. Furthermore, the opportunities for "on the job training" are limited as there are typically only one or two posts in neuropsychology in any one health district. This book is therefore primarily aimed at the clinical psychologist who is either specialising in neuropsychology or who is required to conduct neuropsychological assessments in the course of more general clinical duties. We hope that it will also serve as an introduction to the area for trainee clinical psychologists, as a detailed knowledge of the area is not assumed.

In many other countries the profession of clinical neuropsychology is considerably more developed than is the current situation in the U.K., although the formation of a Special Group in Clinical Neuropsychology within the British Psychological Society is an encouraging development. In the U.S., for example, there are a number of specialised training courses, a credentialling system, and a special division (Division 40) of the American Psychological Association. Despite this, our hope is that the expertise of the contributors and the broad coverage of topics will also make this book of interest and value to clinicians in such countries.

The material is organised into four sections, the first dealing with basic topics. In Chapter 2, Ed Miller provides an overview of the aims of neuropsychological assessment, its rationale and its problems. The WAIS-R and its predecessor the

WAIS continue to occupy a prominent place in the assessment process. The uses and potential misuses of these scales in neuropsychological assessment are covered by John Crawford in Chapter 3. This chapter also provides a detailed evaluation of proposed methods of estimating a client's *premorbid* level of ability. The assessment of handedness, footedness and eyedness can provide the clinician with some clues as to a client's cerebral laterality. The assessment of handedness and other preferences is more complex than many might imagine. Marian Annett (Chapter 4) reviews the various methods and offers practical advice on their use.

The second section of the book is devoted to the assessment of the major cognitive functions. Andrew Mayes and Richard Warburg provide an extensive treatment of memory assessment (Chapter 5) in which the major patterns of memory dysfunction are outlined. The bulk of the chapter is devoted to a critical review of clinical memory tests and guidance on their use. In recent years there has been some concern over the ecological validity of clinical memory tests. Partly in response to this, there have been a number of attempts to make the collection of information on a client's everyday memory problems more systematic through the use of memory failures questionnaires. The use of these with clients and their relatives provide different but complimentary information to formal memory testing. Anne Hickox and Alan Sunderland (Chapter 6) review the available questionnaires/checklists and offer guidance on their use.

Chapter 7 covers the wide range of dysfunctions subsumed under the term visuoperceptive dysfunction. The topics covered include: Colour perception, visuospatial, and visuoconstructive abilities. In common with the other contributors, Graham Beaumont and Jules Davidoff highlight the importance of a unifying conceptual structure as a prerequisite for a rational approach to assessment in their area.

Deficits in face processing can produce severe disruption in a client's ability for social interaction/communication, and screening for their presence is an important part of the neuropsychological assessment process. Haydn Ellis describes the different forms of face processing deficits, and presents methods for their assessment. Unilateral neglect has also been allocated a separate chapter as it straddles the areas of attentional and visuoperceptive dysfunction and yet is clearly very distinct from other disorders that could be subsumed under either heading. Peter Halligan and Ian Robertson detail the various forms of neglect and provide a comprehensive review of methods of assessment.

Sandra Walker (Chapter 10) reviews the background to language dysfunction and presents a number of alternative, and clinically robust, assessment schemes. The model of language organisation which forms a background to this chapter is the classical neurological one. While this model has been criticised by the majority of those active in the area of cognitive neuropsychology, it is the conceptual framework within which most neurologists work. Consequently the practising clinical neuropsychologist has to be familiar with it. Both linguistic and cognitive neuropsychological approaches are discussed, but it is clear that at their current stage of development neither can provide a realistic set of assessment procedures that the practitioner would be happy to adopt. In a companion chapter to that on language dysfunction, Philip Seymour specifies the functional systems underlying reading ability, outlines how they can be disrupted, and offers guidance on methods for their assessment. The approach presented here is very much the cognitive neuropsychological one, and it reflects the fact that in this area both the model of the processes involved in reading, and appropriate techniques for assessing impairment are well developed.

Assessment of the various forms of attentional dysfunction is an important part of the neuropsychological assessment process, particularly in cases of closed head injury. Ed van Zomeren and Wiebo Brouwer (Chapter 12) provide an introduction to this topic and a guide to methods of assessment.

Assessment of cognitive dysfunction arising from frontal lobe injury is one of the most problematic areas in assessment. It is clear that there are very few well-standardised and well-validated tests available to the clinician. Chapter 13 (Denis Parker and John Crawford) evaluates the tests that are available and discusses the changes in behaviour and mood that can follow damage to anatomical areas within the frontal lobe.

The third section of the book is devoted to the major clinical conditions that the clinical neuropsychologist is liable to encounter. The chapters in this section provide a brief introduction to the pathology involved in these conditions and outline current theoretical issues. However, the main emphasis is on the pattern of neuropsychological deficits observed in the various conditions and on the provision of practical guidance on assessment. The topics covered are: closed head injury (Bill McKinlay and John Gray); stroke (Clive Skilbeck); toxic conditions and alcohol and drug abuse (Lindsay Wilson and Klaus Wiedmann); and the dementias (Mike Kopelman and Robin Moris). In these chapters cross-referencing with the section on assessment of cognitive functions is provided.

The final section of the book deals with three supplementary topics: Assessment for medico-legal purposes, computerised assessment, and the use of evoked potentials.

The importance of a detailed neuropsychological assessment as evidence in compensation cases is increasingly being recognised by the medical and legal professions. Bill McKinlay's chapter deals with a number of topics in this area including the admissibility of neuropsychological evidence, report writing and the possibility of faking deficits. A good deal of very practical advice on dealing with court appearances/hostile cross-examination is also offered.

Most if not all clinical neuropsychologists now have access to a desktop computer. The chapter by Sarah Wilson and Tom McMillan assesses the advantages and disadvantages of using computers in assessment. It also details the available software, discusses its applications in various clinical conditions, and provides guidance on software development.

Finally, the chapter by Michael Rugg introduces the area of event-related potential recording. This type of investigation will only be available to a few clinical neuropsychologists since, regrettably, the combination of necessary facilities and expertise is present only at a restricted number of centres. However, it is likely that this non-invasive technique for investigating brain function will prove to be increasingly popular in the future. It does not involve injection of inhalation of radio-labelled pharmaceuticals, as both single photon emission computed tomography (SPECT), and positron emission tomography (PET) require, yet it can provide evidence about the functional state of populations of neurones involved in cognitive activities. This chapter provides a "tutorial" introduction to the area for the clinical neuropsychologist. It is not envisaged that any practitioner will embark on a programme of investigations using these techniques after this concise review, but it should provide them with the necessary background to make the available literature in this important area comprehensible.

Every effort has been made to direct the chapters in this volume towards the practitioner who has some experience with patient assessment but who wishes to gain a readily assimilable grounding in particular areas or issues. Even though we have aimed for a wide coverage of neuropsychological assessment in the book as a whole, each chapter should be capable of being accessed and read as a guide without working through others. Obviously Chapters 2−4 discuss issues which are relevant to all areas of neuropsychological assessment; nevertheless we believe it is possible to read any of the chapters in sections B, C and D, and utilise the knowledge gained without having to refer back to these foundation chapters. This does not deny the importance of interdependencies and conceptual relations between areas, but recognises the reality of how practical demands may direct the search for a concise source of information on a topic.

SECTION A:
BASIC ISSUES

2 Some Basic Principles of Neuropsychological Assessment

Edgar Miller
Department of Clinical Psychology, Addenbrooke's Hospital,
Cambridge CB2 2QQ

INTRODUCTION

Assessment is a central issue in neuropsychology, and much more so than in most other branches of clinical psychology where assessment is often regarded as of little significance. There are doubtless several reasons for this. Amongst these is the fact that psychologists are rather more confident in the measurement of cognitive functioning than in the assessment of disordered personality and mood, which are the characteristic features of more psychiatrically related disorders. In addition, clinical neuropsychologists have not been actively drawn away by developments in psychological treatment as psychological methods for the management of those with neuropsychological impairment are still in an early stage of development (see Miller, 1984; Prigatano, 1986). Finally the question of diagnosis in those with neuropsychological impairments is of more obvious relevance to future management than is the case with psychiatrically related problems.

Despite having become unfashionable in some branches of clinical psychology, assessment is not an issue that will go away. For example, any therapeutic intervention, whether it be surgical, psychological, pharmacological, etc., is based on some form of assessment of the client's problems. Similarly, the effectiveness of any intervention can only be judged in relation to some assessment of change in these problems. What follows from this is that assessment is an issue of critical importance which needs to be considered in a wide context. This book will consider many different aspects of neuro-

7

psychological assessment but it is the purpose of this particular chapter to set out the fundamental issues involved. In doing so it will be assumed that the reader has some familiarity with psychometrics and test theory as set out in the standard texts on the subject (e.g. Anastasi, 1982; Crocker & Algina, 1986; Cronbach, 1984).

In the first place, it is important to ask why an assessment is being carried out. Broadly speaking, assessment in neuropsychology can be carried out with a number of goals in mind.

1. Diagnosis, to determine the underlying nature of the problem. A simple example here is an assessment to determine whether someone with a complaint of memory impairment is suffering from an organic disease of the brain.

2. To delineate the nature of any neuropsychological impairment and its impact on the individual as a means of devising, say, a rehabilitation programme or offering advice as to an individual's suitability to drive a vehicle or return to previous employment.

3. The measurement of change. For example, to determine the consequences of a surgical procedure or the impact of a cognitive training programme.

In addition, assessment may also be carried out for research purposes as when patients with a particular type of lesion are studied to determine the effects of that lesion on psychological functioning. In such circumstances the principles involved are very much those associated with the related clinical assessment as in the aforementioned goal 2.

An important consequence of these different goals of assessment is that the crucial features of the assessment process will vary with the goal. This point will be brought out in greater detail later, but it is fairly obvious that the sensitivity to detect small changes in level of functioning is a much more important characteristic of an instrument used to monitor change as a result of a rehabilitation programme, than is the case for a test used purely for diagnostic purposes.

DIAGNOSTIC ASSESSMENT

The literature on neuropsychological assessment is heavily dominated by discussions on the use of neuropsychological tests to diagnose brain lesions; both their presence and approximate location within the brain. The value of some of this diagnostically oriented assessment is open to fundamental questioning. The past two decades have seen very impressive developments in neuroradiological techniques and, in particular, sophisticated forms of brain scanning. In terms of detecting areas of infarction, the presence of tumours, etc., it would take neuropsychological instruments of extremely impressive validity to compete with radiological techniques in many diagnostic situations. In any case, even if neuropsychologists could locate tumours within the brain as efficiently as the radiologists, surgeons would still require the radiological pictures for other reasons. One of these is simply that when opening a head to operate on a tumour, it is so much easier for the surgeon to rely on films which can give a three dimensional impression of where the pathology is inside the head. In addition the surgeon may need to have some idea of localised blood flow and this can only be revealed by radiological techniques.

Whereas these arguments greatly limit the value of the diagnostic exercise as far as neuropsychology is concerned, some important diagnostic issues still remain. In the first place, sophisticated scanners are not always easily accessible and their use can be expensive, thus making other methods of investigation, including neuropsychology, useful as preliminary screening. It is also the case that not all lesions are readily demonstrated radiologically and that radiological evidence can be equivocal. For example, CT scanning is often unhelpful in the early diagnosis of dementia simply because the overlap between normal brain and mild atrophy is quite considerable. Therefore, neuropsychological assessment is certainly not redundant for diagnostic purposes, even though the range of situations in which it is of real value may have declined.

Requirements of diagnostic instruments

Diagnostic instruments have particular requirements. The most important is a high level of criterion (or discriminative) validity in that the test is able to distinguish the presence and type of lesion reliably enough to be of value in making decisions about individual cases. Construct validity, in the sense of the test embodying relatively pure measures of specific psychological functions, is not an essential feature. For example, the value of the Trail-making Test (see Lezak, 1983) as a diagnostic instrument depends on its ability to detect patients with certain types of brain lesion. Whether failure on this test is due to lowered motor speed in tracing the line, a difficulty in detecting where the next target is, or in planning movements ahead, is not of immediate significance (although knowing the answer to this question might enhance the value of the test for use in other ways).

The technical problems in developing good diagnostic tests, therefore, are those inherent in determining criterion validity. The general principles of test validity are presented by Crocker and Algina (1986) and it is not the intention to rehearse these here. However, one important problem that can arise in determining the validity of diagnostic tests is that of criterion contamination. Direct contamination, whereby the test to be validated is used in determining the validation groups, is an obvious source of error that is readily avoided but can creep in occasionally when diagnostic validity is being determined retrospectively. In other words, the test is used on the basis of an assumption (or preliminary evidence) that it will have some discriminatory power. Subjects assessed may then be reconsidered some time later to see if the test did in fact have validity in the particular diagnostic role for which it was intended.

Indirect contamination (Shapiro et al., 1956) is more subtle and, therefore, can creep into validation unnoticed. This is best described in terms of the following example. A test based on verbal memory may be developed to discriminate subjects with early dementia. Direct contamination, whereby this test is used to determine the status of the validation groups, is easily avoided. However, verbal memory (assessed by means of a formal test or merely on the basis of general clinical examination), may have been used to determine which subjects are demented. If the new test then turns out to have some validity this might be at least partly due to the fact that the same function (verbal memory) was used in determining the criterion groups. In this way spuriously high levels of validity may be obtained.

Yet another way in which the latter may be obtained in some contexts is through the selection of subjects making up criterion groups. It is tempting to use only clear-cut cases of dementia, frontal impairment, etc. These cases may be easier to discriminate than some of the less clear-cut cases that the test will typically be applied to in practice, and test validity in the latter may well be reduced.

These comments only outline some of the problems of determining criterion (or diagnostic validity). For further discussion the reader is referred to Crocker and Algina (1986).

The Big Battery Versus the Individual Approach

One of the major trends in diagnostic assessment in neuropsychology has been the development of large, standard batteries of tests such as the Halstead-Reitan and Luria-Nebraska batteries (e.g. Boll, 1981; Golden, 1981). The former was evolved from Halstead's (1947) quest for "biological intelligence" and consists of a rather odd collection of tests, i.e.: finger oscillation and trail-making tests; tests of sensory-perceptual ability, etc., to which the Wechsler Adult Intelligence Scale and Minnesota Multiphasic Personality Inventory may be added. In contrast, the Luria-Nebraska battery offers a systematic and standardised version of tests described by Luria in his many publications (e.g. Luria, 1966).

The battery approach has its advantages. Ideally the battery offers a range of tests covering the most important aspects of functioning and its use is embedded in an extensive body of validational data. On the negative side, batteries often take a long time to administer and rarely cover everything the examiner might need to assess at a sufficiently detailed level. At their worst, they can encourage a rather mindless "test-bashing" without pausing to consider whether the information that is likely to be obtained is the most useful for the individual case concerned. To be fair, there is some justification in the counter-argument that the mindless use of batteries is more a failure of the examiner than the battery itself.

The alternative is to select from a range of potential instruments, those that will best contribute to answering the diagnostic question that is being posed. Thus, the investigation of a case with a potential frontal lesion might be tackled very differently from one where the presenting question is whether the patient has suffered a small cerebrovascular incident with a consequent fluent dysphasia and little other sign of neurological impairment, as opposed to suffering from schizophrenia with prominent thought disorder. (The writer has encountered a few examples of fluent aphasia initially admitted to psychiatric beds as cases of schizophrenic thought disorder!) This individual-based approach can be more economical as the administration of s small number of key instruments may reveal the answer. It is certainly more flexible, and capable of being almost infinitely adapted to the needs of the particular clinical problem. In addition, it can lead easily into other types of assessment (e.g. with a view to decision-making for future management). One potential disadvantage of the individual approach is that it is sometimes easy to foreclose on the assessment because the answer seems to have been obtained whereas, further test administration might yield information which could significantly modify, or even challenge the original conclusion. Batteries, by forcing the examiner to look at a wide range of functions, are less likely to run into this problem.

Specific Problems with Diagnostic Assessment

One particular complicating factor that arises in all diagnostic assessment is that of base rates (or antecedent probabilities). The significance of these has been outlined by Meehl and Rosen (1955). A test of memory, for example, may discriminate well (i.e. with 90% accuracy) between similarly sized samples of subjects with and without dementia. If it is then applied in a setting where 90% of those examined as possible cases of dementia actually *are* demented, it can be readily understood that simply guessing that every case is demented gives an outcome that is as good as using the test. Following on from this it will be appreciated that the value of the test in detecting dementia in practice then depends on the proportion of relevant subjects assessed who are likely to have dementia (the base rate). The simple mathematical procedures for dealing with variations in base rates are described by Meehl and Rosen (1955) and will not be elaborated further here. The important point to note is that base rates do have an appreciable effect on the diagnostic accuracy of tests and are largely missing in the diagnostic decisions made by many neuropsychologists. One of the very few diagnostic procedures to take base rates into account is the Kendrick Battery for the detection of dementia (Kendrick et al., 1979).

A second set of problems arise around what Walsh (1987) has referred to as "seductive inference". One manifestation of this, as it relates to diagnostic assessment, has been described by Miller (1983). Because poor performance on test T is associated with a lesion at X in the brain it is all too easy to assume that a patient who performs badly on test T must therefore have a lesion at X. As Miller (1983) points out: "...the logical status of this argument is the same as arguing that because a horse meets the test of being a large animal with four legs, then any newly encountered large animal with four legs must be a horse. The newly encountered specimen could of course be a cow or a hippopotamus and still meet the same test." In the same way subjects who do badly on test T may do so for reasons other than having a lesion at X.

This is especially so where the test is complex and capable of being influenced in a number of ways. Miller (1983) cites examples of studies which have assumed that, because some subjects tend to do worse on the Wechsler Performance than the Verbal Scales (e.g. those with dementia and Parkinson's disease), this must indicate that the pathology is predominantly right-sided. Even assuming that right-sided lesions are often associated with lower Performance than Verbal IQs, the evidence cited does not necessarily lead to the conclusion that has been drawn. There are other explanations of a lowered Performance IQ. For example, Performance tests tend to be timed and it could be that the demented and Parkinsonian subjects are allowed down, producing a bigger impact on the Performance scales, or simply that the Performance IQ is less stable and more sensitive to any general decline in functioning.

DECISION MAKING

The most significant development in clinical neuropsychology since the mid-1970s has undoubtedly been the growing interest in the rehabilitation and amelioration of those who have suffered neuropsychological impairments. (e.g. Miller, 1984; Powell, 1981; Prigatano, 1986; Meier et al., 1987). It is likely that the amelioration of the consequences of brain impairment will become the most important application of neuropsychology. In addition, decisions about management may need to be made where the neuropsychologist is not directly involved in implementing any programme. For example, in advising on whether a patient who has had a meningioma removed is likely to be capable of returning successfully to a previous employment, or might be best encouraged to consider some alternative. Assessments in contexts like these require a rather different approach from that considered in the previous section and one which has hitherto been left largely unexplored.

The mechanisms by which recovery can be enhanced remain subject to controversy. However, a strong case can be argued (e.g. Miller, 1984) that, for adults at least, much longer term recovery after the resolution of short-term physiological disturbances like oedema, involves a process of functional adaptation or compensation. In other words, recovery in achieving goals occurs by developing alternative ways of gaining the same end point as, for example, when speech impaired subjects learn cueing strategies to cope with their word finding difficulties (Holland, 1982; Penn & Cleary, 1988). Conclusions about the means by which recovery is achieved need to be based on carefully controlled studies and it is not surprising that the clearest evidence comes from investigations based on animals with experimentally induced lesions. It is interesting to note that the most recent animal research continues to support the notion of compensation as the dominant mechanism underlying recovery (e.g. Rose et al., 1988). Interventions to enhance recovery are likely to be most effective if they try to build on this process of compensation.

If this analysis is correct, it has two important implications for assessment. The first is that assessment has to be concerned not only with the impairments shown by the patient but also with areas of spared, or relatively spared functioning. In this it is unlike diagnostic assessment or the measurement of change, in which the emphasis is heavily on those aspects of functioning that have suffered impairment. This is of course because the development of compensatory strategies depends on knowing what functions remain relatively intact and therefore available to be exploited in compensation. Secondly, if the focus in rehabilitation is on compensation then it is important to identify the handicaps that patients experience in their everyday lives as a result of their neuropsychological impairments. To put it another way, it is not sufficient to identify a memory impairment in terms of performance on particular tests of memory. It is also necessary to identify how that impairment affects ordinary activities. This is simply because a successful compensatory strategy has to be adapted to the circumstances under which the impairment is particularly manifest.

Thus, what is required is an assessment that operates at two levels. At one level the assessment is concerned with identifying the handicaps that the patient experiences (e.g. not being able to find their way around the local shopping centre, or finding that on arrival at the shop, many of the items to be purchased have been forgotten). At the other level, what is required are ways to measure specific neuropsychological impairments that might explain the handicaps, and to identify relatively well-preserved functions that might be exploited in determining compensatory strategies.

Within neuropsychology, little attention has been devoted to the problem of designing instruments to identify handicaps. The Competency Rating Scales described by Prigatano (1986) provide some fairly isolated examples. The identification and measurement of handicap is one area that lends itself to the techniques of behavioural assessment (e.g. Bellack & Hersen, 1988). Apart from this, it is necessary to look at other types of assessment to find useful models. For example, much assessment in the field of learning difficulties (mental handicap) is concerned with the individual's competency in carrying out everyday activities (feeding, dressing, using public transport, etc.). A similar emphasis is found in scales dealing with "Activities of Daily Living" as developed by Occupational Therapists, although the technical sophistication of such instruments is often far from impressive. Yet further examples can be found in scales developed for use with chronic psychiatric patients.

A general approach to assessment not as yet specifically exploited in neuropsychology, and which might prove to be of value is "Criterion-referenced" testing (Glaser, 1963). Most tests, like the conventional intelligence tests, are "Norm-referenced"; that is, they are based on comparison of the individual with a normative sample alleged to be representative of a population. Thus, they yield results enabling the investigator to conclude that the individual is, say, at the 55th percentile in relation to the general population on a test of verbal intelligence but only at the 30th percentile on a test of verbal memory.

To relate the individual to some normative population is not always very informative. This is especially so for many practical, "real-life" skills. Thus, it can be argued that what is most important about patients' abilities to dress themselves or to conduct a conversation is not whether these things are done at a particular level in relation to a reference population (e.g. adults in general), but whether these things can be done at a level of competence to match everyday needs. Criterion-referenced tests systematically consider certain functions and basically ask whether the individual concerned can perform this function to meet a set criterion (e.g. can the individual dress in the morning within 10 minutes totally unaided, putting on all normal indoor clothes and managing all the necessary fastenings?). Criterion-referenced tests also typically break down the activity involved in a main item by means of a set of subsidiary items. If the individual does not meet the overall criterion for dressing then a set of further items is brought in to see if certain types of garments can be put on, the usual kinds of fastenings coped with, etc. Ideally these subsidiary items are arranged to follow those steps by which increased competence in the function covered by the main item would be manifest.

So far criterion-referenced tests have been used largely with children and the mentally handicapped (although some "Activities of Daily Living" scales for handicapped adults can be seen as crude criterion-referenced tests). Nevertheless, criterion-referenced tests have obvious potential value in dealing with clients who have handicaps of all kinds, including neuropsychological impairments. Not only does a well-constructed criterion-referenced test direct attention to matters of practical concern from the client's point of view, but they also provide a good idea of the point at which to start with any rehabilitative intervention. If the patient fails, say, the main item on dressing, and the subsequent items indicate that the main problem is with fastenings (e.g. buttons or shoe laces), then this directs attention to the possibility of some form of retraining programme for fastenings, or even advising on the use of clothing with different forms of fastening (e.g. velcro rather than buttons). It is important to note that, in principle, criterion-referenced tests need not be confined to very basic activities such as dressing and feeding. Criterion-referenced items could, in principle, be developed to deal with different aspects of communication for use with aphasic patients or to cover the various everyday activities that might be adversely affected by an impaired memory.

The analysis of handicaps may in itself provide a good indication as to why performance is breaking down, and also indicate what might be an appropriate strategy to adopt in remediation. Nevertheless it may sometimes be useful to be able to test out hypotheses as to what impairments are producing the handicap and to indicate what functions remain relatively intact. Thus, if the victim of a severe head injury has difficulty in finding his way around the city in which he lives, it might be useful to know whether verbal memory remains reasonably intact before embarking on the strategy of getting the patient to remember the names and order of key features encountered on the way from A to B as an alternative method of navigation not dependent on spatial abilities. Tests for this purpose need to have good construct validity and be good measures of specific aspects of functioning.

In practice a major problem with tests of this kind (tests of memory, spatial ability, etc.) is that few of them are based on up-to-date understanding of the nature of the function itself. For example, there are no really satisfactory tests measuring important aspects of memory as memory would now be conceived by experimental psychologists (e.g. Baddeley, 1986). Of the various functions that might be examined, it is possibly language that is best served by instruments or test batteries which attempt to carefully dissect out different aspects of language (e.g. Goodglass & Kaplan, 1972).

MEASUREMENT OF CHANGE

A common issue in neuropsychological assessment is the measurement of change, either from some premorbid state, or as the result of some form of intervention, such as surgical or other forms of treatment. For example, the question may arise as to whether a patient's memory has declined as a result of a mild head injury, or whether the removal of a small arteriovenous malformation has adversely affected another person's ability to function in a particular way. Often, in looking for change it is not sufficient to know that change in cognitive functioning has occurred, it is also useful to know what particular functions (memory, comprehension of speech, etc.) have declined or, even occasionally, improved. This demands instruments that also have construct validity, (i.e. assumed to be relatively pure measures of a defined function). As indicated in the previous section, good tests of specific functions are not always easy to find. Another technical requirement of instruments to detect change is that they be adequately sensitive to the type and degree of change that is likely to occur.

In principle, there are two possible ways of assessing change which can be referred to as "direct" and "indirect". Indirect methods have evolved because it is not always possible to assess the subject separately on two occasions.

Indirect Measurement of Change

This type of neuropsychological assessment has a long history and has its origins in general tests for "brain damage" when the latter was often conceived as a unitary concept. This has been discussed in detail elsewhere (e.g. Miller, 1977; 1980; Yates, 1956) and the basic issues surrounding the logic of the method have not changed with time. As a consequence only the basic principles need to be outlined here.

In many circumstances the patient is not seen until some pathology (or suspected pathology) has arisen and the requirement is to determine whether some change has occurred from the premorbid state. Only in very few cases will there have been any previous psychological examination of the person that can be used as a base line. Even if there has, the results may not be accessible to the present examiner and where they are, they may not be of much direct relevance to present concerns.

One way round this is to use some form of indirect measurement. This involves applying two sets of procedures. The first is relatively straightforward and involves an assessment of the individual's present state. A second measure is also used which is alleged to be insensitive to change produced by the brain damage and thus can give an indication of the previous status of the individual. Examples of this methodology are: the Babcock-Levy Revised Examination for the Efficiency of Mental Functioning, the Shipley-Hartford Retreat Scale, and the various Wechsler Deterioration Indices (see Miller, 1977; Yates, 1956). Fortunately, these older variants have been largely abandoned. More recently advocated indirect methods of measuring change include: the National Adult Reading Test (Nelson & O'Connell, 1978) and the use of information relating to the individual's education, occupational status, etc., to estimate premorbid IQ.

Whereas indirect methods can be useful, it is important to note that they do have serious limitations. Consider, for example, the use of reading to indicate premorbid IQ. Although the ability to read irregularly spelled English words does correlate highly with IQ and is stable (in that it is relatively uninfluenced by many types of brain pathology), there are limitations to its use in this way. In the first place, the correlation with IQ is less than perfect, resulting in errors in estimated IQ. These errors in estimation will have two sources. One is the lack of perfect reliability in the measures involved. The other is the simple fact that, despite the strong association between IQ and sight reading, there will always be some people whose ability to read obscure words is relatively good for their IQ level and others who are the reverse. The estimate of premorbid IQ therefore, will, be subject to much greater error of measurement than if it had been formally examined, using an intelligence test, in the premorbid state. Secondly, no measure is wholly uninfluenced by brain pathology. In the case of using a reading test to estimate premorbid IQ, the fact that some brain lesions can produce an acquired dyslexia poses a potential problem.

This estimate of premorbid IQ is then related to the IQ as measured at present, itself subject to an appreciable error in measurement. Comparing change between two measures, both of which are liable to contain error, then minimises the accuracy with which change can be detected, let alone measured. These factors inevitably set limits on the validity of indirect measures of decline (for more detailed discussion see Miller, 1977, and also Chapter 3 of this volume for a more optimistic view).

Direct Measurement of Change

In some instances it may be required that change is to be measured across a particular event that has yet to occur, such as the surgical removal of an meningioma. In this case, measures can be applied before and after the intervention, and the degree of change noted. On the surface this seems to be a fairly simple procedure but it is surrounded by a number of difficulties.

In the first place, the timing of assessments may be important. If the intervention is, say, a surgical procedure, then any psychological consequences are likely to vary according to the time elapsing between the procedure and the assessment. In other words, some degree of recovery may well occur. Spontaneous recovery may go on for months and even years and is related to a number of different factors (Miller, 1984). One solution is repeated follow-up testing after varying intervals but this compounds the problems of repeated testing to be described shortly. Even if the change being sought is positive, as following a cognitive retraining package, similar problems will arise as the impact of any programme may be attenuated with time.

A major concern in evaluating change is that performance on neuropsychological tests may vary over time for a number of reasons and that not all of these will reflect any true change in the subject (see Campbell & Stanley, 1966; Cook & Campbell, 1979). Of particular importance in the neuropsychological context are practice effects, which can be quite large. Satisfactory information from test-retest studies is often not available for neuropsychological tests and is essential if the examiner is to be able to judge the likely size of practice effects. The importance of practice effects can be illustrated by the fact that Milner (1958) claimed that right temporal lesions had no effect on Wechsler Performance IQ because the mean change between pre- and post-operative testing was a drop of only 1.4 IQ points − a change which seems trivial and of no real significance. However, Miller (1972) pointed out that the test-retest data available at that time, suggested a gain in the order of 10 or more IQ points on the Performance scale simply as a function of previous exposure to the test. When this is taken into account, Milner's mean drop of 1.4 starts to look like a real decline in

Performance IQ. The relevant statistics for using test-retest data in this way are presented by Payne and Jones (1957).

The designer of tests specially adapted for detecting change faces a paradox. On the one hand it is desirable to have tests that are sensitive to small degrees of change. On the other, highly reliable tests are also advisable in order to reduce the error of measurement since it is difficult to detect change reliably if the original baseline measure is subject to considerable error. The trouble with these two requirements is that they tend to be mutually exclusive as tests with very high test-retest reliability are usually very stable (i.e. relatively insensitive to change). A good example here is provided by the various Wechsler intelligence scales, These have high reliability but also high stability. Generally it is only fairly gross insults to the brain that reveal changes in IQ.

GENERAL COMMENTS

As indicated earlier in this chapter, assessment is something that is not undertaken for its own sake. It is important because it achieves certain goals. Good practice in assessment depends on being clear about the purposes for which any assessment is being carried out and the requirements of any instruments or procedures used in carrying out the assessment. The main discussion in this chapter has then been based on the major assessment goals that the neuropsychologist might wish to achieve. Breaking the material up in this way makes for easier exposition and gives the material some logical coherence. Nevertheless, this subdivision by goals needs some qualification.

Firstly, an assessment undertaken in clinical practice may not be concerned with just one of the general goals identified. Establishing that some change has occurred from a premorbid state and to what degree, may be of value in diagnosis, because it indicates that something must have happened to produce the change, but it may also contribute to later decisions about management as a large decline in memory may have implications for the individual's ability to live independently in the future.

Secondly, the discussion so far has not taken into account one important factor, which is the cost of assessment (where "cost" is considered in its widest sense of the time, effort and expense involved in any assessment). A question that needs to be considered in practice is always whether the cost of gaining any new information is worth the likely yield in increased accuracy of decision-making. Thus, in a given case, will the considerable expenditure of time and effort involved in administering the Halstead-Reitan Battery produce additional information that cannot be equally well obtained in some other way? This leads us into a third issue. In clinical practice, neuropsychological assessment never stands on its own. It is part of a whole procedure of information gathering involving the neurologist's clinical examination, radiological and neuropsychological procedures, etc. Thus, the clinical value of neuropsychological assessment can only be properly judged in a wider context. To take a very simple example, providing neuropsychological evidence of a possible right posterior lesion is rather redundant if general clinical examination and a recent CT scan both point to a space occupying lesion in the right parietal lobe.

As a final point, it should be emphasised that well-conceived assessment is central to effective clinical practice and, indeed, to much neuropsychological research. Following the changing emphasis in clinical practice, future developments in assessment need to be directed towards the kinds of analysis of neuropsychological impairment that can inform useful rehabilitative interventions (e.g. cognitive retraining) or the making of sensible decisions about future management (such as whether particular individuals are capable of returning to live independently on their own in the community). After all, it is the resolution or reduction of the patient's problems that is the ultimate aim of all clinical activity and the clinical value of any assessment is really determined by its eventual contribution to this aim.

REFERENCES

Anastasi, A. (1982). *Psychological testing*-(5th ed.) New York: Macmillan.

Baddeley, A.D. (1986). *Working memory.* Oxford: Oxford University Press.

Bellack, A.S., & Hersen, M. (1988). *Behavioural assessment: A practical handbook.* Oxford: Pergamon.

Boll. T.J. (1981). The Halstead-Reitan neuropsychology battery. In S.B. Filskov & T.J. Boll (Eds.), *Handbook of clinical neuropsychology.* New York: Wiley.

Campbell, D.T., & Stanley, J.C. (1966). *Experimental and quasi-experimental designs for research.* Chicago: Rand McNally.

Cook, T.D., & Campbell, D.T. (1979). *Quasi-experimentation: Design and analysis issues for field settings.* Chicago: Rand McNally.

Crocker, L., & Algina, J. (1986). *An introduction to classical and modern test theory.* New York: Holt, Rinehart & Winston.

Cronbach, L.J. (1984). *Essentials of psychological testing*-(4th ed.) New York: Harper & Row.

Glaser, R. (1963). Instructional technology and the measurement of learning outcomes. *American Psychologist, 18,* 519—521.

Golden, C.J. (1981). A standardised version of Luria's neuropsychological tests: A quantitive and qualitative approach to neuropsychological evaluation. In S.B. Filskov & T.J. Boll (Eds.), *Handbook of clinical neuropsychology.* New York: Wiley.

Goodglass, H., & Kaplan, E. (1972). *Assessment of aphasia and related disorders.* Philadelphia: Lea & Febiger.

Halstead, W.C. (1947). *Brain and intelligence: A quantitative study of the frontal lobes.* Chicago: University of Chicago Press.

Holland, A.L. (1982). Observing functional communication of aphasic patients. *Journal of Speech and Hearing Disorders, 47,* 50—56.

Kendrick, D.C., Gibson, A.J., & Moyes, I.C.A. (1979). The revised Kendrick battery: Clinical studies. *British Journal of Social and Clinical Psychology, 18,* 329—340.

Lezak, M.D. (1983). *Neuropsychology assessment*-(2nd ed.) New York: Oxford University Press.

Luria, A.R. (1966). *Higher cortical functions in man.* New York: Basic Books.

Meehl, P.E., & Rosen, A. (1955). Antecedent probability and the efficiency of psychometric signs, patterns of cutting scores. *Psychological Bulletin, 52,* 194−216.

Meier, M.J., Benton, A.L., & Diller, L. (1987). *Neuropsychological rehabilitation.* Edinburgh: Churchill-Livingstone.

Miller, E. (1972). *Clinical neuropsychology.* Harmondsworth: Penguin.

Miller, E. (1977). *Abnormal ageing.* Chichester: Wiley.

Miller, E. (1980). Cognitive assessment of the older adult. In J.E. Birren & R.B. Sloane (Eds.), *Handbook of mental health and ageing.* Engelwood Cliffs, NJ: Prentice-Hall.

Miller, E. (1983). A note on the interpretation of data derived from neuropsychological tests. *Cortex, 19,* 131−132.

Miller, E. (1984). *Recovery and management of neuropsychological impairments.* Chichester: Wiley.

Milner, B. (1958). Psychological defects produced by temporal lobe excision. *Research Publications of the Association for Research in Nervous and Mental Disease, 36,* 244−257.

Nelson, H.E., & O'Connell, A. (1978). Dementia: The estimation of premorbid intelligence levels using the New Adult Reading Test. *Cortex, 14,* 234−244.

Payne, R.W., & Jones, H.G. (1957). Statistics for the investigation of individual cases. *Journal of Clinical Psychology, 13,* 115−121.

Penn, C., & Cleary, J. (1988). Compensatory strategies in the language of closed head injury patients. *Brain Injury, 2,* 3−17.

Powell, G.E. (1981). *Brain function therapy.* Aldershot: Gower.

Prigatano, G.P. (1986). *Neuropsychological rehabilitation after brain injury.* Baltimore: John Hopkins University Press.

Rose, F.D., Dell, P.A., Love, S., & Davey, M.J. (1988). Environmental enrichment and recovery from a complex go/no go reversal deficit in rats following large unilateral neocortical lesions. *Behavioral Brain Research, 31,* 37−45.

Shapiro, M.B., Post, F., Lofving, B., & Inglis, J. (1956). Memory function in psychiatric patients over sixty: Some methodological and diagnostic implications. *Journal of Mental Science, 102,* 233−247.

Walsh, K. (1987). *Neuropsychology: A clinical approach.* Edinburgh: Churchill-Livingstone.

Yates, A.J. (1956). The use of vocabulary in the measurement of intellectual deterioration. *Journal of Mental Science, 102,* 409−440.

3 Current and Premorbid Intelligence Measures in Neuropsychological Assessment

John R. Crawford
Department of Psychology, University of Aberdeen, AB9 2UB

INTRODUCTION

Most authorities continue to view the Wechsler Adult Intelligence Scales as constituting the core measures in neuropsychological assessment. Lezak (1988) for example describes the Wechsler as, "the workhorse of neuropsychological assessment", and identifies it as "the single most utilized component of the neuropsychological repertory". As the WAIS (Wechsler, 1955) and its successor the WAIS-R (Wechsler, 1981) were not designed with neuropsychological assessment in mind, it is perhaps worth considering why they have achieved this position. Firstly, their standardisation samples are very large and are highly representative of the (U.S.) adult population. Secondly, their scaling, reliability and other psychometric properties are excellent (although the reliabilities of a few subtests leave something to be desired).

Thirdly, in neuropsychological assessment much emphasis is placed on the analysis of discrepancies between tests. Such analysis requires that the tests concerned are on the same scale of measurement, a criteria fulfilled by the 11 Wechsler subtests (although see caveat discussed later regarding the WAIS and IQ gains). Scores on other neuropsychological measures can, in principle, be rendered comparable by converting them to percentiles, z-scores or t-scores (Anastasi, 1988, pp. 84-87). However, given that the quality of the standardisation samples for many neuropsychological measures are poor in terms of their representativeness of the general population, this can be a very dangerous practice. Such score conversions assume that the standardisation samples of the tests to be compared are equivalent in terms of variables that could

21

affect performance (e.g. age, educational level etc.). Therefore, the strength of the Wechsler lies not only in the convenience of having tests on the same scale but also in the fact that they were standardised on the *same* sample.

Rationale for the Detection and Quantification of Impairment

Whether for clinical, medico-legal or research purposes, the detection and quantification of impairment in individual cases is problematic. As there are substantial individual differences in cognitive ability in the general population, simply comparing a client's current test performance with the relevant test norms will be of little value. A particular test score can represent an entirely normal level of functioning for one individual and yet severe impairment for another. Therefore, it is necessary to compare current performance against an *individualised* comparison standard (Lezak, 1983). Test results from a period preceding the point at which neurological disorder or behavioural change raised the suspicion of impairment constitute one obvious comparison standard. However, such information is rarely available. Therefore, the clinician must fall back on some method of estimating a client's *expected* or *premorbid* level of performance.

The most common approach is to use present ability measures and involves two assumptions. Firstly, it is assumed that knowledge of an individual's performance on one cognitive measure will permit some estimation of their performance on another. Probably one of the most robust finding in the history of psychology is that in healthy subjects the correlations between cognitive measures (no matter how diverse) are always positive. Thus, this first assumption has a sound foundation. Secondly, it is assumed that not all tests of cognitive ability will be equally affected by cerebral dysfunction and that some will be almost entirely unaffected. The selection of such tests for use as premorbid indices can be performed *a priori* on the basis of empirical studies. However, in the case of the Wechsler, they will simply be the subtests on which a client obtains their highest scores. Lezak (1983) has termed this the "Best Performance" method. The exception to this occurs when the Digit Symbol, Digit Span or Object Assembly subtests provide the highest scores. These subtests have low inter-correlations with many of the other subtests and therefore will be a poor guide to a client's *general* premorbid ability.

An alternative means of obtaining a comparison standard is to use a test specifically designed to estimate premorbid ability. The most widely used of such tests is the National Adult Reading Test (Nelson, 1982). Such tests have been used to provide a comparison standard for a client's current performance on the Wechsler *when the latter is expressed as an IQ*.

The two methods differ but are complimentary. With the Best Performance method, analysis is conducted at the subtest level. The Wechsler summary

IQs (i.e. Full Scale, Verbal and Performance IQ) very commonly obscure large differences in ability which are observable when the subtest scatter is examined. However, as will be detailed later, the discrepancies between subtests have to be very substantial before the clinician can be confident that they represent impaired functioning. Therefore, in cases where impairment extends across a wide range of abilities, the degree of subtest scatter may not be sufficient to draw conclusions. However, when the scores on the impaired subtests are summed into an IQ (with the accompanying increase in reliability), a statistically significant discrepancy between the *obtained* IQ and the estimated *premorbid* IQ can be revealed. For example, in the present author's experience this is often the case in clients who are subsequently diagnosed as suffering from a dementing illness.

The first major section of this chapter is devoted to the Wechsler Adult Intelligence Scales and assumes some previous familiarity with the WAIS or WAIS-R. The second section will deal with measures developed specifically to estimate *premorbid* ability. Both of these topics are developed further in later chapters in which their clinical applications for specific disorders are discussed. Therefore, the present chapter aims to provide an overview in which the emphasis is placed on the technical aspects of measurement.

THE WECHSLER ADULT SCALES

WAIS or WAIS-R?

The WAIS-R (Wechsler, 1982) was standardised on a representative sample of 1880 Americans during 1976-80. Although broadly similar to its predecessor the WAIS (Wechsler, 1955), the administration and scoring rules for some subtests have been changed and around 20% of item content has been updated (see Reitan & Wolfson, 1990, for a detailed note of these changes). It is to be expected that, in the U.S., the majority of clinicians will have switched from using the WAIS to the WAIS-R. The same is probably true of U.K. clinicians now that the U.K. version of the WAIS-R is available (Lea, 1986).

Some experts on the Wechsler scales consider that this may be premature and potentially dangerous (Bornstein, 1987; Reitan & Wolfson, 1990). Reitan & Wolfson, (1990, p.80), for example point out that, unlike the WAIS, there are as yet no studies "in which the WAIS-R has been shown to be sensitive to cerebral damage".

The most important difference between the WAIS and WAIS-R is in their relative difficulty. Studies conducted in the U.S. and U.K. have demonstrated that the WAIS-R yields IQs that are around half a standard deviation *lower* than the WAIS (e.g. Crawford et al., 1990a; 1990e; Mishra & Brown, 1983; Prifitera & Ryan, 1983; Quereshi & Ostrowski, 1985; Smith, 1983; Urbina,

Golden & Ariel, 1982; Wechsler, 1981). Bornstein (1987) has highlighted the problems this and other differences can present for the clinician. He notes that a considerable reliance is placed on patterns of relationship between the Wechsler and other neuropsychological measures and that (Bornstein, 1987, p.187): "the modifications represented in the WAIS-R alter in an as yet unknown way the pattern of relationships upon which clinicians have come to depend". A particularly serious example of this problem relates to the use of the National Adult Reading Test. The NART was standardised against the WAIS and, as noted, provides an estimate of *premorbid* IQ which is compared with a client's *obtained* IQ (see later). The present author has encountered a number of medico-legal reports in which NART estimates of IQ have been compared with a client's WAIS-R performance. Aside from the difference in content between the WAIS and WAIS-R, the difference in difficulty between the two tests makes this practice unjustifiable and may lead to unwarranted conclusions of impaired functioning (the NART will tend to provide an estimate that is, on average, around half a standard deviation *higher* than the actual WAIS-R IQ in healthy, intact subjects).

Bornstein (1987, p.189) is pessimistic in his assessment of the relative merits of the WAIS and WAIS-R, suggesting that the latter "may unfortunately be more bust than boon to the clinical neuropsychologist". However, in defence of the WAIS-R, and as Bornstein acknowledges, studies of the WAIS-R standardisation sample are now providing very useful base-rate data for the neuropsychologist which was never available for the WAIS. Furthermore, the difference in difficulty, although problematic, should not be seen as casting doubts on the psychometric properties of the WAIS-R. This difference is part of a larger trend and reflects the fact that, at least throughout the westernised world, measured IQ is continually rising. As a result successive standardisation samples routinely outperform their predecessors (Flynn, 1984; 1987). Therefore, the difference observed between the WAIS and WAIS-R actually constitutes one reason for abandoning the WAIS, namely: it yields IQs in the contemporary population that are inflated by around half a standard deviation (i.e. the contemporary population mean on the WAIS is now around 107/108 instead of the desired value of 100).

Furthermore, the indications are that IQ gains are not uniform across all cognitive measures. Tests such as the Raven's Matrices (Raven, 1982), which have been characterised as measuring "fluid" ability, have been subject to massive gains whereas tests which measure "crystallised" ability (e.g. that principally make demands on previously established knowledge), have risen much less dramatically (Flynn, 1984; 1987). This is potentially very serious for neuropsychologists because, as already noted, much of our work relies on the interpretation of discrepancies between tests. Such comparisons assume that the population mean scores are equivalent. Although this assumption was eminently reasonable when the WAIS was standardised, differential rates of IQ gain may mean that there are now inbuilt discrepancies between subjects. For example, if Block Design and Object Assembly have been subject to large gains, the contemporary population mean on these tests could be 13 or more. In contrast, if Vocabulary and Comprehension have essentially remained stable, then their population means will still be around 10. As some authors have suggested that differences not much greater than these can be interpreted in an individual case, it can be seen that there is a danger that unjustified conclusions regarding a client's cognitive status could be drawn.

Factor Structure of the WAIS/WAIS-R

Despite the changes introduced in the WAIS-R, factor analytic studies of its standardisation sample have indicated that it measures the same underlying ability dimensions as the WAIS (see Leckliter, Silverstein & Matarazzo, 1986, for a review). Vocabulary, Information, Comprehension and Similarities load highly on the first factor which has been termed the *verbal* factor. Block Design and Object Assembly load highly on the second factor which has been termed *perceptual organisation* (other Performance subtests load on this factor but to a more modest degree). In three factor solutions, the same two factors emerge, while Arithmetic and Digit Span load on the third factor termed *freedom-from-distractability* or *attention/concentration*.

Encouragingly for U.K. users, the factor structure in samples of the U.K. population is essentially indistinguishable from that found in the standardisation sample (Crawford et al., 1989a; 1990d). This is illustrated in Table 3.1 which presents the factor structure obtained in a U.K. sample of healthy subjects. Coefficients of congruence (the most widely accepted measure of factorial similarity/dissimilarity) are presented at the foot of this table and demonstrate that the factor structure is highly replicable within the U.K. and highly congruent within the U.S. structure.

The crucially important finding for neuropsychologists is that, broadly speaking, the same factor structure has also emerged consistently when the WAIS-R performance of *clinical* samples has been analysed (e.g. Atkinson et al., 1989; see also Leckliter, Silverstein & Matarazzo, 1986, for a review of the earlier literature). Thus, it would appear that when performance on the individual subtests breaks down, it does so according to these underlying dimensions.

The aforementioned findings have two implications. Firstly, they indicate that the allocation of subtests to the Verbal or Performance Scale (within which each subtest is equally weighted in calculating IQs) does not have a sound factorial base. Secondly, they indicate that clinicians should consider using one of the recently available factor score methods for the WAIS-R, e.g. Lawson, Inglis, and Stroud (1983), Gutkin et al. (1984) or Canavan et

TABLE 3.1
Factor Structure Of The WAIS-R In A Healthy UK Sample
(adapted from Crawford, Jack, Morrison, Allan, & Nelson, 1990)

Subtest	Factor I	Factor II	Factor III
Information	0.83	0.21	0.09
Digit Span	0.16	0.07	0.90
Vocabulary	0.87	0.20	0.25
Arithmetic	0.42	0.39	0.51
Comprehension	0.78	0.24	0.32
Similarities	0.71	0.48	0.22
Picture Completion	0.62	0.56	0.10
Picture Arrangement	0.47	0.66	0.09
Block Design	0.28	0.80	0.24
Object Assembly	0.21	0.88	0.02
Digit Symbol	0.17	0.71	0.47
CoC PS vs USA*	0.99	0.97	0.97
CoC PS vs UK	0.99	0.99	0.95

* Coefficients of congruence between the factors obtained in the present
sample (PS) and those obtained from factor analysis of the US standardisation
sample and a previous UK sample.
Loadings greater than 0.50 in italic.

al. (1986). Even if these methods are not used, clearly it would be advisable
to be familiar with the factor structure as it provides a useful framework for
interpretation when examining subtest scatter. One disadvantage of the existing
factor score methods is that they do not calculate the third factor. Many clinicians
find this factor of value in assessment (see Leckliter, Silverstein & Matarrazzo,
1986, for a fuller discussion and examples of research applications of the
freedom-from-distractability factor).

Subtest Scatter

Normal scaled scores (which are summed to derive IQs) should not be used
to examine a client's pattern of subtest scatter because they are not corrected
for age. Instead, raw scores should be converted to age-graded scaled scores
using the tables provided at the back of the WAIS and WAIS-R manuals
(Wechsler, 1955; 1981, pp.139-50). The importance of this is illustrated in
Table 3.2 which presents raw, scaled and age-graded scaled scores on the
WAIS-R for two hypothetical cases (both aged 70 years). For case A, the
large discrepancies between scaled scores could lead to an erroneous conclusion
of impaired function. However, it can be seen from the age-graded scores that
the variations in subtest performance are within normal limits for someone
of this age. In case B, there are large discrepancies between the age-graded

TABLE 3.2
Comparison Of Subtest Scatter Using Normal Scaled Scores
vs Age-Graded Scaled Scores In Two 70 yr-old Subjects

Subtest	Raw score	Normal scaled score	Age-graded scaled score
CASE A			
Information	21	10	12
Digit Span	14	12	12
Vocabulary	56	12	12
Arithmetic	11	9	10
Comprehension	23	11	12
Similarities	17	8	11
Picture Completion	12	6	10
Picture Arrangement	4	7	9
Block Design	13	5	9
Object Assembly	23	4	10
Digit Symbol	25	4	9
CASE B			
Information	17	9	10
Digit Span	15	10	11
Vocabulary	43	9	10
Arithmetic	12	10	11
Comprehension	19	9	10
Similarities	18	9	12
Picture Completion	18	12	17
Picture Arrangement	14	10	15
Block Design	41	12	18
Object Assembly	36	12	17
Digit Symbol	69	12	18

scores. The pattern would indicate an individual of very high premorbid ability who has suffered impairment of verbal abilities. Had the analysis of scatter been based on normal scaled scores, nothing untoward would have been apparent.

The most obvious questions relating to the analysis of Wechsler profiles revolve around the magnitude of subtest discrepancies necessary for meaningful interpretation. A bewildering array of guidance, tables and formulae have been offered in response to these questions but much of it is inappropriate for neuropsychological applications and can in fact be seriously misleading. The reason for this hinges around the distinction between the reliability of a difference and the abnormality of a difference.

To assess whether an observed difference between two tests is reliable (i.e. represents a true difference in ability rather than being the result of measurement error) one must know the standard error of the difference

(SE_{diff}) for the pair. The SE_{diff} is derived from the standard errors of measurement of the two tests which are in turn derived from the tests' reliability coefficients and SDs (see Anastasi, 1988). Having determined the SE_{diff}, a level of significance must be set. Multiplying the SE_{diff} by 1.96 gives the 0.05 level of significance, for example, if the SE_{diff} for any test pair was 3.0 then a difference of 5.9 or more would be significant at the 0.05 level (i.e. there is a 95% probability that the difference is real and not measurement error).

Wechsler (1981) maintained that the less stringent 0.15 level of significance is adequate for comparisons between tests. Table 13 of the WAIS-R manual gives the size of difference between one subtest and any of the others needed for this level of significance. The size of difference varies from comparison to comparison because of the differences in subtest reliabilities. However, rounding the values presented reveals that differences of between 2 and 3 points are required. In this author's view this table should not have been included in the manual as it has a number of serious problems. Firstly, the clinician rarely, if ever, specifies *a priori* which of the 55 possible subtest comparisons they will make. This decision is made upon examination of a client's subtest profile. This, plus the use of the 0.15 level of significance ensures that the probability of making a Type I error using Wechsler's table (i.e. wrongly concluding that the difference is real and not the result of measurement error) is extremely large.

Knight and Godfrey (1984), drawing on work by Davis (1959) and Reynolds (1982), have developed a much more satisfactory method of evaluating the reliability of WAIS-R subtest differences. In order to limit the number of possible comparisons, the individual subtests are compared with the *mean* of all the subtests rather than with every other subtest individually. This procedure permits 11 possible comparisons. A table is presented which gives the difference between any subtest and the mean of all subtests required for three levels of significance (0.1, 0.05, and 0.01). Importantly, these significance levels have been corrected to take into account the effects of multiple comparisons (using the Bonferroni method, e.g. see Kirk, 1968).

Methods such as those developed by Knight and Godfrey (1984) are clearly superior as means of detecting reliable differences between subtests and it cannot be denied that such information is very useful to the neuropsychologist. However, it would be *unjustifiable* to conclude that a client has suffered impairment on the basis of reliable differences alone. To recap, a difference which is reliable simply means that it is real and not the result of measurement error. The vast majority of the healthy population will exhibit such differences between subtests and this will simply be a reflection of the fact that they are stronger on some abilities and weaker on others. Therefore, for the neuropsychologist, the concern is with differences that are not only reliable but also *abnormal*.

Matarazzo et al. (1988) have examined the range of subtest scatter exhibited by the WAIS-R standardisation sample. This study provides indispensable base-rate data for the neuropsychologist and also vividly demonstrates the dangers of relying on reliable differences. As noted, on the basis of Wechsler's table a difference of 2 to 3 points would be reliably different at the 0.15 level. Performing the necessary calculations reveals that, if the more stringent 0.05 level is adopted, then a difference of 5 points (on average) between subtests would be significant (i.e. reliable at the 0.05 level). Matarazzo et al.'s study demonstrated that, in the standardisation sample, the *mean* difference between a subject's highest and lowest subtest score was 6.6 scaled score points. Thus, the vast majority of the healthy population have discrepancies between subtests that are reliably different at the 0.05 level.

Matarazzo et al., provide tables that record the percentage of subjects exhibiting different ranges of scatter. These can be used to determine the range of scatter required to be significantly abnormal at varying levels of significance (the ranges are calculated separately for the Verbal and Performance subtests as well as for all 11 subtests together). When all 11 subtests are considered, a range (i.e. the discrepancy between a client's highest and lowest subtest score) greater than 10 points is required to be significantly abnormal at the 0.05 level and a range greater than 9 for the 0.1 level. The present author has conducted a provisional examination of the subtest range in a healthy sample of the U.K. population and has obtained similar values. The aforementioned figures are based on the standardisation sample as a whole but the range has been found to vary with IQ level (the higher the IQ the larger the range). Tables of the range in different IQ bands are presented and constitute an important source of information for the clinician. It should be stressed that when using these tables the client's *current* IQ should not be used to determine which figures to use but instead this should be based on an estimate of their premorbid IQ (see later).

Finally, it should be noted that the subtest range data presented by Matarazzo et al. (1986), was based unfortunately on normal scaled scores rather than age-graded scores. Although it was reported that the relationship between age and subtest range was weak (although nevertheless significant), it is highly probable that the range necessary to be significantly abnormal will be less when age-graded scaled scores are employed. Base-rate data based on these age-corrected scores would be a considerable asset but these have not been made available.

A further useful index of the abnormality of a subtest profile has been developed by Silverstein (1984). It has similarities to the previously cited method proposed by Godfrey and Knight (1984), in that it is concerned with the deviations of subtests from the mean of the subtests. However, whereas Knight and Godfrey's method evaluated whether a particular subtest was *reliably* different from the mean, Silverstein's method evaluates whether any of the subtests are *abnormally* different. For example, a Block Design score which deviated by more than 3.5 scaled score points from an individual's mean for all five performance subtests would be abnormal in the sense that Silverstein's formula estimates that less than 5% of the standardisation sample exhibited a deviation as large as this (Silverstein, 1984, p.938, Table 3).

A different but important form of base rate data has been provided by Kaufman, McLean and Reynolds (1988). Their study explored the relationship between performance on the 11 WAIS-R subtests and background demographic characteristics in the standardisation sample. The sample was divided into subgroups according to educational level, sex, urban/rural residence etc. and the mean scores in the these subgroups presented in tabular form. Considerable mean differences across subtests were revealed in the discrete subgroups. This data can help guide interpretation of an individual's subtest profile. Take the example of a client who exhibits a moderate to large degree of subtest scatter. If this scatter maps broadly on to the inbuilt discrepancies exhibited by standardisation subjects who have the same demographic characteristics, then the scatter should be considered to be of little clinical significance. In contrast, if the subtest discrepancies depart radically from these mean scores the possibility that the scatter represents impaired functioning should be given very serious consideration.

Before leaving this section it is worth noting that many fellow clinicians have expressed surprise on learning of the magnitude of the subtest discrepancies that occur in the general population. This is probably because few of us have had the opportunity to test large numbers of healthy subjects. This lack of direct experience of the normal limits makes it all the more important that clinicians be familiar with the available base–rate data.

It should also be stressed that if a client's subtest profile is found to be "abnormal" by any of the aforementioned criteria this cannot be taken as definitive evidence of impairment. Rather, as Silverstein (1984) points out, the presence of an abnormal profile is simply a finding which requires explanation. Conclusions as to the presence, nature or extent of cognitive impairment can only be arrived at by integrating WAIS-R findings with other test results and by taking account of both the client's history (personal and medical) and any behavioural observations.

A recent development in the analysis of subtest scatter is the use of methods employing the Mahalanobis Distance (D^2), (Huba, 1985; 1986). Burgess (1991) has applied this method to the analysis of WAIS-R subtests and has made available the source code of a BASIC program for its computation. Unlike other indices of abnormal subtest scatter, the D^2 tests whether the combination of subtests *considered together* is abnormal or not (Burgess, 1991). It takes into account not only the size of the subtest discrepancy but also the correlation between them (thus a discrepancy between two subtests that are highly correlated in the general population will be more likely to produce an abnormal value for D^2 than the same size of discrepancy between two subtests with a low intercorrelation).

VIQ/PIQ Discrepancies

The question of the clinical significance of discrepancies between the Verbal and Performance Scales of the Wechsler has generated a voluminous body of research but no consensus has emerged. Lezak (1983) dismisses the examination of VIQ/PIQ discrepancies as being of no value, whereas Bornstein, Matarazzo and their colleagues (e.g. Matarazzo & Herman, 1985) maintain that they are the best validated Wechsler index of dysfunction and consequently have an important clinical role. Most research on VIQ/PIQ discrepancies has concentrated on their utility as a means of differentiating between left and right hemisphere dysfunction.

Bornstein and Matarazzo (1982) reviewed the WAIS studies conducted prior to 1982 and reported that, with few exceptions (for which reasonably convincing explanations were offered), VIQ was lower than PIQ in patient groups with well-verified left-hemisphere lesions. The opposite pattern was observed in the groups with right-hemisphere lesions. Bornstein (1984) has subsequently demonstrated the same patterns in patients administered the WAIS-R. For those working with individual cases these findings are of limited value as they are based on group means. Where the pattern in individual cases has been examined, a large number of exceptions are found. To summarise the implications of such investigations: A large discrepancy in favour of PIQ is a strong indication of left hemisphere dysfunction but the converse pattern does not necessarily indicate right hemisphere dysfunction. Not surprisingly, given the nature of the PIQ subtests, a significant proportion of cases with LH lesions can be expected to exhibit a PIQ lower than VIQ. It could be argued, that although the pattern VIQ > PIQ is not of localising significance, it still constitutes a useful indicator of impairment. The problem here is that large VIQ/PIQ discrepancies (in both directions) are the norm rather than the exception in the *healthy population*.

Matarazzo and Herman (1985) examined the WAIS-R standardisation sample and reported the percentage of subjects exhibiting varying levels of VIQ/PIQ discrepancies. This study serves to highlight further the importance of the distinction between the abnormality and the reliability of a difference. The previously mentioned table in the WAIS-R manual (Table 13) presents the size of VIQ/PIQ difference necessary to be reliably different from zero at the 0.15 and 0.05 levels. Because the VIQ and PIQ scales are composite measures, they have exceptionally high reliabilities (0.97 and 0.93 respectively). As a result, relatively small differences between the two will be reliable. A discrepancy of 7 IQ points is required for significance at the 0,15 level, a 10-point discrepancy is required for the 0.05 level. Matarazzo and Herman have demonstrated that 30% of the standardisation sample exhibit discrepancies of 10 or more points. For a VIQ/PIQ discrepancy to be significantly *abnormal* at the 0.05 level it would have to be 23 IQ points or more (a discrepancy of 19 is required for a significant abnormality at the 0.1 level). It can be gathered from these findings that, (although when combined with other test results and behavioural observations, VIQ/PIQ discrepancies can be of some value), they are unlikely to detect impairment that is not already discernible from other test results.

A refinement of the VIQ/PIQ index has been proposed by Lawson and Inglis (Lawson & Inglis, 1983; Lawson, Inglis & Stroud, 1983). In place of VIQ and PIQ they use factor scores from principal components analysis. This has considerable appeal as the factor scores represent a subject's relative standing on the underlying ability dimensions consistently identified in factor analytic studies (see earlier). Lawson and Inglis view their index as a measure of the lateralisation dysfunction. Their results indicate that their method can be useful in differentiating left *vs* right hemisphere lesions in males but not females (this is consistent with evidence of lesser functional asymmetry in females although Lawson and Inglis offer another explanation). Although this method has considerable promise, in clinical practice the equivalent of the VIQ > PIQ pattern is liable to be most useful simply as a measure of dysfunction rather than specifically right−hemisphere dysfunction.

Short-forms of the WAIS/WAIS-R

The realities of clinical work are such that short-forms of the Wechsler will be employed because of heavy caseloads. Short-forms have a valid role in the initial screening of clients and when, because of fatigue or a negative attitude to testing, a client is unlikely to complete successfully the full-length version. Furthermore, given limited time, it would certainly be advisable to administer a short-form rather than neglect to examine those cognitive functions not covered by the WAIS-R. If equivocal results are obtained with a short-form then, as Reynolds, Willson and Clark (1983) point out, the omitted subtests can be administered at a later stage.

The various proposed short-forms of the Wechsler scales cane be divided into two categories: those (e.g. Satz & Mogel, 1962) where all subtests are administered but in a shortened form (i.e. only every second or third item); and the more common approach of administering a subtest of the 11 subtests.

The Satz-Mogel has generated considerable interest and numerous studies have indicated that this short-form has high validity in predicting full-length IQs for both the WAIS and WAIS-R. However, the neuropsychologist is primarily interested in examining the pattern of strengths and weaknesses at the subtest level. It has been claimed that the principal advantage of the

Satz-Mogel over the selected subtest approach is that it permits the clinician to examine a client's performance over all of the subtests. However, there is a heavy price to be paid for this. An important factor in determining a test's reliability is its length (i.e. number of items). The effect of lengthening or shortening a test on its reliability can be estimated using the Spearman-Brown prophecy formula (Anastasi, 1988, p.121). In the Satz-Mogel, only 1 in every 3 items are administered for three of the subtests. The effect of this shortening can be illustrated using the Picture Completion subtest as an example. The reliability of this subtest in its full-length form (WAIS-R) is 0.81 (Wechsler, 1981, p.30) but its estimated reliability is only 0.58 in its Satz-Mogel form. Because of this effect on subtest reliability, and because the effect of a Satz-Mogel administration on the subtest means and SDs is largely unknown, it would be inappropriate to interpret subtest differences. This makes it unsuitable for neuropsychological applications.

Consideration will now be given to short-forms in which a subset of the 11 subtests are administered. A large number of such short-forms have been proposed, varying in length from Silverstein's (1982) two-subtest short-form, to the seven-subtest short-form used by Warrington and her colleagues (e.g. Warrington, James & Maciejewski, 1986). Almost all evaluative studies of short-forms have used the correlation with full-length IQs as the sole criteria for judging competing short-forms. However, for the neuropsychologist, other considerations are more important.

Reynolds, Willson and Clark (1983) have developed a four-subtest short-form specifically for neuropsychological applications. This consists of the Information, Arithmetic, Block Design , and Picture Completion subtests. When time is short, the present author uses a modified version of a four-subtest short-form proposed by Britton and Savage (1966). This consists of the Similarities, Comprehension, Block Design, and Object Assembly subtests. This short-form has a reasonably high correlation with full-length IQ but more importantly has high construct validity as a measure of the *verbal* and *perceptual organisation* factors (see previous section on Factor Structure). It is also suitable for use with the elderly and other populations where there is an increased probability of impaired visual acuity. This short-form may be more appropriate for neuropsychological applications than Britton and Savage's original which employed Vocabulary instead of Similarities. Vocabulary tends to fall between two stools in clinical practice in that it is less impairment-sensitive than many of the Wechsler subtests. Because of this it was, previously, widely used as a measure of premorbid ability (Lezak, 1983), but has largely been supplanted in this role by more recently developed measures (e.g. NART, see later). It also takes considerably more time to administer and score than any of the other verbal subtests.

Regression equations for the above short-forms are available if the clinician wishes to obtain estimates of full-length IQs (Crawford et al., 1992; Reynolds,

Willson & Clark, 1983). The use of regression equations is preferable to the conventional method of prorating (i.e. allocating the mean of the administered subtests to those subtests that were omitted to obtain a prorated sum of scaled scores). Because of regression to the mean, the latter approach tends seriously to underestimate full-length IQ for subjects who obtain low subtest scores, and to overestimate IQ in subjects who obtain high scores. Furthermore, with prorating, raw scores must be converted to normal scaled scores (to derive IQs) and age-graded scaled scores (to examine subtest scatter). In contrast, the regression approach estimates IQs from age-graded scaled scores, thereby rendering the calculation of normal scaled scores unnecessary.

Retesting with the Wechsler

Parallel forms of the Wechsler have never been developed so, unfortunately, retesting must be conducted using the same materials. As with any neuro-psychological measure, interpretation of retest data is beset with enormous difficulties. This is mainly because insufficient base-rate data is available to serve as a guide to the range of change in test scores one can expect when no change is cognitive status has occurred. Wechsler (1981) retested 119 subjects drawn from the WAIS-R standardisation sample after 2 to 7 weeks (71 of these subjects were aged between 25-34 years, 48 were aged between 45-54 years). Examination of the means at the two test periods revealed that large practice effects occurred, particularly on the Performance Scale. The magnitude of the change was similar in both age groups; mean changes for FIQ, VIQ and PIQ were 6, 3 and 8 IQ points respectively. In the younger age group the test-retest reliabilities for FIQ, VIQ and PIQ were 0.95, 0.94 and 0.89 respectively. Reliabilities for the individual subtests ranged from a low of 0.72 for Object Assembly to 0.93 for Vocabulary. Similar results were obtained in the older age group.

As a first step towards establishing base-rate data, Matarazzo and Herman (1984) have examined Wechsler's sample in more detail. Their study revealed that, despite the high test-retest reliability coefficients, there was considerable variation from individual to individual in the magnitude of change. Around 5% of the sample showed gains from test to retest of 15 points or more, others (approximately 7%) actually obtained lower scores at retest although (with one exception), the differences were small. The WAIS-R tables provided by Matarazzo and Herman can provide some guidance. However, far more base-rate data is needed before the clinician can feel at all confident in interpreting retest data. Firstly, the test-retest intervals required in clinical practice are considerably longer than the interval used by Matarazzo and Herman. There is also little information on whether an individual's level of ability is systematically related to the size of practice effects. Similarly, although the two age groups examined by Matarazzo and Herman did not differ to any appreciable extent in the size of the practice effects, the limited age range means that the effects of age remain largely unknown.

It is clear that, as is the case for any neuropsychological application of the Wechsler, conclusions regarding change in a client's cognitive status cannot be based solely on Wechsler retest data. Instead, such data must be combined with results from other neuropsychological measures and client interviews/behavioural observations.

Finally, given the difficulties in interpretation when the same version of the Wechsler is used on both occasions, it can be seen that the last thing the clinician wants is to further complicate matters by retesting a client on the WAIS-R if they had originally been tested on the WAIS (see earlier section on differences in difficulty between the two tests).

ESTIMATION OF PREMORBID INTELLIGENCE

The most common approach to estimating premorbid IQ is to use tests of present ability which are considered to be relatively resistant to neurological and psychiatric disorder. A more recent approach involves building multiple regression equations to estimate premorbid IQ from demographic variables known to be related to IQ test performance (e.g. years of education). These approaches, and a method which combines the two, will be evaluated in the following sections.

Estimation of Premorbid IQ with Tests of Present Ability

Currently, the most commonly used measure of premorbid intelligence is the National Adult Reading Test (NART: Nelson, 1982). The NART is a single-word, oral reading test consisting of 50 items. The majority of words are short in length and all are irregular; that is, they do not follow normal grapheme-phoneme correspondence rules (e.g. *ache, gauche*). Because the words are short, subjects do not have to analyse a complex visual stimulus, and because they are irregular, "intelligent guesswork" will not provide the correct pronunciation. Therefore, it has been argued that successful test performance requires previous familiarity with the words but makes minimal demands on current cognitive capacity (Nelson & O'Connell, 1978).

The NART and a short-form WAIS were administered to a standardisation sample of 120 subjects free of neurological disorder. Regression equations were generated to predict WAIS IQ from NART errors. These are presented in the test manual along with tables to assess the probability of a particular size of discrepancy between NART estimated premorbid IQ and current WAIS IQ occurring in the normal population. The NART has rapidly become a widely used test for the estimation of premorbid IQ in clinical and research settings.

This usage has largely preceded research on the basic psychometric properties of the test. Recently, however, a number of studies have begun to address the necessary issues.

A present ability measure must fulfil the following three criteria if it is to qualify as a valid means of estimating premorbid IQ. Firstly, it must have adequate reliability. Secondly, it must correlate highly with IQ (in the normal population). Finally, and most importantly, it must be largely resistant to the effects of neurological and psychiatric disorder. The extent to which the NART meets these three criteria will be addressed in the following.

Reliability of the NART

The NART is one of the most reliable tests used in clinical practice (see Crawford, 1989, for a review). It has high split-half reliability (Crawford et al., 1988b; Nelson 1982), inter-rater reliability (Crawford et al., 1989b; O'Carroll, 1987); and test-retest reliability (O'Carroll, personal communication; Crawford et al., 1989b). A statistically significant practice effect has been reported but this was of a very small magnitude (Crawford et al., 1989b).

Validity of the NART as a Measure of Intelligence

Evidence of the NART's construct validity as a measure of intelligence has been provided by a factor analytic study of the WAIS and NART (Crawford et al., 1989d) in which the NART loaded very highly (0.85) on g (i.e. the first unrotated principal component). Crawford et al. (1989b) examined Nelson's (1982) original standardisation sample and reported that the NART predicted 55%, 60% and 32% of the variance in WAIS Full Scale, Verbal and Performance IQ, respectively. These authors also examined the predictive validity of the NART in a cross-validation sample consisting of 151 healthy subjects administered a *full-length* WAIS (in the standardisation sample a seven-subtest short-form had been used). They reported that NART performance predicted 66%, 72% and 33% of the variance in WAIS FSIQ, VIQ and PIQ, respectively. It can be concluded that the NART has high construct validity as a measure of general ability, is a powerful predictor of WAIS FSIQ and VIQ, but is relatively poor at predicting PIQ.

NART Performance in Neurological and Psychiatric Disorder

Nelson and O'Connell (1978) conducted the first study of NART. They compared the NART and WAIS performance of the NART standardisation sample with a group of patients ($n=40$) who had EMI scan evidence of cortical atrophy. Their results indicated that the atrophy group were severely impaired on the WAIS ($P<0.001$). In contrast, there was no significant difference in NART performance between the two groups. Although these results should be interpreted with caution because of the lack of demographic information on the samples (i.e. years of education), they do suggest that NART performance was unaffected by the presence of cortical atrophy. Following publication of these results, the NART has been widely used in clinical practice to estimate premorbid IQ in a diverse variety of other clinical conditions. It is only relatively recently that the validity of this practice has been investigated.

The most widely employed approach has been to compare the NART performance of clinical groups with that of healthy subjects matched on demographic variables (e.g. Crawford, Besson & Parker, 1988; Hart, Smith & Swash, 1986). In a related design, the NART performance of clinical subjects has been compared with a demographically derived estimate of their expected performance (Egan et al., 1990). This is achieved through the use of a regression model which employs education, social class, age and sex as predictor variables (Crawford et al., 1990b). A correlational design has also been used (e.g. O'Carroll & Gilleard, 1986) and involves computing the correlation between the NART and "impairment" or "dementia" sensitive measures. A significant correlation is taken as evidence that the NART is itself impairment sensitive whereas the opposite is concluded for a non-significant correlation.

Finally, a longitudinal design, which is appropriate for use in progressive conditions, has been employed. O'Carroll, Baikie and Whittick (1987) tested patients with dementia on the NART and retested them after one year. Although dementia severity and physical disability had worsened significantly in the intervening period, NART performance had not. The results obtained in these studies are summarised in Table 3.3. Perusal of this table shows that, although some studies have found evidence of impaired NART performance, overall the NART has shown itself to be surprisingly resistant to the effects of a wide range of disorders.

Prior to the development of the NART, the Vocabulary subtest of the Wechsler Scales was the test most widely used as a premorbid index (Lezak, 1983). In studies that directly compared the NART with Vocabulary, the former has consistently proved to be the more resistant of the two (e.g. Crawford, Besson & Parker, 1988; Crawford et al., 1987; Hart, Smith & Swash, 1986). Given that the two tests are essentially equivalent in the extent to which they meet the other criteria for an index of premorbid IQ (e.g. reliability and validity as a measure of general ability), the NART should be considered the test of choice in estimating premorbid intelligence.

Finally, the rationale underlying the use of premorbid indices is that they will improve the detection and quantification of impairment by providing an individualised standard against which current performance can be compared. Crawford, Hart and Nelson (1990) have tested this rationale in a sample consisting of healthy subjects and patients with dementia/cortical atrophy,

TABLE 3.3
Summary of NART Studies in Clinical Groups

Condition	Authors	Design*	Result
ALCOHOLIC DEMENTIA			
	Crawford, Besson, & Parker (1988)	MS	→
CLOSED HEAD INJURY			
	Crawford, Besson, & Parker (1988)	MS	→
CORTICAL ATROPHY			
	Nelson & O'Connell (1978)	MS	→
DEMENTIA ALZHEIMER TYPE			
	Nebes, Martin, & Horn (1984)	MS	→
	Hart, Smith, & Swash (1986)	MS	↓
	O'Carroll & Gilleard (1986)	C	→
	O'Carroll, Baikie, & Whitick (1987)	L	→
	Crawford, Besson, & Parker (1988)	MS	→
	Stebbins, et al. (1990)	MS	
	moderate/severe		↓
	mild		→
	Sharpe (1990)	MS	→
DEPRESSION			
	Crawford et al. (1987)	MS	→
HIV INFECTION			
	Egan et al.	RM	→
HUNTINGTON'S DISEASE			
	Crawford, Besson, & Parker (1988)	MS	↓
KORSAKOFF PSYCHOSIS			
	Crawford, Besson, & Parker (1988)	MS	↓
MULTI-INFARCT DEMENTIA			
	Crawford, Besson, & Parker (1988)	MS	→
PARKINSON'S DISEASE			
	Lees & Smith (1983)	Ms	→
	Crawford et al. (1988a)	MS/C	→
SCHIZOPHRENIA			
	Crawford et al. (1992)		
	long-term hospitalised	MS	↓
	community resident	MS	→

* MS = matched samples; RM = regression model;
C = correlational; L = longitudinal.
↓ denotes that the results indicated impairment of NART performance; → denotes that the results indicated NART performance was unaffected.

all of whom had been administered the WAIS and NART. Hierarchical discriminant function analysis was used to compare the accuracy of the WAIS in discriminating between the healthy and clinical subjects with the accuracy achieved when the WAIS and the NART were used. Inclusion of the NART significantly improved discrimination. In the case of FSIQ, the WAIS on its own correctly classified 86% of subjects as either healthy or demented; this rose to 96% when the NART was included.

The NART in Clinical Practice

Crawford et al. (1989b) combined the standardisation and cross-validation samples ($n=271$) in order to generate new equations and discrepancy tables. As these equations are based on a larger sample with a wider range of age and IQ, they should be used in preference to the original equations presented in the test manual. As the NART predicted a larger proportion of IQ variance when the full WAIS was the criterion variable, equations and discrepancy tables for the estimation of *full-length* WAIS IQs were also presented; these were necessarily based on the cross-validation sample alone ($n=151$).

In clinical practice, NART estimated IQ is compared with a client's obtained WAIS IQ. A sizable discrepancy in favour of NART estimated IQ suggests a decline from a previously higher level of functioning. For example, when using the full-length WAIS, a discrepancy of 12 IQ points in favour of *estimated* FIQ is statistically significant at the 0.05 level (i.e. less than 5% of healthy subjects exhibit this size of discrepancy).

The NART manual provides equations to estimate premorbid WAIS IQ from the combination of the NART and the Schonell Graded Word Reading Test (Schonell, 1942). Nelson (1982) advises that these equations should be used to estimate premorbid IQ in poor readers (operationally defined as subjects with a NART error score greater than 40). However, analysis of the standardisation and cross-validation samples has indicated that combining the NART and Schonell does not improve prediction in such subjects; this procedure tends to underestimate the true IQ to the extent that the relationship between predicted and obtained IQ becomes non-linear (Crawford et al., 1989b). Therefore, estimates of premorbid IQ should be derived from NART errors *alone*.

The NART and its revised versions (see later) clearly cannot be used in dyslexic patients nor in clients with significant articulatory problems. It would also be unrealistic to suppose that performance on *any* current ability measure would be entirely unaffected by severe cerebral dysfunction. Indeed, a number of the studies reviewed earlier have reported evidence of some deterioration in NART performance. In many cases where NART performance is impaired this is not a serious problem as intellectual deterioration is all too readily apparent, thereby obviating the need for a comparison standard. However, as this is not always the case, it is necessary to exercise clinical judgment in evaluating the likely validity of a client's NART estimate of premorbid IQ. To assist in this evaluation, Crawford et al. (1990b) have developed a regression equation which predicts a client's NART performance from their background demographic details (age, sex, years of education and occupation). A NART error score which exceeds a client's predicted error score by more than 9 points would suggest impaired NART performance, thereby alerting the clinician to the fact that the NART is unlikely to provide a valid estimate of premorbid IQ. In such a situation the clinician could consider obtaining an estimate of premorbid IQ directly from demographic variables (see later).

Beardsall and Brayne (1990) have recently developed a method whereby the full-length NART scores of subjects who are of average to below average reading ability can be predicted from performance on the first half of the test (termed the Short NART). There is only a minimal loss of accuracy in predicting WAIS IQ when the Short NART is used in place of the full-length version (Crawford et al., 1991). This suggests that it can be used with reasonable confidence in clinical practice. However, using the Short NART complicates administration and scoring. Furthermore, Beardsall and Brayne introduced the Short NART because they considered that the full-length version would produce distress or anxiety in poor readers. This view is at variance with the experience of the present author and his colleagues. The NART can in fact provide a boost to morale as it draws on previously established knowledge and does not demand a high degree of cognitive effort. It could also be pointed out that, if a client reacts badly to the NART, it is unlikely that a meaningful assessment could be conducted as more demanding, impairment-sensitive tests would almost certainly provoke more serious distress or anxiety.

Estimating Premorbid WAIS-R IQ: Revised Versions of the NART

A U.K. revision of the NART (NART-R UK) has now been standardised against the WAIS-R (Crawford, 1990; Crawford et al., in preparation). In the light of previous research, a number of changes have been made to the test itself and to the standardisation procedures. Firstly, as superior prediction was achieved when the full-length WAIS was used as the criterion measure, a full-length WAIS-R was administered to the standardisation sample. Secondly, although the overall inter-rater reliability of the NART is high, some individual items have been found to provoke low inter-rater agreement rates (e.g. the inter-rater agreement rate for *aeon* is nearer to chance than to perfect agreement). Furthermore, raters have been found to differ significantly in the strictness/leniency with which they score the NART (Crawford et al., 1989b). Analysis has revealed that the unreliable items were the main cause of these differences. For these reasons, the unreliable items (8) were removed and replaced with reliable alternatives.

The original format of the NART limited its use to clients with reasonable visual acuity. This can be frustrating for the clinician as the NART is commonly used with the elderly. It seemed preferable that the words be organised in a booklet form so that they could be individually presented in a larger, more widely spaced typeface. As Crawford, Parker, and Besson (1988) have noted, this should also serve to reduce attentional demands and therefore be more in keeping with the test's aim of tapping previous word knowledge while minimising the demands on current cognitive capacity. The NART-R UK standardisation sample consisted of 200 subjects and was representative of the adult U.K. population in terms of age, sex and social class. The NART-R predicted 59% of FIQ variance.

A North American revision of the NART has been developed by Blair and Spreen (1989). They standardised this revised version (which consists of 61 items) on 66 healthy subjects administered a full-length WAIS-R. Their revised NART predicted 56% of the variance in FIQ.

Estimating Premorbid IQ with Demographic Variables

It is well-established that a number of demographic variables (e.g. education, social class) have a strong relationship with measured IQ (Matarazzo, 1972). Thus, a knowledge of a client's educational and occupational history can provide the clinician with a rough guide to a client's likely level of premorbid ability. Wilson et al. (1978) attempted to make this process more systematic and objective by building regression equations to predict premorbid WAIS IQ from demographic variables. Using the WAIS (Wechsler, 1955) standardisation sample (n=1700) they regressed WAIS FSIQ, VIQ and PIQ on age, sex, race, education and occupation using a stepwise procedure. Education was the single best predictor of IQ for all the WAIS scales, although all three remaining demographic variables significantly improved predictive accuracy at subsequent steps of the analysis. The equations generated by this procedure predicted 54%, 53% and 42% of the variance in WAIS FSIQ, VIQ and PIQ respectively. In a follow-up study, Wilson, Rosenbaum and Brown (1979) have demonstrated that combining the demographic estimate of premorbid IQ with a subject's current WAIS performance can be of value in discriminating neurological from non-neurological subjects.

There have been a number of cross-validation studies of Wilson et al.'s (1978) equations but the quality of their design has varied considerably. Some studies have concluded that the method is of little utility because, in the samples examined, the equations predicted only a small proportion of IQ variance and systematically overestimated the actual IQ (e.g. Bolter et al., 1982; Klesges et al., 1985). However, these samples consisted of clinically referred subjects (a significant proportion of whom were liable to be cognitively impaired) and are therefore inappropriate for cross-validation purposes. Where adequately designed cross-validation studies have been conducted (most notably Karzmak et al., 1985) the results have lent support to Wilson et al.'s (1978) method. A detailed review of the literature on this topic can be found in Crawford (1989).

Wilson et al.'s (1978) equations have now been used for a number of purposes, for example as a means of determining the premorbid comparability of clinical groups (e.g. Bayles & Tomoeda, 1983; Weingartner, 1983); as a variable in the prediction of outcome after head injury (Williams et al., 1984); and as a means of assessing the degree of intellectual deterioration (e.g. Hamsher & Roberts, 1985). However, as is the case for all of the putative premorbid indices reviewed here, the use of Wilson et al.'s equations are limited to their country of origin as it cannot be assumed that the inter-relationships between the predictor variables and IQ are the same in other countries. To the present author's knowledge, there has only been one attempt outside the U.S. to estimate premorbid IQ with this method. Crawford et al. (1989c) built demographic regression equations for use in the U.K. They administered the WAIS to a sample of 151 subjects free of neurological, psychiatric or sensory disability and recorded their demographic variables (age, sex, education and social class). Using a stepwise procedure, WAIS IQs were regressed on the demographic variables. These variables predicted 50%, 50% and 30% of the variances in FSIQ, VIQ and PIQ respectively. It would appear, then that the demographic method is a reasonable predictor of FSIQ and VIQ in the U.K. However it can be seen that, in common with Wilson et al.'s results the proportion of PIQ variance predicted was unimpressive. It should also be stressed that, to date, the predictive ability of the U.K. equations has not been investigated in a cross-validation sample.

Using the WAIS-R standardisation sample data, Barona, Reynolds, and Chastain (1984) have generated demographic equations for the estimation of premorbid WAIS-R IQ. The predictor variables employed were those used in the original WAIS equations (age, sex, race, education and occupation) plus a further three: urban/rural residence, geographical region and handedness. Despite the availability of these additional predictor variables, the WAIS-R equations predicted substantially less IQ variance than their WAIS counterparts (36%, 38% and 24% for FSIQ, VIQ and PIQ respectively) and had correspondingly larger standard errors of estimate. However, fairly encouraging results have been obtained in a cross-validation study (Eppinger et al., 1987). The equations predicted a substantial proportion of IQ variance in a "neurologically normal" sample, and a highly significant discrepancy in favour of predicted IQ was obtained in a sample of neurological patients. A more recent cross-validation sample (Blair & Spreen, 1989) found a highly significant relationship between demographically estimated IQs and obtained IQs in a sample of 66 healthy subjects. However, the correlations were disappointingly low (i.e. 0.47 for FIQ) although this may have been because the U.S. equations were applied to a sample which was predominantly Canadian.

Barona and Chastain (1986) suggested that the deletion of two subgroups from the standardisation sample would permit more accurate demographic estimation of IQ in the remaining subjects. The first subgroup consisted of subjects between 16 and 19 years of age. Occupational classification of these subjects was on the basis of their head of household because they were not yet steadily employed in full-time occupations. The second subgroup consisted of ethnic minorities. Barona and Chastain argued that, because of the very small numbers of such subjects, coding them for inclusion in the analysis would produce meaningless results. Regression equations were generated from the remaining standardisation sample subjects ($n=1433$). These equations predicted more IQ variance than the initial WAIS-R equations (43%, 47% and 28% for FSIQ, VIQ, and PIQ respectively) and should therefore be used in preference to the originals.

Regression equations to estimate premorbid WAIS-R IQ have recently been built for the U.K. (Crawford, 1990) using the procedure employed for the UK WAIS equations. Demographic variables predicted 53%, 53% and 32% of the variance in FSIQ, VIQ and PIQ respectively. Examination of the standardisation samples ($n=200$) indicated that a discrepancy in favour of predicted IQ of 13 points or more would be significant at the 0.1 level (i.e. less than 10% of the standardisation sample exhibited this size of discrepancy), whereas a discrepancy of 17 points or more would be necessary for significance at the 0.05 level.

NART and Demographic Methods Compared

On present evidence the NART is a more powerful predictor of IQ test performance than demographic methods; i.e. it will predict more IQ variance and its equations will have correspondingly smaller standard errors of estimate. The standardisation sample used to generate the U.K. demographic equations for the WAIS (Crawford et al., 1989c) was also used to cross-validate the NART (Crawford et al., 1989b). It is therefore possible directly to compare the two methods in the same sample. The percentage of predicted WAIS IQ variance and standard errors of estimate for both methods are presented in the first two rows of Table 3.4. It can be seen that there is little to choose between the two methods in terms of predicting PIQ, as both produce fairly disappointing results. However the NART is markedly superior as a predictor of FSIQ and VIQ. A similar pattern of results has been obtained for the WAIS-R

TABLE 3.4

Percentage of WAIS IQ Variance Predicted by the NART, Demographic Variables, and the Combined Method in a Sample of 151 Healthy Subjects

	Full Scale IQ	Verbal IQ	Performance IQ
NART	66 (7.4)	72 (7.5)	33 (9.5)
Demographic equations	50 (9.1)	50 (10.2)	30 (9.8)
NART plus	73 (6.7)	78 (6.8)	39 (9.2)

Note: standard errors of estimate in parentheses

using the revised versions of the NART referred to earlier (Blair & Spreen, 1989; Crawford, 1990).

The lesser predictive ability of demographic methods may be offset by their major advantage: They provide premorbid estimates that are entirely independent of a patient's current cognitive status. Therefore, unlike the NART, there is no danger of the premorbid estimates being subject to decline. The demographic method can also be used with patients for whom the NART would be inappropriate (e.g. dyslexic patients). However, it must constantly be borne in mind that the band of error associated with the demographic approach is considerable. A definitive judgment on the relative clinical utility of the two methods must await future research. Studies directly comparing the ability of the two methods (when paired with measures of current ability) to discriminate between impaired and healthy subjects would clearly be very informative.

Combining the Psychometric and Demographic Approaches

Crawford et al. (1989e) built a multiple regression equation to predict WAIS IQ from the NART and demographic variables in the previously discussed sample of 151 healthy subjects. The aim was to determine whether combining the psychometric and demographic approaches would predict more IQ variance than either method alone. There is considerable covariance between the NART and demographic variables, most notably in education and social class (Crawford et al., 1988b; Crawford et al. 1990b). Clearly then, combining these variables would not have an additive effect on predicted IQ variance. However, it was hypothesised that a cumulative effect would be observed in that demographic variables would mediate the relationship between the NART and IQ.

A stepwise procedure was employed to regress WAIS IQs on the NART and demographic variables (age, sex, social class, and education). For all three WAIS scales, NART errors were the best predictors of IQ. All the demographic variables (except education) significantly increased predicted variance at subsequent steps. The percentage of IQ variance predicted is presented in the bottom row of Table 3.4, from which it can be seen that the combined approach compares very favourably with the results for either the NART or demographic methods alone. This study presented regression equations to obtain the NART/demographic estimate of premorbid IQ in individual cases. Discrepancy tables for obtained vs premorbid IQ were also presented.

Crawford et al. (1990c) investigated the construct validity of the combined NART/demographic estimate by factor analysing it along with the WAIS. The NART/demographic estimate loaded very highly on "g", indeed its loading (0.9) exceeded that of all the WAIS subtests. Crawford et al. (1990f) conducted a cross-validation study using the original NART standardisation sample ($n=120$) and confirmed that the inclusion of demographic variables significantly increases predicted variance. This study also presented equations and discrepancy tables to estimate premorbid IQ for use when Nelson's (1982) seven-subtest short-form is used as the current IQ measure.

The effects of combining the NART-R with demographic variables have not been so encouraging when the WAIS-R has been used as the criterion variable. Blair and Spreen (1989) reported that in their sample of 66 subjects demographic variables did not significantly improve prediction. Crawford (1990) found that although demographic variables did produce a significant increase in predicted IQ variance, the practical gain in accuracy of prediction did not justify the additional effort that would be required in their computation.

REFERENCES

Anastasi, A. (1988). *Psychological Testing* (6th ed.). New York: Macmillan.

Atkinson, L., Cyr. J.J., Doxey, N.C.S., & Vigna, C.M. (1989). Generalizability of WAIS-R factor structure within and between populations. *Journal of Clinical Psychology, 45*, 124–129.

Barona, A., & Chastain, R.L. (1986). An improved estimate of premorbid IQ for blacks and whites on the WAIS-R. *International Journal of Clinical Neuropsychology, 8*, 169–173.

Barona, A., Reynolds, C.R., & Chastain, R. (1984). A demographically based index of premorbid intelligence for the WAIS-R. *Journal of Consulting and Clinical Psychology, 52*, 885–887.

Bayles, K.A., & Tomoeda, C.K. (1983). Confrontation naming impairment in dementia. *Brain and Language, 19*, 98–114.

Beardsall, L., & Brayne, C. (1990). Estimation of verbal intelligence in an elderly community: A prediction analysis using a shortened NART. *British Journal of Clinical Psychology, 29*, 83–90.

Blair, J.R., & Spreen, O. (1989). Predicting premorbid IQ: A revision of the National Adult Reading Test. *The Clinical Neuropsychologist, 3*, 129–136.

Bolter, J., Gouvier, W., Veneklasen, J., & Long, C.J. (1982). Using demographic information to predict premorbid IQ: A test of clinical validity with head trauma patients. *Clinical Neuropsychology, 4*, 171–174.

Bornstein, R.A. (1983). VIQ-PIQ discrepancies on the WAIS-R in patients with uniltateral or bilateral cerebral dysfunction. *Journal of Consulting and Clinical Psychology, 51*, 779–780.

Bornstein, R.A. (1984). Unilateral lesions and the Revised Wechsler Adult Intelligence Scale: No sex differences. *Journal of Consulting and Clinical Psychology, 52*, 604–608.

Bornstein, R.A. (1987). The WAIS-R in clinical practice: Boon or bust? *The Clinical Neuropsychologist, 1*, 185–190.

Bornstein, R.A. & Matarazzo, J.D. (1982). Wechsler VIQ versus PIQ differences in cerebral dysfunction: A literature review with emphasis on sex differences. *Journal of Clinical Neuropsychology, 4*, 319–334.

Britton, P.G., & Savage, R.D. (1966). A short form of the WAIS for use with the aged. *British Journal of Psychiatry, 112*, 417–418.

Burgess, A. (in press). Profile analysis of the Wechsler Intelligence Scales: A new index of subtest scatter. *British Journal of Clinical Psychology.*

Canavan, A.G.M., Dunn, G., & McMillan, T.M. (1986). Principal components of the WAIS-R. *British Journal of Clinical Psychology, 25*, 81–85.

Crawford, J.R. (1989). Estimation of premorbid intelligence: A review of recent developments. In J.R. Crawford & D.M. Parker (Eds.), *Developments in Clinical and Experimental Neuropsychology* (pp. 55–74). New York: Plenum Press.

Crawford, J.R. (1990). *The estimation of premorbid intelligence*. Unpublished PhD thesis, University of Aberdeen.

Crawford, J.R., Allan, K.M., Besson, J.A.O., Cochrane, R.H.B., & Stewart, L.E. (1990a). A comparison of the WAIS and WAIS-R in matched UK samples. *British Journal of Clinical Psychology, 29,* 105–109.

Crawford, J.R., Allan, K.M., Cochrane, R.H.B., & Parker D.M. (1990b). Assessing the validity of NART estimated IQs in the individual case. *British Journal of Clinical Psychology, 29,* 435–436.

Crawford, J.R., Allan, K.M., & Jack, A.M. (1992). Short-forms of the UK WAIS-R: Regression equations and their predictive accuracy in a general population sample. *British Journal of Clinical Psychology, 31,* 191–202.

Crawford, J.R., Allan, K.M., Jack, A.M., Morrison, F.M., & Parker, D.M. (1991). The Short NART: Cross-validation, relationship to IQ and some practical considerations. *British Journal of Clinical Psychology, 30,* 223–229.

Crawford, J.R., Allan, K.M., & Morrison, F.M. *Estimating premorbid WAIS-R IQ: The development of the National Adult Reading Test -Revised (NART-R).* Manuscript in preparation.

Crawford, J.R., Allan, K.M., Stephen, D.W., Parker, D.M., & Besson, J.A.O. (1989a). The Wechsler Adult Intelligence Scale – Revised (WAIS-R): Factor structure in a UK sample. *Personality and Individual Differences, 10,* 1209–1212.

Crawford, J.R., Besson, J.A.O., Bremner, M., Ebmeier, K.P., Cochrane, R.H.B., & Kirkwood, K. (1992). Estimation of premorbid intelligence in schizophrenia. *British Journal of Psychiatry, 161,* 69–74

Crawford, J.R., Besson, J.A.O., & Parker, D.M. (1988). Estimation of premorbid intelligence in organic conditions. *British Journal of Psychiatry, 153,* 178–181.

Crawford, J.R., Besson, J.A.O., Parker, D.M., Sutherland, K.M., & Keen, P.L. (1987). Estimation of premorbid intellectual status in depression. *British Journal of Clinical Psychology, 26,* 313–314.

Crawford, J.R., Cochrane, R.H.B., Besson, J.A.O., Parker, D.M., & Stewart, L.E. (1990c). Premorbid IQ estimates obtained by combining the NART and demographic variables: Construct validity. *Personality and Individual Differences, 11,* 209-210.

Crawford, J.R., Hart, S., & Nelson, H.E. (1990). Improved detection of cognitive impairment with the NART: An investigation employing hierarchical discriminant function analysis. *British Journal of Clinical Psychology, 29,* 239–241.

Crawford, J.R., Jack, A.M., Morrison, F.M., Allan, K.M., & Nelson, H.E. (1990d). The UK factor structure of the WAIS-R is robust and highly congruent with the USA standardisation sample. *Personality and Individual Differences, 11,* 643–644.

Crawford, J.R., Morrison, F.M., Jack, A.M., Cochrane, R.H.B., Allan, K.M., & Besson, J.A.O. (1990e). WAIS vs. WAIS-R in matched UK samples. *Personality and Individual Differences, 11,* 427–428.

Crawford, J.R., Nelson, H.E., Blackmore, L., & Cochrane, R.H.B. (1990f). Estimating premorbid intelligence by combining the NART and demographic variables: An examination of the NART standardisation sample and supplementary equations. *Personality and Individual Differences, 11,* 1153–1157.

Crawford, J.R., Parker, D.M., Stewart, L.E., Besson, J.A.O., & De Lacey, G. (1989b). Prediction of WAIS IQ with the National Adult Reading Test: Cross-validation and extension. *British Journal of Clinical Psychology, 28,* 267–283.

Crawford, J.R., Stewart, L., Calder, S., Ebmeier, K., Mutch, W., & Besson, J. (1988a). Estimation of premorbid intelligence in idiopathic Parkinson's disease. *9th International Symposium on Parkinson's Disease. Israel, Book of Abstracts, 9.*

Crawford, J.R., Stewart, L.E., Cochrane, R.H.B., Foulds, J.A., Besson, J.A.O., & Parker, D.M. (1989c). Estimating premorbid IQ from demographic variables: Regression equations derived from a UK sample. *British Journal of Clinical Psychology, 28,* 275–278.

Crawford, J.R., Stewart, L.E., Cochrane, R.H.B., Parker, D.M., & Besson, J.A.O. (1989d). Construct validity of the National Adult Reading Test: A factor analytic study. *Personality and Individual Differences, 10,* 585–587.

Crawford, J.R., Stewart, L.E., Garthwaite, P.H., Parker, D.M., & Besson, J.A.O. (1988b). The relationship between demographic variables and NART performance in normal subjects. *British Journal of Clinical Psychology, 27,* 181–182.

Crawford, J.R., Stewart, L.E., Parker, D.M., Besson, J.A.O., & Cochrane, R.H.B. (1989e). Estimation of premorbid intelligence: Combining psychometric and demographic approaches improves predictive accuracy. *Personality and Individual Differences, 10,* 793–796.

Davis, F.B. (1959). Interpretation of differences among average and individual test scores. *Journal of Educational Psychology, 50,* 162–170.

Egan, V.G., Crawford, J.R., Brettle, R.P., & Goodwin, G.M. (1990). The Edinburgh cohort of HIV-positive drug users: Current intellectual function is impaired, but not due to early AIDS dementia complex. *AIDS, 4,* 651–656.

Eppinger, M.G., Craig, P.L., Adams, R.L., & Parsons, O.A. (1987). The WAIS-R index for estimating premorbid intelligence: Cross-validation and clinical utility. *Journal of Consulting and Clinical Psychology, 55,* 86–90.

Flynn, J.R. (1984). The mean IQ of Americans: Massive gains 1932 to 1978. *Psychological Bulletin, 95,* 29–51.

Flynn, J.R. (1987). Massive IQ gains in 14 nations: What IQ tests really measure. *Psychological Bulletin, 101,* 171–191.

Gutkin, T.B., Reynolds, C.R., & Galvin, G.A. (1984). Factor analysis of the Wechsler Adult Intelligence Scale-Revised (WAIS-R): An examination of the standardisation sample. *Journal of School Psychology, 22,* 83–93.

Hamsher, K. de S., & Roberts, R. (1985). Memory for recent US Presidents in patients with cerebral disease. *Journal of Clinical and Experimental Neuropsychology, 7,* 1–13.

Hart, S., Smith, C.M., & Swash, M. (1986). Assessing intellectual deterioration. *British Journal of Clinical Psychology, 25,* 119–124.

Huba, G.J. (1985). How unusual is a profile of test scores? *Journal of Psychoeducational Assessment, 4,* 321–325.

Huba, G.J. (1986). Statistics for computer-based test interpretations: Bivariate and multivariate uniqueness. *Educational and Psychological Measurement, 46,* 331–334.

Karzmak, P. Heaton, R.K., Grant, I., & Matthews, C.G. (1985). Use of demographic variables to predict Full Scale IQ: A replication and extension. *Journal of Clinical and Experimental Neuropsychology, 7,* 412–420.

Kaufman, A.S., McLean, J.E., & Reynolds, C.R. (1988). Sex, race, residence, region, and education differences on the 11 WAIS-R subtests. *Journal of Clinical Psychology, 44,* 231–248.

Kelly, M.P., Montgomery, M.L., Felleman, E.S., & Webb, W.W. (1984). WAIS and WAIS-R in a neurologically impaired population. *Journal of Clinical Psychology, 40,* 788–790.

Kirk, R.E. (1968). *Experimental design: Procedures for the behavioral sciences.* Belmont: Brooks/Cole.

Klesges, R.C., Fisher, L., Vasey, M., & Pheley, A. (1985). Predicting adult premorbid functioning levels: Another look. *International Journal of Clinical Neuropsychology, 7,* 1–3.

Knight, R.G., & Godfrey, H.P.D. (1984). Assessing the significance of differences between subtests on the Wechsler Adult Intelligence Scale-Revised. *Journal of Clinical Psychology, 40,* 808–810.

Lawson, J.S., & Inglis, J. (1983). A laterality of cognitive impairment after hemispheric damage: A measure derived from a principal-components analysis of the Wechsler Adult Intelligence Scale. *Journal of Consulting and Clinical Psychology, 51,* 832–840.

Lawson, J.S., Inglis, J., & Stroud, T.W.F. (1983). A laterality index of cognitive impairment after hemispheric damage: A measure derived from a principal-components analysis of the WAIS-R. *Journal of Consulting and Clinical Psychology, 51,* 841–847.

Lea, M. (1986). *A British supplement to the manual of the Wechsler Adult Intelligence Scale – Revised.* San Antonio: Psychological Corporation.

Leckliter, I.N., Silverstein, A.B., & Matarazzo, J.D. (1986). A literature review of factor analytic studies of the WAIS-R. *Journal of Clinical Psychology, 42,* 332–342.

Lees, A.J., & Smith, E. (1983). Cognitive deficits in the early stages of Parkinson's disease. *Brain, 106,* 257–270.

Lezak, M.D. (1983). *Neuropsychological assessment* (2nd ed.). New York: Oxford University Press.

Lezak, M.D. (1988). Neuropsychological tests and assessment techniques. In F. Boller & J. Grafman (Eds.) *Handbook of neuropsychology* (Vol.1, pp. 47–68). Elsevier.

Matarazzo, J.D. (1972). *Wechsler's measurement and appraisal of adult intelligence (5th ed.).* Baltimore: Williams & Wilkins.

Matarazzo, J.D., Daniel, M.H., Prifitera, A., & Herman, D.O. (1988). Inter-subtest scatter in the WAIS-R standardisation sample. *Journal of Clinical Psychology, 44,* 940–950.

Matarazzo, J.D., & Herman, D.O. (1984). Base rate data for the WAIS-R: Test-retest reliability and VIQ-PIQ differences. *Journal of Clinical Neuropsychology, 6,* 351–366.

Matarazzo, J.D., & Herman, D.O. (1985). Clinical uses of the WAIS-R: Base rates of differences between VIQ and PIQ in the WAIS-R standardisation sample. In B. Wolman (Ed.), *Handbook of intelligence: Theories, measurement and applications* (pp. 899–932). New York: Wiley.

Mishra, S.P., & Brown, K.H. (1983). The comparability of WAIS and WAIS-R IQ and subtest scores. *Journal of Clinical Psychology, 39,* 754–757.

Nebes, R.D., Martin, D.C., & Horn, L.C. (1984). Sparing of semantic memory in Alzheimer's disease. *Journal of Abnormal Psychology, 93,* 321–330.

Nelson, H.E., & O'Connell, A. (1978). Dementia: The estimation of premorbid intelligence levels using the new adult reading test. *Cortex, 14,* 234–244.

Nelson, H.E. (1982). *National Adult Reading Test (NART): Test manual.* Windsor: NFER-Nelson.

O'Carroll, R.E., & Gilleard, C.J. (1986). Estimation of premorbid intelligence in dementia. *British Journal of Clinical Psychology, 25,* 157–158.

O'Carroll, R.E. (1987). The inter-rater reliability of the National Adult Reading Test (NART): A pilot study. *British Journal of Clinical Psychology, 26,* 229–230.

O'Carroll, R.E., Baikie, E.M., & Whittick, J.E. (1987). Does the National Adult Reading Test hold in dementia? *British Journal of Clinical Psychology, 26,* 315–316.

Prifitera, A., & Ryan, J.H. (1983). WAIS-R/WAIS comparisons in a clinical sample. *Clinical Neuropsychology, 5,* 97–99.

Quereshi, M.Y., & Ostrowski, M.J. (1985). The comparability of three WAIS's in a college sample. *Journal of Clinical Psychology, 44,* 397–407.

Raven, J.C. (1982). *Revised manual for Raven's Progressive Matrices and Vocabulary Scale.* Windsor: NFER Nelson.

Reitan, R.M., & Wolfson, D. (1990). A consideration of the comparability of the WAIS and WAIS-R. *The Clinical Neuropsychologist, 4,* 80–85.

Reynolds, C.R. (1982). Determining statistically reliable strengths and weaknesses in the performance of single individuals on the Luria-Nebraska Neuropsychology Battery. *Journal of Consulting and Clinical Psychology, 50,* 525–529.

Reynolds, C.R., Willson, V.L., & Clark, P.L. (1983). A four-test short-form of the WAIS-R for clinical screening. *Clinical Neuropsychology, 5,* 111–116.

Satz, P., & Mogel, S. (1962). An abbreviation of the WAIS for clinical use. *Journal of Clinical Psychology, 18,* 77–79.

Schonell, F. (1942). *Backwardness in the basic subjects.* London: Oliver & Boyd.

Sharpe, K.L. (1990). *Estimating premorbid intelligence using the National Adult Reading Test in Newfoundland.* MSc Thesis, Memorial University of Newfoundland.

Silverstein, A.B. (1982). Two and four-subtest short-forms of the Wechsler Adult Intelligence Scale-Revised. *Journal of Consulting and Clinical Psychology, 50,* 415–418.

Silverstein, A.B. (1984). Pattern analysis: The question of abnormality. *Journal of Consulting and Clinical Psychology, 52,* 936–939.

Smith, R.S. (1983). A comparison study of the WAIS and the WAIS-R in a college population. *Journal of Consulting and Clinical Psychology, 51,* 414–419.

Stebbins, G.T., Wilson, R.S., Gilley, D.W., Bernard, B.A., & Fox, J.H. (1988). Use of the National Adult Reading Test to estimate premorbid IQ in dementia. *The Clinical Neuropsychologist, 4,* 18–24.

Urbina, S.P., Golden, C.J., & Ariel, R.N. (1982). WAIS/WAIS-R: Initial comparisons *Clinical Neuropsychology, 4,* 145–146.

Warrington, E.K., James, M., & Maciejewski, C. (1986). The WAIS as a lateralizing and localizing diagnostic instrument: A study of 656 patients with unilateral cerebral lesions. *Neuropsychologia, 24,* 223–239.

Wechsler, D. (1955). *Manual for the Wechsler Adult Intelligence Scale.* New York: Psychological Corporation.

Wechsler, D. (1981). *Manual for the Wechsler Adult Intelligence Scale–Revised.* New York: Psychological Corporation.

Weingartner, H. (1983). Forms of memory failure. *Science, 221,* 380–382.

Williams, J.M., Gomes, F., Drudge, O.W., & Kessler, M. (1984). Predicting outcome from closed head injury by early assessment of trauma severity. *Journal of Neurosurgery, 61,* 581–585.

Wilson, R.S., Rosenbaum, G., & Brown, G. (1979). The problem of premorbid intelligence in neuropsychological assessment. *Journal of Clinical Neuropsychology, 1,* 49–53.

Wilson, R.S., Rosenbaum, G., Brown, G., Rourke, D., Whitman, D., & Grisell, J. (1978). An index of premorbid intelligence. *Journal of Consulting and Clinical Psychology, 46,* 1554–1555.

4

Assessment of Laterality

Marian Annett
Department of Psychology, University of Leicester, Leicester LE1 7RH

INTRODUCTION

In any diagnostic or classificatory process, the proportion of cases identified in the sample tested depends on the methods of examination, the type of subject and the criteria of classification. This is as true of laterality as any other variable, whether continuous like height, or apparently discrete like dwarfism. The example illustrates one of the basic issues about laterality assessment. Newcomers to the field usually assume that laterality is discrete and that it will be a simple matter to count how many people are sinistral (for hand, eye, foot or other asymmetry). However, there are no agreed answers to questions of the type: "How many people are left-handed?", because one of the main outcomes of laterality studies is an enormous variability in estimates of incidence.

For those who believe laterality varies discretely, the differing estimates of incidence pose a difficult problem; one solution is to believe that one's own estimate is correct and everyone else's in error (McManus, 1985). This strategy would put laterality beyond the scope of scientific enquiry because there could be no replicability and consensus. The alternative is to accept that although we talk about laterality as if it were discrete, it makes more sense to regard it as varying continuously (Macsweeney, Gillies, & Zangwill, 1960), and to treat it as amenable to threshold concepts (Annett, 1972). Thus, height is a continuous variable but dwarfism can be treated as a discrete condition, whose ascertainment in a survey of child growth would depend directly on methods, samples and criteria. A chapter on the assessment of laterality must consider

51

the ways in which outcomes are influenced by methods and point out some of the pitfalls that have dogged clinical and research efforts to study asymmetries scientifically. These will be discussed firstly in relation to purposes of laterality assessment and secondly in the light of some specific methods.

Although there is not enough space to discuss theoretical issues as such, decisions about method often involve assumptions about theory and the author's prejudices should be declared. My views on assessment have been reached through the discovery and development of the right shift (RS) theory of handedness and cerebral dominance (Annett, 1972; 1978). A review of the laterality literature and the RS theory (Annett, 1985) is the main reference for material discussed here, unless other specific citations are given. Lateral asymmetries will be discussed with particular reference to handedness as the asymmetry most often tested, but the principles are applicable to other behavioural asymmetries.

PURPOSES OF LATERALITY ASSESSMENT

1. Lateral Asymmetry as a Human Population Characteristic

There are many features of anatomy and function which show lateral biases in humans and other animals. A basic issue in the description of these aspects of human biology is whether the features are universal (i.e. present in all members of the species except for pathological deviations), or whether they are subject to natural variation, or individual differences. Whether pathological or natural, the frequency in the population of the alternate forms is of interest. For example, *situs inversus* of the viscera occurs in about 1 in 10,000 (Norwegian survey conducted by Torgerson, 1950), whereas left-handed writing occurs in about 1 in 10 of modern samples of young people. The difference in frequency makes it clear that left-handedness cannot be caused by the same agent that causes *situs inversus*, a point made by Sir Thomas Browne in the 17th Century.

When laterality is to be assessed as a population characteristic the main problem is finding a sample that is truly representative of the population. The first rule must be to avoid volunteer effects as willingness to take part in a survey of handedness is not likely to be independent of personal and familial laterality. The second rule must be not to rely on undergraduates, as it has recently become clear that intellectual ability is not independent of laterality (Annett & Manning, 1989). How then to get a captive, non-student, representative sample? Fleminger, Dalton and Standage (1977) studied 800 patients attending the Dental Department of Guy's Hospital. Smith (1987) gave questionnaires to passengers at King's Cross and Paddington railway stations. Questions about hand preference were included in a demographic survey of 928 adults resident in a group of Oxfordshire villages (Newcombe et al., 1975), and also as part of a regular telephone survey made twice yearly in Greater Cincinnatti (Lansky, Feinstein & Peterson, 1988).

2. Laterality in Subgroups of the Population

The question of whether laterality varies with characteristics such as sex, age, race, ability, twinning, or dyslexia, has led to much research. The findings for 2083 residents of Cincinnati (cited earlier) show highly significant differences for sex, race and age (females, whites and the 40+ age group being more dextral). Percentages of left-handed writers ranged from 1.6% for older white females to 12.7% for younger white males, with 7.2% for the total sample. With a base-rate of about 7%, very large numbers would be needed for each subgroup to be certain of significant departures from the population mean. However, the range of proportions found in Cincinnatti is sufficient to show that any investigation of laterality in special groups must use controls similar to the target group in all respects except the specific variable of interest; architects, for example, should be compared with a group of professionals of similar age and sex, preferably having attended the same universities. In a recent study of laterality in homosexual men, Lindesay (1987) took as a control group heterosexual men attending the same venereology clinic, which would seem to match for possibly relevant variables other than sexual orientation.

The need to find a demographically similar control group has been slow to be recognised in laterality research, because investigators have assumed that population values are known. In twin research, for example, there was little data on twins and singletons assessed by the same methods (McManus, 1980). However, a demographic survey including questions about twinning and handedness as part of a national study of hearing loss (Davis: personal communication) and data from the National Child Development Survey (Annett, 1987) have now shown that there is a small but consistent increase in sinistrality in twins.

3. Laterality in the Individual Case

It is standard practice in the report of neurological cases to describe the patient as right- or left-handed, but it is rare to see the criteria for this assessment specified. In a report of CT scan findings for lesions associated with aphasias in left-handers, the only information on handedness was that: "Left-handedness was determined by either self-report or family enquiry" (Naeser & Borod, 1986). This does not tell us whether all the patients were sinistral for writing, or whether right-handers with any sinistral tendencies were included in the sample, as is often the case in clinical assessments.

Patients presenting with neurological lesions cannot be observed directly for premorbid hand use and the patient's disabilities may make for a poor informant. Relatives may be unaware of sinistral tendencies unless they were very marked. As sinistrality is not a salient characteristic for most right-handers, it seems likely that left-handedness will be under-reported. However, there is an important further difficulty in that the probability that evidence of sinistrality will be found is proportional to the enthusiasm of the questioner; there are probably few people in the general population who have no sinistral tendencies and no sinistral relatives. In other words if the incidence of left-handedness is 1 in 10 and the patient has ten relatives it is very probable that one will be sinistral.

An important handicap to the analysis of the problem of the relations between hand preference and cerebral dominance for speech has been shifts in criterion of sinistrality, between non-aphasics and aphasics, in the clinical descriptions of cases. In the influential series of Hécaen and Ajuriaguerra (1964), and Gloning and Quatember (1966), all right-brained speakers were reported to be nonright-handed; this was almost certainly due to the generous criteria of sinistrality applied. With more conventional criteria, such as the writing hand, the majority of right-brained speakers were predicted by the RS theory to be *right-handed*, and were found to be so (Annett, 1975; 1985, chap. 14).

The aim of a standard method of assessment for individual cases may be difficult to achieve as the circumstances of enquiry, and reliability of informants, are likely to vary. However, if cases are to be useful for research, it is important to agree a format for the enquiry using objective questions about the hand used for common actions likely to be known to relatives (i.e. writing, use of cutlery and tools). Enquiries about relatives should be standardised with the help of a schematic family tree so that missing, unknown and negative reports can be recorded as systematically and reliably as positive ones. The practice of counting the presence of a sinistral relative as evidence of non-dextrality in the patient is misleading; familial sinistrality should be studied as a variable independently of personal sinistrality.

4. Laterality and Cerebral Dominance

The term "cerebral dominance" is used here as a convenient shorthand for "cerebral hemisphere with main responsibility for speech". Many laterality research reports begin by justifying the work on the grounds of a probable link with cerebral dominance. Asymmetries of perception at the right and left ears and in the right and left visual fields have been popular research topics, on the assumption that these throw light on asymmetries of the cerebral hemispheres. Right ear advantages are reliably found when two different messages are presented simultaneously at the right and left ears in the techniques known as dichotic listening (Kimura, 1961), and dichotic monitoring (Geffen, Traub, & Stierman, 1978). When visual stimuli are presented briefly to one or other side of the midline, reliable advantages are found for words and letters in the right visual field compared with the left visual field (reviewed by Bradshaw &

Nettleton, 1983; Bryden, 1982). "Indices" of cerebral dominance have been claimed for the direction of drawing circles (clockwise or anticlockwise) and for the manner of holding the pen (whether in the normal orientation or inverted with the point toward the writer). Until it is as easy to go for a brain laterality test as for a blood test, "indices" of cerebral dominance will probably continue to be suggested. What do these various measures of laterality have to contribute to the understanding of cerebral dominance in an individual or group?

The RS theory suggests that two sorts of correlation should be distinguished in measures of laterality. The first I will call "by-product" correlations and the second "true" correlations. In the first, the bias to one side (such as right-handedness or -eyedness) is a by-product of some advantage of the left hemisphere, associated with its role in serving speech. Correlations between handedness and brainedness are high in general samples which include many left-brained speakers and right-handers; this is because the bias of the majority to the right hand is a by-product of the factor inducing left hemisphere advantage. The key question is: What happens when samples are restricted to right-brained speakers or to left-handers? In by-product correlations, no association is expected to hold between different types of asymmetry for atypical cases. Thus, in the children of two left-handed parents, and in patients with right hemisphere speech, there should be even biases to either side (on culture free tests of laterality), and moderate biases to dextrality for culturally influenced actions. By the same argument, knowing that someone is left-handed (or atypical for some other asymmetry) does not help to predict that person's hemisphere asymmetry but simply increases the randomness of the probabilities. This follows if all lateral asymmetries arise as chance accidents in the development of the two sides of the body, but some are jointly influenced by the factor inducing left hemisphere speech. A thorough study of associations between a variety of types of lateral asymmetry, including perceptual and behavioural asymmetries, found considerable independence (Eling, 1983).

True correlations arise if two aspects of asymmetry are correlated, even in atypical cases, presumably because both lateralities were influenced by the same developmental accidents, independently of the factor inducing left hemisphere speech. Recent data for students found about 50% of left-handers to be left-footed and the authors suggest that this is predicted by the RS theory (Chapman, Chapman, & Allen, 1987). However, in my own data for consistent left-handers, and in a sample of Canadian Indian children (cited by Peters, 1988), about 80% of sinistrals were left-footed. This would suggest a true correlation between hand and foot asymmetry. Eye preference also may have a true correlation with handedness, though weaker than that for footedness (see further on).

Evidence that dichotic listening asymmetries could be "by-product" rather than true correlates of cerebral dominance can be seen in the findings for patients whose speech laterality was assessed by the carotid amytal method (Strauss,

Gaddes, & Wada, 1987). In ten cases of right hemisphere speech, exactly five showed a typical right ear advantage. If this is true for dichotic listening (long thought to be one of the most probable predictors of cerebral dominance), it must be evident that researchers of atypical laterality should expect randomness to be their main result (see also Annett, 1991). This conclusion seems negative only in the paradigm of a search for the "essence" of left-handedness. It makes sense if chance is the main agent of lateral asymmetries.

The main point being made in this section is that laterality assessment should not be assumed to give direct information about cerebral dominance. Further, it is necessary to evaluate all reports of "true" correlations with cerebral dominance in atypical cases by asking whether there were sufficient numbers to test deviations from the expected base rate of 50/50 bias to each side. With only a dozen subjects, it would be easy to get apparently "statistically significant" departures from a 6/6 split by chance.

METHODS OF LATERALITY ASSESSMENT

The conduct of laterality assessment must be guided by considerations of purpose (discussed earlier), and the suitability of techniques for that purpose; the latter depends on the subject's age, physical and mental status, and the reliability and validity of the methods employed. Harris (1958) describes methods for assessing a number of aspects of lateral asymmetry. There is no special virtue in any particular set of questions or observations, except insofar as they offer a standard for comparison with new samples examined in the same way. It often happens in laterality studies that some previously reported technique is modified slightly, such that the new data reported cannot be compared with that of anyone else. Investigators must always be free to invent new instruments, but a control group is then essential in the research or clinical design.

1. Questionnaire for intelligent adults: The Edinburgh Handedness Inventory (EHI: Oldfield, 1971)

The EHI is the most widely used hand preference questionnaire. It consists of ten hand preference items (writing, drawing, throwing, scissors, toothbrush, knife (without fork), spoon, broom (upper hand) striking match (match), opening box (lid)). Two columns, labelled: "Left" and "Right", are provided and the subject is required to place a "+" in one to indicate the hand preferred for each action; "++" is to be used to indicate very strong preference for that hand; and "+" is to be placed in both columns to indicate indifferent preference for either hand (see Oldfield 1971, Appendix II, for the original layout).

A laterality quotient (LQ) is derived by counting the number of "+"s in each column, calculating the difference between hands as a proportion of total responses, and expressing the proportion as a percentage, negative or positive.

$$LQ = \frac{R - L}{R + L} \cdot 100$$

The range of quotients is -100 to +100, with all possible values in between.
The advantages of this questionnaire are that:

1. It is easily administered to adults of reasonably good intelligence.
2. The scoring system is straightforward and the LQ can be derived even if some answers are missing.
3. The LQ offers an apparently continuous scale of degrees of hand preference between strong left and strong right.

The disadvantages of the EHI are that:

1. It requires a literate, verbally sophisticated respondent who is:
   i. Fully aware of everyday personal hand use.
   ii. Prepared to envisage the hypothetical possibility of using the "other" hand.
   iii. Willing to make a judgement about this hypothetical possibility.
2. The scoring system gives the same value to "writing" as to "broom" and "box lid". Without independent evidence that these are of equal significance for laterality, there is a danger of counting cabbages with coconuts. That is, the simplicity of the LQ may hinder rather than aid the cause of discovering relevant distinctions.
3. A related point is that the willingness to put " + " or " + + " in the columns may vary with the personality of the respondent and the circumstances of testing.

Smith (1987) gave the EHI to patients attending an allergy clinic and obtained controls from the general population by giving the questionnaire to passengers waiting at two large London railway stations (as mentioned earlier) and collecting the forms after a few minutes. Can we be sure that the circumstances of testing, in the rush and bustle of a railway station, would allow respondents to make the imaginary experiments needed to decide whether to place " + " or " + + ", in one or both columns? The finding that allergy clinic patients were more often left-handed than controls depended not on left-handed writers but on a greater proportion of scores in the -40 to 0 range; is it not possible that the more relaxed atmosphere of the clinic made games with " + "s more probable? Consider the number of ways in which a LQ of 0 could be obtained; there could be 5 " + " in each column; or 10 " + " in both columns; or " + + " for 3 "left" items, " + " for 6 "right" items and a "both" response for 1 item; and of course, many more variations. Can all of these patterns of response be equivalent?

McMeekan and Lishman (1975) studied the reliability of the EHI (and the AHQ, further on) on retesting after an interval of 8 − 26 weeks. Changes were found for 12.9% of EHI responses, but as only 2.6% changed between right and left, it can be inferred that there were many changes in the recording of strength of preference for particular items. Bryden (1977) showed that females are more ready than males to use extreme response categories in hand preference questionnaires.

Tan (1988) derived what he terms "Geschwind scores" for the EHI, following a personal suggestion from Norman Geschwind that "++" responses be given a score of 10, "+" a score of 5, and counted as positive in the "Right" column and negative in the "Left" column. This gives a possible range of scores from -100 to +100 as for the original LQ, but only for subjects willing to declare themselves unable to change for any item. The "Geschwind scores" are open to all of the same objections are the LQ and perhaps even more, as the difference between a score of 50 and 100 can be seen to depend entirely on willingness to record "++" as opposed to "+". How could such a judgement of strength of preference be cashed into objective measurement?

Salmaso and Longoni (1985) evaluated the items of the EHI by calculating the probability of an L response in each of 20 LQ classes (divisions of the scale between -100 and +100), for a large sample of Italian university and high school students. They argued that for "good" items, the probability should be approximately linearly related to LQ class. The worst departures from this predicted relationship were "writing" and "drawing", leading Salmaso and Longoni to recommend that these items be dropped and replaced by other items from Oldfield's (1971) original 20-item research instrument. But would anyone wish to make a laterality assessment with "writing hand" excluded? Would not this be Hamlet without the prince?

The attempt of Salmaso and Longoni to improve the EHI is based on assumptions about the mathematical properties of an ideal scale, and the use of empirical data from responses in a restricted subset of the population, to discover how to make the distribution of responses fit the ideal. There is an inherent circularity in this approach. What is needed to break out of the circle is an external criterion of lateral asymmetry against which response patterns can be validated. An example of such an external validation of a LQ (based on seven actions observed in children, calculated according to the LQ formula), was provided by Peters and Durding (1978) who measured the tapping rate of the index fingers of each hand, and plotted the mean difference between hands for subjects grouped for LQ. The relationship was linear except for minor reversals in trend at both extremes, suggesting that those with minor departures from consistent preference are indistinguishable, on this measure of skill, from consistent preference.

In conclusion, it may be noted that although the LQ of the EHI appears to give a continuous scale, there is no independent evidence that it measures some continuous linear function. In practice most researchers subdivided the continuum to distinguish preference subgroups. As the same LQ can be arrived at in several different ways, there is no certainty that subjects with the same LQ are indeed matched for preference.

2. Questionnaire/Observations of Hand Use in Adolescents and Adults: The Annett Handedness Questionnaire (AHQ, Annett, 1970)

The AHQ has been used as a questionnaire in large samples of students, their families and service recruits and as the basis for observations of hand preference in several samples of students and secondary school children. The AHQ must be considered in relation to: (a) The treatment of "either" hand responses and (b) the classification of handedness subgroups.

a. Either Hand Responses

Because the EHI has been criticised earlier for its reliance on subjective judgements of strength of preference, and because confusions have arisen in the use of the AHQ due to the treatment of "either" hand responses, it is necessary to explain the treatment of such responses in some detail.

The questionnaire reproduced in Fig. 4.1 was referred to as Q2 in Annett (1970) because it was the second in a series of three versions, used in a series of studies beginning in 1963 at the University of Aberdeen. Version Q1 (items 1-8 only) asked subjects to indicate how easy it would be to change the hand used for each item on a 3-point scale ("easy", "slightly difficult", "difficult"). The analysis of responses of 730 undergraduates at Aberdeen and Hull found that over 50% of the sample recorded "easy to change" on at least 1 item; there seemed no justification for extending the concept of nonright-handedness so widely, especially when it relied on a personal judgement that could not be made objective in a questionnaire. Some 25–37% of student samples claimed a definite preference for the "other" hand for at least one action, so there was a great quantity of variability to be investigated for definite R and L responses, without the subjectivity of the Es. An attempt was made to discourage E responses by omitting the sentence marked "*" in Q3, but because they continued to be given, it was considered better to reinstate the sentence and avoid ambiguity, at least in the instructions.

Two large studies of hand preferences in schizophrenics appeared to reach very different findings but it turned out that the apparent difference was due to one study counting "eithers" as nondextral; when this difference of classification was removed, there was good agreement between the studies in finding no excess of left-handers among schizophrenics (Taylor et al., 1982). From what has been said earlier, it should be clear that I do *not* believe that modifying the AHQ so as

Handedness research

Name .... Age ....Sex ....
Were you one of twins, triplets at birth or were you single born? ....
Please indicate which hand you habitually use for each of the following activities by
writing R (for right), L (for left), E (for either).*
Which hand do you use:
  1. To write a letter legibly? ....
  2. To throw a ball to hit a target? ....
  3. To hold a racket in tennis, squash or badminton? ....
  4. To hold a match whilst striking it? ....
  5. To cut with scissors? ....
  6. To guide a thread through the eye of a needle (or guide needle on to thread)?
....
  7. At the top of a broom while sweeping? ....
  8. At the top of a shovel when moving sand? ....
  9. To deal playing cards? ....
  10. To hammer a nail into wood? ....
  11. To hold a toothbrush while cleaning your teeth? ....
  12. To unscrew the lid of a jar? ....
If you use the *right hand for all of these actions,* are there any one-handed actions
for which you use the *left hand*? Please record them here ....
....
If you use the *left hand for all of these actions,* are there any one-handed actions for
which you use the *right hand*? Please record them here ....
....
* This instruction was omitted in some versions with the intention of discouraging 'E' responses.

FIG. 4.1.   Annett Handedness Questionnaire (AHQ).

to obtain scores which can be summed to a "scale" (as by Briggs & Nebes, 1975)
is acceptable. Such a treatment is open to all the objections given earlier to the
LQ of the EHI. So, if a continuous numerical score is not to be derived, how are
the enormous numbers of patterns of preference to be reduced to a manageable
number? Further, can it be shown that the patterns have validity against other
criteria of lateral asymmetry?

b. Methods of Classifying Patterns of Questionnaire Response

Faced with the diversity of questionnaire responses the clinician or researcher
may adopt one of the following classification strategies.

i. Right and Left.   For many purposes a dichotomous classification into right/
left, or right/nonright is sufficient. The decision to be made in this case is the

criterion for the definition of the atypical group. The criterion may be response to a single item, such as writing, throwing, or hammering (about 7–10%); it may be to "any one left response" (30–40%); or "all responses left" (2–4%). The smaller percentages tend to give very few cases to analyse, unless samples are large; the larger percentages include relatively weak criteria of sinistrality. Witelson (1985) used the "any left" criterion to good effect for comparisons of *corpus callosum* size between consistent right- *vs* nonright-handers.

ii. Right, Mixed and Left. If the sample is reasonably large, it may be useful to distinguish the three groups: Right- mixed- and left-handers. This classification, using Q1–Q3 (Annett, 1967, and subsequently) has been based on the following rules:

1. Consistent right-handers − No left preference (i.e. R or R + E).
2. Mixed handers − Any combination of R and L (i.e. R, L + E).
3. Consistent left-handers − No right preference (i.e. L or L + E).

The relative proportions of subjects defined in this way were shown to be remarkably consistent between several samples, despite very different incidences, in obeying certain expectations for binomial proportions (Annett, 1967). The proportions of consistent right-, mixed- and consistent left-handers in the Cincinnati survey (cited earlier), 70.0, 27.6 and 2.4 respectively, fit these expectations as fully as the samples described in 1967. This consistency is now interpreted (on the RS theory) as due to the stability of the distance between thresholds for consistent left and consistent right preference along the baseline of the laterality continuum (that is, the distance defining mixed-handedness) when incidences are interpreted as areas under the normal curve (Annett, 1972; 1985).

Using the EHI to distinguish strong left-, mixed- and strong right-handers, Lindesay (1987) obtained evidence that the distribution of lateral asymmetry of homosexual males is less strongly shifted to the right than that of heterosexual males (Annett, 1988). The important point is that the proportions of mixed-handers in these and other samples, (non-human primates, students, and dyslexics) are as expected under the normal distribution curve, as it moves a short distance to the right along the L-R skill continuum. Thus, the three-group classification is useful for answering questions about the comparative shifts to the right of subgroups of the population.

3. Subgroups of Mixed-Handers

The question of whether it is possible to make meaningful distinctions between subgroups of mixed-handers was tackled by asking what patterns of hand preference, as identified through an analysis of over 2000 questionnaire

TABLE 4.1

Hand Preference Classes in Two Samples: Frequency and L-R Peg
Moving Time (1/10s) in Two Sets of Combined Samples of Students and
High-school Children

Preference Class	Annett (1985) (N = 1474)		Annett (1992) (N = 888)	
	%	L-R mean (S.D.)	%	L-R mean (S.D.)
1. Right-consistent	63.0	9.5 (7.3)	56.5	10.1 (7.2)
2. Right-weak left	10.2	9.0 (7.8)	8.7	12.1 (8.0)
3. Right-moderate left	9.6	7.0 (7.3)	12.4	7.1 (6.6)
4. Right-strong left	9.0	3.7 (7.2)	10.7	3.5 (6.5)
5. Reclassified (see Fig. 4.2)				
6. Left-strong right	2.8	-3.7 (7.1)	4.6	-5.4 (8.0)
7. Left-weak right	2.2	-6.8 (7.8)	2.4	-7.6 (8.2)
8. Left-consistent	3.2	-8.0 (7.2)	4.7	-10.4 (8.4)

responses, could be distinguished for relative hand skill on a peg moving task. Table 4.1 shows the classes identified, the percentage of subjects in each class and the mean left minus right (L-R) hand differences for peg moving, for two sets of combined samples (Annett, 1985, Table 11.4; Annett, 1992). Degrees of mixed-hand preference can be distinguished for both right and left mixed-handers. Notice how class 4 matches class 6, and class 3 matches class 7, for peg moving time difference, mirroring the direction of L-R asymmetry in each pair. The reliability of this coordination of hand preference and hand skill was demonstrated by its replication in the several samples (see Annett, 1985, Chapter 11). The new combined samples of Annett (1992) confirm that the subgroups of mixed-hand preference are ordered reliably and systematically for relative hand skill.

The hand preference classes have implications not only for skill, but also for foot and eye preferences. The proportion of subjects with left foot and left eye preference rises fairly linearly through the hand preference classes, as expected if each class represents increased bias to sinistrality (Annett, 1985, Figs. 12.1,

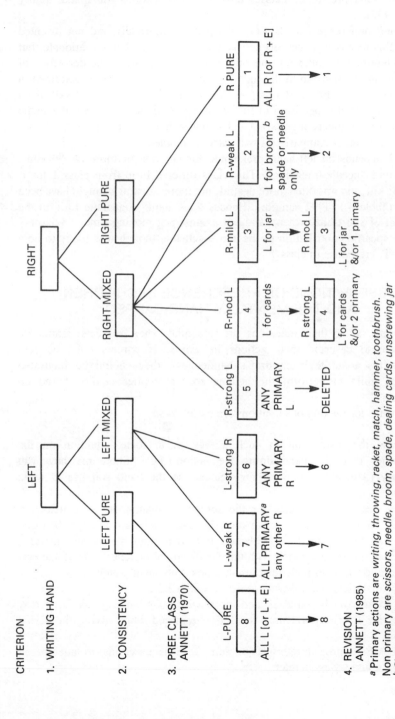

CRITERION

1. WRITING HAND

2. CONSISTENCY

3. PREF. CLASS
ANNETT (1970)

RIGHT

RIGHT PURE

RIGHT MIXED

R PURE
1
ALL R [or R + E]
→ 1

R-weak L
2
L for broom *b*
spade or needle
only
→ 2

R-mild L
3
L for jar
→ R mod L
3
L for jar
&/or 1 primary

R-mod L
4
L for cards
→ R strong L
4
L for cards
&/or 2 primary

R-strong L
5
ANY
PRIMARY
L
→ DELETED

LEFT

LEFT MIXED

LEFT PURE

L-strong R
6
ANY
PRIMARY
R
→ 6

L-weak R
7
ALL PRIMARY*a*
L any other R
→ 7

L-PURE
8
ALL L [or L + E]
→ 8

4. REVISION
ANNETT (1985)

a Primary actions are *writing, throwing, racket, match, hammer, toothbrush.*
Non primary are *scissors, needle, broom, spade, dealing cards, unscrewing jar*
b Classes to the *left* take precedence

FIG. 4.2. A decision tree for hand preference.

63

12.2). The hand preference classes also have implications for spatial ability (Annett, 1992).

The hand preference classes were discovered empirically and not invented *a priori*; this means that they do not have an intuitively obvious rationale, but must be identified by following the rules set out in Fig. 4.2. The derivation of the scheme and its revision in the light of subsequent research was described in Annett (1985, chaps. 10–11). Class 5 tended to be out of line for L-R skill from the beginning and this persisted in further samples. Hence, the revised scheme regroups class 5 subjects in classes 3 and 4, but without renumbering the classes (as this would hinder comparisons with earlier samples).

Class 2 depends on left-hand preference for any one or more of "broom", "shovel" and "needle-threading". This class differed little from class 1 for L − R hand skill, and was often more dextral, not more sinistral as might have been expected (Table 4.1, 1992 sample). Hence, these items contribute little to the assessment of sinistrality when validated against peg moving time. "Scissors" makes no specific contribution to the above scheme, though it is likely to be a frequent "R" response in class 7.

OBSERVATIONS OF PREFERENCE IN CHILDREN AND THE MENTALLY HANDICAPPED

Observations rather than questions are essential when subjects cannot be relied upon to describe their actions in words. If parents must be sent questionnaires about their children's handedness, they should be requested to ask the child to perform the actions so that replies can be based on observation.

Some rules for making observations are as follows:

1. Frame the instruction in such a way as to focus attention on the action rather than the hand doing the action, i.e: "Show me how you write Mary (Sam etc.)" rather than: "Show me the hand you use to write your name".

2. Have real or toy objects for the subject to manipulate as realistically as possible, though common sense must be used for when to say: "Pretend to brush your teeth with this toothbrush, but do not put it into your mouth", and: "Pretend to strike a match with this (real) box of matches". Or, if subjects cannot be relied upon to pretend, present a box with spent matches.

3. Place materials centrally, not closer to one hand.

4. For young or shy children and those with poor language skills, it may be helpful for E briefly to mime the action required while giving the verbal instruction.

5. The whole procedure must be fun. If S is unwilling to attempt an item, leave it and try again later.

Actions observed in two samples of schoolchildren in Hull included pointing to pictures, pretend digging with a child's sand spade, and placing small buttons in a narrow-necked bottle (Annett, 1985, Chap. 10). Annett and Manning (1989) observed 7 actions (the six primary actions listed in Fig. 4.2 plus dealing playing cards) in 5−11 year olds. These 7 actions permit subjects to be classified in all of the hand preference classes except class 2, although the absence of most of the non-primary actions means that the parallel with the classification based on 12 items cannot be precise. However, there is a remarkable similarity between the distribution of hand skill over the classes distinguished in these young children with that found for the new combined samples of high school and undergraduate subjects of Annett (1992). Table 4.2 shows the mean L-R differences for both samples, expressed as a percentage of the total time taken (L − R / L + R)* 100). Notice how classes 4 and 6 mirror each other for L-R hand skill for the

TABLE 4.2

Hand Preference and Hand Skill in Younger and Older Samples: The Similarity of L-R Peg Moving Skill in Younger and Older Ss When the Difference is Measured as ((L-R)/(L + R) × 100)

Preference Class	5−11 yrs. (Annett & Manning 1989) (N = 353) L-R% mean (S.D.)	14 yrs. + (Annett 1992) (N = 888)[a] L-R% mean (S.D.)
1. Right-consistent		5.4 (3.8)
	5.9 (3.6)	
2. Right-weak left		6.4 (4.0)
3. Right-moderate left	4.2 (3.0)	3.8 (3.5)
4. Right-strong left	1.5 (4.3)	1.9 (3.5)
5. See Figure 2.		
6. Left-strong right	−1.5 (3.0)	−2.6 (4.3)
7. Left-weak right	−5.1 (3.2)	−3.9 (4.4)
8. Left-consistent	−5.0 (3.0)	−5.7 (4.3)
TOTAL	4.1 (4.7)	3.8 (4.9)

[a] The same sample described for L-R Time in Table 4.1.

younger sample. This replication of findings for relationships between hand preference and hand skill in younger as well as older subjects suggests that the hand preference classes can be used with some confidence as reliable measures of degrees of relative dextrality and sinistrality along the L-R continuum. Distinctions based on these classes are likely to be more fruitful than those based on arbitrary divisions by laterality quotient.

OTHER ASYMMETRIES

1. Footedness

The literature on foot preference and skill was reviewed by Peters (1988), who argued that tests of foot control have an important role in neurological assessment. Most assessments of preference rely on a single item: Kicking a ball. Porac and Coren (1981) used four items: Kicking, stepping up onto a chair, picking up a pebble with the toes, and putting on the first shoe; all were judged to be valid in showing good agreement between self-report and subsequent observation.

The foot used for 13 tasks was observed in 220 psychology students and all items were significantly correlated with the overall scale of footedness (Chapman, Chapman, & Allen, 1987). The highest correlations were found for items which required the foot to be used to achieve some external goal such as writing one's name in sand, rolling a golf ball round a circle and kicking; in contrast, those requiring strength or balance such as stepping on a stool, or standing on one foot, were less highly correlated with the total scale.

Foot preference is highly correlated with hand preference in the sense that about 90% of right-handers kick with their right foot (96% in consistently right-handed schoolchildren personally observed). The question as to whether this is a true correlation in the sense that consistent left-handers are more likely to kick with the left foot, or whether it is a by-product correlation, with 50/50 preference for left-handers, has been considered earlier. Foot skill has been tested for speed and regularity of tapping in several experiments; right-handers showed advantages for tapping with the right foot, but left-handers showed smaller and inconsistent biases, more often for the right foot than the left (Peters, 1988).

2. Eyedness

Porac and Coren (1981) reviewed measures of eyedness in the sense of proficiency and also preference, as in sighting through a telescope or down a rifle. There are some important points which should be noted about eyedness, in relation to laterality assessment. Firstly, the preferred eye is not necessarily the "best" eye, from the viewpoint of acuity; there is a bias to prefer the right eye for sighting at all levels of relative acuity, except at the extreme of left superiority. Secondly, each eye sends sensory inputs to both cerebral hemispheres and there is no obvious anatomical cause, on the input side, for one eye to be preferred; studies of visual perceptual asymmetries, concern the right and left visual fields, as mentioned previously. The basis of eye preference is unknown, but seems likely to be related to the motor control of muscles involved in eye movement and fixation.

Tests of eye preference used in my research were as follows:

1. Sighting through a hollow tube: The instruction should focus on the object to be looked at, rather than the eye doing the looking; "Look at the clock through this tube", rather than: "Show me the eye with which you would look at the clock...."
2. Sighting a distant vertical line (edge of door, blackboard) through a small hole in a piece of cardboard held at arm's length in both hands; E covers each eye in turn with a small card and asks if the line can still be seen.
3. Sighting a near object such as a pencil held at arm's length through the hole in cardboard held at half arm's length; again, E covers each eye in turn and asks if the pencil can be seen.
4. Sighting the distant line again as in (2), while S brings the cardboard up to the nose, keeping the line in view. To which eye is it brought?

For Open University students testing each other, and for personally tested families, findings for right-, mixed- and left-eye preference on these tests were remarkably consistent between samples. About 37% of right-handers showed some left eye preference and at least 50% of left-handers showed some right eye preference. These proportions demonstrate that so-called "cross-laterality" of hand and eye is a very common phenomenon.

3. A Miscellany of Behavioural Observations

Numerous other behavioural and physical asymmetries can be observed; hand-clasping, arm-folding, the winking eye, the reversing hand in simultaneous drawing, and side of hair parting are among asymmetries that have been included in student practical classes on laterality (reviewed in Annett, 1985, chap. 12). None of these were found to correlate highly with hand preference, and for this reason were not considered worth further attention.

Clinicians and researchers are likely to note with some interest individuals whose hair parting is on the right as opposed to the typical parting on the left, or who gesture while speaking with the left hand rather than the right. It is tempting to treat such characteristics as *signs* of cerebral dominance. There is no good evidence at present that these asymmetries are strongly predictive of hemisphere asymmetry; until true correlations are demonstrated, in the sense discussed earlier, such observations contribute nothing beyond an increased probability of random assortment of asymmetries.

ASSESSMENT OF HAND SKILL

Questions about the relevance of measures of skill, and the types of measures to be used for assessments of laterality are subject to some controversy which cannot be considered in detail here (but see Bishop, 1990). A number of points must be made briefly. Firstly, the preferred hand must be taken to mean, on some definitions at least (Brain, 1945), that hand which is more *able* to perform certain actions which require skill; that is, the hand which is more likely to hammer a flint at the required angle, or to make a small mark on paper in the correct orientation. Preference questionnaires which include actions not requiring skill, such as self-touching movements, or pushing open a door, show little correlation with writing or hammering. Whether such relatively unskilled movements should be regarded as belonging to a separate level of lateral asymmetry (based on gross *vs* fine motor control) has been considered by Beukelaar and Kroonenberg (1983), and Healey, Liederman and Geschwind (1986).

A second important point is that measures of hand skill, on a variety of dexterity tests, have been found to give such high mis-classification rates for hand preference that it has been suggested that hand preference does not depend on differences in skill. However, a coordination of findings for preference and skill was the basis for the classification of levels of weak and strong mixed right and left preferences given in Fig. 4.2. The task used for this purpose in my research is one of peg moving, originally devised for testing hemiplegic children but found very useful for individual testing of all age levels from about 4 years (described in Annett, 1985, chap. 11). The peg moving task is continuing to prove invaluable in current research looking at levels of ability across the whole of the laterality spectrum (Annett & Manning, 1989: 1990a; 1990b). Whereas assessments of hand preference alone are restricted to identifying a small subset of the population, a good measure of hand skill can make important distinctions about degrees of right-handedness. Another measure of hand skill which correlates well with hand preference is speed and consistency of finger tapping (Peters, 1981).

Thirdly, group measures of hand skill have been devised using paper and pencil methods in class (Borod, Koff, & Caron, 1984; Tapley & Bryden, 1985). The use of a pencil in one hand has been highly practised, of course, and it is not surprising to find that such methods generally find relatively poor performance by the "other" hand and distributions which are more biomodal than continuous. However, the development of a group test of hand skill, not subject to this limitation is a goal worth pursuing.

REFERENCES

Annett, M. (1967). The binomial distribution of right, mixed and left handedness. *Quarterly Journal of Experimental Psychology, 19*, 327–333.

Annett, M. (1970). A classification of hand preference by association analysis. *British Journal of Psychology, 61*, 303–321.

Annett, M. (1972). The distribution of manual asymmetry. *British Journal of Psychology, 63*. 343–358.

Annett, M. (1975). Hand preference and the laterality of cerebral speech. *Cortex, 11*, 305–328.

Annett, M. (1978). *A single gene explanation of right and left handedness and brainedness.* Coventry: Lanchester Polytechnic.

Annett, M. (1985). *Left, right, hand and brain: The right shift theory.* London: Lawrence Erlbaum Associates Ltd.

Annett, M. (1987). La latéralité manuelle des jumeaux: Théorie du déplacement à droite. *Bulletin de Psychologie, 40*, 747–754. also published as Handedness in twins: The right shift theory. National Child Development Study, Working paper no.22.

Annett, M. (1988). Comments on Lindesay: Laterality shift in homosexual men. *Neuropsychologia, 26*, 341–343.

Annett, M. (1991). Speech lateralisation and phonological skill. *Cortex, 27*, 583–593.

Annett, M. (1992). Spatial ability in subgroups of left and right handers. *British Journal of Psychology*, in press.

Annett, M., & Manning, M. (1989). The disadvantages of dextrality for intelligence. *British Journal of Psychology, 80*, 213–226.

Annett, M., & Manning M. (1990a). Arithmetic and laterality. *Neuropsychologia, 28*, 61–69.

Annett, M., & Manning, M. (1990b). Reading and a balanced polymorphism for laterality and ability. *Journal of Child Psychology and Psychiatry. 31*, 511–529.

Beukelaar, L.J., & Kroonenberg, P.M. (1983). Toward a conceptualization of hand preference. *British Journal of Psychology, 74*, 33–45.

Bishop, D.V.M. (1990). *Handedness and development disorder.* Mac Keith Press. Oxford: Blackwell Scientific Publications Ltd.

Borod, J.C., Koff, E., & Caron, H.S. (1984). The target test: A brief laterality measure of speech and accuracy. *Perceptual and Motor Skills, 58*, 743–748.

Bradshaw, J.L., & Nettleton, N.C. (1983). *Human cerebral asymmetry.* Englewood Cliffs, NJ: Prentice-Hall.

Brain, W.R. (1945). Speech and handedness. *Lancet, 249*, 837–841.

Briggs, G.G., & Nebes, R.D. (1975). Patterns of hand preference in a student population. *Cortex, 11*, 230–238.

Bryden, M.P. (1977). Measuring handedness with questionnaires. *Neuropsychologia, 15*, 617–624.

Bryden, M.P. (1982). *Laterality: Functional asymmetry in the intact brain.* New York: Academic Press.

Chapman, J.P., Chapman, L.J., & Allen, J.J. (1987). The measurement of foot preference. *Neuropsychologia, 25*, 579–584.

Eling, P. (1983). Comparing different measures of laterality; Do they relate to a single mechanism? *Journal of Clinical Neuropsychology, 5*, 135–147.

Fleminger, J.J., Dalton, R., & Standage, K.F. (1977). Age as a factor in the handedness of adults. *Neuropsychologia, 15*, 471–473.

Geffen, G., Traub, E., & Stierman, I. (1978). Language laterality assessed by unilateral ECT and dichotic monitoring. *Journal of Neurology, Neurosurgery and Psychiatry, 41*, 354–360.

Gillies, S.M., MacSweeney, D.A., & Zangwill, O.L. (1960). A note on some unusual handedness patterns. *Quarterly Journal of Experimental Psychology, 12*, 113–116.

Gloning, K., & Quatember, R. (1966). Statistical evidence of neuropsychological syndromes in left-handed and ambidextrous patients. *Cortex, 2*, 484–488.

Harris, A.J. (1958). *Harris tests of lateral dominance, manual of directions for administration and interpretation* (3rd ed.). New York: Psychological Corporation.

Healey, J.M., Liederman, J., & Geschwind, N. (1986). Handedness is not a unidimensional trait. *Cortex, 22,* 33–53.

Hécaen, H., & Ajuriaguerra, J. (1964). *Left handedness: Manual superiority and cerebral dominance.* New York: Grune and Stratton.

Kimura, D. (1961). Cerebral dominance and the perception of verbal stimuli. *Canadian Journal of Psychology, 15,* 166–171.

Lansky, L.M., Feinstein, H., & Peterson, J.M. (1988). Demography of handedness in two samples of randomly selected adults (*N*=2083). *Neuropsychologia, 26,* 465–477.

Lindesay, J. (1987). Laterality shift in homosexual men. *Neuropsychologia, 25,* 965–969.

McManus, I.C. (1980). Handedness in twins: A critical review. *Neuropsychologia, 18,* 347–355.

McManus, I.C. (1985). Handedness, language dominance and aphasia: A genetic model, *Psychological Medicine,* Monograph supplement 8.

McMeekan, E.R.L., & Lishman, W.A. (1975). Retest reliabilities and interrelationship of the Annett Hand Preference Questionnaire and the Edinburgh Handedness Inventory. *British Journal of Psychology, 66,* 53–60.

Naeser, M.A., & Borod, J.C. (1986). Aphasia in left-handers: Lesion site, lesion side and hemispheric asymmetries on CT. *Neurology, 36,* 471–488.

Newcombe, F.G., Ratcliff, G.G., Carrivivk, P.J., Hiorns, R.W., Harrison, G.A., & Gibson, J.B. (1975). Hand preference and I.Q. in a group of Oxfordshire villages. *Annals of Human Biology, 2,* 235–242.

Oldfield, R.C. (1971). The assessment and analysis of handedness: The Edinburgh Inventory. *Neuropsychologia, 9,* 97–113.

Peters, M. (1981). Handedness: Effects of prolonged practice on between hand performance differences. *Neuropsychologia, 19,* 587–590.

Peters, M. (1988). Footedness: Asymmetries in foot preference and skill and neuropsychological assessment of foot movement. *Psychological Bulletin, 103,* 179–192.

Peters, M., & Durding, B. (1978). Handedness measured by finger tapping: A continuous variable. *Canadian Journal of Psychology, 32,* 257–261.

Porac, C., & Coren, S. (1981). *Lateral preferences and human behavior.* New York. Springer-Verlag.

Salmoso, D., & Longoni, A.M. (1985). Problems in the assessment of hand preference. *Cortex, 21,* 533–549.

Smith, J. (1987). Left-handedness: Its association with allergic disease. *Neuropsychologia, 25,* 665–674.

Strauss, E., Gaddes, W.H., & Wada, J. (1987). Performance on a free-recall verbal dichotic listening task and cerebral dominance determined by the carotid amytal test. *Neuropsychologia, 25,* 747–753.

Tan, U. (1988). The distribution of hand preference in normal men and women. *International Journal of Neuroscience, 41,* 35–55.

Tapley, S.M., & Bryden, M.P. (1985). A group test for the assessment of performance between the hands. *Neuropsychologia, 23,* 215–221.

Taylor, P.J., Dalton, R., Fleminger, J.J., & Lishman, W.A. (1982). Differences between two studies of hand preference in psychiatric patients. *British Journal of Psychiatry, 140,* 166–173.

Torgerson, J. (1950). Situs inversus, asymmetry and twinning. *American Journal of Human Genetics, 2,* 361–370.

Witelson, S.F. (1985). The brain connection: The corpus callosum is larger in left-handers. *Science, 229,* 665-668.

SECTION B:
ASSESSMENT OF MAJOR
PSYCHOLOGICAL FUNCTIONS

5 Memory Assessment in Clinical Practice and Research

Andrew Mayes
Department of Psychology, University of Manchester,
Manchester M13 9PL

Richard Warburg
Department of Clinical Psychology, North Manchester General Hospital,
Manchester M8 6RB

INTRODUCTION

This chapter is about the use of memory assessment procedures with brain-damaged patients for both clinical and research purposes. It is known that lesions in distinct brain regions disturb memory in different ways although our knowledge of how the brain mediates the various aspects of memory and how distinct lesions disrupt separate components of memory is far from complete (Mayes, 1988a). Ideally, we would like to achieve a state in which it was known precisely what brain lesions cause disturbances in distinct components of memory, and to have a clear view with each of these elementary memory disorders of precisely what functional loss has caused the impairment. This is the major aim of research into organic memory disorders. Such understanding will clearly greatly advance our thinking about how the healthy brain mediates memory processes. With this degree of knowledge it would also be possible to select tests that would give a comprehensive profile of a patient's pattern of memory impairment; or examine whether a single component of memory is impaired; and to what degree—or anything between these two extremes. As some memory disorders unquestionably are triggered by reductions in aspects of intelligence, motivation or concentration, a complete understanding of a patient's pattern of memory disorder would also require assessment of pre- and post-morbid intelligence, and of current levels of motivation and concentration.

Types of Organic Memory Disorder

At present, however, our knowledge of how lesions affect the various components of memory and, indeed, of what these components are, is only partial. Five different groups of organic memory disorders have been identified and incompletely characterised. First, posterior association cortex, and, possibly, frontal association cortex lesions cause a variety of material-specific short-term memory disorders (see Mayes, 1988a, for a review). Second, similar lesions can cause impairments in previously very well established memories that most notably include semantic memories (Mayes, 1988a). Third, frontal association cortex lesions disturb those kinds of memory that are most dependent on the ability to plan information processing as well as memory for temporal order and item frequency, which may or may not depend on the ability to plan information processing (Mayes, 1988a). Fourth, there is organic amnesia or, possibly, the organic *amnesias* that are caused by limbic diencephalic and cholinergic basal forebrain lesions (Squire, 1986). Fifth, there is a more heterogeneous group of disorders that include impairments of skill acquisition and retention, of conditioning, and of priming (an indirect form of memory distinct from direct forms such as recall and recognition, and indicated by changes in the way a subject processes recently presented items when they are re-presented). Basal ganglia and cerebellar lesions are among those that affect skill learning and conditioning, and priming may be affected by association cortex lesions and also possibly by those of the basal ganglia (Mayes, 1988a).

Standardised Tests in Research

How is research into organic memory disorders to fulfill its goal of producing a more finely subclassified taxonomy of elementary memory deficits, and of characterising the precise functional impairments that produce these deficits? Clearly it will depend on the use of standard memory tests so that patients in different laboratories can be compared with each other, and on the development of special purpose memory tests that either identify new memory disorders or help identify the functional deficits that underlie those disorders that have already been identified.

Currently, most research on organic memory disorders has been concerned with organic amnesia, its detailed characterisation and the determination of whether or not it comprises several sub-syndromes. Even if one's research interest is solely in amnesia, however, it is vital to know whether the patients studied have non-mnemonic cognitive deficits and other kinds of memory disorder. Thus, Squire and Shimamura (1986) have recently suggested that selectiveness of amnesia should be assessed by the administration of: The Wechsler Adult Intelligence Scale (WAIS), a Dementia Rating Scale, the Boston Naming Test, tests sensitive to frontal lobe lesions, as well as standardised tests sensitive to the memory impairment in amnesia. To these one might add: Measures of short-term memory (tapped by the WAIS), previously well-established semantic memory, and priming. Without the knowledge provided by these tests it is hard to decide whether amnesic patients from different laboratories are truly comparable and so be able to interpret their performance on specially devised memory tests. For example, some Korsakoff amnesics have been found to show improved memory for material on which they have performed semantic rather than physical feature orienting tasks, whereas other Korsakoff patients and amnesics with differing aetiologies have not (Mayes & Meudell, 1983).

The origin of these discrepant results would probably be confidently known if everyone observed the strictures of Squire and Shimamura with regard to the extensive use of standard memory and cognitive tests on patients. But researchers do not only need to characterise their patients on a wide range of memory and cognitive tests, they also need to be able to measure how severely impaired their patients are on various aspects of memory. Once more, without this knowledge it is hard to compare the results in different laboratories. For example, in a recent study McAndrews, Glisky and Schacter (1987) found a difference between two groups of amnesics in how they performed on a task that involved priming to previously novel material. Although the patient groups were indistinguishable with respect to their performance on the Wechlser Memory Scale (WMS), McAndrews et al. argued that one of the groups was more amnesic because they performed significantly worse on specially devised recall and recognition tests. Unfortunately, it would be hard to check their results on other amnesics because these tests are not generally available. Nor can one be completely confident about their validity although poor performance on them did correspond to the experimenters' intuitions. This problem could have been avoided if there were sensitive, standardised tests that measured the severity of amnesia. Future progress of research on amnesia and other memory disorders will therefore depend on obtaining a careful description of patients across a wide range of standardised memory and cognitive tests, and on the availability of tests that can give a precise estimate of how impaired they are on critical memory components.

USES OF MEMORY TESTS FOR CLINICAL PURPOSES

There are four main circumstances in which clinical psychologists need to give memory and other kinds of cognitive assessments. First, they may be asked whether any functional change has taken place. For example, memory and cognition might be measured before and after a shunting procedure is performed, or a patient suspected of dementia might be assessed on a number of occasions over a period of months to confirm that a progressive deterioration was taking place. Second, patients might be referred to a clinical psychologist in order to be assessed for impairment or for diagnostic purposes. The latter will generally involve more than determining whether a patient has impaired memory. For example, patients might be assessed to identify whether their memory problem was caused by frontal lobe lesions or whether it was a relatively pure amnesia, such as Korsakoff's syndrome.

In all these instances it is important for the clinician to discover whether patients' memory deficits can be ascribed to brain lesions or whether the possibility of psychogenic causes exists. Adequate diagnoses of a patient requires more detailed testing than is needed to see whether a patient has shown a functional change, so as to identify a pattern of cognitive and memory performance. Third, patients may be referred for a more detailed case description. For example, a head injury patient might be assessed in order to see whether their cognitive and memory impairments were too severe to allow return to work and to see what would be their likely effect on daily life. Detailed case description is also essential for medico-legal work, where it is important not only to specify cognitive and memory deficits and to show that they are caused by brain lesions, but to assess the chances of spontaneous recovery and the effects on the patient's lifestyle. This last desideratum may be best served by subjective questionnaires that ask patients and their relatives to rate the severity of their impairments and the effects of these on the quality of daily life. Medico-legal work also relates to the fourth purpose for which patients are referred to clinicians, which is assessment for rehabilitation. This involves testing to see whether a patient is likely to respond to rehabilitation and what kind of rehabilitation is likely to be most effective. Assessment of the effects of rehabilitation is a special form of measurement of change as already discussed.

Criteria that Tests must Fulfill

It is clear from the previous discussion that researchers and clinicians use standard memory tests for a variety of different, if overlapping, purposes. No one test is ideal for all these purposes. Choice of test, therefore, depends on matching the features of test to the purpose that one has in mind. Table 5.1 illustrates the range of criteria that standard memory tests could be called on to satisfy if they are to achieve the various aims to which they can be put.

As can be seen the criteria that need to be satisfied vary somewhat depending on the purposes for which the tests are required. These criteria fall into three groups. First, tests need to have suitable norms, which should include means and standard deviations for age- and IQ-matched normal subjects. Such norms are important to have because many aspects of memory decline with age (for still poorly understood reasons). Recall and recognition levels correlate positively with intelligence and organic amnesia is a condition in which recall and recognition are significantly worse than would be expected on the basis of a patient's measured intelligence. Severity of amnesia must,

TABLE 5.1
Properties of Memory Tests Required for Various Purposes

	Norms			Validity				Test Construction					
	Age-related	I.Q. related	Condition-related	Construct(1)	Organicity(2)	Ecological(3)	Sensitivity	Test-retest reliability	Inter-tester reliability	Alternate forms	Speed of difficulty	Range of abnormalities samples	Brevity
Measuring change	–	–	–	++	–	–	+	++	–	++	+	–	++
Examining for impairment & diagnosis	++	++	+	++	–	–	+	–	+	–	++	+	+
Case description	++	++	+	++	+	+	+	–	+	–	++	++	–
Assessment for rehabilitation	+	–	+	+	–	+	–	–	+	+	+	++	–
Research	++	++	++	++	++	+/–	++	++	++	+/–	++	+	–

Key: ++ essential that the test has this feature for this purpose
+ desirable that the test has this feature for this purpose
+/– variable requirement for this feature
– this feature not important for this purpose
(1) Refers to test being a valid measure of appropriate memory function.
(2) Refers to test's ability to indicate presence of organic brain damage.
(3) Refers to test being a valid measure of everyday memory function.

therefore, be measured as the number of standard deviations below the mean that the patient's recall and recognition performance lies for someone of their age and intelligence. Second, tests must be valid and reliable. One kind of validity particularly relevant for clinical purposes is that a test should enable the examiner to determine whether patients will have problems in coping with daily life. Assessment of reliability is, of course, hard with memory tests because, unless memory is severely affected, subjects are likely to show improved performance when retested. Third, tests must satisfy specific requirements without which they will be of limited use. For example, tests of recall and recognition must have a wide range so that subjects with widely varying levels of memory do not perform at floor or ceiling levels, and tests must also be sensitive so that small changes in the underlying organic disturbance cause a change in performance. Whatever their other merits, nearly all existing tests of amnesia lack range and are relatively insensitive.

Problems in Satisfying Criteria

Some of the criteria, listed in Table 5.1, are in tension with each other. That is, if a test satisfies one criterion, it cannot satisfy another with which it is in tension. This tension exists most clearly between the criterion of brevity and those of sensitivity and, perhaps, range. This is because sensitive tests tend to require a large number of items and take some time to administer, and tests that tap a wide range of performance levels whilst avoiding floor and ceiling affects may also have to be given in a series of stages of graded difficulty, a procedure that also takes time. If two or more criteria cannot be simultaneously satisfied, then there can be no memory test or battery that perfectly fulfills all the different clinical and research goals for which tests can be devised. Thus for research purposes it is important to use time-consuming, sensitive tests whereas for some clinical purposes quicker, less sensitive tests are preferable.

In the remaining sections of this chapter we shall assess how well existing standard memory batteries and tests satisfy the criteria, enumerated in Table 5.1, as relevant to the fulfilment of various clinical and research goals. We shall also consider some of the problems in devising special purpose memory tests that are intended to advance our understanding of organic memory disorders, and finally make some recommendations and suggest ways in which testing procedures can be improved in the future.

A REVIEW OF CLINICAL MEMORY TESTS

In this section we discuss a number of existing memory tests and test batteries in relation to the criteria outlined earlier. We do not attempt to review all existing tests—this would probably be an impossible task, given the abundance of memory tests distributed by the major publishers, and *a fortiori*, the number of reports of different memory assessment procedures in the literature. However, an attempt has been made to cover the major tests and batteries likely to be available and in use in a typical psychology department. There are a wide variety of research and clinical situations requiring differing properties of assessment instruments, and our attempt here is perhaps more to facilitate the choice of "horses for courses" than to advocate the use of any one test or combination of tests. As will be discussed presently, most existing memory tests are deficient in some aspects.

Table 5.2 presents in summary form some of the main details of the various memory tests and test batteries under review. Most of the details summarised have been drawn from the original test manuals or papers where the tests were first described. In many instances, further standardisation work, revisions to the original tests, or critiques of the tests exist. We will first consider all of the batteries or tests individually with a brief description of each and some general remarks about its use, and will then discuss the tests generally in relation to the purposes for which tests may be required.

1. Wechsler Memory Scale (WMS)—Wechsler (1945)

The WMS is one of the oldest batteries in current use but it is still used widely. This is probably not on account of its intrinsic properties, which have frequently been criticised (Lezak, 1983, Erickson & Scott, 1977, Prigatano, 1977) but rather because it is convenient in use, widely available, commands an extensive literature, and has some demonstrated neuropsychological validity (e.g. Skilbeck & Woods, 1980).

The WMS is made up of seven subtests: Personal and Current Information—requiring the testee to state their age, date of birth, and the names of four prominent people; Orientation (five questions about year, month, day, location); Mental Control (three timed tasks: counting backwards, repetition of the alphabet, and counting in threes); Logical Memory (immediate repetition of two prose passages); Digit Span (forward and reversed); Visual Reproduction (immediate reproduction of geometrical designs from memory); and Paired-Associate learning (three trials of a list of ten word pairs where the testee has to provide the second word of each pair given the first word).

Administration usually takes about 25 minutes, though this can be longer in difficult cases. There are two alternate forms, though standardisation of form II is poor and its equivalence to form I is doubtful (Lezak, 1983). The test has been criticised on a number of other counts, including the reduction of subtest scores to a single memory quotient, excessive bias towards verbal

TABLE 5.2
Summary Details of Memory Batteries and Tests

Test/battery name	Subtests included	Measures yielded	Standardisation population	No. alternate forms	Typical admin time	Notes
(Old) Wechsler Memory Scale (WMS)	Personal and current info Orientation Mental control Logical memory Digit span Visual reproduction Associate learning	Memory quotient (norms + factors from other sources n n)	Form 1: 200 normal subjects between 20 and 50 Form 2: Adult student groups	2	30 mins	Additional norms available (see text)
Wechsler Memory Scale Revised (WMS-R)	Information and orientation Mental control Figural memory Logical memory Visual paired-associates I & II Visual reproduction I & II Digit Span Visual memory span	Indices of: Verbal memory Visual memory Attention/concentration Delayed recall	360 normal subjects in 6 age groups selected according to US population norms of Race, Geographic Region, Education & IQ	1	50 mins (30 mins without delayed recall)	I-immediate recall II-delayed recall
Rivermead Behavioural Memory Test (RBMT)	Recall of name Recall of belonging Recall of appointment Picture recognition Story recall I & II Delivering message I & II Orientation Date	Screening score Profile score	176 Brain-damaged S's 118 Control S's	4	25 mins	I-immediate recall II-delayed recall
Recognition Memory Test (RMT)	Recognition memory for words Recognition memory for faces	Recognition score (words) Recognition score (faces)	310 control in-patients without cerebral disease 134 patients with right hemisphere lesions 112 patients with left hemisphere lesions	1	15mins	

(continued)

Test/battery name	Subtests included	Measures yielded	Standardisation population	No. alternate forms	Typical admin time	Notes
Adult Memory and Information-Processing Battery (AMPIB)	Story recall I & II Figure recall I & II Word list learning Design learning Information processing A Information processing B	Age related norms ranges, and cut-off scores provided for each subtest	180 normal subjects, selected on basis of age, sex, social class and academic 54 neurological patients of varying aetiology	2	45 mins	I-immediate recall II-delayed recall
Luria-Nebraska Neuropsychological Battery (LNNB)	Word list learning Picture recognition Visual reproduction Rhythm reproduction Hand position reproduction Word repetition (with interference) Sentence repetition (with interference) Story recall Word-picture association	Scaled score	Numerous studies with neurological, control and psychiatric patients	1	15 mins	Part of larger battery
Benton Visual Retention Test (BVRT)	Visual reproduction Admin A: immediate reproduction after 10 seconds presentation Admin B: immediate reproduction after 5 seconds presentation Admin C: copying Admin D: reproduction after 15 secs following 10 secs presentation	No. correct score Error score	Admin A: 600 normal in and out patients-children and adults (aged 8–64) Admin B: 103 medical patients (16–60) with no history of brain disease Admin C: 200 medical patients (adults) + 236 children (6–13)	3	10–15 mins	4 administration methods - ABCD
Auditory-Verbal Learning Test (Rey) (AVLT)	Word list learning (with interference)	Recall score (Trials I-VI)	Manual labourers n=25 Professionals n=30 Students n=47 Elderly labourers (70–90) n=15 Elderly professionals n=15	1	15-20 mins	
Complex figure (Rey) (CFT)	Copying, immediate and delayed reproduction of complex figure	Recall score (various scoring methods available)	Various studies (see Lezak, 1983)	1	10 mins + delay time of 30-45 mins	
Williams Delayed Recall (WDRT)	Recall, prompted recall, and recognition of 9 object pictures	Test score	40 controls (graduates and nursing staff) 25 Neurotic 14 Depressive 22 Alcoholic 20 Organic	1	5 mins + interpolated delay of 10 minutes	

memory functions, absence of a delayed memory task, and an overly inclusive concept of memory function (Lezak, 1983). However, its continuing widespread use, and indeed, the criticism that it has attracted, testify to its importance and its ability to function at least as a screening instrument. Some of its shortcomings may be remedied to some extent by using additional published normative data (Hulicka, 1966, Ivinskis et al., 1971, Ivison, 1977, Klonoff & Kennedy, 1966) and by deriving factor scores, such as those suggested by Kear-Colwell (1973).

2. Wechsler Memory Scale—Revised (WMS-R) —Wechsler (1987)

A number of the criticisms levelled at the original WMS have been addressed in the publication of a revised version of the scale. The original scale has been expanded to include both new subtests (figural memory, visual paired-associates, and visual memory span), and provision has also been made for assessment of delayed recall of logical memory prose passages, verbal and visual paired-associates, and visual reproduction. Changes have also been made to the original subtests (amalgamation of personal and current information subscales, revision of logical memory stories and of scoring criteria, in the administration of paired-associates subtest). Scoring and interpretation have also been revised, and considerably more extensive norms have been provided for both normal and clinical populations, using stratified sampling techniques, for age, sex, race, and geographical region for the U.S. population. Instead of the single Memory Quotient, raw scores on individual subtests are now weighted and converted into scores on composites—verbal memory, visual memory, attention/concentration and delayed recall. (Optionally delayed recall tests can be omitted.) Index scores, derived from the sums of weighted scores on the composites can then be looked up in tables corresponding to the appropriate age group. It is therefore possible both to compare performance on subtests with the population norms for that age group, and also to compare performance between subtests for a particular individual. Extensive information is given in the manual on reliability, validity, and performance of selected clinical groups on the various scales.

The revised WMS therefore appears (potentially) to be considerably more satisfactory in a number of respects than its older brother—particularly in respect of normative data, information on standardisation, validity and reliability, scoring criteria (especially in logical memory), range of memory functions sampled, and provision for clinical interpretation of test results. This has been achieved at the cost of increased administration time, particularly if delayed recall is tested, abandonment of provision of an equivalent alternate form, and increased cost of the test. It is to be expected that a good deal of information on the WMS-R will become available over the coming years. A special issue of *The Clinical Neuropsychologist* (1988, Vol.2, part 2) contains a number of initial validity studies and is recommended reading.

3. Rivermead Behavioural Memory Test (RBMT)
—Wilson, Cockburn, and Baddeley (1985)

The RBMT differs from the majority of published memory tests and batteries in its explicit attempt to sample memory behaviours characteristic of everyday life, rather than the traditional "laboratory-type" learning and memory task. The subtests making up the battery consist of: (i) Remembering a name (given the photograph of a face); (ii) Remembering a belonging (some belonging of the testee is concealed, and the testee has to remember to ask for it back on completion of the test); (iii) Remembering a message after a delay; (iv) An object recognition task (ten pictures of objects are shown, and the testee then has to recognise these out of a set of 20 pictures shown after a delay); (v) A face recognition task (similar to object recognition, but using five faces to be recognised later among five distractors); (vi) A task involving remembering a route round the testing room; and (vi) Recall of a short story, both immediately and after a delay.

The tests are carried out in a fixed order, with intervening presentations filling the interval between presentation and test for previous subtests. The disparate nature of the various tests appears to reduce interference between subtests to minimal proportions, and the whole test can be completed within 25 minutes for most subjects. Face validity is high, and in our experience, the test is acceptable and even enjoyable to the large majority of testees.

Two methods of scoring the test are available: The simpler method consists of deriving a "screening score" by allocating 1 point for an adequate subtest response, and 0 points for a partial or complete failure. The average normal subject will obtain a near-perfect score, and the cut-off is set at three or more failures. The profile score provides a method of weighting raw scores, giving a wider range of scores and less of a ceiling effect than the screening score, though published data on its behaviour or significance are still sparse.

The test was originally standardised on a sample of 176 brain-damaged patients and 118 control subjects. Inter-rater reliability and parallel form reliability studies have been carried out, yielding satisfactory correlations between raters and between forms of the test. Validity studies have been undertaken, by comparing RBMT performance with other memory tests, and by comparison of RBMT test performance with ratings of "forgetting" carried out by therapists, using a checklist of behaviours during sessions. There are variable correlations of RBMT scores with other memory tests but correlations of RBMT scores with the number of memory lapses observed for individual patients suggest that the claim that the RBMT measures everyday memory performance is valid.

4. Recognition Memory Test (RMT)—Warrington (1984)

The RMT was developed with the stated aim: "To standardise and validate a memory test geared to detect minor degrees of memory deficit across a wide range of the adult population". It consists of two subtests: Recognition memory for words (RMW), and recognition memory for faces (RMF). Both subtests are administered in a similar fashion: Fifty words or fifty faces, ("unknown" males), are shown to the testee one at a time for three seconds each. The testee has to respond "yes" or "no" to each word or face depending on whether it is judged "pleasant" or "unpleasant" (this is a device to ensure attention to each item). Following the presentation of fifty words or faces, the testee is required to perform an immediate two-choice recognition task, with distractors drawn from the same pool as the previously presented stimulus item. A recognition paradigm was chosen to ensure comparability between the two parts of the test, and also because it is claimed to be less vulnerable to the effects of anxiety and depression (Coughlan & Hollows, 1984).

The test was standardised on patients with right- and left-hemisphere lesions as well as normal controls. It is therefore a useful measure where it is required to test for a specific verbal or non-verbal memory impairment and to compare the two, although Kapur (1987) has argued that there is a significant verbal component in the face recognition task. It is perhaps less useful as a screening instrument on account of the limited scope of the subtests and the relatively large amount of time needed to administer them.

5. Adult Memory and Information Processing Battery (AMIPB)—Coughlan and Hollows (1985)

The AMIPB represents a further attempt to produce a memory battery with adequate standardisation data on age, IQ, social class, and educational achievements for use with a clinical population. It is perhaps less well-known and widely used than the tests reviewed previously: This may be due more to the facts that it is published by the author, and is not advertised or distributed nationally, than to any intrinsic demerits of the test.

The battery contains six subtests: (1) Story recall (similar to WMS logical memory) but with detailed scoring guidelines; (2) Figure copying and recall (the testee has to copy a complex figure, and then reproduce it from memory immediately and after 30 minutes delay); (3) A word list learning task (a list of fifteen words is presented for immediate recall up to a total of five presentations, followed by a simple presentation of another fifteen-word list with one recall trial, and a further trial of list A; (4) A design learning task where the subject has to reproduce a design connecting dots in a 4x4 array. (Up to five learning trials with the first design are given, followed by a single presentation and recall trial of a second design with a further recall of the first design); (5) Information processing A (the testee has to cancel the highest number in a list consisting of arrays of five two-digit numbers, followed by a motor speed test, where cancellation of numbers alone is required); (6) Information processing B also requires the testee to work through a list of items consisting of four- and five-digit numbers separated by a hyphen, the subject's task being to identify and cancel the digit which is not in the four-digit number. A motor speed task again follows.

Detailed scoring instructions and norms are provided for the test, which exists in two parallel forms. It is not necessary to give all subtests, as norms for individual subtests are provided, together with suggested cut-off points for different age ranges, and percentile figures for obtained scores.

Standardisation was carried out on approximately 180 subjects for each version of the test, and data is provided on age, sex, social class, and academic status for the sample. Additional background data is provided on IQ, mood state, and performance on the RMT. Correlations with other memory tests, test-retest correlations, and inter-test correlations appear to be generally satisfactory. The test was additionally given to 54 neurological patients of varying aetiology, with significantly higher incidence of poor performance of neurological subjects on most measures.

The aforementioned batteries constitute the major memory test batteries which are available for use on clinical populations and appear either to have received extensive use on such populations and/or to have adequate standardisation and validation data. However, this by no means exhausts the range of tests and other assessment devices available, and some additional instruments will now briefly be described.

6. Luria-Nebraska Neuropsychological Examination —Memory Scale (LNMS—Golden et al. (1980)

This scale is part of the larger Luria-Nebraska examination, and in line with the general principles used in this examination, most of its subtests consist of a brief administration of one or two items of a particular task, so this scale samples a relatively wide range of memory functions briefly in contrast to the more usual strategy of repeated observations on a restricted range of tasks. As such, it can be useful for an initial screening battery, though clinicians might usually wish to investigate any apparent deficits shown by this scale in more detail before reaching any firm conclusions, although in principle a cut-off score can be calculated for performance on this scale alone. An additional feature is that it contains tasks which do not appear in other tests, such as asking subjects to predict how many words in a list they are likely to remember, word-picture association, and memory for hand position. Unfortunately, the norms provided in the manual and the construction of the test are not sufficient for confident interpretation of the significance of failures on such tasks.

7. Benton Revised Visual Retention Test (BVRT)
—Benton (1974)

In this test, the testee is shown a series of ten figures to draw from memory. The figures consist of line drawings of geometric shapes, either one or three on a card. Some parts of the stimulus are easily verbalisable ("triangle", "a small square"), others are more complex, but still potentially verbalisable to some degree. ("a vee shape with straight sides at the top"). Various possible administrations exist (see table 5.2), but the most commonly used one, for which most normative data is available is administration A: Presentation of the stimulus for 10 seconds, followed by immediate reproduction on its removal. Responses are scored in terms of number correct and also number of errors, and a detailed analysis of the types of error can be made using guidelines in the manual. The manual gives guidelines for interpretation of both quantitative and qualitative results.

Within the limitations imposed by the single task, the test remains useful as a screening device for memory impairment. The design makes it possible to pick up perseverative errors giving a useful indication of frontal lobe impairment, and in addition, significant visuo-perceptual or visuo-spatial errors are likely to show themselves on this test.

8. Auditory-verbal learning test (AVLT)—Rey (1964)

Of the many word learning tests available, the AVLT is one of the most widely used, as it can give measures of immediate memory span and susceptibility to interference, as well as giving an opportunity to study the strategy used by the testee undergoing a learning task. Five presentations of a 15-word list (list A) are given, each followed by attempted recall. A second 15-word list (list B) is read, followed by a recall trial of this list, and then another recall trial of list A. It is possible to give a delayed recall trial of list A, and also a recognition trial of list A following the last list A recall trial, which can give information about the nature of any recall difficulty that is found, (Lezak, 1983).

The AVLT is perhaps better seen as a test paradigm, rather than a fixed test (in the sense of the remainder of the tests reviewed up to this point). An equivalent form of the AVLT word-lists and recognition test is available if re-testing is required (Crawford, Stewart, & Moore, 1989), and pictorial stimuli could be used instead. The available norms (Lezak, 1983) are perhaps better regarded as aids to diagnostic interpretation than a representative sampling of the clinical or normal population, but as the intention of the test is more as a tool for qualitative analysis of verbal learning and memory than a device for detecting impairment, this is not a serious drawback.

9. Rey-Osterreith Complex Figure Test (CFT)—Rey (1941), Osterreith (1944)

As with the AVLT, this test, using a complex figure originally devised by Rey is perhaps more of a paradigm than a specific test. Various methods of administration and scoring are described in Lezak (1983). Typically, the testee is presented with Rey's complex line drawing and requested to copy it. The original and copy are then removed, and the testee is asked to draw the figure again from memory. A third delayed reproduction trial can then be given.

Various scoring methods have been proposed with the aim of reflecting both qualitative and quantitative aspects of the testee's performance, as the purpose of the test is again to reveal aspects of the testee's learning and recall strategy, as well as to discover any perceptual deficits or difficulties that may be present in organising response. As with the AVLT, the CFT can be a useful test in the hands of an experienced clinician as a diagnostic guide, but will be less useful if a quantitative assessment of the degree of impairment is required.

10. Williams Delayed Recall Test. (Williams—1968)

This test is the main survivor of a battery of tests proposed by Williams for the assessment of memory disorders. It is worth a brief mention as it is easy to give, and although the norms are rudimentary, appears to have clinical validity as a brief screening test. A card with nine line drawings of objects is given to the testee to name, so that total exposure time is around one minute. After a period of ten minutes, the testee is requested to recall as many of the objects as possible. Prompts are then given for those items not recalled. If there still remain unrecalled items, a card with the original nine pictures and nine distractors is shown, and the testee asked to indicate the originals. Different weights are given to items: Recalled, recalled with prompt, recognised, and not recognised or recalled, and an overall score can be calculated. It is also possible to gain a qualitative impression of the relative efficiency of recall, prompted recall, and recognition, which can be valuable for both diagnostic and rehabilitation purposes, though this test on its own cannot be said to provide a definitive analysis.

Do the Tests Fulfill the Criteria?

Having described a number of tests and batteries for the measurement of memory function, in this section we will consider their appropriateness for the various assessment tasks described in the introduction: Measuring change, examining for impairment, diagnosis and case description, rehabilitation, and research.

Assuming that testees will act as their own controls, the major requirements of a test measuring change are: (a) that the test is a valid measure of the type of memory under scrutiny (b) that the test is sensitive to a change in the function of this type of memory; and (c) that the test can be repeatedly administered—implying a need for brevity and for the existence of alternate forms. Criteria (a) and (b) may dictate the use of specially-designed tests; of the standard tests, the RBMT and BVRT have the largest number of alternate forms and are reasonably brief, so from the point of view of criterion (c), they may be the most satisfactory. If memory impairment is severe and retest intervals are not so short, it may be possible to re-administer the same test form repeatedly, in which case existence of alternate forms becomes less important.

Examination for memory impairment requires the ability to detect lowering of memory function relative to some expected level. The question is, therefore, whether the person has a level of memory function commensurate with their age and IQ, and its answer, therefore, requires a test with satisfactory age and IQ norms. The most extensive norms of this type are available with the WMS-R and Luria-Nebraska tests, although the WMS, AMPIB, RMT, and BVRT are also supplied with some norms of this type.

The function of diagnosis goes beyond a simple examination for impairment in that the question at issue is whether a given pattern of impairment reflects the presence of a certain lesion or condition. Examples of such questions are whether an observed memory impairment is functional or organic in origin, whether an impairment reflects a dementing or a depressive illness, or whether a particular condition (e.g. normal pressure hydrocephalus) is present. Sometimes one may wish to use a particular pattern of impairment as a localising sign for a brain lesion. Such diagnostic questions are diverse, and cannot all necessarily be answered by a single test battery. The basic necessity is to have information about the performance of appropriate diagnostic groups on the test in question. With the exceptions of the WMS-R and Luria-Nebraska, information supplied in test manuals on performance of diagnostic groups is usually limited to information about the overall test performance of a fairly heterogeneous group of neurologically impaired patients, indicating recourse to clinical experience or particular articles in the literature where performance of relevant patient groups on a given test has been studied.

We have used the term "case description" for the situation where a general work-up of a patient's impairments and difficulties is required. Specification of memory impairments may be part of a more general review of all aspects of cognitive and perceptual function. What is required here may be an analysis of memory function in both auditory and visual modalities, information about memory function under immediate and delayed test conditions, specification of the relative impairments in recall and recognition, and possibly an analysis of retrograde amnesia and long-term recall. This kind of analysis may be requested, say, in the case of a head injury patient where it is required to know what type of difficulty they may face on discharge or return to employment. In medico-legal cases, where compensation is an issue, it will be particularly important to have a comprehensive description of all aspects of memory function and where possible an indication of how this will influence day-to-day work and leisure functioning and the likely persistence of any impairments found.

No one test of those reviewed is likely to be able to provide a comprehensive case description of this type, though most of the tests can contribute one or more elements. The WMS-R, for example will provide an analysis of verbal and visual memory function, both immediate and delayed. It will also give information about concentration and attention. However, long-term recall and retrograde amnesia are only examined very cursorily, and the relationship of test performance to everyday life function is unclear. There is also no built-in method to examine the relative efficiency of recognition vs recall, and the influence of intervening material or events is difficult to establish. The RBMT appears to have the best-established relationship to everyday memory function in the case of major neurological impairments, but milder cases will perform at ceiling, and the possible influence of minor memory impairments on work performance, which may be significant, will be difficult to establish using this test alone. Again, here, there is no clear method for examining the relative efficiency of recognition vs recall or to analyse long-term recall. As the tests are relatively easy, there is no satisfactory measure of the ability to learn and retain a more complex task. For this purpose, something like the Rey AVLT might be a useful addition, giving a measure of the ability to master a list of items beyond the immediate memory span, with some indication of the learning strategy adopted, and susceptibility to interference. However, the very repetitiveness and difficulty of the AVLT makes it unacceptable to some patients.

As in all assessment situations, the precise questions asked and information sought along with the current abilities of the patient will determine the ultimate choice of measures used. No one test on its own is likely to be sufficient for a comprehensive case description. It is worth noting at this point, for the purposes of the final discussion, that there is no standardised test of long-term recall and analysis of retrograde amnesia, although a number of potentially suitable methods have been described in the literature. No test allows a deliberate analysis of the learning and remembering strategy adopted by the testee, and in most tests, comparison of recall and recognition performance is at best implicit, even though their relative efficiencies may have considerable clinical and practical significance.

We distinguish assessment for rehabilitation purposes from case description because while there is a considerable overlap between the two situations, assessment for rehabilitation introduces a number of additional elements. First, there will be an emphasis on discovery of intact skills and abilities, rather than simply of impairments. Second, there must be some assessment of the subjective importance of particular deficits in planning a rehabilitation programme, as a patient will be more likely to work on areas of function which are important to them. Third, an analysis of existing strategies of learning and memory and the effects of manipulating these strategies is likely to be helpful. Fourth, it will be necessary to establish a baseline and monitor change when implementing a rehabilitation programme. In general, the more a test is able to suggest and predict the success of particular rehabilitative techniques, the more useful it will be in the planning of a rehabilitation programme.

None of the tests or batteries described earlier, or any known to the authors, are particularly satisfactory for rehabilitation purposes. This is not surprising, as all have been designed with assessment of impairment in mind, not its remediation, so none contain any element of assessment of the subjective impact of memory problems. Neither is there any attempt to investigate or manipulate the testee's strategy of approach to the various memory tasks (e.g. Do they use visual imagery in a paired associate learning test? Can they be made to do so? Does this aid recall?). A test such as the RBMT, with its four alternate forms and use of everyday life tasks is likely to be the most useful in monitoring change during a rehabilitation programme, and would provide a useful test of the generalisation of specific rehabilitation tasks. However, no test of those we have reviewed can do more than to provide some indication of the areas that might need to be addressed by a rehabilitation programme, and at present, further experimentation and assessment of a less formal kind is necessary in designing a rehabilitation programme.

Much current research is about amnesia and such work depends on the availability of standardised memory tests from which it is possible to derive sensitive measures of severity of amnesia rather than simply an index of how poor memory is. (Although the two are usually correlated.) No existing test provides a sensitive measure of amnesia. If future ones are to do so, more care will have to be devoted to developing IQ- and age-related norms and longer tests will need to be developed. There are also other ways of increasing sensitivity. For example, forced-choice recognition tests could have more than one foil as this will reduce random variations across test sessions. Development of standard memory tests in the context of research is discussed more fully in the next section.

To summarise the discussion of this section, the most satisfactory role of existing tests is in the area of detection of impairment. Many will also provide information for diagnostic purposes, but there is a lack of formal procedures to detect functional from organic memory impairment, and in general, norms for specific clinical sub-groups are lacking. The length, complexity, and diversity of most test batteries makes them less suitable for monitoring change, where a brief, repeatable measure appropriate to the type of memory function under scrutiny is required. Case description is also reasonably well-served by existing techniques, with the proviso that little of a standardised nature is available to analyse long-term recall and retrograde amnesia, and that there is some question about the relevance of test performance to everyday life memory function. None of the tests appear to have been designed with rehabilitation in mind, and this is probably the area in which all the tests reviewed are weakest, giving little indication about the type of remediation technique, if any, that is likely to prove fruitful.

RESEARCH AND MEMORY TEST DEVELOPMENT

Our understanding of organic memory disorders is still far from complete and the inadequacies of contemporary standardised tests are partially a result of this fact. Future research will increase understanding and hence enable improved standardised memory tests to be developed. This section will consider some of the specific ways in which research can achieve this goal and will discuss the particular problems of developing special purpose memory tests. The focus will be on the amnesic syndrome because this is the most frequently encountered disorder and the one about which most is known.

Problems in Measuring Severity of Amnesia

One of the aims of memory assessment is to determine just how amnesic a patient is. Currently, this aim is very poorly achieved. Assessment faces two kinds of problems. First, how poor a patient's memory is does not correlate perfectly with severity of amnesia. Memory seems to depend on the efficiency of the kinds of processing that are measured by intelligence tests and on the unknown processes that are disturbed in organic amnesics. Although these processes are largely unknown, they appear to be independent of the ones that are tapped by currently used intelligence tests. So, the measured intelligence of some amnesics may show no decline from its premorbid levels despite the fact that their recall and recognition memory is now grossly impaired. Many patients, however, show a decline in both their intelligence and their memory post-morbidly so it becomes a problem to determine what proportion of the memory reduction is caused by amnesia and what proportion by their lowered intelligence. Second, it is still unknown whether amnesia is caused by the loss of one function or whether it comprises several partially correlated functional losses. If the latter possibility obtains, then it would be inappropriate to use one index of amnesic severity. Furthermore, in patients with poor memory and reduced intelligence, if there were several indices, then their calculation might depend on giving a different weighting to the effect of the decline in intelligence.

These problems can be given content by discussing current thinking about the possible heterogeneity of amnesia. It is generally accepted that left-sided limbic-diencephalic lesions selectively cause an amnesia specific to verbalisable material whereas right-sided limbic-diencephalic lesions cause an amnesia for material that is difficult to verbalise (Mayes, 1988a). A patient's assessment should therefore provide a measure of the severity of both material—specific kinds of amnesia. This is useful even in patients with bilateral lesions because impairment is still often significantly more severe for one kind of material than the other. Great care needs to be taken to ensure that memory for the material chosen is only affected by lesions within one hemisphere. This is particularly hard to achieve with difficult-to-verbalise material as is apparent from Kapur's (1987) criticism of Warrington's RMT to the effect that recognition of the faces used in the test is sensitive to left hemisphere lesions because easily describable details external to the faces are visible on the pictures. Assessment of verbal and non-verbal amnesia is also made harder because patients often show differential reductions in verbal and non-verbal intelligence as well as in verbal and non-verbal memory. For example, a patient's recognition of faces may be significantly worse than recognition of words, but there may also be a significantly greater reduction in the WAIS Performance Scale score relative to the Verbal Scale score. In such cases current knowledge does not permit accurate estimation of the severity of verbal and non-verbal amnesia. This is largely because we still do not know to what extent verbal memory is determined by verbal intelligence and to what extent different kinds of non-verbal memory are determined by intelligence measures such as those provided by the Performance Scale of the WAIS. One way of resolving the problem would be to give large numbers of intact people tests of verbal and non-verbal intelligence and memory and then to determine the correlations between the intelligence and memory scores.

Other Possible Amnesic Sub-syndromes

The other kinds of possible heterogeneity of the amnesic syndrome are far more polemical and much more research will be needed before it is known whether or not they are genuine. First, it has been suggested that anterograde and retrograde amnesia are potentially dissociable disorders, caused by lesions to distinct, if overlapping, neural systems (Mayes, 1988a). Second, it has been suggested that amnesias caused by medial temporal limbic system and midline diencephalic lesions are distinct in that only the former is associated with pathologically fast rates of forgetting and also, possibly, a different kind of retrograde amnesia (Mayes, 1988a). Third, Mishkin (1982) has argued that permanent severe amnesia only occurs if there is damage both to a hippocampal-diencephalic circuit and to an amygdala-diencephalic circuit. If appropriately formulated, these dichotomies could each apply to the patient population and so there could be as many as eight sub-syndromes subsumed under the rubric of amnesia. Thus, medial temporal lobe limbic system lesions might cause a hippocampal circuit anterograde amnesia subsyndrome and a retrograde amnesia subsyndrome together with an amygdalar circuit anterograde amnesia subsyndrome and a retrograde amnesia subsyndrome. There might also be the same number of diencephalic subsyndromes. This would mean that a full assessment of an amnesic would require eight indices of severity of impairment, or sixteen if these impairments could take verbal or hard-to-verbalise material-specific forms. Converting level of memory measures into measures of severity of amnesia might present different problems for the different indices. For example, if retrograde and anterograde amnesia are dissociable disorders, then the retrograde amnesia measure might need less adjustment than the anterograde in patients with post-morbidly reduced intelligence. This is because remote memories would have been established when intelligence was intact and are only retrieved with the traumatically reduced processing ability, whereas with anterograde amnesia the affected memories must be both established and retrieved when intelligence has already been reduced.

It remains possible, however, that only the two material specific measures of amnesic severity are necessary and that the other claims of amnesic heterogeneity will not stand up to scrutiny. Examination of the claims depends critically on the use of appropriate non-standardised as well as standardised memory tests. The problems faced in examining the claims will be discussed in some detail because they illustrate the difficulties involved in constructing special purpose memory tests. With respect to the claim that retrograde and anterograde amnesia are dissociable disorders, the aim is to determine whether the two forms of amnesia can occur in isolation and whether, when they occur together, the severity of one correlates poorly with the severity of the other. This aim can be achieved only if the proper measures of severity are used and tests of retrograde and anterograde amnesia are of similar sensitivity, where sensitivity indicates the ability of a test to detect a specified change in the underlying process being measured. To consider the second claim first, it is invalid to conclude that a patient has a selective anterograde amnesia if performance is normal on a very insensitive test of pre-morbid memory. Some attempt must be made to ensure that tests of both pre- and post-morbid memory respond to equally small changes in the underlying memory processes. Even if this is done and the two disorders are dissociable, one may fail to find either in isolation because the lesions responsible for each deficit overlap. Demonstration of the dissociation would then have to rely largely on showing that severity of retrograde and anterograde amnesia do not necessarily correlate in amnesic patients. But failure to find a correlation may result from the fact that brain damage has lowered patients' intelligence and that this necessitates a different correction factor for measures of anterograde and retrograde amnesia. In other words, the measure of severity may be differentially distorted if no allowance is made for the fact that, in patients with lowered intelligence, severity of retrograde amnesia is less influenced by such reductions in current processing abilities than is anterograde amnesia.

As patients will differ in the extent to which brain damage has affected their intelligence, correlations are likely to be artefactually small. Until it is known to what extent changes in intelligence affect retrograde and anterograde amnesia, correlations should only be treated as reliable in patients who have suffered minimal decreases in post-morbid intelligence.

Psychogenic Memory Problems

The examination of the possibility that retrograde and anterograde amnesias are dissociable must also allow for another possibility that is often ignored in research on organic amnesia. That is, the risk that the organic amnesia may be compounded by motivated forgetting, something that can only be identified by using specially devised tests. In other words, the patients may either be suffering from some kind of hysterical amnesia or actually be faking it. This risk is particularly worrying in the few cases of isolated retrograde amnesia that have been reported (see Mayes, 1988a) because hysterical amnesias are usually confined to pre-traumatic events and because it is very hard to think of a convincing organic explanation of such selective memory disturbances. Conscious malingering can, of course, produce the appearance of anterograde amnesia as easily as retrograde, so it is important to have general means of distinguishing between organic and motivated forgetting. Although no standardised tests exist for identifying whether there is an hysterical amnesia or that faking is occurring, special purpose memory tests can be constructed to make such identifications on the basis of two major principles. Both assume that faking and hysterical amnesia work in the same way. The first principle makes use of the fact that people hold erroneous beliefs about memory and that this can lead them to behave in ways not found in organic amnesia. For example, Schacter (1986) has found that fakers do not show the same kind of feeling-of-knowing effect as genuine forgetters. The success of tests that rely on erroneous beliefs in identifying non-organic causes of forgetting depends, of course, on how sophisticated the subjects are. The second principle does not do so because it makes use of the fact that more automatic kinds of memory are hard to fake. A good example of the application of this principle is found in a case study by Kapur et al. (1986) of a patient with an apparent isolated organic retrograde amnesia. The patient's ability to learn a list of "counterfactual" paired names and occupations such as "John Newcombe — actor" was compared with that of a group of matched controls with similar learning ability. The patient learned the list more effectively indicating that unlike the controls he was not accessing information from remote memory about the well-known people in the list. One problem in relying on the second principle in constructing discriminative tests is that not all kinds of "automatic" memory are impaired in amnesics. Indeed, it is a central topic of research as to exactly what kinds of automatic memory are preserved in amnesics and what are not. Some evidence suggests that there are kinds of automatic memory that are preserved in some amnesics, but not others (see Mayes, 1988a, for a review). The creation of good standardised tests to discriminate hysterical from organic amnesia therefore partly depends on characterising the features of organic amnesia more clearly.

Measuring Rate of Forgetting

Assessment of the claim that some amnesics forget pathologically quickly whereas others do not, involves different problems. These primarily concern test construction and have been discussed by Mayes (1986), but it is also important to look at forgetting over a number of different time intervals and to partial out the possible influence of severity of amnesia on forgetting rate (patients with medial temporal lobe lesions might have a qualitatively similar amnesia to patients with medial diencephalic lesions, but one which is usually more severe). The main procedure that has been used to date equates recognition between amnesics and their controls by giving the former learning exposures that can be up to 20 times as long as those allowed controls (Huppert & Piercy, 1978). As lists typically contain 120 or so items and the initial test occurs ten minutes after the last item is shown, patients are actually tested at longer average item-to-test delays than are controls. For example, whereas controls may be tested after an average 12 minute item-to-test delay, some patients may be tested after delays as long as 50 minutes. If controls were tested at such delays, then their recognition might be 10% or more worse than that actually reported.

The technique as currently used, therefore, could be seriously underestimating amnesic forgetting rates, particularly with patients who are most amnesic. There is no perfect solution for this problem, but it is possible to match average item-to-test delay by having the same interval between items during learning exposure, but dividing this interval between exposure proper and engagement in some irrelevant activity. Exposure proper is increased in proportion to how disturbed memory is. There is some evidence that when this procedure is used with patients, who have diencephalic lesions, then they forget faster than controls (Mayes, 1988b), although this has never been found with the unmodified Huppert and Piercy procedure. The initial delay used in this study was only two minutes, however, and this could have been equally significant. Pathologically fast forgetting may be most prevalent immediately following post-presentation distraction with the patients in whom it is found. Indeed, Parkin, and Leng (1988) have found some evidence to support this possibility over the first five minutes following learning. Whichever interval forgetting rate is examined over the procedure should be sensitive to variations in forgetting rate. Unfortunately, there are reasons for believing that available procedures are not sensitive (Politynska, personal communication).

Disproportionate Memory Deficits and Problems with Sensitivity

If Mishkin (1982) is correct and lesions to a hippocampal circuit cause different kinds of memory losses from those caused by lesions to an amygdalar circuit, then a slightly different pattern of impairment would be expected in patients, most of whose damage lies either in hippocampal or amygdalar circuitry. One possibility is that lesions to these circuits cause distinct deficits in aspects of background spatiotemporal memory and that poor memory for these features produces the more general memory loss that is characteristic of amnesia (Mayes, 1988a).

If permanent, severe amnesia is caused by two kinds of dissociable and selective failure of contextual memory, then patients should be disproportionately bad in their memory for such material relative to their memory for "target" information and conversely be normal at those kinds of memory (if they exist) that do not require retrieval of contextual information. Current research is concerned with examining these possibilities. It has to cope with two design and methodological issues. The first is the problem of how to determine whether one kind of memory is more impaired than another (Mayes, 1986; 1988a). This problem partly relates to the second and more general issue of trying to ensure that contrasted tests are of roughly equal sensitivity. Clearly, a form of memory may mistakenly be thought to be preserved in amnesics if the test used to assess it is grossly insensitive. Similarly, if patients appear to be more impaired on one test relative to another, then that might simply be caused by the insensitivity of the second test.

Test sensitivity is affected by many things including floor and ceiling effects, the point on the scale between floor and ceiling where the tested subjects fail, and, most importantly, the proportion of inter-subject variability that is determined by random factors and the proportion that is determined by changes in the process being measured—error and true variance. Calev et al. (1983) have made an interesting attempt to equate the sensitivity of contrasted tests of recognition and recall by designing the two tasks so that they are matched on several statistics, including mean and various measures of variance. In research on forms of memory that may be preserved in amnesics, such as various kinds of priming, it is generally assumed that the tests of priming are not insensitive because scores on them can be affected more strongly than those on recognition or recall tests by applying certain manipulations such as varying delay. Although the conclusion may be correct, the inference is dubious. Priming and recognition may be affected equally (or almost equally) by certain common processes, but evidence also suggests that each is affected by at least one process that does not affect the other form of memory. If varying delay over the range used mainly affects one of these latter processes, then one learns little about the relative sensitivity of the tests of priming and recognition. Only if the commonly influential processes are being manipulated can one make inferences about the relative sensitivity of the two kinds of memory test.

Even if one is fairly sure that the sensitivities of two contrasted memory tests have been matched, one still needs to interpret why patients are more impaired on one of the tests relative to the other. For example, a group of amnesics may perform two standard deviations worse than their controls on a test of recognition and four standard deviations worse on an equally sensitive test of recall. But this pattern of performance might be found in normal people whose memory was equally bad as a result of: Being tested after a long delay; after brief learning exposures; after having to learn much more material; or some combination of these manipulations. The only way to be sure that the amnesic pattern of memory performance is qualitatively distinct from that shown by normal people is to test the normal people under a variety of harder conditions so as to match amnesic-normal performance on one of the tests and then see how the two groups compare on the other test when the learning conditions are repeated. If the amnesics are still worse than their controls on one of the tests, then a *prima facie* case has been made for the view that the cause of their poor memory is qualitatively distinct from that of normal forgetting. However, it would still need to be shown that their performance pattern related to amnesia rather than an incidental additional impairment.

This section has focussed on research into amnesia, but the problems discussed here are likely to crop up when other kinds of memory disorder are examined. For example, research concerned with material-specific semantic memory deficits must take into account how much memory for different kinds of categorical material varies in normal people for reasons that have nothing to do with organic efficiency or damage. Only if great care is applied will research into memory disorders provide a sound basis for improvements in existing standard tests of organic memory deficits. At present, as this section indicates, most work is focussed on amnesia and current research is concerned with: Resolving whether more than one index of amnesia is necessary; how to refine measures of amnesia as opposed to simply impaired memory; and how to develop more sensitive measures of severity of amnesia. But whether one is concerned with standardisation or special purpose memory tests, they all need to satisfy most, or all, of the criteria listed in table one.

FUTURE DIRECTIONS FOR TEST DEVELOPMENT

It is clear from this review and others covering similar territory (Erickson & Scott, 1977; Mayes, 1986) that much work remains to be done in further developing assessment instruments and techniques, both to further our understanding of the nature of memory disorders and for better clinical assessment. In this final section, we summarise our view of the main future developments which in our opinion are needed to meet the needs identified earlier. There are three main types of development we would advocate. The first is the development of standardised measures for the assessment of various aspects of memory disorder which currently have no accepted standard measure:

1. Measures are needed to discriminate organic from non-organic (functional) memory impairment. Functional impairments can range from deliberate faking of poor performance through a loss of confidence and anxiety in a situation which places demands on memory, to frank hysterical amnesia. Experienced clinicians may develop a "feel" for such matters, but more formal assessments are still desirable. A variety of tests have been proposed for identifying memory deficits of psychogenic origin, (Lezak, 1983, p. 618,) which exemplify the first principle (outlined in the research section), that exploits subjects' false knowledge of memory's operation. Future tests should be based on this principle and the second one (described earlier), that tests of automatic memory are hard to fake.

2. There is a need to develop measures of subjective aspects of memory function, particularly of a patient's knowledge of their own memory function and their insight into deficits they may have, and also the subjective importance of the various difficulties they may have. The accuracy of metamemory may have diagnostic significance (Luria, 1966) as well as significance for rehabilitation. A number of questionnaires about everyday memory and metamemory exist (Herrmann, 1984), but none appear to have been sufficiently validated for routine clinical use.

3. A further desirable development would be the availability of standardised tests for retrograde amnesia. A number of different kinds of tests have been developed, including: Public events questionnaires; tasks involving identification of famous people and faces; a price estimation task (Wilson & Cockburn, 1988); and autobiographical schedules (Baddeley & Wilson, 1986) and interviews (Kopelman, Wilson & Baddeley, 1989). Although such measures are inevitably country- and culture-specific, and little is known about the comparability of different measures, there are both theoretical and practical reasons motivating development of such tests. One kind of test that should be easy to update and score could involve forced-choice recognition of famous names and faces. Such tests might be selectivity sensitive to verbal and non-verbal forms of retrograde amnesia, and could easily be expanded to ask further questions about recognised items. If names were selected that were only famous for limited times, (e.g. Lillian Board), the tests could be used to see whether retrograde amnesia is temporally graded.

4. If evidence for the existence of subtypes of organic amnesia continues to grow, it may be necessary to develop specific indices of the various components of the amnesic syndrome. The nature of such possible subtypes has been discussed in the section concerned with research, and to ensure both comparability of different amnesic groups in research studies as well as for diagnostic and rehabilitation purposes, indices of such things as the relative

severity of retrograde and anterograde amnesia, and the rate of forgetting, may be desirable.

5. For rehabilitation purposes, deeper analysis of both normal and impaired subjects' strategies in performing memory tasks may allow both more rational planning of rehabilitation programmes, and also the kind of rehabilitation strategy likely to benefit a given patient. This would imply the development of techniques to investigate the extent to which a patient, both spontaneously and under instruction, would: Attend to the temporal and spatial context of material to be remembered; would categorise material; use visual imagery; or generate cues for recall.

The second main aspect of development we would advocate for both existing memory assessment instruments and for those to be developed, is improved normative data. We need to know more about the behaviour of existing instruments in both normal and impaired populations, for example: The extent to which, in the normal population, verbal memory correlates with verbal IQ and non-verbal memory with performance IQ, and more generally, the relationship between memory and intelligence tests.

Existing methods of collecting such normative data are in many ways time-consuming and cumbersome. Individual research studies and different centres have different protocols and favour different standard tests, or frequently report results of non-standard tests. Clinical psychologists, who have the most day-to-day exposure to amnesic patients frequently have little time to collate and report on the extensive test results lying in their filing cabinets. Such considerations lead us to the final development we would advocate, which is the exploitation of the potential of automated psychological testing and data collection to a much greater degree than before.

Although there are some limitations to automated memory testing (for example, verbal responses cannot be fed directly into the computer at present), these are relatively minor in comparison to the potential benefits. Test administration can be standardised precisely, responses can be timed accurately, and detailed analysis of responses can easily be performed. It is also potentially possible to facilitate large-scale data collection, as clinical testing and test-scoring time is reduced. Standardisation of test and patient description protocols across centres would increase comparability of results, and would also enable clinical psychologists without access to substantial research time and facilities to contribute their data more readily. The fact that tests and normative data exist on magnetic media rather than in printed form means that both modifications and extensions to test protocols and updating of norms becomes considerably easier.

For these reasons we think that the development of an automated test battery for memory impairment will provide an important stimulus to both clinical and research work in this field. Such a battery will need to be flexible and contain a wide variety of measures which can be used both singly and in combination. It should contain not only analogues of the traditional measures of memory function, but also: Measures of the type advocated in this review, such as questionnaires and checklists relating to subjective aspects of memory function and metamemory; dynamic tests of visual and auditory memory which are hard to administer by other than automated means; and suitable screening measures to enable discrimination of perceptual, language, and concentration deficits from memory deficits. Most importantly, perhaps, data handling and storage protocols need to be standardised, so that direct access to data is possible for a number of different research centres, and that development of norms and validation can be facilitated and speeded up.

REFERENCES

Benton, A. L. (1974). *Revised Visual Retention Test.* New York: The Psychological Corporation.
Baddeley, A., & Wilson, B. (1986). Amnesia, autobiographical memory, and confabulation. In D. C. Rubin (Ed.), *Autobiographical Memory.* Cambridge: Cambridge University Press.
Calev, A., Venables, P. H., & Monk, A. H. (1983). Evidence for distinct verbal memory pathologies in severely and mildly disturbed schizophrenics. *Schizophrenia Bulletin, 9,* 247–264.
Coughlan, A. K., & Hollows, S. E. (1984). The use of memory tests in differentiating organic disorder from depression. *British Journal of Psychiatry, 145,* 164–167.
Coughlan, A. K., & Hollows, S. E. (1985). *The Adult Memory and Information Processing Battery* (A. K. Coughlan) St James's University Hospital, Leeds.
Crawford, J.R., Stewart, L.E., & Moore, J.W. (1989). Demonstration of savings on the AVLT and development of a parallel form. *Journal of Clinical and Experimental Neuropsychology. 11,* 975–981.
Erickson, R. C., & Scott, M. L. (1977). Clinical memory testing: A review. *Psychological Bulletin, 84,* 1130–1149.
Golden, L. J., Hammeke, T. A., & Purisch, A. D. (1980). *The Luria-Nebraska Neuropsychological Examination.* Los Angeles: Western Psychological Services.
Herrmann, D. J. (1984). Questionnaires about memory. In J. E. Harris & P. E. Morris (Eds.), *Everyday memory, actions and absent-mindedness* (pp. 133-151). London: Academic Press.
Huppert, F. A., & Piercy, M. (1978). *Dissociation between learning and remembering in organic amnesia, 275,* 317–318.
Ivinskis, A., Allen, S., & Shaw, E. (1971). An extension of Wechsler Memory Scales norms to lower age groups. *Journal of Clinical Psychology, 27,* 354–357.
Ivison, D. J. (1977). The Wechsler Memory Scale: Preliminary findings toward an Australian standardisation. *Australian Psychologist, 12,* 303–312.
Kapur, N. (1987). Some comments on the technical acceptability of Warrington's Recognition Memory Test. *British Journal of Clinical Psychology, 26,* 144–146.
Kapur, N., Heath, P., Meudell, P., & Kennedy, P. (1986). Amnesia can facilitate memory performance: Evidence from a patient with dissociated retrograde amnesia. *Neuropsychologia, 24,* 215–221.
Kear-Colwell, J. J. (1973). The structure of the Wechsler Memory Scale and its relationship to "brain damage". *British Journal of Social and Clinical Psychology, 12,* 384–392.
Klonoff, H., & Kennedy, M. (1966). A comparative study of cognitive functioning in old age. *Journal of Gerontology, 20,* 239–243.
Kopelman, M. D., Wilson, B. A., & Baddeley, A. D. (1989). The autobiographical memory interview: A new assessment of autobiographical and personal semantic memory in amnesic patients. *Journal of Clinical and Experimental Neuropsychology, 11,* 724–744.
Lezak, M. D. (1983). *Neuropsychological assessment.* New York: Oxford University Press.

Luria, A. R. (1966). *Higher cortical functions in man*. London: Tavistock.

McAndrews, M. P., Glisky, E. L., & Schacter, D. L. (1987). When priming persists: Long-lasting implicit memory for a single episode in amnesic patients. *Neuropsychologia, 25,* 497–506.

Mayes, A. R. (1986). Learning and memory disorders and their assessment. *Neuropsychologia, 24,* 25–39.

Mayes, A. R. (1988a). *Human organic memory disorders*. Cambridge: Cambridge University Press.

Mayes, A. R. (1988b). What functional deficits underlie organic amnesia? In M. M. Gruneberg, P. E. Morris & R. N. Sykes (Eds.), *Practical aspects of memory: Current research and issues. vol, 2. Clinical and educational implications*. Chichester: John Wiley.

Mayes, A., & Meudell, P. (1983). Memory in humans and other animals. In A. Mayes (Ed.), *Memory in animals and humans*. Wokingham: Van Nostrand Reinhold.

Mishkin, M. (1982). A memory system in the monkey. *Philosophical Transactions of the Royal Society, 298B,* 85–95.

Osterrieth, P. A. (1944). Le test de copie d'une figure complexe. *Archives de Psychologie, 30,* 206–356.

Parkin, A. J., & Leng, N. R. C. (1988). Comparative studies of human amnesia. In H. Markowitsch (Ed.). *Information processing and the brain*. Toronto: Huber.

Prigatano, G. P. (1977). Wechsler Memory Scale is a poor screening test for brain dysfunction. *Journal of Clinical Psychology, 33,* 722–777.

Rey, A. (1941). L'examen psychologigue dans les cas d'encéphalopathie traumatique. *Archives de Psychologie, 28 (112),* 286–340.

Rey, A. (1964). *L'examen clinique en psychologie*. Paris: Presses Universitaires de France.

Schacter, D. L. (1986). Amnesia and crime: What do we really know? *American Psychologist, 41,* 286–295.

Skilbeck, C. E., & Woods, R. T. (1980). The factorial structure of the Wechsler Memory Scale: Samples of neurological and psychogeriatric patients. *Journal of Clinical Neuropsychology, 2,* 293–300.

Squire, L. R. (1986). Mechanisms of memory. *Science, 232,* 1612–1619.

Squire, L. R., & Shimamura, A. P. (1986). Characterizing amnesic patients for neurobehavioral study. *Behavioral Neuroscience, 100* (6), 866–877.

Warrington, E. K. (1984). *Recognition Memory Test*. Windsor: NFER-NELSON.

Wechsler, D. (1945). A standardised memory scale for clinical use. *Journal of Psychology, 19,* 87–95.

Wechsler, D. (1987). *Wechsler Memory Scale—Revised*. San Antonio: Psychological Corporation.

Williams, M. (1968). The measurement of memory in clinical practice. *British Journal of Social & Clinical Psychology, 7,* 19–34.

Wilson, B. A., & Cockburn, J. (1988). The prices test: A simple test of retrograde amnesia. In M. M. Gruneberg, P. E. Morris & R. N. Sykes (Eds.) *Practical aspects of memory: Current research and issues (Volume 2)*. Chichester: John Wiley and Sons.

Wilson B., Cockburn, J., & Baddeley, A. (1985). *The Rivermead Behavioural Memory Test*. Reading: Thames Valley Test Co.

6 Questionnaire and Checklist Approaches to Assessment of Everyday Memory Problems

Anne Hickox
Clinical Neuropsychologist, Middlesbrough General Hospital,
Middlesbrough, Cleveland TS5 5AZ, U.K.

Alan Sunderland
Lecturer in Clinical Psychology, University of Leicester, Leicester LE1
7RH, U.K.

INTRODUCTION

Measurement and identification of real-life memory problems following brain injury have been the focus of discussion and debate by neuropsychologists over recent years. In particular, it is often reported that a discrepancy exists between the patient's performance in formal psychometric tests and their subjective report of everyday forgetting (Newcombe & Artiola i Fortuny, 1979). Formal tests enable us to measure changes in the patient's performance on highly structured and specific tasks, and may be a sensitive way of detecting change or analysing the nature of the deficit (Sunderland, 1990). However, their lack of relevance to day-to-day memory reduces their clinical significance (Sunderland, Harris, & Baddeley, 1983). Efforts to develop more environmentally relevant assessment methods, such as the Rivermead Behavioural Memory Test (Wilson, Cockburn, & Baddeley, 1985) provide a promising alternative in attempting to bridge the gap between laboratory and real-life performance, and further development of such tests is needed. Such alternatives are scarce, however, and in the main, current neuropsychological assessment lacks such ecological significance, leaving us with the practical question of whether any advice can be given to the patient who reports difficulty in day-to-day memory.

Cognitive rehabilitation strategies are becoming increasingly directed to everyday problems (Wilson, 1987; McKinlay & Hickox, 1988), and highlight the importance to the clinician of having a means of obtaining a clear picture of the patient's experience of everyday memory. This could then be used as a basis from which appropriate rehabilitation and mnemonic strategies can be devised and evaluated. The need for remediation efforts to be aimed at these day-to-day memory failings is particularly apparent in patients with closed head injuries. Not only do they show persistent deficits on formal psychometric tests (Brooks et al., 1987; Levin et al., 1979) but memory is also found to be a significant and persisting problem in the everyday setting, placing the greatest burden on relatives (Brooks et al., 1986), and is a key factor in return to work (Brooks et al., 1987). However, only recently have researchers addressed the task of developing an ecologically valid means of identifying the everyday memory problems of patients.

EVERYDAY MEMORY ASSESSMENT

The simplest way of attempting to investigate everyday memory is to use self-report questionnaires. A number of questionnaires have been devised. These enable patients to describe their real-life experience of memory on scales which usually rate the frequency or severity of the problem. The results are discussed later, with particular attention to their value or limitation for the clinician wishing to measure everyday forgetting, either for research or remedial purposes. The major underlying issue is that of validity: To what extent can a person accurately report on their own everyday performance? It is generally agreed that, because of their subjective nature, memory questionnaire responses are based on "metamemory", that is, a person's belief on their own mnemonic abilities, and the finding of low validity may be due not to weak questionnaire design, but rather to people holding inaccurate beliefs about their actual memory performance (Herrmann et al., 1986; Hultsch, Dixon, & Hertzog, 1985). In a brain-injured population, memory and lack of insight are prominent features, and are likely to compound the difficulty of measuring everyday memory problems by self-report (Kapur & Pearson, 1983).

MEMORY QUESTIONNAIRES

Inventory of Everyday Memory Experiences (IME)

This questionnaire, devised by Herrmann and Neisser (1978) consists of 48 questions (Part F) regarding the frequency of various kinds of everyday forgetting, and 24 questions (Part R) regarding ability to remember early childhood and daily life. Ratings are based on a 7-point scale, ranging from "never" to "always" and from "not at all" to "perfectly" for Part R. A factor analysis of data provided by college students resulted in the emergence of eight factors: Rote memory (e.g. telephone numbers); absentmindedness (e.g. misplacing items); names, people, (e.g. forgetting faces); conversations, errands, retrieval, (e.g. feeling of knowing); and places. Herrmann and Neisser found that the students involved reported most difficulty with rote memory and names, and least difficulty with conversations and people. Women reported better performance than men at remembering childhood experiences. The authors conclude that normal people can give meaningful and discriminating reports of their everyday memory experiences.

These findings are based on a normal population, and it is not known what pattern would be found with brain-injured groups. As Lezak (1976) points out, the IME could be a useful instrument for discriminating such differences, and for making comparisons between recall of recent and remote memories. However, because it was devised for a normal population, there are further drawbacks for using the IME with brain-injured patients. It is a lengthy questionnaire, taking approximately an hour, and may be unwieldy for regular clinical use. A second problem is that many of the questions are repetitious, and may give undue emphasis to problems which, in day-to-day life, the patient may consider trivial in nature. For example, remembering phone numbers may be difficult, but less stressful to the patient than forgetting people's names. In addition, many of the questions, such as those relating to long-term events, may not be particularly useful in assessing problems to which remediation techniques may be aimed. Finally, the validity of the patients' reports remains unestablished.

The Subjective Memory Questionnaire (SMQ)

The Subjective Memory Questionnaire (Bennett-Levy & Powell, 1980) was designed with the aim of confirming and extending the findings of Herrmann and Neisser's Inventory (1978) using a slightly different scoring system. Measurement on 36 of the items is based on a five-point qualitative scale, ranging from "very bad" to "very good", and on seven items a frequency measure "very rarely" to "very often" is used. No time scale was integrated into the rating. Items such as the following are included on the SMQ:

• Names of people (minutes after being introduced).

• Appointments.

• Details of shoe sizes, etc. of parents/husband/wife.

Bennett-Levy and Powell found a sex difference in the reporting of a few items, which they considered to be culturally biased. Like Herrmann and Neisser (1978), the authors show that a self-report questionnaire of memory can be constructed and reliably completed by normal subjects. They found only a weak correlation with laboratory tasks, but stress that this does not imply that either measure is wrong, but that they measure different things. The authors also found that subjects belonging to higher social classes had higher total SMQ scores. McMillan (1984) has replicated and extended the original study, to provide a baseline for different patient groups, as well as confirming the original findings. For clinical use, the attraction of the SMQ is that it is relatively quick and easy for the respondent to complete. Although some of the items included, such as recognising signposts, may not be particularly relevant to brain-injured patients whose lifestyle may still be highly dependent or restricted, this in itself is valuable information to the rehabilitative therapist, and overall the SMQ contains a good variety of day-to-day problems which the patient will recognise.

The Cognitive Failures Questionnaire

This is a more wide-ranging self-report questionnaire (Broadbent et al., 1982) than those so far described. Items cover everyday mistakes in perception, memory and motor function. Broadbent considers that, as with memory, we may find corresponding deficits in choosing strategies in "perceptual selection and overt action", resulting in the familiar phenomenon of absent-mindedness. The questionnaire consists of 25 questions about the frequency with which the respondent has made mistakes over the preceding six-month period. Responses are based on a five-point scale ranging from "never" to "very often". A few examples are:

* Do you find you daydream when you ought to be listening to something?

* Do you read something and find you haven't been thinking about it and must read it again?

* Do you bump into people?

* Do you have trouble making up your mind?

All of the questions were found to positively correlate. The CFQ for Others is designed to be completed by a close relative, with the purpose of identifying those aspects of cognitive failure which are apparent to others. The authors found that respondents' own view of their cognitive failure does tend to be shared by someone in a position to judge. They also studied the relationship of the CFQ to stress, finding that, rather than high levels of stress leading to a high CFQ score, it was the case that high CFQ increases one's vulnerability to stress. However, Broadbent et al., leave open the question of what makes one liable to cognitive failure itself.

Items on the CFQ, while more heterogeneous than the memory questionnaires previously described, do appear to have considerable relevance to the problems of memory, concentration, and poor self-monitoring ability frequently experienced by brain-injured patients. While it is difficult to see how some of the items could be considered targets for simple rehabilitation strategies, they do provide valuable information to the clinician by giving an overall picture of a patient's ability to cope with the demands of day-to-day thinking and action. The relative's questionnaire is a welcome adjunct, and a large discrepancy between the two questionnaires may provide an indication of patients' insight into overt difficulties.

So far, the questionnaires described appear to offer some practical benefit to the clinician wishing to measure everyday memory. The items include behaviours which normal people forget or fail on from time to time, and the rating methods are, on the whole, simple and unstressful to the respondent. The relative's report of overt behaviours which the subject may be unaware of, yet are apparent to others, is particularly useful when working with brain-injured patients who may lack insight. However, because findings so far have been based on the self-report of normal populations, it would not be justifiable to generalise the subjective problems reported to the more severe problems found in patients with brain injury whose memory problems are organically based, although there is considered to be a wide overlap between memory failures reported by non-injured and brain-injured populations (Kapur & Pearson, 1983). Such patients often lack insight, and may be unaware of their own memory failures, and may be unable to remember past memory failings.

The Everyday Memory Questionnaire

Sunderland, Harris, and Baddeley (1983) attempted to tackle these problems directly: In a study of the relationship between memory performance in everyday life and that of laboratory tests; in a group of subjects with normal memory; and two groups of severely head-injured patients. Everyday memory was measured using questionnaires and checklists completed by each subject, and relatives were asked to complete independently corresponding questionnaires and checklists. The questionnaire included 35 items grouped under the headings: "speech", "reading and writing", "faces and places", "actions", and "learning new things". The patient (or relative) was asked to rate how frequently an episode of forgetting had occurred over the past five weeks, on a nine-point scale ranging from several times each day to never. Checklists were also given to patient and relative, containing identical items, but the patient or relative was asked to tick independently whether an item had occurred over the past 24 hours for a period of seven days. Two ticks indicated that an item occurred more than once. Examples from the questionnaire included:

• Forgetting where you have put something. Losing things around the house.

• Forgetting when it was that something happened, for example, whether it was yesterday or last week.

• Letting yourself ramble on to speak about unimportant or irrelevant things.

• Telling someone a story or joke that you have told them once already.

The authors found that, for normal subjects and the long-term head injured group, the relatives' questionnaire did correlate with test performance, but there was less consistency among the subjects' questionnaires of each group. The results suggest that the patient's questionnaire may be inaccurate as a measure of the incidence of memory failures.

As Sunderland et al., point out, responding to the questionnaire is in itself a memory task, so that patients with poorer memories may be less able to recall episodes of forgetting, resulting in low estimates. This suggests that the daily checklist may give more accurate estimates, as the interval between forgetting and recording is shorter. This was found to be the case, with greater differences between head-injured subjects and controls, and significant correlation with other measures. An important point made by the authors is that the more severely injured patients were less likely to be back at work and thus were sheltered by relatives from demanding situations. Conversely, the less seriously injured patients were more likely to be in situations which exposed them to problems and thus error-making.

Head Injury Postal Questionnaire (HIPQ)

The HIPQ (Sunderland & Harris, 1984) is a modified version of the EMQ, which enables it to be self-administered, and includes the 16 items which had been found significantly to discriminate head injured patients from controls, and five "floor" items to check on "halo" effects. The findings suggest that, when completed by relatives, the questionnaire can provide an accurate measure of easily observed aspects of the everyday memory of patients several years after severe head injury. The low validity of the patient's questionnaire again is likely to be due to the inability to recall memory failures, and suggests that a more accurate self-assessment might be achieved by using methods that minimise the demands placed on a patient's memory.

In summary, these studies have shown that normal subjects can give reliable responses to questionnaires concerning their everyday memory performance. This probably reflects the fact that the normal individual has certain clear beliefs about their memory (Herrman et al., 1986). Information about the validity of these responses as a true measure of performance is still patchy but the work with head injured patients suggests that self-report questionnaires should not be regarded as giving accurate information. Relatives' questionnaires and checklists seem to give better results but even here there is need for caution.

In a later study (Sunderland et al., 1986) the questionnaires and checklists which had been used in the studies of head injury were used to try to assess everyday memory in the normal elderly population. No measure was found to have high reliability or validity here; not even the relatives' questionnaire. This may have been due to particular characteristics of the elderly population, but in general it would seem unwise to place too great a weight on the validity of any subjective method of assessing everyday memory.

With these reservations in mind, it would appear that the studies described earlier show that, generally, memory questionnaires correlate poorly with formal psychometric tests. More recently devised questionnaires do appear, however, to be reasonably reliable when completed by normal subjects, or by the relatives of head injured patients. Questionnaires completed by patients that are several years post-injury also appear to have some validity. Daily checklists completed by these patients again appear to be quite reliable.

Memory Questionnaires in Clinical Practice

In clinical practice, it would appear that the use of retrospective questionnaires may be particularly valuable when completed by the relative for the patient. They may be used as a means of tapping the frequency and type of failure noted by relatives, and, when re-administered after a period of time, say, when further formal testing is carried out, can indicate changes in the severity of everyday memory problems. In research, they may provide a means of discriminating between different brain-injured populations. For a number of reasons the clinician may choose to give a memory questionnaire to the patient, for example, as an initial screen of some specific incidents of forgetting on which remedial techniques might be planned, or when the memory impairment is not very severe. However, it should be borne in mind that accuracy is likely to be limited by: a) Lack of insight; and b) the demands that the questionnaire places on memory.

Memory Checklists in Clinical Practice

Memory checklists may be a better option for self-report of everyday memory. From the aforementioned studies, it appears that four factors are particularly important in gaining a degree of accuracy in self-report by these patients. These are:

1. The items should be easy to understand and relevant to the patient's day-to-day life.
2. The rating system should place minimum demand on the patient's ability to remember, i.e. the interval between the episode of forgetting and recording each failure should be brief.

3. The patient and relative should be aided in adopting a system which maximises their chances of referring to the checklist at regular intervals, and results in greater accuracy.

4. Patients and relatives should each complete checklists either separately or jointly, to ensure a record of episodes observed both subjectively and objectively.

The usefulness of checklists in clinical practice is demonstrated in a current study of severely head injured out-patients in which frequency counts on memory checklists are used as the main dependent measures. This study has been previously described elsewhere (McKinlay & Hickox, 1988) and will only be described briefly here as it relates to this chapter. Using a multiple baseline across subjects' design, the study aims to evaluate the effectiveness of simple mnemonic strategies taught to severely head injured adult out-patients, Relatives are closely involved as co-therapists. In view of the lack of real-life prediction available from tests and the evidence that patients' retrospective questionnaires are not valid (Sunderland, Harris, & Baddeley, 1983), the main outcome measures are checklists of "real-life" memory failures. Clinical psychometric assessments of IQ, memory and concentration are included, as are questionnaires regarding the patient's memory failures (Broadbent et al., 1982; Sunderland, Harris, & Gleave, 1984).

The randomly assigned baseline period (ranging from four to eight weeks) is the independent variable, and changes attributable to treatment should occur always and only after the baseline has ended and treatment has begun. During the baseline period, the frequency of memory failures is recorded using a checklist completed jointly by relatives and patients. The record is made at the time of the failure, by whomever observed it. If a failure occurs more than once, the total number of times it occurs is noted.

A standard Memory Checklist (MCL) was devised for the study, compiled from items which severely head injured patients and their relatives reported most often on interviews at the beginning of the study. Alternatively, an individual checklist, based on the patient's most frequently reported failure may be used, which can include more idiosyncratic concerns, e.g. forgetting dreams.

The patient and relative are provided with MCLs to complete each day, and are instructed to record a memory failure as soon as it is noticed by one or the other. If an item occurs more than once, this is to be noted. In cases where there is a high degree of memory failure, a daily checklist is used, being more manageable, and perhaps less discouraging to the patient than the weekly checklist, which allows one sheet per week with columns for each day of the week. The sheets are collected at the end of the baseline period, and the weekly totals recorded. At the onset of treatment, the checklists are still kept, but the instructions now are to record failures which occur either through failure to use a strategy or despite its use. In this way, the effectiveness of compensatory memory strategies can be evaluated throughout the treatment period. At two-months follow-up, the checklists are posted to the patient for completion over a fortnight, to enable the therapist to check on whether the use of memory aids has been maintained.

The Memory Checklist can be used for a simple, relatively unstressful dependent measure in research; in this case, on the effectiveness of mnemonics in the day-to-day setting, in which the MCL is used to provide a measure of daily frequency of forgetting, and a similar use of checklists based on EMQ items was applied by Wilson in evaluating mnemonic strategies (Wilson, 1987). Concurrently, the MCL can be used to target problems for remediation, e.g. losing concentration while reading would suggest PQRST would be helpful. In the clinical setting, memory checklists may be given to the patient and relative to complete, say for a week following formal testing, to identify day-to-day difficulties, and problems which persist or relapse during treatment can be readily identified. Its value is in its brevity and relevance to the patient, enabling it to be completed regularly be minimising the interval between forgetting and recording.

The Problem of Under-reporting

As suggested in previous studies using memory questionnaires, disagreement between the head-injured patient and the relative is common, due to under-reporting by the patient. This is most likely to be the result of: 1) Forgetting to record; and 2) lack of insight or denial.

The first problem results from the task of being asked to remember what one has forgotten, the greater the interval between forgetting and recording, the more likely it is that the patient will fail to note episodes of forgetting. This is supported by Wilkins and Baddeley (1978) who suggest that it may be compounded by the absence of a strategy or cue to remember failures. While the retrospective nature of memory questionnaires does not lend itself to such strategies, in memory checklists the problem of forgetting to record maybe minimised by devising a means of reminding the patient to record memory failures as soon as possible after they occur. Prompting by the relative is one obvious solution, but is not always practical or desirable. Keeping the checklist in a conspicuous place, or using wristwatch alarms may help to ensure that the interval between forgetting and recording the failure is not loo long. Nevertheless, the nature of the task makes it very likely that both memory questionnaires and checklists are providing an underestimate if kept solely by either patient or relative, and there may be failures (subjective or objective) which may not be noticed.

As treatment progresses, and possibly more demands are made on the patient's memory, perhaps as that person becomes more socially active, an increase in the variety of failures may be observed. Increased insight as treatment progresses may also result in more failures being recorded, and patients may comment that they had been forgetting, but had failed to acknowledge it. This is not a particular problem, for although initially an increase may appear, with treatment this should decline, as mnemonic strategies compensate for the greater demands on memory. A recent study lends qualified support to the hypothesis that such awareness of deficits actually results in greater response to treatment (Lam et al., 1988). The author's findings suggest that clients who are unaware of their deficits would benefit from intervention which helps them recognise their problems. As insight increases, a more active learning approach can be introduced.

In summary, the need for reliable means of assessing everyday memory is of considerable importance to the clinical neuropsychologist. Whilst formal memory tasks are becoming more sensitive to discriminating the nature of impairment, they need to be complemented by everyday measures in order for assessment to be complete. Simulation tests (Crook & Larrabee, 1988; Wilson, Cockburn, & Baddeley, 1985) are promising indicators for future developments. Memory questionnaires and checklists, particularly when completed by both patient and relative, appear to offer a practical means of such ecological assessment. A number of these have been described, and they have been found to be valuable in highlighting problems of insight, as well as assessing and evaluating the target problems to which simple memory strategies may be aimed. It is hoped that such measures will enable us to be more flexible in our approach than formal memory tests have so far allowed.

REFERENCES

Bennett-Levy, J., & Powell, G. E. (1980). The subjective memory questionnaire (SMQ). An investigation into the self-reporting of "real-life" memory skills. *British Journal of Social and Clinical Psychology, 19*, 177–188.

Broadbent, D. E., Cooper, P. F., Fitzgerald, P., & Parkes, K. R. (1982). The cognitive failures questionnaire (CFQ) and its correlates. *British Journal of Clinical Psychology, 21*, 1–16.

Brooks, N., Campsie, L., Symington, C., Beattie, A., & McKinlay, W. (1986). The five year outcome of severe blunt head injury: A relative's view. *Journal of Neurology, Neurosurgery and Psychiatry, 49*, 764–770.

Brooks, N., McKinlay, W., Symington, C., Beattie, A., & Campsie, L. (1987). Return to work within the first seven years of severe head injury. *Brain Injury, 1*, 5–19.

Crook, T. H., & Larrabee, G. J. (1988). Interrelationships among everyday memory tests: Stability of factor structure with age. *Neuropsychology, 2*(1) 1–12.

Herrmann, D. J., Grubs, L., Sigmundi, R. A., & Grueneich, R. (1986). Awareness of memory ability before and after relevant memory experience. *Human Learning, 5*, 91–107.

Herrmann, D. J., & Neisser, U. (1978). An inventory of everyday memory experiences. In M. M. Gruneberg, P. S. Harris, & R. Sykes, (Eds.), *Practical aspects of memory*. London: Academic Press.

Hultsch, D. F., Dixon, R. A., & Hertzog, C. (1985). Memory perceptions and memory performance in adulthood and aging. *Canadian Journal on Aging, 4*, 179–187.

Kapur, N., & Pearson, D. (1983). Memory symptoms and memory performance of neurological patients. *British Journal of Psychology, 74*, 409–415.

Lam, C. S., McMahon, B. T., Priddy, D. A., & Gehred-Schultz, A. (1988). Deficit awareness and treatment performance among traumatic head injury adults. *Brain Injury, 2*, 235–242.

Levin, H. S. et al. (1979). Long-term neuropsychological outcome of closed-head injury. *Journal of Neurosurgery, 50*, 412–422.

Lezak, M. D. (1976). *Neuropsychological assessment.* New York: Oxford University Press.

McKinlay, W. W., & Hickox, A. (1988). How can families help? *Journal of Head Trauma Rehabilitation, 3*(4) 64–72.

MacMillan, T. M. (1984). Investigation of everyday memory in normal subjects using the subjective memory questionnaire (SMQ). *Cortex, 20,* 333–347.

Newcombe, F., & Artiola i Fortuny, L. (1979). Problems and perspectives in the evaluation of psychological deficits after cerebral lesions. *International Rehabilitation Medicine, 1,* 182–192.

Sunderland, A. (1990). Clinical memory assessment–Matching the method to the aim. In D. Tupper & K. Cicerone, (Eds.), *The neuropsychology of everyday life: Assessment and basic competencies (Foundations of neuropsychology series).* Norwell Mass.: Kluwer Academic Publishers.

Sunderland, A., Harris, J. E., & Baddeley, A. D. (1988). Do laboratory tests predict everyday memory? A neuropsychological study. *Journal of Verbal Learning and Verbal Behaviour, 22,* 341–357.

Sunderland, A., Harris, J. E., & Gleave, J. (1984). Memory failures in everyday life following severe head injury. *Journal of Clinical Neuropsychology, 6,* 127–142.

Sunderland, A., Watts, K., & Baddeley, A. D. (1986). Subjective memory assessment and performance in elderly adults. *Journal of Gerontology, 41,* 376–384.

Wilkins, A. J., & Baddeley, A. D. (1978). Remembering to recall in everyday life: An approach to absent-mindedness. In M. M. Gruneberg, P. S. Harris, & R. Sykes *Practical aspects of memory.* London: Academic Press.

Wilson, B. A. (1987). *Rehabilitation of memory.* London: The Guildford Press.

Wilson, B. A., Cockburn, J., & Baddeley, A. D. (1985). *The Rivermead Behavioural Memory Test.* Reading: Thames Valley Test Company.

7

Assessment of Visuo-Perceptual Dysfunction

J. Graham Beaumont and Jules B. Davidoff
Department of Psychology, University College of Swansea, Wales

INTRODUCTION

The assessment of visuo-perceptual dysfunction is one of the more difficult areas of investigation for the practising clinical neuropsychologist. Although there are many tests, often of a good standard, they do not form a standardised battery around which an organised approach to assessment can be formulated. If one of the major batteries is used, as is rare in Britain although much more common in North America, some aspects of visuo-perceptual function will be addressed, although in a rather preliminary fashion. If a battery of this type is not employed, then assessment of this area relies upon the initiative of the clinician in selecting appropriate tests. As a result, we have the impression that the assessment of visuo-perceptual dysfunction is often cursory and inadequate by comparison with other areas of clinical investigation. There are a number of reasons for this.

One reason is that the clinical question is often poorly formulated. While there may be good tests available, they do not relate to each other and the results cannot be related back to a coherent theory of visuo-perceptual function. However, it is not the case that little is known about normal and abnormal visual function; the neuropsychology of vision is one of the more advanced fields of neuropsychology. The problem for the practising neuropsychologist is that without a clear and unifying conceptual structure it is hard to organise a rational assessment approach. It is difficult to give a clear and concise account for the organisation of visuo-perceptual functions in the brain, and it is, in consequence, difficult to arrive at a clinically useful description of the problems which a given patient may have in this area of function. By comparison, when faced with the need to assess, for example, reading ability or memory function, there is a fairly clear and limited set of choices which the clinician will make. This is not so for visuo-perceptual dysfunction, and as a result clinicians lack a clearly structured approach to the problem.

A second reason is that assessment in this area involves a rather uncomfortable mix of behavioural neurology and the psychometric neuropsychological approach, tests of copying [simple copying vs. Bender Gestalt Test] to assess visuoconstructive abilities being an obvious example. The behavioural-neurological testing procedures rely upon the assumption that there is a discontinuity between normal and abnormal performance and that the two can be (fairly) easily distinguished: The patient can perform the task or not. By contrast, the psychometrically-based tests rely upon classical mental test theory and involve the use of normative standardisation as the conceptual basis of the assessment. There is nothing inherently wrong in mixing these approaches where appropriate, but it demands that the clinician be clear about which approach is currently being employed, and why it is appropriate at that stage of the investigation.

Lastly, it is difficult to assess visual functions without involving some form of verbal or gestural response. Motor performance is often closely linked with perceptual function, as are aspects of attention, memory and spatial orientation. As a result it is often difficult to extract the purely visuo-perceptual aspects from the other (higher level) functional factors involved in the patient's performance.

In the following we shall attempt to summarise some of the more common contemporary practices, with some pointers to what seems most clinically useful among currently available test procedures. We shall also try to show how the more recent cognitive-neuropsychological approaches can be applied in this area, and how the development of cognitive theories may be opening up new clinical opportunities through the restructuring of available assessment techniques. Here, visuo-perceptual dysfunction is taken to include basic visual functions and to extend to certain aspects of spatial function and visual agnosia (in that it is difficult to delimit the area precisely). As they are treated elsewhere in the book, face perception and visual neglect have been excluded.

Given the space available here it is difficult to give more than a brief introduction, and readers wishing to pursue the topic in more depth are urged to consult the further reading list given at the end of the chapter. However, it is worth mentioning that a discussion of the historical background to assessment in this area is to be found in Heilman and Valenstein (1985), and also that no discussion of assessment procedures should fail to acknowledge Lezak (1983) as the established authority to whom we are all greatly in debt.

TRADITIONAL ASSESSMENT APPROACHES

Basic Visual Processes

The assessment of basic visual processes is probably the most technically difficult of all areas of neuropsychological assessment, and it is rarely performed adequately by clinical neuropsychologists. There are two reasons for this.

The first is that visual deficits cover a large number of stimulus dimensions: Location, size, brightness, contrast, movement, colour, temporal distribution, and stimulus complexity. In certain patients (for example in the recovery from stroke), they may also be variable — even over quite short periods of time. In addition there are rare cases in which patients report visual distortions: They may see objects as too small (micropsia); too large (macropsia); at a great distance (teleopsia) or even repeated (polyopsia). Object boundaries may become distorted or displaced, with fluctuations in intensity or clarity of vision. In addition, visual events may perseverate (palinopsia) in a most bizarre way, or even be "replayed" a number of times so that the patient sees a visual event as being repeated. (Milner & Teuber, 1968, provide an excellent discussion of many of these rare phenomena.) There is also the possible complication of blindsight (Weiskrantz, 1986) by which a patient may be able to locate and discriminate between stimuli, yet outside conscious awareness, through operation of the secondary (subcortical) visual system.

The point to be made is that simple confrontational testing of the visual fields is an unacceptably crude assessment of the patient's visual function, and, even more carefully conducted perimetry may fail to identify visual problems from which the patient suffers. Heilman and Valenstein (1985) recommend the assessment of detection thresholds, local adaptation time, flicker fusion, movement after-effect, tachistoscopic presentation, luminance discrimination, and depth perception (they recommend use of the Julesz figures, which are available in the TNO Test: TNO, 1972). They also recommend more careful psychophysical assessment where the opportunity arises. Even these are unlikely to exhaust the potential difficulties which a patient may exhibit.

The second reason why this kind of assessment is often inadequate is that clinical neuropsychologists generally lack the training and resources to conduct this kind of thorough investigation, and it is, in consequence, rarely performed.

Tests of *visual recognition* are more commonly employed, and the tests developed by Warrington and Taylor (1973) are widely known and used. The stimuli are distorted in one of two ways: By being either dramatically enlarged, or photographed from unusual angles (Unconventional Views; Fig. 7.4). Both tests discriminate between brain-damaged and control subjects, and the Unconventional Views task also discriminates left- from right-sided lesions. Taylor and Warrington (1973) also provide examples of tests of size, length, shading and other stimulus dimensions. The neuropsychology of visual recognition is a complex issue and is discussed at greater length later.

In addition the ability to match or identify shapes is sometimes tested by requiring the patient to draw the object either from a model or from memory, although this inevitably introduces constructional aspects for all but the most simple stimuli. Performance on the WAIS Picture Completion subtest may also be a preliminary indication of difficulties in figural recognition. A way of pursuing this difficulty is to use one of the picture vocabulary tests. (The English Picture Vocabulary Test: Brimer & Dunn, 1963; Peabody Picture Vocabulary Test: Dunn, 1965; or the Picture Vocabulary component of the Stanford-Binet). The linguistic response component can be eliminated by using elements from the Leiter International Performance Scale (Leiter, 1969). The Stanford-Binet also provides Discrimination of Forms (level IV), while the first sequence of twelve items of the Raven's Standard Progressive Matrices (Raven, Court & Raven, 1977) may also provide evidence of simple recognition difficulties in an otherwise intelligent patient.

Visual Organisation and Inference

Visual organisation is normally tested in one of two ways: By using either incomplete or fragmented visual stimuli. Ambiguous stimuli (such as the Rorschach plates), are also used in North America (see Lezak, 1983), but the British rejection of projective tests extends to their use as neuropsychological stimuli.

The most well-known incomplete visual stimuli come from the Picture Completion subtest of the WAIS. However, they are regarded as being relatively resistant to the effects of perceptual dysfunction, presumably because they are so highly structured. They will, nevertheless, reveal severe impairments. Similar comments apply to the Mutilated Pictures subtest of the Stanford-Binet (level VI).

More specifically developed for the purpose are the various tests of perceptual closure, which include: the Street Completion Test (Street, 1931); the Mooney Closure Test (Mooney & Ferguson, 1951); and the Gestalt Completion Test (Ekstrom et al., 1976); all using various forms of incomplete picture. However, Wasserstein (1980) found poor inter-correlations among these tests with regard to "normals", although they do discriminate patients from controls. Wasserstein produced a new test out of items drawn from two of the above tests which, additionally, has the ability to lateralise lesions producing a deficit. Norms would have to be obtained before using these tests with older subjects.

The most useful set of incomplete stimuli are, however, the Gollin Incomplete Figures (Gollin, 1960) which comprise 20 sets of stimuli, each set being a progressively more complete representation of the object from that of barely suggestive through to the complete drawing. The test is easy to administer and score, and whereas not highly sensitive to right posterior lesions, appears to be tapping more than the extraction of perceptual features (Warrington & Rabin, 1970).

Fragmented visual stimuli are employed in two other well-known tests. The Hooper Visual Organisation Test (Hooper, 1958; see Fig.7.1) was originally devised for the general detection of organic impairment, in which role it has been found (like many such tests) to provide a high level of false negatives, although rarely yielding false positive results. However, it can be used for identifying specific deficits and is especially useful in detecting the kind of fragmentation occasionally seen in patients with right frontal lesions. These patients will, in general, perform quite well (i.e. they understand the task), but on items where there is a relatively distinct and (falsely) identifiable fragment, will tend to base their response on that single element. The Revised Minnesota Paper Form Board Test (Likert & Quasha, 1970), has also been used, but performance may be particularly sensitive to subjects' cognitive strategies (Lezak, 1983).

Visual inference has traditionally been assessed by one of the figure-ground tasks. The Gottschaldt Embedded Figures Test is familiar to most students of psychology, and there is a similar tradition in the use of overlapping figures from the work of Poppelreuter during the First World War, through to Luria's procedures. If adopting a behavioural-neurological approach in the style of Luria (see Christensen, 1979) then these tests may be of value, as may the Visual Closure subtest from the ITPA (Illinois Test of Psycholinguistic Abilities: Kirk, McCarthy & Kirk, 1968). Other stimuli are to be found in the Southern California Figure-Ground Perceptual Test (Ayres, 1966), and there are normative data on this test for children.

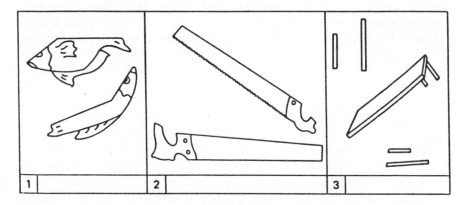

FIG. 7.1. Three easy items from the Hooper Visual Organisation Test. (VOT). Copyright © 1957 renewed by H. Elson Hooper. Reprinted by permission of the publisher, Western Psychological Services, 12031 Wilshire Boulevard, Los Angeles, California 90025, U.S.A.

The most clinically useful of the tests for visual inference which employ fragmented visual stimuli, in terms of its ease of administration and its psychometric properties, is the Closure Flexibility (Concealed Figures) test (Thurstone & Jeffrey, 1982) which is a modern multiple-choice version derived ultimately from the work of Gottschaldt. The subject is required to select the more complex figure which contains the simpler unembedded stimulus. The existence of a clinical literature associated with the task is an added bonus (e.g. Corkin, 1979; Russo & Vignolo, 1967).

Tests of closure and completion involve some degree of visual synthesis and have been used in the investigation of simultaneous agnosia (simultanagnosia). There has been a long debate about the integrity of this defect and its conceptual status, but there is no doubt that visual synthesis is an important aspect of perception, and that deficient synthesis may be revealed in tests which involve incomplete, mutilated or embedded figures.

Colour Perception and Recognition

By contrast, the assessment of colour perception and recognition appears relatively straightforward; perhaps deceptively so. It is important to remember, however, that before proceeding to test a patient and infer a disorder of colour vision, the clinician must be confident that the patient had no abnormality of colour vision before acquiring the relevant lesion. Congenital abnormalities of colour vision are not uncommon, especially among males and it is possible, if unlikely, that a patient could reach adulthood without becoming aware of one of the less severe disorders of colour perception.

The basic assessment of colour perception is known to most students of psychology. It is usually assessed by tests that require the mental construction of shapes from coloured spots that are equally bright. The Ishihara is the most commonly used of these tests, and includes shapes that can be traced without being explicitly named. There are similar alternatives (Dvorine Plates: Dvorine, 1953; H-R-R Pseudoisochromatic Plates: Hardy et al., 1955). The Farnsworth-Munsell 100-Hue and Dichotomous Test for Color Vision (Farnsworth, 1943) is also clinically useful. In this test the colours are represented on small counters which have to be arranged in sequence, involving quite subtle discriminations. In its full form the test is particularly arduous, although it does give a more precise assessment than the aforementioned tests, and discriminates between congenital and acquired disorders. The test, therefore, provides a sensitive nonverbal assessment for a purely sensory disorder, as well as the material for assessing colour agnosias through verbal response or by other tasks.

De Renzi and Spinnler (1967) have produced a short Color Perception Battery which includes the Ishihara plates, but also includes tests of colour matching, colour naming, pointing to colour, colour drawing, and memory for colour. The battery seems able to discriminate those patients whose difficulty stems from a purely perceptual disorder and those with aphasic involvement, from those with other forms of the loss of knowledge concerning object colours.

The distinction between loss of colour knowledge and colour anomia is clearly an important one and is often tested rather informally by requiring the patient to colour in drawings. Slightly more standardised procedures have been developed (Damasio et al., 1979; Lhermitte et al., 1969); they consist of two basic tests derived from Lewandowsky (see Davidoff & Fodor, 1989). Colouring of Pictures requires the patient to select the appropriate crayon from a standard set to colour a line drawing of an object with a dominant colour association, such as a banana. The companion test: Wrongly Coloured Pictures, demands that the subject identify a line drawing which has been coloured in an inappropriate colour. Varney (1982) has also reported a set of line drawings for which the appropriate colour must be selected in a four-choice selection, also eliminating the requirement of verbal response from the task.

Visual Scanning

Visual scanning is often associated with disorders of neglect, which are treated elsewhere in this volume, but some mention of the function is appropriate here.

The test that has had a particular vogue in this area is Elithorn's Perceptual Maze Test (Elithorn et al., 1964; see Fig.7.2) which has been widely used, although its use may now be declining. It was originally conceived as a nonverbal test of general intelligence, comparable to the Raven's Matrices tests, but has proved less successful than the latter in that role. A typical version of the test involves a series of V-shaped lattices with points randomly placed at various intersections of the lattice. The subject must trace from the top to the bottom

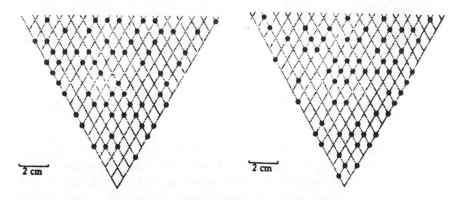

FIG. 7.2.   Two lattices from the Elithorn Perceptual Maze test. Reproduced by kind permission of the publishers, The British Psychological Society.

of the lattice, passing through as many of the points as possible but without doubling-back at any intersection.

The test obviously invokes a number of functions, not all purely perceptual, for the patient must keep track of various potential routes and the point counts associated with them, as well as choosing among the alternatives. Reasons for failure on the task may not be perceptual: For example, frontal lobe patients may fail because they ignore the rules rather than because they fail to plan the route or adequately to scan the display. In addition not all patients may be capable of understanding the task, performance on which also has a significant correlation with intelligence (Colonna & Faglioni, 1966). However, the test does discriminate well between brain-damaged patients and normal subjects, and is more affected by right than by left hemisphere lesions. This may provide a useful part of an investigation of visuo-perceptual functions.

An explicit Visual Search task is available in the Repeatable-Cognitive-Perceptual-Motor Battery (which is derived from the Halstead-Reitan Neuropsychological Battery). It involves searching for small chequered stimulus matrices within a set of larger matrices arranged around the central stimulus matrices. A useful aspect is that it has been reported as being one of the tests capable of reflecting the effects of changing medication in epileptics (Lewis & Kupke, 1977).

Visual tracking tasks may also be used as a measure of visual scanning abilities, and Talland's Line Tracing task (Talland, 1965) is a typical example. The format would be familiar to the reader of children's comics, where the child is asked to find which line the bunny must follow to get back to its burrow, and the difficulty is manipulated by varying the number of lines involved. This is a task which most normal subjects complete without difficulty and serious failure would normally indicate some deficit of visual scanning.

Visuospatial Functions

Visuospatial function clearly has two aspects which involve: (a) personal and (b) extrapersonal orientation, and also psychological components which are not only visuo-perceptual. Many of the tests are firmly in the tradition of behavioural neurology.

Personal orientation includes body orientation and certain aspects of right-left orientation. Body orientation is normally part of the neurological examination, but a more extended and systematic development is provided by Semmes and Weinstein (Semmes et al., 1963; Weinstein, 1964) as the Personal Orientation Test. This requires, by a standard set of commands, that the patient: Touch body parts names by the examiner; name parts touched by the examiner; touch parts which the examiner names on the examiner's body; imitate touches made by the examiner; and make touches indicated by schematic diagrams. The last three of these sections all involve visuo-perceptual components, and a specific deficit on them may indicate a visuo-perceptual disorder, although it is obvious that neglect, apraxic difficulties and disturbances of the body schema may also be involved.

Right-left orientation may be tested in a similar fashion, and Heilman and Valenstein (1985, Table 6-2), present a set of tests which allows for a systematic analysis of this function. One subset of these tests involves the repetition of the tests assessing orientation by the patient towards the patient's own body, but without visual guidance (by closing the eyes, or blindfolding the patient). In this way the particular contribution of the visuo-perceptual process to right-left orientation can be assessed.

In terms of extrapersonal orientation, one of the few formal tests available is the Standardised Road Map Test of Direction Sense (Money, 1976), and in a computer-based version (Beaumont & French, 1987). The test subject watches the examiner trace a route around a schematic "street plan" in pencil. The examiner then goes over the route again and at each turning the subject must indicate whether a right or a left turn is made in the route. It is possible to distinguish direction of turn on the route from direction of turn with respect to the subject's personal orientation. The test was originally constructed to study developmental aspects of the function, but it is fairly easy for normals, and gross failure indicates a deficit of right-left orientation which might have a visuo-perceptual basis.

Considering the contribution of more basic perceptual processes to extra-personal spatial perception, the Judgement of Line Orientation task (Benton et al., 1983), which tests angulation by requiring a patient to match samples to lines arranged as radii around a semi-circle is a valid task. Judgement of direction (Benton et al., 1975); distance (Hécaen & Angelergues, 1963); and the role of depth perception (Hamsher, 1978); all have visuo-perceptual aspects, although there are almost no formal tests available of these higher-level visuospatial abilities.

Visuoconstructive Abilities

Constructional functions have received a great deal of attention in neuro-psychology and generally also have visuo-perceptual aspects. From the point of view of practical assessment, they are best considered in terms of: drawing and copying; two-dimensional construction; and three-dimensional construction. A good theoretical discussion of the neuropsychology of constructional abilities appears in Heilman and Valenstein (1985).

Drawing, either as copying or as free drawing, is used in the practice of some clinical neuropsychologists, but has little to recommend it. The analysis of drawings is a difficult business, largely because so many factors may influence the final production. Diagnostically, drawing is a complex situation. The more formal versions of drawing the human figure in the Draw-a-Person and the

House-Tree-Person Tests are difficult to score. Partly as a consequence of this they have poor reliability and questionnable validity and they are best avoided. Asking the patient to draw a bicycle may be useful, particularly if it is followed by a discussion with the patient of the elements of the drawing and how they relate to the structure and mechanics of a bicycle; and Lezak (1983, Table 13-6) gives a useful scoring protocol for bicycle drawings. Similarly, asking the patient to draw a clock-face or a daisy may reveal perceptual distortions, but they are likely to be signs of neglect through unilateral inattention.

Copying tests are available in more standardised forms, although they vary greatly in their utility. The most widely known must be the Bender Gestalt Test, which has applications in the area of personality as well as in its role in neuropsychology. The nine designs of the original test have been used in a variety of ways, and the administration procedure developed for Hutt's (1977) revision is probably the one which can be recommended. However, for neuropsychological purposes, Hain's (1964) scoring procedure is more appropriate, and has norms available for brain-damaged and normal groups (reported in Lezak, 1983, Tables 13-1 & 13-2). Not all cerebral lesions produce impairments on the test because performance may be normal with left frontal lesions, but severe dysfunction is likely to indicate parietal involvement, probably on the right.

Canter has developed a Background Interference Procedure as a development of the Bender Gestalt (see Heaton, Baade, & Johnson, 1978). The procedure involves making normal copies, and then further copies on a sheet already covered with bold curved lines. It appears more powerful as a screening device than the Bender Gestalt alone, and may also be used with elderly subjects.

The Minnesota Percepto-Diagnostic Test uses two of the Bender-Gestalt figures (Fuller & Laird, 1963), but does not seem to be of great utility; similarly the Benton Visual Retention Test: Copy Administration (Benton, 1974), seems less useful than other tests, (although it possesses the virtue of three alternate forms).

Particularly useful as an alternative to the Bender Gestalt, however, is the Complex Figure Test: Copy Administration (Fig. 7.3), also known as the Rey Figure or the Rey-Osterreith Figure (Osterreith, 1944). It also has a parallel version (Taylor, 1979). Its scoring procedure is more reliable (see Lezak, 1983), for protocols for both figures), and reasonably adequate norms are available for normal subjects and for various brain-damaged groups. It is probably to be recommended as the best of the copying tests.

Two-dimensional construction tests have been based upon Kohs blocks, and the best-known is the Block Design subtest of the WAIS. As the norms for this are so good, it is the clear choice for a test of this type, although the original Kohs Blocks provides a number of items at a higher level of difficulty than are available in the WAIS subtest (Arthur, 1947).

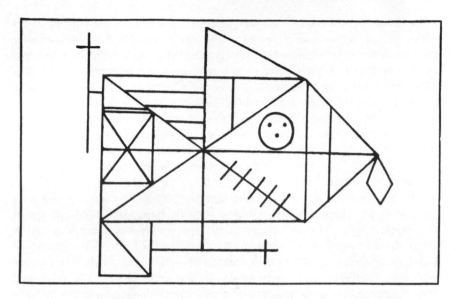

FIG. 7.3.   Rey Complex Figure (Osterrieth, 1944). Reproduced by kind permission
of the publisher, Médecine et Hygiène, Geneva.

The one alternative to the blocks tasks is the Stick Construction task
(Butters & Barton, 1970). It has the advantage of requiring both normal and
rotated copying and is quick and easy to administer. The task is sensitive to
postcentral lesions and can provide lateralising signs.

Similarly there are two tests of *three-dimensional construction*. The first
comprises the two subtests drawn from the 1960 Revision of the Stanford-Binet:
Tower (level II), and Bridge (level III). Failure on either of these easy tasks is
evidence of a significant impairment. More commonly used is the Test of Three-
Dimensional Block Construction (Benton et al., 1983), in which the patient is
required to construct, using various shaped blocks, copies from either a model
of similar blocks or from a photograph. The test is sensitive at moderate as well
as severe levels of impairment and can provide evidence of lateralisation.

Visual Agnosia

The patient with visual agnosia fails to respond appropriately to visually
presented material even though visual sensory processing, language, and
general intelligence are sufficiently normal not to account for the patient's
poor recognition. There has been a long and continuing debate about the
classification of visual agnosias, and good introductions are to be found in
both Hécaen and Albert (1978), and Heilman and Valenstein (1985) (and see
the following).

Examination of the range of visual agnosic difficulties is a complex subject which cannot be adequately treated in the space available here. A particular problem is the discrimination between agnosic and aphasic difficulties. pointers are that the former are more likely to be confined to a single modality, whereas additional aphasic signs (most likely a word-finding difficulty), are commonly associated with the latter. Apraxic difficulties may also be confused with visual agnosia. If the patient is unable to follow commands which do not involve objects, or to demonstrate the use of objects which are not within vision, then the problem is likely to be an apraxic one. This can account for an apparent agnosic difficulty if the patient fails to demonstrate the use of an object which is visually presented.

The examination of the suspected agnosic patient proceeds by requiring the patient to recognise forms: Objects, figures, faces, signs and colours. If the patient fails to identify certain forms, the opportunity must be given to demonstrate recognition by matching, or by drawing the form. Correct matching and drawing then suggest normal perceptual processing but a deficit at a higher associative level. However, the possibility of perceptual-motor impairments and their potential effect upon matching or drawing performance must also be taken into account.

COGNITIVE NEUROPSYCHOLOGICAL APPROACHES

The *ad hoc* nature of current clinical assessment of visuo-perceptual functions can be seen in the previous summary. It is the hope of cognitive neuropsychology to give a more principled account upon which future testing can be based. Current models of vision in cognitive neuropsychology stress the critical role played by mental representations used for object recognition. These models of object recognition have two main stages. They are; firstly, the formation of a temporary representation, and secondly, its match to a description in long-term storage. Model-based approaches to neuropsychological testing, ask of any loss of function: Where in the processing chain does an impairment occur? It is useful to consider standard neuropsychological tests within theoretical frameworks even though they were often designed to assess perceptual abilities from a more atheoretical perspective. One should ask whether the test considers impairments to the formation of the temporary representation, the match to long-term storage or the permanent object descriptions.

Presumably, when colour vision, form perception, or other "basic" percepts are assessed as impaired after a cortical lesion, it is the temporary representation created from the visual input which is faulty. However, when testing the loss of colour vision by the Ishihara, or form perception by Poppelreuter's test, there is a hidden assumption that the loss takes place while other functions remain intact. Most available tests of perceptual function have, therefore, an implicit theoretical stance. In particular, the tests are the neuropsychological extension of a modular input theory. That assumption needs to be examined. To consider the extent to which those carrying out neuropsychological assessment need worry about the validity of the assumption, an account of the formation of the temporary representation will be given.

Pictorial Register

The retina receives patterns of light energy that change both spatially and temporally. Temporary representations are created from these luminance and chromatic differences. The representations are held in a buffer store which has been given various names. As a generic for all the alternatives, the term: Pictorial Register, will be used. The pictorial register incorporates, or results from, a more direct sensory store called "iconic" memory (Sperling, 1960). Iconic storage is said to have different properties (Phillips, 1974), from the more durable short-term pictorial register. However, the distinctions have been disputed (Coltheart, 1983). The pictorial register also operates as the short-term visual memory store known as the visuospatial scratch pad (Baddeley & Hitch, 1974). Maintenance of information in the pictorial register involves the visual memory maps found in the frontal lobes (Goldman-Rakic, 1987); these are part of a neural network connected to the "where" and "what" systems of the posterior cortex (Mishkin, Ungerleider, & Macko, 1983). A different register deals with auditory material (Brooks, 1968; Logic, 1986).

As its name implies, the contents of the register are pictorial. Posner and Keele (1967) talk of a visual code, which can survive for up to 25 seconds (Kroll et al., (1970). The visual code has interesting properties. Subjects are particularly quick to assess that two simultaneous or successive stimuli are identical (Bertelson, 1961). Non-identical shapes which differ only by orientation are also easy to match (Kelter et al., 1984), but less facilitation occurs compared to an identical repetition (Bartram, 1973). Thus, the pictorial register is the site at which unmediated visual information is represented. The central theoretical issue concerning the pictorial register is whether its contents are formed from isolated input modules. Neuropsychology provides some of the best evidence for independent loss of colour, motion etc. However, those patients in which only one of these modules has been lost are very rare. They are, nevertheless, theoretically important disorders. Perhaps the best-known are the loss of colour and form perception.

Modular Input to the Pictorial Register

Acquired achromatopsia (selective and complete loss of colour vision), of a central origin was first reported in the nineteenth century. An early case, though not the first (see Zihl & Von Cramon, 1986), documented by Verrey in

1888 (Damasio & Damasio, 1986) is most interesting. In his patient, there was a lesion of the infra-calcarine region involving the lingual gyrus and underlying white matter resulting in achromatopsia confined to one visual field. There was little damage to area 17, therefore visual reception was generally good. The lesion was relatively shallow so there was very little disturbance of other cortical sites and hence no other cognitive impairments. The patient was, therefore, able to be his own control and compare his normal colour vision to his achromatopsia. Until comparatively recently, nineteenth century reports of achromatopsia were not part of received opinion in the medical establishment. Neither Holmes (1918), nor Teuber, Battersby and Bender (1960) observed any achromatopsia in their large-scale studies of missile wounds to the brain to which they attributed a central origin. There are several reasons for their unwillingness to admit the possibility of acquired achromatopsia (see Damasio & Damasio, 1986). However, in more recent times, reports of cases where patients claim that "everything appears in various shades of grey" (Critchley, 1965; Meadows, 1974; Pallis, 1955), have had more widespread acceptance. Meadows, in what is still the largest survey, compared 14 cases of achromatopsia (some dyschromatopsic), with the intention of finding the anatomical locus and concommitant symptoms which they all shared. His survey found that all patients had visual field defects, especially for the left upper quadrant, usually with some loss of acuity. The critical lesion affected the anterior inferior part of the occipital lobe. Prosopagnosia (disorder of face recognition), and topographical disorientation were very common accompanying symptoms – presumably from lesions to anatomically close regions. A most informative description of the anatomy and associated symptoms for acquired achromatopsia comes from two cases reported by Damasio et al. (1980).

Acquired achromatopsia provides some of the best evidence for input modularity in the visual system. Further support for modularity comes from the selective loss of other functions. While being extremely rare, selective loss can occur for both motion (Zihl, von Cramon, & Mai, 1983), and stereopsis (Riddoch, 1917). A series of patients with occipital lobe lesions collected by Warrington (1985) shows the breakdown of these modular systems most clearly. Every possible double dissociation between colour discrimination, shape discrimination, visual acuity, and visual location estimation, was reported. While it is more common in cases of severe brain damage to lose both the ability to recognise colours and form, Warrington's cases are by no means the only reports of dissociation. Lissauer (1890; Shallice & Jackson, 1988), in his classic paper on disorders of object recognition noted that his patient had normal colour vision. In another similar case where colour vision was intact, objects were considered to be identical if they had the same colour (Marin, Glenn, & Rafal, 1983). Most remarkable of all, patients have been reported who can discriminate colour considerably better than lightness (Milner & Heywood, 1989; Rovamo, Hyvarinen, & Hari, 1982). These findings argue strongly that the temporary representation is formed from independent input modules.

The function of the input modules is to produce shapes that are potentially matchable to descriptions in long-term storage. The investigation of impaired shape perception is most often considered under the heading of apperceptive disorders of perception, following the classic paper of Lissauer (1890; Shallice & Jackson, 1988). Apperception refers to those perceptual processes, in the terminology of information processing, that go towards forming the temporary representation. Most disorders of object recognition are of the apperceptive type and may not be as rare as commonly thought. Poppelreuter (in Lange, 1936/1989) showed, from observations on a large sample, that apperceptive disorders could be shown in most cases of occipital lobe damage if the patient was put under time pressure. The functional contribution of the input modules to shape perception is not made clear in accounts of apperception. Thus, without a clear definition of its boundary conditions, it is no surprise to find concern about the variety of symptoms taken to demonstrate an apperceptive disorder. Poetzl (1928; Levine, 1978), for example, described Lissauer's case as if it were an attentional problem. Other definitions have depended on reasonable acuity but an inability to copy (Benson & Greenberg, 1969). Recent neuropsychological research, however, has tried to make clearer the different processing disorders which are present in disturbed apperception (Charnallet et al., 1988). It has been helped by drawing on ideas formulated in models of computer vision (Marr, 1982). Transposing Lissauer's scheme to Marr's theory of object recognition, apperceptive disorders include failures up to and including the formation of a 3-D temporary representation. Testing ought, therefore, to examine the formation of a 3-D model (Warrington & James, 1986), which could be impaired by many factors including: Sensory loss (Campion, 1987); disorders of stereoscopic vision (Riddoch, 1917); and spatial transform processes (Humphreys & Riddoch, 1984; Warrington & Taylor, 1973). Apperceptive disorders should also cover the incorrect match of the intact 3-D model to intact representations in long-term storage.

"Computer vision" research has given both modular and non-modular accounts of shape representation at the pictorial register. On the modular account (Marr, 1982), the representation is the end-product of a multistage process in which information (tokens) at different places in the visual field is constructed into surfaces. These surfaces, produced from several modular inputs, are held at what Marr called a 2½D sketch. The surfaces are then used to construct descriptions of shapes without any reference to object knowledge. The first constructed description is viewer-centred. The final 3-D model or object-centred representation allows the surfaces of objects to be specified independently of the viewer's position. The non-modular account dispenses with the 2½D sketch. The shape of a surface cannot be accurately determined from the luminance gradients within the surface (Barrow & Tenenbaum, 1978; Todd & Mingolla, 1983);

therefore, the boundary must be defined first. Boundaries are not formed from several modular systems but from the output of neurons differentially sensitive to all aspects of the input. Grossberg and Mingolla (1985), proposed that the temporary representation of an object is formed by the cooperation of two systems, namely: boundary contours and feature contours. The non-modular account has the implication that selective impairments for "basic" perceptual functions will never be absolute.

Implications for Testing "Basic" Visual Functions

The argument that double dissociation implies modular function is a popular one in neuropsychology. Shallice (1988) has cogently argued that the reasoning is based more on parsimony than logical necessity. It is logically possible for damage to non-modular systems also to produce double dissociations and thus appear to be modular. However, the argument becomes rather involved when the dissociation is profound. The dissociation between colour and form shown in neuropsychology can, in fact, be fairly sharp for preserved form perception with achromatopsia, even though there is usually some object recognition impairment. The implication of a non-modular input system is that the neuropsychologist is made aware of the limiting conditions for test validity. These limitations may not, in general, cause concern but it is important that they are known. For example, in using the Ishihara Test, one is asking for the formation of chromatic boundaries. Failure on the test need not imply loss of chromatic boundary formation, but of a more general problem with all boundaries. Failure could also imply a problem with achromatic surface perception, this being a likely consequence of non-modular input to the pictorial register. Indeed, there is no reported case where the discrimination of surface greys is absolutely perfect (but see Heywood, Wilson, & Cowey, 1987). It is also possible to succeed at the Ishihara Test while having no colour vision. At distances greater than normally tested, it is possible to form boundaries by the input into boundary forming systems more generally concerned with luminance (Mollon et al., 1980).

Not all failure at tests assessing "basic" functions necessarily indicates a problem in forming the temporary representation at the pictorial register. It is important to be aware that tests of basic visual functions require intact spatial abilities, otherwise false conclusions can be drawn. For example, failure at the Farnsworth Munsell test may not be due to an inability to form chromatic boundaries but rather in the ordering of the sequence of boundaried surfaces (Zihl et al., 1988). Tests are therefore required to assess the ability to carry out spatial computations on the temporary representation. They demand the matching and alignment of what might otherwise be perfectly formed temporary representations. Some of the problems with respect to modular functioning might also (theoretically), apply. When we use the Benton Test of Line Orientation we are explicitly assuming that the lack of colour is unimportant, as are the stationary and 2-D aspects of the display. However, as the test assesses not so much the formation, as the spatial organisation of the representations, it is probably correct not be concerned about these assumptions.

The Match to Descriptions in Long-Term Storage

Marr believed that the extraction of principal axes was critical for the construction of the object-centred view. His belief was based, in part, on clinical observations concerning object recognition (Warrington & Taylor, 1978). Warrington and Taylor (1973) found that patients with right parietal lesions were particularly impaired on object recognition tasks. The patients had difficulty in recognising objects from what they called an "unconventional" view but not from "conventional" views (Fig. 7.4). There are several interpretations of their patients' disorders that might highlight disordered apperception rather than impairments of long-term storage. For example, the formation of a 3-D representation could be impaired. The effect of right parietal lesions could be to allow the formation of only those representations that retain the main axis. Alternatively, these patients may fail to recognise an object from a particular view because of the omission of a salient feature from the representation at the pictorial register (Warrington & James, 1986). The problem, for these patients, could also be impaired access to representations in long-term storage (see Riddoch & Humphreys, 1987a).

Temporary representations contain both local and global features; it is reasonable to presume that access to the permanent representations might

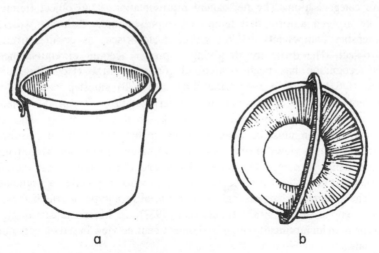

a   b

FIG. 7.4.   Unconventional Views of Objects Test: an everyday item is presented in (a) conventional and (b) unconventional representation (Beaumont, 1983). Reproduced by kind permission of the publisher, Blackwell Scientific Publications.

proceed from either (Humphreys & Riddoch, 1987). In the normal person there is preferential access from global features or, in the terms of the Grossberg and Mingolla (1985) model, large-scale boundary contours. Thus, a brain-damaged patient has been reported who was able to categorise objects from boundary information (Riddoch & Humphreys, 1987a), but was unable to integrate the detail sufficiently with the outline in order to achieve within-category recognition. Internal object detail hindered the patient in his attempt to recognise an object and, unlike normal subjects, he found silhouettes easier than line drawings. Riddoch and Humphreys argue that the patient's recognition difficulties were probably due to his inability to access the descriptions in long-term memory. However, since he could draw quite well from memory, the permanent storage of visual knowledge was probably intact.

Long-term Storage

Object recognition is a classification problem that has been tackled by researchers from two main directions. Some are more concerned with the perceptual problems and others by the place of object recognition in cognition. Computer vision theorists are mostly in the former category; they try to solve problems of edge extraction and resolving stereoscopic images rather than those of modelling human object recognition. Thus, with some exceptions (see Ullman, 1984; 1989), current algorithms for object recognition concentrate on the formation of the initial representations at the pictorial register. Nevertheless, computer vision models must propose some sort of template against which the temporary representation is matched. The primary and most difficult task is to achieve categorisation. The permanent representation of an object (template) must be in such a form that temporary representations differing widely in their sensory components are recognised (categorised) as coming from the same object. The difficulty in giving a proper account of equivalence in object recognition has been recognised for some time (Hoeffding, 1891); Neisser (1967) called it the "Hoeffding step". To sidestep concerns with the nature of object description in long-term storage, it can be called an entry level representation (Jolicoeur, Gluck, & Kosslyn, 1984). The entry level representation must be determined by spatial and/or visual coordinates as there are certain views of objects which are harder, and which some patients find impossible, to recognise. Palmer, Rosch and Chase (1981) have, therefore, suggested that entry level representations are in what they called a "canonical" form. The "canonical" representation is a visual prototype of which there are several versions (Marr, 1982; Biederman, 1987). In Marr's terminology, the prototype is an hierarchically organised object-centred view based on generalised cone shapes.

One relatively straightforward approach to the investigation of entry level representations is simply to demand categorisation of a stimulus as an object or non-object (Kroll & Potter, 1984; Riddoch & Humphreys, 1987b). In these studies, non-objects were constructed from random shapes or from parts of real objects (a wolf's head on a sheep's body would be categorised as a non-object). Activation of the entry level representation is affected by its connections to other entry level representations. Kroll and Potter (1984) found that object decisions were made easier by the prior presentation of a related object. Non-replications (Lupker, 1988) of the Kroll and Potter (1984) priming effect may result from task demands encouraging independent responses to each presentation.

Agnosic Disorders of Object Recognition

The term visual agnosia makes a distinction between a loss of knowledge from vision compared to that derived from touch and other modalities. By definition, the disorder will not involve problems with verbal comprehension (Hécaen et al., 1974; Rubens & Benson, 1971), and patients with word comprehension difficulties are not necessarily agnosic for visual stimuli (Benson, 1979; Warrington & McCarthy, 1983). However, the term visual agnosia suggests a unitary disorder and requires a considerable amount of unpacking (Humphreys & Riddoch, 1989). Lissauer distinguished between apperceptive disorders of object recognition and those based on impairments of association. Apperceptive disorders can be considered as inabilities to form temporary representations (see earlier). The diagnosis of an associative visual disorder assumes intact temporary representations and must result from damage to, or problems in, accessing stored object knowledge. It is necessary to discuss whether the impairment arises from damaged entry level systems and/or associated stored knowledge.

Damaged entry level representations would prevent recognition from the intact integration of boundary contours with feature contours (Grossberg & Mingolla, 1985). Thus, disorders at the entry level are probably involved in the poor object recognition of many cases that have been described as visual agnosia (Adler, 1944; Davidoff & Wilson, 1985; Sartori & Job, 1988). These patients could provide quite detailed non-visual information from a question, but showed that they had no detailed knowledge of what objects looked like. The patient of Davidoff and Wilson, for example, could count the number of legs in a picture but, if they were not shown, the correct answer would not be given. A swan pictured floating on a pond was said to have no legs visible but "four legs, I think, below the water". In a less extreme case, the patient of Schwartz, Marin and Saffran (1979) no longer knew the visual difference between a dog and a cat. Depending on the amount of detail that is required to differentiate objects at the entry level, most of the aforementioned patients could be assessed to have intact "semantics" but impaired entry level representations, enough information might trickle through to make possible some judgements from other knowledge structures. There seems no other way of explaining the successful performance on matching visually dissimilar pictures, according to the functions of the object, by patients with apperceptive disorders (Warrington & James, 1988). In fact, the amount of information that needs to be extracted to perform what appear to be complex visual tasks may be quite small. Marin, Glenn and Rafal (1983), for example, described a patient with very impaired picture recognition who was able to drive around and function moderately well in familiar surroundings.

The existence of visual agnosia, i.e. disorder of recognition without apperceptive disorder, was controversial at the time of Lissauer (Mauthner, 1881 and Simerling, 1890 − quoted in Levine, 1978), and those doubts have continued (Bay, 1953; Campion, 1987). Visual agnosia implies a dual representation of stored knowledge which is to some theorists unsatisfactory. To avoid proposing dual coding for knowledge representations, it is necessary to argue (Riddoch & Humphreys, 1987a), that studies which show separate impairments of stored knowledge for pictures and words (Warrington, 1975), are contaminated by differences at their respective entry level. Such arguments are often persuasive. However, the proposal *for* multiple and *against* unitary storage does not rest entirely (or even mainly) on visual agnosia. It is at least equally supported by a parallel line of neuropsychological research showing highly specific "semantic" impairments (Warrington, 1975; Warrington & Shallice, 1984). These impairments can be both modality- and category-specific.

Implications for Testing Object Recognition

Many tests of perceptual function (Street Completion Test, Gollin Figures, Hooper Visual Organisation Test, Minnesota Paper Form Board Test, Hidden Figure Tests, Overlapping Figure Tests; see earlier) are multidetermined. They are, in part, measuring the intact nature of the temporary representation at the pictorial register. However, to some degree all of them also require some access to stored knowledge concerning objects. Attempts have been made to clarify the processes involved (see Lezak, 1983). These clarifications have as yet been somewhat *ad hoc* relying, for example, on presumed functions impaired by damage to particular anatomical sites. The future of these tests must await a clearer indication of the perceptual functions involved in their successful completion. The provision of satisfactory tests of entry level and associated object knowledge is also still awaited.

CONCLUSION

We have attempted to review current practice in the clinical neuropsychological assessment of visuo-perceptual dysfunction, and also to show how an appraisal of current theoretical advances in the understanding of normal visuo-perceptual function has fundamental implications for the kinds of assessment which may be conducted in the future. Human neuropsychology is undergoing a period of rapid and radical change and we have yet to see how useful will be the developments which arise out of the cognitive neuropsychological approach.

Whatever the techniques which are yet to be developed, the provision of more valid cognitive models of normal function must be of benefit to clinical practice in assessment. As the ultimate goal of any neuropsychological assessment is an accurate description of the patient's psychological state (whether with the aim of diagnosis, of management, or of rehabilitation), this can only be successfully achieved if well-elaborated and valid models of normal performance are available. One of the great achievements of neuropsychology over the past two decades has been the collaboration between cognitive psychology and neuropsychology to improve and develop such models.

At least in the field of the assessment of visuo-perceptual disorders, investigatory techniques have always been, to some degree, based upon some functional analysis or model of the relevant performance. This is by contrast with the assessment of general intellectual function where the models have been essentially psychometric, or of aphasia where the models have often been taxonomic (although there are exceptions, for example, the Aachen Aphasia Test is based on prior linguistic principles: Huber et al., 1983). This is, of course, only broadly true as a generalisation, but it illustrates that the approaches adopted in different areas of neuropsychological assessment have had distinctive characteristics which have partly determined the validity and utility of the techniques employed.

The problem currently facing us is that the technology of assessment has generally failed to keep pace with the development of theory in neuropsychology, as in other areas such as neurophysiology. What we need now are new techniques intimately based upon recent advances in our understanding of visual-perceptual processes. No doubt they will emerge given time.

FURTHER READING

Beaumont, J. G. (1983). *Introduction to neuropsychology*. Oxford: Blackwell Scientific.

De Renzi, E. (1982). *Disorders of space exploration and cognition*. Chichester: Wiley.

Ellis, A. W., & Young, A. W. (1988). *Human cognitive neuropsychology*. Hillsdale, NJ: Lawrence Erlbaum Associates Inc.

Golden, C. J., & Vicente, P. J. (Eds.), (1983). *Foundations of clinical neuropsychology*. New York: Plenum Press.

Hécaen, H. J., & Albert, M. L. (1978). *Human neuropsychology*. New York: Wiley.

Heilman, K. M., & Valenstein, E. (Eds.), (1985). *Clinical neuropsychology* (2nd ed.). New York: Oxford University Press.

Lezak, M. D. (1983) *Neuropsychological assessment* (2nd ed.). New York: Oxford University Press.

Stiles-Davis, J., Kritchevsky, M., & Bellugi, U. (Eds.), (1988). *Spatial cognition: Brain bases and development*. Hillsdale, NJ: Lawrence Erlbaum Associates Inc.

Walsh, K. W. (1978) *Neuropsychology: A clinical approach*. Edinburgh: Churchill-Livingstone.

REFERENCES

Adler, A. (1944). Disintegration and restoration of optic recognition in visual agnosia. *Archives of Neurology and Psychiatry, 51,* 243–259.

Arthur, G. A. (1947). *A Point Scale of Performance Tests. Revised Form II.* New York: Psychological Corporation.

Ayres, A. J. (1966). *Southern California Figure-Ground Visual Perception Test. Manual.* Los Angeles: Western Psychological Services.

Baddeley, A. D., & Hitch, G. (1974). Working memory. In. G. Bower (Ed.), *The psychology of learning and motivation. Attention and performance VIII.* New York: Academic Press.

Barrow, H. G., & Tenenbaum, J. M. (1978). Recovering intrinsic scene characteristics from images. In A. Hanson & E. Riseman (Eds.), *Computer vision systems.* New York: Academic Press.

Bartram, D. J. (1973). The effects of familiarity and practice on naming picutres of objects. *Memory and Cognition, 1,* 101–105.

Bay, E. (1953). Disturbances of visual perception and their examination. *Brain, 76,* 515–550.

Beaumont, J.G. (1983). *Introduction to neuropsychology.* Oxford: Blackwell Scientific Publications.

Beaumont, J. G., & French, C. C. (1987). A clinical field study of eight automated psychometric procedures: The Leicester/DHSS project. *International Journal of Man-Machine Studies, 26,* 661–682.

Benson, D. F. (1979). *Aphasia, alexia and agraphia.* New York: Churchill-Livingstone.

Benson, D. F., & Greenberg, J. P. (1969). Visual form agnosia. *Archives of Neurology, 20.* 82–89.

Benton, A. L. (1974). *The Revised Visual Retention Test.* (4th ed.). New York: Psychological Corporation.

Benton, A. L., Hannary, H. J., & Varney, N. R. (1975). Visual perception of line direction in patients with unilateral brain disease, *Neurology, 25.* 907–910.

Benton, A. L., Hamsher, K. de S., Varney, N. R., & Spreen, O. (1983). *Contributions to neuropsychological assessment.* New York: Oxford University Press.

Bertelson, P. (1961). Sequential redundancy and speed in a two-choice responding task. *Quarterly Journal of Experimental Psychology, 12,* 90–102.

Biederman, I. (1987). Recognition-by-components: A theory of human image understanding. *Psychological Review, 94,* 115–145.

Brimer, M. A., & Dunn, L. M. (1963). *English Picture Vocabulary Tests.* London: National Foundation for Educational Research.

Brooks, L. R. (1968). Spatial and verbal components in the act of recall. *Canadian Journal of Psychology, 22,* 349–368.

Butters, N., & Barton, M. (1970). Effect of parietal lobe damage on the performance of reversible operations in space. *Neuropsychologia, 8,* 205–214.

Campion, J. (1987). Apperceptive agnosia: The specification and description of constructs. In G. W. Humphreys & M. J. Riddoch (Eds.), *Visual object processing: A cognitive neuropsychological approach.* London: Lawrence Erlbaum Associates Ltd.

Charnallet, A., Carbonnel, S, & Pettal, J. (1988). Right visual hemiagnosia: A single case report. *Cortex, 24,* 347–355.

Christensen, A-L. (1979). *Luria's Neuropsychological Investigation. Test.* (2nd ed.). Copenhagen: Munksgaard.

Colonna, A., & Faglioni, P. (1966). The performance of hemisphere-damaged patients on spatial intelligence tests. *Cortex, 2,* 293–307.

Coltheart, M. (1983). Iconic memory. *Philosophical Transactions of the Royal Society of London, B302,* 283–294.

Corkin, S. (1979). Hidden-Figures-Test performance: Lasting effects of unilateral penetrating head injury and transient effects of bilateral cingulotomy. *Neuropsychologia, 17,* 585–605.

Critchley, M. (1965). Acquired anomalies of colour perception of central origin. *Brain, 88,* 711-724.

Damasio, A. R., & Damasio, H. (1986). Hemianopia, hemiachromatopsia and the mechanisms of alexia. *Cortex, 22,* 161–169.

Damasio, A. R., McKee, J., & Damasio, H. (1979). Determinants of performance in color anomia. *Brain and Language, 7,* 74–85.

Damasio, A. R., Yamada, T., Damasio, H., Corbett, J., & McKee, J. (1980). Central achromatopsia: Behavioral, anatomic and physiologic aspects. *Neurology, 30,* 1064–1071.

Davidoff, J. B., & Fodor, G. (1989). An annotated translation of Lewandowsky (1908). *Cognitive Neuropsychology, 6,* 165–177.

Davidoff, J. B., & Wilson, B. (1985). A case of visual agnosia showing a disorder of pre-semantic visual classification. *Cortex, 21,* 121–134.

De Renzi, E., & Spinnler, H. (1967). Impaired performance on color tasks in patients with hemispheric damage. *Cortex, 3,* 194–217.

Dunn, L. M. (1965). *Expanded Manual for the Peabody Picture Vocabulary Test.* Minneapolis: American Guidance Service.

Dvorine, I. (1953). *Dvorine pseudo-isochromatic plates.* (2nd ed.). Baltimore, MD: Waverly Press.

Ekstrom, R. B., French, J. W., Harman, H. H., & Dermen, D. (1976). *Manual for Kit of Factor-Referenced Cognitive Tests.* Princeton, NJ: Educational Testing Service.

Elithorn, A., Jones, D., Kerr, M., & Lee, D. (1964). The effects of the variation of two physical parameters on empirical difficulty in a perceptual maze test. *British Journal of Psychology, 55,* 31–37.

Farnsworth, D. (1943). Farnsworth-Munsell 100-Hue and Dichotomous Test for Color Vision. *Journal of the Optical Society of America, 33,* 568–578.

Fuller, G. B., & Laird, J. T. (1963). The Minnesota Percepto-Diagnostic Test. *Journal of Clinical Psychology,* (Suppl. 16).

Goldman-Rakic, P. S. (1987). Circuitry of the primate prefrontal cortex and the regulation of behaviour by representational knowledge. In E. Plum (Ed.), *Handbook of physiology, the nervous system, higher functions of the brain, I*(V), 373–417. Bethesda, MD: American Physiological Society.

Gollin, E. S. (1960). Developmental studies of visual recognition of incomplete objects. *Perceptual and Motor Skills 11,* 289–298.

Grossberg, S., & Mingolla, E. (1985). Neural dynamics of form perception: Boundary completion, illusory figures, and neon color spreading. *Psycholoigcal Review, 92,* 173–211.

Hain, J. D. (1964). The Bender Gestalt test: A scoring method for identifying brain damage. *Journal of Consulting Psychology, 28,* 34–40.

Hamsher, H. De S. (1978). Stereopsis and unilateral brain disease. *Investigative Ophthalmology, 4,* 336–343.

Hardy, C. H., Rand, G., & Rittler, J. M. C. (1955). *H-R-R pseudoisochromatic plates.* Buffalo, NT: American Optical Co.

Heaton, R. K., Baade, L. E., & Johnson, K. L. (1978). Neuropsychological test results associated with psychiatric disorders in adults. *Psychological Bulletin, 85,* 141–162.

Hécaen, H., & Albert, M. L. (1978). *Human neuropsychology.* New York: Wiley.

Hécaen, H., & Angelergues, R. (1963). *La cécité psychique.* Paris: Masson et Cie.

Heilman, K. M., & Valenstein, E. (Eds.). (1985). *Clinical neuropsychology* (2nd ed.). New York: Oxford University Press.

Heywood, C. A., Wilson, B., & Cowey, A. (1987). A case study of cortical colour "blindness" with relatively intact achromatic discrimination. *Journal of Neurology, Neurosurgery and Psychiatry, 50,* 22–29.

Hoeffding, A. (1891). *Outlines of psychology.* London/New York: MacMillan.

Hooper, H. E. (1958). *The Hooper Visual Organization Test. Manual* Los Angeles: Western Psychological Services.

Huber, W., Poeck, K., Weniger, D., & Willmes, K. (1983). *Der Aachener Aphasie Test (AAT)*. Goettingen: Hogrefe.

Humphreys, G. W., & Riddoch, M. J. (1984). Routes to object constancy: Implications from neurological impairments of object constancy. *Quarterly Journal of Experimental Psychology, 36A*, 385–415.

Humphreys, G. W., & Riddoch, M. J. (1987). The fractionation of visual agnosia. In G. W. Humphreys & M. J. Riddoch (Eds.), *Visual object processing: A cognitive neuropsychological approach*. London: Lawrence Erlbaum Associates Ltd.

Hutt, M. L. (1977). *The Hutt Adaptation of the Bender-Gestalt Test* (3rd ed.). New York: Grune and Stratton.

Jolicoeur, P., Gluck, M. A., & Kosslyn, S. M. (1984). Pictures and names: Making the connection. *Cognitive Psychology, 16*, 243–275.

Kelter, S., Groetzbach, H., Freiheit, R., Hoehle, B., Wutzig, G., & Diesch, E. (1984). Object identification: The mental representation of physical and conceptual attributes. *Memory and Cognition, 12*, 123–133.

Kirk, S. A., McCarthy, J. J., & Kirk, W. D. (1968). *Illinois Test of Psycholinguistic Abilities. Examiner's Menual* (rev. ed.). Urbana, IL: University of Illinois Press.

Kroll, J. F., & Potter, M. C. (1984). Recognising words, pictures and concepts: A comparison of lexical, object and reality decisions. *Journal of Verbal Learning and Verbal Behavior, 23*, 39–66.

Kroll, N. E., Parks, T., Parkinson, S. R., Bieber, S. L., & Johnson, A. L. (1970). Short-term memory while shadowing: Recall of visually and aurally presented letters. *Journal of Experimental Psychology, 85*, 220–224.

Lange, J. (1936/1989). Agnosia and apraxia. In J. W. Brown (Ed.), *Agnosia and apraxia: Selected papers of Liepmann, Lange and Poetzl*. New York: Institute for Research in Behavioral Neuroscience.

Leiter, R. G. (1969). *Examiner's Manual for the Leiter International Performance Scale*. Chicago: Stoelting.

Levine, D. (1978). Prosopagnosia and visual object agnosia: A behavioral study. *Brain and Language, 5*, 341–365.

Lewis, R., & Kupke, T. (1977). *The Lafayette Clinic repeatable neuropsychological test battery: Its development and research applications*. Paper presented at the Southeastern Psychological Association, Hollywood, FL.

Lezak, M. D. (1983). *Neuropsychological assessment* (2nd ed.). New York: Oxford University Press.

Lhermitte, F., Chain, F., Aron, D., Leblanc, M., & Souty, O. (1969). Troubles de la vision dans les lesions du cerveau. *Revue Neurologique, 121*, 1–29.

Likert, R., & Quasha, W. H. (1970). *The Revised Minnesota Paper Form Board Test. Manual*. New York: Psychological Corporation.

Lissauer, H. (1890). Ein Fall von Seelenblindheit nebst einem Beitrage zur Theorie derselben. *Archiv fuer Psychiatrie und Nervenkrankheiten, 21*, 222–270.

Logie, R. H. (1986). Visuo-spatial processing in working memory. *Quarterly Journal of Experimental Psychology, 38A*, 349–368.

Lupker, S. J. (1988). Picture naming: An investigation of the nature of categorical priming. *Journal of Experimental Psychology: Learning, Memory and Cognition, 14*, 444–455.

Marin, O. S. M., Glenn, C. G., & Rafal, R. D. (1983). Visual problem solving in the absence of lexical semantics: Evidence from dementia. *Brain and Cognition, 2*, 285–311.

Marr, D. (1982). *Vision: A computational investigation into the human representation and processing of visual information*. San Francisco: W. H. Freeman.

Meadows, J. C. (1974). Disturbed perception of colours associated with localised cerebral lesions. *Brain, 97*, 615–632.

Milner, A. D., & Heywood, C. A. (1989). A disorder of lightness discrimination in a case of visual form agnosia. *Cortex*, *25*, 489–494.

Milner, B., & Teuber, H-L. (1968). Alteration of perception and memory in man: Reflections on methods. In L. Lwiskrantz (Ed.), *Analysis of behavioural change*. (pp. 268–375). New York: Harper and Row.

Mishkin, M., Ungerleider, L. G., & Macko, K. A. (1983). Object vision and spatial vision: Two cortical pathways. *Trends in the Neurosciences*, *6*, 414–417.

Mollon, J. D., Newcombe, F., Polden, P. G., & Ratcliff, G. (1980). On the presence of three cone mechanisms in a case of total achromatopsia. In G. Verriest, (Ed.), *Colour vision deficiencies*. (pp. 130–135). Bristol: V. Hilger.

Money, J. (1976). *A Standardized Road Map Test of Direction Sense: Manual*. San Rafael, CA: Academic Therapy.

Mooney, C. M., & Ferguson, G. A. (1951). A new closure test. *Canadian Journal of Psychology*, *5*, 129–133.

Neisser, U. (1967). *Cognitive psychology*. New York: Appleton Century Crofts.

Osterreith, P. A. (1944). La test de copie d'une figure complexe. *Archives de Psychologie*, *30*, 206–356.

Pallis, C. A. (1955). Impaired identification of faces and places with agnosia for colours. *Journal of Neurology, Neurosurgery and Psychiatry*, *18*, 212–224.

Palmer, S. E., Rosch, E., & Chase, P. (1981). Canonical perspective and the perception of objects. In J. Long & A. D. Baddeley (Eds.), *Attention and performance*, *IX*, Hillsdale, NJ: Lawrence Erlbaum Associates Inc.

Phillips, W. S. (1974). On the distinction between sensory storage and short term visual memory. *Perception and Psychophysics*, *16*, 283–290.

Posner, M. I., & Keele, S. W. (1967). Decay of visual information from a single letter. *Science*, *158*, 137–139.

Raven, J. C., Court, J. H., & Raven, J. (1977). *Manual for Raven's Progressive Matrices and Vocabulary Scales*. London: H. K. Lewis.

Riddoch, G. (1917). Dissociation of visual perception due to occipital injuries, with especial reference to appreciation of movements. *Brain*, *40*, 15–57.

Riddoch, M. J., & Humphreys, G. W. (1987a). A case of integrative visual agnosia. *Brain*, *110*, 1413–1462.

Riddoch, M. J., & Humphreys, A. W. (1987b). Visual object processing in optic aphasia: A case of semantic access agnosia. *Cognitive Neuropsychology*, *4*, 131–185.

Rovamo, J. Hyvarinen, L., & Hari, R. (1982). Human vision without luminance-contrast system: Selective recovery of the red-green colour-contrast system from acquired blindness. In *Colour vision deficiencies VI* (pp. 457–466). The Hague: W. Junk.

Rubens, A., & Benson, D. (1971). Associative visual agnosia. *Archives of Neurology*, *24*, 305–316.

Russo, M., & Vignolo, L. A. (1967). Visual figure-ground discrimination in patients with unilateral cerebral disease. *Cortex*, *3*, 118–127.

Sartori, G., & Job, R. (1988). The oyster with four legs: A neuropsychological study on the interaction of visual and semantic information. *Cognitive Neuropsychology*, *5*, 105–132.

Schwartz, M. F., Marin, O. S. M., & Saffran, E. M. (1979). Dissociations of language in dementia: A case study. *Brain and Language*, *7*, 277–306.

Semmes, J., Weinstein, S., Ghent, L., & Teuber, H-L. (1963). Correlates of impaired orientation in personal and extrapersonal space. *Brain*, *86*, 747–772.

Shallice, T. (1988). *From neuropsychology to mental structure*. Cambridge: Cambridge University Press.

Shallice, T., & Jackson, M. (1988). Lissauer on agnosia. *Cognitive Neuropsychology*, *5*, 153–192.

Sperling, G. (1960). The information available in brief visual presentations. *Psychological Monographs*, *74*, (11, Whole no. 498).

Street, R. F. (1931). *A Gestalt Completion Test.* Contributions to Education, No. 481. New York: Bureau of Publications, teachers College, Columbia University.

Talland, G. A. (1965). *Deranged memory.* New York: Academic Press.

Taylor, A. M., & Warrington, E. K. (1973). Visual discrimination in patients with localized brain lesions. *Cortex, 9,* 82–93.

Taylor, L. B. (1979). Psychological assessment of neurosurgical patients. In T. Rasmussen & R. Marino (Eds.), *Functional Neurosurgery.* New York: Raven Press.

Thurstone, L. L., & Jeffrey, T. E. (1982). *Closure flexibility (Concealed figures).* Park Ridge, IL: London House Press.

Todd, J. T., & Mingolla, E. (1983). Perception of surface curvature and direction of illumination from patterns of shading. *Journal of Experimental Psychology: Human Perception and Performance, 9,* 583–595.

TNO (1972). *TNO Test of Stereoscopic Vision.* Utrecht: Lameris.

Ullman, S. (1984). Visual routines. *Cognition, 18,* 97–159.

Ullman, S. (1989). Aligning pictorial descriptions: An approach to object recognition. *Cognition, 32,* 193–254.

Varney, N. R. (1982). Colour association and "colour amnesia" in aphasia. *Journal, of Neurology, Neurosurgery and Psychiatry, 45,* 248–252.

Warrington, E. K. (1975). The selective impairment of semantic memory. *Quarterly Journal of Experimental Psychology, 27,* 635–657.

Warrington, E. K. (1985). Visual deficits associated with occipital lobe lesions in man. In C. Chagas, R. Gatass & C. Gross (Eds.), *Pattern recognition mechanisms* (pp. 247–261). Berlin: Springer-Verlag.

Warrington, E. K., & James, M. (1986). Visual object recognition in patients with right hemisphere lesions: Axes or features. *Perception, 15,* 355–366.

Warrington, E. K., & James, M. (1988). Visual apperceptive agnosia: A clinico-anatomical study of three cases. *Cortex, 24,* 13–32.

Warrington, E. K., & McCarthy, R. (1983). Category specific access dysphasia, *Brain 106,* 859–878.

Warrington, E. K., & Rabin, P. (1970). Perceptual matching in patients with cerebral lesions. *Neuropsychologia, 8,* 475–487.

Warrington, E. K., & Shallice, T. (1984). Category specific semantic impairments. *Brain, 107,* 829–853.

Warrington, E. K., & Taylor, A. M. (1973). The contribution of the right parietal lobe to object recognition. *Cortex, 9,* 152–164.

Warrington, E. K., & Taylor, A. M. (1978). Two categorical stages of object recognition. *Perception, 7,* 695–705.

Wasserstein, J. (1980). *Differentiation of perceptual closure: Implications for right hemisphere functions.* Unpublished doctoral dissertation. New York: City University of New York.

Weiskrantz, L. (1986). *Blindsight: A case study and implications.* Oxford: Oxford University Press.

Zihl, J. Roth, W. Kerkhoff, G., & Heywood, C. A. (1988). The influence of homonymous visual field disorders on colour sorting performance in the FM 100-hue test. *Neuropsychologia, 26,* 869–876.

Zihl, J., & Von Cramon, D. (1986). *Zerebrale Sehstoerung.* Stuttgart: Kohlhammer.

Zihl, J. von Cramon, D. & Mai, N. (1983). Selective disturbance of movement vision after bilateral brain damage. *Brain, 106,* 313–340.

8 Assessment of Deficits in Facial Processing

Hadyn D. Ellis
School of Psychology, University of Wales College of Cardiff,
P.O. Box 901, Cardiff, CF1 3YG

INTRODUCTION

Faces are extremely important socio-biological objects. They indicate age, sex, race and identity, emotional state, health, and they also play an important role in communication. Our ability to discriminate among faces is quite impressive: Even identical twins seen together usually can be distinguished by the minutest of differences (Ellis, 1981).

Given the perceptual/cognitive skills underlying the categorisation of faces alone, their identification and the decoding of any muscular patterns revealed by them, it is, perhaps, surprising that faces have not been more extensively employed in neuropsychological tests. One would imagine that brain damage may easily disrupt the smooth operation of such finely-tuned processes involved in any of the aforementioned face-processing skills and that, therefore, tests designed to measure such impairments ought to have evolved universally for clinical use. However, as we shall see later, there have been a number of attempts in recent years to measure impairments in face-processing abilities, there have been very few commercially available tests published (e.g. Benton et al., 1978; Warrington 1984).

Many other face processing tests have been used for research purposes but these are characterised mainly by being *ad hoc* and largely unsupported by extensive normative data. Initially, this short review will concentrate mainly on two of the commercially available tests before discussing some of the other tests that have been described in the literature. Lezak (1983),

141

and Kapur (1988) also provide useful descriptions of some of the topics to be covered here.

THE BENTON FACIAL RECOGNITION TEST (1978)

The Benton Facial Recognition Test (BFRT) is something of a misnomer: It is better thought of as a face-matching test rather than a recognition test as it does not involve memory. Instead, as Fig. 8.1 indicates, the individual being tested is required to find a target face from among a set of six alternatives exposed simultaneously (Benton et al., 1978). There are two forms of the test: The Long and the Short Form. The Long Form comprises 22 items divided into three parts:

1. *Matching front views (identical)* – 3 male and 3 female targets, each included once among 6 similar alternatives.
2. *Matching front views to roughly ³/₄ profile view* – 4 male and 4 female targets each to be matched with 3 of 6 alternatives shown in various views, approximating ³/₄ profiles facing both left and right.
3. *Matching front views to faces under different lighting conditions* – 4 male and 4 female targets each of which is shown 3 times in a matrix of 6 faces.

In the Long Form the maximum total score is 54. The Short Form of the BFRT has a maximum total score of 27.

Benton et al. (1978) have standardised the BFRT with 286 normal adults and 266 normal children. Average performance is in the range 43-46. Any score below 40 may indicate pathological performance but defective performance is considered for scores below 38 (a score exceeded by 96.5% of normal subjects).

Not surprisingly, Hamsher, Levin, and Benton (1979) found that patients with right posterior lesions have the highest proportion of defective scores (0.53). They also noted that patients with left posterior damage and aphasia plus comprehension difficulties were also prone to defective BFRT scores (0.44).

Levin and Benton (1977) demonstrated the wider potential of the BFRT when they administered it to 44 psychiatric patients whose symptoms could be interpreted as arising either from an organic or a functional aetiology. Only one patient scored in the defective range, supporting, they claim, the usefulness of the BFRT for discriminating between neurological and "pseudoneurological" patients. However, since nonaphasic left hemisphere damaged patients also tend to score within the normal range (Hamsher et al., 1979), it seems premature to be too certain about the diagnostic value of the BFRT for such screening purposes.

Prosopagnosia

One of the other caveats to bear in mind regarding the BFRT is that it has often been reported that prosopagnosic patients score within the normal range (e.g. Bauer, 1984; Young & Ellis, 1989). But in order to do so they appear to have to adopt a piecemeal search strategy whereby they compare the target face feature by feature with each face in the matrix. This, of course, takes time and, because there is no temporal measure in the BFRT, a normal score may mask abnormal performance.

The fact that prosopagnosics may be able to match faces is not inconsistent with the model of face processing proposed by Bruce and Young (1986). They argued that what they term "directed visual processing", a module that derives information from a face concerning its owner's sex, race, age etc., is independent of other modules concerned with the recognition of familiar faces. It may also support matching unfamiliar faces. Therefore, it is not surprising that prosopagnosics, who have damage to one or more face recognition modules, may, nonetheless, manage to match faces — although why they should need to employ an atypical strategy to do this is not entirely explained.

It is perhaps worthwhile mentioning at this point another face matching test described by Warrington (1982). Figure 8.2 illustrates the type of items employed. The full test involves 20 pairs of faces on full-face pose and one $^3/_4$ pose, half of which are same and half different. Warrington (1982) reports that, compared with controls who average around 95% correct, patients with right hemisphere damage score poorly (averaging around 82% correct). There are no data to indicate whether Warrington's face matching test correlates significantly with the BFRT.

Warrington Face Recognition Memory Test (1984)

The Warrington Face Recognition Test (WFRT), which is a true test of recognition, is part of a two-stage memory test, the other half of which involves memory for words. Warrington's (1984) overall intention was to produce a test "geared to detect minor degrees of memory deficit"; and she chose to use material-specific tests to achieve this.

The WFRT comprises photographs of 100 unfamiliar faces, half of which are each presented for 3 sec. In order to ensure full attention, subjects are required to make a binary "pleasant" or "not pleasant" judgement about each one. Immediately afterwards each of the 50 test faces is paired with one of 50 distractor faces and the subject is required to choose which of these was shown earlier.

Warrington provides norms for adults of different ages. The average range is 84-90% correct which is slightly higher than the scores of a right hemisphere

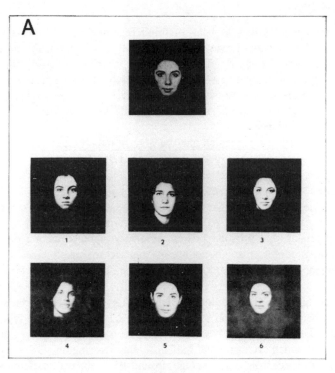

A

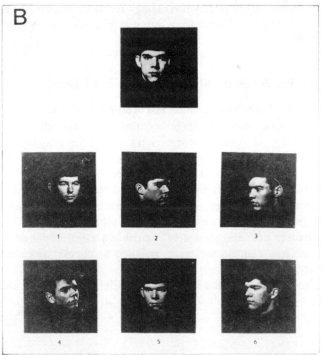

B

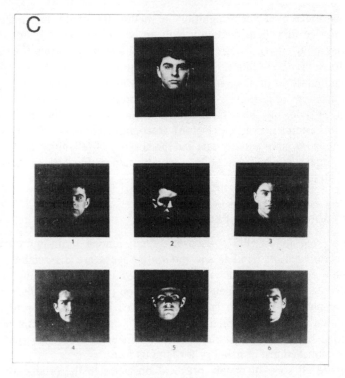

FIG. 8.1.   Test of Facial Recognition (Benton and Van Allen, 1968; Benton et al., 1983). These photographs illustrate the three parts of the test: A. Matching of identical front-views. B. Matching of front-view with three-quarter view. C. Matching of front-view under different lighting conditions. (Reproduced with kind permission of A.Benton)

lesion group (79.4%), but not particularly different from a left hemisphere lesion group (83.6%) − though both patient groups' scores were significantly lower than normals'. The right temporal and right parietal subgroups tended to contain most patients with problems on the WFRT (i.e. scoring at the level of 5% or less than the normal population).

The WFRT has not been used extensively in research. Clearly, it is limited in sensitivity and in the amount of information it can reveal. (Admittedly, in clinical use it would probably be administered in conjunction with the word memory test and therefore be more informative than when given alone.)

The problem with using a two-alternative forced choice memory test is that it confounds recognition of what has been presented with recognition of something that appears novel. In other words, on any trial subjects may choose an item, not because they recognise it but because the other item paired with it may look decidedly novel.

In most research on face recognition the method favoured is to present a target set and then to mix them randomly with an equal number of distractor faces. In this way both hits (i.e. correct recognitions) and false alarms (i.e. incorrect recognitions) may be separately measured or combined using statistical decision theory techniques to produce independent measures of memory sensitivity and decision criterion (e.g. Banks, 1970). This technique would have the additional advantage of requiring fewer faces to be shown at presentation and test. Kapur (1987) in his comments on Warrington's Recognition Memory Test notes that it is handicapped by poor validity data and the absence of reliability data. Moreover the photographs include details of dress which could enable testees to adopt verbal encoding strategies.

Recognition of Familiar Faces

Warrington and James (1967) discovered that, among brain-injured subjects, the ability to identify familiar and unfamiliar faces are dissociable – as we should now expect from Bruce and Young's (1986) model. Although there are few published tests of unfamiliar face recognition (Warrington, 1984), there are even fewer published tests for familiar faces. Leaving aside the problems, both practical and, possibly, theoretical, in using faces of individuals personally known to a patient, it is, at first glance, somewhat surprising that there is no well-established test of memory for famous faces.

There are all sorts of mainly practical obstacles to the production of such a test, ranging from considerations of copyright to the much more intractible problem arising from the evanescent quality of fame: i.e. today's celebrities may

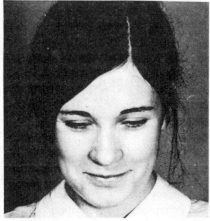

FIG. 8.2.   Example from Warrington's Face Matching test. (Reproduced with kind permission of E. Warrington).

be tomorrow's has-beens. Moreover, people's faces change with age so that even those who remain in the public eye for a considerable amount of time may not be so easily recognised from an old photograph.

Accordingly, most investigators have tended to construct *ad hoc* tests of famous face recognition, establishing data from control subjects appropriate for the patients being examined. Often these are single cases, suffering from some degree of prosopagnosia (e.g. Bauer, 1984; Bruyer et al., 1983). In other studies they are dementing patients (e.g. Crawford et al., 1986; Kurucz & Feldmar, 1979). With amnesic patients tests of their ability to recognise the celebrities of a particular decade have been employed in order to establish the retrograde extent of the memory disorder (e.g. Albert, Butters, & Levin, 1979). The face test used by Albert and her co-workers which forms part of the Boston Remote Memory Battery, contains 180 faces of famous people who achieved fame in one of six decades (1920s-1970s). Of these, 29 are shown in youthful and more contemporary photographs to form an old-young subtest. Albert's test has been used effectively with Korsakoff patients who show a gradient of accuracy (being worse with more modern celebrities); whereas controls show an essentially flat function between accuracy and decade of fame.

Other interesting techniques for measuring familiar face recognition ability have been developed by Young and his associates (e.g. Hanley, Young, & Pearson, in press). For example they have established two sets of celebrities: Set 1 comprises the faces of 20 very well-known people (e.g. Margaret Thatcher and John Wayne); Set 2 contains 20 "low familiarity" faces (e.g. Marlene Dietrich and Max Bygraves); and Set 3 is made up of 20 unfamiliar faces. Each set has been given to a number of control subjects at The Radcliffe Infirmary, Oxford, and so it is possible to match groups of equivalent age etc. The task requires first that each face is rated for familiarity, using a 7-point scale ranging from 1 ("totally unfamiliar") to 7 ("highly familiar"); second, that the person's profession is given; and third that their name is supplied. Thus, the test measures performance at different stages along the information processing chain leading to complete recognition of a face and, as such, has distinct advantages (both clinically and theoretically), over simpler tests of face memory.

Recognition of Emotional Expression

The ability to identify faces and recognise emotional expressions appears to be dissociable (Crawford et al., 1986; Ellis, 1983; Kurucz & Feldmar, 1979). It is important, therefore to employ separate tests of these abilities — but this is rarely done. DeKosky et al. (1980), are among the small group of researchers who have attempted to measure deficits in the ability to recognise emotional expressions. They compared right and left hemisphere damaged patients with controls on a task in which four faces were presented, depicting: anger, happiness, sorrow and indifference. The right hemisphere group performed worst on this task.

It is worth noting in passing that rather more work on affect recognition has appeared in the psychiatric literature. Morrison, Bellack, and Mueser (1988), present a recent review of efforts to measure deficits in the interpersonal skills of schizophrenics and other categories of psychiatric disorder by using tests of emotional expression recognition. They point out that most investigations use either stimuli developed by Izard (1971) or by Ekman, Friesen, and Ellsworth (1972), and that the comparability of the two sets of stimuli is unknown, making generalisation difficult. Equally, when investigators use their own stimuli, there is a problem of comparison with the results of others using different material (e.g. Mandal, 1987).

One easy objection to the use of any photographs of expressions or other social cues, whether posed or natural, is that normally we see dynamic faces. Giannini et al. (1984) describe their own attempts to overcome this by using videotaped faces surreptitiously recorded when interacting with a slot machine. Their interest was in assessing the social-cue recognition ability of a case of Mobius' Syndrome (a condition resulting, among other things, in the sufferer being unable to display facial expressions). Giannini et al., found that the patient was not only unable to "send" messages of affect, but was totally unable to "read" the faces to determine information from the non-verbal cues available.

CONCLUSIONS

Although there exists tests of face processing skills, some of which are accompanied by respectable normative data, there is a clear need for a more theory-driven approach. This would allow a more sensitive analysis of any deficits in an individual's ability to recognise and name familiar faces; learn new faces; draw inferences from faces (see DeRenzi et al., in press, for an age ordering test); and even to differentiate faces from other objects (see Newcombe's 1979, use of Mooney faces). At the same time attention needs to be paid to the response requirements of different tests which, themselves, may introduce artefacts. We are close to being able to design such a test battery. The approach by Young and his co-workers which goes much of the way towards meeting these criteria has already been adopted by others and has proved very useful (See Flude, Ellis, & Kay, in press). It cannot be long before a similar, more extensive battery complete with adequate norms, becomes available to all clinicians interested in measuring deficits in face processing.

ACKNOWLEDGEMENTS

I am grateful to Andrew Young, Narinder Kapur and John Crawford for their help in preparing this chapter. My work is currently funded by ESRC Programme Award (XC15250003). I should like to thank Arthur Benton (and

OUP) and Elizabeth Warrington for allowing me to reproduce Figs. 8.1 and 8.2, respectively.

REFERENCES

Albert, M. S., Butters, N., & Levin, J. (1979). Temporal gradients in the retrograde amnesia of patients with Korsakoff's disease. *Archives of Neurology, 36*, 211–216.

Banks, W. P. (1970). Signal detection theory and human memory. *Psychological Bulletin, 74*, 81–99.

Bauer, R. M. (1984). Autonomic recognition of names and faces: A neuropsychological application of the Guilty Knowledge Test. *Neuropsychologia, 22*, 457–469.

Benton, A. L., Hamsher, K., Varney, N. R., & Spreen, O. (1978). *Contributions to neurological assessment*. New York: Oxford University Press.

Bruce, V., & Young, A. (1986). Understanding face recognition. *British Journal of Psychology, 77*, 305–327.

Bruyer, R., Laterre, C., Seron, X., Feyereisen, P., Strypstein, E., Pierrand, E., & Rectem, D. (1983). A case of prosopagnosia with some preserved covert remembrance of familiar faces. *Brain and Cognition, 2*, 257–284.

Crawford, J. R., Besson, J. A. O., Ellis, H. D., Parker, D. M., Salzen, E., Gemell, H. G., Sharp, P. F., Beavan, D. J., & Smith, F., W. (1986). Facial processing in the dementias. In H. Ellis, M. Jeeves, F. Newcombe & A. Young (Eds.), *Aspects of face processing*. Dordrecht: Martinus Nijhoff

DeKosky, S. T., Heilman, K. M., Bowers, D., & Valenstein, E. (1980). Recognition and discrimination of emotional faces and pictures. *Brain and Language, 9*, 206–214.

DeRenzi, E., Gonacini, M. G., & Faglioni, P. (in press). Right posterior brain-damaged patients are poor at assessing the age of a face. *Neuropsychologia*.

Ellis, H. D. (1981). In G. Davies, H. Ellis & J. Shepherd (Eds.), *Perceiving and remembering faces: Introduction*. London: Academic Press.

Ellis, H. D. (1983). The role of the right hemisphere in face perception. In A. Young (Ed.), *Functions of the right cerebral hemisphere*. London: Academic Press.

Ekman, P., Friesen, W. V., & Ellsworth, P. (1972). *Emotion in the human face*. Elmsford, New York: Pergamon Press.

Flude, B., Ellis, A. W., & Kay, J. (in press). Face processing and name retrieval in an anomic aphasic: Names are stored separately from semantic information about familiar people. *Brain and Cognition*.

Giannini, A. J., Tamulonis, D., Giannini, M. C., Loisella, R. H., & Spiritos, G. (1984). Defective response to social cues in Mobius Syndrome. *The Journal of Nervous and Mental Disease, 172*, 174–175.

Hamsher, K., Levin, H. S., & Benton, A. L. (1979). Facial recognition in patients with focal brain lesions. *Archives of Neurology, 36*, 837–839.

Hanley, J. R., Young, A. W., & Pearson, N. A. (in press). Defective recognition of familiar people. *Cognitive Neuropsychology*.

Izard, C. E. (1971). *The face of emotion*. New York: Appleton. Century Crafts.

Kapur, N. (1987). Some comments on the technical acceptability of Warrington's Recognition Memory Test. *British Journal of Clinical Psychology, 26*, 144–146.

Kapur, N. (1988). *Memory disorders in clinical practice*. London: Butterworths.

Kurucz, J., & Feldmar, G. (1979). Prosopo-affective agnosia as a symptom of cerebral organic disease. *Journal of the American Geriatrics Society, 27*, 225–230.

Levin, H. S., & Benton, A. C. (1977). Facial recognition in "pseudoneurological" patients. *Journal of Nervous and Mental Diseases, 164*, 135–138.

Lezak, M. D. (1983). *Neuropsychological assessment* (2nd ed). New York: Oxford University Press.

Mandal, M. K. (1987). Decoding of facial emotions in terms of expressiveness by schizophrenics and depressives. *Psychiatry, 50,* 371–376.

Morrison, R. L., Bellack, A. S., & Meuser, K. T. (1988). Deficits in facial affect recognition and schizophrenia. *Schizophrenia Bulletin, 14,* 67–83.

Newcombe, F. (1979). The processing of visual information in prosopagnosia and acquired dyslexia: Functional versus physiological interpretation. In D. Oborne, M. Gruneberg & R. Eiser (Eds.), *Research in psychology and medicine.* London: Academic Press.

Warrington, E. K. (1982). Neurological studies of object recognition. *Philosophical Transactions of the Royal Society London, B298,* 15–33.

Warrington, E. K. (1984). *Recognition memory test manual.* London: NFER-Nelson.

Warrington, E. K., & James, M. (1967). Disorders of visual perception in patients with localised cerebral lesions. *Neuropsycholia, 5,* 140–142.

Young, A. W., & Ellis, H. D. (1989). Childhood prosopagnosia. *Brain and Cognition, 9,* 16–47.

9 The Assessment of Unilateral Neglect

Peter W. Halligan
Neuropsychology Unit, University Department of Clinical Neurology,
The Radcliffe Infirmary and Rivermead Rehabilitation Centre, Oxford

Ian H. Robertson
MRC Applied Psychology Unit, Cambridge

INTRODUCTION

Unilateral neglect has become one of the most exciting topics of modern clinical neuropsychology. This is evident from the growing number of texts concerned with the phenomenon, (Bisiach & Vallar, 1988; De Renzi, 1982; Freidland & Weinstein, 1977; Heilman, Watson, & Valstein, 1985a; Jeannerod, 1987; Mesulam, 1985). The study of neglect has theoretical implications for those interested in spatial processing (Bisiach, Luzzatti, & Perani, 1979) and attention (Posner, Walker, Freidrick, & Rafal, 1984; Robertson, 1989). It also has practical significance for the clinical management of those patients whose behaviours serve as major barriers to recovery (Diller & Weinberg, 1977; Kinsella & Ford, 1980; Robertson et al., 1990).

Unilateral neglect or hemi-inattention are both terms commonly used in clinical neurology to refer to the constellation of heterogenous and often debilitating behaviours characterised by the patient's failure to orientate, respond to, or report salient stimuli appearing on the side contralateral to a cerebral lesion. In the absence of any widely accepted definition, neglect was described in the early neurological reports rather loosely as a disturbance of visuo-spatial functioning within a larger syndrome thought to be peculiar to the damaged right hemisphere (Benton, 1982; Brain, 1941). The classical description, nevertheless, indicated that the phenomenon could not be explained solely in terms of generalised intellectual deterioration, sensory, or motor dysfunction (Friedland & Weinstein, 1977; Werth, Von Cramon, & Zihl, 1986). It is worth stressing however, that, not unlike other neuropsychological phenomena, neglect describes a clinically isolated conceptual construct commonly found within a much larger set of interacting, sensory, motor, and psychological deficits associated with acquired brain damage (Gordon & Diller, 1983). As such, the condition should not be considered a single invariant pattern of dysfunction, any more than the term aphasia labels one form of language disorder.

Many factors conspired towards the relative obscurity of neglect until the early 70s (cf. Bisiach & Berti, 1987), not least, difficulties in conceptualising and attempting to explain this predominantly lateralised behaviour in patients who otherwise retained impressive verbal and cognitive abilities. Furthermore, "... an important feature of hemi-inattention is that the manifestations are selective. Neglect phenomena are variable with different content; neglect is not an all or none phenomenon...thus the manifestations of hemi-inattention cannot be elicited with the same consistency as evidence of sensory or motor deficits alone". (Weinstein & Friedland, 1977).

One consequence of this variability has been the profusion of terms used to describe the condition. Indeed, the fostering of misleading interpretations may well have been facilitated by the use of the term "neglect" itself (Pineas, 1931), which describes an involuntary lack of awareness, whereas normal usage suggests a voluntary decision not to respond. A review of the literature reveals that the study of neglect has been hampered by the absence of any widely acceptable definition, assessment procedure, or neuropsychological explanation (Baynes, Holtzman, & Volpe, 1986; Campbell & Oxbury, 1976; Halligan, Marshall, & Wade, 1989; Johnston & Diller, 1986). In many cases neglect has tended to be defined by the particular *tests* employed to detect it.

From a clinical perspective, neglect has been singled out in several studies (e.g. Fullerton, McSherry, & Stout, 1986; Kinsella & Ford, 1985), as a negative prognostic factor which has profound effects upon the assessment and rehabilitation of other functions, (Wade et al., 1985; Gordon & Diller, 1983; Oxbury, Campbell, & Oxbury, 1974). Functionally, visual neglect imposes limitations on the degree of active participation in retraining programmes (Piasetsky et al., 1982), and has been associated with poor performance on functional recovery measures (Kinsella & Ford, 1980, 1985; Denes et al., 1982).

This chapter will not attempt to evaluate the current theories of neglect; this can be readily found in De Renzi (1982), Heilman et al. (1985a), Rizzollatti and Camarda (1987), and Bisiach and Valler (1988). Instead, we propose to clarify some of the current nomenclature, and review some of the tests and practicalities involved in assessing neglect.

CLINICAL PRESENTATION OF NEGLECT

The presence of spatial neglect following right hemisphere damage can be diagnosed simply by observing the patient's behaviour in their everyday environment. In severe cases the patient may behave as if one side of space has suddenly ceased to exist. Neglect may encompass several modalities. In the acute phase, neglect is associated with marked deviation of the head, eyes and trunk towards the ipsilesional side. The patient may fail to recognise their contralesional limbs as their own, may respond only when addressed from the ipsilesional side, and, in general, attend only to those people and events located on the non-affected side. The early stages are typically associated with a dense hemiplegia, which can be further complicated by a denial of the problem (anosognosia), or an equally striking emotional change, where the patient tends to minimise or rationalise the problem (anosdiaphoria). Examination of eye saccades in scanning during visual tasks indicates that eye movements are often restricted to the ipsilesional side (Girotti et al., 1983; Ishiai, Furukawa, & Tsukageshi, 1987; Rubens, 1985), despite the fact that occulmotor examination often reveals normal extraocular movement (Mesulan, 1985). In the majority of cases these symptoms resolve within the first few weeks; however, a preference for right-sided stimuli can continue for several months (Campbell & Oxbury, 1976; Colombo, De Renzi, & Gentilleni, 1982).

Behavioural manifestations commonly associated with spatial neglect are listed in Table 9.1. The list is by no means exhaustive and has been adapted from Gordon and Diller (1983). Patients may shave, dress or groom only the right side of their body; they may fail to eat food placed on the left side, fill out one half of a form, neglect to wear one sleeve or slipper, forget to place one foot on the footplate of the wheelchair and often lose their way while travelling between hospital departments.

It is therefore not surprising that such patients manifest difficulties with such basic skills as reading, writing, drawing and communication. The drawings themselves often include adequate representations of the right side, with the left side entirely omitted. Many of these patients remain debilitated across a wide range of naturalistic behaviours (Piasetsky et al., 1982) and from an assessment point of view neglect has been shown to have an adverse effect on most tests of perceptual processing (Gordon & Diller, 1983; Wade et al., 1985).

NATURE OF THE PHENOMENON

It is unlikely that neglect is a unitary phenomenon and within the clinical sphere it is more commonly used as a blanket term that describes a family of partially-separable yet conceptually related behaviours. (Heilman,

TABLE 9.1
Some Behavioural Manifestations of Visual Neglect

The patient may:

1) **Grooming:**
   a) Shave only one side of their face/wash only one side of their body.
   b) Experience difficulty in dressing/undressing.
   c) Apply make-up to one side.
   d) Experience difficulties with personal toileting.

2 **Perceptuo-motor Skills:**
   a) Omit, distort or misplace part of an object when copying or drawing.
   b) Omit letters and/or words from one side of the page while reading (Neglect dyslexia).
   c) Position text over on the right hand side when writing, revealing omissions of letters and words in written text.

3) **Time:**
   a) Experience difficulty in telling the time from a conventional analogue clockface.
   b) Have difficulty estimating time.

4) **Activities of Daily Living:**
   a) Experience difficulty in walking due to collisions with other patients and objects located on the left side; may frequently lose their way within hospital or rehabilitation settings as a result of neglecting left sided turns.
   b) Experience an increased number of accidents especially while transferring from wheelchair (Diller & Weinberg, 1977).
   c) Reveal difficulties in preparing simple meals in the kitchen.
   d) Ignore food on one side of the plate.
   e) Ignore items on a menu located on the affected side.
   f) Experience difficulty dialling the phone, shopping, watching TV and playing board games, e.g. chess (Cherrington, 1974).
   g) Display a tendency to over-attend to the 'good' side — sometimes failing to respond to people talking on the left side.

Valenstein, & Watson, 1984; Mesulam, 1981). One indication, however, of the confusion that currently surrounds the subject can be seen in the diversity of competing theories offered to explain neglect (Rizzolatti & Camarda, 1987).

One reason for this spectrum of theories is that neglect, and in particular, visual neglect, does not appear to be an all or none phenomenon. It can probably be best conceptualised as a heterogenous spatial disorder whose behavioural manifestations can be found along a continuum of severity and qualitative types (Behrmann et al., 1990). For example, recent reviews suggest that the presentation of neglect is far from simply a neglect of hemi-space with respect to the patient's bodily midline (Ladavas, 1987). Rather it may encompass:

1. Neglect of space with respect to particular features within a larger, more complex array. In Fig. 9.1 the left side of the woman is neglected although all or part of the stimulus placed further to the left is reproduced (and also neglected).

2. Neglect of representational space, as in the case of those tasks involving mental imagery. Bisiach and Luzzatti (1978), have shown that patients may describe (from long-term memory) only the right side of a familiar scene, in this case the respective views of the Piazza del Duomo in Milan. Similar examples have been described by Messeruli (see Bisiach & Berti, 1986): the Place Neuve in Geneva; and by Lhermitte, Cambier and Elghozi (1981): Place de la Concorde, Paris; Barbut and Gazzaniga (1987): a map of the U.S., and Meador et al. (1987): a street map of a town.

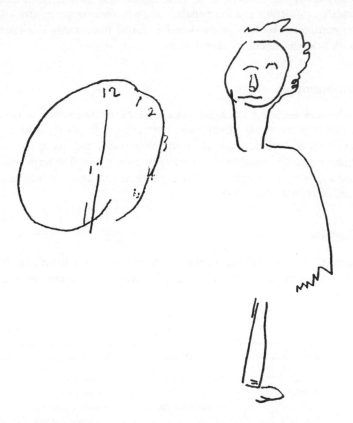

FIG. 9.1. "Object-centred neglect": Drawing of a clock face and a woman by a patient with visual neglect.

These observations suggest the relative independence of visual neglect from retinopic correspondence, a position that has more recently received support from the work of Bradshaw et al. (1987), Calvanio, Petrone, and Levine (1987), and Ladavas (1987).

The current literature suggests that neglect may encompass several sensory modalities and involve features of personal, peripersonal, extrapersonal and imagined space, (Halsband, Gruhn, & Ettlinger, 1985; De Renzi, 1982; Rizzolatti & Camarda, 1987). A summary of the spatial domains and sensory-motor factors affected are shown in Table 9.2.

TYPES OF NEGLECT IDENTIFIED

The major components of unilateral neglect, which often appear together, have nonetheless been shown to be dissociable, and include hemi-inattention, hypokinesia, extinction and hemispatial neglect. Anosognosia and allesthesia are also considered by some authors to be related phenomena (Heilman et al., 1985a). A brief discussion of each follows:

Hemi-inattention

This collective term describes the patient's lack of awareness or response to tactile, auditory, or visual stimuli unless attention is explicitly drawn to them. This can refer to both personal (hemisomatognosia), and extrapersonal space, and cannot be totally explained by sensory or motor loss. The term refers to the lateralised failure of ambient attentional processes to attract selective or serial attention. (Posner & Rafal, 1987).

Hypokensia

Hypokensia, or "intentional neglect", describes the patient's inability or delay in initiating a movement into the hemispace, contra-lateral to the

TABLE 9.2

Input Modalities	Spatial Domains	Output Modalities
Visual	Personal Space	Motor Limb/eye
Tactile		movements
Auditory	Peripersonal space	Initiation Latency
Olfactory		Response Latency
Kinesthetic/	Extrapersonal space	
Proproceptive		

lesion. (Coslett et al., 1990; Heilman et al., 1983; Valenstein & Heilman, 1981). The condition can be distinguished from more clinical impairments of the pyramidal system. The condition readily applies to head, eyes and torso movements, where patients manifest a reluctance to initiate movements towards the affected side.

Motor Neglect

This describes the absence or poverty of movements in a patient who, upon examination, does not appear to have motor loss on the side contralateral to the lesion (Critchley, 1953). Such patients may in response raise only one hand to the examiner's request to raise both hands. Laplane et al. (1983) has defined the condition as an under-utilisation of the limb contralateral to the lesion. When attention is focused on the limb in question the patient performs adequately (Heilman et al., 1979).

Hemispatial Neglect

This term describes what many regard as the classical symptoms of the neglect patient's performance. Drawing and constructional tasks remain among the clearest ways of illustrating this curious and often variable phenomenon. Requested to copy or draw a simple object, e.g. a clock (Fig. 9.2), the patient, besides confining the drawing to the right side of the page, will either grossly distort or omit the entire left side of the object (Critchley, 1953). Similar phenomena can be found when patients are asked to read or write (cf. Fig. 9.3). On tasks such as line bisection, the patient will position the perceived midpoint significantly to the right of the objective middle (Schenkenberg, et al., 1980). When requested to scan an array of stimuli and cross out designated members, items located to the left are seemingly ignored (Diller & Weinberg, 1977; Mesulam, 1985).

Allesthesia

This describes the patient's perceived displacement of a stimulus applied to the contralateral side over to the ipsilateral side. The disorder may occur in the auditory (alloacusis) tactile or visual modality. A recent example of allesthesia in the visual modality has been documented by Joanette and Brouchon (1984). In their case an interesting interaction appeared between the side of space upon which the stimulus appeared and the arm that was used. Only when the right arm was used in response to

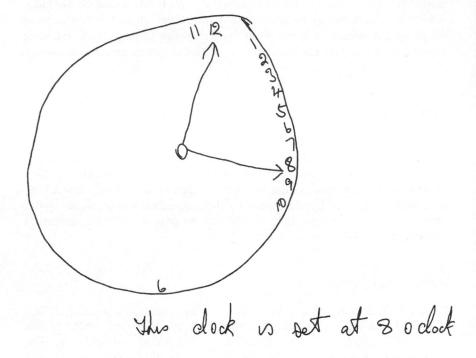

This clock is set at 8 o'clock

FIG. 9.2.   Left-sided neglect and right-sided contra-positioning on a clock face drawing.

a left-sided stimulus did the allesthesia appear. When the left arm was used in response to the same stimulus on the same side, there was no allesthesic response.

Anosognosia

This was first described by Babinski (1914), and typically refers to patients with left hemiplegia who appear unaware of their paralysis. Other forms of anosognosia have been described for aphasia, blindness (Antons syndrome), and hemianopia (Bisiach et al., 1986). Like neglect, the condition appears to vary along a continuum of severity from total denial to an inappropriate lack of concern (anosdiaphoria). Cuttings' (1978) study of anosognosic phenomena in a group of acute stroke patients suggests that the condition is not uncommon among right hemiplegics. The condition is typically associated with gross sensory loss, visual spatial deficits, and personal/extrapersonal neglect. However, Bisiach et al. (1986) have reported instances of double dissociation from neglect. Like

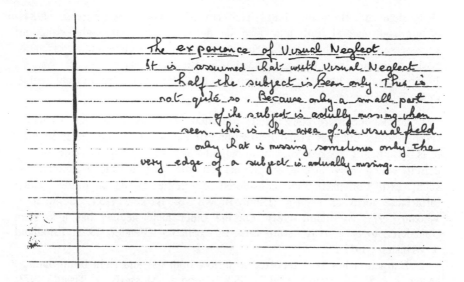

FIG. 9.3. Patient's description of her neglect. Note the positioning of the text on the right side of the page.

neglect, anosognosia cannot be explained solely in terms of sensory loss; many patients with severe sensory loss have no anosognosia. Furthermore, it may resolve in patients who continue to manifest sensory deficits or neglect features (Hier et al., 1983).

Extinction

The relationship between extinction and visual neglect has been the source of much discussion. (Freidland & Weinstein, 1977; Halligan, Marshall, & Wade, 1990; Halsband, Gruhn, & Ettlinger, 1985; Karnath, 1988; Milner, 1987).

Rapsak, Watson and Heilman (1987) state that extinction refers to the phenomenon whereby a patient fails "to respond to one of two simultaneously presented stimuli; despite the fact that each stimulus is correctly detected and localized in isolation". The condition has been observed in several modalities and was studied extensively by both Bender (1952), and Critchley (1949).

Extinction can also be seen in normal adults. Benton and Levin (1972), and Bender (1952) have reported that about half of the normal subjects tested exhibited extinction on the first exposure to the test. Furthermore, the condition is not only reserved for sensory input, motor extinction

(Valenstein & Heilman, 1981; Heilman, Valenstein & Watson, 1984), of the contralateral limb may also be demonstrated. Although extinction, as assessed on double simultaneous stimulation, currently enjoys a major position within the "neglect syndrome" (Heilman, Valenstein, & Watson, 1985b; Mesulam, 1985), the condition may be differentiated from visual neglect in the following ways:

1. Unlike the more conspicuous presentation of visual neglect, Critchley (1953), points out that visual inattention, or extinction, is not detected until it is specifically looked for; most patients and staff being unaware of any deficit which may arouse suspicions on the part of the examiner. As such, extinction has been considered by some to be a milder, often intractable form of neglect (Denny-Brown, & Barker, 1954; Heilman & Watson, 1977; Mesulam, 1981). On the other hand neglect has also been considered to be a more severe form of extinction (Bender, 1952; Friedland & Weinstein, 1977).

2. Extinction has been reported to follow both left and right brain damage (Allen, 1948; De Renzi et al., 1984; Gainotti, Messerli & Tissot, 1972; Weinstein & Freidland, 1977).

3. Unlike neglect, which does not require competing stimuli, visual extinction is an elicited response requiring fixation of gaze and occurs within the parameters of the visual field.

4. Although evidence exists indicating an association between the two phenomena, several studies have reported dissociations (e.g., Ettlinger, Warrington, & Zangwill, 1957; Ferro, Kertesz, & Black, 1987; Vallar & Perani, 1987; Zihl & Von Cramon, 1979). Furthermore, recent studies by Ogden (1985) and Halligan et al. (1990) describe double dissociations that support the position of Schwartz, et al. (1979), who argues for caution in applying findings derived from extinction to those of neglect.

AETIOLOGY AND NEUROPATHOLOGY

The most common cause of unilateral neglect tends to be vascular or tumoral in nature, although the phenomenon has been reported after other pathologies. These include: *Head injury* (McFie, Piercy & Zangwill, 1950; Rosenberger, 1974); *Parkinsons disease* (Villerdita, Smirni, & Zappala, 1983); *Right temporal lobe seizures* (Heilman & Howell, 1980); *Right unilateral ECT* (Heilman, Valenstein, & Watson, 1985); and *Right ventrolateral thalamotomy* (Vilki, 1980).

For the most part, the responsible lesions in neglect involve the right parietal lobes (Heilman et al. 1983), although lesions of the dorsolateral frontal lobe, cingulate gyrus, neostriatrium, and thalamus have also been documented, (Damasio, Damasio, & Ching Chui, 1980; Healton et al.,

1982; Rizzolatti & Gallese, 1988). Some authors have reported unilateral neglect after left hemisphere lesions (Albert, 1973; Ogden, 1985; and Gainotti et al., 1986); however, most reports agree that right-sided neglect is both less common and less severe than left-sided neglect. (Denes et al., 1982, De Renzi, 1982).

TOP-DOWN/BOTTOM-UP PROCESSING DEFICIT

As a contralesional disorder, spatial neglect manifests a misleading similarity to many sensory/motor disorders. While the classical descriptions (Weinstein & Freidland, 1977), indicate that the phenomenon cannot be explained solely in terms of primary disorders, the suggestion has been made that many symptoms of neglect may be secondary to more basic sensory or motor disorders (Battersby et al., 1956; Gianutsos & Matheson, 1987). This suspicion is perhaps best illustrated in the case of visual field deficits. The association is not altogether surprising as many patients who demonstrate neglect have lesions which typically involve, or pass close to, areas of the visual cortex or supragericulate pathways. However, the two disorders are operationally distinct and, notwithstanding the acute stages after brain insult, the behaviour associated with both disorders appears qualitatively distinct (Critchley, 1953).

Although sensory loss, such as homonomous hemianopia, may, in the acute stages of recovery, exacerbate some symptoms of visual neglect, many patients with reportedly intact fields continue to manifest florid symptoms of visual neglect (Halligan, Marshall, & Wade, 1990; Hier et al., 1983; Karnath & Hartze, 1987; Ogden, 1985; Mesulam, 1985; Oxbury, Campbell, & Oxbury, 1974). These clinical findings are supported by detailed visual field and occulographic studies (Girotti et al., 1983; Ishiai et al., 1987; Meienberg, 1983; Meienberg et al., 1981), which have shown that, unlike the hemianopic neglect patient, most hemianopics employ a consistent set of compensatory scanning strategies to locate and fixate objects on the affected side.

Furthermore, Albert (1973), Ogden (1985), and more recently Vallar and Perani (1987), have reported double dissociations between the two disorders. The recovery rates between the two conditions are often dissimilar (Hier et al., 1983; Meienberg et al., 1986). As to other occulographic factors (cf. De Renzi, 1982) it remains (Bisiach & Berti, 1987), "a well established fact that clear manifestations of unilateral neglect can be found dissociable from clinically detectable occulomotor impairments..."

These findings indicate the limitations of attempting to explain many forms of visual neglect at an infracognitive level. Indeed, much of the thrust behind sensory explanation rests with the misconception that confuses visual and spatial field (Jeannerod, 1987).

NATURAL HISTORY

Few studies have attempted to document the extent and time course of recovery from neglect. Fortunately, for the majority of patients the clinical evidence suggests that severe symptoms are often transitory and rarely persist beyond the acute phase (Columbo, De Renzi, & Gentilleni, 1982; Sunderland, Wade, & Langton-Hewer, 1987).

However, for a small number of patients it appears that features of neglect can continue to be insidiously disruptive long after the apparent resolution of the more florid symptoms (Campbell & Oxbury, 1976). Lawson (1962) describes two cases with neglect up to two years post-insult. Robertson et al. (1990) found that of 33 subjects still showing neglect, on average, 15 weeks post-stroke, 23 continued to show visual neglect 9 weeks later, and at least 19 of *these* were still exhibiting it a further six months after that. Other studies have reported symptoms of neglect lasting for 9 weeks (Hier et al., 1983); 6 months (Denes et al., 1982); 10 months (Columbo et al., 1982); 18 months (Kinsella & Ford, 1985) and up to 4 years (Kotila et al., 1986). Studies such as Zarit and Kahn (1974), describe features of neglect that have persisted for up to 12 years. The difficulty in interpreting many of these studies lies in the problem of patient selection, and the types of measures and criteria used (Sunderland et al., 1987). Campbell and Oxbury (1976) indicated that in some cases, the resolution of neglect on drawing tasks may be more apparent than real and that more subtle signs of the condition may continue to persist.

Incidence of Neglect

Despite its often striking presentation, the reported incidence of neglect is far from clear. In the absence of any widely agreed operational definition, all studies reporting the frequency of visual neglect have to be considered within the context of the particular criteria, definition, and tests employed. The incidence figures reflect the sensitivity of the various tests used (Piasetsky, 1981), together with the influence of aetiology (Bisiach & Vallar, 1988). The multiplicity of tests, coupled with the fact that the selection criteria for many of the subject cohorts investigated were based solely on unilateral cerebral lesions with little control over aetiology, time post onset, and lesion size, highlights the difficulty of making comparisons between studies (Sunderland et al., 1987). This can be seen clearly from a selective review of the reported incidences of visual neglect (Table 9.3).

For example, Hier et al.'s (1983) study of right brain-damaged patients found a prevalence rate of 85% using omissions on the Rey Ostereith figure copy, in a group of stroke patients seen within 7 days. A similar study by Vallar and Perani (1986) with right hemisphere-damaged patients of similar aetiology, found a prevalence rate of 43% using a simple circle cancellation task with patients seen within a mean interval post-onset of 7 days. Furthermore, in the absence of an acceptable operational definition, many, often cross-model, assessment techniques have been used (cf. Vallar & Perani, 1987), apparently with the implicit assumption that the same underlying deficit is being tapped.

ASSESSMENT OF NEGLECT

Although neglect has been shown to occur in several modalities, Halsband, Gruhn, and Ettlinger (1985), point out that "...it is uncertain whether neglect can still be regarded as a unitary defect, or whether different processes are disturbed in association with different forms of neglect". From a clinical point of view hemispatial neglect can be singled out as the most striking form, and by far the greatest number of tests and investigations have involved this type.

In the acute stages after brain damage, the symptoms of neglect are obvious even to the casual observer, and testing at this stage provides a useful audit of the patient's specific problems in everyday situations. In order to avoid any precipitous diagnosis of neglect it is necessary to differentiate neglect from primary sensory (hemianopia), and/or motor deficits (hemiparesis), as sensory motor loss may be the most obvious explanation for some of the patient's initial behaviour (Werth, Von Cramon, & Zihl, 1986). The diagnosis of neglect, therefore, should be reserved for those conditions not directly explained by more obvious motor and sensory deficits (Gianutsos & Matheson, 1987). In the acute phase, this may be difficult as the standard clinical neurological examination is unlikely to reveal many of the characteristic features of neglect (Chakravorty, 1982). However, several bedside clinical tests have been used, and, more recently, small batteries of tests have been devised to evaluate the heterogenous nature of neglect.

TABLE 9.3

Incidence (%)	N	Authors
12	136	Smith, Akhtar, and Garraway (1983).
24	106	Horner, Massey, Woodruff, Chase, and Dawson (1989).
36	97	Bisiach, Perani, Vallar, and Berti (1986).
41	172	Gianotti, D'Erme, Monteleone, and Silveri (1986).
43	290	Zarit and Kahn (1974).
50	101	Ogden (1985).
61	70	Leicester, Sidman, Stoddard, and Mohr (1969).
72	29	Levine, Warrach, Berowitz, and Calvanio (1986).
85	41	Heir, Mondock, and Caplan (1983).
95	40	Sckenkerberg, Bradford, and Ajax (1980).

As neglect is often associated with homonymous hemianopia (Vallar & Perani, 1986) and other occulomotor disorders (De Renzi, 1982), which can potentially affect the patient's condition, a careful examination of the patient's visual fields, acuity and eye movements is important (Gianutsos & Matheson, 1987). Some patients experience insight into their deficit, and the integrity of macular vision and congruity of field deficit appears to be an important factor in this respect (Gianutsos & Matheson, 1987). Unawareness of hemianopia appears to occur more often when macular vision is spared (Critchley, 1953).

The characteristic feature of visual neglect appear to be the patient's apparent inability to compensate by turning their head or eyes towards the affected side, as most hemianopic patients quickly learn to do (De Renzi, 1982; Critchley, 1953). A sensory explanation is difficult to sustain at this stage as the mere loss of sensory information does not in itself require the patient to cease exploring the affected side (Bisiach et al., 1981). Moreover, a visual field deficit may be confined to one quadrant whereas neglect may involve the whole hemispace (De Renzi, 1982). The simple bed-side test, devised by Meienberg (1983), which assesses saccadic eye movements, has shown that unlike hemianopia patients, the neglect patient's failure to compensate can be deduced from their apparent inability to predict target movements on the affected side.

VISUAL NEGLECT (HEMISPATIAL NEGLECT)

At present there exists a wide range of tests, all of which claim to be measuring the same condition. However, few of these have been standardised and little is known about the relationship between such tests (Halligan et al., 1991; Keenan, 1981; Wilson, Cockburn, & Halligan, 1987a). Several sources (Heilman et al., 1984; Mesulam, 1985), have suggested the initial use of double simultaneous stimulation in the absence of a primary sensory loss as a useful clinical method for diagnosing visual neglect. However, in the absence of a clear relationship between the elicited response of extinction and the more flagrant symptoms of hemispatial neglect, the equivalence of these measures must remain open to question (Schwartz et al., 1979). Clinical experience suggests that it is by no means the case that all patients who demonstrate visual extinction (in the absence of a visual field deficit), will necessarily exhibit the more florid forms of neglect behaviour.

Besides extinction tests (Isaacs, 1971; Smith et al., 1983), several other quantifiable tests have been developed and these typically require a motor response with the ipsilesional limb.

Many of these are un-standardised and, on their own, do not appear to adequately sample the diversity of neglect behaviours other than to indicate the extent of impaired lateralised performance.

Tests of visual neglect can be divided into the following:

1. Bedside Tests

Observing the patient during the standard examination of functional activities often reveals evidence of visual neglect. If the patient is asked to describe their room or immediate surroundings or pick up a series of items from the table in front of them, they will typically ignore features on the left-hand side (Stone et al., 1991). Visitors and friends are often ignored if they approach from the affected side. Complaints about eyesight or glasses are commonly put forward by the patients as an explanation for their reluctance to read or watch television.

2. Copying/Drawing Tests

These are among the simplest but most popular forms of tests used. (Battersby et al., 1956; Columbo et al., 1976; Critchley, 1953; Gainotti et al., 1970; Horner et al., 1989; Isaacs, 1971; Ogden, 1985; Oxbury et al., 1974; Zarit & Kahn, 1974).

The patient is given a pen and piece of paper which is positioned in front of their midsaggital plane. The patient is instructed to copy line drawings of e.g. a four-pointed star, Greek cross, butterfly, cube, simple map, geometric shapes or more complex scenes composed of several items. The patient may be asked to draw from memory a freehand picture of e.g. a flower, house, clock face, map of the country or locality with which they are familiar.

In most cases the neglect patient's performance demonstrates a striking omission of the left side of an object or group of objects. The patient usually places the drawing to the right of the page. Although drawing and copying tasks appear similar, dissociations between them have been observed; this is not surprising as copying relies heavily upon visual sensation whereas freehand drawing relies on a mental representation from memory and is devoid of immediate input up to the point of executing the task.

3. Visual Search and Cancellation Tests

These tests have shown themselves to be sensitive indicators of hemispatial neglect. Since Albert's line crossing test in 1973 several different types of this test have been published. Albert's (1973) line crossing test was one of the first standardised tests and required the patient to cross out 40 apparently random lines (2.5 cm long) on a sheet of paper (20 x 26 cm). This simple detection task has been adapted and used by several authors investigating the condition (Bisiach et al., 1986; Halligan et al., 1991; Karnath & Harze 1986; Kinsella & Ford, 1980; Levine et al., 1986; Ogden, 1985; Villerdita, 1987).

Cancellation tests are more complex and differ as to the number and type of target stimuli used. (Diller & Weinberg, 1977; Wade et al., 1988). Mesulam (1985) devised four tests which require the patient to scan random and structured arrays of verbal and non-verbal items. Neglect patients typically begin

Test sensitivity (Hemispatial neglect)

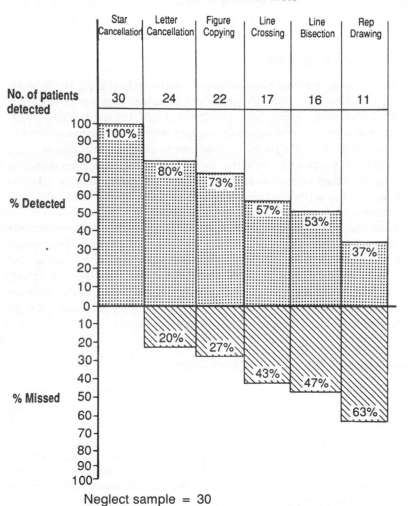

FIG. 9.4.   The relative "sensitivities" of the six conventional screening tests of the *Behavioural Inattention Test*.

their search in the centre or to the right of the display (Marshall & Halligan, 1989). Mesulam also reports that such patients display more omissions on the non-verbal version, and when the items are randomly, as opposed to systematically, structured. Cancellation tasks were found to be a sensitive indicator, revealing neglect when comparable tests such as line crossing were performed normally. Recently Halligan et al. (1988) showed that individual tests of visual neglect could differ substantially in their sensitivity. Star cancellation (see Fig. 9.4) was the most sensitive measure of neglect.

4. Line Bisection

Another sensitive test of neglect, this requires the patient to estimate and indicate the midpoint of a group of horizontal lines of varying length. The neglect patient, unlike controls who deviate slightly to the left (Bradshaw et al., 1985; Scarisbrick, Tweedy, & Kuslanski, 1987), tends to bisect the line towards the ipsilesional side (Columbo et al., 1976; Schenkenberg et al., 1980; Zarit & Kahn, 1974). Placing the target lines in left or right hemispace or cueing the patient to the left or right end of the line has been shown to enhance or reduce the overall displacement (Heilman et al., 1979; Riddoch & Humphreys, 1983). The great advantage of line bisection lies in its simplicity, ease of quantification and repeatability. However, it is advisable to utilise line lengths greater than 6 inches (152mm), as clear evidence of rightward displacement appears to occur as a function of line length for most patients (Halligan & Marshall, 1988; Marshall & Halligan, 1990).

5. Quantitative Assessments

As patients are often variable in the ways they manifest neglect, several authors have felt it necessary to use more than one test (Halligan et al., 1989; Ogden, 1985a). For example, Caplan (1987) found that 11 (4 LBD and 7 RBD) patients who exhibited significant attentional bias on *Raven's Coloured Progressive Matrices* and *Making Familiar Faces Test*, were able to perform a reading test without error. On the other hand, 10 (5 RBD and 5 LBD) patients, while demonstrating clear-cut omissions on a sensitive reading test, showed no significant position preference on either of the perceptual tests or on more general occupational therapy tasks. Similar dissociations include those reported by Bisiach et al., 1986; and Piercy et al., 1960.

Several neglect batteries have been described (Ferro & Kertesz, 1984; Horner et al., 1989; Rosselli et al., 1985). Ogden (1985) used five pencil-and-paper tests (line crossing, clock numbers, necker cube, five-pointed star, and a scene copying), to assess hemi-neglect and found that several tests were more sensitive than others. However, most large batteries test several modalities of neglect. One of the most recent, comprehensive investigations of unilateral neglect was reported by Halsband, Gruhn, and Ettlinger (1985). Their investigation involved quantitative tests of visual, auditory, tactile, kinaesthetic, motor and conceptual neglect and illustrated interesting dissociations that suggested different functional sub-components of neglect.

One of the main groups involved in the assessment and treatment of perceptual disorders such as neglect, over the past 15 years, is located at the New York University Medical Centre. Their quantitative battery of assessments samples four major areas (Gordon et al., 1984) and included:

1. Tests of Visual Scanning Deficits and Visual inattention.
2. Test of ADL/Skills.
3. Test of Sensory/motor Integration Tests.
4. Tests of Perceptual Integration.

6. Behavioural Inattention Test

A recently published test battery that also emphasises a quantitative approach is the *Behavioural Inattention Test* (Wilson, Cockburn, & Halligan, 1987b). The traditional assessment of visual neglect has tended to focus on a variety of single perceptual motor tasks which, while providing information about the presence and type of neglect, could not be easily related to the specific difficulties encountered in everyday life (Caplan, 1982; Hart & Hayden, 1986). The rehabilitation prospects of brain-damaged patients are rendered more realistic if considerations of their behavioural strengths and weaknesses are assessed within a functional framework. The *Behavioural Inattention Test* (BIT), by clearly pinpointing potentially disruptive aspects, enables resources to be directed more effectively to functionally relevant areas. Behavioural dependent measures provide a useful method of evaluating therapeutic and patient success irrespective of the theoretical orientation taken (Halligan et al., 1991).

The *Behavioural Inattention Test* (BIT) comprises a number of subtests, selected by psychologists and occupational therapists familiar with the real world problems faced by many patients with visual neglect. The practical selection of these items were determined by their quantitative testability and relevance to daily life (Table 9.4).

The test battery has the additional advantage of incorporating a standardised version of six conventional tests. The BIT was standardised on a group of 80 stroke patients and 50 controls. Validity, parallel form and inter-reliability all proved to be high.

CONCLUSION

Neglect probably consists of a constellation of inter-related disorders which can be difficult to disentangle. Until recently, well-standardised tests have not been available, though even as these appear there remains a need for careful

TABLE 9.4
Behavioural Inattention Test (Wilson et al. 1987b)

(A) Conventional Tests	(B) Behavioural Tests
Line Crossing	Picture Scanning
Letter Cancellation	Telephone Dialling
Star Cancellatin	Menu Reading
Figure and Shape Copying	Article Reading
Line Bisection	Telling/Setting the Time
Representational Drawing	Card Sorting
	Address and Sentence Copying
	Map Navigation
	Card Sorting

neuropsychological analysis of the nature of the problems underlying lateralised attentional loss. Only thorough assessments such as these are likely to provide a sound basis for effective rehabilitation.

ACKNOWLEDGEMENTS

The preparation of this chapter was supported by grants from the Stroke Association and Remedi (PWH).

REFERENCES

Albert, M.L. (1973). A simple test for visual neglect. *Neurology, 23*, 658–664.

Allen, I.M. (1948). Unilateral Visual Inattention. *New Zealand Medical Journal, 47*, 605–617.

Babinski, M.J. (1914). Contribution a l'etude des troubles mentaux dans l'hemiplegia organique cerebrale. *Revue Neurologique, 27*, 845–848.

Barbut, D., & Gazzaniga, M. (1987). Disturbances in conceptual space involving language and speech. *Brain, 110*, 1487–1496.

Battersby, W.S., Bender, M.B., & Pollack, M. (1956). Unilateral Spatial Agnosia (inattention) in patients with cerebral lesions. *Brain, 79*, 68–93.

Baynes, K., Holtzman, J.D., & Volpe, B.T. (1986). Components of visual attention. *Brain, 109*, 99–114.

Behrmann, M., Moscovitch, M., Black, S., & Mozer, M. (1990). Perceptual and conceptual mechanisms in neglect dyslexia. *Brain, 113*, 1163–1183.

Bender, M.B. (1952). *Disorders of Perception*. Springfield, IL., C.C. Thomas.

Benton, A. (1982). Spatial thinking in neurological patients: Historical aspects. In M. Potegal (Ed.). *Spatial Abilities: Development and Physiological Foundations*. New York: Academic Press.

Benton, A.L., & Levin, H.S. (1972). An experimental study of obscuration. *Neurology, 22*, 1176–1181.

Bisiach, E., & Bertie, A. (1986). Representational impairment as a factor in neglect. In K. Poeck, H.J. Freund, & H. Ganshirt (Eds.). *Neurology*. Berlin: Springer-Verlag.

Bisiach, E. & Berti, A. (1987). Dyschiria: An attempt at its systemic explanation. In M. Jeannerod (Ed.). *Neurophysiological and Neuropsychological Aspects of Spatial Neglect*. North-Holland: Elsevier Science.

Bisiach, E., Capitani, E., Luzzatti, C., & Perani, D. (1981). Brain and conscious representation of outside reality. *Neuropsychologia, 19*, 543–551.

Bisiach, E., & Luzzatti, C. (1978). Unilateral neglect of representational space. *Cortex, 14*, 129–133.

Bisiach, E., Luzzatti, C., & Perani, D. (1979). Unilateral neglect, representational schema and consciousness. *Brain, 102*, 609–618.

Bisiach, E., Vallar, G., Perani, D., Papagno, C. & Berti, A. (1986). Unawareness of disease following lesions of the right hemisphere: Anosagnosia for hemiplegia and anosagnosia for hemianopia. *Neuropsychologia, 24*, 471–482.

Bisiach, E., & Vallar, G. (1988). Hemineglect in humans. In F. Bollar & J. Grafman, (Eds.). *Handbook of Neuropsychology* Amsterdam: Elsevier Science.

Bradshaw, J.L., Nettleton, N.C., Pierson, J.M., Wilson, L.E., & Nathan, G. (1987). Coordinates of extracorporeal space. In M. Jeannerod (Ed.). *Neurophysiological and neuropsychological aspects of spatial neglect*. Amsterdam: Elsevier.

Brain, W.R. (1941). Visual disorientation and special reference to lesions of the right cerebral hemisphere. *Brain, 64*, 244–272.

Calvanio, R., Petrone, P.N., & Levine, D.N. (1987). Left visual spatial neglect is both environment-centred and body centred. *Neurology, 37*, 1179–1183.

Campbell, D.C., & Oxbury, J.M. (1976). Recovery from unilateral visuospatial neglect. *Cortex, 12*, 303–312.

Caplan, B. (1982). Neuropsychology in rehabilitation: Its role in evaluation and intervention. *Archives of Physical Medicine and Rehabilitation, 63*, 362–366.

Caplan, B. (1987). Assessment of unilateral neglect: A new reading test. *Journal of Clinical and Experimental Neuropsychology, 9*, 359–364.

Chakravorty, N.K., (1982). Parietal lobe syndrome due to cerebrovascular accidents. *Practitioner, 266*, 129–131.

Cherrington, M. (1974). Visual neglect in a chess player. *Journal of Nervous and Mental Disease, 159*, 145–147.

Columbo, A., De Renzi, E., & Faglioni, P. (1976). The occurrence of visual neglect in patients with unilateral cerebral disease. *Cortex, 12*, 221–231.

Columbo, A., De Renzi, E., & Gentilleni, M. (1982). The time course of visual hemi-inattention. *Archiv für Psychiatrie Nervenkrankheiten, 231*, 539–546.

Coslett, H.B., Bower, D., Fitzpatrick, E., Haws, B., & Heilman, K. (1990). Directional hypokinesia and hemispatial attention in neglect. *Brain, 113*, 475–486.

Critchley, M. (1949). The phenomenon of tactile inattention with special reference to parietal lesions. *Brain, 72*, 538–561.

Critchley, M. (1953). *The Parietal Lobes*. New York: Hafner.

Cuttings, J. (1978). The study of anosagnosia. *Journal of Neurology, Neurosurgery and Psychiatry, 41*, 548–555.

Damasio, A.R., Damasio, H., & Chui, H.C. (1980). Neglect following damage to frontal lobe or basal ganglia. *Neuropsychologia, 18*, 123–132.

Denes, G., Semeza, C., Stoppa, E., & Lis, A. (1982). Unilateral spatial neglect and recovery from hemiplegia. *Brain, 105*, 543–552.

Denny-Brown, D., & Barker, B. (1954). Amorphosynthesis from left parietal lesion. *Archives of Neurology, 71*, 303–313.

De Renzi, E. (1982). *Disorders of Space Exploration and Cognition*. New York: Wiley.

De Renzi, E., Gentillini, M., & Pattacini, F. (1984). Auditory extinction following hemisphere damage. Neuropsychologia, 22, 733–744.

Diller, L., & Weinberg, J. (1977). Hemi-inattention in rehabilitation; The evolution of a rational remediation programme. In E.A. Weinstein & R.P. Friedland (Eds.). Advances in Neurology, 18, 63–82.

Ettlinger, G., Warrington, E., & Zangwill, O., (1957). A further study of visual and spatial agnosia. Brain, 80, 335–361.

Ferro, J., & Kertesz, A., (1984). Posterior internal capsule infarction associated with neglect. Archives of Neurology, 41, 422–424.

Ferro, J.M., Kertesz, A., & Black, S.E. (1987). Subcortical neglect: Quantification, anatomy and recovery. Neurology, 37, 1487–1492.

Friedland, R.P., & Weinstein, E.A. (1977). Hemi-inattention and hemisphere specialization: Introduction and historical review. In E.A. Weinstein & R.P. Friedland (Eds.), Advances in Neurology, 18, 1–31.

Fullerton, K.J., McSherry, D., & Stout, R.W. (1986). Albert's Test; A neglected test of perceptual neglect. Lancet, 1 430–432.

Gainotti, G., D'Erme, P., Monteleone, D., & Silveri, M.C. (1986). Mechanisms of unilateral spatial neglect in relation to laterality of cerebral lesions. Brain, 109, 559–612.

Gainotti, G., Messerli, P., & Tissot, R. (1972). Qualitative analysis of unilateral spatial neglect in relation to laterality of cerebral lesions. Journal of Neurology, Neurosurgery and Psychiatry, 35, 545–550.

Gainotti, G., & Tiacci, C. (1970). Patterns of drawing disabilities in right and left hemisphere patients. Neuropsychologia, 8, 379–384.

Gianutsos, R., & Matheson, P. (1987). The rehabilitation of visual perceptual disorders attributable to brain injury. In M. Meier, A. Benton, & L. Diller (Eds.). Neuropsychological Rehabilitation. London: Churchill-Livingstone.

Girotti, G., Casazza, M., Musicco, M., & Avanzini, G. (1983). Occulomotor disorders in cortical lesions in man: The role of unilateral neglect. Neuropsychologia, 21, 543–553.

Goldenberg, G. (1986). Neglect in a patient with partial callosal disconnection. Neuropsychologia, 24 (3), 397–403.

Gordon, W., & Diller, L. (1983). Stroke, coping with a cognitive defect. In T.E. Burish & L.A. Bradley (Eds.). Coping with chronic disease. San Diego: Academic Press.

Gordon, W.A., Hibbard, M.R., Egelko, S., Diller, L., Shaver, M.S., Lieberman, A., & Ragnarsson, K. (1985). Perceptual remediation in patients with right brain damage: A comprehensive programme. Archives of Physical Medicine and Rehabilitation, 66, 353–359.

Gordon, W.A., Ruckdeschel-Hibbard, M., Elgelko, S., Diller, L., Simmens, S., Langer, K., Sano, M., Orazem, J., & Weinberg, J. (1984). Evaluation of the deficits associated with right brain damage: Normative data on the Institute of Rehabilitation Medicine Test Battery. New York: New York University Medical Centre, Dept. of Behavioural Sciences, 400 East 34th Street, New York, N.Y. 10016.

Gordon, W., Ruckdeschel-Hibbard, M., Elgelko, S., Weinberg, J., Diller, L., Slaver, M., & Piasetsky, E. (1986). Techniques for the treatment of visual neglect and spatial inattention in right brain damage individuals. Research and Training Centre on Head Trauma and Stroke, 400 East 34th Street, New York, N.Y. 10016.

Halligan, P.W., Cockburn, J., & Wilson, B. (1991). The behavioural assessment of visual neglect. Neuropsychological Rehabilitation, 1, 5–32.

Halligan, P.W., & Marshall, J.C. (1988). How long is a piece of string? A study of line bisection in a case of visual neglect. Cortex, 24, 321–328.

Halligan, P.W., Marshall, J.C., & Wade, D.T. (1989). Visuospatial Neglect: Underlying factors and test sensitivity. Lancet, 2, 908–911.

Halligan, P.W., Marshall, J.C., & Wade, D.T. (1990). Do visual field deficits exacerbate visuospatial neglect? *Journal of Neurology, Neurosurgery and Psychiatry, 53,* 487—491.

Halsband, V., Gruhn, S., & Ettlinger, G. (1985). Unilateral spatial neglect and defective performance in one half of space. *International Journal of Neuroscience, 28,* 173—195.

Hart, T., & Hayden, M.E. (1986). The ecological validity of neuropsychological assessment and remediation. In B.P. Uzzell, & Y. Gross (Eds.). *Clinical neuropsychology of intervention.* Boston: Nijhoff.

Healton, E.B., Navarro, C., Bressman, S., & Brust, J.C.M., (1982). Subcortical Neglect, *Neurology, 32,* 776—778.

Heilman, K., Bowers, D., Valenstein, E., & Watson, R.T. (1986). The right hemisphere: Neuropsychological functions. *Journal of Neurosurgery, 64,* 693—704.

Heilman, K.M., Bowers, D., Coslett, H.B., Whelan, H., & Watson, R.T. (1985). Directional hypokinesis: Prolonged reaction times for leftward movements in patients with right hemisphere lesions and neglect. *Neurology, 35,* 855—859.

Heilman, K.M., & Howell, G.J. (1980). Seizure induced neglect. *Journal of Neurology, Neurosurgery and Psychiatry, 43,* 1035—1040.

Heilman, K.M., & Valenstein, E. (1979). Mechanisms underlying hemispatial neglect. *Annals of Neurology, 5,* 166—170.

Heilman, K., Valenstein, E., & Watson, R.T. (1984). Neglect and related disorders. *Seminars in Neurology, 4* (2).

Heilman, K.M., Valenstein, E., & Watson, R.T. (1985b). The neglect syndrome. In J.A.M. Fredricks. (Ed.). *Handbook of Clinical Neurology, 1, (45): Clinical Neuropsychology.* Amsterdam: Elsevier.

Heilman, K.M., & Watson, R.T. (1977). Mechanisms underlying the unilateral neglect syndrome. In E.A. Weinstein & R.P. Friedland (Eds.). *Advances in Neurology, 18,* 93—106.

Heilman, K.M., Watson, R.T., & Valenstein, E. (1985a). Neglect and related disorders. In K.M. Heilman & E. Valenstein (Eds.). *Clinical Neuropsychology, (pp. 243—293).* New York: Oxford University Press.

Heilman, K., Watson, R., Valenstein, E., & Damasio, A. (1983). Localization of lesions in neglect. In A. Kertesz (Ed.). *Localization in Neuropsychology.* New York: Academic Press, 471—492.

Hier, D.B., Mondlock, J.R., & Caplan, L.R. (1983). Behavioural abnormalities after right hemisphere stroke. *Neurology, 33,* 337—344.

Horner, J., Massey, E., Woodruff, W., Chase, K., & Dawson, D. (1989). Task-dependent neglect: Computerized tomography size and locus correlations. *Journal of Neuropsychological Rehabilitation, 3,* 7—13.

Isaacs, B. (1971). Identification of disabilities in the stroke patient. *Modern Geriatrics, 1,* 390—402.

Ishiai, S., Furukawa, T., & Tsukagoshi, H. (1987). Eye fixation patterns in homonymous hemanopia and unilateral spatial neglect. *Neuropsychologia, 25,* 675—679.

Jeannerod, M. (Ed.) (1987). *Neurophysiological and neuropsychological aspects of spatial neglect.* North-Holland: Elsevier Science Publishers.

Joanette, Y., & Brouchon, M. (1984). Visual allesthesia in manual pointing: Some evidence for a sensorimotor cerebral organization. *Brain and Cognition, 3,* 152—165.

Johnston, C., & Diller, L. (1986). Exploratory eye movements and visual hemi-neglect. *Journal of Clinical and Experimental Neuropsychology, 8, (1),* 93—101.

Karnath, H.O. (1988). Deficits of attention in acute and recovered visual hemineglect. *Neuropsychologia, 26 (1),* 27—43.

Karnath, H.O., & Hartze, W. (1987). Residual information processing in the neglected visual field. *Journal of Neurology, 234,* 180—184.

Keenan, E. (1981). *Unilateral neglect: A study of the relationship between performance on perceptual task and corresponding difficulties in the everyday lives of patients with right hemisphere damage.* Unpublished B.P.S. dissertation.

Kimura, P. (1967). Cerebral dominance and the perception of verbal stimuli. *Canadian Journal of Psychology, 15*, 166–171.

Kinsella, G., & Ford, B. (1980). Acute recovery patterns in stroke patients. *Medical Journal of Australia, 2*, 663–666.

Kinsella, G., & Ford, B. (1985). Hemi-inattention and the recovery patterns of stroke patients. *International Rehabilitation Medicine, 7*, 102–106.

Kotila, M., Niemi, M., & Laaksonin, R. (1986). Four-year prognosis of stroke patients with visuospatial attention. *Scandinavian Journal of Rehabilitation Medicine, 18*, 177–179.

Ladavas, E. (1987). Is the hemispatial deficit produced by right parietal lobe damage associated with retinal on gravitational co-ordinates? *Brain, 110*, 167–180.

Laplane, D., & Degos, J.D. (1983). Motor Neglect. *Journal of Neurology, Neurosurgery and Psychiatry, 46*, 152–158.

Lawson, I.R. (1962). Visual-spatial neglect in lesions of the right cerebral hemisphere. *Neurology, 12*, 23–33.

Leicester, J., Sidman, H., Stoddard, L.J., Mohr, J.P. (1969). Some determinants of visual neglect. *Journal of Neurology, Neurosurgery and Psychiatry, 32*, 580–587.

Levine, D.N., Warach, J.D., Berowitz, L., & Calvanio, R. (1986). Left spatial neglect: Effects of lesion size and premorbid brain atrophy on severity and recovery following right-cerebral infarction. *Neurology, 36*, 362–366.

Lhermitte, F., Cambier, J., & Elghozi, D. (1981). Thalamic control of lateralized hemisphere function. In C. Loeb. (Ed.), *Studies in Cerebrovascular Disease*. Milan: Masson, Italia.

Marshall, J., & Halligan, P. (1989). Does the midsaggital plane play any privileged role in "left" neglect? *Cognitive Neuropsychology, 6*, 403–422.

Marshall, J., & Halligan, P. (1990). Line bisection in a case of visual neglect: Psychological studies with implications for theory. *Cognitive Neuropsychology, 7*, 107–130.

McFie, J., Piercy, M.F., & Zangwill, D. (1950). Visual spatial agnosia associated with lesions of the right hemisphere. *Brain, 73*, 167–190.

Meador, K.J., Loring, D.W., Bowers, D., & Heilman, K.M. (1987). Remote memory and neglect syndrome. *Neurology, 37*, 522–526.

Meienberg, O. (1983). Clinical examination of saccadic eye movements in hemianopia. *Neurology, 33*, 1311–1315.

Meienberg, O., Harrer, M., & Wehren, C. (1986). Oculographic diagnosis of hemineglect in patients with homonymous hemianopia. *Journal of Neurology, Neurosurgery and Psychiatry, 233*, 97–101.

Meienberg, O., Zangemeister, W.H., Rosenberg, M., Hoyt, W.F., & Start, L. (1981). Saccadic eye movements strategies in patients with homonymous hemianopia. *Annals of Neurology, 9*, 537–544.

Mesulam, M.M. (1981). A cortical network for directed attention and unilateral neglect. *Annals of Neurology, 10*, 309–325.

Mesulam, M.M. (Ed.). (1985). *Principles of behavioural neurology*. Philadelphia: F.A. Davis.

Milner, D. (1987). Animal models for the syndrome of spatial neglect. In M. Jeannerod (Ed.). *Neurophysiological and neuropsychological aspects of spatial neglect*. Amsterdam: Elsevier.

Ogden, J.A. (1985). Anterior-posterior interhemispheric differences in the loci of lesions producing visual hemi-neglect. *Brain and Cognition, 4*, 59–75.

Oxbury, J.M., Campbell, D.C., & Oxbury, S.M. (1974). Unilateral spatial neglect and impairment of spatial analysis and visual perception. *Brain, 97*, 551–564.

Piasetsky, E. (1981). *A study of pathological asymmetries in visual spatial attention in unilaterally brain-damaged stroke patients*. Unpublished Ph.D. City of New York: New York.

Piasetsky, E.B., Ben Yishay, Y., Weinberg, J., & Diller, L. (1982). The systematic remediation of specific disorders: Selective applications of methods derived in a clinical research setting. In L.E. Trexler (Ed.). *Cognitive Rehabilitation*. New York: Plenum.

Piercy, M., Hecaen, H., & Ajuriaguerra, J. De. (1960). Constructional apraxia associated with unilateral cerebral lesions − left and right sided cases compared. *Brain, 83*, 225−242.

Pineas, H. (1931). Ein Fall Non Raumlicher Orientierungsstorung mit Dyschirie. *Zeitschrift fuer die Gesamte Neurologie und Psychologie, 133*, 180−195.

Posner, M.I., & Rafal, R.D. (1987). Cognitive theories of attention and rehabilitation of attentional deficits. In R.J. Meier, L. Diller, & A.S.C. Benton (Eds.). *Neuropsychological rehabilitation*. London: Churchill-Livingstone.

Posner, M.I., Walker, J.A., Friedrick, F.J., & Rafal, R.D. (1984). Effects of parietal injury on covert orienting of attention. *The Journal of Neuroscience, 4*, 1863−1874.

Rapsak, S.Z., Watson, R.T., & Heilman, K. (1987). Hemispace—Visual field interactions in visual extinction. *Journal of Neurology, Neurosurgery and Psychiatry, 50*, 1117−1124.

Riddoch, M.J., & Humphreys, G.L. (1983). The effect of curing on unilateral neglect. *Neuropsychogia, 21*, 589−599.

Rizzolatti, G., & Camarda, R. (1987). Neural circuits for spatial attention and unilateral neglect. In M. Jeannerod (Ed.), *Neurophysiological and neuropsychological aspects of spatial neglect*. North-Holland: Elsevier Science.

Rizzolatti, G., & Gallese, V. (1988). Mechanisms and theories of spatial neglect. In F. Boller, J. Grafman (Eds.). *Handbook of neuropsychology, Vol. 1*. Amsterdam: Elsevier.

Robertson, I. (1989). Anomalies in the laterality of omissions in unilateral left visual neglect: Implications for an attentional theory of neglect. *Neuropsychologia, 27*, 157−165.

Robertson, I., Gray, J., Pentland, B., & Waite, L. (1990). Microcomputer-based rehabilitation for unilateral left visual neglect: A randomized controlled trial. *Archives of Physical Medicine and Rehabilitation, 71*, 663−668.

Rosenberger, P. (1974). Discrimination aspects of visual hemi-inattention. *Neurology, 24*, 17−23.

Rosselli, M., Rosselli, A., Vergara, I., & Ardila, A. (1985). Topography of hemi-inattention syndrome. *International Journal of Neuroscience, 27*, 165−172.

Rubens, A.B. (1985). Caloric stimulation and unilateral visual neglect. *Neurology, 35*, 1019−1024.

Scarisbrick, D., Tweedy, J.R., & Kushanski, G. (1987). Hand preference and performance effects on line bisection. *Neuropsychologia, 25*, 695−699.

Schenkenberg, T., Bradford, D.C., & Ajax, E.T. (1980). Line bisection and unilateral visual neglect in patients with neurological impairment. *Neurology, 30*, 509−517.

Schwartz, A.S., Matchok, P.L., Kreinick, C.J., & Flynn, R.E. (1979). The asymmetric lateralization of tactile extinction in patients with unilateral cerebral dysfunction. *Brain, 102*, 669−684.

Smith, D.L., Akhtar, A.J., & Garraway, W.M. (1983). Proprioception and spatial neglect after stroke. *Age Ageing, 12*, 63−69.

Stone, S.P., Wilson, B., Wroot, A., Halligan, P.W., Lange, L.S., Marshall, J.C., & Greenwood, R.J. (1991). The assessment of visuospatial neglect after acute stroke. *Journal of Neurology, Neurosurgery and Psychiatry, 54*, 345−350.

Sunderland, A., Wade, D.W., & Langton-Hewer, R. (1987). The natural history of visual neglect after stroke. *International Disabilities Studies, 9*, 60−65.

Valenstein, E., & Heilman, K. (1981). Unilateral hypokinesia and motor extinction. *Neurology, 31*, 445−448.

Vallar, G., & Perani, D. (1986). The anatomy of unilateral neglect after right hemisphere stroke lesions. A clinical CT scan correlation study in man. *Neuropsychologia, 24*, 609−622.

Vallar, G., & Perani, D. (1987). The anatomy of spatial neglect in humans. In J.M. Jeannerod (Ed.). *Neurophysiological and neuropsychological aspects of spatial neglect*. North-Holland: Elsevier Science.

Vilki, J. (1980). Visual hemi-inattention after ventrolateral thalamotomy. *Neuropsychologia, 27 (4)*, 399−408.

Villerdita, C. (1987). Tactile exploration of space and visual neglect in brain-damaged patients. *Journal of Neurology, Neurosurgery and Psychiatry, 234*, 292−297.

Villerdita, C., Smirni, P., & Zappala, G. (1983). Visual neglect in Parkinsons Disease. *Archives of Neurology*, 40, 737–739.

Wade, D.T., Langton-Hewer, R., Skilbeck, C.E., & David, R.M. (1985). *Stroke – A critical approach to diagnosis, treatment and management.* London: Chapman and Hall.

Wade, D.T., Wood, V.A., & Hewer, R.L. (1988). Recovery of cognitive function soon after stroke: A study of visual neglect, attention span and verbal recall. *Journal of Neurology, Neurosurgery and Psychiatry*, 51, 10–13.

Weinstein, E.A., & Friedland, R.P. (Eds.). (1977). Hemi-inattention and hemisphere specialization. *Advances in Neurology*, 18, New York: Raven Press.

Werth, R., Von Cramon, D., & Zihl, J. (1986). Neglect: Phanomene halbeitiger vernachlassigung nach hirnshadigung. *Fortschritte der Neurologie-Psychiatrie*, 54, 21–22.

Wilson, B.A., Cockburn, J., & Halligan, P.W. (1987a). Development of a behavioural test of visuo–spatial neglect. *Archives of Physical Medicine and Rehabilitation*, 68, 98–102.

Wilson, B.A., Cockburn, J., & Halligan, P.W. (1987b). *Behavioural Inattention Test.* Thames Valley Test Company, 34–36 High Street, Titchfield, Fareham, Hants.

Zarit, S., & Kahn, R. (1974). Impairment and adaption in chronic disabilities: Spatial inattention. *Journal of Nervous and Mental Disease*, 159, 63–72.

Zihl, J., & Von Cramon, D. (1979). The contribution of the "second" visual system to directed visual attention in man. *Brain*, 102, 835–856.

10 Assessment of Language Dysfunction

Sandra Walker
Department of Geriatric Medicine, University of Glasgow, Southern
General Hospital, Govan Road, Glasgow GS1 4TF

INTRODUCTION

Communication by speech is a strictly human characteristic. No other species has evolved such a means of communication. For language to emerge from the signal and sound systems common to many species, the human brain had to evolve to a point whereby it could integrate the vocalisations of the speech organs and also decipher and store linguistic data. Evolution of language was dependent on the development of underlying psychological functions. Language and symbolic activity probably evolved in an integrated way. We can look to the conceptual development from infancy to maturity to see this parallelism (simplified in Fig. 10.1) and their interrelated and integrated components (Chapey, 1981, after Muma).

Communication through the symbolised rules of utterance construction and usage, then, is a socially interactive convention. Thus (Carroll (1964) states:

> Language is a socially institutionalised sign system. It is the result of centuries of gradual development and change at the hands of many generations of species, but at any one point of history it exists as a set pattern of behaviour learned and exploited in varying degrees by each member of the speech community in which it is used.

Language is viewed, therefore, as one of the highest and most complex of cerebral functions, and subsequently language breakdown or dysfunction as one of the most sensitive indicators of brain damage or change.

177

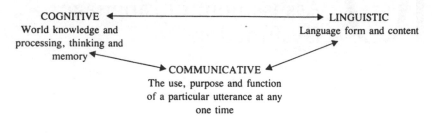

FIG. 10.1

The main theme of this chapter addresses the question of how brain damage can disrupt the use and system of language in adults (aphasiology), by focusing on the clinical investigation of aphasia and its concommitants. It is recognised, of course, that there are children for whom development of language does not conform to the broad spectrum of normality and for whom the description 'developmental dysphasia' might apply. Similarly there will be children who, like adults, acquire aphasia after they have developed language or during the normal period of language development. The unique patterns of disruption and developmental progression in children is beyond the scope of this review.

Before we can begin to evaluate the communication impaired patient, we must appreciate not only some linguistic concepts and terminology but also the basic anatomical organisation of language function. The description of the language system which follows uses broadly the classical neurological model. It is important to use a model such as this because it is the one commonly understood by neurologists and speech therapists. For those who wish to understand the functional neuropsychology of language, excellent reviews are provided by Ellis and Young (1988) and Shallice (1988).

THE BRAIN LANGUAGE SPEECH CONNECTION

Cortical Language Areas

In the dominant hemisphere of the brain the principal regions involved in language can be viewed in relation to the Sylvian fissure (Fig 10.2); concealed within the latter is a region of cortex which probably has an important role in language functions: the insula. Broca's area lies anterior to, and Wernicke's area lies posterior to the Sylvian fissure. It should be noted that Broca's area is used here as a shorthand for a system which includes parts of the insula and perhaps some subcortical regions, as well as the classical inferior frontal pars opercularis (Mohr, 1976). Likewise, Wernicke's region should be understood as referring to a posterior language region whose boundary is rather indefinite (Bogen & Bogen, 1976). Broca's area lies in the region of the motor association cortex lying anterior to the face region of the motor cortex. Since representation of the tongue, lips, jaw, soft palate and vocal cords is at the lower end of the precentral gyrus, these speech production muscles have representation directly in front of Broca's area. This allows for an output from Broca's area to be conveyed to the facial area of motor cortex (and to the corresponding area in the other hemisphere), then downwards via the motor tract to the required musculature.

Wernicke's area can be argued to be a region of auditory association cortex, lying next to the primary and secondary auditory cortex on the upper surface of the temporal lobe. An auditory stimulus received in the auditory cortex (the hearing cortex), is then decoded or deciphered in Wernicke's area.

Broca's and Wernicke's areas are connected by long association fibres which include the arcuate fasciculus and probably also tracts running through the insula. A further important area is the temporo-parieto-occipital junction: the angular gyrus. This clearing house is concerned with visual and auditory stimuli associations. Hence the visual stimulus can evoke an auditory association. (See Fig. 10.2)

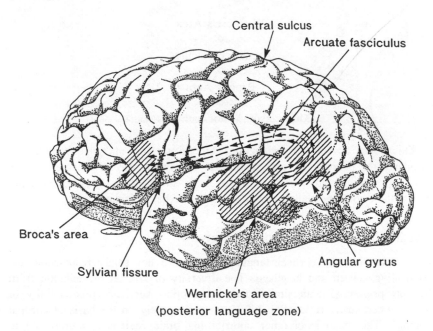

FIG 10.2.   Lateral view of the left hemisphere.

Visual Cortex

⇕

Visual Association Cortex

⇕

Angular Gyrus

⇕

Auditory Association Cortex (Wernicke's Area)

⇕

(The primary receptive areas—visual and auditory cortex
have no direct connections, but communicate via their
neighbouring association areas).

Thus, in order to relate the object *hat* with the name "hat" the visual stimulus of the object has to be processed correctly and the appropriate auditory association has to be made. the pathway can then be continued so that the word "hat" may be uttered, e.g.:

Visual Cortex

⇕

Visual Association Cortex

⇕

Angular Gyrus

⇕

Wernicke's Area

⇕

Arcuate Fasciculus

⇕

Broca's Area

⇕

(Motor strip, Motor pathways, etc.)

This route covers comprehension, repetition, and utterance production. Similarly the pathway for oral reading is usually by way of Wernicke's area onward to Broca's area, and the motor strip, in that the words seen usually arouse their common auditory association before being spoken.

Integrating Structures and Function

It is clear that the cortical language areas are not solely responsible for controlling speech and language. The diversity of clinical presentation from patients presenting with similar trauma, support such non-predictability of effect, when structure/function links are made purely on the basis of cortical damage. The anatomy of other contributing brain regions is represented in Fig. 10.3.

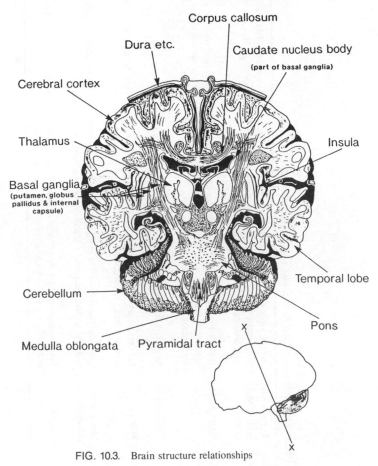

FIG. 10.3.   Brain structure relationships

Control of speech and language is complex because it involves simultaneous integrations of many cortical and subcortical structures. To explain this complexity of function, two functional divisions of brain can be made:

1. The function of the most recently developed and largest subdivision of the forebrain: the *Neocortex*.

2. The supporting non-cortical structures of the forebrain, the basal ganglia and the thalamus and *Hindbrain* (medulla oblongata and cerebellum).

The contribution of these brain areas is summarised in Table 10.1.

CLASSIC LOCALISATION OF DAMAGE

The effect of lesions in these main language areas gives rise to three major classic aphasic syndromes.

TABLE 10.1

Table Giving Parts of the Brain and Their Associated Language Functions

Cortex Concerned with the reception and recognition of other's speech, as well as the formulation, initiation and control of own.	Cortical lobes with speech areas	All the lobes are important in language processes since any sensory mnestic information may make connection with the language association areas. See Fig. 10.1 for the organisation of the language areas.
Subcortical Structures Concerned with the organisation and relay of sensory and motor impulses to and from the cortex	Basal ganglia	Involved in the control of the muscles of the face, larynx, tongue and pharynx and synchronisation with respiration. Damage to them may lead to lack of co-ordination in articulation, gesture and facial expression.
	Thalamus	Organises and relays sensory data on the way to the cortex.
	Midbrain	On the sensory side it contains relay stations concerned with sight and hearing. Similarly, on the motor side it carries the pyramidal and extra-pyramidal tracts.
	Medulla oblongata	Contains motor nuclei for controlling basic body functions, such as breathing, together with the motor and sensory tracts connecting with the midbrain.
	Cerebellum	The control centre for continuous muscular movements and co-ordination. Damage to it results in speech which is jerky, and unco-ordinated.

Wernicke's Aphasia

Wernicke's area, within the posterior language zone, appears to be of central importance in the comprehension and production of language through both speech and writing. When the auditory stimulus for spoken language reaches the primary auditory cortex it is heard because the patient is not deaf, but appropriate processing cannot occur in Wernicke's area because it is damaged and comprehension is impaired. The patient cannot repeat the heard stimulus, and reading is also impaired as comprehension of the written word depends on access to a semantic system which appears to involve the posterior language zone. Language production, too, is disrupted because this is dependent on arousing a central language processor. Similarly the patient will write incorrectly, frequently omitting content words. Thus, all four modalities of language: Comprehension of spoken language; comprehension of written language; use of language through speech; and use of language through writing; are affected by a lesion in Wernicke's area. Breakdown of comprehension resulting from such a lesion is of major communicative importance. The plentifully fluent, grammatically erroneous output, together with lack of insight (and often orientation and mood disturbance), present as a classic jargon aphasia pattern.

Broca's Aphasia

The nature of Broca's aphasia is more controversial. According to the classical model, a focal lesion in this area should preserve comprehension of spoken and written language whereas selection and production of the specific speech sounds for communication are disturbed. The muscles remain innervated from the motor cortex but the cortical selection and production of the sounds of speech are disturbed, and a slow, laborious pattern of speech results. There is also evidence that Broca's area has a grammatical function, and the Broca's aphasic exhibits grammatical errors in comprehension and production. Typically, function words (grammatical framework words more than meaning carrying words) the articles, auxiliary verbs, prepositions etc., and grammatical inflections (verb endings, plural endings), are omitted not only in spontaneous speech but also on repetition. Some word finding difficulties will be present. Errors in writing will broadly parallel those in the speech of a Broca's aphasic. There is a range of severity in this syndrome and some suggestion that when damage is restricted to narrowly defined Broca's area (area 44) the disturbance may be transient, but with wider and deeper injury the disturbance is more profound and persistent.

Conduction Aphasia

Classically, damage to the Arcuate Fasciculus, the link between the otherwise intact Broca's and Wernicke's areas, was said to produce conduction aphasia. Thus Wernicke's area can no longer communicate with Broca's area which particularly affects repetition. Broca's area can also function, but without the influence of Wernicke's area is unable to do appropriately. Availability of grammar is reduced at a higher level with many paraphasic naming errors, especially of the phonemic type, being produced. This also hinders reading aloud. Patients are aware and frequently attempt to self-correct their errors.

The problem with this explanation of conduction aphasia is that if the route from posterior to anterior language areas was seriously impaired one would expect more widespread disruption of verbal communication than is apparent in the typical conduction aphasia patient. Modern accounts of this syndrome instead, stress the presence of a deficit in short-term auditory memory because of damage to the inferior-anterior parietal cortex, the latter producing the deficit in repetition often accompanied by a phoneme—requiring problem as a result of damage to the posterior edge of Wernicke's region (see Shallice, 1988, for a review).

This picture of the classic aphasic syndromes was widened by the influence of the Boston School in the Seventies. At least two further syndromes are now accepted into aphasia typology.

Global Aphasia

Large pre- and post- Rolandic lesions damaging much of the fronto-temporo-parietal areas and with many concommitants (hemiplegia, hemianopia) pre-dispose patients to severe impairment across all language modalities. Output is non-fluent, restricted to a few word utterances at best, which are slowly and inaccurately produced, or one sound or syllable at worst, often repetitively uttered. A severe comprehension deficit distinguishes the global aphasic from the Broca's type. Written (read) language is meaningless and written production may be absent or limited as in speech production.

Anomic Aphasia

This category of aphasia is less clearly defined linguistically and anatomically but is generally associated with posterior lesions involving the angular gyrus and inferior parietal lobule. Auditory comprehension appears intact except if highly sensitive tests are applied. The sign of the anomic is word-finding difficulty, and particularly retrieval of less common word items. The grammatical framework remains, and a fluent output includes circumlocutions to compensate for missing items or indefinite term usage, i.e: 'thing', 'this', 'that', for specific meaning words. This word-finding problem is disproportionate to reduced abilities in the other modalities and may be manifest variably in reading and writing, according to the focus of lesion.

In recent years, with advances in brain scanning, it has been hypothesised that whereas the common language features in aphasia are associated with temporo-parietal changes, the distinguishing features between syndromes are associated with the nature and extent of changes taking place in regions such as the subcortical and pre-frontal regions.

The basic communicative functions: Conversational fluency, auditory comprehension, confrontation naming and repetition; can be used as markers to describe broadly the major aphasic types based on anatomic localisation. Two separate reviews are shown in Table 10.2. The minor variations, more in degree of presentation than presence or absence of feature, probably reflects the assessment bias of the workers concerned.

Aphasia-related Sequelae

There can be a number of focal concommitants attendant on acquired brain damage, which themselves constitute or contribute to communication impairment. Those worthy of particular attention are: *Dysarthria, Apraxia and Agnosia*. The contribution of the right hemisphere to communication and hence the outcome of right hemisphere damage is also considered here.

Praxis

Dyspraxia or apraxia of speech is a term used by speech pathologists which according to Behan (1989) is avoided to a great extent by neurologists. This is in part due to difficulty in its precise definition and also doubt as to its

TABLE 10.2
Résumé of Speech/Language Characteristics of Major (Boston) Aphasic Types

Aphasia type	Conversational Speech	Repetition	Naming (Confrontation)	Auditory Comprehension
Broca	Non-fluent (−)	Abnormal (=)	Abnormal (=)	Good (+)
Wernicke	Fluent paraphasic (+)	Abnormal (−)	Abnormal (−)	Abnormal (−)
Conduction	Fluent paraphasic (−)	Abnormal (−)	Usually good (=)	Good (+)
Anomic	Fluent (+)	Normal (+)	Abnormal (−)	Good (+)

Written Description from McNeil (1982) after Benson (1979)
Symbol Code. Lesser (1978)

KEY: + intact
      − impaired
      = limited proportional to other impairments

existence as a distinct or separate entity from aphasia. Thought to be present in a large proportion of aphasic patients, the picture is compounded further because testing for dyspraxia is frequently complicated by the co-existence of a severe comprehension deficit. The term dyspraxia generally acknowledges a failure of purposeful movement in the absence of any paralysis or paresis of the musculature involved; automatic or involuntary acts remaining uncompromised. Hence the locus of damage is assumed to be at the higher cortical planning or executive level rather than at the peripheral motor speech level.

Oral dyspraxia (buccofacial), therefore, would describe failure to make purposeful movement involving the facial muscles. The patient might be unable to: 'Show me how you blow' or 'Purse your lips', but might spontaneously put out a match. Similarly, in articulatory dyspraxia the patient may be unable to purposefully make articulations of the tongue, lips, palate and sequence speech sounds to form words. The resulting errors are inconsistently variable (though not necessarily without logical anatomic/phonemic pattern).

> e.g. Target *Book:* 'pook' 'boot' 'poot'
> 'pool' 'pood' 'bood', etc.

Testing for this phenomenon is often integrated into other procedures (Western Aphasia Battery), or as supplementary tasks (i.e. Boston Diagnostic Aphasia Examination). Limb, dressing, and constructional dyspraxia are other non-communication manifestations of disturbed praxis.

Motor Speech Difficulty or Dysarthria

Dysarthria (anarthria) by contrast arises from damage to the motor speech pathways from the motor strip in the cortex via the pyramidal, extra pyramidal and spinal nerve tracts, with contributions from the cerebellum and basal ganglia system. Depending on the locus of damage the outcome may be variable degrees of spasticity, paralysis, paresis or weakness in the muscles for speech and facial movement and may affect the primary functions of chewing and swallowing. The mark of the dysarthric patient is the drooling of saliva and slurring of speech, although a wide diversity of type and degree of dysarthria is encountered reflecting the severity and location of neurological insult.

Dysarthria tests examine the respiratory phonatory, articulatory and prosodic mechanisms as well as the functions of mastication and deglutition. The dysarthria assessment tests which are routinely available include the Frenchay Dysarthria Assessment (Enderby, 1983), and the Robertson Dysarthria Profile (Robertson, 1983).

Agnosia

Angosia (see Chapter 7), might simply be defined as an inability to attach meaning to sensory impressions, whereby a person may see but not perceive any, or only, specific visual stimuli (visual agnosia), or hear but not perceive any, or only, isolated auditory stimuli (auditory agnosia). The presence of such perceptual deficits can complicate interpretation of language test results. This requires targeted testing in order to specify the exact nature of the perceptual breakdown, i.e. the Rivermead Perceptual Assessment Battery (Winting et al., 1985).

The Right Hemisphere

Until fairly recently it was accepted that the left hemisphere alone, in the vast majority of the population, could communicate with language. Hence, it was often referred to as the speech hemisphere, and indeed Sperry (1970), described it as the "talking hemisphere". Experimental investigations over recent years have demonstrated that the right hemisphere has a linguistic capacity area in those who, in classical terms, were left-hemisphere dominant for language, and in spite of its inability to "speak".

Tachistoscopic experiments and often investigations with split-brain patients, confirm that it has some ideational existence of its own, recognising, for example, the meanings of certain spoken and written words. This can be good in respect of common object recognition, but is less impressive for verbs. The basis and degree of right-hemisphere language capabilities is, however, controversial (Gazzaniga, 1983; Zaidel, 1983). Recently, much attention has been given to the emotional or affective function of the right hemisphere, specific to language encompassing its influence on attitudes and emotions. (Bryan, 1988).

Heilman, Scholes, and Watson (1975); Tucker, Watson, and Heilman (1977); and Ross, Harney, and de Lacoste-Utamsing (1981), all suggest that these particular aspects of language appear to be principally governed by the right hemisphere and allow spoken language to acquire affective tone through prosody and gesturing. Without them the expression and comprehension of affectively charged speech may be seriously impaired. It is proposed that the right hemisphere controls affective language and behaviour and that this management is organised in an analogous fashion to the left hemisphere's role in propositional language. Specific right hemisphere functions relating to communication are shown in Table 10.3.

In general terms the previously held concept of the minor role of the right hemisphere is no longer acceptable. Above and beyond the affective use of prosody in this hemisphere is its capacity to process specifically linguistic prosody. Impairment of this capacity can be expected to have a fundamental effect on communication and as a result will again require specifically focused assessment. It is also hypothesised that in rehabilitation, right hemisphere compensation may be one of the major factors in the process of language recovery in many aphasic patients for whom the right hemisphere may be the primary information processing mechanism available.

TABLE 10.3
Right Hemisphere Specialised Processes which Directly or
Indirectly Affect Communication

Directly Affected Processes	Indirectly Affected Processes
Reception of emotionally intoned speech	Facial Recognition
Production of emotionally intoned speech	Holistic processing
Cadence	Visuo-spatial reasoning
Affective gesturing	Gross musical processing
	Copying figures
	Non-verbal memory

(Bayles, 1987)

OVERVIEW

In aphasiology clinicians always acknowledge and are vigilant as to the possibility of these complex factors and other possible co-existing features when assessing language functions as the causes of any performance deficit are likely to be multifactorial.

Linguistic Aspects of Aphasiology

Linguistics, or the scientific study of language, is an umbrella term for a group of related and ever-changing theories. Historically, linguists have looked to the normal development and the abnormal breakdown of speech and language function in order to test theories.

Linguistics has described communication in terms of different organisational levels, providing a basic, often hierarchical, framework for the analysis of the components of language. Aphasiology offers a rich source of experimental material with which to examine and develop this notion of linguistic levels and models.

Three basic levels can be considered, and these are shown in Table 10.4.

TABLE 10.4
Communication

Phonology: The sound system of speech	Syntax or grammar: The structural arrangement of sentences	Semantics: The level of lexical meaning

Whilst convenient, it must be stressed that it is virtually impossible to isolate (and hence evaluate) each level as a separate autonomous entity, as stated by Lesser (1978): "the separation of these levels has sometimes been objected to as a misleading avoidance of the complexities of the interwoven fabric of language", however, "this notion of separable levels is proving a productive one in asphasiology". This latter view has been especially the focus of cognitive neuropsychologists investigating human information processing models, and will receive further attention subsequently.

Each of the levels can be subdivided and some or several subdivisions can be investigated through applied linguistic testing strategies to assess the individual's competence within and between levels or modalities. The inter-relationship of the spoken to written or read levels is being developed elsewhere in this book (Chapter 11). Language assessment would aim to consider all of the psycholinguistic and sociolinguistic components to a greater or lesser extent. The former describing how the brain damage has affected the cognitive processes involved in language, and the latter considering the repercussions of that damage in terms of how it affects the impaired person's day-to-day communicative function. Table 10.5 describes some of the linguistic divisions used in aphasiology.

The primary role of the speech pathologist or clinician is to diagnose the type of communication disorder and compare it to similar clinical presentations

TABLE 10.5
Some Linguistic Divisions as Used in the Analysis of Aphasic Language

Level	Description	Examples of term
Phonology	Prosodic	Intonation, Stress
	Phonetic	Aspiration, Fronting
	Phonemic	Distinctive features
	Morphemic	Inflections
	Syntactic structure (surface)	Noun phrase, Verb, Clause
Syntax (grammar)	Transformation	Passive, Interrogative
	Syntactic structure (deep)	Subject, Object
	Case relations/Deep relations	Agent, Instrument, Functions
Semantics	Syntagmatic sense relations	Selectional restrictions
		Collocational restriction
	Paradigmatic sense relations (lexical-semantics)	Fields, Features, Networks
	Discourse (structure and sense relationships across sentences)	Intersentential anaphoric pronouns, Presuppositions
Communication	Verbal structure of communication	Assertion, Stream Analysis
		Support elements
	Non-verbal communication	Kinesics, Proxemics, Eye-contact, Social role
		(Lesser, 1978)

Reproduced by kind permission of the publisher, Whurr Cole Publishers and the author.

that permit prognostic judgement and therapeutic intervention. Subsequently, assessment establishes an objective baseline upon which response to therapy or change over time can be measured and monitored.

Areas of Communicative Interest or Focus

The areas of linguistic function in Aphasiology are usually investigated by focusing assessment on broader areas of communication, namely verbal expression and verbal reception, and assessing a range of tasks from simple single word repetition or naming, to more complex paragraph comprehension or construction. It is virtually impossible to devise a test focused solely on language. The problem of test construction is not one of selecting valid tasks, as these are fairly well agreed on, requiring systematic testing of the input modality used in receiving instruction, the input modality of the actual stimulus and the output modality of the response (Porch, 1967). Subtests are normally included which require relationships within and between the modalities of speech, reading, listening and writing, e.g. spoken (heard) word to written (read) word, or written (read) word to picture, etc. Interaction of phonetic, lexical, or grammatical function may be simultaneously investigated in a single task or isolated for single function examination. The major problem of test construction is more one of achieving a procedure fulfilling, as Chapey (1981), notes: all the "hallmarks of a quality assessment". Kertesz (1988) describes how, from clinical experience with aphasics and from the standards of construction from other psychological tests, an ideal aphasia test would have the following hallmarks:

1. It explores all potentially disturbed language modalities.
2. The subtests should discriminate between clinically relevant aphasia types.
3. The test items should include a range of difficulty in order to examine a representative range or severity of deficit (construct validity).
4. There should be enough items to eliminate most of the day-to-day and test-to-test variability (internal consistency).
5. The test items should measure the same factor (subtest internal consistency).
6. The administration and scoring should be standardised (inter-tester and intra-rater reliability).
7. The effect of intelligence, education and memory should be minimised to achieve, as specifically as possible, a test of language (content validity).
8. It should discriminate between normals, aphasics and non-aphasic brain-damaged individuals (criterion validity).
9. The length should be practical (administration in one or two sittings).
10. The test should measure the efficiency of communication (functional validity).

In these respects Benton (1967) suggests that development of specific aphasia tests paralleled similar developments in psychometric standardisation in the 1950s and 1960s.

Clinical practice has created the demand for assessments that fulfil as many of such hallmarks as possible.

The Goals of Assessment

Chapey (1981) summarises the goals of assessment under three headings:

1. Etiologic goals. These involve determining the presence of aphasia and identifying and defining factors which have precipitated or are perpetuating the impairment, and so determining if they can be reduced, changed or eliminated.

2. Linguistic/Cognitive/Communicative goals. These involve behavioural analyses which specify the nature and extent of abilities and deficits in that particular behaviour. This involves the ability to comprehend the content and form of spoken language; ability to produce the content and form of verbal language; ability to produce cognitive behaviour; and ability to communicate, i.e. use language for various functions.

*3. Intervention Goals.*These determine suitability for therapy and/or prognosis in therapy, they analyse ability to learn or profit from intervention, and specify and prioritise the series of intervention goals.

Many major tests having considered the aforementioned goals and hallmarks have focused their design on the following criteria:

1. Detection.
2. Localisation.
3. Prognostic judgement.
4. Classification of syndrome.
5. Classification of severity.
6. Focus for therapeutic intervention.
7. Measurement of status change.
8. Differential diagnosis.

Many tests can be evaluated against these standards as shown in Table 10.6.

THE LANGUAGE ASSESSMENT REPERTOIRE

Assessments of language might be considered under the following headings:

1. Classic multimodal or multidimensional batteries and screening tests.
2. Target or task-specific tests.

TABLE 10.6
Major Tests: Purpose/Design

Test	Defect Confirm	Localise Lesion	Predict Outcome	Classify Syndrome	Classify Severity	Focus Therapy	Measure Change	Termination Criteria	Differential Diagnosis
BDAE	X	X		X	X	X			
MTDDA	X		X	X	X	X	X		X
Examining for aphasia (Eisenson)	X				X	X			
PICA (Porch)	X	X	X	X	X	X	X	X	X
WAB	X	X	X	X	X	X	X		X

from McNeil (*op cit*)

Key: BDAE: Boston Diagnostic Aphasia Examination
MTDDA: Minnesota Test for Differential Diagnosis of Aphasia
PICA: Porch Index of Communicative Ability
WAB: Western Aphasia Battery

3. The cognitive neuropsychological targeted approach.
4. Functional assessments.
5. Tests for specific etiologic groups, i.e. dementias.

STANDARD ASSESSMENTS AND SCREENING TESTS

Focusing attention on differentiating abnormalities of language ability led to the traditional classification of aphasic syndromes previously described. Such classification evolved to recognise anything from two to eight varieties of aphasia. However, there is currently a sufficient measure of agreement as to the main features of the major aphasia types. Historically, the rationale for aphasia testing has been dynamic, reflecting different needs against a theoretical standpoint or the evolving theoretical constraints of the day. The changing fashion in tests reflecting the constraints current at the time, or the bias of the designer is illustrated in Table 10.7.

CLASSIC MULTIMODAL/MULTIDIMENSIONAL TESTS

Against this background, assessments of a multidimensional or multimodality nature can either be: (i) extensive battery procedures, or (ii) shorter screening procedures, selections of which are shown in Table 10.8.

TABLE 10.7
Aphasia Tests Illustrating Chronologically Distinctive, Theoretical Concepts of Aphasia

1. *Eisenson (1954) Examining for Aphasia:*
   In practice it is useful to distinguish *three classes of aphasia*
   1. Predominantly expressive
   2. Predominantly receptive
   3. Amnesic

2. *Schuell (1965) Minnesota Test for Differential Diagnosis of Aphasia (MTDDA):*
   Aphasia is one dimensional, and can properly only be classified by severity, and by whether or not it is accompanied by other symptoms, i.e. sensorimotor or visual deficits.

3. *Goodglass, Kaplan (1972) Boston Dianostic Aphasia Examination (BDAE):*
   There are several aphasias:
   Broca: Conduction: Wernicke: Anomic: Transcortical sensory: Transcortical motor

TABLE 10.8
Classic Multimodal/Multidimensional Batteries and Screening Tests

Name of Test	Author
1. (i)	
a. Minnesota Test for the Differential Diagnosis of Aphasia (MTDDA)	Schuell (1965)
b. Porch Index of Communicative Ability (PICA)	Porch (1967)
c. Boston Diagnostic Aphasia Examination (BDAE)	Goodglass, Kaplan (1972)
d. Western Aphasia Battery (NAB)	Kertesz (1982)
1. (ii)	
a. Aphasia Screening Test (AST)	Whurr (1972)
b. Shortened Schuell	Thompson & Enderby (1979)
c. Very Shortened Schuell	Powell, Bailley & Clark (1980)
d. Frenchay Aphasia Screening Test (FAST)	Enderby, Wood & Wade (1976)

DESCRIPTION OF SELECTED PROCEDURES

1. Extensive/Batteries

(a). The Minnesota Test for Differential Diagnosis of Aphasia (1965, rev. 1973).

Author	Hildred Schuell University of Minnesota Press U.S.A.
Supplier	NFER-Nelson, Windsor, U.K.
Auditory Disturbances	Recognising common words Discriminating paired words Recognising letters Identifying items named serially Understanding sentences Following directions Understanding a paragraph Repeating digits Repeating sentences
Visual, Reading Disturbances	Matching forms Matching letters

	Matching words to pictures
	Matching printed to spoken words
	Reading comprehension sentence
	Reading rate sentences
	Oral reading words
	Oral reading sentences
Speech and language	Imitating gross movements
Disturbances	Rapid alternating movements
	Repeating monosyllables
	Repeating phrases
	Counting to 20
	Days of week
	Completing sentences
	Answering simple questions
	Giving biographical information
	Expressing ideas
	Producing sentences
	Describing picture
	Naming pictures
	Defining words
	Re-telling paragraph
Visuomotor, Writing	Copying Greek letters
Disturbances	Writing Nos. to 20
	Reproducing wheel
	Reproducing letters
	Writing letters to dictation
	Writing spelling
	Oral spelling
	Producing written sentences
	Writing sentences to dictation
	Writing a paragraph
Numerical relations and	Making change
arithmetic	Setting clock
	Simple numerical combinations
	Written problems

Scoring: Essentially a pass/fail scoring, although some descriptive qualitative scores are provided for paragraph writing and picture description. Total scores per section can be graphically presented as percentages of achievement possible, patterns of which identify five major and two minor aphasias according to severity and type. This procedure is still widely used but its popularity decreased subsequent to the appearance of BDAE and WAB. Criticism relates to certain parts of its qualitative scoring which fails to reflect adequately error typology, e.g. "sounds normal but not quite". It also required British amendments (Davies & Grunwell, 1973) to eliminate much of its Americanese. Many therapists make use of the subtest form in related therapeutic tasks.

b. The Porch Index of Communicative Ability (1967, rev. 1971)

Author	Bruce Porch
Publisher (U.S.)	Consulting Psychologists Press
	55 College Avenue, Palo Alto, Calif. 94306
	U.S.A.
U.K.	NFER-Nelson, Windsor, U.K.
Content	The same 10 common objects, e.g. toothbrush, comb, are used throughout all 18 subtests.

Production

subtest	IV	Spontaneous verbal naming
	IX	Verbal closure naming
	XII	Verbal repetition naming
	B	Graphic repetition naming
	C	Graphic repetition naming
	D	Graphic repetition spelling
	E	Graphic copying
	F	Graphic copying

Comprehension

Subtest	X	Recognition of objects named
	VIII	Matching pictures of objects to objects
	XI	Matching objects

Content/Form

Production

Subtest	I	Verbal description object use
Subtest	A	Graphic description object use

Comprehension

Subtest	II	Gestural description object use
	III	Gestural description object use

VI   Recognition of object by description of function
V   Reading comprehension
VII Reading comprehension

Scoring: The degree to which each response deviates from the norm provides norm-referenced scores. Deviations consider: accuracy, responsiveness, completeness, promptness, and production efficiency hence scoring is multidimensional. Percent scores from a large aphasic sample are provided. Each subtest has a mean score, and total for verbal, gestural and graphic modalities collectively provide an overall mean score. These have diagnostic, prognostic and therapeutic significance.

(It should be noted that clinical use of this procedure normally requires a degree of training to achieve administrative consistency and accuracy.)

c. The Boston Diagnostic Aphasia Examination ⊃ established

Authors	Goodglass, Kaplan. (1972)
Publisher	Lee & Febiger. Philadelphia, Penn. 19106, U.S.A.

also:

The Computerised Boston

Authors	Code C, Heer M, and Scofield J. (1989)
Publisher	FAR Communications, Kibworth, Leics, LE80 NE, U.K.

Content

Production

Test II   Oral Expression:
Part B − Automatised sequences
Part D − Repetition of words
Part E − Word reading
Part G − Responsive naming
Part H − Visual confrontation naming
Part J − Body part naming
Part K − Animal naming

Test V   Writing:
Part B − Recall of written symbols
Part C − Written word-finding

Comprehension

> Test II   Auditory Comprehension:
> Part A — Word discrimination
> Part B — Body part identification
>
> Test IV   Understanding Written Language:
> Part A — Symbol and word production
> Part B — Phonetic association
> Part C — Word-picture matching

Form

Production

> Test III   Oral Expression: Part A — Oral agility

Content/Form

Production

> Test I   Conversational and Expository speech or
>
> Test III   Auditory Comprehension:
> Part C — Commands
> Part D — Complex Idential Methods
>
> Test IV   Understanding Written Language
> Part D — Reading Sentences and Paragraphs
>
> Test V   Writing:
> Part A — Mechanics of Writing
> Part D — Written Formulation

Comprehension

> Test I   Conversational and Expository Speech or
> Auditory comprehension:
> Part C — Commands
> Part D — Complex Idential Methods
>
> Test IV   Understanding Written Language:
> Part D — Reading Sentences and Paragraphs

Scoring   Norm-referenced scores are based on degree of deviation from the norm, then computed against performance standards of aphasics, and hence into major aphasic classifications approximately localising areas of cerebral insult. This remains one of the most popular aphasic tests in clinical practice in the U.K. However, competent administration does require a degree of training to achieve interscorer reliability and interpretation. Many of the original test materials were criticised as unsuitable for specific client groups, i.e. the elderly. These have been modified in more recent versions.

Supplementary Tests

BDAE also makes provision for separate assessment of apraxia, arithmetic problems, and visuospatial disturbances.

d. The Western Aphasia Battery (1982)

[handwritten: could mention this as being one of the other commonly used tests]

Author	Andrew Kertesz
Publisher	The Psychological Corporation
	Harcourt Brace, Jovanovich, Inc., U.S.A.

Unit 1

Spontaneous Speech	Scored by:
	(a) information content
	(b) fluency, grammatical competence and paraphasias.
Auditory Verbal comprehension	Yes/No questions
	Auditory word recognition
	Sequential commands
Repetition	Single word to multiple clauses
Naming	Object naming
	Word fluency
	Sentence completion
	Responsive speech (Wh. Questions)

Unit 2

Reading	Reading comprehension of sentences
	Reading commands
	Written commands
	Written word − object choice matching
	Written word − picture choice matching
	Pictorial stimulus − written word
	Spoken word − written word
	Letter discrimination
	Spelled word recognition
	Spelling
Writing	On request

Written output (written picture description)
Writing to dictation
Writing dictated or visually presented words
Alphabet and numbers
Dictated letters and numbers
Copying words of a sentence

Apraxia   Upper limb
Facial
Instrumental
Complex

Constructional, Visuospatial, Calculation Tasks

Raven's Coloured Progressive Matrices

Scoring: The Western Aphasia Battery evaluates the main language functions together with non-verbal skills, i.e. drawing, block design, and praxis. It can be administered in one hour to most patients or split into sections. Oral language tests constitute an independent unit, reading, writing, calculation, and praxis constitute a second. Scoring provides an overall measure of severity as an aphasia quotient (AQ) using the oral tests, and cortical quotient (CQ) from non-verbal scores. Patients are then classified according to eight aphasic types (Global, Broca's, Isolation, Transcortical Motor, Wernicke's, Transcortical Sensory, Conduction, Anomic).

The procedure is easily administered and interpreted without specific training. In conjunction with the author's textbook (Kertesz, 1979), reporting prognostic/outcome studies should be accorded more widespread recognition. It remains more favoured by neuro-psychologists than speech pathologists because of many of the aforementioned features.

2. Screening Tests

Shorter screening tests confirm diagnostic impressions and allow for prognostication. Brevity of testing according to Thorum (1981), does appear to influence the choice of test rather than necessarily the suitability of the procedure or theoretical constraints of its design. Indeed, Beele, Davies, and Muller (1984) found that many experienced clinicians only part administer standard tests, thus confirming the view of Thompson and Enderby (1979) that test constructors tend to be over inclusive and test users more selective and practical. Kertesz (1988) suggests also that many screening tests invariably may not fully satisfy all the hallmarks of a quality assessment with regard to research analysis or reliable baselines.

a. Aphasia Screening Test

Author	R. Whurr (1974)
Publisher	Whurr Publishers Ltd., 19b Compton Terrace, London, N1 2UN, U.K.
Tests of Receptive Functions	The same five items are incorporated in each subtest
Pre-Assessment Test	Four subtests to assess visual perceptual function (because of emphasis on visual channel for test materials).
Reading test	Matching numbers Matching letters Matching words Matching sentences Matching written words to pictures Matching written sentences to pictures Carrying out simple written commands Carrying out complex written commands
Auditory Language Tests	Selecting pictures Selecting colours Selecting numbers Selecting letters Selecting words Selecting sentences Carrying out simple oral commands Carrying out complex oral commands
Speech Tests	Repetition sounds Repetition groups of sounds Repetition words Repetition sentences Repetition sequences alphabet Repetition sequences days of week Repetition sequences months of year Repetition sequences 1–20 Reading aloud letters Reading aloud words Reading aloud sentences
Language Tests	Naming objects Naming colours Naming body parts

	Oral description, object use
	Oral description, action pictures
	Oral description, composite picture

Writing Tests   Copying letters
Copying words
Copying sentences
Writing to dictation — Numbers
Writing to dictation — Letters
Writing to dictation — Words
Writing to dictation — Sentences
Writing object names
Written description, object use
Written description, action pictures
Written description, composite pictures

The aim of the AST is to provide an objective measure of language disturbance. A five-point scoring system is used throughout on a pass/fail basis.

A summary record form is a profile grid giving a visual interpretation of results and space for written account. Scores for receptive function (total 100) and expressive function (total 150) can also be calculated as percentages. Therapists have reported (Beele et al., 1984) that the graphs provide easily readable profiles which aid interpretation when writing reports or discussing the patient's abilities with staff and relatives.

The profile can define areas of disturbance useful in planning treatment and provides an objective measure for test-retest situations. The test is not timed, and is designed for avoidance of fatigue in patients in the early stages of recovery.

Extensive clinical evaluations have been carried out using this procedure. In audit studies it is repeatedly the most favoured evaluation used in clinical practice in the U.K.

(A children's version: the Children's Acquired Aphasia Screening test, which identifies language disturbances in the brain damaged child, is also available.)

b. The Shortened version of the MTDDA (Thompson, Enderby, 1979)

The shortened version resulted from item analysis of the original Schuell test, using the "best items" in each case. Best items were judged on a factor analysis of efficiency, and the poorest discriminators according to simplicity or over-ease, discarded. In spite of analyses suggesting elimination of certain complete subtests, and because of their informative clinical nature, all the original subtests were salvaged. The resulting procedure retained both the larger number of prime items, and a smaller number of marginal ones. Five items per subtest were retained reducing the total items by more than half.

The resulting shorter test has not compromised the procedure's ability to reveal individual patient strengths and weaknesses.
(The shortened version scoresheet and marking scale is available from Dr. P. Enderby, Frenchay Hospital, Bristol, U.K.).

c. The Very Shortened Schuell (Powell, Bailey & Clerk 1980)

A further reduction in redundancy on the MTDDA provides a useful brief screening procedure which has been shown to correlate highly with the full test battery,. The purpose was to detect the presence of a degree of general aphasia, the resulting procedure misdiagnosing only a small percentage of the most minimally impaired. One subtest from each of four major modalities from the original full procedure is retained.

Auditory	Subtest A4: Identifying objects named serially
Reading	Subtest B8: Oral reading of words
Naming	Subtest C3: Naming pictures
Writing	Subtest D6: Written spelling
Scoring:	On a pass/fail scoring system. A cut-off point of 3+ errors indicates that further, more extensive testing, is required.

The procedure is frequently chosen in research projects or audits where screening the language skills of a population group is necessary.

d. Frenchay Aphasia Screening Test

Author	P. Enderby, V. Wood, D. Wade
Supplier	NFER-Nelson, Oxford, U.K.
Comprehension	Simple to complex instructions viz. picture Simple to complex instructions viz. shapes
Expression	Picture verbal description (naming focus if unable to comply) Animal naming
Reading	Read silent instructions and respond
Writing	Written picture description

Qualitative and quantitative scoring provides a raw score and cut-offs confirm the presence of aphasia. Age norms for those above/below 60 years are provided. The administration time is 3-10 minutes. The authors recommended that failure to reach the cut-offs indicated the need for comprehensive language assessment. The design of materials may prove difficult for certain patients, e.g.

although focused on elderly clients, the authors have not sufficiently considered the effect of sensory changes of ageing in the materials used.

Target or Task-specific Tests

In order to satisfy the clinical need for accurate description of the communication-impaired, additional information further to comprehensive, or screening procedures, may be required. It has been shown (Beele et al., 1984), that no one test satisfies the needs of all therapists or patients and that: "Given the range of behaviours in question, no one test would be able to convey every area in sufficient depth". Further, if a screening assessment is the only measure employed (for example, early post-onset) it is likely that other task-specific tests would be essential as a complement but not a substitute for standard investigations.

Selected specific tests of expression, reception and naming, as well as praxis and right hemisphere function, are briefly described in Table 10.9.

The Cognitive Neuropsychological Targeted Approach

In clinical practice procedures can be loosely adhered to and modified to suit individual patients or therapists' needs (Beele et al., 1984). So, too, with ideas on the conceptualisation of aphasia. As knowledge of linguistics and aphasiology increased, so testing became subject to change, often modifying an original theoretical framework and bringing with it an increasingly empirical, progressively atheoretical appearance to systems and types. This was compounded by a weight of opinion which concluded that language processing could be investigated with equal validity in normal and in brain-damaged subjects (Coltheart, 1967; cited Ellis & Young, 1988, p. 314).

The search for a psychologically strong theory required that the aphasic categories we chose to employ are supported by a psycholinguistically appropriate model of language processing. Thus, the cognitive neuropsychology approach has gained prominence. Most recently, specifically constructed experimental tests have been developed reflecting these views and thus the Cognitive Neuropsychology "school" established.

Aims of Cognitive Neuropsychology are:

1. To explain patterns of impaired and intact performance following brain injury, including patterns of errors in terms of impairment to one or more components of a theoretical model of normal intact cognitive processing.

2. To produce detailed refined descriptions of the abilities and disabilities of the individual patients.

3. To produce motivated targeted therapies.

TABLE 10.9
Task Specific Procedures

Focus of Communicative Interest	Title	Author	Description
1. Reception of Language	The Token Test	De Renzi & Vignolo (1962) (Revised McNeil Prescot, 1978)	A sensitive tool to determine minimal receptive language loss in adults, where impairment not obvious in conversation. (A children's version is also available, Di Simoni, 1978.)
	Test for Reception of Grammar (TROG)	Bishop. (1982)	Designed for children, applicable to adults also. Multiple choice test of understanding of grammatical contrasts in English. Provides quantitative and qualitative information.
2. Grammatical Construction	The Story Completion Test	Goodglass et al., (1972)	Test to elicit various syntactic constructions using contextual information as part of an expression task.
3. Naming	Boston Naming Test	Kaplan, Goodglass & Weintraub (1983) (Revised Nicholas et al., 1989)	Confrontation naming from line drawings with American cultural bias. Useful in that it provides information on effect of cueing – phonemic/semantic on performance. (Original normative data up to 59 yrs revised to provide quantitative scoring and norms 59–95 yrs.)
	Graded Naming Test	Warrington McKenna (1983)	Useful confrontation (line drawings) naming test, provides also for estimate of premorbid intelligence using correlation data. Does not provide for qualitative analysis of errors.
4. Praxis	Boston (BDAE) supplemental	Goodglass and Kaplan (1972)	Provides subtests for constructional and ideational apraxia.
5. Right Hemisphere Function	Right Hemisphere Test Battery	Bryan (1989)	Comprehensively assesses semantic processing, spoken/written metaphor appreciation, humour, inference, prosody. Discrimates R/L damaged aphasics and normal subjects.

205

4. To draw conclusions about the nature of normal cognitive processes from observed neuropsychological patterns.

5. To provide theoretical models of the components of language processing, whose localisation might be determined by lesion studies, i.e. Regional Cerebral Blood Flow (CRBF).

As yet the approaches have concentrated on models and targeted therapies at the single word level and mainly in single case or small group studies (Table 10.10). Reading and written language function, and their focal or isolated disorders have also been vigorously investigated.

These models most easily apply to patients with relatively specific problems being least suitable for patients with dynamic, inconsistent performances, i.e. Global or Wernicke's Aphasics.

Some aspects of sentence production are receiving similar targeted identification and remediation (Byng, 1986; Byng and Black, 1989; Jones, 1986). The problem with this approach for the clinician is the need to treat each patient as totally unique, often constructing a specific group of tests for that patient. This can prove costly in terms of time, and demands a level of expertise that may be beyond the capabilities of a clinician working without the necessary back-up. It is possible that future developments in this area will lead to the development of a new group of tests together with a system of testing which may be of great practical value.

Functional Assessment

Cognitive neuropsychology has as yet little to say about the natural parameters of communication, of spoken interaction and language in context, leading Lesser (1987) to suggest that there was a need to "look beyond" the "synthetic clinical tasks" and include the contribution of sociolinguistics and pragmatics. Specific assessment of *functional communication* and other pragmatic approaches, i.e. *discourse analysis* and *field observation* are necessary in order to consider how language-impaired individuals communicate in their social setting.

Three more routinely available functional procedures are:

1. The Functional Communication Profile (FCP) (Sarno, 1969).
2. Communicative Abilities in Daily Living (CADL) (Holland 1980).
3. The Edinburgh Functional Communication Profile (EFCP) (Skinner, Wirz, Thompson, & Davidson, 1984).

1. Functional Communication Profile (1969)

Author   M.T. Sarno
Publisher   Institute of Rehabilitation Medicine
                      New York University Medical Centre

TABLE 10.10

Name	Author	Description
1. Psycholinguistic Assessment of Language Processing in Aphasia (PALPA)	Kay et al. (in press)	40 item phonological word picture matching task requiring distinctive feature contrast/identification. Also available for written form presentation.
2. Pyramids and Palm Trees Test (PAT)	Howard & Orchard-Lisle (1984)	52 item tests of inter semantics based on judgement of association – (pictorial version). Can also be presented in spoken form (auditory version).
3. Consonant-vowel (CV) Discrimination Test	Franklin (1989)	Same-different judgement task of spoken c.v. (consonant/vowel) pairs. (40 items)., i.e. /ta va/
4. Easy Lexical Decision Test	Coltheart (1980)	Real word/non word decision test involving single letter changes, i.e. boy. doy. Auditory (spoken form) and written versions are available.
5. High-Low Imageability Synonym Matching Test	Coltheart (1980)	Paired synonym/semantically non-related words of high imageability *cash/money* or *cash/fight* low imageability (abstract) *detection/discovery* on a judgemental task, e.g. *fight: money*, which is synonym for *cash*. Auditory and written presentations used.
6. Imageability/Frequency Repetition Test	Howard (1985) cited Franklin (1989) *op cit*	80 word task comprising high image, high frequency (i.e. answer) low image high frequency words (i.e. river) high image low frequency words (i.e. pole) low image low frequency words (i.e. plead) to be repeated after tester.

400 East 34th Street
New York, New York 10016

Content

Production

Movement

Ability to indicate 'yes' and 'no'
Indicating floor to elevator operator
Saying greeting
Saying own name
Saying nouns
Saying verbs

Reading

Reading single words

Comprehension

Understanding

Understanding own name
Awareness of speech
Recognition of family names
Recognition of names of familiar objects

Form

Production

Speaking

Saying non-verb combinations
Saying phrases (non-automatic)
Saying short complete sentences
  (Non-automatic)
Saying long sentences (non-automatic)

Comprehension
Understanding

Awareness of emotional voice tone
Understanding action verbs

Content/Form

Production

Speaking

Giving directions
Speaking on the telephone

Comprehension

Understanding

Understanding verbal directions
Understanding simple conversation with one person

Understanding television
Understanding conversation with more than
one person
Understanding movies
Understanding complicated verbal directions

Reading   Understanding rapid complex conversations
Reading rehabilitation programme card
Reading street signs
Reading newspaper headlines
Reading letters
Reading newspaper articles
Reading magazines
Reading books

Scoring   Norm referenced ratings on a 5 point scale giving behaviour:
normal; good; fair; poor; absent. Overall language ability can
be described in terms of a percentage score.

Communicative Abilities in Daily Living (CADL) (1980)

Author   A.L. Holland
Publisher   University Park Press, 233 E.Redwood St.,
Baltimore, Md. 21202

Content/Form   Writing
Production   Social conventions, greetings

Comprehension   Reading
Social conventions, greetings

Cognition
Thinking   Untangling cause-effect relationships
Using numbers to estimate, calculate, judge
time
Humour, absurdity, metaphor
Divergence

Use   Role playing
Speech acts: explaining
correcting misinformation
informing
requesting
negotiating
advising
reporting

Makes use of verbal and non-verbal contexts to interpret verbal and non-verbal material.

Also considers Deixix i.e. movement related or dependent communication.

Scoring   Norm referenced citing mode on a 3-point scale: against fail; partial success; or success. Maximum 135 (on 68 items).

Edinburgh Functional Communication Profile (1984)

Authors   Skinner, C., Wirz, S., Thompson, I., & Davidson, J.

Publishers   Winslow Press, 23 Horn St., Winslow, Bucks MK18 3AP

Communicative Contexts

1. *Greeting*

2. *Acknowledging*   Yes/No response
                            Confirmation

3. *Responding*   To non-verbal requests
                            To closed questions
                            To open questions
                            By description

4. *Requesting*   Object transfer
                            Initiates communication

5. *Prepositional*   Objects transfer
                            Initiates communication

6. *Problem Solving*

Scoring   Each function is scored according to five modalities: Speech, Gesture (including formal signing), Facial Expression, Vocal response (non-word), written response, and against various dimensions of response: No response, inappropriate, inadequate, stereotyped − the non-communicating responses; or adequate, qualified, elaborate, − the communicating responses. This provides a profile of the overall pattern of functional communication.

Field Observation and Discourse

Social and behavioural scientists have extensively applied systematic field observation to record various aspects of people's day-to-day social interaction. Language pathologists have also taken this approach in the area of language acquisition and more recently although to a lesser extent, in aphasiology. Holland (1982) suggested that because knowledge of the aphasic patient's communication is restricted to formal testing, experimental manipulation, family or patient discussion or knowledge from patients/families, there is need to expand our understanding of aphasic patients by exploring the usefulness of systematic observation in natural settings, especially the home environment. Whilst a worthy concept, the idea of two hours of observation per person and subsequent analysis (considered sufficiently representative), may be impractical, even with the advent of video recording. Holland (1982) is one of the few workers to pursue this approach, using an observing procedure concerned with the frequency and form of successful and failed verbal and non-verbal communicative acts. Holland's observational categories form the following checklist:

Verbal Output:

Form	Verbal lubricant/social convention, asks questions, makes requests, answers questions, requests or volunteers information
Style	Agrees, disagrees teases, uses humour/sarcasm metaphor
Conversational dominance	Interrupts/changes topic
Correctional strategies	Corrects, clarifies, requests
Metalinguistics	Comments on own speaking Responds to phonemic cues
Non-verbal output	Spatial indicators Direct verbal referent Gestures to maintain conversation Humour Affect/state
Others	Talks on phone Talks to pets Talks to self Responds to household sounds Sings Speaks in foreign language

Holland (1982) concludes that such "observation is a quantitatively productive means for knowing an aphasic better".

A less specific communication scale which has been used in field observation of the elderly is the Holden Communication Scale for the Elderly (Holden & Woods, 1982).

This rates on a five-point scale aspects of: Conversation, awareness/knowledge, and overall communication. Although less linguistically, and more behaviourally focused, it is useful in clinically increasing awareness of professionals and carers in the range and variety of communication variables and interactions (see Table 10.11).

Discourse

Discourse analysis offers another means of describing more naturally produced communication, making use of an elicited sample, for example: through picture description or a spontaneous sample occurring in conversation. The latter may be less than spontaneous in that the aphasic's conversation, too, may require to be elicited in a semi-structured or structured way.

Breakdown of the elements of cohesion and coherence within utterances (microstructure) and between utterances (macrostructure) form the basis for various approaches whose aim is to capture the interactive contribution of context, semantics and syntax as linguistic competence.

At a simplistic level, Grice (1975) proposed five maxims as being the basic requirements of conversation:

1. Co-operation: Mutual order and politeness, i.e. turn-taking etc.
2. Quality: Truthful; appropriately substantiated.
3. Quantity: Neither too much nor too little, i.e. fluency.
4. Relevance: Pertinence to the situation.
5. Manner: Perspicuity, i.e. easy to understand.

These can be used to provide an introductory focus for breakdown of conversation.

Discourse analysis has long been of interest in psychiatric disorders, particularly in schizophrenia and more recently dementias, although Davies and Wilcox (1981) concentrated extensively on the use of discourse and other pragmatic approaches in the description and management of acquired communication deficits.

Patry (1987, after Charroles) used three rules to describe coherence breakdown in a story telling task:

1. *Semantic Progression:*   The semantic content of discourse must develop what is already stated and add new pieces of information to it, i.e. *absence of repetitious discourse.*

TABLE 10.11

Holden Communication Scale for the Elderly

	0	1	2	3	4
Conversation					
Response	Initiates conversation deeply involved with anyone	Good for those familiar to him/her	Fair response to those close by. No initiation of conversation	Rather confused Poor comprehension	Rarely or never converses
Interest in past events	Long full account of past events	Fairly good description	Short. Description a little confused	Confused or disinterested	No response
Pleasure	Shows real pleasure in situation/achievement	Smiles and shows interest	Variable response, slight smile, vague interest	Rarely shows even a smile	No response or just weeps
Humour	Creates situations or tells funny story on own initiative	Enjoys comic situations or stories	Needs an explanation and encouragement to respond	Vague smile, simply copies others	No response or negativistic
Awareness/Knowledge					
Names	Knows most peoples' names on ward	Knows a few names	Needs constant reminder	Knows own name only	Forgotten even own name
General Orientation	Knows day, month, time, weather & whereabouts	Can forget one or two items	Usually gets two right but tries	Vague, may guess one	Very confused
General Knowledge	Good on current events, generally able	Outstanding events only. Fair on general knowledge	No current knowledge. Poor general information	Confused about many things. Gets anxious and upset	Confused about everything. Does not respond
Ability to join in games etc.	Joins in games and activities with ease	Requires careful instructions but	Can only join simple activities	Becomes anxious and upset	Cannot or will not join in

(Continued)

TABLE 10.11
(Continued)

	0	1	2	3	4
Communication					
Speech	No known difficulty	Slight hesitation or odd wording	Very few words, mainly automatic phrases	Inappropriate words, odd sounds. Nodding	Little or no verbalisation
Attempts	Communicates with ease	Tries hard to speak clearly	Tries to draw — gesticulates needs, etc.	Euphoric laugh. Weeping, aggressive movements	No attempt
Interest and response to objects	Responds with interest and comment	Despite difficulties shows interest	Shows some interest, but rather vague	Weeps, rejects, shows aggression	No response. No comprehension
Success in communication	Clearly understood	Uses gestures and sounds effectively	Understanding restricted to a few people	Becomes frustrated and angry	Makes no attempt

(Holden & Wood, 1982)
Reprinted by permission of the publisher, Churchill Livingstone.

2. *Non-contradiction:*   A given piece of information in a discourse must not contradict the content of a previous or subsequent piece, i.e. *absence of contradictory discourse.*

3. *Relation:*   Discourse must make the connection between the facts it expresses clearly so that the listener understands them, i.e. *absence of shattered discourse.*

At a more microstructural level, Nicholas et al. (1985) described fourteen characteristics as being the marks of the discourse of dementing speakers, focusing on errors of reference or omission, and of fluency: The so-called "empty speech" characteristics (Table 10.12).

The CAMDEX (Roth et al., 1986) includes a picture description for discourse analysis in the CAMCOG subtests focussing on quantity and quality of

TABLE 10.12
Empty Speech Characteristics of Alzheimer's Dementia (Nicholas et al., 1985)

Descriptive	Example
1. Empty phrases	And so on, something like that
2. Indefinite terms	Something; stuff; thing
3. Deiectic terms	This; that; here
4. Pronouns without antecedents	He/she with no referent in conversation
5. Comments on task not stimulus	
6. Neologism	Literally use of a new (non-dictionary) word
7. Literal paraphasic	Word sound error, i.e. *"sair"* for "chair"
8. Unrelated verbal paraphasia	i.e. *"gun"* for handle
9. Semantic paraphasia	i.e. *"stool"* for "chair"
10. Verbal phonological paraphasia	i.e. *"red"* for "bed"
11. Repetition of words or phrases	
12. Personal value judgement of stimulus	
13. *"and"* used frequently to conjoin sentences	
14. Absence of other conjunctions. Hence prolonged continuation of clauses reduced and cohesion breaks down	

utterance in terms of percentage of utterances containing errors (which are then rated) and types of errors including elision, repetition, etc. It is recommended that this subtest should be scored by someone with skill in linguistic analysis.

Etiologically Focused Communication Assessment

Finally, because language dissolution reflects many different etiologies for which most of the previously described measures are suitable (C.V.A., head injury, epilepsy, etc.), there will always be controversy when applying tests of language abnormality to normal subjects or subjects for whom the procedure was not originally conceived or standardised. (Hence the cognitive neuropsychology argument for a universal model.) *Dementias* are one such area of debate where the impaired language disorder might be viewed as a variation of classical aphasic syndromes and, it is suggested, can be assessed using the same tools (Au, Albert, & Obler, 1988; Walker, 1988). While others believe the term aphasia (and the diagnostic tools) to be inappropriate. Bayles and Kaszniak (1987) state that whilst providing valuable information, aphasia test batteries were not necessarily designed for the differential diagnosis of aphasia and dementia. As a result considerable effort has been made by these authors to develop a unique testing procedure for this patient group. This follows some early work by Phillips (1982) and more recently by Weeks (1988). The latter focused on one specific language task (repetition of anomalous sentences) to differentiate dementia from other organic illnesses of old age. The possibility of performance masking by focal language or motor speech deficit or praxis for speech appears not to have been considered in the design of this procedure.

Bayles and Kaszniak (1987) evolved their "designer" test: The Arizona Battery of Communication Disorders of Dementia (ABC), to include the common aphasia subtests of language breakdown such as: Fluency, Auditory Comprehension, Reading, Writing, Naming, Repetition, Spontaneous language (see Table 10.13).

The ABC differs in that it additionally permits examination of verbal and non-verbal memory, visuospatial construction, orientation, and linguistic reasoning. As yet, the procedure is not available in the U.K. but the authors have reported that their procedure reveals dementia performance profiles which are uniquely distinct between mild and moderate dementias and from those of aphasic patients.

Timescale and Sequence of Assessment

Assessment of language impairment or ability is a multifaceted one, requiring a repertoire of tests applied at different stages and for different reasons.

At onset, *a screening procedure* may be used as a quick, non-fatiguing method giving a descriptive and sometimes prescriptive indication of the areas of linguistic interest. These areas might be further investigated by

TABLE 10.13
Arizona Battery for Communication Disorders (ABC) of
Dementia (Bayles & Kazniak 1987)

| Mode of Response | | Task |
Oral	Non-oral	
		Sensory perception
×	×	Auditory Discrimination
		Receptive Language
×	×	Peabody Picture Vocabulary Test
		Reading Comprehension
	×	* Words
	×	* Sentences
	×	* Paragraphs
		Sentence Disambiguation
	×	* Non-oral
		Expressive language
×	×	Oral Description of Objects
	×	Pantomime Expression
	×	Drawing
×		FAS Verbal Fluency
		Sentence Disambiguation
		* Oral
×		Oral Discourse
	×	Written Discourse
		Receptive/expressive
×		Repetition
		Orientation and memory
×	×	Mental Status Test (MST)
		Story retelling
×	×	* Immediate
×	×	* Delayed
	×	Recognition Memory
	×	* Spatial
×		* Verbal

(Bayles and Kaszniak (1987))

specific targeted tests. Once neurological stability is achieved a *standard clinical aphasia test* would be used, possibly complemented by *a functional communication assessment* and/or *any supplemental or targeted tests* required to specify more accurately the patient's actual and potential language ability, and to formulate longer-term goals for management.

RECOMMENDATIONS

It seems not unreasonable to suggest that the expertise of speech pathologists most routinely using such procedures might aid us in our selection.

Based on a rating of popularity by clinical usefulness (Table 10.14), the following are suggested:

1. *Multimodal/Multidimensional full battery*

   Boston Diagnostic Aphasia Examination
   or:
   Minnesota Test for Differential Diagnosis of Aphasia
   or:
   Western Aphasia Battery*

2. *Multimodal Screening Tests*
   Aphasia Screening Test
   or:
   Shortened Schuell

3. *Functional Assessment*
   Edinburgh Functional Communication Profile*

* Not included in Beeles' Study

CONCLUSION

The suggestions made in this chapter should act as a reasonable guide to those who have not yet developed an approach to assessment based on wide experience.

TABLE 10.14
Rank Order Most Popular Aphasic Tests in Speech
Therapy Practice in U.K. (Beeles et al., 1984)

Test	*% Therapist Selection*
Aphasia Screening Test (Whurr)	74%
Boston Diagnostic Aphasia Examination (BDAE)	66%
Shortened version of Schuells MTDDA	49%
Minnesota Test, Differential Diagnosis of Aphasia (MTDDA)	46%
Token Test (De Renzi & Vignolo)	31%
Porch Index of Communicative Ability (PICA)	12%
Others	23%

Specific advice from experienced neuropsychologists, aphasiologists and speech therapists can usually be obtained with a little effort, and one should bear in mind the advice of Chapey (1981):

> Unfortunately there is no simple solution to the problem of assessing the speech and language assets and liabilities of adult aphasic patients. The final decision is left to each aphasiologist to determine which of the procedures discussed in this chapter are the most appropriate for a particular patient and clinical setting.

REFERENCES

Au, R., Albert, M.L., & Obler, L.K. (1988). The relation of aphasia to dementia. *Aphasiology, 2 (2),* 161-174.

Bayles, K.A., & Kaszniak, A.W. (1987). *Communication and cognition in normal ageing and dementia.* New York, London: Taylor, Francis.

Beele, K.A., Davies, E., & Muller, D. (1984). Therapists' view on the clinical usefulness of four aphasia tests. *British Journal of Disorders of Communication, 19,* 151-178.

Behan, P. (1989). *Cases in neurogenic communicative disorders* (Book Review) (Eds. Dwarkin & Hartman). In *British Journal of Disorders of Communication, 24 (2),* 209.

Benton, A.L. (1967). Problems of test construction in the field of aphasia. *Cortex, 6,* 32-36.

Bishop, D. (1982). *Test for Reception of Grammar.* Oxford: MRC and Oxford: Thos. Leach.

Bogen, J.E., & Bogen, G.M. (1976). Wernickes' region — where is it? *Annals of the New York Academy of Sciences, 280,* 834-843.

Bryan, K. (1988). Assessment of language disorders after right hemisphere damage. *British Journal of Disorders of Communication, 23 (2),* 111-125.

Bryan, K. (1989). *The right hemisphere test battery.* Kibworth, U.K.: Far Communications.

Byng, S. (1986). *Sentence processing deficits in aphasia: Investigated remediation.* Unpublished doctoral thesis, University of London.

Byng, S., & Black, M. (1989). Some aspects of sentence production in aphasia. *Aphasiology, 3 (3),* 241-264.

Carrol, J. (1984). *Language and thought.* Engelwood Cliffs, N.J.: Prentice-Hall.

Chapey, R. (1981). *Language intervention strategies in adult aphasia.* Baltimore: Williams & Wilkins.

Code, C., Heer, M., & Scofield, J. (1989). *The computerised Boston.* Kibworth, Leicester: FAR Communications.

Coltheart, M. (1980). *Analysing acquired disorders of reading.* (Unpublished, monograph).

Coltheart, M. (1986). Cognitive neuropsychology. In M. Posner & O.S. Marin (Eds.). *Attention and Performance XI.* Hillsdale, N.J.: Lawrence Erlbaum Associates Inc.

Davis, C., & Grunwell, P. (1973). British amendments to an American test for Aphasia. *British Journal of Disorders of Communication, 8 (2),* 189.

Davies, G.A., & Wilcox, J.M. (1981). Incorporating parameters of natural communication in aphasia treatment. In Chapey, R. (Ed.), *Language Intervention Strategies in Adult Aphasia* (pp. 159-174).

De Renzi, E., & Vignolo, L. (1962). The Token Test: A sensitive test to detect receptive disturbances in aphasics. *Brain, 85,* 665-678.

Di Simoni, F. (1978). *The Token Test for children.* Oxford: NFER-Nelson.

Eisenson, J. (1954). *Examining for aphasia.* New York: Psychological Corporation.

Ellis, A.W., & Young, A.W. (1988). *Human cognitive neuropsychology.* London: Lawrence Erlbaum Associates Ltd.

Enderby, P. (1983). *Frenchay dysarthria assessment and computer differential analysis.* Oxford: NFER-Nelson.

Enderby, P., Wood, V., & Wade, D. (1987). *Frenchay aphasia screening test.* Oxford: NFER-Nelson.

Franklin, S. (1989). Dissociations in auditory word comprehension: Evidence from nine non-fluent aphasic patients. *Aphasiology, 3,* 189-207.

Gazzaniga, M.S. (1983). Right hemisphere language following brain bisection: A 20 year perspective. *American Psychologist, 38,* 525-537.

Goodglass, H., & Kaplan, E. (1972). *Boston Diagnostic Aphasia Examination.* Philadelphia: Lea & Febiger.

Goodglass, H., Gleason, J.B., Bernholz, N.A., & Hyde, M.R. (1972). Some linguistic structures in the speech of a Brocas aphasic. *Cortex, 8,* 191-212.

Grice, H.P. (1975). Logic and conversation. In Cole & Morgan (Eds.), Syntax and Semantics. Speech Acts. *New York Seminar Press, 3,* 41-58.

Heilman, K.M., Scholes, R., & Watson, R.T. (1975). Auditory affective agnosia: Disturbed comprehension of affective speech. *Journal of Neurology, Neurosurgery and Psychiatry, 38,* 69-72.

Holden, V., & Woods, R. (1982). *Reality orientation.* London: Churchill-Livingstone.

Holland, A.L. (1980). *Communicative abilities in daily living.* Baltimore: University Park Press.

Holland, A. (1982). Observing functional communication of aphasic adults. *Journal of Speech and Hearing Disorders, 47,* 50-56.

Howard, D., & Orchard Lisle, V. (1984). On the origin of semantic errors in naming: Evidence from the case of a global aphasic. *Cognitive Neuropsychology, 1,* 163-190.

Jones, E. (1986). Building the foundations for sentence production in a non-fluent aphasic. *British Journal of Disorders of Communication, 21,* 63-82.

Kaplan, E., Goodglass, H., & Weintraub (1983). *The Boston naming test.* Philadelphia: Lea & Febiger.

Kay, J., Lesser, R., & Coltheart, M. (in press). *Psycholinguistic assessment of language processing in aphasia.* Hove: Lawrence Erlbaum Associates Ltd.

Kertesz, A. (1982). *Western aphasia battery.* San Antonio: The Psychological Corporation Inc.

Kertesz, A. (1989). Is there a need for standardised aphasia tests? Why, how, what and when to test aphasics. *Aphasiology, 2 (3/4),* 313-318.

Kertesz, A. (1979). *Aphasia and associated disorders.* New York: Grune and Stratton.

Lesser, R. (1978). *Linguistic investigations of aphasia.* London: Ed. Arnold (2nd Edition, London: Whurr Publishers).

Lesser, R. (1987). Cognitive neuropsychological influences on aphasia therapy. *Aphasiology, 1 (3),* 189-200.

Mohr, J.R. (1976). Brocas' area and Brocas' aphasia. In H. Whitaker & H.A. Whitaker. *Studies in Neurolinguistics, Vol. 1,* New York: Academic Press.

McKenna, P., Warrington, E. (1983). *Graded naming test.* Oxford: NFER-Nelson.

McNeil, A.R., & Prescot, T.E. (1978). *Revised token test.* Baltimore: University Park Press.

McNeil, A.R. (1984). Current concepts in adult aphasia. *International Journal of Rehabilitation Medicine, 6,* 128-134.

Nicholas, M., Obler, L.K., Albert, M.L., & Helm Estabrook, N. (1985). Empty speech in Alzheimer's dementia and in non-fluent aphasia. *Journal of Speech and Hearing Disorders, 25,* 405-410.

Nicholas, L.E., Brookshire, R.H., & McLennan, D.L. (1989). Revised administration and scoring procedure for the BNT and norms for non-brain damaged adults. *Aphasiology, 3 (6),* 569-580.

Patry, R. (1989). *Language dementia and discourse analysis.* Paper presented at the conference on Language in Dementia, Ottawa Civic Hospital.

Phillips, A. (1974). *Dysphasia/dementia screening test.* (Available from Briggs Unit, Brighton General Hospital, Brighton BN2 3EW, U.K.

Porch, B.E. (1967). *Porch Index of Communicative Ability — Theory and development.* Palo Alto, U.S.A.: Consulting Psychologists Press.

Powell, G., Bailey, S., & Clark, E. (1980). A very shortened version of the Minnesota Aphasia Test. *British Journal of Clinical Psychology, 19,* 189-194.

Robertson, S. (1983). *Dysarthria profile.* Oxford: Winslow Press.

Ross, E.D., Harney, J.H., & de Lacost-Utamsing, C. (1981). How the brain integrates affective and propositional language into unified behavioural function: Hypothesis bases on clinco-anatomic evidence. *Archives of Neurology, 38,* 745-748.

Roth, M., Tym, C., Mountjoy, L.Q., Huppert, F.A., Hendrie, M., Verma, S., & Goddard, R. (1986). CAMDEX — a standardised instrument for the diagnosis of mental disorders in the elderly. *British Journal of Psychiatry, 149,* 698-709.

Sarno, M.T. (1969). *The functional communication profile — Manual of directions.* New York: New York Medical Centre.

Schuell, H. (1965). *Minnesota Test for Differential Diagnosis of Aphasia.* Minnesota: University of Minnesota Press.

Skinner, C., Wirz, S., Thompson, I., & Davidson, J. (1984). *Edinburgh Functional Communication Profile.* Oxford: Winslow Press.

Shallice, T. (1988). *From neuropsychology to mental structure.* New York: Cambridge University Press.

Sperry, R.W. (1970). Perception in the absence of neocortical commisures. In *Perception and its disorders. The Association for Research in Nervous and Mental Disorders, 48.*

Thompson, J., Enderby, P. (1979). Is all your Schuell really necessary? *British Journal of Disorders of Communication, 14,* 195-201.

Thorum, A.R. (1981). *Language assessment instruments.* Springfield, Il: C.C. Thomas.

Tucker, D.M., Watson, R.T., & Heilman, K.M. (1977). Discrimination and evocation of affectively intoned speech in patients with right parietal disease. *Archives of Neurology, 27,* 947-950.

Walker, S.A. (1988). Dementia and dysphasia: Like asking a blind man to describe an elephant. *Aphasiology, 2 (2),* 145-180.

Weeks, D. (1988). *The Anomalous sentences repetition test.* Oxford: NFER-Nelson.

Winting, S., Lincoln, N., Bhavani, G., & Cockburn, J. (1985). *Rivermead Perceptual Assessment Battery.* Windsor: NFER-Nelson Publishing Co. Ltd.

Whurr, R. (1972). *Aphasia Screening Test.* London: Cole and Whurr.

Zaidel, E. (1983) A response to Gazzaniga: Language in the right hemisphere, convergent perspectives. *American Psychologist, 38,* 342-346.

11 The Assessment of Reading Disorders

Philip H K Seymour
University of Dundee, Scotland

INTRODUCTION

It is a well-established fact that neurological damage can affect the systems required for reading and writing, producing an acquired dyslexia or dysgraphia (Shallice, 1988). These conditions can also occur in a developmental (congenital) form where they appear as a difficulty in learning to read or spell in childhood (Critchley, 1970). This chapter will focus on the assessment of disturbances of the reading process. A deficit in this area may be evident from the reports of patients and their families, or from informal requests to read samples of text. It can be verified by the application of standardised reading tests which are based on age norms, and which relate the patient's performance to a specific level of reading development. using either single word recognition measures or the reading and comprehension of text (see, for example, Neale, 1966, and Schonell & Schonell, 1956).

In recent times the interest in acquired dyslexia has been concerned less with the verification of the presence of a reading problem *per se* than with the diagnosis of the locus of the damage within a functionally defined cognitive system. The objective of the assessment has been to determine which components of the system are damaged and to what degree, and also to analyse the more or less preserved reading functions which remain available. I will take the view that the assessment of acquired dyslexia is a matter of cognitive diagnostics of this kind.

The essential requirements for a diagnostic investigation consist of:

1. A *model* of the "functional architecture" of the cognitive system which represents the processing components and their inter-connections.

2. A methodology, consisting of tasks, stimulus categories and indicators of process, which make reference to the model and which can be used to determine the availability or functional level of particular components or pathways.

In this chapter I will outline a brief account of the information processing framework which has dominated recent studies of the acquired dyslexias. I will then discuss the experimental procedures which can be deployed in attempts to probe the components of the reading system.

FUNCTIONAL ARCHITECTURE

The idea of using an information processing model as a framework for the interpretation of the acquired dyslexias was originally put forward by Marshall and Newcombe (1973). They proposed that the pathway between printed input and spoken output included: (1) peripheral processes of visual analysis and recognition; (2) two central processes, concerned respectively with semantic interpretation and letter-sound translation; and (3) an output process, involving storage of spoken word forms and the control of articulation. The framework was related to the *logogen model* formulated by Morton (1969). In subsequent research it has been superseded by an elaborated version developed by Morton (1980); Patterson and Shewell (1987); Morton and Patterson (1980); and, most comprehensively, by Ellis and Young (1988). Figure 11.1 reproduces Ellis and Young's version.

Reading is based on the formation of an *orthographic system* which is specialised for the analysis and identification of printed forms. In Ellis and Young's scheme this system is sub-divided into a number of components, including: (1) a visual analysis process; (2) a word recognition system (visual input lexicon); and (3) a process of letter-sound (grapheme-phoneme) conversion. These components have been highlighted in Fig. 11.1. I will define the reading system as consisting of these three components together with their input and output pathways, especially the links from the visual lexicon to the semantic system and to the speech output lexicon, and from grapheme-phoneme conversion to the phonemic level of the speech output processes. Strictly speaking, a dyslexia, defined as a disorder of *reading,* is a disorder which is localised within one or more of these components or pathways.

PSYCHOLINGUISTIC METHOD

Marshall and Newcombe (1973) laid the foundations for a psycholinguistic method of analysing acquired disorders of reading. Their procedure involved the presentation of lists of words which sampled contrasting linguistic properties, including: (1) the frequency of occurrence of words in the language (as

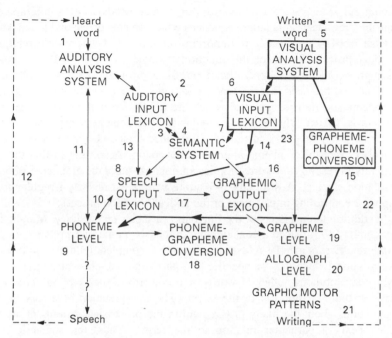

FIG. 11.1 Modular information processing model proposed by Ellis and Young (1988) as a framework for analysis disorders of language. The orthographic input systems and pathways required for reading have been highlighted.

determined by published counts, such as Carroll, Davies, & Richman, 1971; Kucera & Francis, 1967; Thorndike & Lorge, 1944); (2) the syntactic function (form class) of the word (i.e. its part of speech); (3) the concrete or abstract nature of its meaning (as indicated by rating studies, e.g. Paivio, Yuille, & Madigan, 1968). Other factors which are important are the length of the word (in letters or other units), and the nature of the correspondence between its letters and its pronunciation, which may be straightforward (regular), derivable from rules, or exceptional (irregular). Part of Marshall and Newcombe's method involved tests for effects of these variations on reading accuracy. The effects were interpreted by reference to assumptions about the location (in the processing model), of the influence of the variable in question. For example, if concreteness is assumed to be a property of the semantic component of the model, a large or atypical influence of this variable might be taken to imply: (1) an involvement of the semantic process in reading; and/or (2) a disturbance of that process.

Since the publication of Marshall and Newcombe's paper it has become evident that the linguistic variation of predominant importance is the factor of *lexicality*, that is, the distinction between real words, which are familiar and meaningful, and so-called non-words (or pseudo-words), i.e. orthographically plausible, pronounceable letter sequences which do not correspond to any known English word. This variable is important on account of its possible relation to the dual process format of the functional model (see Fig. 11.1). A standard assumption, maintained by Coltheart (1980), Morton and Patterson (1980), and many others, has been that the logogen systems (lexicons) are word-specific (or morpheme-specific) recognisers, which are implicated in the correct reading of real words, particularly those of irregular spelling-sound correspondence. Non-words have no logogens and must be translated to speech via the second (non-lexical) process of grapheme-phoneme conversion. According to this theory, a difficulty in reading non-words implies an impairment of the grapheme-phoneme translation channel. A difficulty in reading words, particularly irregular forms, implies a contrasting impairment of the lexical-semantic process.

In addition to the effects of the linguistic variables on accuracy, Marshall and Newcombe (1973) placed a considerable emphasis on the interpretation of *error responses*. Errors may be refusals, indicating a complete failure of information transmission (which may be specific to a particular sub-class of items), or may involve substitutions, either of words or non-words, which can be classified in terms of their relationship to the target. The interpretation of errors involves assumptions about the likely origin, within the processing system, of an error which bears a particular relation to the target. Thus, the semantic errors produced by Marshall and Newcombe's patient, G.R., are assumed to originate in the semantic system, and to imply a reading process which is mediated by that system.

A further index, not examined by Marshall and Newcombe, is the *reaction time* for correct responses. This is a sensitive index of information transmission which can be helpful in establishing whether or not a particular process functions in a strictly normal fashion (see, for example, Seymour, 1986). This can be considered both in terms of the overall level of the reaction time (including the form of the reaction time distribution), and also for the magnitude of particular effects. For example, an exaggeration of the effect of word length on reaction time might indicate an atypical commitment to serial processing.

The measurement of reaction times raises some technical problems which can readily be solved by the use of a microcomputer combined with a voice switch and key-press unit. In my own view, the reaction time measure adds significantly to the diagnostic power of the cognitive method and should, if at all possible, be included in an assessment procedure.

SYNDROMES vs. FUNCTIONS

Before proceeding to a more detailed discussion, we need to consider a general point about the objectives of the assessment procedures. When Marshall and Newcombe (1973) reported their pioneering investigation they represented contrasts (defined in terms of psycholinguistic effects and error patterns), among their six patients by the coinage of the following quasi-descriptive labels:

1. *Visual dyslexia*, referring to a disturbance of the visual analysis system, resulting in errors attributable to mis-identification of letters.

2. *Surface dyslexia*, resulting from an impairment of the lexical-semantic process, with reading forced to proceed via the grapheme-phoneme translation process, giving rise to errors of stress assignment and letter-sound conversion, especially for silent letters or ambiguous letters.

3. *Deep dyslexia*, a disturbance of the grapheme-phoneme process, which resulted in reading via the semantic process, producing effects of semantic variables, such as concreteness and part of speech, and errors of lexical, syntactic or semantic substitution.

This approach was widely adopted and led to the assumption that there were a number of distinctive *types* of acquired dyslexia, each characterised by a particular pattern of preserved and impaired function. An important addition to Marshall and Newcombe's list was the discovery of *phonological dyslexia* by Beauvois and Dérouesné (1979), a condition involving damage to the grapheme-phoneme process, resulting in loss of ability to read non-words, but with preservation of word reading unaccompanied by the semantic features noted in the cases of deep dyslexia.

The introduction of these labels led to the view that the acquired dyslexias could be described by reference to several distinct types or *syndromes*, each involving the occurrence of a set of defining symptoms (see, for example, the discussions of "deep dyslexia" and "surface dyslexia" by Coltheart, 1980, and by Coltheart et al., 1983). This general approach has its parallel in treatments of the developmental dyslexias, e.g. in the classification of cases into *dysphonetic* (phonological) and *dyseidetic* (surface) types by Boder (1973).

If this syndrome-oriented approach is adopted, it appears that the objective of a cognitive assessment is to assign an individual patient to one or another of the standard categories. Thus, Coltheart (1981) published a series of word and non-word lists which could be applied to cases of acquired dyslexia, and presented the tree diagram shown in Fig. 11.2 as an aid to the allocation of cases to one of a set of mutually exclusive categories, depending on the occurrence of a defining symptom.

The syndrome approach was effectively criticised by Ellis (1987). The main problem is that a complex system, of the kind set out in Fig. 11.1, is vulnerable to numerous variations in the location and severity of damage. To attempt to force these variations into a restricted set of categories is to invite over-simplification and stereotyping, particularly in the presumption that the observation of a defining symptom reliably implies the status of

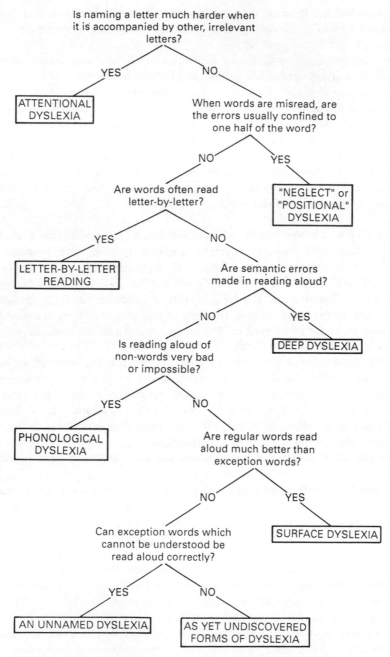

FIG. 11.2 Scheme for assignment of cases to categories of acquired dyslexia proposed by Coltheart (1981).

other processes. A more realistic approach, which I will maintain in this chapter, is one which sees assessment as an attempt to determine the status of each of a number of functional systems (see Seymour, 1986). The general distinction between peripheral and central functions advocated by Shallice and Warrington (1980) seems helpful in this regard. Thus, using the terms of the model in Fig. 11.1, we can say that the objective of an assessment procedure for acquired dyslexia should be to determine the status of a peripheral system concerned with the visual analysis and identification of printed forms and of central systems required for access to meaning or to phonology via lexical and sub-lexical processes.

In a system-oriented approach, the assessment procedure is directed towards the determination of the status of particular functions. It follows that the term "dyslexia" should also be considered to refer to a system rather than to the overall processing configuration displayed by a patient (Seymour, 1986). This usage, which seems consistent with Shallice and Warrington's distinction between single and multiple component disorders, allows that an individual patient may display more than one dyslexia, e.g. a disturbance of visual processing (a visual dyslexia) combined with a disturbance of grapheme-phoneme translation (a phonological dyslexia).

Accordingly, in this discussion I will avoid reference to types or syndromes of acquired dyslexia and will concentrate on the procedures which can be used to probe each of the four functional systems identified in Fig. 11.1.

ACCESS TO PHONOLOGY

The principal task used to assess the process of relating visual input to speech output involves the oral reading (vocalisation) of words or non-words presented one at a time without a supporting context. Measures can be taken of the accuracy and latency of response and the errors produced can be categorised and interpreted. The distinction between words and non-words (the factor of *lexicality*) is the variable of primary interest. Other psycholinguistic factors of relevance include: frequency of usage of words, concreteness, spelling-to-sound regularity, and length. The assessment procedure, therefore, consists of matched lists of words and non-words (i.e. lists which are equated for lengths of items, and the orthographic structures from which the items are composed), possibly including a balanced variation of frequency, regularity, or concreteness within the word set.

According to the model in Fig. 11.1, the visual-phonological conversion may be mediated by a lexical or sub-lexical process. The outcome of the word/non-word reading assessment can be interpreted as evidence of an impairment which has its primary effect on one or the other of these underlying processes.

a. Sub-lexical Impairment as Primary Feature

A major difficulty in non-word reading is frequently interpreted as evidence of an impairment of the sub-lexical (grapheme-phoneme) process. This could occur in a "pure" (single component) form, or might be accompanied by other impairments, including damage to the lexical route to phonology.

Outcome 1

> The patient fails badly in attempts at non-word reading but succeeds when reading familiar words of equivalent orthographic structure.

This outcome implies the presence of an isolated "phonological dyslexia". In order to localise the effect in the grapheme-phoneme conversion process, it would be desirable to demonstrate: (1) absence of a visual processing impairment (see later for a discussion of visual processor tests); and (2) absence of a general output difficulty relating to non-words. The task of repeating auditory non-words is usually applied in order to exclude the output interpretation. If the errors made on non-words are predominantly refusals or lexical substitutions this will suggest abolition of the translation process. The occurrence of some non-word responses, combined with a degree of structural relation to the target, suggests the presence of a partially preserved malfunctioning sub-lexical process.

A question may arise as to whether the preserved reading via the lexical route is "direct" or mediated by semantics. A semantic involvement would be suggested by the occurrence of effects (on reaction time or accuracy) of psycholinguistic factors such as concreteness or part of speech. In order to determine whether or not the preserved word reading is entirely normal, it would be desirable to obtain latency measures and to establish: (1) that the general level of the vocal reaction time fell within a normal range; (2) that the effect of word length was not excessive; and (3) that the relation between frequency and regularity was not atypical.

Outcome 2

> The patient fails badly on the non-word lists and also makes errors on the word lists.

This implies loss of the sub-lexical procedure combined with some damage to the lexical process. It can be anticipated that the preserved word reading will not be fully "normal" (indexed by the errors, elevated reaction time levels, or exaggerated effects of length or other variables).

b. Lexical-semantic Impairment as a Primary Feature

The converse of the aforementioned cases is a situation in which the lexical-semantic routes to phonology appear relatively more severely impaired than the grapheme-phoneme channel.

Outcome 3

The patient succeeds in non-word reading but has difficulty with words, especially those with irregular spelling and/or low frequency of usage.

This pattern implies the preservation of the sub-lexical (grapheme-phoneme translation) process combined with damage to the lexical-semantic process. To verify that the translation function was operating normally it would be necessary to establish that error rates and vocal reaction times for non-word reading fell within normal limits and that there was no excessive effect of non-word length. The nature of the deficit in word reading might be determined by examining the impact of frequency and regularity on error rates. If the only words correctly read at each frequency level are regular, this could imply total abolition of the lexical process, with all targets being processed via the grapheme-phoneme translation process. If, as is more likely, some irregular words are read correctly, and if these come from the higher frequency ranges, then the implication is that the lexical process is partially damaged, and that it is the less familiar forms which are most vulnerable. If words which cannot be recognised are processed sub-lexically, it is expected that errors should consist predominantly of "regularisations" (i.e. pronouncing an irregular word as it is written), or incorrect assignment of stress. If some words are processed lexically, a proportion of errors may be substitutions of visually similar words, and some effects of semantic variables may be obtained.

Outcome 4

The patient fails with words (especially irregular forms) and also makes errors with non-words.

This pattern implies a multiple component disorder, in which damage to the lexical process is accompanied by an impairment of the sub-lexical process. The sub-lexical impairment should be detectable as an increase in the latency of non-word reading combined with letter-sound translation errors (e.g. omissions, additions, substitutions of sounds, failure to apply consonant softening or vowel lengthening rules).

Conclusion

These four possible outcomes represent differing distributions of impairments across the lexical and sub-lexical processes involved in visual-phonological conversion. They allow for "pure" phonological or lexical impairments, and for combined impairments in which one or the other aspect is considered to predominate.

ACCESS TO SEMANTICS

As was noted in the previous section, indirect evidence of the involvement of semantic processing in oral reading can be derived from a study of errors and effects of semantic variables. In order to assess the semantic route directly, it is usual to employ classification tasks of one kind or another in which the patient makes a decision on the basis of a comparison of semantic properties of the target items.

In Fig. 11.1, the process of semantic access is represented as consisting of a number of steps, including: (1) the initial recognition of the target word; (2) access to the semantic system; and (3) the retrieval of conceptual representations. Comparison and decision processes are additionally required to support a Yes/No ("true" or "false") response.

a. Initial Recognition

In order to determine whether or not words can be recognised at an initial (logogen) level, it is convenient to use a "lexical decision" task. The patient is presented with a series of words and non-words, and is required to classify real words by a positive (Yes) response, and non-words by a negative (No) response. The discrimination should be quite demanding. Hence, the non-words should be orthographically legal and pronounceable forms. A commonly used procedure is to create non-words by re-arrangement of the orthographic components of the words. Performance can be assessed in terms of the accuracy levels of the two responses and the latency of the reaction.

Abolition of the recognition process will be indicated by chance performance on the lexical decision task. As this could reflect random responding, yielding a 50% error rate on both words and non-words, or a non-discriminatory bias towards one response or the other, it is appropriate to index accuracy by calculation of a d' measure. Preservation of the logogen system will be suggested by high levels of discrimination (falling within the relevant normal range). It would also be desirable to show that reaction time levels were normal and that any effects of frequency, regularity and length were not atypically large.

b. Access to Semantics

An access failure could result from a disconnection between the recognition and semantic levels or from a loss of content within the semantic system itself. A disturbance of the latter type is not strictly a "dyslexia" but needs to be excluded in order to sustain an orthographic interpretation of an access defect. This is best done by varying the modality of presentation of the semantic task, e.g. by comparing written word input with auditory input, pictured objects, tactile objects, or environmental sounds.

Most semantic tasks involve the presentation of two or more targets, either simultaneously or in succession, together with an instruction to indicate whether or not the items correspond with respect to some dimension of stored knowledge. This can be stated in terms of superordinate class membership (Both animals?); the possession of a common property (Both red?); or equivalent standing on a dimension of variation (Both larger than a chair?). Alternatively, classes or properties can be specified in advance, and individual targets can be classified as members or non-members. Another procedure is to present three (or more) items and to ask the patient to select the odd-man-out, i.e. the item which differs from the others on a semantic dimension. In all of these situations, the semantic similarity of the concepts, and hence the difficulty of the discrimination required, can be varied.

Whatever procedure is adopted, the use of formally equivalent tasks with different input modes should indicate whether a failure of semantic processing generalises across modalities, implying abolition of concepts held in a central semantic store, or whether the failure appears specific to written input, suggesting an access failure due to damage to the pathway from the logogens to the semantic system.

VISUAL FUNCTIONS

The reading process may also be impaired at a "peripheral" level, i.e. in terms of the visual processing of print which occurs prior to the attainment of the logogen (word recognition) level. Damage at this level can be inferred from performance on vocalisation or semantic judgement tasks or examined more directly using visual comparison tasks of various kinds.

a. Indirect Measures

A visual processing impairment can be inferred from a study of the errors which occur in oral reading or from an indication that reading accuracy or latency are affected by variations which appear, prima facie, to refer to the visual processor.

Errors. The argument that an error category relates to the visual processing level can be strengthened by a demonstration that it recurs across variations which refer to the higher processing levels. Thus, the effect should be observable in both word and non-word reading, and should occur in lexical and semantic decision tasks as well as in vocalisation tasks.

If the patient consistently neglects one side of visual space errors may show a *positional* effect, with errors located predominantly towards the left or right end of the letter array. The effect might be specific to print or could be part of a more general visuospatial disturbance. To establish this point, standard procedures for assessing neglect (line bisection, copying, cancellation, etc.), might be applied (see chapter 9). Ideally, these should be procedurally close to the reading task, involving identification of rows of numbers, objects or other symbols. Obviously, it will also be essential to determine the extent and nature of the visual field defects which accompany the neglect dyslexia.

A second possibility is that particular *letters* are consistently mis-identified. If so, presentation of single letters for naming or sounding should reveal a consistent error pattern which is sustained irrespective of target type (word or non-word); task (vocalisation, lexical or semantic decision); or letter position.

Processing Disturbances. The earlier stages of recognition include attentional processes which select groups of letters for higher-level processing. These can be thought of as:

1. Analytic functions, required for isolation of letters from a larger array.
2. Synthetic functions, involved in grouping letters together in blocks.

The extreme possibilities are: (1) analytic focus on a single letter; and (2) synthesis of the entire letter array. There are numerous intermediate possibilities where letters are isolated from the larger array but synthesised as a block for further processing.

A disturbance of the analytic process is suggested if the patient has difficulty in identifying single letters when they are embedded in an array. Identification of letters presented in isolation should be unimpaired (i.e. no general letter recognition deficit). The target letter can be marked by colour, a fixed position, or a pointer (cf. Shallice & Warrington, 1977). A disturbance of this kind can be referred to as a "visual attentional dyslexia".

An impairment of the synthetic process is best detected by a measurement of the effect of *word length* on the reaction time for correct responses to words or non-words. If word length is systematically varied, and if a sufficiently large number of observations is taken, the effect of length can be expressed as the slope of the line of best fit (using a least squares procedure or other appropriate statistical method), and a formal test for the linearity of the time/length relationship can be made. An impairment of the synthetic process will be indexed by an excessive effect of word length (defined in terms of the estimate of processing time per letter). Absence of an impairment will be suggested if the effects of length are slight and within a normal range. In my own work with developmental cases, I concluded that effects in the range of 200 ms/letter or more were indicative of an impairment of the synthetic process (Seymour, 1986). Neurological cases of "word-form dyslexia" (letter-by-letter reading) are likely to show much slower processing rates (Warrington & Shallice,

1980). It is, of course, expected that the effect should generalise across materials (words vs non-words), and across tasks (vocalisation and decision).

Format Distortions. The word length variation can be combined with other factors which limit the operations of the visual processor. These include: reductions in legibility by the use of handwritten targets, limited exposure time, backward masking, superimposition of "visual noise" or removal of parts of letters. Another possibility is to introduce a spatial distortion of the array by re-arrangement of the letters in zigzag, diagonal, vertical (or other) formats, by alternation of case, or by introduction of extraneous forms between letters. In general, large effects of these manipulations indicate the presence of a disturbance of the visual processor. Tolerance of the distortions, or their resolution with normal time costs (cf. Seymour, 1987), suggest efficiency of visual processing.

Some of the effects may have a specific significance. For example, very slow resolution of vertical distortions may index an impairment of the analytic process, on the assumption that this is needed to recode the spatial format of the array prior to orthographic recognition (Seymour & MacGregor, 1984). However, it has to be admitted that the detailed interpretation of many of these visual effects remains an open question.

b. Direct Measures

An alternative approach is to employ visual matching tasks which require the patient to make "same-different" judgements based on a comparison of visual properties of letter arrays. Two procedures can be considered, which will be referred to as: (1) the letter comparison task; and (2) the array comparison task.

Letter Comparison Task. The patient is presented with displays consisting of two or more letters and must indicate whether the letters are all the same or whether any differences are present. Efficiency is indexed by error levels and reaction times. The decision can be based on physical identity or on categorical (nominal) identity. The ability to match alternative physical forms of letters (e.g. upper vs lower case versions), is thought to tap a level of "abstract letter identities" which defines the input code for the word recognition process. Hence, the letter comparison task, conducted with both physical and nominal identity instructions, might be used to tap an early level of visual feature analysis (physical identity matching), and the higher abstract letter identity level (nominal identity matching).

The use of larger letter arrays, combined with systematic variation in the location of a single discrepant item, would allow tests for positional effects at these two levels in investigations of neglect dyslexia.

Array Comparison Task. In this procedure two arrays of letters are presented simultaneously, usually one above the other, and the patient is instructed to respond "Yes" if the arrays are identical (i.e. contain the same letters in the same positions), and "No" if there are any differences. The number of letters in the arrays, the number and positions of the differences, and whether the comparison is of physical features or nominal identities, can all be varied. The performance indicators are the error levels and reaction times for the two responses.

If the comparison is nominal (upper *vs* lower case), the task may be seen as an assessment of the abstract letter identity level. More generally, it assesses the availability and functional rate of a systematic visual comparison process, possibly involving a serial self-terminating procedure. The underlying processing mode can be determined from a consideration of the pattern of reaction times. The critical variable here is the position of the difference when the arrays differ by only one letter. The location of this single difference can be varied systematically. If the comparison involves a serial self-terminating scan which proceeds from left to right across the arrays, "different" reaction times should be an increasing function of the position of the difference, and "same" reaction times should always be greater than the slowest "different" reaction time. In practice, normal subjects often show departures from this idealised pattern. An impairment of the analytic function of the visual processor will be suggested by a general elevation of the reaction time or error rates, or, more specifically, by an excessively slow position of difference function. The variation in the position of the difference may also be exploited in studies of neglect dyslexia.

CONCLUSION

This chapter has been guided by the proposition that an assessment procedure for acquired (or childhood) dyslexia needs to be based on an information processing framework which identifies the members of the subset of modules and pathways that form the input side of the orthographic component of a larger cognitive system (see Fig. 11.1). The assessment procedure involves the superimposition onto this framework of a range of assumptions regarding the location (within the functional model) of task requirements, stimulus variations, origins of errors, and reaction time and accuracy effects.

A previously held view has been that an objective of assessment is to allocate patients to one of a number of possible types of acquired (or developmental) dyslexia. This view is explicitly rejected in the present discussion. Instead, it is argued that the assessment consists of procedures which focus on regions of the orthographic system and which can be applied to determine the operational status and mode of functioning of each component.

The cognitive assessment techniques I have described do not, as yet, exist as a "package" of generally accepted procedures, based on agreed lists of items, and supported by normative tables of ranges of scores from representative control groups. Clearly, it would be entirely practical to assemble such a package on the basis of current knowledge. Given the desirability of including reaction time measures in the assessment, it would be sensible to establish the package on a microcomputer. However, until this has been done clinicians who wish to make a comprehensive cognitive analysis of reading functions in individual cases of neurological (or developmental) impairment, remain in the position of needing to assemble their own materials or cull lists and procedures from the published case reports (see volumes on "deep dyslexia" and "surface dyslexia" edited by Coltheart, Patterson, & Marshall, 1980; and by Patterson, Marshall, & Coltheart, 1985). Kay, Lesser, and Coltheart (1992) have assembled a set of carefully matched lists which should form the basis of a comprehensive procedure for assessing the components of the cognitive model in the future.

A more general question concerns the utility of a detailed diagnostic procedure of the kind I have described. The initial interest in the acquired dyslexias was in part motivated by the belief that neuropsychological studies of patients with interesting combinations of preserved and impaired functions might provide information relevant to the task of developing a generally applicable cognitive theory of reading processes (Ellis, 1987; Ellis & Young, 1988; Marshall & Newcombe, 1973). This belief led to the publication of a range of case studies and much theoretical debate (cf. Coltheart, Patterson, & Marshall, 1980; Patterson, Coltheart, & Marshall, 1985). The application of a similar approach to developmental disorders of reading followed soon after (Seymour, 1986). Collectively, the published studies are probably sufficient to establish the main arguments in favour of functional heterogeneity within the acquired and developmental populations, and also the major distinctions between: (1) peripheral and central systems; (2) lexical and sub-lexical processes; and (3) phonological and semantic access. It seems likely, therefore, that the theoretical justification for a further proliferation of case studies is diminishing.

The availability of a standard assessment programme could be helpful in establishing the distribution of impairments within particular populations of neurological patients or children. Studies of this kind could show which disturbances are predominant and also what associations or dissociations typically occur. Again, however, there would be a decreasing need to repeat such investigations once a few had been reported for sufficiently large samples of cases. Indeed, investigations of this kind, conducted with normal as well as disturbed populations, would constitute a standardisation of the assessment procedure.

The necessity for detailed cognitive diagnostics in a clinical setting demands careful consideration. The most obvious relevance is in relation to rehabilitation and remediation. The relevance of a diagnostic assessment depends on a theory of the relation between a specific pattern of impairment and preservation of function and the likely impact of particular training/educational methods. Such connections are hardly well established at the present time. However, an assessment procedure offers a method of monitoring and evaluating remediation in a standard fashion, and it seems probable that this application stands as the main justification for the formal construction of a cognitive assessment package for the dyslexias.

REFERENCES

Beauvois, M-F., & Dérouesné, J. (1979). Phonological alexia: Three dissociations. *Journal of Neurology, Neurosurgery and Psychiatry, 42,* 1115-1124.

Boder, E. (1973). Developmental dyslexia: A diagnostic approach based on three atypical reading-spelling patterns. *Developmental Medicine and Child Neurology, 21,* 504-514.

Carroll, J.B., Davies, P., & Richman, B. (1971). *The American Heritage Word Frequency Book.* Boston: Houghton Mifflin.

Coltheart, M. (1980). Reading, phonological recoding, and deep dyslexia. In M. Coltheart, K. Patterson, & J.C. Marshall (Eds.), *Deep dyslexia.* London: Routledge & Kegan Paul.

Coltheart, M. (1981). *Analysing acquired disorders of reading.* Unpublished paper, Birkbeck College, London.

Coltheart, M., Patterson, K., & Marshall, J.C. (1980). *Deep dyslexia.* London: Routledge & Kegan Paul.

Coltheart, M., Masterson, J., Byng, S., Prior, M., & Riddoch, J. (1983). Surface dyslexia. *Quarterly Journal of Experimental Psychology, 35A,* 469-495.

Critchley, M. (1970). *The dyslexic child.* London: Heinemann.

Ellis, A.W. (1987). Intimations of modularity, or, the modularity of mind: Doing cognitive neuropsychology without syndromes. In M. Coltheart, G. Sartori, & R. Job (Eds.), *The cognitive neuropsychology of language.* London: Lawrence Erlbaum Associates Ltd.

Ellis, A.W., & Young, A.W. (1988). *Human cognitive neuropsychology.* London: Lawrence Erlbaum Associates Ltd.

Kay, J., Lesser, R., & Coltheart, M. (1992). *PALPA.* London: Lawrence Erlbaum Associates Ltd.

Kucera, H., & Francis, W.N. (1967). *Computational analysis of present day American English.* Providence: Brown University Press.

Marshall, J.C., & Newcombe, F. (1973). Patterns of paralexia: A psycholinguistic approach. *Journal of Psycholinguistic Research, 2,* 175-199.

Morton, J. (1969). The interaction of information in word recognition. *Psychological Review, 76,* 165-178.

Morton, J. (1980). The logogen model and orthographic structure. In U. Frith (Ed.), *Cognitive processes in spelling.* London: Academic Press.

Morton, J., & Patterson, K.E. (1980). A new attempt at an interpretation, or, an attempt at a new interpretation. In M. Coltheart, K. Patterson, & J.C. Marshall (Eds.), *Deep dyslexia.* London: Routledge & Kegan Paul.

Neale, M.D. (1966). *Neale analysis of reading ability.* London: Macmillan.

Newcombe, F., & Marshall, J.C. (1980). Transcoding and lexical stabilisation in deep dyslexia. In M. Coltheart, K. Patterson, & J.C. Marshall (Eds.), *Deep dyslexia.* London: Routledge & Kegan Paul.

Paivio, A., Yuille, J.C., & Madigan, S. (1968). Concreteness, imagery and meaningfulness values for 925 nouns. *Journal of Experimental Psychology Monograph, 76,* (1, Pt 2).

Patterson, K.E., & Shewell, C. (1987). Speak and spell: Dissociations and word class effects. In M. Coltheart, G. Sartori, & R. Job (Eds.), *The cognitive neuropsychology of language.* London: Lawrence Erlbaum Associates Ltd.

Patterson, K.E., Coltheart, M., & Marshall, J.C. (Eds.). (1985). *Surface dyslexia: Neuropsychological and cognitive studies of phonological reading*. London: Lawrence Erlbaum Associates Ltd.

Schonell, G.B., & Schonell, F.E. (1956). *Diagnostic and attainment testing*. Edinburgh: Oliver & Boyd.

Seymour, P.H.K. (1986). *Cognitive analysis of dyslexia*. London: Routledge & Kegan Paul.

Seymour, P.H.K. (1987). Word recognition processes: An analysis based on format distortion effects. In J. Beech and A. Colley (Eds.), *Cognitive approaches to reading*, Chichester: Wiley.

Seymour, P.H.K., and McGregor, C.J. (1984). Developmental dyslexia: A cognitive experimental analysis of phonological morphemic and visual impairments. *Cognitive Neuropsychology, 1*, 43–82.

Shallice, T. (1988). *From neuropsychology to mental structure*. Cambridge: Cambridge University Press.

Shallice, T., & Warrington, E.K. (1977). The possible role of selective attention in acquired dyslexia. *Neuropsychologia, 15*, 34-41.

Shallice, T., & Warrington, E.K. (1980). Single and multiple component central dyslexic syndromes. In M. Coltheart, K. Patterson, & J.C. Marshall (Eds.), *Deep dyslexia*. London: Routledge & Kegan Paul.

Thorndike, E.L., & Lorge, I. (1944). *The Teacher's Word Book of 30,000 Words*. New York: Columbia University Press.

Warrington, E.K., & Shallice, T. (1980). Word-form dyslexia. *Brain, 103*, 99-112.

12

Assessment of Attention

Adriaan H. van Zomeren
Department of Neurology J-1, University Hospital, Groningen, The
Netherlands

Weibo H. Brouwer
Traffic Research Centre, Rijksuniversiteit Groningen, Haren,
The Netherlands

> *You are talking about attention as if it is a known active entity that*
> *sits somewhere and pays out things. Yet, it is only a metaphor. It*
> *is a term that has really not been defined sufficiently but that is*
> *used to label a very complex set of processes.... I think at some*
> *point we have to understand what we mean when we use the word*
> *attention as the subject of a sentence.*
>
> —*E. Donchin (1984).*

INTRODUCTION

The aforementioned quotation stems from a workshop on event-related brain potentials as tools in the study of cognitive function, held in Carmel, California. Apparently, there was some semantic confusion among the experts gathered there, which should serve as a warning for the writers and the readers of the present chapter. The problem is, that whereas "attention" is used in daily language in a variety of ways, psychologists and other neuroscientists have given different definitions of the concept. Hence, to avoid confusion when talking about the assessment of attention, our terminology should be as clear and consistent as possible.

In common language, attention is mostly used to indicate the "paying of attention" to a particular source of information, e.g. traffic lights, or the voice of a lecturer in an academic setting. In this sense, attention is closely related with

241

perception, and especially with the direction of perception. Without consulting psychological handbooks, every layperson knows that the perception of others can be manipulated by calling "Attention please!", or by introducing elements that will catch the eye, like flashing lights in a display window, or a fluttering flag in front of a hamburger joint. Apart from this directivity in perception, common language also describes attention as a matter of degree or quantity, in that it can be said that someone is paying little attention to their environment. Next, the dimension of effort can be distinguished in the daily use of the word attention, for example, when it is said that a person is concentrating hard on a task. Finally, the layperson obviously had some knowledge of time-on-task effects: no-one is surprised when attention falters should an audience be confronted with a dull lecture, or the reader with a boring text. Also, it is recognised that fatigue will have an effect on the attention of a person who is working for a longer period of time on a given task.

Cognitive psychology has incorporated and elaborated these various meanings of attention, and added a few concepts of its own. The net result is, that no single, correct definition of attention can be given. As Donchin (1984) pointed out, the word may refer to several dimensions or processes in human and animal behaviour. The next section will attempt to list the various concepts of attention, before we turn to the essential question of this chapter: How to measure attention.

CONCEPTS OF ATTENTION

Alertness

A basic biological aspect of attention is alertness, defined by Posner (1975) as a hypothetical state of the central nervous system which affects general receptivity to stimulation. This state may vary from a very low level in sleep to a high level in wakefulness. A distinction can be made between phasic and tonic changes in alertness.

A *phasic* change in alertness can be provoked by means of a warning signal, in an experimental paradigm in the laboratory, or by a meaningful signal in daily life. The effect is the same in both situations: the subject becomes alerted and receptive to external stimulation. In the laboratory it has been demonstrated that this phasic change reveals itself in electrophysiological indices. (See Chapter 19 for a full discussion of electrophysiological indices.) The best known of these is the Contingent Negative Variation in the EEG (Walter et al., 1964). When a subject is presented with a warning signal, and instructed to react to an imperative signal that follows, that person's EEG will show slow negative shifts in widespread cortical regions, but most notably in frontal areas. This slow potential became known as CNV or Expectancy Wave. Later research indicated that CNV is made up of two components, one reflecting preparation for action, and the other, stimulus anticipation (Brunia & Damen, 1988). The motor preparation component is largest over the hemisphere contralateral to the movement side, i.e. contralateral to the hand that is used in the reaction. However, the stimulus anticipation component is larger over the right hemisphere, irrespective of the hand to be used in responding.

On the other hand, *tonic* changes of alertness occur slowly and involuntarily, resulting from physiological changes in the organism. An important factor in this respect is the diurnal rhythm, and another well-known phenomenon is the post-lunch dip marked by a decline in performance on some tasks. In the present chapter, however, a specific kind of change in tonic alertness is essential. Alertness tends to decline within half an hour when subjects are engaged in monotonous tasks. Mackworth (1950) was the first to demonstrate that signal detection decreases rapidly in boring task situations, and this aspect of attention has been studied extensively under the heading of "vigilance".

Alertness is maintained by the first functional unit in the brain, as described by Luria (1973). This is the unit for regulating cortical tone, waking, and mental states. The structures maintaining and regulating cortical tone do not lie in the cortex itself, but in the subcortex and brain stem. In fact, the brain stem reticular formation can be considered as the cornerstone of the whole functional unit. The subcortical structures have a double relationship with the cortex, both influencing its tone, and themselves experiencing its regulatory influence. (In particular, the medial and orbital prefrontal cortex projects on the subcortical system.) Cortical tone and wakefulness are maintained by means of three kinds of stimulation: external stimulation, internal stimulation like hunger and pain, and input from the cortex. The latter stimulation is especially important in humans, who are able to stay awake even when outside stimulation is reduced to a minimum and no internal stimulation is bothering them. For example, anxiety may prevent people from falling asleep, and sense of duty may keep a sentinel or guard awake. It will be clear that this cortical input supplies a link between one aspect of attention, i.e. alertness, and factors like drive and motivation.

A study by Salazar et al. (1986) suggests that the functional unit maintaining alertness is not functioning symmetrically, despite its anatomical symmetry. These investigators studied loss of consciousness in soldiers wounded in Vietnam, mainly by low-velocity fragment wounds from explosive devices, i.e. shell-splinters penetrating the skull. Of soldiers wounded this way, 53% had no, or only momentary, loss of consciousness. Further analysis revealed that there was a preponderance of left hemisphere lesions in those with prolonged unconsciousness. Brain structures much more commonly involved in soldiers with prolonged unconsciousness included the area of the posterior limb of the left internal capsule, the hypothalamus, the left basal forebrain, and the midbrain. On the basis of this finding Salazar et al. (1986) suggest that "wakefulness" or the tonic component of arousal, is maintained by the left hemisphere. This would be in line with Luria's view that many human psychological processes, including consciousness, are organised on a verbal basis and are linked to language processes. Salazar et al. (1986) believe that an intimate working relationship between the left hemisphere and brainstem centres such as the reticular activating system (RAS), could explain the loss of consciousness by acute injury in this hemisphere. On the other hand, the right hemisphere functions with a habituation bias more suited to phasic attention and orienting to novelty. Hence, a comparable acute injury to the right hemisphere would not disrupt the function of RAS and "wakefulness".

Neglect

Even if the two hemispheres play different roles in the maintaining of alertness, it may be stated that alertness normally results in a symmetrical orientation on the external world. In other words, it makes no difference whether a sudden event occurs in the left or right visual field, or whether an itch occurs on the left or right side of our body. However, this symmetry can be disturbed by lesions of the brain. Even in the absence of primary sensory deficits, people with circumscribed brain lesions may display a tendency to neglect one half of their environment or body. This is known as hemi-inattention or half-sided neglect (see Chapter 9 for a review of this area). Heilman et al. (1985) define the neglect syndrome as a unilateral defect in the orienting response. Mesulam (1981) states that unilateral neglect reflects a disturbance in the spatial distribution of directed attention. Research with monkeys and humans suggests that four cerebral regions provide an integrated network for the modulation of attention within extrapersonal space. A posterior parietal component provides an internal sensory map. A limbic component in the cingulate gyrus regulates the spatial distribution of motivational valence. A frontal component coordinates the motor programmes for exploration, scanning, reaching and fixating. Finally, a reticular component provides the underlying level of arousal and vigilance.

This network is functioning asymmetrically. In human beings, unilateral neglect syndromes are more frequent and severe after lesions in the right hemisphere. The attentional functions of the right hemisphere seem to span *both* hemispaces, while the left hemisphere seems to contain the neural apparatus mostly for contralateral attention. Hence, the evidence indicates that the right hemisphere of dextrals has a functional specialisation for the distribution of directed attention within extrapersonal space.

Focused Attention

Once a subject is alert and receptive to stimulation, the problem of selection arises. A person simply cannot deal with all the information coming in through his senses and stored in his long-term memory. In a way, this implies that attention is always selective for two reasons. First, from an ergonomic point of view the bulk of the stimulation from the external world is irrelevant for the task at hand. Secondly, human beings have a limited processing capacity, and are thereby forced to select the most relevant information in order to reach satisfactory task performance. This selectivity is usually studied under the name of focused attention, in the domains of auditory and visual perception.

Selectivity implies that there must be alternatives to attend to. A global distinction can be made between selection within one category of stimuli, and selection from different sources of information. In the first case, the subject is confronted with stimuli in one sensory modality that are classified as target and non-target stimuli. An example from daily life would be the picking of currants, where the colour of the berries is the discriminant feature. On a somewhat higher cognitive level, the correction of printer's proofs is an example of focused attention as the search is directed to lacking or incorrect letters. In the second case, selectivity must be described in terms of concurrent sources of information. The best-known example would be the cocktail party phenomenon, which illustrates that we can selectively listen to one voice in the presence of many others. Of course, the different sources of information can also be of different modalities, for example when someone is reading while ignoring a speaker on the radio nearby.

Closely related to focused attention is the concept of *distraction*. Our selective perception can be disturbed by responses to stimuli that are, at that particular moment, irrelevant for task performance. In fact, we have a large repertoire of automatic attention responses that may interrupt an activity. Some of these tendencies are obviously inborn and useful in a biological sense. The sudden appearance of a strong stimulus, be it a loud bang or a movement in the periphery of our visual field, almost inevitably results in an orienting reaction towards the source of this stimulation. This is a basic mechanism, and for saccadic eye movements to peripheral stimuli it is assumed that it is realised by lower visual structures like the superior colliculus. Buchtel and colleagues (Buchtel & Guitton, 1980; Buchtel, 1987) have demonstrated that the frontal lobes are essential for the suppression of reflex-like saccades to irrelevant visual stimuli. This seems to imply that the frontal lobes play an important role in focusing when visual distractors are present.

Automatic response tendencies can also be the result of learning or con-ditioning. For example, it is hard to ignore a ringing telephone, and virtually impossible not to hear your own name when it is spoken in your presence.

Experimental psychology usually investigates focused attention by manipu-lating distraction, i.e. by adding irrelevant stimulation in a task situation. A well-known method is the dichotic listening task, where two sources of information are presented with an instruction to focus on one of them. In the visual domain focused attention is sometimes operationalised as visual search, where target stimuli have to be detected in a field of distractors more or less resembling the targets. A special case is the Colour Word Test as devised by Stroop (1935).

This test consists of stimuli with two dimensions, colour and verbal meaning. For example, the word "red" may be printed in green letters. Subjects are required to focus on the colour of the words and to name these colours, while ignoring the conflicting word meaning. On the basis of work by Perret (1974), and Holst and Vilkki(1988) with neurological patients, it is probable that the left frontal lobe plays an essential role in this form of focused attention.

Divided Attention

Even when subjects are attending to task-relevant signals alone, they often have to pay attention to more than one source of information. An example would be the participant of a conference who is both listening to a speaker and looking at the slides that illustrate the lecture. Moreover, in daily life one may be forced to perform two tasks simultaneously, like driving a car while at the same time having a conversation with a passenger. In such situations it may become clear that the human information processing system has a limited capacity. In other words, we only have a certain amount of attention to pay. The result is that combination of tasks may lead to a decline in performance in one or both of the tasks.

The core of the problem is that the controlled processing of information is serial in nature. According to Shiffrin and Schneider (1977) there are two modes of processing, i.e. automatic *vs* controlled. Automatic processing is fast and parallel, and has an almost unlimited capacity. It is partly based on inborn capacities, like the ability to perceive symmetry in a visual pattern, and partly on learning processes. Reading, for example, is an activity which is to a high degree automatised, as we tend to pick up the meaning of a line of text with only a few saccades. On the other hand, controlled processing is slow and serial, and is necessary to perform tasks that are not routine. In this mode of processing a bottleneck is involved, as we can only perform one basic operation at a time in our working memory.

When subjects are confronted with a dual task, or with a task requiring the processing of information from various sources, their performance will be determined by two factors: the *capacity* of controlled processing, and the *strategy* that is used to divide the available capacity over the subtasks or sources of information. Particularly when the processing system is overloaded, a dividing strategy may restrict the negative effects by allocating available processing capacity mainly to the most relevant task or information.

Sustained Attention

In the previous section an implicit notion can be found to the effect that focused attention and divided attention cannot logically be conceived as entirely separate processes. Even when subjects are dividing their attention, they are still acting selectively by ignoring all stimulation that is irrelevant to the two tasks or activities that they are trying to combine. In a similar vein, sustained attention cannot be seen as a separate entity. If performance over longer periods of time is studied (minutes or hours) we are in fact dealing with sustained focusing, sustained dividing, or both. Still, it is ecologically useful to consider what happens in a sustained performance as our duties in daily life practically always demand a prolonged effort. Three topics will be dealt with in this context: time-on-task effects, lapses of attention, and intra-individual variability.

Time-on-task Effects. When a subject is engaged in a certain activity, that person's performance may change over time. It may improve for a while due to a practice effect, or it may decline through fatigue, boredom or drowsiness. Psychologists have been interested mainly in negative effects of time-on-task, inspired as they were by practical problems of decreasing vigilance in people working in monotonous situations. The early work in this domain (Mackworth, 1950) stemmed directly from a concern about decreasing efficiency of military personnel in watchkeeping with radar and sonar. In present psychological research a distinction can be made between the more or less "classical" vigilance tasks, and in monitoring tasks. Originally, the term vigilance referred to sustained attention in a low-event-rate situation, in a room with a low level of stimulation (soundproofed and dimly lit). Such situations may provoke drowsiness in the subjects, and falling asleep in a vigilance experiment is, although undesirable, not unusual. On the other hand, subjects may be presented with a continuous stream of stimuli in which they have to detect target stimuli, in a situation which is not sleep-provoking. The latter kind of task can be characterised by the term: Monitoring.

Although this section is dealing with sustained attention, the time-on-task effect relates the topic with alertness as discussed earlier. Decreasing vigilance in a monotonous task situation is the manifestation of decreased alertness. Due to a lack of sensory stimulation, a tonic change in alertness occurs that may result in drowsiness or even sleep − unless the subject can keep awake through an iron sense of duty, or fear of the experimenter. As noted in a previous section, there are obvious links between the regulation of consciousness, particularly wakefulness, and language functions. Thoughts may keep us awake, and, in fact, often do.

Lapses of Attention. These are phasic changes in alertness, resulting in a decreased receptivity to stimulation. As the word lapse suggests, these are short periods, lasting a few seconds at the most. Lapses of attention are usually operationalised as response omissions in a continuous task, or as extremely long reaction times in a continuous RT task. In the latter case the criterion for a lapse is a reaction time exceeding the mean by at least two standard deviations. Like the time-on-task effects, lapses of attention are related to alertness in a physiological way. Lapses have been demonstrated in normal subjects after sleep deprivation; they are, for example, a potential source of danger during long car drives at night. Lapses of attention have also been documented in groups of neurological patients, i.e. in narcoleptics and epileptics (Aarts et al., 1984; Townsend & Johnson, 1979; Valley & Broughton, 1983).

Intra-individual Variability. Even when a subject stays alert and active in a task situation, some variability in that person's performance level may be noted. The accuracy of responses, or the speed of responding, will seldom be constant. This intra-individual variability has been studied mostly in continuous RT tasks.

Supervisory Attentional Control

A relatively new concept in the study of attention is Supervisory Attentional Control (SAC). In the section on Divided Attention, it was already pointed out that an effective allocation of processing capacity in a complex task requires some kind of strategy. The use of a control strategy is likewise required in tasks that are primarily loading on Focused or Sustained Attention. Practically all our activities are consciously monitored by control strategies. Such strategies will determine, for example, when attention will be shifted to other aspects of the stimulus situation, or how responses are sequenced. In this sense, flexibility of attention is an aspect of supervisory control.

Luria (1966) and Lezak (1982) have introduced the concept of "executive functions of the brain". These functions are: planning, programming, regulation and verification of goal-directed behaviour. There is ample evidence, both from animal and human studies, that the prefrontal cortex is the neuro-anatomical substrate of these functions. Hence, on logical grounds it may be assumed that the prefrontal areas are important for Supervisory Attentional Control. Direct evidence for this assumption stems from work by Shallice (1982), who developed an information processing model in which a so-called Supervisory Attentional System supervises the running of highly specialised routine programmes. Such programmes or schemas are activated in any mental activity, as any activity is at least partly based on routine. However, the question of which schemas will be activated in a given task situation depends on two qualitatively distinct processes: Contention scheduling, and the influence of the Supervisory System.

Contention Scheduling quickly selects schemas from the strongest perceptual triggers, or from the output of previously run schemas. Contention scheduling is, therefore, mainly dependent on automatic processing of information, and most effective in the performance of well-trained tasks. On the other hand, the Supervisory system is responsible for controlled processing and the selection of alternative schemes. With some effort, the supervisory system can suppress contention scheduling and allow the subject to concentrate on a non-routine aspect of the stimulus material. The correction of printer's proofs can illustrate the control exerted by SAS. Normal reading is to a large extent automatised by a learning stage that began in our school age, and that resulted in a fast and efficient process: when a skilled reader is confronted with a text, that person immediately perceives semantic meaning, without even realising that the process started with the perception of little black figures, grouped in horizontal lines on a white background. However, Supervisory Attentional Control enables us to take one step back in this reading process when we want to check the text for misprints. The routine reading of semantic meaning is then replaced by "reading" at a lower level, i.e. the search for abnormalities in the combination of letters into words. It is even wise to ignore the meaning of the text completely, as this may distract us from the task of proof correction. In more conventional terms, supervisory control enables us to concentrate on the level of orthography.

Shallice studied the integrity of Supervisory Attentional Control by means of a test called the Tower of London. This test is derived from an Oriental puzzle game, the Tower of Hanoi, and has been widely used in the study of artificial intelligence to simulate problem-solving. Subjects are required to manipulate coloured beads, placed on three sticks, in order to construct a certain pattern. The task is basically a look-ahead puzzle or a test of planning, as the goal can only be achieved by dividing the task into subtasks. It is essential to suppress moves that apparently solve a detail of the problem presented, in favour of a planning of the correct number and sequence of moves. Shallice found a specific deficit on the Tower of London in neurological patients with lesions of the left frontal lobe. He concluded that patients with such lesions may be impaired in a general programming system, and this seems to confirm the ideas formulated by clinical neuropsychological investigators such as Luria and Lezak.

THE ASSESSMENT OF ATTENTION

From the preceding pages two things will have become clear: attention cannot be caught in a single definition, and attention cannot be related to a single cerebral structure. Logically, then, attention cannot be assessed with a single test. The problem of the present chapter could even be formulated more strongly with the statement: *there are no tests of attention.*

The point is, that one can only assess a certain aspect of human behaviour with special interest for its attentional component. One may study the auditory perception of brain-damaged subjects, while being interested in the selective character of their responses. Or one may study their efficiency of signal detection in a boring situation, stating that one is testing their sustained attention. In essence, the effect of a certain task variable (duration, discriminability etc.), on performance tells us something about a certain aspect of attention. However, as a particular task is never assessing "attention" only, intervening variables may influence performance and obscure the role of the attentional component. For example, a motor deficit may mimick the effect of slow information processing.

To make things even more complicated, a particular test may be described by some investigators as a test of short-term memory, and by others as a test of attention. Digit Span, for example, is usually considered as a test of immediate memory but appeared in a study by Wade et al. (1988) as a test of attention. Likewise Stuss et al. (1987) discussed a Brown-Peterson test of auditory short-term memory in a comparison of "three tests of attention". This should not be considered as wrong or inconsistent: the point is that attention and memory can hardly be discriminated when we look at information processing, particularly in working memory. Information in our working memory will be kept there for some seconds, and this aspect justifies the use of the word memory. At the same time, the information presents a load to the limited processing capacity of the system, and can therefore also be discussed in terms of attention. Moreover, the operations that are carried out on this information in working memory are based on rules and strategies laid down in long-term memory. The constant interaction between working memory and long-term memory thus forms a second indication of the fact that memory and attention are intertwined in a way that makes a distinction between the two concepts rather artificial at times.

A second problem is, that each test will inevitably tap several aspects of attention. Thus, if we describe in the following a test that seems fit to study the capacity to divide attention, it should not be forgotten that the subject in this particular situation has to display alertness, will be perceiving selectively, and will have to sustain attention for at least several minutes to finish the test. Finally, one can be sure that the subject's Supervisory Attentional Control is active during the testing session. And let us hope that the subject will show no lapses of attention, as a result of lack of sleep in the preceding night. Therefore, statements about one particular aspect of attention can only be made after manipulation of task variables. By varying the load on one aspect and recording the effect on task performance, an impairment in this aspect could be demonstrated.

Finally, it must be stressed here that the assessment of attention has long been neglected in psychology. The very word "attention" was practically absent, from the rise of Behaviourism until the publications of Mackworth on vigilance around 1950. Although attentional concepts from then on returned to cognitive psychology, especially in the framework of information processing models, the word attention was seldom seen or heard in fields of applied psychology such as clinical and neuropsychology. Even in 1978, when Walsh published his valuable *Neuropsychology: A clinical approach*, the word was completely absent in the book's index. In other well-known handbooks, attention is often casually mentioned in the text, without being treated as a separate topic; Lezak's handbook (1983) is an exception, dedicating a section to several forms of attention. At present, the scene is changing and attention is making its comeback in neuropsychology.

Nevertheless, there is an arrears. In the domains of intelligence and memory, numerous tests can be found with satisfactory information on their psychometric qualities, reliability and validity. Unfortunately, this is not the case in the domain of attention, and never will be. By the very complexity of the topic, investigation of attentional deficits will always demand a special methodology, be it at least the combination of data from different tests. Moreover, many of the methods of assessment to be described in the following have hardly outgrown their experimental stage, and hardly deserve the name of "test". This results in a remarkable gap between clinical practice and the limited number of available "tests of attention". Many practical professionals will rely on their clinical eye and make impressionistic statements about attention in their patients. In fact, there is nothing wrong with that approach. As well as being able to detect a mild aphasia by simply listening to a patient, we may detect hemi-neglect by carefully looking at a patient's behaviour in the testing situation. After all, sophisticated laboratory techniques are not yet available in many institutions.

Therefore, the review of assessment methods will be an attempt to list all available techniques, whether or not they deserve the formal name of "test".

Alertness

A *phasic* change in alertness, provoked by a warning signal, can be assessed on two levels: the electrophysiological one, and the behavioural one. Electrophysiologically, a phasic increase of alertness will manifest itself in the CNV, and this can be split up in a motor preparation component and a stimulus anticipation component, with the paradigm described by Brunia and Damen (1988). Normative data for these assessment techniques are not yet available, and may never be so because of practical problems like differences in set-up and equipment.

On the behavioural level the effect of a phasic increase in alertness can be assessed by comparing reaction times with and without a warning signal within one subject. A warning signal increases speed of reaction in simple RT tasks, by reducing time uncertainty (Theios, 1975). It is assumed that this effect is based on response preparation between warning signal and imperative stimulus. Hence, the difference between warned and unwarned RT more or less parallels the motor preparation as registered in the CNV. However, for this method normative data are also missing, implying that clinical investigators would have to collect such data in their own settings before statements about this aspect of alertness are possible.

The recording of *tonic changes* in alertness would be even harder to realise in a clinical setting, as it demands long registrations with high technology equipment. Still, these tonic changes have limited clinical relevance, and in most cases observation of a patient can supply some information on a present state of alertness. In the Neurobehavioural Rating Scale, devised by Levin et al. (1987) the first of the 27 items is called Inattention/Reduced Alertness. This aspect of behaviour must be assessed on a 7-point scale with the help of the following descriptions: "Fails to sustain attention, easily distracted; fails to notice aspects of environment, difficulty directing attention, decreased alertness". For the sake of exercise, the reader might try to identify which aspects of attention as described in the theoretical introduction (earlier), are featuring in these guidelines for observation.

In theory, a tonic decline in alertness might occur during a single test or one testing session. In fact, such changes are even deliberately provoked in low event-rate situations like vigilance tasks. However, we prefer to discuss the assessment of such changes in the section on Sustained Attention.

Hemi-neglect

Inattention to one half of the personal space occurs most frequently in the visual sphere, although it can also manifest itself in hemi-somatagnosia or inattention to one half of the patient's own body (see Chapter 9). Visual hemi-neglect can exist without visual field defects. This dissociation is most apparent in the case of visual extinction: a patient may be able to perceive a given stimulus when it is presented in isolation in one half of the patient's visual field, but no longer note the same stimulus when it is presented simultaneously with an identical stimulus at the exact opposite position in the other half of the visual field. Like hemi-neglect, this extinction phenomenon is more often found in the left half field than in the right (Lezak, 1983).

Observation of a patient's behaviour may already reveal hemi-neglect. When walking around they may bump into furniture on the left side, or against the left doorpost. During testing, they may fail to note material on one half of the table, or start reading in the middle of a line of text. In an intelligence test like the Raven Progressive Matrices, that presents a multiple-choice response method, the patient may fail to find the right alternative when it is depicted in the left half of the array. Formal testing of the phenomenon may begin with drawing and copying: in drawings the patient will show a tendency to neglect the left half, for example the points of a star on that side. Neglect may also become apparent when the patient has to copy complex figures like the Rey-Osterrieth (1944).

The next approach makes use of visual search. The patient is presented with an array of stimuli in which target stimuli have to be detected, and tick them with a pencil. Albert's Test consists of a collection of one-inch lines randomly distributed over a 21 x 30 cm sheet of paper (Albert, 1973; Vanier et al., 1990). A more sensitive test was devised by Gauthier et al. (1989): in this Bells Test, 315 stimuli, all familiar figures such as house, horse, key etc., are randomly distributed over a sheet of paper measuring 20 x 26 cm. Thirty-five of the stimuli are targets (bells) and have to be circled by the subject, the others being distractors. Although apparently random, the bells among the distractors are organised into seven columns. Vanier et al. (1990) compared the discrimination power of Albert's Test and the Bells Test, and found that the latter worked far better. In a group of 47 right-hemisphere stroke patients, the Albert's Test detected 7 cases of neglect (15%) whereas the Bells Test identified 22 patients with neglect (47%). Both tests showed a gradient of omissions, the percentages of missed targets being higher in the extreme left column and diminishing from left to right. The Bells Test allowed a finer gradient of omissions than the Albert's Test.

In the two tasks described previously, the field of search is unstructured. More widely used are tests in which targets and distractors are arranged in horizontal lines. A well-known example is the Letter Cancellation Task (Diller & Weinberg, 1977; Lezak, 1983), which consists of rows of letters randomly interspersed with a designated target letter. Strategy of search is derived from the reading process, as subjects are searching from left to right, line by line from top to bottom. The performance is scored for errors and for time to complete; Diller and Weinberg supply some normative data. Their stroke patients with right-hemisphere lesions were not much slower than control subjects but had many more errors – always of omission and usually on the left side of the page. Patients with left-hemisphere lesions made few errors but worked much more slowly than controls. Digit Cancellation Tasks have also been described as useful in the assessment of hemi-neglect. Wade et al. (1988) applied this method in a study of cognitive recovery after stroke and present normative data for elderly subjects. The authors expressed performance as a percentage, dividing the number of correctly cancelled digits on one side by the number correctly cancelled on the other side. With this method, all normal subjects scored between 90–100%. Wade et al., conclude that the use of this relative percentage score is a simple way of scoring visual neglect. A retest of 12 elderly subjects, two to four weeks after their first assessment, indicated that this test had an acceptable reliability.

Reading itself can be used as a test of visual neglect. When presented with a text, patients may skip the first word of the next line. This indicates that the well-trained habit of picking up the beginning of the next line "at a glance" is disturbed by damage to their right hemisphere. Caplan (1987) has refined this method of investigation by introducing his Indented Paragraph Reading Test. This is a passage consisting of 30 lines, glorifying the beauty of trees. The left-hand margin is intentionally constructed to be highly variable. The first word of each line is indented between 0 and 25 spaces, with the amount of indentation being unpredictable from one line to the next. The layout of the text thus precludes the possibility that a neglecting subject could form a compensatory "spatial set", as each refixation from the end of one line to the beginning of the next requires a separate act of controlled scanning. Caplan reports that in some cases patients with neglect showed their impairment on this task only, and he considers the test as a valuable screening measure.

A more extensive series of tests aimed at hemi-neglect is combined in the Rivermead Behavioural Inattention Battery (Wilson et al., 1987). This battery has an apparent ecological validity, as it makes use of standardised tests derived directly from daily life situations (see Chapter 9). Moreover, the battery has been published with satisfactory normative information.

Focused Attention

Focused attention can be operationalised as selectivity in perceiving and responding. Hence, an enormous number of tasks could be used to approach this aspect of cognitive functioning. In practice, focused attention is usually assessed in the auditory and visual domain only.

Auditory focused attention can be tested with the method of dichotic listening. Two different messages can be fed by earphones simultaneously into both ears of a subject, while one message is indicated as the target one, and the other as the distractor. Gronwall and Sampson (1974) have applied this method in the study of focused attention after mild head injury. To check their ability to listen selectively, subjects were instructed to shadow the target message, that is, to repeat it word by word while listening. This can be done with lists of isolated words, or with meaningful texts. Performance can be scored as the number of correctly shadowed elements, or as knowledge of content when questions are asked afterwards about a meaningful text. Impaired focused attention or a negative effect of the distractor message can be concluded: when shadowing is worse than in a single-message condition; when knowledge of content decreases; or when intrusions from the irrelevant message are noted in the shadowing. Task difficulty can easily be altered, by varying the resemblance between target and non-target message, either physically (for example, male vs female voice), phonologically, or semantically. An extensive amount of literature from cognitive psychology is available on this topic, but unfortunately few clinical neuropsychological studies have been aimed directly at the aspect of focused attention.

Normative data are not available, but the impression exists that auditory focused attention is usually perfect in normal subjects, resulting in ceiling effects when they are required to listen selectively in a dichotic stimulation task. In daily life, the cocktail party phenomenon illustrates the efficiency of selective listening to a (more or less) meaningful message in the presence of potentially distracting other messages.

Visual focused attention is usually operationalised as visual search. Target stimuli have to be found in a field of distractor stimuli, all stimuli usually being arranged in horizontal rows. These tasks are self-paced, although the instruction almost always requires subjects to complete the task as quickly as possible. The Letter Cancellation Task and the Digit Cancellation Task described earlier are well-known examples. In Europe two more varieties are used: the Bourdon-Wiersma and the Brickenkamp test.

The Brickenkamp (1981) presents rows of b's and d's, some of these letters being labelled with primes. The target stimulus is the letter d. The Bourdon-Wiersma (Grewel, 1953) uses groups of dots, either 3, 4 or 5, as stimuli. Subjects have to check each row as quickly as possible, crossing out groups of 4 dots. For both the Brickenkamp and the Bourdon-Wiersma, norms are available on speed and efficiency of target detection.

In the tests described so far, the visual search of the subject is almost completely guided by the structure of the stimulus field presented to that person. That is, just as in normal reading, their gaze simply follows the horizontal lines of stimuli, in search of targets. This is not the case in the Trailmaking Test (Reitan, 1958) in which circles, numbered from 1 to 25, are randomly distributed on a page. The circles have to be connected by a line, beginning in circle 1, as quickly as possible. Lezak presents in her handbook (1984) detailed norm tables for the interpretation of results. These tables reflect a clear effect of age on Trailmaking, older subjects being slower. This effect has been confirmed by Stuss et al. (1987) who supply additional normative information.

Focused attention can also be assessed with a special kind of visual search via the Embedded Figures Test. This test has been developed from Gottschaldt's Hidden Figures Test (1928). It demands that the subject discovers a simple figure embedded in a complex pattern. This is clearly an example of selective perception, as the combination of a few relevant lines has to be seen against the background of a multitude of irrelevant ones. Thurstone (1944) stated that successful performance in normals was related to the ability to form a perceptual closure against some distraction. The test has been shown to be sensitive to brain lesions in a variety of locations, and caused by various aetiologies (Lezak, 1983; Talland, 1965; Teuber et al., 1960).

Finally, as described on page 245, the Stroop paradigm can be used to assess a form of focused attention.

Divided Attention

The ability to divide attention is determined by two factors: processing capacity and strategic control. The first of these is easier to assess in a clinical setting than the second one. Processing capacity depends largely on speed of processing, and psychology has always been apt to measure duration of behaviour. Speed of information processing can be assessed with a variety of tasks, although care must be taken that demands on the motor system are kept at a minimum. A suitable method is the recording of choice reaction times (Blackburn & Benton, 1955; Bruhn & Parsons, 1971; Miller, 1970; Norrman & Svahn, 1961; van Zomeren & Deelman, 1978). Thirty to forty trials are sufficient, after some ten practice trials, to calculate the median as a stable index for the central tendency in an individual's reactions. Visual stimuli have been most popular, as they are more easy to present and manipulate in space. In recent years the introduction of computerised assessment has facilitated the recording and calculating of reaction times (RT).

Nevertheless, if the recording of RT is impossible in a given clinical setting, there are alternative methods available for a global assessment of speed of information processing. For example, speeded tasks like reading of word lists, or colour naming as used as a pre-condition in the Stroop Test (Stroop, 1935) can give the investigator some idea about the mental speed of a patient. The subtest Digit Symbols from the Wechsler Adult Intelligence Scale is likewise useful, as is its counterpart the Symbol Digit Modalities Test (Smith, 1973). The latter test demands translation of symbols into digits, and has the advantage, in comparison with Digit Symbols from the WAIS, that no unfamiliar symbols have to be written. The SDMT also provides norms on various age groups (Lezak, 1983). As noted earlier one should be very careful regarding motor problems when judging speed of information processing; a dysarthria may impede reading speed, and a mild hemi-paresis may prolong visual RT, or the performance on any paper-and-pencil test, even when speed of information processing is in itself normal.

If we move to more complex tasks, tests are available that are clearly tapping the ability to divide attention. Divided attention can be operationalised by combining two tasks into one test, or by combining two sources of information, both relevant to the same task. The best-known test of divided attention so far is the Paced Auditory Serial Addition Task or PASAT, as devised by Gronwall and Sampson (1974). The authors describe their test as follows (p.26):

A random series of digits from 1 to 9 is presented to the subject, who is instructed to add pairs of numbers such that each number is added to the one immediately preceding it. The second digit is added to the first, the third to the second, and so on. To be correct, a response must be made before presentation of the next stimulus. PASAT thus yields an estimate of the subject's ability to register sensory input, respond verbally, and retain and use a complex set of instructions. He must also hold each item after processing, retrieve the held item for addition to the next digit, and perform at an externally determined pace.

Stated otherwise, the subject has to perform several subtasks within one test, under a considerable time pressure. At a low rate of presentation, say one digit in every four seconds, the task is still fairly easy for normal subjects. When rate of presentation increases to, for example, one digit per two seconds, subjects begin to make errors as their processing capacity is exceeded. Some normative data for PASAT can be derived from work by Gronwall and her co-workers, mainly on the effects of head injury (Gronwall, 1977; Gronwall & Wrightson, 1974; and Stuss et al., 1987; 1988). Rate of presentation is, of course, critical in this test. Gronwall's own publications suggest that an inter-stimulus interval of two seconds discriminates best between normal controls and subjects who had sustained mild head injuries. PASAT has also been proven useful for monitoring recovery after such injuries, by retesting patients in the course of several weeks or months. However, findings on retest should be corrected for a practice effect that was demonstrated by Stuss et al. (1987).

Gronwall and Wrightson (1981) have claimed that PASAT performance was not significantly correlated with either general intelligence or arithmetical ability. This view has been challenged by Egan (1988) who found a correlation of 0.63 between PASAT scores and IQ on Raven's Standard Progressive Matrices, in a non-clinical group of 28 young adults. In our own department (Bruins & Van Nieuwenhuizen, 1990), we found a Pearson correlation of 0.40 (P = 0.012) between Raven-IQ and PASAT scores in a group of 32 normal subjects. In addition, a correlation of 0.42 was found between PASAT and the speed of making additions (adding three numbers under 100, during one minute). Moreover, in this group women performed significantly better than men. Stuss et al. (1987) also report a positive correlation between years of education and PASAT performance. These findings suggest that norm tables for PASAT should control for level of education, intelligence, and, possibly, sex.

As another example of a divided attention task, the Trailmaking Test as devised by Reitan (1958) should be mentioned. As described earlier, the subject has to connect circles sequentially in this test, by drawing lines between them with a pencil, starting at circle 1. Although this is primarily a visual search task, it can also be considered a divided attention task, as the subject must keep track of the numbers while searching for the next circle. The required dividing of attention is even clearer in part B, where two kinds of circles are presented: thirteen circles containing the numbers from 1 to 13, and 12 circles containing the letters from A to L. The subject now has to connect the circles again (hence, the same motor activity is required as in part A), but alternating from letters to numbers. Thus, the sequence becomes 1-A-2-B-3-C etc. In this second part of the Trailmaking Test the patient's working memory is loaded with a double task of keeping track, i.e. keeping in mind both the alphabet and the counting. Extensive normative data for several age groups have been presented by Davies (1968; also in Lezak, 1983) and Stuss et al. (1987).

Of course, numerous tasks can be found or devised that demand divided attention. Particularly, the experimental combination of tasks has resulted in a whole new dual task methodology. However, as the emphasis in that approach is firmly on strategy, it seems more adequate to discuss this field under the heading of Supervisory Attentional Control (see the following).

Sustained Attention

In a testing session covering a few hours, the observable behaviour of a patient may display changes that are not recorded by the separate tests. It is worthwhile, therefore, to pay attention to those changes by means of the clinical eye. During the session, a patient may become less talkative and less alert, particularly in the short intervals between tests when left alone for a minute. Such changes can be viewed as indicating a global decline in attention, or receptivity to information from outside. Observation of these effects has a practical relevance when statements are expected from the psychologist about a patient's chances of resuming former work. In their job, too, the patient will have to maintain an adequate level of alertness for at least several hours.

Of course, it is hard to differentiate here between effects of "fatigue", decreasing motivation and attentional deficits. Unfortunately, fatigue is hard to define and record, and usually remains a purely subjective phenomenon. As soon as an experimenter tries to operationalise "fatigue" the focus will probably be on decline in task performance (decreasing speed of responding, increasing error rate). However, the approach then gets a somewhat circular character, as these same indices are supposed to reflect deficits in sustained attention. It seems, then, that we will have to accept the fact that fatigue, motivation and attention are intertwined in such a way that it is impossible to dissect them. Instead, the clinical investigator may look at three aspects of sustained attention: time-on-task effects, lapses of attention and intra-individual variability.

Time-on-task Effects. As every task has an attentional aspect, in principle every test can be extended to cover 15 minutes and claimed to assess "sustained attention". In practice, two categories of tasks have been used widely to study attention over time periods of up to one hour, i.e. vigilance and monitoring. The study of vigilance started with the classical investigations of N.H. Mackworth (1950) who placed his subjects "alone in a cubicle for two hours, watching a clock hand jerking round in regular jumps, one jump a second, one hundred jumps per revolution. The signal was a jump of twice the usual distance. The interval between successive signals varied from 0.75 to 10 minutes (!), twelve signals being presented each half hour." (J.F. Mackworth, 1970). It will be clear that this classical vigilance task presented an extremely boring situation to the subjects. Vigilance tests of such long duration are, however, hardly feasible in a clinical setting. Fortunately, if one is interested in time-on-task effects half an hour seems to be enough to provoke a decrease of signal detection, as was demonstrated by Brouwer and Van Wolffelaar (1985) in a study of severely head-injured subjects. Still, the setting up of a vigilance task is a laborious enterprise, and therefore commercially available tests of monitoring clearly play a more important role in current clinical neuropsychology.

In the terminology of this chapter, *monitoring* refers to a situation in which clear signals are presented at a high rate, and at a high signal to non-signal event ratio. In the classical Mackworth experiment, only one out of 150 signals was a target, but in monitoring tasks one out of ten stimuli may be a target. The most widely used test of monitoring is probably the Continuous Performance Test as devised by Rosvold and Mirsky (Rosvold et al., 1956). In this test the subject is facing a visual display that presents a random series of letters, the letters coming into view at approximately 0.92 sec intervals. The subject is instructed to press a button when the stimulus is an A. In a second condition, the subject is instructed to react only to the A if it is preceded by an X — which in fact means that the X will serve as a warning signal that it is sometimes followed by the target stimulus, and sometimes not. The Continuous Performance Test has been used with patient groups of various neurological etiologies, among them epileptics and head-injured patients (Greber & Perret, 1985).

Working with tests of vigilance or monitoring contains a special pitfall. The problem is that poor performance on such a test is not proof of poor vigilance or poor monitoring. Of course, brain-damaged subjects will often do poorly on these tests, demonstrating slow reactions, or missing more signals than people with intact brains. However, if they maintain their original level of performance, doing the best they can, there is no reason at all to speak of "decreased vigilance". The only essential point is the presence or absence of a time-on-task effect, particularly a steady decline in level of performance not found in normal subjects.

Both in vigilance and monitoring the pace of stimulus presentation is fixed and determined by the experimenter. This is not the case in cancellation tasks, which form another possible approach of sustained attention. Lezak (1983) characterises these tests as follows (p.548):

> These paper-and-pencil tests require visual selectivity at fast speed on a repetitive motor response task. They assess many functions, not least of which is the capacity for sustained attention. Visual scanning and activation and inhibition of rapid responses are also necessary to the successful performance of cancellation tasks. Lowered scores on these tasks can reflect the general response slowing and inattentiveness of diffuse damage or acute brain conditions, or more specific defects of response shifting and motor smoothness or of unilateral neglect.

This quotation once more illustrates that it is virtually impossible to devise a test that assesses only one aspect of attention in its pure form. From a clinical point of view, the cancellation tasks have the advantage that subjects determine their own rate of working and their own speed/accuracy trade-off. This facilitates generalisation of test findings to real-life situations such as monotonous low-level office work.

Some cancellation tasks have already been mentioned in the section on focused attention and visual search. The Bourdon-Wiersma, the Letter Cancellation Task (Diller et al., 1974), and the Digit Vigilance Test (Lewis & Kupke, 1977), can all be used as tests of sustained attention. In our own laboratory we doubled the duration of the Bourdon simply by combining two test forms, in order to get a task of at least 15 minutes duration. Some normative data are available for the aforementioned tests.

Lapses of attention. In sustained attention tasks with a high response frequency, lapses of attention may manifest themselves as a lacking response or series of responses. In continuous RT tasks, lapses are defined as reaction times that exceed the mean with at least two standard deviations. Lapses can, in principle, also be recorded in self-paced cancellation tasks. Particularly when the task consists of blocks or rows of stimuli a lapse of attention may manifest itself in a clear increase of time per block. In the Bourdon-Wiersma, time in seconds is recorded per line of 25 dot configurations, normal times ranging from 10 to 14 seconds per line. The definition of a lapse is, of course, more or less arbitrary, although in this case the criterion might be a deviation of 2 seconds or more from average time per line.

Intra-individual Variability. In a sustained attention task the variability of a subject's responses can be analysed. The easiest dimension of behaviour for such an analysis would be the speed of responding. In continuous RT tasks, intra-individual variability (IIV) can be readily calculated over blocks of a certain duration. The question remains as to which index of variability will work best? The standard deviation should not be the index of choice, in our experience, as RT distributions are highly skewed to the slower side by incidental extremely slow reactions or responses in which the push-button as a target is not hit at the first attempt. For that reason, we preferred the use of the median as index of central tendency, and the inter-quartile deviation or Q as index of variability. This Q is calculated as half the distance between the 25th and 75th percentage in the distribution of a subject's RT's. Other investigators (Bruhn & Parson, 1977) have suggested that the difference between the 10th and 90th percentage is a more sensitive index, as the use of Q implies a serious reduction of information used from the distribution. Benton (1986) has reviewed the use of RT indices, including variability measures, in neuropsychology.

Of course, time is not the only dimension along which variability can be analysed. Quality of response or efficiency of signal detection might as well be considered in blocks during a sustained attention task. For the sake of completeness, it must be noted that IIV could be used for the assessment of time-on-task effects. Instead of looking at a decline in performance one might as well study changes in variability in prolonged task conditions.

Regarding the relation between IIV and lapses of attention, it can be stated that lapses are merely one possible aspect in IIV. In principle, however, the concepts are independent: even when a subject shows no lapses of attention at all, performance on the task will show some variability from response to response.

Supervisory Attentional Control

There exists as yet no tradition in clinical neuropsychology of assessing this aspect of attention. In a way, the activity of SAC can already be discerned in the performance of subjects on some of the tests mentioned earlier. The Stroop effect, for example, with its strong response interference, clearly taps the integrity of supervisory control. In self-paced cancellation tasks subjects must find their own personal balance between speed and accuracy, and it is conceivable that here, too, higher cognitive elements like strategies are important. Some tests that are assumed to assess "frontal functions" or the executive functions, apparently touch on supervisory control, particularly if they require the subject to be attentive to changes in stimulation. For example, subjects must react flexibly in changes in feedback from the experimenter when the Wisconsin Card Sorting is used (see Chapter 13).

Techniques that pretend to test supervisory control directly are not yet available in a clinically useful form. Hence, clinical neuropsychologists must rely, first of all, on their own observations to make an estimate of how subjects cope with tasks that exceed their processing capacity or that force them to determine priorities when an optimal task performance can no longer be maintained. It is to be hoped that cognitive psychology will contribute to and participate in clinical investigations, resulting in the development of useful tests for the assessment of supervisory control. Particularly, one might think of testing adaptive strategies in task situations with a stepwise increasing load on subjects, and systematic feedback on their level of performance.

Some attempts of assessing Supervisory Attentional Control have been published already. Shallice (1982) described the use of his Tower of London in a study of problem solving by patients with unilateral localised brain lesions. It might well be asked, whether a puzzle of this kind is still concerned with "attention" or whether it is just testing the ability of intelligent thinking. Indeed, has the introduction of SAC widened the concept of attention still further, bringing it close to the concept of intelligence? However, as stated in the theoretical introduction, attention cannot be studied in isolation, and it is evident that subjects labouring on the Tower of London must be attentive to approaches of a problem that are not readily offered by the stimulus pattern presented to them. The Tower of London as described by Shallice can easily be constructed on the basis of his publication from 1982.

Another approach of supervisory control can be realised with a dual-task methodology. This field has seen some new developments, inspired by a method of analysis offered by Somberg and Salthouse (1982). They describe an analysis of Performance Operating Characteristic (POC) for dual-task situations. The essence of their approach is that subjects are instructed to vary their emphasis on the two tasks involved: emphasis is first laid on task A, then on task B, and finally the instruction requires subjects to try to give equal weight to both tasks. These instructions result in shifts in attention allocating strategies, represented by points in a POC curve. The method also enables the calculation of Divided Attention Costs, and therefore seems to hold a promise in the further exploration of attentional deficits in neurological patients. Brouwer et al. (1989) applied the method in a study of 15 survivors of severe head injury, combining a dot-counting task and a lane-tracking task in a simple car simulator. Both the dot-counting task and the road were presented on a video screen facing the subjects. Results were somewhat surprising: although the head-injured patients were performing worse than control subjects on both tasks, the combination of tasks did not reveal extra divided attention costs in the patient group. However, this may have been an effect of patient selection. All 15 patients were active car drivers again, and they were tested many years after injury. This could imply that they have been a positive selection from the general population of head-injury survivors. The fact that these patients had not made themselves conspicuous by an increase in their traffic violations and accidents might well indicate that they were quite able to combine tasks in a daily life activity like car driving, which in itself contains a multitude of subtasks.

THE PRACTICAL APPROACH

In accordance with the practical aim of this book, the present chapter should close with useful guidelines for the assessment of attention in the individual neurological patient. That is easier said than done, because of the variety of symptoms resulting from a variety of etiologies. An epileptic patient definitely presents a picture that is very different from a patient with Alzheimer's Disease or a CVA, and thus general statements are hardly justified. Another problem is the time of investigation when brain damage has been acute, through CVA, head injury, cerebral anoxia etc. In a very early stage, alertness may be the aspect of attention most affected, most patients even being comatose. In the recovery process alertness may slowly increase until patients are aware again of their environment. It may then be found that they are stimulus-bound, or reacting to objects in their environment without being driven by intentions from themselves. In fact, this can also be considered as a form of distractibility, when, for example, the patient grasps the investigator's pen instead of answering their questions. In a later stage, the patient may be behaving adequately, but then be hindered mainly by divided attention deficits, due to mental slowness. In cases of focal brain damage, be it acute by CVA or developing slowly by a neoplasm, Supervisory Attentional Control may be deficient if the lesion is located in the left frontal lobe.

Nevertheless, it can safely be stated that the assessment of attentional aspects in a patient should begin with observation of behaviour, from the very first moment of contact. Level of alertness can be estimated, and a normal reaction of the patient on the appearance of the investigator should be an increase of this alertness. Likewise it can be observed whether the patient shows an interest in the testing situation, manifesting itself in exploratory eye movements and questions. Hemi-neglect is another attentional deficit that may be noted, or at least suspected, by sheer observation. Next, within a few minutes the investigator can get an impression of an aspect that used to be called "span of attention", i.e.: How long can the patient maintain an adequate level of alertness, adequately attending to the testing situation? Finally, it can be observed whether the patient is distractible, reacting to irrelevant sounds from outside the room or to irrelevant features of the testing material.

Of the aspects of attention that can be assessed with standardised tests, at least one seems to be relevant for all subjects with cerebral lesions and diseases. *Mental slowness* is an aspecific but very frequent result of brain damage (Benton, 1986; Hicks & Birren, 1970). In a readily visible form, it even got a name of its own in psychiatry and neurology, i.e. bradyphrenia. However, even if the behaviour of the patient is not regarded as slow in a normal conversation, there may be a delay in the actions that can be revealed with speeded tests, if adequate age-adjusted norms are available. As stated before, such slowness may cause Divided Attention Deficits in many daily activities. Next, when a focal lesion is suspected in a given patient, *hemi-neglect* should be looked for with one of the visual search tasks or reading tasks as described in a previous section (and more fully described in Chapter 9). In patients with diffuse brain damage, caused by Alzheimer or severe head injury, such tests will seldom be useful. Finally, *time-on-task effects* may be a relevant aspect for patients of varying etiologies. In order to increase the ecological validity a task in the laboratory should last at least a quarter of an hour, and preferably up to one hour – although we run here into the ethical problem of how boring one can get in the assessment of a patient for whom the task at hand has no face validity. *Lapses of attention* might be worthwhile investigating in epileptic and narcoleptic patients.

The clinical interview should not be forgotten as a potential source of information about a patient's attentional problems. Also, an interview with a relative, partner or caretaker may be very useful in this regard. However, when questioning people about the complex phenomena gathered under the global term "attention" the investigator should be very cautious in avoiding semantic confusion, and try to specify both the questions asked and the answers received. One day, when interviewing a patient, we asked him whether he had a memory problem. His answer was: "Oh no, my memory is perfect — the only problem is that I forget everything." He probably referred to his memory for the past as being perfect. Anyway, this incident contains a warning that psychologist and patient may be thinking of quite different things when questions are asked about attention, distractibility, alertness etc. The authors of this chapter would be happy if the present text would at least reduce partially the semantic confusion between psychologists, or between psychologists and professionals in related disciplines.

REFERENCES

Aarts, J.H.P., Binnie, C.D., Smit, A.M., & Wilkins, A.J. (1984). Selective cognitive impairment during focal and generalized epileptiform EEG activity. *Brain, 107*, 293–308.
Albert, M.L. (1973). A simple test of visual neglect. *Neurology, 23*, 658–664.
Benton, A.L. (1986). Reaction time in brain disease: Some reflections. *Cortex, 22*, 129–140.
Blackburn, H.L., & Benton, A.L. (1955). Simple and choice reaction time in cerebral disease. *Confinia Neurologica, 15*, 327–338.
Brickenkamp, R. (1981). *Test d2, Aufmerksamkeits-Belastungstest.* Hogrefe-Verlag: Goettingen.
Brouwer, W.H., & Van Wolffelaar, P.C. (1985). Sustained attention and sustained effort after closed head injury. *Cortex, 21*, 111–119.
Brouwer, W.H., Ponds, R.W.H.M., Van Wolffelaar, P.C., & Van Zomeren, A.H. (1989). Divided attention 5 to 10 years after closed head injury. *Cortex, 25*, 219–230.
Bruhn, P., & Parsons, O.A. (1971). Continuous reaction time in brain damage. *Cortex, 7*, 278.
Bruhn, P., & Parsons, O.A. (1977). Reaction time variability in epileptic and brain-damaged patients. *Cortex, 14*, 373–384.
Bruins, R., & Van Nieuwenhuizen, C.H. (1990). *PASAT is PVSAT? Projectverslag, internal report,* Dept. Neuropsychology, State University Groningen.
Brunia, C., & Damen (1988). Distribution of slow brain potentials related to motor preparation and stimulus anticipation in a time estimation task. *Electroencephalography and Clinical Neurophysiology, 69*, 234–243.
Buchtel, H.A., & Guitton, D. (1980) Saccadic eye movements in patients with discrete unilateral frontal-lobe removals. *Abstracts of the Society of Neuroscience, 6*, 316.
Buchtel, H.A. (1987). Attention and vigilance after head trauma. In H.S. Levin, J. Grafman, & H.M. Eisenberg (Eds.), *Neurobehavioral recovery from head injury.* Oxford University Press: New York.
Caplan, B. (1987). Assessment of unilateral neglect: A new reading test. *Journal of Clinical and Experimental Neuropsychology, 9*, 359–364.
Davies, A. (1968). The influence of age on Trailmaking Test performance. *Journal of Clinical Psychology, 24*, 96–98.
Diller, L., Ben-Yishay, Y., Gerstman, L.J., Goodkin, R., Gordon, W., & Weinberg, J. (1974). *Studies in cognition and rehabilitation in hemiplegia.* (Rehabilitation Monograph No. 50), New York: New York University Medical Center.
Diller, L., & Weinberg, J. (1977) Hemi-inattention in rehabilitation: The Evolution of a rational remediation program. In E.A. Weinstein & R.P. Friedland (Eds.), *Advances in Neurology, 10.* New York: Raven Press.
Donchin, E. (1984). *Attention and Performance.* New York: Appleton-Century-Crofts.
Egan, V. (1988). PASAT: Observed correlations with IQ. *Personal Individual Differences, 9*, 179–180.
Gauthier, L., Dehaut, F., & Joannette, Y. (1989). The Bells Test: A quantitative and qualitative test for visual neglect. *International Journal of Clinical Neuropsychology, 11*, 49–54.

Gottschaldt, K. (1928). Ueber den Einfluss der Erfahrung auf die Wahrnehmung von Figuren. *Psychologische Forschungen, 8,* 18–317.

Greber, R., & Perret, E. (1985). Attention and short-term memory disorders after brain stem lesions. *Proceedings of an E.B.B.S. workshop,* Zurich.

Grewel, F. (1953). Le test de Bourdon-Wiersma. *Folia Psychiatrica Neurologica Neurochirurgica Neerlandica, 56,* 694.

Gronwall, D., & Sampson, H. (1974). *The psychological effects of concussion.* Auckland: Auckland University Press.

Gronwall, D., & Wrightson, P. (1974). Delayed recovery of intellectual function after minor head injury. *Lancet, 2,* 995–997.

Gronwall, D. (1977). Paced Auditory Serial Addition Task: A measure of recovery from concussion. *Perceptual and Motor Skills, 44,* 367–373.

Heilman, K.M., Watson, R.T., & Valenstein, E. (1985). Neglect and related disorders. In K.M. Heilman & E. Valenstein (Eds.), *Clinical Neuropsychology.* New York: Oxford University Press.

Hicks, L., & Birren, J.E. (1970). Aging, brain damage and psychomotor slowing. *Psychological Bulletin, 74,* 377–396.

Holst, P., & Vilkki, J. (1988). Effect of frontal medial lesions on performance on the Stroop Test and Word Fluency Tasks. *Journal of Clinical and Experimental Neuropsychology, 10,* 79–80.

Levin, H.S., High, W.M., Goethe, K.E. (1987). The neurobehavioral rating scale: Assessment of the behavioral sequelae of head injury by the clinician. *Journal of Neurology, Neurosurgery and Psychiatry, 50,* 183–193.

Lewis, R., & Kupke, T. (1977). *The Lafayette Clinic repeatable neuropsychological test battery.* Paper presented at the Southeastern Psychological Association, Hollywood, FL.

Lezak, M.D. (1982). The problems of assessing executive functions. *International Journal of Psychology, 17,* 281–297.

Lezak, M.D. (1983). *Neuropsychological Assessment.* New York: Oxford University Press.

Luria, A.R. (1966). *Higher cortical functions in man.* London: Tavistock.

Luria, A.R. (1973). *The working brain.* London: Penguin.

Mackworth, N.H. (1950). Researches in the measurement of human performance. MRC Special Report 268. In H.A. Sinaiko (Ed.), *1961, Selected papers on human factors in the design and use of control systems,* (pp. 174–331). London: Dover.

Mackworth, J.F. (1970). *Vigilance and attention: A signal detection approach.* Harmondsworth: Penguin.

Mesulam, M.M. (1981). A cortical network for directed attention and unilateral neglect. *Annals of Neurology 10,* 309–325.

Miller, E. (1970). Simple and choice reaction time following severe head injury. *Cortex, 6,* 121–127.

Norrman, B., & Svahn, K. (1961). A follow-up study of severe brain injuries. *Acta Psychiatrica Scandinavica, 37,* 236–264.

Osterrieth, P.A. (1944). Le test de copie d'une figure complexe. *Archives de Psychologie, 30,* 206–356.

Perret, E. (1974). The left frontal lobe in man and the suppression of habitual responses in verbal categorical behavior. *Neuropsychologia, 12,* 323–330.

Posner, M.I. (1975). The psychobiology of attention. In M.S. Gazzaniga & C. Blakemore (Ed.), *Handbook of Psychobiology* (pp. 441–480). New York: Academic Press.

Reitan, R.M. (1958). Validity of the Trailmaking Test as an indication of organic brain damage. *Perceptual Motor Skills, 8,* 271–276.

Rosvold, H.E., Mirsky, A.F., Sarason, I., Bransome, E.D., & Beck, L.H. (1956). A Continuous Performance Test of brain damage. *Journal of Consulting Psychology, 20,* 343–350.

Salazar, A.M., Grafman, J.H., Vance, S.C., Weingartner, H., Dillon, J.D., & Ludlow, C. (1986). Consciousness and amnesia after penetrating head injury: Neurology and anatomy. *Neurology, 36,* 178–187.

Shallice, T. (1982). Specific impairments of planning. In D.E. Broadbent & L. Weiskrantz (Eds.), *The neuropsychology of cognitive function,* 199–209. London: The Royal Society.

Shiffrin, R.M., & Schneider, W. (1977). Controlled and automatic human information processing: II. Perceptual learning, automatic attending and a general theory. *Psychological Review, 84,* 127–190.

Smith, A. (1973). *Symbol Digits Modalities Test: Manual.* Los Angeles: Western Psychological Services.

Somberg, B.L., & Salthouse, T.A. (1982). Divided Attention abilities in young and old adults. *Journal of Experimental Psychology, 8,* 651– 663.

Stroop, J.R. (1935). Studies of interference in serial verbal reactions. *Journal of Experimental Psychology, 18,* 643–662.

Stuss, D.T., Stethem, L.L., & Poirier, C.A. (1987). Comparison of three tests of attention and rapid information processing across six age groups. *Clinical Neuropsychology, 1,* 139–152.

Stuss, D.T., Stethem, L.L., & Pelchat, G. (1988). Three tests of attention and rapid information processing: An extension. *Clinical Neuropsychology, 2,* 246–250.

Talland, G.A. (1965). *Deranged memory.* New York: Academic Press.

Teuber, H-L., Battersby, W.S., & Bender, M.B. (1960). *Visual field defects after penetrating missile wounds of the brain.* Cambridge, Mass.; Published for the Commonwealth Fund by Harvard University Press.

Theios, J. (1975). The components of response latency in simple human information processing tasks. In P.M.A. Rabbitt & S. Dornic (Eds.) *Attention and performance, V,* New York: Academic Press.

Thurstone, L.L. (1944). *A factorial study of perception.* Chicago: University of Chicago Press.

Townsend, R.F., & Johnson, L.C. (1979). Relation of frequency-analyzed EEG to monitoring behaviour. *Electroencephalography and Clinical Neurophysiology, 47,* 272–279.

Valley, V., & Broughton, R. (1983). The physiological (EEG) nature of drowsiness and its relation to performance deficits in narcoleptics. *Electroencephalography and Clinical Neurophysiology, 55,* 243–251.

Vanier, M., Gauthier, L., Lambert, J., Pepin, E., Robillard, A., Dubouloz, C.J., Gagnon, R., & Joannette, Y. (1990). Evaluation of left visuospatial neglect: Norms and discrimination power of two tests. *Neuropsychology, 4,* 87–96.

Wade, D.T., Wood, V.A., & Langton Hewer, R. (1988). Recovery of cognitive function soon after stroke: A study of visual neglect, attention span and verbal recall. *Journal of Neurology, Neurosurgery and Psychiatry, 51,* 10–13.

Walsh, K.W. (1978). *Neuropsychology, a clinical approach.* Edinburgh: Churchill-Livingstone.

Walter, W.G., Cooper, R., Aldridge, V., McCallum, W.C., & Winter, A.L. (1964). Contingent negative variation: An electric sign of sensorymotor association and expectancy in the human brain. *Nature, 203,* 380–384.

Wilson, B.A., Cockburn, J., & Halligan, P. (1987). The development of a behavioral test of visuospatial neglect. *Archives of Physical Medicine and Rehabilitation, 68,* 98–102.

Van Zomeren, A.H., & Deelman, B.G. (1978). Long-term recovery of visual reaction time after closed head injury. *Journal of Neurology, Neurosurgery and Psychiatry, 41,* 452–457.

13

Assessment of Frontal Lobe Dysfunction

Denis M. Parker and John R. Crawford
Department of Psychology, University of Aberdeen

INTRODUCTION

The titles of the majority of chapters in this section refer to functional impairments of behaviour involving for example, language, memory, or attention. This is the only chapter that makes reference to an anatomical region, a fact which reflects one of the problems of dealing with frontal lobe dysfunction. As defined anatomically the frontal lobes comprise brain structures which are rostral to the central sulcus and the Sylvian fissure, and make up a third of the entire cerebral cortex (see Fig. 13.1) As long ago as 1925 Brodmann had identified thirteen anatomically distinct regions within the human frontal cortex. They include systems which are implicated in an enormous range and complexity of behaviours from motor control to social behaviour. Damage to frontal structures may produce at one extreme paralysis and spasticity, and at the other an adynamic, asocial individual who nevertheless when assessed by routine psychometric instruments appears cognitively intact. Given the diversity of behaviours which may be affected by frontal damage, to speak of a "frontal syndrome" is extremely misleading. Studies of regional cerebral metabolism have identified seventeen *functionally* distinct areas within frontal cortex, excluding cingulate and orbital cortex, and have led Roland (1984) to conclude that in humans any structured processing of information requires the involvement of one or more regions within the frontal zone.

Over the years there have been many attempts to summarise the role of the frontal lobes in behaviour. Preserving the individual's cognitive and emotional equilibrium (Damasio, 1979); a complex feedback system (Pribram, 1973); integrating behaviour over time (Fuster, 1980); providing the cortical representation of the limbic system (Nauta, 1971); and regulating behaviour guided by internal models (Goldman-Rakic, 1987), are a few of the broad descriptors used by theorists in an attempt to *precis* the essence of their viewpoints. However, and this has already been implied earlier, no one view can satisfactorily encompass the diversity of affective, cognitive and motivational changes which can follow frontal damage. This being the case, and given that the aim of this chapter is to provide a guide to clinical appraisal, we will adopt an atheoretical approach, but one which tries to indicate the broad categories of impairment that are routinely found. A large number of studies have been conducted on frontally injured patients but there are in fact few tests that have sufficient empirical support for the neuropsychologist to feel happy with their sensitivity and reliability.

ANATOMICAL AND STRUCTURAL FACTORS

If we were to make a quick sketch of the relationships between various regions of the cortex and broad categories of psychological function, then one very obvious pattern would be apparent. The cortical tissue which falls behind the central sulcus and below the Sylvian fissure is, roughly speaking, concerned with the interpretation of sensory input. Systems involved in audition, vision, somaethesis, kinaethesis and the cognitive elaboration of these processes are located here, and damage to these systems produces a variety of disorders which can be understood as disorders of interpretation. Once we move forward of this boundary we encounter systems that are concerned with actions, whether this is direct, as in the case of the motor and pre-motor systems, or indirect, as appears to be the case with much of the pre-frontal cortex.

The frontal cortex immediately in front of the central fissure contains the main output control mechanisms of the motor system. These areas, indicated by crosshatching and stippling in Fig. 13.1, include the motor cortex, the pre-motor and supplementary motor-cortex, the frontal eye fields and Brocas' area. Given the fact that a substantial portion of frontal cortex is involved with motor control it is not surprising that a varied pattern of motor disturbance can be found after injury. As well as direct motor effects resulting in paralysis and spasticity, a number of other disturbances can be evident. Changes in muscle tone are evident with damage close to the premotor areas and these reveal themselves in reflex-like opposition to passive limb manoeuvring by the examiner. Damage to the supplementary motor area may initially produce mutism which later resolves into a pattern suggestive of transcortical motor aphasia (Chapter 10); there may also be difficulties initiating activities of the upper limbs, sometimes called "motor neglect" (Laplane & Degos, 1983). A variety of abnormalities of gait and posture have also been reported (Damasio, 1985). A group of disorders which may result from a loss of normal inhibitory control exercised by the frontal system may also be present singly or in combination. These include the grasp, groping, snout and suck reflexes and loss of sphincter control (in the context of this latter disorder it is interesting that patients are usually unconcerned about it). Finally, bilateral damage to the anterior cingulate cortex may produce akinetic mutism a transitory state in which the return of speech is marked by whispering and hoarseness and not by aphasic or dysarthric symptoms. Further details on these and other motor consequences of frontal damage may be found in Brown (1985) and Damasio (1985).

The prefrontal cortex includes all other cortex (all the non-filled regions indicated in Fig. 13.1) in the lobe. It comprises the medial, orbital (those areas above the orbits of the eyes) lateral and polar areas. These regions have rich connections with posterior association cortex, with the limbic system, parts of the corpus striatum (caudate and putamen), hypothalamus and mesencephalon. Given the wide pattern of connections with systems involved in sensory, mnestic, motivational and motor processing it is hardly surprising that it has been impossible to define a narrow role for this region. However, broadly speaking the cognitive deficits following frontal damage frequently involve disruption of an action system, either through failure to initiate appropriate activity, or to integrate relevant information into the system guiding the current action. Affective and motivational changes following frontal injury are also frequently present, but currently there seems to be no adequate theoretical or procedural scheme for relating these changes to those evident in cognition. These rather "soft" patterns of impairment may pass unnoticed where the pathology has an insidious onset (e.g. tumours, Pick's disease), but be much more obvious after a stroke or head injury.

THE FRONTAL LOBE PATIENT

The *variability* in the pattern of behavioural impairment in frontal lobe patients appears to be more conspicuous than in those with temporal, parietal or occipital damage. In part this impression may reflect the lack of an accepted categorisation for frontal syndromes but the inter-patient contrast in temperament is often striking, as is the fluctuation in mood and sociability within a particular patient over time. Perhaps it is the intra-patient variability in mood that has contributed to the impression of the "oddness" of some frontal damage patients; the pattern of disability in patients with posterior damage remains relatively constant and their reaction to their illness seems appropriate. The brief case descriptions which follow are included simply to give an impression of the range of behavioural dysfunction which may follow frontal damage and which are often apparent before any systematic assessment has been carried out.

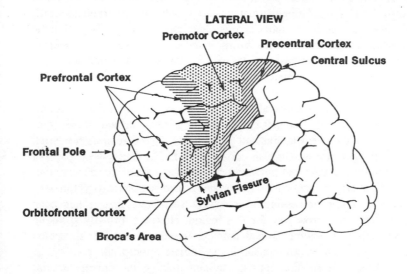

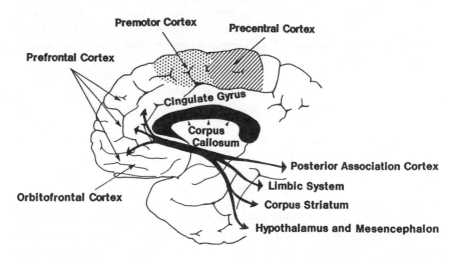

FIG. 13.1.   Lateral and medial views of the brain showing the gross subdivisions and connections of the frontal cortex.

Case 1. A 27-year-old man sustained a head injury in an industrial accident which resulted in complete loss of vision in his left eye and damage to the left frontal lobe. A CT scan showed localised gliosis over the left frontal region and enlargement of the anterior horn of the left lateral ventricle. A year after the accident his full scale WAIS IQ was 80 (Verbal, 85; Performance, 76); he showed no aphasic disturbance and was oriented in person, time and place. Verbal Fluency performance was at the 15th percentile level and on the Wisconsin Card Sorting Task he attained three categories. However, his demeanour gave one little confidence that his test scores genuinely tapped available cognitive resources. His facial expression was one of sadness/depression, sometimes appearing almost anxious, and spontaneity was totally lacking. Personal details and test performance were elicited only with continuous prompting but he was not overtly uncooperative, only rather inattentive/apathetic. His family described him as a previously cheerful, humorous, sociable person and he had a long-standing relationship with a girlfriend prior to the accident. They described his current disposition as gloomy and occasionally irritable. He was either "distant" or ill at ease in social gatherings, often getting up and leaving a social or family gathering without a word. His sleep pattern was disturbed and he often spent large parts of the night awake. Tasks he agreed to carry out were not performed, and for visits to hospital for assessments he had to be organised and transported in the same manner as a young child. The relationship with his girlfriend had ceased. The patient himself said that he was unable to understand what was happening when he was with a group of people; he could not follow the conversation or the pattern of social gestures. In a one-to-one situation he said he did not have this difficulty (in fact the interviewer had to be directive to keep a conversation moving). Five years later his pattern of cognitive performance, his asocial disposition and apathy remained unchanged.

Case 2. A 46-year-old engineer had sustained a head injury involving frontal damage in a mountaineering accident. A man of high intellectual ability (estimated post-accident IQ 125, based on Raven's Progressive Matrices and Mill Hill Vocabulary Scale), he was oriented in time, place and person, had no aphasic difficulty, showed normal learning of supraspan digit and spatial sequences but showed impairment on the Rey Auditory Verbal Learning Task (Rey, 1964). His Verbal Fluency performance was within normal limits but his performance on the Wisconsin Card Sorting Test, given his intellectual level, was just acceptable at four categories, yet achieving this level caused him considerable difficulty. His attitude in the interview was judged to be mildly euphoric although a family member reported that emotionally he was quite labile; inappropriate explosive outbursts of temper on some occasions and tearfulness on others. His major difficulties occurred with the supervisory and administrative aspects of his employment where his failure to organise and schedule work and to respond to requests for information led to (inappropriate) disciplinary action by his employers. His ability to respond to immediate, short duration emergencies of a technical character were unaffected. A family member reported his increased distractibility and failure to return to the task at hand following interruption.

Because of the variability in personality/temperament among the population at large it is essential to obtain information about the patients' behaviour and life-style before their illness. Most of us have known individuals whose personal demeanour would have brought to mind the possibility of frontal pathology if we had encountered them in a clinical setting, yet because we know the individual's history, a cerebral insult can be excluded as an explanation of their behaviour. In both of the cases outlined earlier the contrast between the patients' behaviour before and after their respective injuries was clearly apparent to family members. These two examples also expose a particular problem of frontal lobe research: that of making a judgement of the severity of the impairment in the context of the prevailing level of intellectual functioning. While the pattern of behavioural dysfunction following frontal pathology is usually encountered by the clinical neuropsychologist in patients with a diagnosis of tumour, stroke or head injury it can often be a major factor in diffuse cerebral degeneration, as is shown in the following case where the presenting symptoms were highly suggestive of frontal lobe disease.

Case 3. A 54-year-old higher education teacher was referred for investigation following expressions of concern by his wife and employer. His wife had noticed his behaviour becoming markedly self-centred and withdrawn, with lack of concern for her or their children, irresponsibility in both financial and personal commitments, and a pattern of social behaviour which was disinhibited and inappropriate. His sleep pattern was disrupted and when he rose in the early hours of the morning he indulged in aimless activity. His employer was concerned about his ability to perform his job satisfactorily. When seen in the clinic he was affable and unconcerned about the reasons for his being there. Neuropsychological assessment, which took place in the patient's home not because of *deliberate* avoidance of appointments at the clinic, but because some distraction always intervened to lead him to another location, provided evidence of serious intellectual deterioration given his record of academic achievement. He was oriented in time, place and person but showed evidence of an impoverished knowledge of current affairs. His WAIS Verbal IQ was assessed as 67 and Performance IQ, 82. His primary and secondary memory were seriously impaired and he showed some evidence of aphasic and dysgraphic problems. Performance on the Wisconsin Card Sorting Test and on Word Fluency was disastrous. He showed no concern when his intellectual difficulties were discussed. Magnetic Resonance Imaging and a cerebral blood flow (SPECT) scan showed generalised cerebral degeneration with severe atrophy in the frontal areas, dilation of the anterior horns of the lateral ventricles and degeneration of the heads of the caudate nuclei. The pattern of findings led to a diagnosis of Pick's disease.

Patients with frontal damage can usually be characterised as generally apathetic and indifferent, even if for short periods they may show restlessness, excitement or aggression. Although they show a lack of both initiative and spontaneity, impulsive behaviour does occur (and can be clearly evident in test performance), and may be a cause of concern to their immediate family, for example when a previously careful patient commits himself to a foolhardy business venture or buys a couple of caravans with no other apparent motive than a childlike attraction to their features. They rarely show evidence of anxiety (although see Case 1); and lack of real concern about the effect of their illness on their life-style is apparent, even in the context of their delivery of a reasonably accurate personal history (usually drawn out by repeated questioning). Their behaviour is largely determined by objects and events which impinge on them immediately (Lhermitte, 1986a;b). As a result their attention may be easily captured by some passing event; someone walking past the window or a noise in the corridor outside often leads to the abandonment of the task at hand and they may not resume without prompting. Where patients show humour it tends to be juvenile, vulgar or inappropriate.

Lack of sensitivity in social situations is extremely common, and may include appalling eating habits, caustic remarks about or abuse of individuals within earshot, getting up and leaving small social gatherings without a word or switching on a radio or T.V. loudly during a conversation, inappropriate affective outbursts etc. Sometimes left frontal patients appear to fail to grasp the structure of conversational interaction among a group of people and report that they are unable to follow the content of the exchanges. Aggressive responses to frustration or attempts at control by family members are not uncommon. Given the pattern of stresses that these kinds of behaviour can induce it is perhaps not surprising that the destruction of family life or marital breakdown may follow.

The question of frontal lobe involvement in antisocial as opposed to asocial behaviour has been raised occasionally (Buikhuisen, 1987; Cloninger, 1987; Pontius, 1972; Yeudall & Fromm-Auch, 1979). The origin of the hypothesis of a connection between delinquency and criminality lies in the observation of poor inhibition and impulsiveness in frontal damage patients. However, while some of the trends are suggestive, the connection remains unproven (Kandel & Freed, 1989).

ASSESSING COGNITIVE DYSFUNCTION

As has been indicated earlier, cognitive impairment is only one aspect of the pattern of deficit seen in frontal lobe patients. However, investigators have been rather more successful at identifying and quantifying cognitive impairments than in pinning down the changes in personality, mood and social behaviour which often follow frontal injury. In this section we will concentrate on those tests that have consistently shown defective performance in frontal damage patients but before we do so two important issues must be explored.

It is frequently pointed out that standard intelligence tests are insensitive to frontal lobe damage. Ever since Hebb's (1939) use of the Stanford-Binet in four cases of left frontal lobe damage, the utility of the IQ assessment in the frontal battery has been questioned. However, it has been clear since the 1950s that minor but significant falls in IQ do occur (Milner, 1964; Smith, 1966; Tow, 1955), and that the Wechsler scales (Wechsler-Bellevue; Wechsler, 1944: WAIS; Wechsler, 1955: WAIS-R; Wechsler, 1981), are more useful than the Stanford-Binet in neuropsychological assessment. Furthermore, left frontal damage in general produces larger falls in IQ than right-sided damage (Smith, 1966). There is also some evidence that orbital damage produces minimal impairment of IQ scores (Girgis, 1971) and so it appears likely that dorsolateral damage is responsible for the deficits that do occur. However, there is often a mismatch between the 5 to 10 IQ points that may sometimes be lost and the inability of the patient to resume a normal life. This may be particularly striking when scores on Full Scale WAIS IQ may be 113 or 118 (Blumer & Benson, 1975), or even 125 (Damasio, 1985), and yet the patients show serious problems of adjustment. On the other hand substantial falls in IQ following serious pathology do occur (see, for example, Lhermitte, Derouesne & Signoret, 1972), and it is obviously crucial to evaluate the patient's performance on a range of specialised tests against an estimate of their current level of functioning. It is extremely significant whether or not the difficulties a particular patient encounters are against the background of a normal level of intellectual and mnestic functioning.

The second issue which needs to be briefly addressed is that of memory pathology following frontal damage. This question is examined in detail in Chapter 5. Here we will simply observe that an adequate performance on routine memory assessment instruments (e.g. Russell, 1975: WMS-R) is often obtained with frontal patients except where damage is very extensive or involves large parts of the inferior medial areas or damage to the anterior communicating artery (Damasio et al., 1985). However, a restricted impairment of recency discrimination, in the sense of "which of these two pictures or words have you encountered most recently?" may prove to be a diagnostically useful feature of some kinds of frontal impairment (Milner, 1982).

Tests of Fluency

Tests of fluency should enable one to assess the readiness with which subjects can produce variable behaviour. A noticeable feature of frontal patients is that they lack dynamism, speaking little and spending a lot of time sitting, and perhaps most of their waking time watching television. While lack of speech could be a sign of dysphasia, with prefrontal damage this is not the case as these patients can respond appropriately when addressed, and scores on most items which assess verbal competence fall within normal limits. The failure to *initiate* appropriate behaviour is one of the frontal patients' greatest inadequacies and is often a significant factor in their inadequate rehabilitation.

The *Controlled Oral Word Association Test* (Benton 1968; Benton & Hamsher, 1976) is probably the most widely used formal test of frontal dysfunction. This reflects the fact that it is quick and easy to use, has available norms and has proved a reliable discriminator of frontal from non-frontal patients.

In its original version the letters used were F, A, and S (Benton, 1968). Subsequently, Benton and Hamsher (1976; 1978) provided normative data for two letter sets, KFL and PRW. These were selected to vary within each set the frequency of English words commencing with each letter. Thus C indicates many words, F is less frequent, and L less frequent still.

In order to administer the test the subject is told to say as many words as possible beginning with a letter of the alphabet provided by the examiner. Proper nouns, numbers or changing the suffix of a word are not allowed. In order to ensure that the subject understands the instructions and to provide a "warm-up" a letter which is a very high frequency word initial, "S", is provided and the sample trial stopped when two or three appropriate words have been spoken. The score is the total of all acceptable words spoken (a cassette recorder is useful!) during three one-minute trials initiated by presentation, in order, of each of the letters in the selected triad. This total score is then adjusted according to age, years of education and the patient's sex (Benton & Hamsher, 1978).

This test, particularly in its initial FAS version (Benton, 1968), has been found to be very sensitive to frontal lobe damage. Benton (1968) initially found that on average left frontal patients generated 30% fewer words than right frontals but that bilateral frontal damage produced the most severe impairment of all. The fact that oral verbal fluency as assessed in this way is sensitive to frontal damage, and left frontal in particular, has been confirmed by a number of studies (Bornstein, 1986; Miceli et al., 1981; Perret, 1974; Raimer & Hecaen, 1970). The sensitivity of the test probably resides in the fact that the generation of lists of words on the basis of their initial letter is an unusual activity (except for lexicographers) and demands that subjects devise their own strategy. Where subjects are asked to provide lists of semantically related items from well-established categories, such as animal, object or plant names (Newcombe, 1969), a deficit specifically related to frontal injury may not appear although these type of tests are very sensitive to left hemisphere damage.

Deficits in fluency of this type appear to be connected with pathology of the lateral prefrontal region. Spreen and Benton (1969) found that damage to the inferior medial white matter, which principally serves the orbital region, resulted in marginal effects on patients' fluency on the FAS version of the test.

A catastrophically low score on verbal fluency provides unequivocal evidence of impairment. However, the clinical neuropsychologist also needs to detect more subtle impairments of fluency. This is not an easy task because of the wide variation in linguistic skills in the population as a whole. An illustration of this point is provided by Borkowski, Benton and Spreen (1967) who reported that the fluency performance of brain-damaged subjects of above-average IQ exceeded that of below-average controls. It is desirable then to obtain some sort of individualised standard against which a patient's current fluency performance can be compared (Lezak, 1983). Benton and Hamsher's (1978) approach to this problem is to introduce corrections to an individual's CFL score on the basis of their age, years of education and sex. Another approach is to take advantage of the co-variation between fluency performance and general verbal ability (e.g. Miller, 1984; Crawford, Moore & Cameron, 1992). Crawford et al. present a regression equation to estimate premorbid performance on the FAS fluency test from performance on the National Adult Reading test (Nelson, 1982: NART). The NART has high construct validity as a measure of verbal intelligence (Crawford et al., 1989) and has proved to be surprisingly resistant to the effects of cerebral dysfunction (see Chapter 3); it therefore provides a measure of the patient's *premorbid* ability. Using this method, the measure of interest is the discrepancy between the *obtained* fluency score and the NART *predicted* fluency score. A relatively poor fluency performance would not be taken to indicate impairment if the NART indicated that a subject was of below-average premorbid ability. Conversely, a fluency score which was around or just below the population mean would be suggestive of impairment if the NART indicated a clearly above-average premorbid ability.

Where patients have difficulties speaking (e.g. dysarthria) then a written fluency task can be used. The Thurstone Word Fluency Task (Thurstone & Thurstone, 1962) requires that subjects write as many words as possible beginning with the letter S in five minutes and then as many four-letter words as possible beginning with the letter C in four minutes. Left frontally damaged patients show particular difficulty with this task (Milner, 1974; Pendelton et al., 1982) producing fewer than 45 words in the total 9 minutes writing time.

The two aforementioned fluency tasks are tied to language and are both more sensitive to left than right frontal damage. A sensitive non-verbal test of fluency would be particularly useful but we have found the only candidate, the Design Fluency Test (Jones-Gotman & Milner, 1977) unsatisfactory. It is difficult to score; some controls find it difficult while others (controls) produce what could easily be categorised as high perseveration scores as they generate a large number of designs with very small variations on a basic theme. A test of gesture fluency has been described by Jason (1985) which might be developed into a clinically useful test.

Tests of Categorisation

The second most widely used test of frontal dysfunction is The Wisconsin Card Sorting Test (WCST) devised by Grant and Berg (1948). The development of this test followed a report by Weigl (1941) that brain-damaged patients showed difficulty in mastering a colour/form categorisation task and that this deficit was of greatest severity in frontal patients. While this conclusion was challenged (McFie & Piercy, 1952; Teuber, Battesby, & Bender, 1951), Milner's (1963) study, which included 71 patients studied both before and after surgery and a further 23 patients who were studied only post-operatively, provided clear evidence of the involvement of frontal structures in successful mastering of this task. The task is a difficult one for the patient because it involves discovering rules on which the categorisation is based, realising when the rules have been arbitrarily changed and changing their behaviour accordingly. It is not surprising then that many patients find the task unpleasant and a few may refuse to complete it, particularly when given in the form used by Milner (1963).

The WCST has been administered in different ways by different investigators. Teuber et al. (1951) changed the categorisation rule independently of the patient's response, and Lezak (1983) uses a slightly different procedure from that used by Milner (1963). Two versions of the test will be described here, that used by Milner (1963) and The Modified Card Sorting Test (MCST) as developed by Nelson (1976).

In the Milner (1963) version of the task, four stimulus cards whose faces show one red triangle, two green stars, three yellow crosses and four blue circles, respectively, are placed in a row on the table before the subjects (see Fig. 13.2), and they are required to sort a stack of response cards on the basis of criteria decided by the examiner. Subjects are given a pack of 128 response cards made up of two sets of 64 cards. Each of these sets contain all possible combinations of colour (red, green, yellow or blue); form (triangle, star, cross or circle); and number (one, two, three or four coloured shapes). The subjects' task is to place each response card underneath one of the four stimulus cards. They must judge for themselves where they think they should be placed as the examiner will only inform them whether the placement is "right" or "wrong". No other help is given to the subject. Subjects must make what use they can of this information in order to get as many cards correctly placed as possible. If, for example, a subject turns over a response card which reveals two red triangles (see Fig. 13.2) then this can be placed beneath card 1 on the basis of its shape and colour, or card 2 on the basis of the number of shapes. If, on the other hand, the card a subject turns over contains two blue stars it may be placed with card 2 on the basis of both number and shape, or with card 4 on the basis of its colour.

If the subject places the two red triangles below card 1 and the examiner replies "right" then this information is ambiguous because the subject does not know whether the sorting criterion is colour or form. If the two blue stars are placed with card 2 and a correct response is indicated then the patient does not know whether the category is shape or number. In these cases it is only on the basis of more than one sorting response that the subject can ascertain which criterion is being used. This ambiguity is a real problem for subjects because in each set of 64 cards, 40 contain this kind of ambiguity. As the subject proceeds through the pack they must generate successive guesses about the criterion for sorting and adjust their responses appropriately when the examiner changes the criterion.

The examiner chooses colour as the first categorisation criterion; all card placements which do not correspond with the stimulus cards on the basis of colour are labelled "wrong". If and when the subject has placed ten consecutive cards correctly the sorting criterion shifts to form; no warning of this shift is given to the subject who at this point finds the responses which would previously have been labelled "right" are now labelled "wrong". Following ten consecutive correct responses to form, the categorisation principle is changed to number; then it returns to colour and so on. In Milner's procedure the sorting continues until six successful categories (two each of colour, form and number) have been achieved or until all 128 cards have been sorted. Lezak's (1983) method is a modification of this; the subject is asked after four consecutive correct runs of ten (allowing a couple of errors each time for the changed criterion) what the general principle being applied is, and the task is discontinued if an accurate account is provided. The task is also counted as being completed successfully if the subject gives a spontaneous report of the underlying principle, for example: "When I discover how to sort correctly you change the rules. It can be colour or form or number". The statement of the rule must be accompanied by unequivocal evidence of correct categorisation behaviour as some frontal patients may state the rule verbally but continue to make perseverative responses to the previously correct but now inappropriate category; an example of the verbal-action dissociation following frontal lobe damage discussed by Luria and Homskaya (1964).

Two measures of the subjects' performance are usually derived. The first is the number of categories attained. This measure refers to the number of successful runs of ten correct responses. Malmo (1974) and Moscovitch (1976) reported a score of four or more categories achieved as representing successful performance. In Milner's (1963) study the dorsolateral frontal patients obtained an average post-operative score on this measure of 1.37, while the orbital/temporal patients scored an average of 5 and the posterior cortex group scored a mean of 4.52. In Heaton's (1981) standardisation sample it is notable that his focal frontal group ($n = 43$) achieved an average of 3.1 categories with a standard deviation of 2.3, while the focal non-frontal group ($n = 35$) achieved a mean of 4.3 categories with a standard deviation of 2.2. Thus, there is a substantial overlap between these distributions, and because Heaton did not

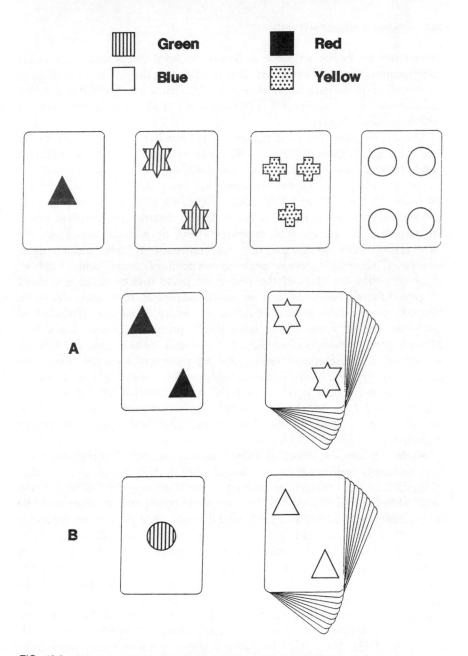

Green   Red

Blue   Yellow

A

B

FIG. 13.2. Showing the testing arrangement for the WCST and MCST. In A the set of cards, similar to those used in the WCST, contains many items that share more than one attribute with the stimulus cards e.g. if the two triangles are placed with the red triangle stimulus card and it is labelled correct, is it because of the colour or the shape of its patterns? In B the cards used in the MCST are not ambiguous because any card in the response set can share a maximum of only one attribute with the cards in the stimulus set.

differentiate his frontal sample (e.g. into dorsolateral and orbital), care in the interpretation of results is required. It is possible that the standard deviation of the frontal group has been enlarged because of the inclusion of orbital and medial cases who would not be expected to show deficits on this task as severely as those with dorsolateral damage.

The second commonly used measure is the number of perseverative errors (see Flashman, Horner & Freides, 1991 for an exhaustive discussion of scoring perseverative errors). These refer to errors subjects make when they continue to sort according to a hypothesis which has been labelled "wrong" by the examiner. In the first sort this would occur when a subject continues to sort on the basis of an incorrect guess. In this instance perseverative errors are recorded for the class of responses (form or number) for which the most errors occur during the first ten responses; if there are an equal number of incorrect responses made on the basis of "form" and "number" hypotheses then the class of the first error made decides those designated as perseverative. Following one or more successful sorts (ten successive correct), perseverative errors would occur where a subject continued to categorise on the basis of the immediately preceding correct hypothesis. Milner's (1963) post-operatively tested dorsolateral frontal patients made an average of 57 perseverative errors, the orbital/temporal patients made, on average, 11 and the cortical non-frontals made a mean of 16. However, once again the results of Heaton's (1981) standardisation sample argue for caution as the mean number of perseverative errors were 38.5 (sd = 29.6) and 22.6 (sd = 19.2) for the focal frontal and focal non-frontal groups respectively.

While the selective effect of frontal lesions on WCST performance has been repeatedly confirmed, the question of whether there is a differential effect of hemisphere locus remains unresolved. It might be expected that because the cards differ in terms of number, colour and form, non-verbal processes might be differentially involved and so right frontal damage might prove more disruptive than left. However, the task is a complex one and verbal mediation is likely. Milner (1963) pointed out that although she found no differences between hemisphere site of lesion and performance, because the quantity of tissue removed was smaller in the left hemisphere cases, this suggested that the task may be more susceptible to left frontal damage. Drewe (1974) found a tendency for right frontal injury to produce greater deficits than left. This (latter) slight tendency has emerged in some studies (Robinson et al., 1980; Bornstein, 1986), but it does not seem a clinically useful effect particularly as at least one study in addition to Milner's has found the opposite effect (Taylor, 1979).

The Modified Card Sorting Test (described fully in Nelson, 1976) was developed to allow use of a less stressful testing instrument for the patient and to make the interpretation of patients' responses straightforward. Whichever classification the patient chooses to use for the first two sorts (provided they are different) are accepted as correct and the patient is told when the correct category has changed:- "The rules have now changed and I want you to find another rule". The card set is reduced to 24 and comprises those cards which are unambiguous in that on placing any one response card it can share only one attribute with three of the stimulus cards (colour, form or number), and be unrelated to the fourth stimulus card (see Fig. 13.2). Furthermore, subjects are required to make only six consecutive correct responses to attain a category.

The MCST uses a 48-card pack (two sets of 24) and the same four stimulus cards placed in the same order as the WCST. Whichever category scheme the patient selects (colour, form or number) on the first response, provided that the card is not placed beneath the unrelated stimulus card, is accepted as correct and remains the correct rule for the first category. Once six consecutive correct responses are made the subject is told that the rule has changed. Provided that the next sorting category chosen by the subject is one of the remaining two then that is accepted by the examiner as the correct rule. The final category then, is the one remaining. After the attainment of three categories they are each repeated again *in the original order*.

Responses are recorded according to the category shared with the stimulus card or as a "random" sort if it is assigned to the unrelated stimulus card. Performance is scored in terms of categories achieved (maximum six) and percentage perseverative errors, i.e. perseverative errors/total errors × 100. It should be noted, however, that a perseverative error in the MCST is not the same as in the WCST. In the latter a perseverative error is usually a response made by sorting to the preceding correct category. In Nelson's MCST a perseverative error is one in the same category as the immediately preceding incorrect response and is thus an estimate of short-range perseveration.

Because scoring the WCST and the MCST requires that the examiner keep track of where the subject is and demands that perseverative errors are clearly identified, an unambiguous system of recording the patient's responses is essential. Lezak (1983, p.490) gives an example of a useful transcription system, while the version of the test produced by Psychological Assessment Resources Inc. (Heaton, 1981) provides standard record forms which make recording easy. On the basis of currently available standardisation data and the number of studies in which it has been used, the WCST is a more useful test instrument than the MCST.

The data available on the WCST argue that a very poor performance is usually clinically significant. There are, however, exceptions as some intellectually able individuals (at least as assessed by university degree results) can fail the test and there is also at least one published report of an individual with dorsolateral frontal damage who showed superior performance on this test (Heck & Bryer, 1986).

Miscellaneous Tests

Whereas the aforementioned tests are the most frequently used and most clinically useful for frontal assessment there are a variety of other procedures that have been claimed to show specific sensitivity to frontal damage. However, at present the evidence for these claims is weak either because of the equivocal nature of the supporting evidence or because lack of data from a reasonable standardisation sample limits the confidence that a clinician can invest in them.

Because impairments of planning and purposive behaviour, together with a tendency towards impulsiveness are frequently noted features of frontally damaged patients, then maze tests should be a particularly appropriate technique for quantifying frontal dysfunction. Whereas maze tests have indeed been found to be sensitive to frontal impairment (Malmo, 1948; Milner, 1964; Smith, 1960; Tow, 1955; Walsh, 1978), they appear to be less popular than they ought to be. The only significant drawback of the Porteus Maze Test (Porteus, 1965) is that it is untimed and some patients may take an inordinate amount of time to complete the series of mazes. It does have the advantage of having norms available (although somewhat outdated). In addition, because it allows the assessment of both the patient's cognitive performance (through their attainment of a certain "test age") and the quality of their approach to the task (whether or not they violate rules), it has the potential to become an extremely useful form of assessment.

Impairment of the kind of executive planning functions which are probably tapped by maze performance (and also perhaps by the Block Design Test, see later) have also been reported by Shallice (1982) using a version of the Tower of Hanoi problem, the Tower of London test. The Tower of London test may be graded in difficulty and thus allow a scaling of the degree of impairment in frontal patients. Shallice reported significant impairments on this task following left frontal lesions. Unfortunately a later study (see Shallice, 1988, p.347) failed to confirm this effect. This failure to replicate findings is not an unusual feature of frontal lobe research and is discussed at several points in Stuss and Benson (1986). It probably reflects features in the patient sample related to lesion location and size but it may also reflect aspects of the patient's personal cognitive history; any premorbid familiarity with problem-solving tasks might lower the demand of the task sufficiently to wipe out differences between the patient groups.

Two tests, Picture Arrangement (PA) and Block Design (BD), which form part of the *Wechsler Adult Intelligence Scale* — WAIS (Wechsler, 1955) have been claimed to be sensitive to right frontal impairment. Since the WAIS or the WAIS-R (Wechsler, 1981) is likely to form part of any assessment procedure, extra information that may be gleaned from their subtests may be a very efficient use of available data. McFie and Piercy (1952b) found greatest impairment in Picture Arrangement (PA) with right frontal lesions and while this claim has been supported by some (McCullough, 1950; Sheer & Shuttleworth, 1952) but not by others (Meier & French, 1966; Milner, 1954), McFie and Thompson (1972) have produced supporting evidence for their case. In order to perform this test adequately the subject must remain sensitive to quite subtle information in the pictures as well as to the structure of a story or sequence of events; Luria (1966) has argued that this kind of comprehension of event structure may be seriously impaired after frontal injury. In a total series of 143 patients, those with right hemisphere, and in particular temporal lobe, damage showed the lowest overall scaled scores on this test, a result similar to that reported by others, e.g. Long and Brown (1979). However, the tendency to leave the pictures in the order presented and to offer this as a solution to the problem occurred significantly more often in the right frontal than in the other right hemisphere groups (McFie & Thompson, 1972). This observation was supported by Walsh (1978). Warrington, James, and Maciejewski (1986), in a retrospective study of 656 patients with cerebral lesions, found a significantly worse performance on PA in the right hemisphere group but with the most impaired performance in the right parietal and parieto-occipital groups. Data on the measure indicative of leaving the presented order unchanged (McFie & Thompson, 1972), was not reported in Warrington et al.'s study, but it is worth noting that the performance of the right frontal group on the PA test was as good as that of left frontals whereas in McFie and Thompson's series they were two points lower. This finding does not give one confidence in McFie and Thompson's measure; it is difficult to see how the alleged tendency following right frontal damage to leave the presented order unaltered would not result in greater relative impairment for this group, because even random alterations to the presented order would increase the probability of getting the order correct. It must be said, however, that this apathetic approach to unfamiliar material (simply leaving the material unchanged after a few cursory adjustments) is typical of frontal patients and seems as likely to arise from left as from right hemisphere lesions.

The second WAIS subtest which may give an indication of frontal damage is Block Design (BD). Frontal patients may fail because they do not correct errors or attend to only restricted portions of the design (Lezak, 1983). They may also fail because they cannot construct a suitable plan which relates the outlines of the blocks to the contours on the target design which cross the borders of individual blocks. Where the failure to perform satisfactorily on this test is noted, and disturbed visuo-spatial perception can be excluded as a causative factor, then a disturbance of executive planning (a high level apraxia) attributable to frontal dysfunction may be implicated. This was neatly demonstrated by Walsh (1976) who showed that by dividing up the target design so that the outline of the individual blocks was apparent, the performance of frontal patients, whose general intelligence had not been adversely affected by surgery but whose Block Design performance had been impaired, was markedly improved with this kind of assistance.

A number of tests which may be sensitive to frontal dysfunction have been reported over the years but all currently lack reliable normative data and also require more extensive empirical support for the view that they indicate frontal type impairment. The Proverbs Test (Gorham, 1956; Fogel, 1965) and The Temporal Orientation Test (Benton, Van Allen & Fogel, 1964) are possible candidate tests for a frontal battery. The Proverbs Test has written and multiple choice forms and, like the Temporal Orientation Test, was found by Benton (1968) to be sensitive to bilateral frontal damage. However, modern norms and a full investigation of the effects of focal regional damage are needed. A simple attention test developed by Wilkins, Shallice, and McCarthy (1987), which involves counting auditory or tactile stimuli delivered at a number of different rates (1-7 *Hz*) and which appears to be selectively sensitive to right frontal injury, may prove useful in future investigations, but again independent support for its utility is needed.

Perret (1974), in a sample of Swiss neurosurgical patients, reported a significantly greater performance deficit in frontal as opposed to patients with damage to other regions on the Stroop Test. This test measures interference between printed colour names and hue of the ink in which the names are printed. While this study is interesting and suggestive, because it provides a possible measure of patients' ability to inhibit interfering response tendencies, it used a non-standard version of the test and performance was clearly related to Verbal IQ (left and right frontal groups had the lowest scores of any of the patient groups at 88.1 and 91.9 respectively). Clearly we cannot yet conclude that enhanced Stroop interference is a *sine qua non* of frontal damage. However, the Stroop and other tests mentioned here are all tests which do not require elaborate special apparatus, such as would be needed for an investigation of conditional associative learning (Petrides, 1985), and are easy to use in a clinical setting. Thus, there is a possibility of easily developing these, and other "low technology" tests (for example Petrides & Milner, 1983; Smith & Milner, 1984) for clinical use.

Given the impact that Luria (1966; 1973) has had on thinking concerning frontal lobe function it is surprising that his methods have not developed into widely used tests. There are probably two reasons for this. The first may be the bias towards an "actuarial" type of assessment in much clinical neuropsychology which does not sit easily with the way in which the individual patients' responses determine the course of the investigations with Luria's methods. The second is the volume of clinical experience which is necessary in order to feel confident with his techniques. There is also a suspicion that the clear-cut dissociations which are alleged to mark frontal impairment in some of Luria's writings, for example, the dissociation between verbal knowledge and motor control, are rather infrequent, at least in their more dramatic manifestations, and may not be the result of frontal injury alone (Canavan, Janota, & Schurr, 1985; Drewe, 1975). A version of Luria's procedures have been developed by Christensen (1979) and a battery developed from them by Golden, Hammeke and Purisch (1980). The use of these instruments would require a special section; the reader is referred to Lezak's (1983) excellent critical appraisal of them.

The Category Test from the Halstead-Reitan Battery (Reitan & Davison, 1974) was originally claimed to be sensitive to frontal dysfunction (Halstead, 1947). It is likely that this time-consuming test is not a good procedure for determining frontal impairment (Bornstein, 1986) although, because it is cognitively demanding and likely to be unfamiliar to the patient, it is sensitive to cerebral injury in general (Chapman & Wolff, 1959).

In summarising the effectiveness of the available instruments for cognitive appraisal of frontal dysfunction it must be concluded that there are few tests in which the clinician can invest a great deal of confidence. Verbal fluency, whether oral or written, and categorisation ability as assessed by the WCST (or MCST) together with careful monitoring of the patient's pattern of performance on the WAIS-R subtests, particularly their attitude to the more unfamiliar performance items, will form the backbone of this part of the assessment.

MOOD AND PERSONALITY

Following the initial descriptions of frontal damage in the last century it became apparent that changes in personality are the most evident to the casual observer. Obviously disturbances in general intellect, as assessed in IQ, alterations in attentiveness/distractibility, and the degree of organisation patients exercise over their lives will contribute to their demeanour and affect the impression left with the examiner. However, we will concentrate here on the changes in mood and disposition which are often evident in frontal patients. Changes in mood and personality are in fact the rule after frontal injury and in a significant proportion of cases may be severe enough to be classified as a disturbance. Hécaen (1964) found that in a sample of 131 cases of frontal tumour, 51 (39%) could be so classified. The most common symptoms, in order, were: euphoria (19.8%), irritability (16.0%) and depression (10.7%).

Kretschmer (1956) grouped frontal patients into three syndrome groups; a disinhibited group, associated with orbital lesions, in which an impulsive, emotionally labile, euphoric and sometimes jocular disposition was combined with poor judgement and distractibility; an apathetic group, associated with dorsolateral lesions, in whom occasional angry or aggressive eruptions could occur but where psychomotor retardation and indifference were usual; and finally, an akinetic group associated with medio-basal lesions, who showed a serious impairment of spontaneous behaviour often combined with incontinence and motor weakness. The disinhibited group probably corresponds to the pseudopsychopathic, while the apathetic group probably corresponds to the pseudodepressed categories of Blumer and Benson (1975), who also linked these syndromes with orbital and lateral convexity regions respectively.

Such divisions in the symptomatology of frontal patients appear to be generally agreed (Cummings, 1985) but the anatomical-behavioural association is not at all clear. There is probably most agreement concerning the akinetic behaviour, which at its most extreme may result in akinetic-mutism, and its association with medio-basal frontal structures (Brown, 1985). The association of an apathetic/pseudodepressed group with lateral convexity lesions, and an uninhibited/pseudopsychopathic group with orbital lesions does not appear to be warranted on the basis of available evidence. Robinson et al. (1984) used three separate scales to assess mood in a sample of stroke patients and found depressive symptoms were significantly worse in left frontal patients than in other groups. Furthermore, the severity of the depression score correlated with proximity to the frontal pole in the group with left hemisphere injury. These findings were supported by the results of a Russian investigation of 140 patients with frontal tumours (Bely, 1985). The association of left frontal pathology with depressive symptoms was confirmed but additionally the presence of euphoria and lack of insight with right frontal pathology was noted. The distinctiveness of the syndromes is not in dispute and on balance there is reasonable evidence linking the apathetic/pseudodepressed group with the left frontal regions and the uninhibited/pseudopsychopathic group with the right frontal regions. This will probably turn out to be an oversimplification but in any case the presence of these symptom clusters should not blind us to the fact that a substantial proportion of frontal patients will show mixtures of all three patterns.

The study of Robinson et al. (1984) confirms the appropriateness of using psychiatric instruments to assess mood in cases of frontal pathology. Traditional personality assessment instruments such as the MMPI (Dahlstrom et al., 1975) or Eysenck Personality Questionnaire (Eysenck & Eysenck, 1975) have not been very helpful as neuropsychological instruments (see Powell, 1980, for a review). On present evidence it appears that psychiatric instruments like the Hamilton Depression Scale (Hamilton, 1960), the Zung Depression Scale (Zung, 1965) and the Present State Examination (Wing, Cooper, & Sartorius 1974) hold promise for exploring mood and attitudinal factors in frontal patients. However, in comparison to the large number of investigations of cognitive impairments following frontal injury, systematic studies of affective change are sparse.

CONCLUSION

The major conclusion that one can fairly reach following a review of assessment procedures for frontal damage is that there are disappointingly few sensitive and reliable tests which the clinical neuropsychologist can depend on. Perhaps more than in other areas of dysfunction, (for example, language or memory where systematic, theoretically structured and reasonably comprehensive groups of tests can be administered), assessment of frontal impairment forces the clinician to rely on informed judgement. The patients' behaviour in social interactions, in the family environment, at work, their disposition and reactions in the interview or testing situation, are all factors which must be seen, along with their performance on formal tests, as leading to an estimate of the severity of the impairment and to useful recommendations for dealing with their problems. Much of this data must be obtained from careful questioning of family, nursing staff, employers and occasionally friends of the patient. The contrast which may often be apparent between patients' achievement in straightforward cognitive tests and the changes in their success in managing their lives will usually be sufficient to alert the clinician to the possibility of frontal dysfunction. However, where damage occurs in one or more of a number of functional systems, e.g. mnestic, praxic, linguistic, perceptual etc, as well as those which utilise these processes to govern behaviour (frontal) then, given the present state of knowledge, the problem of disentangling the neuropsychological failures which underlie the disruptions of everyday behaviour will probably prove impossible.

REFERENCES

Bely, B.I. (1985). Psychic disorders in patients with unilateral frontal tumours. *Zhurnal Nevropatologii i Psikhiatrii, 85,* 224-232.

Benton, A.L. (1968). Differential behavioural effects in frontal lobe disease. *Neuropsychologia, 6,* 53-60.

Benton, A.L., & Hamsher, K. de S. (1976). *Multilingual aphasia examination.* Iowa City: University of Iowa.

Benton, A.L., & Hamsher, K. de S. (1978). *Multilingual aphasia examination. Manual* (rev. ed.) Iowa City: University of Iowa.

Benton, A.L., Van Allen, M.W., & Fogel, M.L. (1964). Temporal orientation in cerebral disease. *Journal of Nervous and Mental Disease, 139,* 110-119.

Blumer, D., & Benson, D.F. (1975). Personality changes with frontal and temporal lobe lesions. In D.F. Benson & D. Blumer (Eds.), *Psychiatric aspects of neurological disease, 1.* New York: Grune and Stratton.

Borkowski, J.G., Benton, A.L., & Spreen, O. (1967). Word fluency and brain damage. *Neuropsychologia, 5,* 135-140.

Bornstein, R.A. (1986). Contributions of various neuropsychological measures to detection of frontal lobe impairment. *The International Journal of Clinical Neuropsychology, 3,* 18-22.

Brown, J.W. (1985). Frontal lobe syndromes. In P.J. Vinken, G.W. Bruyn, & H.L. Klawans (Eds.), *Handbook of clinical neurology: Vol. 45. Clinical Neuropsychology.* Amsterdam: Elsevier Science Publishers.

Buikhuisen, W. (1987). Cerebral dysfunction and persistent juvenile delinquency. In S.A. Mednick, T.E. Moffitt, & S.A. Stack (Eds.), *The causes of crime: New biological approaches.* Cambridge: Cambridge University Press.

Canavan, A.G., Janota, I., & Schurr, P.H. (1985). Luria's frontal syndrome: Psychological and anatomical considerations. *Journal of Neurology, Neurosurgery and Psychiatry, 48,* 1049-1053.

Chapman, L.F., & Wolff, H.G. (1959). The cerebral hemispheres and the highest integrative functions of man. *Archives of Neurology, 1,* 357-424.

Christensen, A.-L. (1979). *Luria's neuropsychological investigation. Text.* (2nd ed.). Copenhagen: Munksgaard.

Cloninger, C.R. (1987). Pharmacological approaches to the treatment of antisocial behavior. In S.A. Mednick, T.E. Moffitt, & S.A. Stack (Eds.), *The causes of crime: New biological approaches.* Cambridge: Cambridge University Press.

Crawford, J.R., Moore, J.W., & Cameron, I.M. (1992). Verbal fluency: A NART-based equation for the estimation of premorbid performance. *British Journal of Clinical Psychology, 31,* in press.

Crawford, J.R., Stewart, L.E., Cochrane, R.H.B., Parker, D.M., & Besson, J.A.O. (1989). Construct validity of the National Adult Reading Test: A factor analytic study. *Personality and Individual Differences, 10,* 793-796.

Cummings, J.L. (1985). *Clinical neuropsychiatry.* New York: Grune and Stratton.

Dahlstrom, W.G., Welsh, G.S., & Dahlstrom, L.E. (1975). *An MMPI handbook.* Minneapolis: University of Minnesota Press.

Damasio, A.R. (1979). The frontal lobes. In K.M. Heilman & E. Valenstein (Eds.), *Clinical neuropsychology.* Oxford: Oxford University Press.

Damasio, A.R. (1985). The frontal lobes. In K.M. Heilman & E. Valenstein (Eds.), *Clinical neuropsychology.* Oxford: Oxford University Press.

Damasio, A.R., Graff-Radford, N.R., Eslinger, P.J., Damasio, H., & Kassell, N. (1985). Amnesia following basal forebrain lesions. *Archives of Neurology, 42,* 263-271.

Drewe, E.A. (1974). The effect of type and area of lesion on Wisconsin Card Sorting Test performance. *Cortex, 10,* 159-170.

Drewe, E.A. (1975). An experimental investigation of Luria's theory on the effects of frontal lobe lesions in man. *Neuropsychologia, 13,* 421-429.

Eysenck, H.J., & Eysenck, S.G. (1975). *Manual of the Eysenck Personality Questionnaire.* London: Hodder and Stoughton.

Flashman, L.A., Horner, M.D. & Freides, D. (1991). Note on scoring perseveration on the Winconsin Card Sorting Test. *The Clinical Neuropsychologist, 5,* 190-194.

Fogel, M.L. (1965). The Proverbs Test in the appraisal of cerebral disease. *Journal of General Psychiatry, 72,* 269-275.

Fuster, J.M. (1980). *The prefrontal cortex. Anatomy, physiology and neuropsychology of the frontal lobe.* New York: Raven Press.

Girgis, M. (1971). The orbital surface of the frontal lobe of the brain and mental disorders. *Acta Psychiatrica Scandanavica (Supplement), 222,* 1-58.

Golden, C.J., Hammeke, T.A., & Purisch, A.D. (1980). *Manual for the Luria-Nebraska Neuropsychological Battery.* Los Angeles: Western Psychological Services.

Goldman-Rakic, P.S. (1987). Circuitry of primate prefrontal cortex and regulation of behavior by representational memory. In V.B. Mountcastle, F. Plum, & S.R. Geiger (Eds.), *Handbook of physiology, Vol. V, Higher functions of the brain, Part 1.* Bethesda: American Physiological Society.

Gorham, D.R. (1956). A Proverbs Test for clinical and experimental use. *Psychological Reports, 1,* 1-12.

Grant, D., & Berg, E.A. (1948). A behavioral analysis of degree of reinforcement and ease of shifting to new responses in a Weigl-type card-sorting problem. *Journal of Experimental Psychology, 38,* 404-411.

Halstead, W.C. (1947). *Brain and intelligence.* Chicago: University of Chicago Press.

Hamilton, M.A. (1960). A rating scale for depression. *Journal of Neurology, Neurosurgery and Psychiatry, 23,* 56-62.

Heaton, R.K. (1981). *Wisconsin Card Sorting Test Manual.* Odessa, FL: Psychological Assessment Resources.

Hebb, D.O. (1939). Intelligence in man after large removals of cerebral tissue: Report of four left frontal cases. *Journal of General Psychology, 21,* 73-87.

Hécaen, H. (1964). Mental symptoms associated with tumours of the frontal lobe. In J.M. Warren & K. Akert (Eds.), *The frontal granular cortex and behaviour*, New York: McGraw-Hill.

Heck, E.T., & Bryer, J.B. (1986). Superior sorting and categorizing ability in a case of bilateral frontal atrophy: An exception to the rule. *Journal of Clinical and Experimental Neuropsychology, 8,* 313-316.

Jason, G.W. (1985). Gesture fluency after focal cortical lesions. *Neuropsychologia, 23,* 463-481.

Jones-Gotman, M., & Milner, B. (1977). Design fluency: The invention of nonsense drawings after focal cortical lesions. *Neuropsychologia, 15,* 653-674.

Kandel, E., & Freed, D. (1989). Frontal lobe dysfunction and antisocial behavior: A review. *Journal of Clinical Psychology, 45,* 404-413.

Laplane, D., & Degos, J. (1983). Motor neglect. *Journal of Neurology, Neurosurgery and Psychiatry, 46,* 152-158.

Kretschmer, E. (1956). Lokalisation und Beurteilung psychophysischer Syndrome bei Hirnverletzen. In E. Rehwald (Ed.), *Das Hirntrauma.* Stuttgart: Theime.

Lezak, M.D. (1983). *Neuropsychological Assessment.* Oxford: Oxford University Press.

Lhermitte, F. (1986b). Human autonomy and the frontal lobes: I. Imitation and utilisation behavior: A neuropsychological study of 75 patients. *Annals of Neurology, 19,* 326-334.

Lhermitte, F. (1986b). Human autonomy and the frontal lobes: II. Patient behavior in complex and social situations. The "environmental dependency syndrome". *Annals of Neurology, 19,* 335-343.

Lhermitte, F., Derouesne, J., & Signoret, J.L. (1972). Analyse neuropsychologique et differenciation du syndrome frontal. *Revue Neurologique, 126,* 164-178.

Long, C.J., & Brown, D.A. (1979). *Analysis of temporal cortex dysfunction by neuropsychological techniques.* Paper presented at the American Psychological Association Convention, New York. Quoted in Lezak (1983).

Luria, A.R. (1966). *Higher cortical functions in man.* New York: Basic Books.

Luria, A.R. (1973). *The working brain.* London: Penguin.

Luria, A.R., & Homskaya, E.D. (1964). Disturbances of the regulative role of speech with frontal lesions. In J.M. Warren, & K. Akert (Eds.), *The frontal granular cortex and behavior.* New York: McGraw-Hill.

Malmo, H.P. (1974). On frontal lobe functions: Psychiatric patient controls. *Cortex, 10,* 231-237.

Malmo, R.B. (1948). Psychological aspects of frontal gyrectomy and frontal lobotomy in mental patients. *Research Publications of the Association for Research on Nervous and Mental Disease, 27,* 537-564.

McCullough, M.W. (1950). Wechsler-Bellvue changes following prefrontal lobotomy. *Journal of Clinical Psychology, 6,* 270-273.

McFie, J., & Piercy, M.F. (1952a). The relation of laterality of lesion to performance on Weigl's sorting test. *Journal of Mental Science, 98,* 299-305.

McFie, J., & Piercy, M.F. (1952b). Intellectual impairment with localised cerebral lesions. *Brain, 75,* 292-311.

McFie, J., & Thompson, J.A. (1972). Picture arrangement: A measure of frontal lobe function? *British Journal of Psychiatry, 121,* 547-552.

Meier, M.J., & French, L.A. (1966). Longitudinal assessment of intellectual functioning after temporal lobectomy. *Journal of Clinical Psychology, 22,* 22-27.

Miceli, G., Caltagirone, C., Gainotti, G., Masullo, C., & Silveri, M.C. (1981). Neuropsychological correlates of localized cerebral lesions in non-aphasic brain-damaged patients. *Journal of Clinical Neuropsychology, 3,* 53-63.

Miller, E. (1984). Verbal fluency as a function of a measure of verbal intelligence and in relation to different types of cerebral pathology. *British Journal of Clinical Psychology, 23,* 53-57.

Milner, B. (1954). Intellectual functions of the temporal lobes. *Psychological Bulletin, 51,* 46-52.

Milner, B. (1963). Effects of different brain lesions on card sorting. *Archives of Neurology,* 9, 90-100.

Milner, B. (1964). Some effects of frontal lobectomy in man. In J.M. Warren & K. Akert (Eds.), *The frontal granular cortex and behavior.* New York: McGraw-Hill.

Milner, B. (1974). Hemisphere specialisation: Scope and limits. In F.O. Schmitt & F.G. Worden (Eds.), *The neurosciences third study program.* Cambridge, Mass.: Massachusetts Institute of Technology Press.

Milner, B. (1982). Some cognitive effects of frontal-lobe lesions in man. *Philosophical Transactions of the Royal Society of London, 298B,* 211-226.

Moscovitch, M. (1976). *Differential effects of unilateral temporal and frontal lobe damage on memory performance.* Paper presented at the fourth annual meeting of the International Neuropsychological Society, Toronto. Quoted in Lezak, (1983).

Nauta, W.J.H. (1971). The problem of the frontal lobe: A reinterpretation. *Journal of Psychiatric Research, 8,* 167-187.

Nelson, H.E. (1976). A modified card sorting test sensitive to frontal defects. *Cortex, 12,* 313-324.

Nelson, H.E. (1982). *The National Adult Reading Scale (NART): Test Manual.* Windsor: NFER-Nelson.

Newcombe, F. (1969). *Missile wounds of the brain.* London: Oxford University Press.

Perret, E. (1974). The left frontal lobe of man and the suppression of habitual responses in verbal categorical behaviour. *Neuropsychologia, 12,* 323-330.

Pendleton, M.G., Heaton, R.K., Lehman, R.A.W., & Hulihan, D. (1982). Diagnostic utility of the Thurstone Word Fluency Test in neuropsychological evaluations. *Journal of Clinical Neuropsychology, 4,* 307-317.

Petrides, M. (1985). Deficits on conditional associative-learning tasks after frontal- and temporal-lobe lesions in man. *Neuropsychologia, 23,* 601-604.

Petrides, M., & Milner, B. (1983). Deficits on subject-ordered tasks after frontal- and temporal-lobe lesions in man. *Neuropsychologia, 20,* 249-262.

Pontius, A.A. (1972). Neurological aspects in some types of delinquency, especially among juveniles. *Adolescence, 7,* 289-308.

Porteus, S.D. (1965). *Porteus Maze Test. Fifty years application.* Palo Alto, Calif.: Pacific Books.

Pribram, K.H. (1973). The primate frontal cortex – executive of the brain. In K.H. Pribram & A.R. Luria (Eds.), *Psychophysiology of the frontal lobes.* New York: Academic Press.

Powell, G.E. (1980). *Brain and personality.* Farnborough: Gower.

Raimer, A.M., & Hécaen, H. (1970). Role respectif des atteintes frontales et de la lateralisation lesionelle dans les deficits de la "fluence verbale". *Revue Neurologique, 123,* 17-22.

Reitan, R.M., & Davison, L.A. (1974). *Clinical neuropsychology: Current status and applications.* New York: Hemisphere.

Rey, A. (1964). *L'examen clinique en psychologie.* Paris: Presses Universitaire de France.

Robinson, A.L., Heaton, R.K., Lehman, R.A.W., & Stilson, D.W. (1980). The utility of the Wisconsin Card Sorting Test in detecting and localizing frontal lobe lesions. *Journal of Consulting and Clinical Psychology, 48,* 605-614.

Robinson, R.G., Kubos, K.L., Starr, L.B., Rao, K., & Price, T.R. (1984). Mood disorders in stroke patients. *Brain, 107,* 81-93.

Roland, P.E. (1984). Metabolic measurements of the working frontal cortex in man. *Trends in Neurosciences, 7,* 430-435.

Russell, E.W. (1975). A multiple scoring method for the assessment of complex memory functions. *Journal of Consulting and Clinical Psychology, 43,* 800-809.

Shallice, T. (1982). Specific impairments of planning. *Philosophical Transactions of the Royal Society of London, 298B,* 199-209.

Shallice, T. (1988). *From neuropsychology to mental structure.* Cambridge: Cambridge University Press.

Sheer, D.E., & Shuttleworth, M. (1952). Psychometric studies. In F.A. Mettler (Ed.), *Psychosurgical problems.* London: Routledge and Kegan Paul.

Smith, A. (1960). Changes in Porteus Maze scores of brain-operated schizophrenics after an eight year interval. *Journal of Mental Science, 106,* 967-978.

Smith, A. (1966). Intellectual functions in patients with lateralized frontal tumors. *Journal of Neurology, Neurosurgery and Psychiatry, 29,* 52-59.

Smith, M.L., & Milner, B. (1984). Differential effects of frontal-lobe lesions on cognitive estimation and spatial memory. *Neuropsychologia, 22,* 697-705.

Spreen, O., & Benton, A.L. (1969). *Neurosensory Center Comprehensive Examination for Aphasia.* Victoria, BC: Neuropsychological Laboratory, Department of Psychology, University of Victoria.

Stuss, D.T., & Benson, D.F. (1986). *The frontal lobes.* New York: Raven Press.

Taylor, L.B. (1979). Psychological assessment of neurosurgical patients. In T. Rasmussen & R. Markino (Eds.), *Functional neurosurgery,* New York: Raven Press.

Teuber, H.-L., Battersby, W.S., & Bender, M.B. (1951). Performance of complex visual tasks after cerebral lesions. *Journal of Nervous and Mental Disease, 114,* 413-429.

Thurstone, L.L., & Thurstone, T.G. (1962). *Primary mental abilities.* Chicago: Science Research Associates.

Tow, P.M. (1955). *Personality changes following frontal leucotomy.* London: Oxford University Press.

Walsh, K.W. (1976). Neuropsychological aspects of modified leucotomy. In W.H. Sweet (Ed.), *Neurosurgical treatment in psychiatry, pain and epilepsy.* Baltimore: University Park Press.

Walsh, K.W. (1978). *Neuropsychology: A clinical approach.* Edinburgh: Churchill-Livingstone.

Warrington, E.K., James, M., & Macjiewski, C. (1986). The WAIS as a lateralizing and localizing diagnostic instrument: A study of 656 patients with unilateral cerebral lesions. *Neuropsychologia, 24,* 223-239.

Wechsler, D. (1944). *The measurement of adult intelligence.* (3rd ed.). Baltimore: Williams and Wilkins.

Wechsler, D. (1955). *Wechsler Adult Intelligence Scale. Manual.* New York: Psychological Corporation.

Wechsler, D. (1981). *WAIS-R manual.* New York: Psychological Corporation.

Weigl, E. (1941). On the psychology of so-called processes of abstraction. *Journal of Abnormal and Social Psychology, 36,* 3-33.

Wilkins, A.J., Shallice, T. & McCarthy, R, (1987). Frontal lesions and sustained attention. *Neuropsychologia, 25,* 359-365.

Wing, J.K., Cooper, E., & Sartorius, N. (1974). *Measurement and classification of psychiatric symptoms.* Cambridge: Cambridge University Press.

Yeudall, L.T., & Fromm-Auch, D. (1979). Neuropsychological impairments in various psychopathological populations. In J. Gruzelier & P. Flor-Henry (Eds.), *Hemisphere asymmetries of function and psychopathology.* New York: Elsevier/North-Holland.

Zung, W.W.K. (1965). A self-rating depression scale. *Archives of General Psychiatry, 12,* 63-70.

SECTION C:
MAJOR CLINICAL DISORDERS

14 The Neuropsychological Assessment of Dementia

Robin G. Morris
Neuropsychology Unit, Department of Psychology, Institute of
Psychiatry, De Crespigny Park, Denmark Hill, LONDON SE5

Michael D. Kopelman
Academic Unit of Psychiatry, United Medical and Dental Schools of
Guy's and St. Thomas's Hospitals, Lambeth Palace Road, London,
SE1 7EH

INTRODUCTION: HISTORY, MEDICAL AND PSYCHIATRIC DIAGNOSIS

The neuropsychological assessment of dementia occurs within a wider context of the clinical evaluation of patients in terms of neurological, psychiatric and physical disability. Although misdiagnoses remain common (e.g. Garcia et al., 1981; Ron et al., 1979), particularly in identifying the cause of dementia (Hamer et al., 1988), recent studies do seem to indicate that the greater the care that is paid to overall assessment of patients, the greater the probability of getting the diagnosis right (Terry & Katzman, 1983; Sulkava et al., 1983; Wade et al., 1987). Neuropsychological studies in the 1960s and 1970s often appeared to assume that, if only the appropriate test or test "battery" could be developed, that test *by itself* would enable us to differentiate dementing from non-dementing patients. Such an assumption has now been abandoned by most clinical psychologists and formal psychological testing is seen to take its place within an array of different types of assessment (Eslinger et al., 1984). In this respect, for example, attempts to systematise and collate the results of clinical assessment, such as the CAMDEX (Cambridge Index of Mental Disorder in the Elderly; Roth et al., 1986), represent an important advance.

The information that is sought in evaluating middle-aged or elderly patients complaining of progressive memory impairment is outlined in Tables 14.1A to 14.1E. The most common group of dementias are the degenerative disorders such as Alzheimer's disease, Pick's disease, dementia associated with Parkinson's disease, and Huntingdon's disease. The second most common group is formed by the vascular dementias, namely multi-infarct dementia, Binswanger's subcortical progressive encephalopathy and dementia which follows major "strokes" (Cerebro-vascular accidents). Other important causes of dementia include hydrocephalus (particularly the so-called normal pressure hydrocephalus), infection (e.g. Creutzfeldt-Jakob disease, AIDS), head injury, metabolic disease (e.g. hypothyroidism, Cushing's disease), toxins (including alcohol, aluminium and lead), nutritional depletion (especially vitamins B6 and B12), and tumours (intracranial groups and extra-cranial carcinoma, which may be undiagnosed when the dementia first becomes apparent). In addition the differentiation of an authentic dementia from so-called "pseudodementia" (most commonly, depressive pseudodementia) can often be difficult, (see e.g. Mahendra, 1985, or Lishman, 1987 for further discussion). Tables 14.1A to 14.1E indicate how particular items in the clinical assessment may give clues to the underlying nature of dementia. In more detailed and elaborated form, such clues might eventually be incorporated into a computerised algorithm for diagnosis. The particular contribution of the electroencephalogram (E.E.G.) and neuroradiological investigations will be discussed in more detail in the next section.

Procedures such as the CAMDEX (Roth et al., 1986) provide a method of collating this type of information systematically, although it is inevitably time-consuming. The CAMDEX, for example, incorporates a history from a relative or carer as well as from the patient, the results of physical examination and investigations, and a brief neuropsychological assessment, called the Cambridge Cognitive Examination (CAMCOG). It provides a means of quantifying the severity of impairment along several possible scales, a "cut-off" point for the diagnosis of dementia, as well as guidelines for the classification of patients between the various subtypes of dementia. It has been validated against current clinical diagnosis, but is awaiting validation using autopsy and biopsy evidence (Roth et al., 1986). An alternative is the Geriatric Mental State, a standardised clinical interview which, when combined with AGECAT, a computerised diagnostic procedure, classifies elderly patients under the main diagnostic categories, e.g. "pervasive dementia" or "depression" (Copeland et al., 1986). It is not as extensive in its history-taking as CAMDEX and, as yet, cannot distinguish between subtypes of dementia. However, the potential of these techniques, when combined with the results of neuropsychological assessment and validated against autopsy studies, will be in enabling us to specify more precisely which variables are of the greatest predictive value in determining particular diagnoses.

Various attempts have been made to specify more precisely clinical criteria for the presence of dementia. Those in DSM-III-R (American Psychiatric Association, 1987) are fairly broad, leaving plenty of scope for individual interpretation. Khatchachurian (1985) essentially provides a discussion document

TABLE 14.1A
Clinical Assessment of Memory Impairments in Middle-Aged or
Elderly Subjects

History

Onset:

   _____   sudden (? vascular episode)
   _____   progressive (? Alzheimer's disease)
   _____   stepwise (? multi-infarct dementia)

Symptoms:

   _____   activities of daily living (e.g. dressing)
   _____   at work (e.g. failure in technical drawing)
   _____   in the home (e.g. leaves taps on)

Other psychological complaints:

   _____   perceptual
   _____   attention and concentration
   _____   language, especially naming and word finding
   _____   cognition (e.g. in mental calculation)
   _____   affective, especially depression or anxiety
   _____   personality/behavioural change
                   (? Pick's disease, Frontal lobe dementia or
                   AIDS-related dementia)
   _____   mental slowing (? Parkinson's, ? AIDS, ? depression)
   _____   i.e. the globality of the cognitive and behavioural change

Other physical complaints:

   _____   motor/sensory (? vascular dementia)
   _____   ataxia/incontinence (? normal pressure hydrocephalus)
   _____   abnormal movements (? Huntingdon's, ? Parkinson's)
   _____   wasting (? carcinoma ? AIDS)

---

of the relevant issues and current state of knowledge. McKhann et al. (1984) provide criteria for the presence of "definite", "probable" and "possible" Alzheimer's disease, which are the most useful; but research findings (e.g. Terry & Katzman, 1983; Wade et al., 1987) would appear to indicate that the thoroughness and care with which clinical information has been gathered are more important in determining the accuracy of diagnosis than the particular set of diagnostic criteria used.

ELECTROENCEPHALOGRAPHIC (E.E.G.) AND NEURORADIOLOGICAL INVESTIGATIONS

Despite advances in neuroradiology, the E.E.G. can still be useful in cases of diagnostic uncertainty. In presenile Alzheimer's disease, a slowing and reduction of alpha rhythm, particularly in the temporal lobes, followed by

TABLE 14.1B

Background Information

Family history:

_____   Alzheimer's
_____   hypertension (? multi-infarct dementia)
_____   affective disorder (? pseudodementia)
_____   Huntingdon's disease (autosomal dominant)
_____   Parkinson's disease
_____   Down's syndrome (associated with Alzheimer's)

Personal history:

_____   education (baseline level of function)
_____   occupation − (baseline level of function and possible
            environmental hazards)
_____   alcohol abuse (? Korsakoff ? alcoholic dementia)
_____   cigarette smoking (? undiagnosed carcinoma)
_____   drug abuse (? AIDS)

Past medical and psychiatric history:

_____   previous episodes of amnesia (? vascular or epileptic
            disorders)
_____   hypertension (? multi-infarct dementia)
_____   'stroke' or other vascular disorder
_____   head injury/epilepsy (associated with increased rates of
            dementia)
_____   affective disorder (? pseudodementia)
_____   E.C.T./anti-cholinergic or other medication affecting
            memory

the appearance of theta and delta rhythm, is commonly seen (e.g. Letamendia & Pampiglione, 1958). In presenile and senile patients, more recent studies have shown that the degree of E.E.G. abnormality can be predictive of the severity of cognitive impairment, mortality at one year follow-up, plaque and tangle count at autopsy, and the extent of neuronal loss (Kaszniak et al., 1979; Muller & Schwartz, 1978; Rae-Grant et al., 1987). On the other hand, one recent study reported 14% false negatives and 27% false positives in terms of the presences of "E.E.G. abnormalities" in dementing patients and controls (Rae-Grant et al., 1987). In Creutzfeldt-Jakob's disease, a characteristic sequence of E.E.G. abnormalities is seen in the presence of little or no change on a Computerised Axial Tomography (CT) Scan (Chaiofalo et al., 1980).

The CT scan can be particularly valuable in demonstrating infarcts in multi-infarct dementia, disproportionate ventricular enlargement in normal pressure hydrocephalus, loss of the characteristic convexities of the heads of the caudate nuclei in Huntingdon's disease, and focal frontal and temporal atrophy in Pick's

TABLE 14.1C

Physical Examination

General Examination:
_____ endocrine disorder (e.g. ? thyroid disease, Cushing's)
_____ wasting (undiagnosed carcinoma, AIDS)
_____ Kaposi's nodules (AIDS)

Respiratory System:
_____ chest infection (organic confusional state)
_____ pneumonitis (AIDS)

Cardiovascular System:
_____ hypertension
_____ cardiac/carotid lesions
_____ peripheral circulation

Abdomen:
_____ chronic liver disease
_____ (? alcohol abuse ? secondary to abdominal carcinoma)

Neurological:
_____ focal signs (? multi-infarct)
_____ extrapyramidal signs (? Parkinson's or Alzheimer's)
_____ ataxia (? hydrocephalus)
_____ raised intracranial pressure (? hydrocephalus)
_____ primitive reflexes (said to indicate 'frontal' involvement)
_____ Wernicke features
_____ (? Korsakoff's syndrome or alcoholic dementia)

---

disease. In Alzheimer-type dementia, there is usually evidence of ventricular enlargement and sulcal and fissure widening; but one study, using various methods of assessment, reported misclassification of patients and controls in approximately 20% of cases (Jacoby & Levy, 1980). Sequential evidence of ventricular and/or sulcal enlargement through time is more reliable, and has been shown to correlate with the rate of cognitive deterioration (Luxenberg et al., 1987; Naguib & Levy, 1982). MRI can be used for indicating changes in periventricular white matter and hippocampal and amygdaloid abnormalities. Abnormalities of T_1 and T_2 relaxation times have been demonstrated in dementia (Besson et al., 1990).

In the United Kingdom, SPECT and PET remain, at present, essentially research procedures; but enough information has been gathered to ensure that, as these techniques become more widely available, they will undoubtedly contribute to diagnostic practice. In Alzheimer-type dementia, the most pronounced reductions in regional blood flow and oxygen utilisation occur in the temporal and parietal lobes; this also tends to occur in multi-infarct dementia, although the findings in individual cases are more variable according to the sites of local

TABLE 14.1D

Clinical Assessment of Mental State

Appearance and Behaviour:

_____ apathetic/unkempt (? frontal lobe involvement)
_____ loss of initiative (? frontal lobe involvement)
_____ disinhibition (? frontal lobe involvement)
_____ psychomotor retardation (? depression)

Mood:

_____ euphoric/labile/inappropriate (? frontal)
_____ depression (? pseudodementia)
_____ anxiety (very non-specific)

Abnormal phenomena:

_____ psychotic/paranoid features (tend to appear relatively late in dementia, and are associated with temporo-parietal pathology)

Cognition:

_____ orientation (time, place, person)
_____ memory, especially new learning and remote memory
_____ language, especially naming and comprehension
_____ mental calculation (e.g. coping with money and change)
_____ drawing/copying (affected early in Alzheimer's disease)
_____ other apraxias (e.g. dressing)

Self-appraisal:

_____ 'insight' (preserved in early Alzheimer's disease; lost at later stages)

infarction (see e.g. Frackowiak et al., 1981; Johnson et al., 1987; Rogers et al., 1986).

PSYCHOLOGICAL TESTS IN DEMENTIA

In this context, psychological assessment aims to establish both the general level of current functioning and particular areas of deficit, and to compare current performance with previous or estimated premorbid levels of abilities. The particular purpose of any given assessment may vary from diagnosis to an evaluation of disability with a veiw to management (Woods & Britton, 1985). Furthermore, the practical aspects of test administration require careful thought when dealing with an elderly client group, who may have a different attitude to assessment from younger people (Comfort, 1978; Miller, 1980; Morris et al., 1987). These factors weigh heavily in the choice and development of assessment procedures and merit a separate discussion before reviewing the specific procedures.

TABLE 14.1E

Physical Investigations

Blood tests:
full blood count (? anaemia from any cause): erythrocyte sedimentation rate. urea. electrolytes (? systemic disease); liver function tests (? alcohol abuse/abdominal disease); random blood sugar (? diabetes); thyroid function tests; V.D.R.L. (? neurosyphilis); B12, folate (? subacute combined degeneration of the cord with dementia); H.I.V. antibody status (? AIDS)

General:

    _____ chest x-ray (pneumonitis in AIDS; unsuspected carcinomas, especially in smokers)

    _____ electrocardiogram (especially if multi-infarct dementia suspected)

Neurological:

    _____ Computerised Tomography scan (for cortical atrophy, focal infarcts, hydrocephalus, caudate atrophy, etc.)

    _____ Electro-encephalogram (usually shows bitemporal slow waves in young-onset Alzheimer's disease; more specific changes in Creutzfeldt-Jakob disease)

    _____ Magnetic Resonance Imaging (MRI)*

    _____ Single photon emission tomography (SPECT)*

    _____ Positron emission tomography (PET)*

    * as available

One of the purposes of neuropsychological assessment of dementia is to identify a progressive deterioration in mental functioning. A difficulty is that a variety of "non-organic" disorders can produce a generalised impairment on cognitive assessment (see e.g. Folstein et al., 1975), producing a risk of "false positive" diagnoses, although this risk is offset when the results of neuropsychological tests are combined with those of other investigations (Eslinger et al., 1984). A second purpose is to determine the severity of dementia, and a variety of procedures have been developed for this purpose. Firstly, there are the brief screening procedures, the dementia rating scales that consist of rapid cognitive tests, which are designed to provide a rapid method of investigation and are used mostly by geriatricians, neurologists and psychiatrists. In some cases, these tests have been supplemented by behaviour rating scales and additional tests of neuropsychological functioning to provide a more comprehensive set of measures (Blessed et al., 1968; Folstein et al., 1975; Hughes et al., 1982). More detailed psychological assessment is usually conducted by neuropsychologists using tests that explore psychological functioning in more detail. If assessment is to be made with a view to management, then it is likely to be more useful if it spans a wide range of functioning and has some predictive validity in terms of assessing the degree of disability of the patients (McPherson et al., 1985).

Psychological tests are also used in the *differential* diagnosis of dementia by examining the profile of test performance in dementia. Distinctions are made on the basis of test performance in dementia, other organic disorders, and functional disorders (Kopelman 1986; Miller, 1980). A frequent problem is the differentiation of a "true" pseudodementia, and specific batteries of tests have been developed to deal with this, such as the Kendrick Cognitive Tests for the Elderly (Kendrick, 1985). As will be seen later, psychological tests are less successful in achieving this aim for a variety of reasons.

More recently, it has been shown that even within Alzheimer's disease there are likely to be subgroups of patients in which different types of neuropsychological deficits predominate (e.g. Jorm, 1985). In particular, there is evidence that patients with Alzheimer-type dementia younger than 65 years tend to a greater prevalence of language disorder (Filley et al., 1986; Seltzer, & Sherwin, 1983). It has been suggested recently, that impairment in syntactic ability frequently occurs in early onset cases affecting comprehension of sentences and written expression (Becker et al., 1988). Other research claims that language disorder and apraxia are particularly associated with a familial form of Alzheimer's disease, forming a distinct clinical entity (Breitner & Folstein, 1984; Folstein & Breitner, 1981). These findings only serve to illustrate the complexity of assessment of dementia at the early stages, where not only is it sometimes difficult to distinguish between different causes of cognitive impairment but to ascertain different patterns of presentation.

THE TESTING ENVIRONMENT

An intention of neuropsychological assessment is to obtain the optimal performance of the person, thereby providing an indication of their true capabilities (Heaton & Heaton, 1981). For a variety of reasons, this is difficult to achieve with dementia patients. For a patient to comply with the testing procedures they should have some understanding of the broad aims and purpose of the investigation. This is not always possible with older patients who may perceive psychological testing as impersonal and something that is very threatening. Furthermore, dementia patients, by the nature of their impairment, are likely to be confused and have limited insight into their disability. They will also take longer to adjust to a novel environment, and procedures that are not readily understood are in danger of being rejected as a result (Morris et al., 1987). To offset these problems it is necessary to take longer in the preliminary interactions with the patient to establish a good rapport.

More severely impaired patients may not be able to communicate their dissatisfaction with the testing session verbally, and careful attention should be paid to non-verbal clues such as increasing restlessness and anxiety. For example, it is best to back off at the first hints of a refusal to attempt a test, than to continue and risk terminating the testing session. People with dementia may be constantly exposed to failure in their everyday living activities and if this experience is repeated in the testing session, then the motivation of a patient can rapidly decline. Thus, it is important to tailor the testing procedures to suit the capabilities of the patients. A common misconception is that an unpleasant experience in a testing session will be forgotten by dementia patients because of the nature of their memory impairment. However, even though the patient may not remember the experience, it can alter their attitude on subsequent occasions – an observation that is consistent with the finding that affective reactions to events and "implicit" memory are relatively preserved in amnesia and dementia (Johnson et al., 1985; Knopman & Nissen, 1987; Morris & Kopelman, 1986).

Finally, a feature of working with elderly patients is that they are more likely to suffer from sensory impairments, such as visual defects or hearing impairment. It is well-established that the presence of sensory impairments is inversely correlated with performance on psychometric tests (O'Neill & Calhoun, 1975). It should be noted that sensory impairments can substantially compound the problems of a patient who is confused or disorientated, and result in a much reduced level of functioning. This factor can easily be overlooked, particularly if sensory impairments are uncorrected or if patients attempt to compensate for their disability by guessing. As well as deficits with the peripheral sensory apparatus there is also evidence in Alzheimer's disease of impairment at the level of the sensory cortex. Central auditory function may be impaired because of temporal pathology that includes the primary auditory reception area (DeLeon et al., 1983; Grimes et al., 1985). Studies of iconic memory functioning by Schlotterer et al. (1983) indicate that the central aspects of visual processing are impaired, possibly at the level of the striate cortex. To some extent these problems can be overcome by using auditory or visual material that is easily discriminable and by ensuring that sensory deficits are corrected where possible in a patient.

SCREENING ASSESSMENT PROCEDURES

A substantial number of brief cognitive tests have been developed that provide an approximate measure of severity and "cut-off" points for identifying possible cases of dementia. These tests, which often form part of the neurological and psychiatric procedures referred to earlier, are designed to be quick to administer and acceptable to patients with varying degrees of impairment. Perhaps the most widely used procedure is the Dementia Rating Scale (Hughes et al., 1982) and the variations of this scale that have been developed (Cooper & Bickel, 1984; Holden & Woods, 1982). The widely used Blessed Scale (Blessed et al., 1968) includes questions concerning spatial and temporal orientation as well as past personal and current information. It also includes tests of mental control, such as counting backwards from 20 down to 1, and a brief test of learning and recall, that involves remembering an address after a short delay.

The Mini Mental State Examination (MMSE) (Folstein et al., 1975; Thal et al., 1986) takes 5-10 minutes to administer and includes brief tests of language functioning and praxis (copying designs). A composite score may be obtained and those who score 23 or less out of 30 are considered to be intellectually impaired. It is notable that in a community study only approximately one third of people scoring below this threshold were diagnosed as having dementia, the rest having either no disorder or other psychiatric problems. However, no-one scoring above 23 was subsequently diagnosed as having dementia (Folstein et al., 1985). Not surprisingly, performance on the MMSE tends to be highly correlated with variations of the Dementia Rating Scale (Fillenbaum et al., 1987; Thal et al., 1986).

A variant of the MMSE is the more recent Cambridge Cognitive Examination (CAMCOG), which forms part of the CAMDEX (Roth et al., 1986). The CAMCOG is essentially an expansion of the MMSE to form a mini neuropsychological test battery including tests of orientation, language, memory, praxis, attention, abstract thinking, calculation and perception. For example, the perceptual test involves recognising photographs of objects taken from unusual angles. The memory assessment is expanded to include items that determine remote memory functioning as well as recall and recognition memory. The extra items in the schedule appear to have made it more sensitive to milder degrees of cognitive impairment, and more accurate in detection. Part of the reason for this is that the CAMCOG has a greater range and is less subject to ceiling effects in performance. The CAMCOG has been validated against clinical diagnosis on samples of patients with Alzheimer-type dementia, multi-infarct dementia, depression and delirium. This has produced promising results, although further investigations using autopsy criteria for diagnosis need to be carried out.

The two brief assessment procedures most favoured by clinical psychologists in the United Kingdom for assessment of dementia are the Clifton Assessment Procedures for the Elderly (CAPE) (Pattie & Gilleard, 1979), and the Kendrick Cognitive Tests for the Elderly (Kendrick, 1985). The CAPE includes a Behavioural Rating Scale and a Cognitive Assessment Scale (CAS), the combined scores of which are used to grade patients in terms of the degree of support they would need. The CAS contains items concerning personal information, temporal orientation and simple mental control, comprising speed and accuracy in counting from 1 to 20 and reciting the alphabet. It includes a reading test, with words of a wider frequency range than the National Adult Reading Test, and simple writing test, in which the person has to write their own name. Gibson's Spiral Maze is added to provide a rapid test of psychomotor skills. This is a spiral design printed on a card in the form of a maze, which the patient has to trace though using a pen. Taken together these components of the CAS distinguish between different degrees of disability, although individual items from the test have been shown to be less reliable (McPherson et al., 1985; 1986; Pattie, 1981).

The Kendrick Battery was designed with the particular aim of diagnosing dementia, and differentiating the cognitive impairments of dementia and depression. It consists of two subtests, an Object Learning Test (OLT) and Digit Copying Test (DCT). The OLT is essentially a test of immediate recall, requiring the patient to study sets of line drawings of objects and recall the names of the objects. There are four sets of drawings with parallel forms for repeated assessment, and a "memory quotient" can be obtained from a subjective score in terms of age-related norms. This test is coupled with the Digit Copying Test, developed originally by Kendrick (1965), a speed test in which the patient copies a series of digits in writing. Both tests are sensitive to dementia, whilst the DCT is more sensitive to depression, enabling it to differentiate between the two disorders (Kendrick et al., 1979). A feature of the procedure is that data is provided for the discriminative power of the test when repeated after an interval of approximately six weeks. This increases the discrimination between depression and dementia, because the demented patients are more likely to remain stable in indicating a deficit in both tasks. Another feature is that Bayesian statistics are used to take into account the baseline probability of occurrence of depression or dementia in a psychogeriatric setting. It has been shown to have a diagnostic discrimination accuracy of over 90%, but this may be an overestimate of how well the battery performs in differentiating difficult cases (see later). However, the Kendrick battery is frequently used by neuropsychologists working with the elderly, because of its speed of administration and acceptability to patients, particularly those who would not cooperate with a more extensive neuropsychological test battery.

An obvious criticism of these procedures is that their brevity does not allow them to provide valid information about detailed neuropsychological functions. More extensive assessment is likely to yield information about the pattern of breakdown in cognitive functioning, although the usefulness of this extra information has to be carefully weighed against the extra time needed for assessment. The following sections are devoted to more extensive neuropsychological investigation of dementia that might follow initial screening, particularly for patients who are at the early stages of the disorder. The procedures that will be described contrast the test battery approach exemplified in the assessment of general intellectual assessment with a more flexible approach used to explore particular facets of cognitive function. In the present chapter, the latter approach will be illustrated with reference to the assessment of memory impairment (see Reiten, 1986, and McKenna & Warrington, 1986, for further examples of these contrasting approaches).

STRATEGIES FOR NEUROPSYCHOLOGICAL ASSESSMENT

As with other types of neuropsychological investigation, it is usual to start with a basic battery, covering the primary dimensions of intellectual abilities, and then to proceed to hypothesis testing regarding the nature of particular cognitive deficits (Lezak, 1983). In dementia, a basic assessment of intellectual functioning can provide a foundation for the remainder of the assessment. Furthermore, the basic set of tests can be used for repeated assessment, an important indicator in the reliable measurement of the presence and rate of cognitive decline (Morris & Fulling, 1988). A basic set of tests might include a method of estimating premorbid intellectual functioning, such as the National Adult Reading Test (NART) (Nelson, 1982), an assessment of current intellectual functioning such as the revised Wechsler Adult Intelligence Scale (WAIS-R) (Wechsler, 1981), and a method of determining the general level of memory performance, for example, by use of the revised Wechsler Memory Scale (WMS) (Psychological Corporation, 1988; Wechsler, 1945). Supplementary tests can then be used in a flexible fashion to explore further particular deficits which have been identified in the basic assessment.

ASSESSMENT OF PREMORBID INTELLECTUAL FUNCTIONING

Although estimation of premorbid intelligence is covered in the chapter by Crawford (Chapter 3), it will also be discussed here, as it is such an important aspect of the assessment of dementia. Because dementia is a progressive disorder an estimate of premorbid intelligence is a very useful marker by which to judge the extent of intellectual decline. Moreover, people who have a higher level of premorbid intelligence tend to do better on tests of particular cognitive functions and therefore it can be important to have some estimate of premorbid intellectual ability with which to judge whether any individual cognitive function is impaired. For example, memory abilities tend to be greater in people who have a higher premorbid intelligence (e.g. Eysenck & Halstead, 1945). A fall in memory performance from a high starting point may not be detected unless an estimate of premorbid intelligence is available. Having said this, it is important to note that *repeated* assessments of general or particular cognitive functions, demonstrating deterioration through time, are a much more reliable way of diagnosing dementia than are comparisons of performance on a single occasion of testing with an estimate of premorbid function (cf. the discussion of CT Scans on P.X.)

The development of the NART has provided a useful index of premorbid intelligence, replacing the Mill Hill Vocabulary Test (MHVT) (cf. Kendrick, 1964) and WAIS Vocabulary Test, both of which are known to decline following the onset of dementia (Crawford, 1989; Davies et al., 1981; Kendrick et al.,

1979; Miller, 1977). The NART required subjects to read a series of irregularly spelt words, such that a correct response cannot be arrived at by using the phonology alone. This test was found to be comparatively insensitive to the effects of dementia in a sample of patients aged between 20 and 70 years (Nelson & O'Connell, 1978). Using a regression equation it is possible to estimate premorbid intelligence from the NART score as the scale has been standardised against the WAIS (Nelson, 1982; Nelson & O'Connell, 1978) and a revised version against the WAIS-R (see Chapter 3). This means that it is possible to assess the degree of decline in intellectual functioning by looking at the difference between the predicted IQ from the NART and that obtained using the WAIS or WAIS-R. The test has more recently been validated on elderly Alzheimer-type patients by Crawford et al. (1988); Kopelman (1986a); Nebes et al. (1984); and Sahakian et al. (1988), who found no difference in performance between the patients and elderly controls. In contrast, Hart et al. (1986) found a slight deficit in their elderly Alzheimer-type dementia patients. One of the difficulties of validating this test is that there is no adequate alternative estimate of premorbid intelligence on which to base a comparison between an experimental and control group, with the exception of the demographic approach outlined in Chapter 3. Unless there is a truly random selection of patient controls, biases in one group or the other can distort the pattern of results. Another method of validation is to conduct a longitudinal study on dementia patients and see whether the NART score holds up. A study by O'Carroll et al. (1987) indicates no decline for dementia patients on the NART after a delay of one year, in comparison to a significant decline on the MHVT and CAPE. Further longitudinal studies of this sort would be extremely useful in interpreting performance on this test.

Thus, there is evidence that the NART is relatively insensitive to dementia and a useful predictor of premorbid intelligence in dementing patients. It is not unusual to find patients who are severely impaired on other psychometric tests, but still produce a high score on the NART. Despite this, the present version of the NART does have some limitations, for it is unsuitable for patients with speech production difficulties and has as yet not been standardised on a large enough sample of the elderly. It is also relatively poor at making discriminations in the very high or below average bands of intelligence.

ASSESSMENT OF CURRENT INTELLECTUAL FUNCTIONING

To obtain an assessment of intellectual functioning the WAIS or WAIS-R is commonly used (see Chapter 3), although an alternative has been to use the Mill Hill Vocabulary Test (MHVT) combined with Raven's Progressive Matrices (Kendrick et al., 1965; Kendrick & Post, 1967; Raven et al, 1977). WAIS profiles have been the subject of much research with several studies indicating that particular subtests on the WAIS are more sensitive to brain damage. Several studies report that the Performance subtests are more vulnerable to dementia giving rise to a Verbal-Performance discrepancy (Miller, 1977; Morris, 1987b; Ron et al., 1979; Savage et al., 1973). This finding should be interpreted with caution, because not all dementing patients deteriorate in this way. Some show a uniform pattern of decrement, some may have had superior verbal intelligence premorbidly, and occasionally Verbal Intelligence may even deteriorate faster than Performance.

Similar difficulties arise in the use of other indices of deterioration that have been considered in relation to dementia. For example the WAIS deterioration index (Wechsler, 1958) has been used by Savage et al. (1973) to explore the WAIS profiles of a mixed sample of elderly patients with Alzheimer-type and multi-infarct dementia. The quotient is calculated on the basis of subtests that are likely to hold up (Vocabulary, Information, Picture Completion and Object Assembly) versus those that are said not to hold (Digit Span, Similarities, Digit Symbol and Block Design). The quotient successfully classified 52% of the patients as having significant intellectual impairment, but 7% of a control sample were wrongly classified as well. This compared with the Verbal-Performance discrepancy, where a cut-off point of fifteen correctly classified 29% of patients with dementia, and 17% of controls as having intellectual impairment. Attempts to distinguish between dementia and "functional" disorders on the basis of WAIS profiles should be viewed with even greater caution. In the Savage et al. (1973) study, a significant proportion of patients with functional disorders would be misclassified using the Verbal-Performance Discrepancy or the WAIS Deterioration Quotient. Studies by Whitehead (1973), McFie (1975) and Miller (1977), show that there is considerable overlap between WAIS profiles associated with functional disorders and dementia.

More recently, interest has focused on a particular WAIS profile that has been hypothesised as being characteristic of Alzheimer-type dementia (Brinkman & Braun, 1984; Fuld, 1984). This profile, which was derived from Drachman's work on the effects of cholinergic "blockade" in healthy subjects (Drachman & Leavit, 1974; Drachman, 1977) consists of the following formula:

$$A \rangle B \rangle C \leqslant = D. A \rangle D$$

Where A = ((Information + Vocabulary) / 2)
      B = ((Similarities + Digit Span) / 2)
      C = ((Digit Symbol + Block Design) / 2)
      D = (Object Assembly)

Fuld (1984) found that approximately 50% of her Alzheimer-type dementia sample conformed to this pattern, whereas only 7% of a control group demonstrated the profile. Similarly, in a replication study by Brinkman and Braun (1984), 56% of the Alzheimer-type dementia patients had the profile, compared with less than 5% of a comparison of group of patients with multi-infarct dementia. Less encouragingly, Filley et al. (1987) report that only 29% of their Alzheimer-type dementia patients conformed to the pattern, compared to a rate of 2.4% in a healthy elderly control population. They also found that it occurred in 18% of patients who had been referred for the evaluation of dementia, but who on follow-up did not have Alzheimer's disease. In addition, Satz et al. (1987) reported that 12% of his sample of normal elderly people revealed this WAIS pattern.

Even if the most optimistic estimates of specificity are used to interpret WAIS profiles, a very high proportion of patients with dementia (of Alzheimer-type dementia in the case of the Fuld formula) will not conform to the predicted pattern. So for individual patients, the WAIS profiles should only be taken as *one* source of evidence concerning the presence of dementia but, as discussed earlier, they form only part of a wider array of assessments. Consequently, attempts to validate them in isolation, although useful, remain somewhat artificial. To a large extent, the profiles produced by test batteries such as the WAIS do not correspond to impairments in individual functions. Thus, further exploratory investigation is needed with a flexible use of testing procedures, to follow up impairments in different areas of function in, for example: memory, language and praxis.

MEMORY AND LEARNING

We shall use memory function to illustrate this more flexible approach to the assessment of specific cognitive functions, as memory is perhaps the most characteristic feature of dementia in the early stages. Yet the memory impairment associated with dementia is more complex than in the pure amnesias and theoretical studies are just beginning to map out the different areas of dysfunction (Morris, 1989; Morris, 1991; Morris & Kopelman, 1986). One complication is that the impairments in other aspects of information processing will impinge on and interact with amnestic deficits. For example, attention deficits which are evident in dementia will impair the ability to maintain material in immediate memory following distraction (Kopelman, 1985; Morris, 1986), and impairments in semantic processing will affect the encoding of material in longer-term memory (Corkin, 1982).

Clinical tests of memory tend not to reflect these complexities to any great extent, nor the boundaries between different types of memories as defined by recent developments in cognitive neuropsychology (see Mayes & Warburg, Chapter 5). Furthermore, the development of novel memory tests specifically for use in patients with dementia has been somewhat limited. Table 14.2 shows some of the tests of memory and learning used with dementia patients, selected because they meet the basic criteria that: (1) they have been standardised on an

TABLE 14.2
Clinical Tests of Memory and Learning used with Dementia Patients

Memory Test	Aspects of memory investigated
Anomalous Sentence Repetition Test (Weeks, 1988)	Immediate verbal recall of sentences
Auditory Verbal Learning Test (Rey, 1964)	Recall and recognition of verbal material
Benton Visual Retention Test (Benton, 1974)	Visual short-term memory for abstract line drawings
Fuld Object Memory Test (1980)	Immediate memory for objects using verbal recognition and recall with selective reminding
Kendrick Test Battery: Object Learning Test (Kendrick, 1985)	Immediate verbal recall of pictorial objects
New York University Memory (Randt, 1980)	Verbal memory span Verbal memory (immediate and delayed recall) Incidental memory Associative learning Picture recognition (immediate and delayed)
Paired Associate Learning Test (Inglis, 1959)	New verbal learning
Recognition Memory Test (Warrington, 1984)	Immediate word and face recognition
Rivermead Behavioural Memory Test (Wilson et al., 1985)	Includes ecologically valid tests
Selective Reminding Test (Bushke & Fuld, 1974)	Free recall of word lists with selective reminding between learning trials
Wechsler Memory Scale	
Wechsler (1945) (Psychological Corporation, 1988)	Rote memory Verbal memory span Immediate verbal and visual memory Associative learning
Russell's Revised Version (Russell, 1975; 1988)	Verbal and visual memory (immediate and delayed)

elderly population; (2) are relatively acceptable for the patients with at least mild dementia; and (3) are currently used by clinicians with dementia patients.

There are three main memory test batteries currently used with dementia patients, namely the Wechsler Memory Scale (WMS) (Wechsler, 1945; 1984); Russell's modification of this scale (Russell, 1975; 1988); and the New York University Memory Test (Randt et al., 1980). The WMS is heavily weighted towards the assessment of verbal memory and learning and is used to derive a Memory Quotient (MQ). This quotient can be compared with the patient's WAIS IQ score to derive an estimate of the relative extent of the memory deficit. Norms for the elderly are available (Cauthen, 1977; Hulicka, 1966) and it has been validated in patients with dementia (Kear-Colwell, 1973; Skilbeck & Woods, 1980). The modified version (Russell, 1975), which comprises immediate and delayed versions of the Logical Memory Test and Visual Reproduction subtests of the WMS has also been standardised on the elderly (Haaland et al, 1983) and is sensitive to impairment in patients with mild dementia (Brinkman et al., 1983; Logue & Wyrick, 1979). The New York University Memory Test (Osbourne et al., 1982; Randt et al., 1980) includes measurements of memory span, immediate and delayed verbal recall, incidental memory, pictorial recognition memory and associative learning. This test has been the least well-researched, although it does distinguish reasonably well between elderly people with progressive memory loss and controls (Osbourne et al., 1982).

In addition, two further memory batteries, the Rivermead Memory Test Battery (Wilson et al., 1985) and the Recognition Memory Test (Warrington, 1984). The "Rivermead" which now includes its norms for the elderly, includes tests that are more "ecologically" valid, such as having to remember to do a particular task when cued by a bell and recalling a route traced around a room. The Recognition Memory Test includes tests of forced-choice verbal and facial recognition memory. The patient is presented with a series of 50 either words or faces and then has to recognise these out of a series of distractor items. This test battery can prove quite demanding for dementia patients, partly because orientating instructions require patients to rate the items as "pleasant" or "unpleasant" within three seconds. Many dementia patients are unable to do this within the time limit and can find this part of the test aversive.

These tests serve to illustrate some of the issues concerning memory test development in this population. One problem, particularly pertinent in the case of the WMS is that test performance correlates with intellectual ability (Hulicka, 1966; Kear-Colwell, 1973). In relation to dementia, this would appear to complicate assessment of memory dysfunction, as it could be argued that performance on the WMS would be "contaminated" by intellectual decline. However, as Mayes (1986) has suggested, there is no accepted theoretical reason why memory functioning should be wholly independent of intelligence. This relates to the earlier observation that aspects of memory such as the encoding and retrieval of information are affected by the manner in which information is processed, which in turn relates to intellectual ability. Thus, a generalised deterioration in intellectual functioning is likely to affect memory functioning indirectly. The situation is complicated further by specific neuropsychological impairments that might affect memory abilities. For example, the naming impairment associated with Alzheimer-type dementia (Appell et al., 1982) is likely to affect a patient's ability on a memory test using objects with verbal recall.

For this reason, an overall score from a memory battery may not be particularly useful for assessing dementia, because it ignores the complexities of the mnemonic deficit. An alternative is to look at the components of the test and see how they relate to memory functioning. Kear-Colwell (1973) conducted a factor analysis on patients' performance on the WMS and reliably identified three factors, namely: immediate learning and recall; attention and concentration; and information and orientation. The factor structure held up in a subsequent analysis in elderly psychiatric patients by Skillbeck and Woods (1980), with the addition of a fourth factor termed "visual short-term memory". Joint factor analysis of the WAIS and WMS scores by Larabee et al. (1983) highlights why WMS performance correlates with intelligence; the attention/concentration factor overlaps with Digit span on the WAIS and the WMS Visual Reproduction test is highly loaded on the WAIS perceptual organisation factor. Larrabee et al. (1985) have also found that using Russell's (1975) delayed version of Logical Memory and Visual Reproduction weakens the correlation with the WAIS, possibly because it makes the memory scale assess purer measures of retention.

The remaining tests are individual tests of specific memory functions, developed mainly because they are thought to be sensitive to brain damage or dementia. The Anomalous Sentence Test (Weeks, 1988) involves the repetition of anomalous sentences and is thought to rely on primary or working memory (Kopelman, 1986b). Kopelman (1986b) found that performance on a test of this type could distinguish dementing patients from depressed patients and patients with other types of organic amnesia. This result is similar to that found by Weeks (1988) who was able to reliably distinguish between patients with dementia and depression, with the latter group showing no impairment. Weeks (1986) also found that the number of errors made by patients correlated with the degree of cortical atrophy on CT scan. In the visual domain, the Benton Visual Retention Test provides an alternative to the WMS visual reproduction test, standardised in elderly subjects (Crookes & McDonald, 1972).

The Fuld Object Memory Test (1980), the Object Learning Test (Kendrick, 1985) (discussed earlier), the Selective Reminding Test (Bushke & Fulde, 1974) and the Auditory Verbal Learning Test (Rey, 1964) all involve secondary memory, requiring verbal responses. The former requires the patient to identify objects hidden in a bag, which are subsequently shown. This has the advantage that there is a greater chance of the dementia patient attending to the material at the encoding stage. Recall of the objects is attempted after a filled delay and further learning trials follow using the selective reminding technique developed by Buschke and Fuld (1974). This test is also claimed to differentiate between dementia and depression, and is suitable for mildly impaired patients. The Selective Reminding Test (Buschke & Fuld, 1974) involves free recall of word lists with "selective reminding" of omitted or erroneous items between trials: this technique has been used with the elderly and in many drug studies. Similar in kind, the Auditory Verbal Learning Test (described by Lezak, 1983) requires free recall of auditorily presented words, with repetition of word lists over four trials to assess learning. An interference trial ensues with a different set of words, followed by a recall and recognition memory test for the first list. Again, this is suitable for mildly impaired dementia patients, and may prove too demanding for patients with moderate to severe dementia.

Various tests of associative learning have been developed, in which the patient has to achieve a criterion level of correct responding. Some versions of this test, involving the learning of unrelated word pairs, were particularly stressful for elderly patients. More acceptable versions using semantically related word pairs are available (Davies et al., 1977; Inglis, 1959; Little et al., 1987; Whitehead, 1973; 1977) and these discriminate reasonably well between patients with dementia and normal controls.

In addition, there are various tests of remote memory, which have been developed for research purposes (e.g. Kopelman, 1989; Kopelman et al., 1989; Sagar et al., 1988; Sanders & Warrington, 1971; Stevens, 1979; Wilson & Cochburn, 1988). Although retrograde amnesia is a particularly important component of the memory disorder in dementia, only one of these tests has been standardised in large populations (Stevens, 1979); and because the material in remote memory tests becomes outdated relatively rapidly, this test is in need of revision.

Certain aspects of semantic memory also need to be assessed, particularly as a naming and word-finding deficit occurs early in dementia (Huff et al., 1986; Kirschner et al, 1984). Various specialist tests have been developed for research purposes; but the most widely used test probably remains Verbal Fluency, which requires the retrieval of words to a letter or category cue. There is considerable information available concerning the performance of dementing patients on this test, including comparative data with the performance of other patient groups (e.g. Hart et al., 1988; Kopelman, 1989; Miller, 1984).

Finally, mention should be made of subjective memory assessment schedules (Bennett-Levy & Powell, 1980; Parkin et al., 1988; Squire & Zouzounis, 1988; Sunderland et al., 1983). The usual finding is that correlations between subjective ratings of memory and objective test performance tend to be low, but that relatives' ratings tend to correlate better with objective test performance than do the patients' own ratings (e.g. Sunderland et al., 1983). The Sunderland Scale was developed for use in head injury patients, but has now been used in an elderly sample (Sunderland et al., 1986). Squire and Zouzounis (1988) have reported different patterns of complaint about memory on a self-rating scale between depressives, depressed patients following ECT, Korsakoff patients, and other amnesic patients. They suggest that such a schedule may be helpful in the diagnosis of pseudodementia.

In summary, the tests described earlier either have been developed as general purpose memory test batteries or as specific tests, sensitive to dementia. The advantage of this approach is that the pragmatics of assessment, brevity and acceptability, have been addressed, but the limitation is that the psychological structure of memory has largely been ignored. Many of the tests cross the boundaries of different types of memory and do not facilitate a descriptive account of memory impairment. Future tests, which are suitable for the assessment of dementia and take into account recent advances in cognitive neuropsychology are needed in this context.

CONCLUSION

We have discussed the clinical assessment of patients with possible dementia, including E.E.G. and neuroradiological investigations, particular problems in conducting neuropsychological tests with elderly subjects, dementia rating scales, the assessment of premorbid and current intelligence, and particular approaches to the investigation of memory deficits. The principles involved in the assessment of language, perceptual impairments, constructional difficulties, and praxis remain essentially similar to those involved in the assessment of memory; using a flexible approach which allows for the particular test constraints of assessing elderly and dementing patients, the types of tests discussed in other chapters of this book can be adapted for use in dementia.

Although it has been increasingly recognised that no one aspect of an assessment can be viewed in isolation, and that "validation" studies which do so have their limitations, the systematic collection of clinical information (Roth et al., 1986), and the computerised evaluation of findings in the "mental state" (Copeland et al., 1986) have only just begun. Future investigations need to combine this type of information with that from the most discriminating neuropsychological tests, and to use biopsy or autopsy data (rather than concurrent clinical judgements) as validating criteria for diagnoses. By such means, we should be able to develop flow charts and computerised algorithms in an attempt to improve further our diagnostic predictions.

REFERENCES

American Psychiatric Association. (1987). *Diagnostic and statistical manual of mental disorders* (3rd ed.). Washington DC: Author.

Appell, J., Kertesz, A., & Fishman, M.A. (1982). A study of language functioning in Alzheimer's disease. *Brain & Language, 17*, 73-91.

Becker, J.T., Hugg, J., Nebes, R.D., Holland, A., & Boller, F. (1988). Neuropsychological function in Alzheimer's disease: Pattern of impairment and rates of progression. *Archives of Neurology, 45*, 263-268.

Bennett-Levy, J., & Powell, G.E. (1980). The subjective memory questionnaire (SMQ). *British Journal of Social and Clinical Psychology, 146*, 31-35.

Benton, A.L. (1974). *The revised Benton Visual Retention Test* (4th ed.) New York: Psychological Corporation.

Besson, J.A.O., Crawford, J.R., Parker, D.M., Ebmeier, K.P., Best, P.V., Gemmell, H.G., Sharp, P.F., & Smith, F.W. (1990). Multimodal imaging in Alzheimer's disease: The relationship between MRI, SPECT, cognitive and pathological changes. *British Journal of Psychiatry, 157*, 216-220.

Blessed, G., Tomlinson, B.E., & Roth, M. (1968). The association between quantitative measures of dementia and of senile change in the cerebral grey matter of elderly subjects. *British Journal of Psychiatry, 114*, 497-811.

Breitner, J.C.S., & Folstein, M.F. (1984). Familial Alzheimer Dementia: A prevalent disorder with specific clinical features. *Psychological Medicine, 14*, 63-80.

Brinkman, S.D., & Braun, P. (1984). Classification of dementia patients by a WAIS profile related to central cholinergic deficiencies. *Journal of Clinical Neuropsychology, 6*, 393-400.

Brinkman, S.D., Largen, J.W., Gerganoff, S., & Pomara, N. (1983). Russell's revised Wechsler Memory Scale in the evaluation of dementia. *Journal of Clinical Psychology, 39*, 989-993.

Buschke, H., & Fuld, P.A. (1974). Evaluating storage, retention and retrieval in disordered memory and learning. *Neurology, 11*, 1019-1025.

Cauthen, N.R. (1977). Extension of the Wechsler Memory Scale Norms to older age groups. *Journal of Clinical Psychology, 33*, 208-211.

Chaiofalo, N., Fuentes, A., & Falvev, S. (1980). Serial E.E.G. findings in 27 cases of Creutzfeldt-Jakob disease. *Archives of Neurology, 37*, 143-145.

Comfort, A. (1978). Non-threatening mental testing of the elderly. *Journal of the American Geriatrics Society, 26*, 261-262.

Cooper, B., & Bickel, H. (1984). Population screening and the early detection of dementing disorders in old age: A review. *Psychological Medicine, 14*, 81-95.

Copeland, J.R.M., Dewey, M.E., & Griffith-Jones, H.M. (1986). A computerised diagnostic system and case nomenclature for elderly subjects: GMS and AGECAT. *Psychological Medicine, 16*, 89-99.

Corkin, S. (1982). Some relationships between global amnesias and the memory impairments in Alzheimer's disease. In S. Corkin, K.L. Davis, J.H. Growden, E. Usdin, & R.J. Wurtman (Eds.), *Alzheimer's disease: A report of research in progress*. New York: Raven Press.

Crawford, J.R. (1989). Estimation of premorbid intelligence: A review of recent developments. In J.R. Crawford & D.M. Parker (Eds.), *Developments in clinical and experimental neuropsychology* (pp. 55-74). New York: Plenum Press.

Crawford, J.R., Besson, J.A.O., & Parker, D.M., (1988). Estimation of premorbid intelligence in organic conditions. *British Journal of Psychiatry, 153*, 178-181.

Crookes, T.G., & McDonald, K.G. (1972). Benton's Visual Retention Test in the differentiation of depression and early dementia. *British Journal of Social and Clinical Psychology, 11*, 66-69.

Davies, A.D., Spelman, M.S., & Davies, M.G. (1981). Combining psychometric data on brain damage and the influence of aging. *Perceptual and Motor Skills, 52*, 583-592.

Davies, G., Hamilton, S., Hendrickson, D.E., Levy, R., & Post, F. (1977). The effect of cyclandelate in depressed and demented patients: A controlled study in psychogeriatric patients. *Age and Ageing, 6*, 156-162.

DeLeon, M.J., Ferris, J.H., & George, A.E., et al. (1983). Computed tomography and positron emission transaxial tomography evaluations of normal aging and Alzheimer's disease. *Journal of Cerebral Blood Flow Metabolism, 3*, 391-394.

Drachman, D.A., & Leavitt, J. (1974). Human memory and the cholinergic system. *Archives of Neurology, 30*, 113-121.

Drachman, D.A. (1977). Memory and cognitive function in man: Does the cholinergic system have a specific role? *Neurology, 27*, 783-790.

Eslinger, P.J., Damasio, H., Graff-Radford, N., & Damasio, A. (1984). Examining the relationship between computed tomography and neuropsychological measures in normal and demented elderly. *Journal of Neurology, Neurosurgery and Psychiatry, 47*, 1319-1325.

Eysenck, H.J., & Halstead, H. (1945). The memory function: A factorial study of fifteen clinical tests. *American Journal of Psychiatry, 102*, 174-180.

Fillenbaum, G.G., Heyman, A., Wilkinson, W.E., & Haynes, C.S. (1987). Comparison of two screening tests in Alzheimer's Disease. *Archives of Neurology, 44*, 924-927.

Filley, C.M., Kelly, J., & Heaton, R.K. (1986). Neuropsychological features of early- and late-onset Alzheimer's disease. *Archives of Neurology, 40*, 143-146.

Filley, C.M., Kobayashi, J., & Heaton, R.K. (1987). Wechsler Intelligence Scale Profiles, the cholinergic system and Alzheimer's disease. *Journal of Clinical and Experimental Neuropsychology, 9*, 180-186.

Folstein, M.F., Folstein, S.E., & McHugh, P.R. (1975). Mini-mental state: A practical method for grading the cognitive state of patient for clinician. *Journal of Psychiatry Research, 12*, 189-198.

Folstein, M.F., & Breitner, J.C.S. (1981). Language disorder predicts familial Alzheimer's disease. *John Hopkins Medical Journal, 149*, 145-147.

Frackowiak, R.S.J., Pozzilli, C., Legg, N.J., du Boulay, G.H., Marshall, J., Lenzi, G.L., & Jones, T. (1981). Regional cerebral oxygen supply and utilization in dementia: A clinical and physiological study with oxygen 15 and positron tomography. *Brain, 104*, 753-778.

Fuld, P.A. (1984). Test profile of cholinergic dysfunction and Alzheimer-type dementia. *Journal of Clinical Neuropsychology, 6*, 380-392.

Fuld, P.A. (1980). *Object Memory Evaluation Test.* Windsor: NFER-Nelson.

Garcia, C.A., Reding, M.J., & Blass, J.P. (1981). Overdiagnosis of dementia. *Journal of the American Geriatric Society, 29*, 407-410.

Grimes, A.M., Grady, C.L., Foster, N.L., Sunderland, T., & Patronas, N.J. (1985). Central auditory function in Alzheimer's disease. *Neurology, 35*, 352-358.

Haaland, K.Y., Linn, R.T., Hunt, W.C., & Goodwin, J.S. (1983). A normative study of Russell's variant of the Wechsler Memory Scale. *Journal of Clinical Neuropsychology, 51*, 878-881.

Hamer, A.C., Honavar, M., Lantos, P.L., Hastie, I.R., Kellett, J.R., & Millard, P.H. (1988). Diagnosing dementia: Do we get it right? *British Medical Journal, 297*, 894-896.

Hart, S., Smith, C.M., & Swash, M. (1986). Assessing intellectual deterioration. *British Journal of Clinical Psychology, 25*, 119-124.

Hart, S., Smith, C.M., & Swash, M. (1988). Word fluency in patients with early dementia of the Alzheimer's type. *British Journal of Clinical Psychology, 27*, 115-124.

Heaton, S.R., & Heaton, R.K. (1981). Testing the impaired patient. In S.B. Filskov & T.J. Boll (Eds.), *Handbook of clinical neuropsychology.* New York: Wiley-Interscience.

Holden, U.P., & Woods, R.T. (1982). *Reality orientation: Psychological approaches to the confused elderly.* New York: Churchill-Livingstone.

Huff, F.J., Corkin, S., & Growdon, J.H. (1986). Semantic impairment and anomia in Alzheimer's disease. *Brain & Language, 28*, 235-244.

Hughes, C.P., Berg, L., Danziger, W.L., Coben, L.A., & Martin, R.L. (1982). A new clinical scale for the staging of dementia. *British Journal of Psychiatry, 140*, 566-572.

Hulicka, I.M. (1966). Age differences in Wechsler Memory Scale scores. *Journal of Genetic Psychology, 109*, 135-145.

Jacoby, R.J., & Levy, R. (1980). Computed tomography in the elderly: 2. Senile dementia. *British Journal of Psychiatry, 136*, 256-259.

Johnson, M.K., Kim, J.K., & Risse, G. (1985). Do alcoholic Korsakoff's syndrome patients acquire affective reactions? *Journal of Experimental Psychology: Learning, Memory & Cognition, 11*, 23-36.

Johnson, K.A., Mueller, S.T., Walshe, T.M., English, R.J., & Holman, B.L. (1987). Cerebral perfusion imaging in Alzheimer's disease. *Archives of Neurology, 44*, 165-168.

Jorm, A.F. (1985). Subtypes of Alzheimer's disease: A conceptual analysis and critical review. *Psychological Medicine, 15*, 543-553.

Kaszniak, A.W., Garron, D.C., Fox, J.H., Bergen, D., & Huckman, M. (1979). Cerebral atrophy, EEG slowing, age, education, and cognitive functioning in suspected dementia. *Neurology, 29*, 1273-1279.

Kear-Colwell, J.J. (1973). The structure of the Wechsler Memory Scale and its relationship to "brain damage". *British Journal of Social and Clinical Psychology, 12*, 384-392.

Kendrick, D.C. (1964). The assessment of premorbid level of intelligence in elderly patients suffering from diffuse brain pathology. *Psychological Reports, 15*, 188.

Kendrick, D.C. (1965). Speed and learning in the diagnosis of diffuse brain damage in elderly subjects: A Bayesian Statistical approach. *British Journal of Social and Clinical Psychology, 4*, 141-148.

Kendrick, D.C. (1985). *Kendrick cognitive tests for the elderly.* Windsor: NFER-Nelson.

Kendrick, D.C., Gibson, A.J., & Moyes, C.A. (1979). The Revised Kendrick Battery: Clinical studies. *British Journal of Social and Clinical Psychology, 18*, 329-340.

Kendrick, D.C. and Post, F. (1967). Differences in cognitive status between healthy, psychiatrically ill and diffusely brain-damaged elderly patients. **British Journal of Psychiatry, 113, 424-433.**

Khatchachurian, Z.S. (1985). Diagnosis of Alzheimer's disease. *Archives of Neurology, 42*, 1097-1105.

Kirschner, H.S., Webb, W.G., & Kelly, M.P. (1984). The naming disorder in dementia. *Neuropsychologia, 22*, 23-30.

Kopelman, M.D. (1985). Rates of forgetting in Alzheimer-type dementia and Korsakoff's syndrome. *Neuropsychologia, 23*, 623-638.

Kopelman, M.D. (1986a). Clinical tests of memory. *British Journal of Psychiatry, 148*, 517-525.

Kopelman, M.D. (1986b). Recall of anomalous sentences in dementia and amnesia. *Brain and Language, 29*, 154-170.

Kopelman, M.D. (1989). Remote and autobiographical memory, temporal context memory, and frontal atrophy in Korsakoff and Alzheimer patients. *Neuropsychologia, 27*, 437-460.

Kopelman, M.D., Wilson, B.A., & Baddeley, A.D. (1989). The Autobiographical Memory Interview: A new assessment of autobiographical and personal semantic memory in amnesic patients. *Journal of Clinical and Experimental Neuropsychology, 11*, 724-744

Knopman, D.S., & Nissen, M.J. (1987). Implicit learning in patients with probable Alzheimer's disease. *Neurology, 37*, 784-788.

Larabee, G.J., Kane, R.L., & Schuck, J.R. (1983). Factor analysis of the WAIS and Wechsler Memory Scale: An analysis of the construct validity of the Wechsler Memory Scale. *Journal of Clinical Neuropsychology, 5*, 159-168.

Larabee, G.J., Kane, R.L., Schuick, J.R., & Francis, D.J. (1985). Construct validity of various memory testing procedures. *Journal of Clinical and Experimental Neuropsychology, 8*, 275-284.

Letemendia, F., & Pampiglione, G. (1958). Clinical and electroencephalographic observations in Alzheimer's disease. *Journal of Neurology, Neurosurgery & Psychiatry, 21*, 167-176.

Lezak, M.D. (1983). *Neuropsychological assessment* (2nd ed.). New York: Oxford University Press.

Lishman, W.A. (1987). *Organic psychiatry: The psychological consequences of cerebral disorder.* (2nd ed.). Oxford: Blackwell Scientific Publications.

Little, A., Hemsley, D., & Volans, J. (1987). Comparison of current levels of performance and scores based on change as diagnostic discriminators among the elderly. *British Journal of Clinical Psychology, 26,* 135-140.

Logue, P., & Wyrick, L. (1979). Initial validation of Russell's Revised Wechsler Memory Scale: A comparison of normal aging versus dementia. *Journal of Consulting and Clinical Psychology, 47,* 176-178.

Luxenberg, J.S., Haxby, J.V., Creasy, H., Sundarah, M., & Rapaport, S.I. (1987). Rate of ventricular enlargement in dementia of the Alzheimer-tye correlates with rate of neuropsychological deterioration. *Neurology, 37,* 1135-1140.

Mahendra, B. (1985). Depression and dementia: The multi-faceted relationship. *Psychological Medicine, 15,* 227-236.

Mayes, A.R. (1986). Learning and memory disorders and their assessment. *Neuropsychologia, 24,* 25-39.

McKenna, P., & Warrington, E.K. (1986). The analytic approach to neuropsychological assessment. In I. Grant & K.M. Adams (Eds.), *Neuropsychological assessment of neuropsychiatric disorders,* Oxford: Oxford University Press.

McKhann, G., Druckman, D., Folstein, M., Katzman, R., Price, D., & Studlan, M. (1984). Clinical diagnosis of Alzheimer's disease: Reports of the NINCDS-ADRA work group under auspices of Department of Health and Human Services task force on Alzheimer's disease. *Neurology, 34,* 939-949.

McPherson, F.M., Gamsu, C.V., Kiemle, G., Ritchie, S.M., Stanley, A.M., & Tregaskis, D. (1985). The concurrent validity of the survey version of the Clifton Assessment Procedures for the Elderly (CAPE). *British Journal of Clinical Psychology, 24,* 83-91.

McPherson, F.M., Gamsu, C.V., Cockram, L.L., & Gormley, A.J. (1986). Inter-scorer agreement in scoring errors on the Pm (Maze) test of the CAPE. *British Journal of Clinical Psychology, 25,* 225-226.

McPhie, J. (1975). *Assessment of organic intellectual impairment.* London: Academic Press.

Miller, E. (1977). *Abnormal ageing.* Chichester: Wiley.

Miller, E. (1980). Cognitive assessment of the older adult. In J.E. Birren & R.B. Sloane (Eds.), *Handbook of mental health and ageing.* Englewood Cliffs, NJ: Prentice Hall Inc.

Miller, E. (1984). Verbal fluency as a function of a measure of verbal intelligence and in relation to different types of cerebral pathology. *British Journal of Clinical Psychology, 23,* 53-57.

Morris, R.G. (1986). Short-term forgetting in senile dementia of the Alzheimer's type. *Cognitive Neuropsychology, 3,* 77-97.

Morris, R.G. (1987a). Identity matching and oddity learning in patients with moderate to severe Alzheimer-type dementia. *The Quarterly Journal of Experimental Psychology, 39B,* 215-227.

Morris, R.G. (1987b). Articulatory rehearsal in Alzheimer-type dementia. *Brain and Language, 30,* 251-362.

Morris, R.G. (1989). Neuropsychological aspects of dementia. *Current Opinions in Psychiatry, 2,* 66-71.

Morris, R.G. (1991). Neuropsychological studies of memory functioning in Alzheimer-type dementia. In J. Weinmann & J. Hunter (Eds.), *Memory: Neurochemical and Abnormal Perspectives.* London: Harwood Academic.

Morris, R.G., & Kopelman, M.D. (1986). The memory deficits in Alzheimer-type dementia: A review. *Quarterly Journal of Experimental Psychology, 38,* 575-602.

Morris, R.G., Evenden, J.L., Sahakian, B.J., & Robbins, T.W. (1987). Computer-aided assessment of dementia: Comparative studies of Alzheimer-type dementia and Parkinson's disease. In S.M.

Stahl, S.D. Iversen, & E.C. Goodman, (Eds.), *Cognitive Neurochemistry*. Oxford: Oxford University Press.

Morris, J.C., & Fulling, K. (1988). Early Alzheimer's disease: Diagnostic considerations. *Archives of Neurology, 45*, 345-349.

Muller, H.F., & Schwartz, G. (1978). Electro encephalograms and autopsy findings in geropsychiatry. *Journal of Gerontology, 33*, 504-513.

Neary, D., Snowden, J.S., Bowen, D.M., Sims, N.R., Mann, D.M.A., Benton, J.S., Northen, B., Yates, P.D., & Davison, A.N. (1986). Neuropsychiatric syndromes in presensile dementia due to cerebral atrophy. *Journal of Neurology, Neurosurgery & Psychiatry, 49*, 163-179.

Naguib, M., & Levy, R. (1982). CT scanning in senile dementia: A follow-up of survivors. *British Journal of Psychiatry, 141*, 618-620.

Nebes, R.D., Martin, D.C., & Horn, L.C. (1984). Sparing of semantic memory in Alzheimer's disease. *Journal of Abnormal Psychology, 93*, 321-330.

Nelson, H.E. (1982). *National Adult Reading Test. (NART): Test Manual.*Windsor: NFER-Nelson.

Nelson, H.E., & O'Connell, A. (1978). Dementia: The estimation of premorbid intelligence levels using the New Adult Reading Test. *Cortex, 14*, 234-244.

O'Carroll, R.E., Baikie, E.M., & Whittick, J.E. (1987). Does the National Adult Reading Test hold in dementia? *British Journal of Clinical Psychology, 26*, 315-316.

O'Neill, P.M., & Calhoun, K.S. (1975). Sensory deficits and behavioural deterioration in senescence. *Journal of Abnormal Psychology, 84*, 579-582.

Osbourne, D.P., Brown, E.R., & Randt, C.T. (1982). Qualitative changes in memory function: Aging and dementia. In S. Corkin, K.L. Davis, J.H. Growden, E. Usdin, & R.J. Wurtman (Eds.), *Alzheimer's disease: A report in progress*. New York: Ravens Press.

Parkin, A.J., Bell, W.P., & Leng, N.R.C. (1988). A study of metamemory in amnesic and normal adults. *Cortex, 4*, 143-148.

Pattie, A.H. (1981). A survey version of the Clifton Assessment Procedures for the Elderly (CAPE). *British Journal of Clinical Psychology, 20*, 173-178.

Pattie, A.H., & Gilleard, C.J. (1979). *Manual for the Clifton Assessment Procedures for the Elderly. (CAPE)*. Sevenoaks: Hodder and Stoughton Educational.

Rae-Grant, A., Blume, W., Lau, C., Hachinski, V.C., Fisman, M., & Merskey. (1987). The electroencephalogram in Alzheimer-type dementia. *Archives of Neurology, 44*, 50-54.

Randt, C.T., Brown, E.R., & Osbourne, D.P. (1980). A memory test for longitudinal measurement of mild to moderate deficits. *Clinical Neuropsychology, 2*, 184-194.

Raven, J.C., Court, J.H., & Raven, J. (1977). *Manual for the Coloured Progressive Matrices*. London: H.K. Lewis.

Reitan, R.M. (1986). Theoretical and methodological bases of Halstead-Reitan Test Battery. In I. Grant & K.M. Adams (Eds.). *Neuropsychological Assessment of Neuropsychiatric Disorders*. Oxford: Oxford University Press.

Rey, A. (1964). *L'examen clinique en psychologie*. Paris: Presses Universaires de France.

Rogers, R.L., Meyer, J.S., Mortel, K.F., Mahurin, R.K., & Judd, B.W. (1986). Decreased cerebral blood flow precedes multi-infarct dementia, but follows senile dementia of Alzheimer type. *Neurology, 36*, 1-6.

Russell, W.R. (1975). A multiple scoring method for the assessment of complex memory functions. *Journal of Consulting and Clinical Psychology, 43*, 800-809.

Russell, W.R. (1988). Renorming Russell's version of the Wechsler Memory Scale. *Journal of Clinical and Experimental Neuropsychology, 10*, 235-249.

Ron, M.A., Toone, B.K., Garralda, M.E., & Lishman, W.A. (1979). Diagnostic accuracy in presenile dementia. *British Journal of Psychiatry, 134*, 161-168.

Roth, M., Tym, E., Mountjoy, C.Q., Huppert, F.A., Hendrie, H., Verma, S., & Goddard, R. (1986). A standardised instrument for the diagnosis of mental disorder in the elderly with special reference to the early detection of dementia. *British Journal of Psychiatry, 149*, 698-709.

Sagar, H., Cohen, N.J., Sullivan, E.V., Corkin, S., & Growdon, J.H. (1988). Remote memory function in Alzheimer's disease and Parkinson's disease. *Brain, 111,* 185-205.

Sahakian, B.J., Morris, R.G., Evenden, J.L., Heald, A., Levy, R., Philpot, M., & Robbins, T.W.R. (1988). A comparative study of visuo-spatial memory and learning in Alzheimer-type dementia and Parkinson's disease. *Brain, 111,* 695-718.

Sanders, H., & Warrington, E.K. (1971). Memory for remote events in amnesic patients. *Brain, 94,* 661-668.

Satz, P., Van Gorp, W.G., Soper, H.V., & Mitrushina, M. (1987). WAIS-R marker for dementia of the Alzheimer's type? An empirical and statistical induction test. *Journal of Clinical and Experimental Neuropsychology, 9,* 767-774.

Savage, R.D., Britton, P.G., Bolton, N., & Hall, E.H. (1973). *Intellectual functioning in the aged.* London: Methuen.

Schlotterer, G., Moscovitch, M., & Crapper-McLachlan, D. (1983). Visual processing deficits as assessed by spatial frequency contrast sensitivity and backward masking in normal aging and Alzheimer's disease. *Brain, 107,* 309-325.

Seltzer, B., & Sherwin, I. (1983). A comparison of clinical features of early- and late-onset primary degenerative dementia. *Archives of Neurology, 40,* 143-146.

Skillbeck, C., & Woods, R.T. (1980). The factorial structure of the Wechsler Memory Scale: Samples of neurological and psychogeriatric patients. *Journal of Clinical Neuropsychology, 2,* 293-300.

Squire, L.R., & Zouzounis, J.A. (1988). Self ratings of memory dysfunction. *Journal of Clinical & Experimental Psychology, 101,* 727-738.

Stevens, M. (1979). Famous personalities' test: A test for measuring remote memory. *Bulletin of the British Psychological Society, 32,* 211.

Sulkava, R., Haltia, M., Paetan, A., Wikstrom, J., & Palo, J. (1983). Accuracy of clinical diagnosis in primary degenerative dementia: Correlation with neuropathological findings. *Journal of Neurology, Neurosurgery & Psychiatry, 46,* 497-506.

Sunderland, A., Harris, J.E., & Baddeley, A.D. (1983). Do laboratory tests predict everyday memory? *Journal of Verbal Learning and Verbal Behavior, 22,* 341-357.

Sunderland, A., Watts, K., Baddeley, A.D., & Harris, J.E. (1986). Subjective memory assessment and test performance in elderly adults. *Journal of Gerontology, 41,* 376-384.

Terry, R.D., & Katzman, R. (1983). Senile dementia of the Alzheimer-type. *Annals of Neurology, 14,* 497-506.

Thal, L.J., Grundman, M., & Golden, R. (1986). Alzheimer's disease: A correlational analysis of the Blessed Information-Memory-Concentration Test and the Mini-Mental State Exam. *Neurology, 36,* 262-264.

Wade, J.P.H., Mirsen, T.R., Hachinski, V.C., Fisman, M., Lau, C., & Merskey, H. (1987). The clinical diagnosis of Alzheimer's disease. *Archives of Neurology, 44,* 24-29.

Warrington, E.K. (1984). *The Recognition Memory Test.* Windsor: NFER-Nelson.

Wechsler, D. (1945). A standardised memory scale for clinical use. *The Journal of Psychology, 19,* 97-95.

Wechsler, D. (1958). *The measurement and appraisal of adult intelligence.* Baltimore: Williams & Williams.

Wechsler, D. (1981). *WAIS-R Manual.* New York: Psychological Corporation.

Wechsler, D. (1984). *The Wechsler Memory Scale − Revised.* New York: Psychological Corporation.

Weeks, D. (1986). The Anomalous Sentences Repetition Test: Replication and validation study. *Journal of Clinical Psychology, 42,* 635-638.

Weeks, D. (1988). *The Anomalous Sentences Repetition Test.* Windsor: NFER-Nelson.

Whitehead, A. (1973). The pattern of WAIS performance in elderly psychiatric patients. *British Journal of Psychiatry, 12,* 435-436.

Whitehead, A. (1977). The clinical psychologist's role in assessment and management. In A.D. Isaacs & F. Post (Eds.), *Studies in geriatric psychiatry.* Chichester: Wiley.

Wilson, B., & Cockburn, J. (1988). The Prices' test: A simple test of retrograde amnesia. In M.M. Gruneberg, P.E. Morris, & R.N. Sykes (Eds.), *Practical aspects of memory: Current research and issues, 2,* Chichester: Wiley.

Wilson, B.A., Cockburn, J., & Baddeley, A.D.B. (1985). *The Rivermead behavioural memory test manual.* Reading: Thames Valley Test Company.

Woods, R.T., & Britton, P.G. (1985). *Clinical psychology with the elderly.* London: Croom Helm.

15

Neuropsychological Assessment in Alcohol, Drug Abuse and Toxic Conditions

J.T.L. Wilson and K.D. Wiedmann
Department of Psychology, University of Stirling, Stirling FK9 4LA

This chapter is concerned with neuropsychological assessment of patients exposed to agents which have, or may have, harmful effects on the nervous system. Exposure may arise in a number of ways: by intentional abuse of a substance, through prolonged use under medical supervision, by accidental exposure to a toxin, by occupational exposure, etc. Although toxic conditions are usually treated as a coherent group in neurological texts, the manner of exposure is of importance when considering the psychological effects of these agents. In general, intentional substance abusers form a large and distinctive category of patients: there is often a history of psychiatric problems, poor nutrition and poor health care. The focus in the present chapter is on the cognitive and behavioural changes which can be attributed to the effects of toxic agents, and the neuropsychological measures appropriate for assessing people who have been exposed.

ALCOHOLISM

Neuropsychological assessment of patients with a history of alcoholism is typically carried out to determine whether there is evidence of organic changes. Such evidence is important in determining prognosis, in counselling patients, and in designing appropriate treatment programmes. Patients with a long-term history of substance abuse invariably have considerable psychiatric problems: for example, anxiety and depression are almost universal features of alcoholic patients. Psychiatric difficulties are given precedence in most treatment regimes, and neuropsychological aspects tend, therefore, to be accorded secondary importance. Although these relative priorities are generally appropriate, it is to be regretted that neuropsychological assessment is sometimes omitted completely from treatment programmes for these patients. Patients may be enrolled in a programme which they are cognitively incapable of following. Neuropsychological assessment can screen for these patients and allow resources to be more effectively directed.

Withdrawal of alcohol is usually followed by a period of obvious disturbance of physical and psychological functions. Symptoms of withdrawal include: sweating, nausea, anxiety, craving for alcohol, tremor, confusion, and hallucinations (Gross, Lewis & Hastey, 1974). The last three of these symptoms are the classic indications of delirium tremens. Contrary to popular opinion delirium tremens is not common among alcoholics, only developing in around 5% of hospitalised cases. During withdrawal, symptoms fluctuate in intensity, rather than increasing and subsiding smoothly. In most patients the acute phase is over in two days or so, and only in severe cases will withdrawal symptoms last for seven days or more. It is clearly inappropriate to attempt neuropsychological examination while physical signs of withdrawal are present. Accurate assessment of neuropsychological status is not in fact possible until several weeks of abstinence.

The physical symptoms of withdrawal usually subside quite quickly but transient impairments of intellectual and memory functions remain for the first few weeks after cessation of drinking. There is clear evidence of short-term recovery of psychological functions after withdrawal. Goldman (1983), reviewing the literature on recovery, notes that while abilities on verbal measures of vocabulary are generally unimpaired in alcoholics, new verbal learning remains impaired for the first week or two of abstinence and then, in non-deteriorated alcoholics, often recovers. The subclinical effects of withdrawal thus persist for several weeks, and it is important that treatment programmes should not place too great intellectual demands on the alcoholic during this period.

After the initial period of rapid recovery many alcoholics are left with residual deficits. The severity of these deficits can vary from impairment of an isolated cognitive function to global impairment of intellect and memory. Horvarth (1975) reported that of 1100 patients seen at an Australian centre for the treatment of alcoholism, 100 had chronic organic syndromes indicated by progressive impairment of memory, intellectual deficits and personality deterioration. Thus, patients with severe persisting impairment form less than 10% of the alcoholic population. Of the remaining patients perhaps half will show deficits in particular areas of intellectual functioning which do not recover despite prolonged abstinence. While the neuropsychological deficits in deteriorated alcoholics are relatively obvious, persisting impairment in non-deteriorated patients is usually only revealed by formal neuropsychological testing.

General Intellectual Abilities in Alcoholics

The most commonly used clinical measures are the Wechsler Adult Intelligence Scale (WAIS) and, in the U.S., the Halstead-Reitan Neuropsychological Battery (HRNB). There is now a considerable body of literature on the performance of non-deteriorated alcoholics on these measures, spanning patients from a variety of different countries and cultural backgrounds. A review of transcultural findings indicates a consistent pattern of sparing and deficit on performance of particular tasks (Loberg & Miller, 1986).

Parsons and Farr (1981) reviewed the results of fifteen studies using the HRNB and eight studies which had used the WAIS. These studies showed that alcoholics are typically impaired on the Performance measures of the WAIS and much less often on the Verbal measures. The subtests on which performance is most often impaired are Digit Symbol, Block Design, Picture Arrangement and Object Assembly, while performance is usually in the normal range on Vocabulary, Digit Span and Similarities. On the Halstead-Reitan battery alcoholics perform most poorly on the Category Test, Tactual Performance Test Time, and Part B of the Trail-making Test.

A study by Long and McLachlan (1974) provides a good example of the pattern of impairment found in alcoholics. Long and McLachlan (1974) tested 22 detoxified alcoholics and 22 controls matched for age, education, and verbal IQ on both Wechsler-Bellevue and Halstead-Reitan batteries. Alcoholics performed significantly more poorly than controls on Object Assembly, Digit Symbol, Block Design, Tactual Performance Test, Tapping with left and right hands, and Trail-making Parts A and B. However, in general the size of the differences between alcoholics and controls was not great. Thus, although there were reliable differences between the groups, there was also a considerable overlap in the scores obtained by alcoholics and controls. This finding is typical of studies of alcoholics. Long and McLachlan (1974) followed up 17 of the alcoholics after one year of abstinence and found evidence of improvement. Comparison with initial testing showed improvement on Block Design, Digit Symbol, Category Test, Tactual Performance Test, and Tapping with left and right hands. A weakness is that Long and McLachlan (1974) did not control for practice effects, but the study illustrates the potential reversibility of alcoholic deficits (since confirmed by other investigators).

In summary, although group studies indicate reliable differences on WAIS and Halstead-Reitan subtests, by no means all alcoholics are impaired on these measures. There are great individual differences in the alcoholic population, and considerable overlap between alcoholics and controls. There is overwhelming evidence that sober alcoholics show neuropsychological impairment, but the degree of impairment is in general quite small, and less than for most brain-damaged patient populations.

Memory Impairment in Alcoholics

There is evidence that alcoholics may show impairment of visual and verbal memory. Deficits are most clearly demonstrated on specifically devised, demanding tests of memory (Bowden, 1988; Ryan & Butters, 1980). The task devised by Ryan and Butters (1980) involved learning 10 pairs of unrelated nouns which were presented to the patient at a rate of one pair every two seconds. The subject was tested by giving them the first word in each pair as a retrieval cue. The presentation-test procedure was repeated four times yielding a total score out of 40. Alcoholics are also consistently impaired on recall of the Rey-Osterrieth figure. Miglioli et al. (1979) found that the performance of alcoholics remained impaired on this test two months after cessation of drinking.

Memory impairment is often poorly demonstrated by conventional tests such as the Wechsler Memory Scale (WMS) (Parsons & Prigatano, 1977). The memory quotient from the WMS reflects overall performance on subtests involving distinct aspects of memory. However, abilities such as memory span and memory for old over-learned material are typically unaffected by mild or moderate brain damage of the kind encountered in alcoholics. Nixon et al. (1987) compared 60 alcoholics and 60 controls, matched for age, education and score on a vocabulary test, and found that alcoholics were impaired on both immediate and delayed recall on the Logical Memory and Visual Reproduction subtests. This study thus indicates that selected WMS subtests emphasizing acquisition of new information are sensitive to alcoholic impairment.

Impairments of memory and learning are of particular clinical relevance because they may directly affect the efficacy of treatment programmes. An issue which is raised by memory deficits is whether there is a continuum of impairment in alcoholics. The presence of such deficits in non-Korsakoff alcoholics suggests that there may be a continuum of memory impairment due to alcohol (Ryback, 1971). An implication of this view is that there will be patients in a borderline region who are not Korsakoff alcoholics but who nonetheless have clinically significant memory problems. There is controversy concerning the continuity hypothesis (Butters & Granholm, 1987); however, even if the hypothesis proves misguided, there is clearly a case for formal memory testing to identify alcoholics with learning impairment.

Other Approaches to Assessing Alcoholics

It is clear from the literature on alcoholic deficits that experimental measures are often more revealing than traditional tests, however, such procedures are not well-integrated with clinical assessment. A possible way in which this might be achieved is by implementing experimental procedures as part of a computer-based battery. Acker, Acker, and Shaw (1984) describe a series of computer-based tests designed to facilitate automated assessment of alcoholics. The tests implemented were Little Men (mental rotation), Symbol Digit Coding, Visuo-perceptual analysis, Verbal memory, Spatial memory, and the Bexley/Maudsley Category Test. A potential advantage of such a system is that it could allow screening of large numbers of alcoholics for intellectual and memory deficits. Another approach to computer-based assessment is described by Wilson et al. (1988), who used a series of procedures designed to assess various aspects of visual processing in alcoholics. They found a persisting deficit in a task involving visual detection of rapid changes. It is to be hoped that further work in this area will allow neuropsychological assessment of alcoholics to routinely extend beyond the commonly used measures such as the WAIS, WMS and HRNB.

Models of Alcoholic Deficits

The typical pattern of test results is often interpreted as evidence that alcoholics have impaired abstracting ability (Category Test); visuo-spatial abilities (Block Design, Picture Arrangement and Object Assembly); and psychomotor co-ordination (Digit Symbol). However, caution must be exercised with regard to the interpretation of results from individual subtests of these psychological batteries. Such tests often involve a range of abilities, and it is problematic to infer a specific cognitive deficit. For example, the Performance measures of the WAIS are all timed tests. In addition they involve visuo-spatial problem-solving, and are novel. Therefore it is not clear which aspects of the tests gives rise to impaired performance in alcoholics. A further complicating factor is that alcoholics can suffer from peripheral neuropathy and this may also interfere with their ability to perform tasks under time pressure. Controversy also surrounds the most appropriate neuropsychological model for alcoholic deficits. Premature aging (Kleinknecht & Goldstein, 1972); right hemisphere dysfunction (Jones & Parsons, 1971); and frontal-limbic-diencephalic dysfunction (Tarter, 1975), have all been suggested as accounting for the pattern of impairment found in alcoholics. Evidence can be presented in favour of each of these hypotheses; however, one must be particularly wary of arguments based on WAIS and HRNB results which assume localisation of these subtests. Perhaps the most widely accepted current proposal is that alcoholics have diffuse cerebral damage (Parsons & Leber, 1981). It is to be hoped that further research using modern neuroimaging techniques may reveal more specific substrates for the psychological deficits found in alcoholics.

Effect of Other Clinical Variables

In general the effects of age are more important than drinking variables such as total alcohol intake, duration of problem drinking, or daily consumption (Grant,

Adams & Reed, 1984). Relationships between cognitive impairment and drinking variables tend to be weak and inconsistent. However, there is a consensus that cognitive impairment is much less common in younger patients (Adams & Grant, 1986; Grant et al., 1984; Hesselbrock et al., 1985), and, in particular, in alcoholics below 40 years of age. The alcoholic population is predominantly male, and there have been few well-matched studies of sex differences. However, the evidence available suggests that the neuropsychological deficits shown by female alcoholics are similar to those found in males (Fabian, Parsons, & Silberstein, 1981).

Anxiety and depression, as already indicated, and other psychiatric disorders are a component of alcoholism, and are related to the course and outcome of treatment (Penick et al., 1985). It is clear that anxiety and depression alone do not account for all neuropsychological deficits in alcoholics, but the interaction between psychiatric and neuropsychological factors has not been clearly established. There is also evidence that neuropsychological deficits similar to those found in alcoholics are found in non-alcoholic offspring of alcoholics, thus raising the possibility of premorbid neuropsychological impairment in this population (Parsons, 1987).

Deteriorated Alcoholics

A small, but significant proportion of alcoholics show profound intellectual impairment. This category includes patients who suffer from Korsakoff's psychosis. However, only about one in five deteriorated alcoholics show the circumscribed memory deficit typical of Korsakoff's psychosis, the rest are globally intellectually impaired (Horvath, 1975).

The key neuropsychological feature of Korsakoff's syndrome is amnesia, which is disproportionate to any intellectual deficit. A convenient way of specifying this discrepancy is in the difference between IQ (as measured by the WAIS), and Memory Quotient (MQ) (as measured by the WMS). In cases of Korsakoff's psychosis this difference will be at least one standard deviation, that is, 15 points, and can be much greater. These patients show severe anterograde amnesia, and consequently perform very poorly on WMS subtests involving new learning. They also usually show retrograde amnesia, and will exhibit disorientation to a greater or lesser extent. Poor performance on the Information and Orientation subtests of the WMS is a hallmark of genuine Korsakoff patients, distinguishing them from sober alcoholics with memory deficits. However, short-term memory performance is unaffected, and consequently Digit Span is normal. Affective disorders are evident in more than half of Korsakoff patients with depression being the most common change. Most reports indicate that the WAIS deficits observed in non-Korsakoff alcoholics are also observed in Korsakoff's syndrome (Malerstein & Belden, 1968), however, some work suggests that, providing cases are carefully selected, IQ is unimpaired

(Cutting, 1978). For a more extensive discussion of the assessment of patients with memory disorders see Mayes and Warburg (Chapter 5).

It is generally accepted that Korsakoff's syndrome is linked to thiamine deficiency, perhaps in combination with other factors such as genetic endowment. However, controversy surrounds the relationship between Korsakoff's syndrome and other forms of alcoholic impairment, and the extent to which these patients form a special and distinct subgroup (Tuck et al., 1984). Thus, for example, the role of nutritional factors in the impairments found in non-deteriorated alcoholics is unclear.

The alcoholic dements who make up the bulk of deteriorated alcoholics have not been studied in any depth, and a clear and consistent definition of alcoholic dementia has not been forthcoming. In clinical practice it is not uncommon for the distinction between alcoholic dementia and Korsakoff's syndrome to be blurred. In contrast to the latter, alcoholic dements show clear impairment of intellect on measures such as the WAIS, and, indeed, impairment may well be so profound that formal assessment is difficult or impossible.

ABUSE OF PSYCHOACTIVE DRUGS

Apart from alcohol the most commonly abused substances are: stimulants (amphetamine, cocaine); narcotics (morphine, heroin); psychedelics (LSD); cannabis; sedatives (barbiturates, benzodiazepines), and inhalants. The latter form a distinct category and will be considered in the next section. A detailed description of the classification and acute effects of psychoactive drugs is contained in Julien (1988). There have been few well-controlled studies of the neuropsychological effects of chronic drug abuse, and in general, research has not clearly established that abuse of single classes of drugs leads to neuropsychological impairment (Parsons & Farr, 1981). This may be because these substances are not individually toxic at the doses commonly used, on the other hand it may reflect the difficulty of carrying out research in this area. Most drug abuse is polydrug abuse, and it is, therefore, difficult to determine the toxicity of specific drugs.

The evidence that polydrug abuse is associated with neuropsychological impairment is more convincing than for abuse of single classes of drugs but by no means conclusive. Grant et al. (1978), carried out a large-scale study of polydrug abusers. They tested 151 polydrug users on the WAIS and HRNB and compared them with psychiatric patients and non-patient controls. Substances used included alcohol, sedatives, narcotics and cannabis, and the mean age of the group was 25.5 years. The findings indicated that 37% of drug users were impaired on the HRNB on initial testing, and 34% were impaired at three-months follow-up. However, 26% of psychiatric controls were also judged to be impaired, suggesting that psychiatric factors among the polydrug abusers could account for neuropsychological impairment. Grant et al. (1978) argue against such an interpretation, pointing to a deficit on measures of language found in drug users but not amongst psychiatric patients. Another possibility is that neuropsychological impairment among polydrug users is due to pre-drug use deficits. Grant et al. (1978) also argue against this idea, but it is difficult to exclude premorbid deficits as an interpretation of their findings.

The question of whether abuse of psychoactive drugs leads to neuropsychological impairment thus remains open. Nonetheless, it is the case that there are clinical reports of profound deterioration after prolonged drug use. Such reports may derive from a number of factors: assessment during withdrawal or recovery from acute effects, failure to allow for premorbid level of functioning, a history of head injury or alcohol abuse, and a history of poor nutrition and health. Therefore, assessment of these patients should include taking a careful history, and the neuropsychologist should be alive to the possibility of acute effects of drug use. In the past few years the issue of poor health in this population has come into prominence, and, particularly, the risk of AIDS among intravenous drug abusers. It is possible that some earlier reports of neuropsychological deterioration in this population reflected unrecognized AIDS-related cognitive impairment.

AIDS was first identified as a discrete syndrome in the early 1980s. It has been claimed that intellectual decline may sometimes be the first presenting symptom in AIDS, and cognitive impairment and dementia are common features of the disease. Levy, Bredesen, and Rosenblum (1985), describe a cohort of AIDS sufferers and other HIV-infected individuals, who had shown neurological symptoms. Upon examination of 318 patients they found neurological abnormalities in 39%, and changes in the brains of 73% of autopsied patients. Price et al. (1988) suggest that AIDS-dementia complex (ADC) is caused directly by the HIV virus, thus making it distinct from other outward symptoms of AIDS, which are caused by secondary infections. Early cognitive complaints often consist of loss of concentration, poor memory for new information, and mental slowness. There are relatively few neuropsychological studies of ADC published to date, though several large-scale studies are ongoing. Further work will establish more clearly the nature of the neuropsychological deficits found, at what stage of the disease they emerge, and whether there is a unique neuropsychological profile associated with AIDS.

VOLATILE SUBSTANCE EXPOSURE

The literature on exposure to volatile substances includes studies of both incidental exposure in industry, and deliberate abuse of solvents. Solvents used in industry include: styrene, toluene, n-hexane, methyl n-butyl ketone, trichloroethylene, carbon tetrachloride and chloroform (Baker, Smith, & Landrigan, 1985). The main solvents in adhesives abused for recreational purposes are toluene and acetone (Watson, 1982). Although a heterogeneous group, most solvents are volatile, lipophilic, and have central nervous depressant effects. Problems in studying both industrial exposure and deliberate abuse include exposure to multiple substances and difficulties in defining the extent of exposure. The literature for neither area is entirely consistent, and indeed in both there has been debate about whether exposure in fact leads to detectable brain damage.

Industrial Exposure to Solvents

Industrial workers may be exposed to a wide variety of solvents, for example, in painting, boat building, shoe manufacturing, printing, and dry cleaning. A series of studies in Scandinavian countries in the 1970s gave rise to widespread concern that exposure may have toxic effects on the nervous system (Axelson, Hane, & Hogstedt, 1976; Haenninen et al., 1976).

However, other studies have failed to find effects of industrial exposure (Cherry et al., 1985). Nevertheless, there does appear to be a consensus that, at least in a small proportion of the population at risk, exposure to solvents produces organic changes. A report from the World Health Organisation (1985) defined two types of disorder due to long-term exposure to solvents: an organic affective disorder, and a chronic toxic encephalopathy. The first is marked by disorders of mood, while the second is indicated by fatiguability, poor memory, concentration difficulties, loss of initiative and personality change. However, the relationship between these disorders has not been clarified, and other classifications may prove more satisfactory (Waldron, 1986). A study by Haenninen et al. (1976) of painters suggests that the most sensitive neuropsychological measures are Block Design, Similarities, and Digit Span from the WAIS; and Logical Memory and Associative Learning from the WMS.

Volatile Substance Abuse

The literature on volatile substance abuse has been reviewed by Ron (1986) who concluded that evidence of permanent brain damage in abusers was inconclusive. Ron (1986) expressed a number of criticisms of studies of volatile substance abuse, and her negative conclusion reflects these shortcomings in published studies. The literature on solvent abuse is reminiscent of the literature on substance abuse in general: there are isolated reports of clear neuropsychological impairment, but group studies often find little, if any, difference between users and controls.

In part, the failure to find effects of abuse may be because group studies have tended to concentrate on users who do not have a prolonged history of abuse.

An exception is a study by Fornazzari et al. (1983) who investigated a group of 24 chronic solvent abusers with a mean age of 23 years and a mean duration of 6.3 years of solvent abuse. All subjects had used solvents, mainly toluene, for at least one year. CT scanning revealed evidence of cerebellar atrophy, together with the presence of some cortical and ventricular abnormalities. Neurological abnormalities, such as ataxia and tremor, were found in just under 50% of subjects. Fornazzari et al. (1983) did not test a control group, but divided subjects into those impaired and unimpaired on neurological testing. The impaired group performed poorly on a range of psychological measures including the WAIS and WMS. Fornazzari et al. (1983) concluded that chronic solvent abusers show profound impairment of motor control together with some impairment of intellectual and memory capacity.

Evidence of long-term recoverability after solvent abuse is largely absent. Recovery in a single case has been reported by Wiedmann et al. (1987). They noted considerable recovery of psychological functions assessed by a computerised battery over a period of 18 months. However, even after 18 months of abstinence their subject was impaired on tests of psychomotor speed, and MRI at this time indicated signs of cerebellar atrophy.

In summary, both cognitive and affective disorders have been documented in people exposed to solvents. The affective problems have most commonly been attributed to premorbid factors in abusers, whereas in industrial workers they have been attributed directly to the effects of exposure. Some solvents appear to produce relatively specific effects: exposure to n-hexane and methyl n-butyl ketone can result in peripheral neuropathy, while toluene exposure is associated with cerebellar dysfunction. However, there is also evidence of diffuse and often subtle cerebral dysfunction.

EXPOSURE TO OTHER NEUROTOXINS

There are numerous other agents which have toxic effects on the central and peripheral nervous system. The list includes metals, organophosphorous and organochlorine insecticides and other toxic chemicals, carbon monoxide, pharmaceuticals, electric shock, bacterial toxins, and bites and stings. Toxic effects may arise as a result of acute poisoning, or from prolonged subacute exposure. Poisoning may result in a generalised impairment of memory and attention resulting in an acute confusional state, which later apparently resolves when the agent responsible is removed (Heilman, Valenstein, & Watson, 1985). During the acute stage patients may be disorientated and show difficulty in following verbal commands (Lee & Hamsher, 1988). The long-term effects of toxic agents are often subtle and the value of neuropsychological testing after suspected exposure has been clearly demonstrated: effects are often difficult to detect by any other means. For many agents information concerning the long-term neuropsychological effects of exposure is limited. This is a very heterogeneous group of substances and effects range from being quite specific, e.g. on the visual system, to generalised intellectual impairment.

For an extensive list of neurotoxic agents the reader is referred to neurological texts such as that by Walton (1985). The following examples are indicative of agents for which industrial exposure has been studied neuropsychologically.

Metals

Metals with neurotoxic effects include: lead, mercury, arsenic, bismuth, cadmium, manganese, gold and aluminium. These metals are toxic to the central nervous system if present in excess, but the problem arises in defining threshold values for neuropsychological and psychiatric disorders. As examples, lead and mercury are considered here. It has been known for many years that high levels of lead in the blood can produce encephalopathy with concomitant impairment of memory and cognition. However, controversy surrounds the issue of low-level lead exposure and central nervous system dysfunction. Some studies have reported an association between cognitive deficits and occupational exposure to lead (Baker et al., 1985), while other studies have failed to find an association (Parkinson et al., 1986). In studies with positive findings the problems most often reported are in memory, visuo-motor function, and mood. High levels of mercury exposure can produce profound sensory and motor impairment, as found, for example, in Minamata disease. However, concern has also been expressed regarding low-level mercury exposure. Uzzell and Oler (1986) studied the effects of long-term exposure in thirteen dental nurses with elevated head mercury levels. They found that the nurses were poorer on memory for recurrent figures, but not on subtests of the WAIS or a range of other neuropsychological findings. The most striking finding was heightened distress as indicated by the SCL-90 self-report questionnaire, particularly in the categories of obsessive compulsion, anxiety, and psychoticism. This work suggests that low-level mercury exposure may lead to mild cognitive changes, together with more marked affective disturbance.

Organophosphorous and Organochlorine Insecticides

Some organophosphorous and organochlorine compounds are highly neurotoxic, and include the so-called "nerve gases". Effects of intoxication in industrial workers have been demonstrated. For example, Savage et al., (1988), studied 100 cases with a history of acute organophosphate poisoning and 100 matched controls (Savage et al., 1988). There was little difference between the groups on neurological examination, but significant differences emerged on neuropsychological tests, including subtests of the HRNB and WAIS. The exposed group also showed higher levels of distress as indicated by the MMPI and patients' and relatives' questionnaires.

Assessment after Industrial Exposure to Neurotoxins

Clearly, it is not possible to prescribe a test battery which is appropriate in assessing the effects of every form of toxic exposure. However, proposals have been made concerning tests suitable for monitoring industrial exposure. Valciukas and Lilis (1980) used only four tests: Block Design (WAIS), Digit Symbol (WAIS), Embedded Figures Test, and Santa Ana Dexterity Test (a pegboard task). Although it has the advantage of brevity, the tests used by Valciukas and Lilis (1980) clearly lack comprehensiveness. The test selection can be particularly criticised for failure to include any measures of memory or learning. Baker et al. (1983) suggest a battery consisting of the following ten items: Digit Span (WMS); Associate Learning (WMS); Digit Symbol (WAIS); Block Design (WAIS); Similarities (WAIS); Vocabulary (WAIS); Digit Symbol Recall; Continuous Performance Test; Santa Ana Dexterity Test; and Profile of Mood States. The Digit Symbol Recall task consists of completing a row of items from memory after the standard administration sequence of the Digit Symbol subtest. A more extensive battery of tests has been proposed by Ryan and colleagues: the Pittsburgh Occupational Exposures Test Battery (POET), (Ryan et al., 1987). The POET consists of the following items: Information (WAIS-R); Similarities (WAIS-R); Digit Span (WAIS-R); Digit Symbol (WAIS-R); Picture Completion (WAIS-R); Block Design (WAIS-R); Visual Reproduction (WMS) immediate and delayed; Associative Learning (WMS) immediate and delayed; Symbol-Digit Learning (Ryan & Butters, 1980); Incidental Memory (recall of nine symbols from Digit Symbol test); Recurring Words; Boston Embedded Figures; Mental Rotation; Trail-making Parts A and B (HRNB); and the Grooved Pegboard. Ryan et al. (1987) provide normative data on these tests for a group of 182 blue-collar workers. A disadvantage of the POET is that some of the tests require an Audio Viewer, and, consequently, they are not widely available. However, the neuropsychologist who wishes to assess an individual case of toxic exposure will be readily able to select an appropriate subset of the battery.

CONCLUSIONS

Although this is a heterogeneous field a number of common themes emerge in the assessment of alcohol and drug abuse, and toxic conditions. First, profound impairment due to toxic exposure is unusual, and, when it occurs, is distinctive. The majority of people exposed may appear to have little or no impairment: neuropsychological testing, however, can reveal subtle deficits in such a population. Thus, formal neuropsychological testing is important, and the detection of deficits may involve screening quite large numbers of people. Second, information concerning background factors should be collected and used before reaching any conclusions concerning organic impairment. It is important to take a careful history with respect to the substances to which the person has been exposed, and also investigate factors such as nutrition and general health. The possibility of a preceding neurological condition such as head injury should not be overlooked. Possible acute effects should be avoided by allowing a sufficient time to elapse before assessment. Information on age and premorbid ability (see Chapter 4) must be gathered and used when assessing the extent of any impairment. Third, the overall picture in this population is of mild to moderate diffuse brain damage, and this should be reflected in the selection of appropriate tests. The WAIS (or WAIS-R), WMS (or WMS-R), and HRNB, traditionally form the basis of clinical assessment of this population. The neuropsychologist may wish to select subtests thought to be particularly affected by diffuse brain damage. There is a clear need for tasks to be developed which are specific to different toxic conditions, are sensitive to suspected abnormalities, and which can be used repeatedly to monitor progress. It is to be hoped that experimental measures will gradually augment and replace the traditional neuropsychological measures. Finally, affective disorders are a feature noted in both substance abusers, and those incidentally exposed to neurotoxins. To what extent such disorders are organically based remains unclear in many cases, however, they should not be ignored.

REFERENCES

Adams, K.M., & Grant, I. (1986). Influence of premorbid risk factors on neuropsychological performance in alcoholics. *Journal of Clinical and Experimental Neuropsychology, 8*, 362-370.

Acker, C., Acker, W., & Shaw, G.K. (1984). Assessment of cognitive function in alcoholics by computer: A control study. *Alcohol & Alcoholism, 3*, 223-233.

Axelson, O., Hane, M., & Hogstedt C. (1976). A case-referent study of neuropsychiatric disorders among workers exposed to solvents. *Scandinavian Journal of Work, Environment and Health, 2*, 14-20.

Baker, E.L., Feldman, R.G., White, R.F., Harley, J.P., Dinse, G., & Berkey, C.S. (1983). Monitoring neurotoxins in industry: Development of a neurobehavioral test battery. *Journal of Occupational Medicine, 25*, 125-130.

Baker, E.L., Smith, T.J., & Landrigan, P.J. (1985). The neurotoxicity of industrial solvents. *American Journal of Industrial Medicine, 8*, 207-217.

Baker, E.L., White, R.F., Pothier, L.J., Berkey, C.S., Dinse, G.E., Travers, P.H., Harley, J.P., & Feldman, R.G. (1985). Occupational lead neurotoxicity: Improvement in behavioural effects after reduction of exposure. *British Journal of Industrial Medicine, 42*, 507-516.

Bowden, S.C. (1988). Learning in young alcoholics. *Journal of Clinical and Experimental Neuropsychology, 10*, 157-168.

Butters, N., & Granholm, E. (1987). The continuity hypothesis: Some conclusions and their implications for the etiology and neuropathology of alcoholic Korsakoff's syndrome. In O.A. Parsons, N. Butters, & P.E. Nathan (Eds.), *Neuropsychology of alcoholism: Implications for diagnosis and treatment*. New York: Guilford Press.

Cherry, N., Hutchins, H., Pace, T., & Waldron, H.A. (1985). Neurobehavioural effects of repeated occupational exposure to toluene and paint solvents. *British Journal of Industrial Medicine, 42*, 291-300.

Cutting, J. (1978). The relationship between Korsakov's syndrome and alcoholic dementia. *British Journal of Psychiatry, 132*, 240-251.

Fabian, M.S., Parsons, O.A., & Silberstein, J.A. (1981). Impaired perceptual-cognitive functioning in alcoholic women: Cross-validated findings. *Journal of Studies on Alcohol, 42,* 217-229.

Fornazzari, L., Wilkinson, D.A., Kapur, B.M., & Carlen, P.L. (1983). Cerebellar, cortical and functional impairment in toluene abusers. *Acta Neurologica Scandinavica, 67,* 319-329.

Goldman, M.S. (1983). Cognitive impairment in chronic alcoholics: Some cause for optimism. *American Psychologist, 10,* 1045-1054.

Grant, I., Adams, K.M., Carlin, A.S., Rennick, P.M., Judd, L.L., & Schoof, K. (1978). The collaborative neuropsychological study of polydrug abusers. *Archives of General Psychiatry, 35,* 1063-1074.

Grant, I., Adams, K.M., & Reed, R. (1984). Aging, abstinence, and medical risk factors in the prediction of neuropsychological deficit among long-term alcoholics. *Archives of General Psychiatry, 41,* 710-718.

Gross, M.M., Lewis, E., & Hastey, J. (1974). Acute alcohol withdrawal syndrome. In B. Kissin & H. Begleiter (Eds.), *The biology of alcoholism: Vol. 3. Clinical pathology.* New York: Plenum.

Haenninen, H., Eskelin, L., Husman, K., & Nurminen, M. (1976). Behavioral effects of long-term exposure to a mixture of organic solvents. *Scandinavian Journal of Work, Environment and Health, 4,* 240-255.

Heilman, K.M., Valenstein, E., & Wastson, R.T. (1985). Behavioral aspects of neurological disease: Attentional, intentional and emotional disorders. In A.B. Baker & R.J. Jount (Eds.), *Clinical neurology.* (Vol.2, pp. 1-29). Philadelphia: Harper and Row.

Hesselbrock, M.N., Weidenman, M.A., & Reed, H.B.C. (1985). Effect of age, sex, drinking history and antisocial personality on neuropsychology of alcoholics. *Journal of Studies on Alcohol, 46,* 313-320.

Horvath, T.B. (1975). Clinical spectrum and epidemiological features of alcoholic dementia. In J.G. Rankin (Ed.), *Alcohol, drugs and brain damage (pp. 1-16).* Toronto: Addiction Research Foundation.

Jones, B., & Parsons, O.A. (1971). Impairment of abstracting ability in chronic alcoholics. *Archives of General Psychiatry, 24,* 71-75.

Julien, R.M. (1988). *A primer of drug action* (5th ed.) New York: Freeman.

Kleinknecht, R., & Goldstein, S. (1972). Neuropsychological deficits associated with alcoholism: A review and discussion. *Quarterly Journal of Studies on Alcohol, 33,* 999-1019.

Lee, G.P., & Hamsher, K. de S. (1988). Neuropsychological findings in toxicometabolic confusional states. *Journal of Clinical and Experimental Psychology, 10,* 769-778.

Levy, R.M., Bredesen, D.E., & Rosenblum, M.L. (1985). Neurological manifestations of the acquired immunodeficiency sydrome (AIDS): Experience at UCSF and review of the literature. *Journal of Neurosurgery, 62,* 475-495.

Loberg, T., & Miller, W.R. (1986). Personality, cognitive, and neuropsychological correlates of harmful alcohol consumption: A cross-national comparison of clinical samples. *Annals of the New York Academy of Sciences, 472,* 75-97.

Long, J.A., & McLachlan, J.F.C. (1974). Abstract reasoning and perceptual-motor efficiency in alcoholics: Impairment and reversibility. *Quarterly Journal of Studies on Alcohol, 35,* 1220-1229.

Malerstein, A.J., & Belden, E. (1968). WAIS, SILS and PPVT in Korsakoff's syndrome. *Archives of General Psychiatry, 19,* 743-750.

Miglioli, M., Buchtel, H.A., Campanini, T., & De Risio, C. (1979). Cerebral hemispheric lateralization of cognitive deficits due to alcoholism. *Journal of Nervous and Mental Disease, 167,* 212-217.

Nixon, S.J., Kujawski, A., Parsons, O.A., & Yohman, J.R. (1987). Semantic (verbal) and figural memory impairment in alcoholics. *Journal of Clinical and Experimental Neuropsychology, 9,* 311-322.

Parkinson, D.K., Ryan, C., Bromet, E.J., & Connell, M.M. (1986). A psychiatric epidemiologic study of occupational lead exposure. *American Journal of Epidemiology, 123*, 261-269.

Parsons, O.A. (1987). Neuropsychological consequences of alcohol abuse: Many questions – some answers. In O.A. Parsons, N. Butters, & P.E. Nathan (Eds.), *Neuropsychology of alcoholism: Implications for diagnosis and treatment.* New York: Guilford Press.

Parsons, O.A., & Farr, S.P. (1981). The neuropsychology of alcohol and drug use. In S.B. Filskov & T.J. Boll (Eds.), *Handbook of Clinical Neuropsychology* (pp. 320-365). New York: Wiley.

Parsons, O.A., & Leber, W.R. (1981). The relationship between cognitive dysfunction and brain damage in alcoholics: Causal, interactive, or epiphenomenal? *Alcoholism: Clinical and Experimental Research, 5*, 326-343.

Parsons, O.A., & Prigatano, G.P. (1977). Memory functioning in alcoholics. In I.M. Birnbaum & E.S. Parker (Eds.), *Alcohol and human memory* (pp 185-194). Hillsdale, N.J.: Lawrence Erlbaum Associates Inc.

Penick, E.C., Powell, B.J., Othmer, E., Bingham, S.F., Rice, A.S., & Liese, B.S. (1985). Subtyping alcoholics by coexisting psychiatric syndromes: Course, family history, outcome. In D.W. Goodwin, R.T. Van Dusen, & S.A. Mednick (Eds.), *Longitudinal research in alcoholism* (pp. 449-469). Boston: Kluwer-Nijoff.

Price, R.W., Sidtis, J.J., Navia, B.A., Pumarola-Sune, & Ornitz, D.B. (1988). The AIDS Dementia Complex. In Rosenblum, M.L., Levy, R.M., & Bredesen, D.E. (Eds.), *AIDS and the nervous system.* Raven Press: New York.

Ron, M.A. (1986). Volatile substance abuse: A review of possible long-term neurological, intellectual, and psychiatric sequelae. *British Journal of Psychiatry, 148*, 235-246.

Ryan, C., & Butters, N. (1980). Learning and memory impairments in young and old alcoholics: Evidence for the premature aging hypothesis. *Alcoholism: Clinical and Experimental Research, 4*, 288-293.

Ryan, C.M., Morrow, L.A., Bromet, E.J., & Parkinson, D.K. (1987). Assessment of neuro-psychological dysfunction in the workplace: Normative data from the Pittsburgh Occupational Exposures Test Battery. *Journal of Clinical and Experimental Neuropsychology, 9*, 665-679.

Ryback, R. (1971). The continuum and specificity of the effects of alcohol on memory: A review. *Quarterly Journal of Studies on Alcohol, 32*, 995-1016.

Savage, E.P., Keefe, T.J., Mounce, L.M., Heaton, R.K., Lewis, J.A., & Burcar, P.J. (1988). Chronic neurological sequelae of acute organophosphate pesticide poisoning. *Archives of Environmental Health, 43*, 38-45.

Tarter, R. (1975). Psychological deficits in chronic alcoholics: A review. *International Journal of the Addictions, 10*, 327-368.

Tuck, R.R., Brew, B.J., Britton, A.M., & Loewy, J. (1984). Alcohol and brain damage. *British Journal of Addiction, 79*, 251-259.

Uzzell, B., & Oler, J. (1986). Chronic low-level Hg exposure and neuropsychological functioning. *Journal of Clinical and Experimental Neuropsychology, 8*, 581-593.

Valciukas, J.A., & Lilis, R. (1980). Psychometric techniques in environmental research. *Environmental Research, 21*, 275-297.

Waldron, H.A. (1986). Solvents and the brain. *British Journal of Industrial Medicine, 43*, 75-83.

Walton, J. (1985). *Brain's diseases of the nervous system* (9th ed.). Oxford: Oxford University Press.

Watson, J.M. (1982). Solvent abuse: Presentation and clinical diagnosis. *Human Toxicology, 1*, 249-256.

Wiedmann, K.D., Power, K.G., Wilson, J.T.L., & Hadley, D.M. (1987). Recovery from chronic solvent abuse. *Journal of Neurology, Neurosurgery and Psychiatry, 50*, 1712-1713.

Wilson, J.T.L., Wiedmann, K.D., Phillips, W.A., & Brooks, D.N. (1988). Visual event perception in alcoholics. *Journal of Clinical and Experimental Neuropsychology, 10*, 222-234.

World Health Organization. (1985). *Environmental health: 6. Chronic effects of organic solvents on the central nervous system.* Copenhagen: WHO.

16 Neuropsychological Assessment in Stroke

Clive Skilbeck
Psychology Director and Consultant Neuropsychologist,
Newcastle Health Authority, Royal Victoria Infirmary,
Newcastle upon Tyne, NE1 4LP.

INTRODUCTION: CLINICAL BACKGROUND TO STROKE

Definition and Diagnosis

Stroke is an interruption in the brain's blood supply, vascular in origin, which is characterised by rapid onset and persistence of neurological symptoms beyond 24 hours. Its definition includes the blocking of an artery (thrombosis, or embolism) to produce tissue infarction in the brain, and the spontaneous bleeding from an artery producing intracerebral or subarachnoid haemorrhage. As the definition does not include specification of particular cerebral blood vessels or area/amount of cerebral damage, a highly varied pattern of symptoms may be seen following stroke. These include hemiplegic limbs, loss of consciousness, and cognitive/intellectual deficits (e.g. communication and perceptual deficits). The diagnosis of stroke is usually a clinical one, most often made by a GP, rather than being based upon hospital laboratory studies or neuroradiological examination. The range of possible symptoms associated with a stroke complicates its diagnosis; Wade et al. (1985) suggested the following frequencies of neurological deficits:

Depression of Consciousness   30%−40%

Loss of motor power   50%−80%

| Dysphasia | 30% |
| Sensory disturbance | 25% |

In spite of this, the diagnosis of stroke is generally reliable. Transient Ischaemic Attacks (TIAs) will present initially as stroke, but resolution of the neurological symptoms within 24 hours clarifies this diagnosis. Otherwise, misdiagnosis is rare, tending to involve post-epileptic weakness or cerebral tumour. In addition to the correct diagnosis of stroke, it can be important to identify which type of stroke has occurred — thrombosis, embolism, or haemorrhage. It is necessary to be reasonably confident that a stroke is not haemorrhagic before considering the use of an anticoagulant agent in treatment. A CT scan carried out soon after stroke will reliably identify an haemorrhagic source. Clinically, haemorrhage tends to be associated with initial coma, vomiting, or neck stiffness (and not with a history of hypertension, TIA, or previous stroke). Attempts at further discrimination between thrombosis and embolism are generally unreliable.

Epidemiology, Incidence, and Risk Factors

Population studies provide the best information on the incidence of stroke, though they are difficult to organise and costly to implement. They rely upon good co-operation to obtain complete reporting of strokes, and those patients who fail to consult their GP will still be missed. The best U.K. information available on the incidence of stroke was provided by Wade et al. (1985) who noted an incidence of approximately 1.7 — 2.0/1000/year in their large study of almost 1000 patients. This incidence indicates that stroke is a relatively common disease. The Wade et al. (1985) data is equivalent to about five new cases per year for a GP, or about 450 cases each year in an "average" U.K. health district (of approximately 250,000 people). Discrimination between each different type of stroke is not reliable, but probably only 15% are caused by haemorrhage.

Sources of epidemiological bias exists. A higher level of reporting those strokes which affect communication abilities might be expected, given that these are easier to identify. Some strokes may be missed if they cause death so rapidly that hospital admission does not occur. Similarly, very mild strokes (particularly those without associated weakness) will be missed if patients do not seek help from their GP.

There are various risk factors associated with a stroke. Of course, elderly people are at a greater risk of the disease, with those over 85 years of age probably showing an incidence of 4% per annum. Any arterial disease raises the probability of a stroke occurring. Approximately one-half of stroke patients have pre-existing hypertension, and about three-quarters have a history of cardiac problems. Diabetes, probably through its association with arterial disease, is also a risk factor. As might be expected, having suffered a previous stroke increases the risk of a further stroke, at about 10% per year. A similar risk is associated with a history of TIA.

ASSESSMENT ISSUES

Purposes

As indicated earlier, stroke is a clinical medical diagnosis and the contribution of neuropsychological assessment is not primarily a diagnostic one. In the situation of an inadequate history for the patient and indefinite medical findings, a neuropsychological profile of particular cognitive deficits will help determine if a stroke has occurred, though such cases should be infrequent. More often, neuropsychological assessment following stroke is undertaken for the following reasons:

1. To provide prognostic information. In addition, to monitor the rate and extent of natural recovery from stroke or improvement under therapy. As medical treatments have little to offer post-stroke recovery, therapy will usually be that provided by physiotherapy, occupational therapy, speech therapy, or neuropsychology.

2. To provide a baseline profile of cognitive functions against which to assess subsequent natural recovery and to judge the outcome of any intervention.

3. To provide a basis on which to plan any cognitive remediation interventions.

4. To provide a source of advice regarding suitable placement or long-term care following termination of active rehabilitation. This guidance can be used to help care staff and relatives gain a better understanding of the stroke patient's cognitive deficits and competencies and, therefore, to behave appropriately. The profile can also be used to "design" a suitable environment for the patient (or at least point to the more important limitations which a proposed environment may impose upon the patient).

The data obtained from the neuropsychological assessment must be interpreted in the light of the patient's premorbid cognitive status, expectations of cognitive performance generated from available age-related normative data, and level(s) of cognitive dysfunction noted in other stroke patients. Obviously, the particular reasons why a patient is being assessed will determine when neuropsychological assessment is carried out. For example, an initial baseline assessment against which to judge subsequent natural, or therapy-based, recovery will be carried out soon after stroke. However, the patient's physical condition may not permit neuropsychological testing in the early days following stroke. Similarly, as almost 50% of those patients who die following stroke will do so in the first month (see Wade et al., 1985, for brief review), it may be sensibly pragmatic for the neuropsychologist to delay seeing very severe patients until at least the second month post-stroke.

As recovery of acquired deficits, including those in cognitive areas, appear to plateau approximately six months post-stroke (Skilbeck et al., 1983), assessment with regard to long-term cognitive impairment in a patient can be performed around this point.

Type and Severity of Cognitive Deficit

Unfortunately, stroke is a very wide-ranging vascular disease. Its various potential processes (haemorrhage, thrombosis, embolism) and the fact that it can compromise the blood supply to any area of the brain means that an extremely wide range of cognitive deficits, of varying severity, can be observed following stroke. There is, therefore, no typical pattern of cognitive deficit to be expected as a result of stroke. The particular cognitive profile noted will depend on which vessels are involved in the stroke, and the particular site of the thrombosis, embolism, or haemorrhage. The cognitive deficit seen will thus relate to the general principles of brain organisation and the localisation/lateralisation of cognitive functions. Having said this, there are a number of neuropsychological deficits which have come to be generally associated with stroke, due to their frequency of occurrence. These deficits, termed inattention or neglect, constitute perceptual dysfunctions and are discussed later in more detail. Severity of impairment shows some correlation with the amount of brain tissue damaged in the stroke. Section 3 will consider the range of cognitive deficits seen following stroke, and will offer suggestions of particular neuropsychological tests that might be employed to assess them.

Neuropsychological Tests

As indicated in the introduction to this chapter, stroke is usually a disease of later life. The average age of people who suffer a stroke is approximately 70 years. For this reason, psychologists have to be particularly careful to select assessment tasks which will be suitable for an older population. The quality of normative data available on neuropsychological tests frequently weakens as older age groups are considered (Wechsler Adult Intelligence Scale (WAIS): Wechsler, 1955); sometimes, the test manual information for people aged 70 years and over simply does not exist (e.g. Wechsler Memory Scale (WMS): Wechsler, 1945) and "expected" performance for this group has to be extrapolated or judged clinically. Perhaps more than is necessary for younger patients, the neuropsychologist has to be flexible in assembling a variety of tests which will cover the full range of suspected cognitive deficits, and will be appropriate to use with older people. This issue is addressed separately later.

Stroke or Cerebral Vascular Disease?

Although the occurrence of a stroke may be the trigger in a referral for a neuropsychologist opinion, stroke should not be regarded as a totally discrete, one-off event. Stroke is very often "just" an end point in a pre-existing (and frequently long-standing) history of cerebral-vascular disease: A referred stroke victim may have had a 10-year history of hypertension and increasing vascular insufficiency, with recent episodes of TIAs, which has culminated finally in a stroke and referral to the neuropsychologist for assessment. The amount of available research to guide us on neuropsychological assessment in the general area of cerebral-vascular disease (rather than stroke specifically) is more limited, though a number of helpful studies are available.

Neuropsychological examination of a 70-year-old person following stroke may reveal cognitive deficits acquired as a result of earlier stroke(s), and careful judgement is required in separating any recent cognitive dysfunction from that already existing at the time of the later stroke. This task is likely to be more difficult in the case of demonstrated pre-existing TIA's. Delaney, Wallace, and Egelko (1980), using Halstead-Reitan, WAIS, and WMS, demonstrated a range of cognitive deficits in patients with TIA's (but who had not suffered a stroke) when compared with age-matched controlled subjects. Although there were not significant differences in relation to basic perceptual, motor, and language functions, the TIA group showed deficits in verbal fluency, perceptual-motor co-ordination, reasoning, and complex memory. The findings of Dull et al. (1982), using a similar test battery, indicated a strong correlation between the duration of the longest ischaemic episode and the degree of neuropsychological impairment produced. Finally, it cannot be assumed that because a patient with cerebral vascular disease has no neurological symptoms that there will be no detectable cognitive impairments. Ponsford, Donnan, and Walsh (1980) studied a small group of vertebrobasilar insufficiency patients, over half of whom were free of physical neurological signs, and noted mild memory deficits (using a range of memory tests).

NEUROPSYCHOLOGICAL ASSESSMENT IN STROKE

Although there is a strong neuropsychological tradition (particularly in North America) of using standard, fixed, test batteries for assessment, a more flexible approach is to be preferred in stroke, for a number of reasons. Purely implementing a predetermined pattern of tests is less conducive to consideration of the specific patient's problems and needs. Starting with a "clean sheet of paper" should assist the neuropsychologist examiner in focusing down upon the patient as an individual, thereby assisting in the process of compiling an appropriate collection of neuropsychology tests to meet the assessment purpose(s).

General Intellectual Level

Estimation of premorbid IQ level frequently arises in neuropsychological assessment (see Chapter 3 for detailed discussion). This can generally be achieved in a number of ways, including reference to educational history, examination success, etc. These sources of information are, however, not readily available for the "average" stroke patient in 1990 who probably left school in 1934: the School Examination System at that time varied enormously across the country. The National Adult Reading Test (NART: Nelson, 1982) was developed from research undertaken with elderly people (in relation to dementia). It is based upon the finding that word reading ability and IQ correlate very highly (0.75) in adults. The NART takes only a few minutes to administer and its score is not confounded by age or social class effects. Subsequent research on the NART (e.g. Crawford et al., 1989) has improved the available normative data and confirmed a correlation between NART error score and WAIS IQ. Besides offering a quick and valid method of predicting premorbid IQ, which is extremely useful when working with an elderly brain-damaged group such as stroke patients, the NART has been shown to be robust in the face of significant intellectual deterioration. The NART can, therefore, assist the clinician to interpret the scores obtained by their patients on memory, perceptual, and intellectual tests. In relation to the latter, tables supplied with the NART allow the psychologist to compare their patient's obtained verbal IQ and performance IQ with that predicted from the NART, and to calculate the probability of finding any noted level of predicted IQ-observed IQ discrepancy in the general population. The only obvious area of contra-indication for use of the NART is where the nature of the patient's stroke is considered to invalidate its employment; for example, posterior left hemisphere strokes may produce specific dyslexic deficits (see Chapter 11). Similarly, visual field defects or visual neglect (see p.345, and Chapter 9) may compromise the value of the NART.

A test of intellectual function which can be particularly appropriate for communication-impaired stroke patients is Raven's Progressive Matrices (RPM) and Coloured Matrices (RCM) scales (Raven, 1977). The scales require the patient to identify from a multiple choice array the particular small pattern piece which completes the larger stimulus design. Verbal expression is not necessary for responding (the patient may point at their selection), and the test can be administered to stroke patients who have gross verbal receptive deficits (simple gestures by the clinician can demonstrate the principles of the test very satisfactorily). For adults, the RPM version offers norms covering the 20-65 age range, and the RCM, upwards from 65 years. The test is, therefore, suitable for use with older patients, and its minimal communication requirements and basic motor response make it very appropriate to use with stroke patients, who often have aphasic or hemiplegic deficits. Its brief administration time is also an advantage. Although the test is based upon visual perceptual/reasoning abilities, tables are available (Peck, 1970) to convert raw scores into percentages and IQs. The RCM and RPM generally show test-retest reliability coefficients of 0.8 or above, and the RCM appears differentially-sensitive to right hemisphere damage, as might be expected given its visuospatial basis (although this finding does not hold for the RPM).

The particular suitability of the Raven's Scales for use with stroke patients has often led to them being used in research. For example, David and Skilbeck (1984) found the RPM correlated significantly with communication ability in aphasic stroke patients, and also noted the indication of a poor prognosis for low scores soon after stroke. Presence of vision neglect (see next section) can adversely affect a stroke patient's score, due to positional preference being shown for items in the right-hand part of the multiple choice array (Lezak, 1983).

Of course, WAIS and WAIS-R sub-tests are often used in assessing intellectual functioning post-stroke. Relationships between site of lesion and a profile of subtest results have been intensively investigated over the years, with specific subtests contributing lateralisation and localisation information (see, for example, Lezak, 1983; McFie, 1975). Skilbeck (1990) offered a summary, whilst stressing that interpretation of a patient's subtest scores need to take account of qualitative clinical observational data, other relevant information from the patient's history, and all available neuropsychological test data. Whilst a stroke patient suffering a left hemisphere stroke is likely to show a differential depression of verbal IQ, given the large majority of the population who are left-hemisphere dominant for language, a stroke involving either hemisphere may impair performance IQ due to its inclusion of timed performance in scoring some items. Particular contribution of WAIS subtests to the description of cognitive deficits following stroke are outlined later in the appropriate sections.

Perceptual Dysfunction

Visual Neglect. A wide range of perceptual deficits can be observed following stroke, amongst which neglect or inattention is often thought of as being "characteristic" of stroke. In visual neglect or inattention, the patient ignores the left side of visual space, behaving as if it did not exist. Visual neglect is a common sequel to posterior right hemisphere stroke: Diller and Weinberg (1977) recorded a 40% frequency of visual neglect (with visual neglect following left hemisphere stroke being rare). In their research, Hier, Mondlock, and Caplan

(1983) studied 41 patients with right hemisphere stroke and reported a very high (85%) frequency of visual neglect immediately after stroke (on average patients were tested within the first week following stroke). The detailed description of various aspects of neglect is provided in Chapter 9 by Peter Halligan and Ian Robertson, accompanied by some theoretical considerations. Halligan and Robertson also offer some information on testing for visual neglect. As these authors indicate, a severe neglect disturbance will be apparent to behavioural observation — the patient will ignore objects and people in their left visual space, tending to bump into the door jamb on the left-hand side of the door, or tripping over furniture to the left side. In extreme cases, the patient may be observed at meal times to ignore food on the left side of the plate and eat only food to the right of the mid line of the plate. Testing, as opposed to observing, visual neglect has a long history, and has often been simple in nature. For many years junior doctors have been taught to ask a patient suspected of showing left-sided visual neglect to insert the numbers on a clock face. Figure 16.1 illustrates the attempt to do so by a 68-year-old man (A.L.) who suffered a large right hemisphere stroke approximately two months prior to testing.

By being unaware of the existence of the left side of visual space A.L. had to place all of the numbers to the right of the clock visual mid-point, thereby cramming them all into the right hand side of the clock face.

In addition to the clock face, patients may also be asked to copy a Greek cross. Figure 16.2 shows the type of response often seen in patients with unilateral visual neglect. Interpretation of the drawing produced may be complicated by the presence of a co-existing constructional disturbance, which can also lead to a marked distortion of the drawing response. In their population study of stroke, Wade, Skilbeck, and Langton-Hewer (1989) employed copy-drawing of a Greek cross in their set of cognitive assessment tests. Of the 361 patients assessable within one week of their stroke, 45% (n = 119) of patients failed to satisfactorily copy the Greek cross, with 36 of these 119 patients showing visual neglect on other tests. Of the patients who failed, 20% had died by the six-month follow-up and 26% were still unable to produce an adequate copy of the cross. Thus, at six-month follow-up of stroke survivors, 9% of the whole stroke sample were still unable to copy the cross satisfactorily.

One of the issues in using clock face or Greek cross tasks to process visual neglect is their subjective nature: reliable, quantitative scoring methods are not available for them, thereby making neuropsychologists uncomfortable about their use.

Introduction of the Line Bisection test (Albert, 1973), described by Halligan and Robertson in this volume, added a quantitative dimension to scoring: the neuropsychologist could measure the percentage error (deviation from the line's midpoint), of the patient's response when attempting to mark the centre of the line.

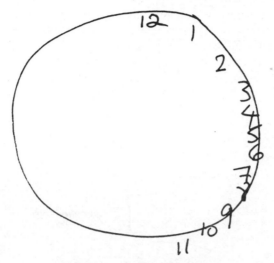

FIG. 16.1.   Clock face, patient A.L.

Figure 16.3 reproduces the results of patient A.W., who suffered a right hemisphere stroke three months prior to assessment. In failing to appreciate the left side of external space, the patient estimated the midpoint of the line to be far to the right of the real midpoint. The introduction of a quantitative scoring system allowed the development of a "severity" dimension, and also provided an index against which to gauge improvement/recovery over time. Skilbeck computer-automated the line bisection approach (Norris et al., 1985) to add the scoring dimension of response timing, and to allow the easier assessment of patients with hemiplegia.

The development of cancellation tasks offered both accuracy and response speed measures (see Halligan & Robertson, this volume, for brief review). Typically, the stroke patient has to search through rows of quasi-random series of letters or numbers crossing out targets. Figure 16.4 illustrates that a right hemisphere stroke patient with neglect will tend to miss the targets to the left side of the visual mid-point.

Many techniques for assessing neglect are unstandardised, but the Behavioural Inattention Test (BIT: Wilson, Cockburn, & Halligan, 1987) has the advantage of employing standard materials and offering normative data on 80 stroke patients and 50 control subjects. Amongst other subtests, the BIT includes untimed versions of the line bisection and letter cancellation tasks, as well as copy-drawing. The reference sample of stroke patients in the BIT was rather young (mean age 56 years) to be typical, and patients were quite intelligent (mean IQ 109), although the test represents a major advance in the assessment of visual neglect. Additional valuable clinical data on its use will rapidly accumulate

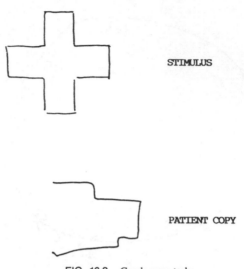

STIMULUS

PATIENT COPY

FIG. 16.2.   Greek cross task.

in the coming years. Further information on the BIT and its subtests are provided by Halligan and Robertson in Chapter 9.

Neglect in stroke is not a phenomenon limited to the visual modality. Lateralised inattention can also affect body awareness, features of this being similar to the visual findings in that it is more frequently seen in the form of right hemisphere stroke with an associated contra-lateral left-sided lack of body awareness. Hécaen and Albert (1978) suggested an impaired awareness of the left side of the body is present in 30% of patients suffering a right posterior hemisphere stroke, with 4% being the equivalent figure as a result of left hemisphere stroke lesions. As with visual neglect, impaired body awareness has great implications for rehabilitation therapists, given that a patient may be ignoring the left side of their body when washing, dressing, applying make-up, or shaving; in the most severe cases, patients may deny that their left arm, or the left side of their body, even belongs to them.

Webster et al. (1989) noted that right hemisphere neglecting stroke patients perform significantly more poorly in terms of colliding with objects on their left side when in a wheelchair than did right hemisphere non-neglecting stroke patients. Interestingly though, the non-neglecting right hemisphere group performed more poorly than the non-neglecting left hemisphere stroke patients. The authors argued that this latter finding did not stem from a subtle, undetected neglect in the non-neglecting right hemisphere stroke group, although this remains a possibility. Webster and his co-workers speculated on reduced accuracy of visual judgement of distance as a possible reason for their findings.

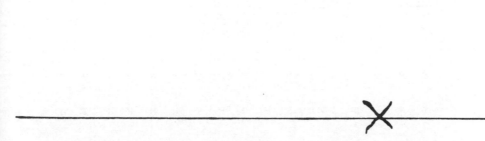

FIG. 16.3.   Line bisection, patient A.W.

Somatic Disorders.   The disturbances in body awareness noted in stroke are not necessarily unilateral. The impairment could be lateralised or bilateral, and Benton (1959), provided some simple clinical tests to assess the patient's ability to name and localise parts of their body, including:

1. Pointing to parts of own body to command (e.g. "point to your left ear").
2. Pointing to parts of the psychologist's body to command.
3. Moving parts of own body to command.
4. Touching one part of own body with another (e.g. "touch your left ear with your right hand").

Benton (1959), introduced a shortened 20-item version of his original test (Benton et al., 1983) and reported on the performance of some patients with brain damage. The presence of aphasic disturbance obviously confounds interpretation of the findings, but for non-aphasic patients deficit scores in relation to "pointing to parts of the psychologist's body" were:

Bilateral damage: 27% of patients showed deficit.
Right hemisphere damage: 35% of patients showed deficit.
Left hemisphere damage: 10% of patients showed deficit.

In terms of the above categories of testing, bilateral damage tended to yield a generalised deficit (38%), although non-aphasic patients with left

```
Targets      = B, E
Hits         = B, E
Misses        B  E
```

S E L P B T U E X B B S G E O U E

B X A D Z B E M O E T B H R F E L

E C H B A R L B F B M P B N E B O

FIG. 16.4.   Letter cancellation task.

hemisphere damage and right hemisphere patients did not show deficits in relation to localisation on their own bodies.

Judgement of Spatial Orientation and Other Aspects of Visual Reception. The personal/body and visual orientation deficits, termed unilateral neglect when affecting only one side of the visual space/body, may also be observed in a more general form: an overall difficulty with right-left orientation. The recently developed Rivermead Perceptual Assessment Battery (RPAB: Whiting et al., 1985) allows examination of this aspect of perceptual functioning, particularly via its body image and right/left copying of shapes and words subtests. The full list of 16 subtest areas is listed, and briefly discussed, in Wade et al. (1985). The RPAB is particularly suitable for use with stroke patients, as its original patient group included 41 stroke patients (20 right hemisphere, 18 left hemisphere, 3 bilateral strokes). The RPAB manual also offers correlations with some other neuropsychological tests. For stroke patients with hemiplegic dominant arms, the required motor response for completing some right-left testing (copy-drawing, placement of small pieces of test material) on the RPAB can be difficult. The right-left orientation task ("Little Men") included in the Bexley-Maudsley Automated Psychology Screening Computer Tests (BMAPS: Acker & Acker, 1982) is particularly suitable for hemiplegic stroke patients, requiring only a simple button-press to indicate "left" or "right". The test consists of a schematic figure displayed on the microcomputer's monitor screen. The figure may appear the right way up, upside-down, facing the patient, or facing away from the patient, so providing four positions in space. In whatever position the figure appears, it holds a package in one of its hands. The patient's task is to decide as quickly as possible which hand holds the package, and to indicate this via one of two response buttons. This test has the advantage of providing a measure of response speed for each spatial orientation position, as well as accuracy data. Such visuospatial deficits may also be identified via WAIS (or WAIS-R) subtest performance, particularly Block Design. The RPAB Cube-copying subtest (Whiting et al., 1985) is very similar to the block design subtest, and offers strong evidence that right hemisphere stroke patients perform significantly poorer than normal control subjects ($P < 0.001$) and left hemisphere stroke patients ($P < 0.01$).

Benton and his group have developed a number of specific visual perceptual tests that are particularly appropriate for use with stroke patients because of their simplicity of instruction and basic response requirements (Benton et al., 1983). The Judgement of Line Orientation test requires a patient to identify which two lines, from an array, have the same orientation in two-dimensional space as two stimulus lines. The test has two parallel forms, each consisting of 30 pairs of stimulus lines. Most of the patient reference data was originally provided from stroke patients (62%), the results showing a very strong relationship (as would be expected) between a visual orientation difficulty and damage to the right hemisphere. The highest impairment rate was noted for patients with posterior right-hemisphere damage and an associated visual field defect. Benton's Visual Form Discrimination test is suitable for stroke patients, responses being based upon a simple matching of the provided multiple choice response array with the presented stimulus geometric shape. The subtest data offered includes control group results in the 55-75 years age range, and patient data (Benton et al., 1985) reflects the highest impairment frequency (78%) in the posterior right hemisphere damage subgroup.

Facial recognition is a complex visual perceptual function. As a pure dissociated deficit its incidence is extremely rare, although it often occurs in the presence of other perceptual deficits. Benton's Facial Recognition test (Benton et al., 1983) offers a very good procedure for examining this aspect of visual perceptual ability in stroke patients, given that a simple pointing, or simple verbal, response is all that is required from the patient. For each item the patient is presented with a stimulus photograph of a person's face, accompanied by six other photographs, one of which is also of the stimulus person. The patient is asked to identify the matching face from the array, raw scores subsequently being corrected according to age (the norms include 65-75 year-old subjects) and number of years of education. Excluding those patients showing a verbal comprehension defect, patients with right posterior hemisphere damage show the highest frequency of deficit (53%), followed by those with right anterior hemisphere lesions (26%). In the absence of a verbal comprehension deficit, aphasic and non-aphasic left hemisphere patient sub-groups yield no examples of deficient performance.

Although it has been extensively discussed in neuropsychological texts visual object agnosia (the failure to recognise common objects from their visual characteristics), is actually very rare (seen in less than 1% of all patients sustaining cortical lesions, according to Hécaen & Albert, 1978). To be defined it needs to be noted separately from any visual perceptual impairment, and other possibly confounding problems such as a naming deficit or general confusion need to be excluded.

A number of tests of communication ability include items relating to object recognition, and the RPAB (Whiting et al., 1985) contains a number of subtests relevant to the assessment of agnosia (e.g. object matching, size recognition, and figure-ground discrimination).

Constructional Disturbance. Perceptual-motor difficulties, particularly con-structional deficits, are frequently seen following right-hemisphere damage, especially if this damage involves the parietal lobe. The deficit is a disturbance in the organisation and synthesis of separate visuospatial elements into a coherent whole which can then be linked to motor output. Constructional deficit following left parietal lesions is far less common, and usually less severe in nature. Binder (1982) noted different constructional difficulties, depending on the side of lesion – right-hemisphere damage led to more severe distortions when copying the Rey Complex Figure (see Lezak, 1983), whilst left-hemisphere damage produced an odd sequencing of drawing (and delay in completing the right side of the figure), but not necesarily an impaired finished copy. Hier et al. (1983) noted a 93% frequency of constructional deficits in their study of right hemisphere stroke patients. This is very high, probably because they assess their patients within one week of stroke, other studies reporting a 37%-67% rate of constructional deficit in right-hemisphere damage (e.g. Rey Figure; see Lezak, 1983). Of course, even the latter range represents a very high frequency.

WAIS-R Block Design subtest performance offers a very good measure of constructional disturbance, as does the copying of a Greek cross, or other visual shapes. Benton et al. 1983, developed parallel forms of a three-dimensional block construction task to assess constructional apraxic disturbances. Both block model and photographic versions were provided; on both, right-hemisphere damage is associated with a high probability of deficit, consistent with general clinical neuropsychological findings. The copying subtests of the RPAB (shape, words, 3-D, cube) can also be used to examine constructional disturbance, although this test fails to discriminate between a left- and a right-hemisphere basis for the dysfunction.

The aforementioned visual perceptual deficits are important to assess ad-equately in stroke, particularly because of their implications for the activities of therapists wishing to rehabilitate ADL aspects of the person's functioning. Of course, the deficits also need a good assessment description if a cognitive remediation programme is being considered, in order to identify which deficits to target, and in which order. The important role of the right hemisphere more generally in visual perceptual processing has been confirmed on a number of occasions. For example, Walcott et al. (1990) observe significantly poorer performance from right hemisphere stroke patients (compared with a left hemisphere stroke group) on a letter-matching task where perceptual degrading of the stimuli was involved.

A number of tactual or "touch" perception disorders can occur as a result of stroke, often in concert with the visual deficits outlined earlier. The range of assessment methods and tests to investigate tactual difficulties is currently poorly developed compared with those available for examining visual perceptual deficits. Finger agnosia refers to a deficit of tactile perception, in which the affected person cannot localise/identify from which finger a touch sensation emanates. Benton's approach to testing for this type of deficit (Benton et al., 1983) does not require a verbal response from the patient (to avoid confounding problems of aphasia). Benton's reference data included information on the performance of right- and left-hemisphere damaged subjects, most of whom were suffering from vascular disease. These data show that left arm unilateral deficits were only seen in right-hemisphere patients (21%), with right arm faulty tactile perception being noted in left non-aphasic patients (33%), and a small number of patients with bilateral cerebral damage (5%). Whilst no bilateral symmetrical faulty perception was observed in left-hemisphere patients, such a disturbance was found in 11% of right-hemisphere patients, and 55% of bilaterally damaged patients.

In tactile spatial agnosia or astereognosis, the patient is unable to recognise objects by touch alone. This disturbance usually occurs in the presence of other perceptual deficits. The presence and degree of impairment can be assessed using the Halstead-Reitan form board from the Halstead-Reitan Neuropsychological Test Battery (see Reitan & Davison, 1974), into which the blindfolded patient has to fit a number of different shaped pieces of wood. Response time scores in relation to left-hand, right-hand, and both-hands performance are obtained, and the patient's recall of the spatial position in the board of each wooden piece is also tested. Benton et al. (1983) employed a box into which the patient places their hand. Ten cards with sandpaper geometric shapes attached are presented to the patient inside the box, one-by-one. For each, the patient has to identify the shape they are touching by pointing to its match on a multiple choice array mounted on a card outside of the box. Response time is also measured, and two parallel forms are available. The test is accompanied by data on normal adult performance, including samples of 61-70 year-old people and those in the 71-80 year-age range. The age-related nature of these normative data makes the test particularly suitable for stroke patients, and the provision of some patient reference data (predominantly from patients with vascular disease) is extremely helpful.

Memory Dysfunction

As pointed out earlier in this chapter, stroke may affect a number of vessels or sites within the brain, and so there is no one specific pattern of cognitive deficit which typifies it. The pattern and severity of memory dysfunction seen following stroke will depend on the site and the extent of the stroke suffered. This section will, therefore, concentrate more upon suggesting suitable memory tasks for use with an elderly population, rather than on linking lesion site with expected profile of memory impairment (see also Chapter 5 in this volume).

Brief Screening Tests.   A number of brief tests of memory functioning have been used with stroke patients. Although they suffer from a number of drawbacks often associated with "screening" instruments (e.g. limited coverage of areas of memory, small number of items employed, lack of reliability or validity information, no linkage with an underlying model of memory), these brief tests can be useful with a stroke population whose average age is 70 years and who may be in poor physical and cognitive condition soon after their stroke. Probably the best example of this type of test is the Memory and Information test, which correlates with neuropathological findings in dementia (Blessed, Tomlinson, & Roth, 1968), and has been shortened to ten items (the Mental Test Scale: MTS), by Hodkinson (1972).

Table 16.1 lists these items and shows that the essential feature of the test is the measurement of personal information (items 1, 6), and current orientation in time and place (2, 4, 5, 7). Three items (8, 9, 10) access long-term memory, and only one item (3) relates to new learning. Each item correctly answered scores one point. Despite its limitations, Wade et al. (1989) found it useful in their population study of stroke: they noted an initial level of satisfactory orientation (scores 7-10) in only 45% of their subjects within a week of stroke, although this rose to 73% by the six-month follow-up. Patients

TABLE 16.1
Mental Test Scale

---

1. Age of patient
2. Time now (to nearest hour)
3. Address given: 42 West Street (for recall at end of test)
4. Name of hospital (or if at home, city district)
5. Current year
6. Date of birth of patient
7. Current month
8. Years of 1st (or 2nd) World War
9. Name of current monarch
10. Count backwards from 20 to 1

---

who were "confused" on the MTS (scores 0-6) were also much more likely to show initial urinary incontinence, sensory inattention, and severe physical dependence, thereby suggesting a possible predictive use for the MTS in terms of initial impairments and areas requiring rehabilitation.

Another test requiring only a short administration time is the Mini-Mental State, which has been shown to be useful in gaining information from neurological patients in areas of memory and other cognitive functions (Dick et al., 1984).

Wechsler Memory Scale (WMS: Wechsler, 1945). At first sight the WMS appears a poor instrument to assess memory in elderly people, as the original normative data in its manual did not include information on patients aged 50 years and older. However, considerable research effort has been directed towards its "rehabilitation" as a screening test for memory dysfunction. Some of these efforts have improved its appropriateness for neurological patients in general, and elderly patients in particular. For example, Skilbeck and Woods (1980), using samples of neurological patients and psychogeriatric patients, observed a factor structure in neurological patients identical to that found in non-brain damaged samples. Lezak (1983) provides a review of the use of the WMS for different age groups, including elderly people. The WMS offers information on: "learning/recall", covering short-term memory (Visual Reproduction, Logical Memory subtests) and learning (Associate Learning subtests); "attention/concentration" (Mental Control, Digit Span); and "information/orientation" (Information, Orientation subtests). The WMS can also provide a measure of incidental learning of information from both visual and verbal short-term memory by the examiner seeking delayed recall scores from the patient in relation to the Visual Reproduction and Logical Memory subtests (without prior warning) 30 minutes after initial testing.

Information on the span of immediate memory can, of course, also be obtained from the Digit Span subtest of the WAIS-R, and, in addition, the Mental Arithmetic subtest can provide some information on memory processing.

Serial Digit Learning Test (Benton et al., 1983). Benton produced a Digit Learning Test which is appropriate for elderly stroke patients because it includes a version (SD8) particularly devised for people who are age 65-74 years and/or who have a poor educational background. The test offers a percentage score distribution against which to judge patients' performance, and also provides reference data which suggests serial digit learning deficits are more frequently seen in patients with bilateral damage to the cerebral hemispheres (60%), compared with left-hemisphere (36%) and right-hemisphere (25%) subgroups. If the new learning criterion is not met sooner (correct recall on two consecutive trials), the test can be administered for up to 12 trials before discontinuing. Given the nature of the test material, parallel versions of the test are very easy to construct. The Benton Serial Digit Learning test offers an easily obtained overall measure of learning, and "learning curve" data.

Rey Auditory Verbal Learning Test (AVLT: Lezak, 1983). Like the Serial Digit Learning Test, the AVLT also allows "learning curve" information to be gained across five trials of a 15-word list. The test offers information on initial learning/immediate memory on the first trial of the list and examines the effects of interference (both proactive and retroactive) via the introduction of a second list (for one trial) after learning has been attempted on the five trials of the first list. The test also includes a recognition dimension. Some normative data are available for elderly people (see Lezak, 1983), and clinical experience suggests that the AVLT is appropriate for stroke patients in whom a language deficit is not suspected. Lezak (1983) offered some reference data for brain-damaged subjects, and Pearlson et al. (1985) employed the AVLT in their study of elderly people. Crawford, Stewart, and Moore (1989) demonstrated that sequential use of parallel versions of the AVLT does not yield practice effects (thereby making this a suitable instrument for measuring memory recovery over time following stroke), although a repeated administration of the *same* version, after approximately four weeks, produces significant improvement (practice effects). Coughlan and Hollows' (1985) Adult Memory and Information Processing Battery (AMIPB) includes parallel versions of the AVLT, accompanied by normative data that encompasses elderly subjects. Lezak (1983) described a pictorial equivalent of the AVLT, which should also prove useful with stroke patients.

Other Memory Tests. There are a number of tests of visual short-term memory available for clinical use — for example, the Visual Reproduction subtest from the WMS, the Benton VRT (Benton, 1974) and the Rey Complex Figure (see description in Lezak, 1983), all of which involve a motor component (i.e. drawing) in testing recall. This can complicate interpretation of results in stroke patients who have a hemiplegia of their dominant arm. Multiple choice visual recognition seems particularly appropriate for such stroke patients. Benton and his co-workers did develop a multiple choice form of his Benton VRT (Benton, Hamsher, & Stone, 1977) although this has, inexplicably, failed to find favour amongst clinical neuropsychologists.

Acker and Acker (1982) included a multiple choice visual memory task in their computer-administered tests, although clinical experience suggests that the difficulty level of the material (abstract visual patterns) is too high for an elderly stroke population. However, Warrington (1984) has provided a visual recognition test based upon photographs of faces. Although the task is demanding for stroke patients (there are 50 photographs to be recognised), this test avoids the skilled motor component of many visual memory tests. Warrington provided some normative data in the 55-70 year age range, and linkage with Raven's PM (see p.344). She also offered some clinical reference data, 31% of the patient sample having suffered cerebral vascular disease.

The AMIPB (Coughlan & Hollows, 1985) includes parallel versions of both a visual memory task (with copy, immediate recall, and delayed recall components, being similar to the Rey Complex Figure) and the design learning task. Whilst both of these tasks include a motor component in testing recall, Design Learning only requires short straight lines to be reproduced and, unusually, offers "learning curve" data for visual material. Coughlan and Hollows (1985) included some normative data for these tests to cover the 61-75 years age range. Whilst the authors did not report data on any brain-damaged patients' samples, they do offer suggested cut-off scores to indicate performances which are "well below average" (below the 10th percentage), and "abnormal" (two standard deviations, or more, below the mean).

Finally, Wilson et al. (1989) reported on the development and validation of a battery of subtests: the Rivermead Behavioural Memory Test (RBMT), designed to examine everyday memory functioning. As indicated earlier, one purpose of neuropsychological assessment of stroke patients is to offer a baseline against which natural recovery or remedial intervention can be judged. The ultimate test of the extent of cognitive recovery, or rehabilitation, is performance in "real life", and the RBMT offers a number of useful subtests in this regard (e.g. remembering appointment, remembering a new route, delivering a message). In the original patient group studies by Wilson and her colleagues, stroke was the most frequent diagnosis, and the RBMT's level of subtest difficulty should make it generally applicable with this patient subgroup. Additional data on the RBMT's characteristics will accrue in the next few years, enhancing its utility.

Although it might be considered that stroke patients and their carers could be in the best position to determine their own memory deficits, few self-report measures are available for use. An exception is the Subjective Memory Questionnaire (SMQ: Bennett-Leby & Powell, 1980), which asks people to rate their memory functioning in "real-life" areas such as memory for appointments, telephone numbers, people's names, etc. Given the ease with which it can be completed, the SMQ appears appropriate for subjective assessment of memory impairment in stroke from either patient or carer.

OTHER COGNITIVE FUNCTIONS

Although it is impossible within this chapter to refer to all other possible cognitive functions which may be disturbed as a result of stroke, a few are worthy of mention.

Information processing speed can be impaired by a stroke in any cerebral area. One index of this deficit is the patient's age scales score on the WAIS-R Digit Symbol subtest relative to other performance subtest age-scale results, although fine motor control is required for this task, often making it unsuitable for hemiplegic stroke patients. The AMIPB (Coughlan & Hollows, 1985) information processing test requires a much simpler response (crossing out the chosen response) and is, therefore, often preferable for this patient group. The Symbol Digit subtest of Acker and Acker (1982) from the BMAPS also improves on the WAIS version, requiring only a button press as the response.

There are few tests that aim to measure motor skill alone − most often this function is observed as part of a visuomotor task (such as WAIS-R Digit Symbol, or Visual Short-Term Memory Recall testing). However, the finger-tapping test from the Halstead-Reitan Battery (see Reitan & Davison, 1974) purely accesses fine motor control. It is a simple test, with clear instructions, and is suitable for use with stroke patients given its normative support and clinical validation with a large number of brain-damaged patient groups. Another possibility is the Purdue Pegboard Test (reviewed by Lezak, 1983) which only takes a few minutes to administer, and involves the patient placing small metal pegs into holes drilled into a board. Reference data are available in relation to sex, dominant and non-dominant hand performance, and left- or right-hemisphere damage.

The concept of "reasoning ability" covers a number of aspects of reasoning. Information on the stroke patient's verbal abstracting ability can be gained from the Similarities subtest age-scale score of the WAIS-R relative to other verbal subtest results, and on the patient's visual sequential reasoning skill from the Picture Arrangement subtest. The former can be depressed by a left hemisphere stroke, particularly if this involves the posterior part of the temporal lobe, and a poor score on the latter may reflect a stroke which implicates the anterior portion of the right hemisphere. Concept formation ability may be affected by a stroke involving the frontal lobe(s). This ability has often been assessed using either the Wisconsin Card Sorting test (Milner, 1963), or the Category test from the Halstead-Reitan Battery (see Reitan & Davison, 1974). However, both tend to have a long administration time with elderly people, and probably the Modified Card Sorting test (Nelson, 1976) is to be preferred. This is a shortened version of the Wisconsin CST. Sherrill (1985) addressed the issue of the length of the Halstead-Reitan Category Test (208 items), developing a 120-item short form which correlates 0.98 with the original. This short form would seem to be more appropriate for elderly stroke patients, if concept formation is being investigated via this type of test. Bornstein and Leason (1985) demonstrated that performance on the Verbal Concept Attainment Test is differentially impaired by left frontal damage (the most frequent diagnosis in their patients' subgroup was stroke), and that it also provided normative data on 360 normal controls. As the test simply requires the patient to identify one word from each line of a set of lines that shows some conceptual relationship with the others (see Table 16.2), this test should be suitable for stroke patients.

Due to limitations on space, it is not possible to discuss the assessment of communication dysfunction in stroke within this chapter (however, see

TABLE 16.2
Verbal Concept Attainment Test

Close	Lunch	Oil	*Drum*
Fence	*Flute*	Open	Picnic
Horn	Lung	Seed	Coal
Head	*Piano*	Shirt	Water

(see Bornstein & Leason, 1985)

Chapter 10 in this book for information on the assessment of language dysfunction). Wade et al. (1985) considered language dysfunction in stroke in some detail, including reviews of the various available formal tests of aphasia (included the Schuell, the Boston, the Western Aphasia Battery, and the Porch Index of Communicated Abilities).

SUMMARY

Stroke is a common neurological disease, an "average" U.K. Health District being expected to note about 450 cases each year. Neuropsychological assessment in stroke is not usually undertaken for diagnostic purposes, but rather to offer prognostic data or baseline information against which to judge natural recovery or a planned cognitive rehabilitation intervention. However, as stroke may affect a number of cerebral blood vessels, there is no definitive or typical pattern of cognitive deficit. In addition stroke is generally considered to be a disease of later life, and choice of neuropsychological assessment instruments needs to take into consideration whether elderly people are able satisfactorily to attempt the tests, and whether relevant normative and patient reference data are available for the tests. In general, neuropsychological evaluation following a major stroke will include examination of intellectual functioning, memory functions, and a range of perceptual abilities. If any deficit can be said to be characteristic of (right hemisphere) stroke, then neglect is often regarded as such. Depending on the site and extent of the stroke, the neuropsychologist may wish to undertake additional testing, for example, in the area of reasoning abilties.

REFERENCES

Acker, W., & Acker, C. (1982). *Bexley-Maudsley automated psychological screening and Bexley-Maudsley category sorting test.* Windsor: NFER-Nelson.
Albert, M.L. (1973). A simple test of visual neglect. *Neurology, 23,* 653-664.

Benton, A.L. (1974). *The revised visual Retention Test: Clinical and experimental applications.* New York: Psychological Corporation.

Benton, A.L. (1959). *Right-left discrimination and finger-localization: Development and pathology.* New York: Hoeber-Harper.

Benton, A.L., K. de Hamsher, & Stone, F.B. (1977). *Visual retention test: Multiple choice form 1.* Iowa: Iowa City Hospital.

Benton, A.L., Hamsher, K., Varney, N.R., & Spreen, O. (1983). *Contributions to neuropsychological assessment.* New York-London: Oxford University Press.

Binder, L.M. (1982). Constructional strategies on complex figure drawings after unilateral brain damage. *Journal of Clinical Neuropsychology, 4,* 51-58.

Blessed, G., Tomlinson, B.E., & Roth, M. (1968). The association between quantitative measures of dementia and of senile change in the cerebral grey matter of elderly subjects. *British Journal of Psychiatry, 114,* 797-811.

Bornstein, R.A., & Leason, M. (1985). Effects of localised lesions on the verbal concept attainment test. *Journal of Clinical & Experimental Neuropsychology, 7,* 421-429.

Coughlin, A.K., & Hollows, S.E. (1985). *The adult memory and information processing battery (AMIPB).* Leeds: St James' University Hospital.

Crawford, J.R., Parker, D.M., Stewart, L.E., Besson, V.A.O., & De Lacy, G. (1989). Prediction of WAIS IQ with the national adult reading test: Cross-validation and extension. *British Journal of Clinical Psychology, 28,* 267-274.

Crawford, J.R., Stewart, L.E., & Moore, J.W. (1989). Demonstration of Savings on the AVLT & Development of a Parallel Form. *Journal of Clinical & Experimental Neuropsychology, 11,* 975-981.

David, R.M., & Skilbeck, C.E. (1984). Raven's IQ and language recovery following stroke. *Journal of Clinical Neuropsychology, 6,* 302-308.

Delaney, R.C., Wallace, J.D., & Egelko, S. (1980). Transient cerebral ischaemic attacks and neuro psychological deficit. *Journal of Clinical Neuropsychology, 2,* 107-114.

Dick, J.P.R., Guiloff, R.J., Stewart, A., Bielawska, C., Paul, E.A., & Marsden, C.D. (1984). Mini-mental state examination in neurological patients. *Journal of Neurology, Neurosurgery & Psychiatry, 47,* 496-499.

Diller, L., & Weinberg, J. (1977). Hemi-inattention in rehabilitation: The evolution of a rational remediation programme. In E.A. Weinstein & R.P. Friedland (Eds.), *Advances in Neurology, vol 18,.* New York: Raven Press.

Dull, R.A., Brown, G., Adams, K.M., Shatz, M.W., Diaz, F.G., & Ausman, J.I. (1982). Preoperative neurobehavioural impairment in cerebral revascularization candidates. *Journal of Clinical Neuropsychology, 4,* 151-166.

Hécaen, H., & Albert, M.L. (1978). *Human neuropsychology.* London: Wiley.

Hier, D.B., Mondlock, J., & Caplan, L.R. (1983). Behavioural abnormalities after right hemisphere stroke. *Neurology, 33,* 337-344.

Hodkinson, H.M. (1972). Evaluation of a mental test score for assessment of mental impairment in the elderly. *Age & Ageing, 1,* 233-238.

Lezak, M.D. (1983). *Neuropsychological assessment* (2nd Ed.). New York-London: Oxford University Press.

McFie, J. (1975). *Assessment of organic intellectual impairment.* London: Academic Press.

Milner, B. (1963). Effects of different brain lesions on card sorting. *Archives of Neurology, 9,* 90-100.

Nelson, H.E. (1976). A modified card sorting test sensitive to frontal lobe defects. *Cortex, 12,* 313-324.

Nelson, H. (1982). *The national adult reading test.* Windsor: NFER-Nelson.

Norris, D., Skilbeck, C.E., Hayward, A.E., & Torpy, D.M. (1985). *Microcomputers in Clinical Practice.* London: Wiley.

Pearlson, G.D., Kim, W.S., & Speedie, L.J. (1985). *Regional CT evaluation values and cognitive task performance in elderly demented, depressed, and normal individuals.* Paper presented at 14th Annual International Neuropsychological Society meeting, Denver, CO.

Peck, D.F. (1970). The conversion of progressive matrices and Mill Hill vocabulary raw scores into deviation IQs. *Journal of Clinical Psychology, 26,* 67-70.

Ponsford, J.L., Donnan, G.A., & Walsh, K.W. (1980). Disorders of memory in vertebrobasilar disease. *Journal of Clinical Neuropsychology, 4,* 267-276.

Raven, J.C. (1977). *Manuals for Raven's progressive and coloured matrices.* London: Lewis & Co.

Reitan, R.M., & Davison, L.A. (Eds.). (1974). *Clinical neuropsychology: Current status and applications.* Washington DC: Winston-Wiley.

Sherrill, R.E. (1985). Comparison of three short forms of the category test. *Journal of Clinical & Experimental Neuropsychology, 7,* 231-238.

Skilbeck, C.E. (1990). The assessment of intelligence and cognitive abilities across the life span. In J. Beech & L. Harding (Eds.), *Neuropsychological Assessment,* Windsor: NFER-Nelson.

Skilbeck, C.E., Wade, D.T., Langton-Hewer, R., & Wood, V.A. (1983). Recovery after stroke. *Journal of Neurology, Neurosurgery & Psychiatry, 46,* 5-8.

Skilbeck, C.E., & Woods, R.T. (1980). The factorial structure of the WMS: Samples of neurological and psychogeriatric patients. *Journal of Clinical Neuropsychology, 4,* 293-300.

Wade, D.T., Langton-Hewer, R., Skilbeck, C.E., Bainton, D., & Burns-Cox, C. (1985, February). Controlled trial of a home-care service for acute stroke patients. *Lancet,* 323-326.

Wade, D.T., Langton-Hewer, R., Skilbeck, C.E., & David, R.M. (1985). *Stroke: A critical approach to diagnosis, treatment, and management.* London: Chapman & Hall Medical.

Wade, D.T., Skilbeck, C.E., & Langton-Hewer, R. (1989). Selected cognitive losses after stroke. Frequency recovery, and prognostic importance. *International Disability Studies, 11,* 34-39.

Warrington, E.K. (1984). *The recognition memory test: Manual.* Windsor: NFER-Nelson.

Webster, J.S., Cottam, G., Gouvier, W.D., Blanton, P., Beissel, G.F., & Wofford, J. (1989). Wheelchair obstacle course performance in right CVA victims. *Journal of Clinical & Experimental Neuropsychology, 11,* 295-310.

Wechsler, D. (1945). A standardised memory scale for clinical use. *Journal of Psychology, 19,* 87-95.

Wechsler, D. (1955). *Manual for the Wechsler adult intelligence scale.* New York: Psychol. Corp.

Whiting, S., Lincoln, N., Bhavnani, G., & Cockburn, J. (1985). The Rivermead perceptual assessment battery: Manual. Windsor: NFER-Nelson.

Wilson, B., Cockburn, J., Baddeley, A., & Hiorns, R. (1989). The development and validation of a test battery for detecting and monitoring everyday memory problems. *Journal of Clinical & Experimental Neuropsychology, 11,* 855-870.

Wilson, B., Cockburn, J., & Halligan, P. (1987). *The behavioural inattention test: Manual.* Fareham: Thames Valley Test Co.

Walcott, C.L., Saul, R.E., Hellige, J.B., & Kumar, S. (1990). Effects of stimulus degradation on letter-matching performance of left and right hemispheric stroke patients. *Journal of Clinical and Experimental Neuropsychology, 12,* 222-234.

17

Assessment of the Severely Head-Injured

William W. McKinlay
Chartered Psychologist, Case Management Services Ltd, 17A Main Street, Balerno, Edinburgh EH14 7EQ; Consulting Neuropsychologist, Scotcare Brain Injury Rehabilitation Unit, Newmains, Lanarkshire.

John M. Gray
Consultant Neuropsychologist, Newcastle Mental Health NHS Trust, Newcastle General Hospital, Newcastle-upon-Tyne.

INTRODUCTION

There are several reasons for carrying out a neuropsychological assessment of an individual who has sustained a severe head injury. Appropriate aims of neuropsychological assessment include:

1. To describe in detail the consequences of the injury in terms of cognitive function and emotional status.
2. To help make an estimate of prognosis, something that will be very important to patient and family in order that appropriate plans are made for the future.
3. To plan rehabilitation or placement on the basis of accurate knowledge of the patient's strengths and limitations.
4. To plan return to work or the finding of alternative employment on the basis of accurate knowledge of the patient's capabilities.
5. In some instances, to carry out a "medico-legal" assessment in relation to a legal action for damages.
6. By means of serial assessment, to monitor progress or to evaluate the effects of training or treatments, for example in the course of research projects.

When an individual is referred who has sustained severe traumatic brain injury (TBI), it will already be established that there has been damage to the

363

brain. Therefore, the focus of the assessment is to document the nature and extent of cognitive and psychosocial difficulties and intact abilities, and not to assess for "presence or absence of brain damage".

This chapter is concerned with a formal and fairly detailed neuropsychological assessment. There are many other roles for the neuropsychologist in relation to the head injured. In rehabilitation settings, in programmes for the amelioration of memory difficulties, or in anger management treatments, a variety of methods of assessment will be brought to bear to analyse the problem and evaluate progress. These, however, are outside the scope of the present chapter.

Neuropsychological assessment of the severely head-injured is important because such cases are relatively common causes of continuing significant disability. There have been many studies of prevalence, but one which gives a clear overall picture, while being broadly consistent with the literature in general, is that of Miller and Jones (1985). They reported on the adult head-injured drawn in one year from a population base of 1.2 million. There were 93 cases with "severe" injuries in terms of Glasgow Coma Scale scores (*vide infra*) on admission, of whom 51 survived. Thirty-three of the latter were severely disabled or vegetative at one month post-injury in terms of the Glasgow Outcome Scale (discussed later). Of the 210 cases who initially had "moderate" injuries, a proportion developed complications whereby eight died and 33 were severely disabled or vegetative at one month post-injury; and of the 1616 with "minor" injuries initially, 7 died and 50 were severely disabled or vegetative at one month. Adding together all those who were severely disabled or vegetative one month post-injury gives a total of 116 cases. All of these are very likely indeed to have significant long-term effects of injury, and, moreover, a proportion of those less severely disabled at one month will also have handicapping *sequelae*.

As there is a large peak in the number of new head-injured patients from the late teens to early thirties (Field, 1976), and as life expectancy is only very slightly reduced, this means that there is a sizeable pool of young disabled people who have been handicapped by head injury.

It should also be noted that the great bulk of civilian head injuries are "blunt" head injuries. The latter involves the head being violently shaken or buffeted as a result of blows or collisions: there is, therefore, a rapid change in velocity and the brain tissue is shaken inside the skull. The considerations that apply in such cases are, in many respects, not the same as those which apply to penetrating head injury where the skull and brain are penetrated by a missile such as a bullet or shrapnel, or where a pointed object is thrust into the brain.

UNDERSTANDING WHAT TO ASSESS

Any comprehensive assessment must take into account the range of deficits and difficulties which are likely to be present after a head injury. It is well to remember the dictum that "absence of evidence is not evidence of absence": in other words if one uses inappropriate tests (and many standard tests are inappropriate for head injury), and fails to find evidence of deficit, this does not mean that there *is* no deficit.

The range of deficits found after head injury may be summed up under the broad headings of physical, cognitive and psychosocial deficits.

Physical Deficits

Whereas physical deficits are not the direct concern of psychologists, it should be borne in mind that they may have psychological effects. Moreover, physical impairments which in themselves are not of major importance may *in combination with* cognitive impairments lead to the patient's job prospects being very much curtailed. For example, there may be cognitive impairments which in themselves do not make the patient unemployable but which leave open the possibility of routine physical work; however, where physical deficits including neuromuscular impairments or lack of stamina occur in combination with the cognitive deficits, the effect may be to close off even that possible avenue of employment. Another example is that when post-traumatic epilepsy occurs, it may be an important source of anxiety and place major restrictions on lifestyle (see Jennett, 1983).

Cognitive Deficits

Cognitive deficits are particularly important because they are a key barrier to the resumption of employment (Brooks et al., 1987). To understand the nature of these deficits, it is helpful to remember that the characteristic neuropathological picture is of *diffuse* rather than *focal* insult to the brain. Widespread and patchy diffuse axonal injury is highly characteristic of closed head injury in addition to which there may be ischaemic or hypoxic damage, infection, or haematoma which may lead to distortion and compression of brain tissues over a wide area (e.g. Adams et al., 1980).

Whereas in other conditions, such as penetrating head injury or stroke, there may be complete destruction of a particular area of the brain, the picture in closed head injury is different, with widespread but patchy, and often microscopic, damage. Rather than losing a capacity (such as language, or movement of a limb) completely, there is, instead, reduced efficiency over a wide range of functions. Neuropsychologically, this manifests itself as a reduction in: attention, mental speed and capacity for new learning and for unfamiliar tasks (e.g. Brooks, 1984; Van Zomeren & Brouwer, 1990), rather than a *complete* destruction of a particular capacity, such as that for speech or the capacity to carry out visuospatial tasks.

Psychosocial Deficits

Finally, psychosocial deficits are important. The most persistent and troublesome in causing distress and "burden" to families, disrupting the resumption of normal activities, and preventing return to work include: poor control of temper, difficulty with memory and concentration, and disturbed social behaviour (Brooks et al., 1987; McKinlay et al., 1981).

NATURE AND SEVERITY OF INJURY

Severity of head injury is, generally speaking, measured in one of two ways: by initial Glasgow Coma Scale (GCS) total score (Teasdale & Jennett, 1974), or by duration of post-traumatic amnesia (PTA), (see Teasdale & Brooks, 1985). The GCS is a method of objectively and reliably measuring the level of responsiveness after traumatic brain injury and is known to relate to outcome (Jennett & Teasdale, 1981).

The GCS is made up of three components (see Table 17.1). Predictions can be made from any individual component although the total score is best. If that is unavailable, the best single predictor is the motor scale, hence highest motor score is sometimes recorded in the notes. Individuals with a GCS total score of 3-8 after resuscitation are often said to have "severe" injuries; where GCS is 9-12 the injury is "moderate"; and where 13-15 the injury is "minor". This

TABLE 17.1
The Glasgow Coma Scale

Eye Opening	
spontaneous	4
to speech	3
to pain stimulus	2
nil	1
Best Motor Response	
obeys commands	6
localizes pain	5
withdraws from pain	4
abnormal flexion	3
extensor response	2
nil	1
Verbal Response	
orientated	5
confused conversation	4
inappropriate words	3
incomprehensible sounds	2
nil	1

applies only to closed head injuries: where the injury is a penetrating one, there may be serious damage to the brain which is not reflected in reduced GCS scores. Moreover, even in closed head injury, there are dangers in taking the GCS score as more than a rough and preliminary guide, and this is discussed later.

Generally speaking, in an uncomplicated head injury, GCS total score will increase gradually as the patient becomes more responsive, although there may be some minor fluctuations according to the sleep/wakefulness cycle. However, in a proportion of cases GCS deteriorates quite markedly; this is an indication of secondary complications. In these circumstances, the lower GCS should be taken into account when considering the severity of the insult to the brain.

The second key index of severity of brain injury is duration of post-traumatic amnesia (PTA). If an individual has been struck on the head at, say, 10.00am on Tuesday and has sustained a significant head injury, there will be a period starting before the point of injury (for example, 9.30am) and ending some time after (for example, 10.00am on Thursday) which will not be recalled. In this case, we should say that retrograde amnesia (RA) is 30 minutes, and PTA, 2 days. Head injuries may be categorised into mild, moderate, severe, very severe and extremely severe on the basis of PTA duration according to the criteria of Russell (1971) as expanded by Jennett and Teasdale (1981) (see Table 17.2).

PTA is a very important index of the severity of injury and a powerful predictor of outcome. The concept was propounded by Russell in 1932 (see Russell, 1971), who proposed that the duration of PTA would provide an

TABLE 17.2
Significance of PTA

Less than 5 minutes: "very mild"
5 to 60 minutes: "mild"
1 to 24 hours: "moderate"
1 to 7 days: "severe"
1 to 4 weeks: "very severe"
More than 4 weeks: "extremely severe"

These descriptions were suggested by Jennett and Teasdale (1981) and are an extension of Russell's descriptions (see Russell, 1971). The apparent overlap between categories is not worrying when it is borne in mind that it is the order or magnitude (was PTA minutes, days, weeks?) that is important, rather than very precise distinctions (was PTA 5 minutes or 6 minutes?).

estimate of the quantum of damage to the brain. What is meant by PTA is sometimes misunderstood, but Russell's definition is quite clear. PTA starts at *the point of impact* and finishes with the recovery of *continuous memory.* Therefore, PTA includes the period of coma or unconsciousness *and* isolated "islands of memory". Islands of memory do *not* signal the end of PTA, but rather it is the recovery of ongoing memory, of a continuous sense of events, that signals the end of PTA. The assessment of PTA is discussed later in the chapter. PTA is not an alternative to the GCS, and indeed Jennett — one of the authors of the GCS — has been one of the leading advocates of the use of PTA. The reader is referred to Russell (1971) and Teasdale and Brooks (1985) for a fuller discussion of the traumatic amnesias.

It is not simply severity of injury that matters: nature of injury also matters with certain features, notably the presence of subdural haematoma (Gennarelli et al., 1982) being associated with worse outcome for equivalent levels of GCS scores.

A number of imaging techniques are now in widespread use. Two are particularly notable: CT scans and MRI scans. CT scans are an unreliable guide to the extent of eventual cerebral damage, especially when they are carried out immediately after the impact. They are widely used to check that there are no intracranial haematomas developing, and, in that role, they have transformed the prospects of post-head injury patients as a whole. However, an early "normal" scan does not mean that there is no brain damage, and it is a misinterpretation to think so. Late scans — some months after injury — will very often show damage that was not evident in early scans in the form of widening ventricles or sulci representing diffuse cortical atrophy caused by late death of cells which were damaged in the injury or in subsequent complications. Moreover, it is late scans which are related to the neuropsychological outcome (Wilson et al., 1988). MRI scans can identify aspects of injury, notably in this context contusional injury, which are not found on CT scanning, and which, at least in some instances, are found alongside cognitive impairments (e.g. Levin et al., 1987).

After the acute medical emergencies are over, the process of recovery is charted by the patient's gradually increasing level of responsiveness. There are several recovery scales including notably the Glasgow Coma Scale and the Galveston Orientation and Amnesia Test (Levin et al., 1979).

Recovery Rates

Neuropsychological testing should be done in the context of a knowledge of the eventual recovery rates for different functions and of the inter-individual variability for any one function. Brooks has, for example, shown that recovery curves may be constructed for IQ and memory, which show a decelerating rate of recovery with a virtual plateau reached between 1 and 2 years. However, he has also shown that individual variation is very large and that the group recovery curves do not apply to many individuals (Brooks et al., 1984). It is also worth noting that for traditionally "unitary" functions, including movement and language, recovery seems to plateau sooner than for overall psychological adjustment, which presumably involves integrating said functions.

ASSESSMENT

1. Records

Assessment should begin with a review of the records to determine the nature and severity of injury. Knowing whether the injury was of overwhelming severity, was in a range from which fairly good recovery is possible, or was minor, will enable the examiner to approach the assessment with relevant questions in mind. For those with injuries of very great severity, the questions will be likely to revolve around level of dependency, whereas in those with less severe injuries the detection of subtle yet potentially important deficits is the task of the examiner. A psychological picture that is broadly consistent with severity of injury will also be convincing in a medico-legal setting, whereas great disability after relatively minor injury raises problems of explanation.

2. Interview with Patient

The neuropsychological assessment should continue with an interview of the patient. This will include the patient's report of how they are feeling, of particular problems being encountered and of what help is being sought. Generally, one would also seek information on premorbid adjustment and the educational/employment level which had been attained in relation to assessment of premorbid intelligence.

Two very important matters which should be addressed at this point are the duration of retrograde and, more particularly, post-traumatic amnesia. Retrograde amnesia (RA) is very variable in length and although the presence of a period of RA is characteristic of severe head injury, there is not a good correlation between the length of RA and the severity of the injury to the brain or eventual outcome. (Teasdale & Brooks, 1985). The period of retrograde amnesia shows some shrinkage over time, although it will finally reach an irreducible minimum. The period of post-traumatic amnesia (PTA), on the other hand, is, as already outlined, a very important index of the severity of injury. Some psychologists find the concept of PTA a difficult one, as it does not fit well with their concepts of memory. However, despite the difficulties in assessing it, PTA remains one of the most useful extant measures of severity, and until or unless something better is developed, will continue to be a benchmark of severity (see Jennett & Teasdale, 1981).

The assessment of PTA is carried out by careful retrospective interviewing. The patient is asked what is the first thing to be remembered after injury and if things are remembered continuously from then on. It may, for example, happen that the patient remembers being in hospital for two or three days before transfer elsewhere: if the case record shows that the patient was in hospital for three weeks before transfer, it is likely, therefore, that PTA is of the order of two and a half weeks. Equally, there may be some particular event – a birthday, a relative's birthday, an item of news on television – which occurred at or just after the time of their first memory and which allows approximate dating of it. It is not important to distinguish, for example, between a PTA of 19 or 21 days. It is important rather to establish its *order of magnitude*.

Another method of assessing or corroborating evidence on PTA is to examine the case notes for evidence of the patient's orientation. If the patient has been well-managed medically there should be regular reports of whether the patient was responsive and orientated in person, place and time. Although the evidence is not unequivocal, probably the best conclusion that can be drawn is that PTA will not have ended while the patient was less than fully orientated; but PTA will not necessarily have ended immediately the patient became orientated – there may be a modest time lag between the two.

As regards severity of injury, the Glasgow Coma Scale is, of course, the other key index and has already been outlined. There are likely to be observations or charts in the original clinical notes which record the GCS regularly in the period following injury.

The major part of the interview will concern the range of changes generally known as "psychosocial" effects of head injury. Both patient and relatives should be questioned separately about these, and further discussion of psychosocial effects is provided towards the end of the chapter.

3. Mental Status Examination

The mental state examination in neuropsychology is very similar to that used in psychiatry but much shorter. This is because much of the data which could be obtained from the mental status examination is obtained in a much fuller and more objective form by psychometric testing. However, any assessment of the patient should begin with a brief examination of the basic parameters of cognitive and social behaviour.

This has two basic functions: firstly, to provide some matrix within which the results of the test can be interpreted, and secondly, to be sure that tests can in fact be administered to certain patients in certain states. It is clearly no good administering a test which is dependent on a set of highly complex verbal instructions to someone who is confused or aphasic. Mental status examination uses data from two sources. Firstly, much information is obtained by observation of the patient's behaviour and performance in simple tasks. Secondly, direct questioning reveals the content of the patient's thoughts and experience. The data could be organised in the following manner:

1. Appearance. As in psychiatry, the examiner notes the patient's dress, grooming, carriage, facial expression, eye contact, level of activity, mannerisms and any unusual movements. In a neuropsychological examination particular attention should be paid to the continuity of rapport, involuntary movements, wandering unattended hands, etc.

2. Orientation. This may be assessed informally, or, better, by using a standard procedure such as the Mini Mental State Examination (Folstein, Folstein, & McHugh, 1975), or the appropriate subtest from the Wechsler Memory Scale − Revised (Wechsler, 1987).

3. Speech. Observations are made of both delivery and content of speech. The examiner is looking for relatively low level problems such as dysarthria, dysphonia, etc., as well as specific language problems like aphasia, and problems to do with the content and control of speech arising, perhaps, from disinhibition, frontal lobe syndrome, perseveration, etc.

4. Thinking. Overt thinking disturbance should be noted. Many of the categories used in psychiatry will be relevant here. Basically one is looking for such things as mental confusion, poverty, circumstantiality, incoherence and stickiness.

5. Attention and Concentration. These may be assessed at basic level by such procedures as serial sevens and backward digit span. The examiner should also note whether the patient can shift mental set flexibly from one task to another (often a problem with frontal lobe-damaged patients), or is unduly susceptible to distraction, such as noises from outside the room.

6. Memory. Of course, this will be formally tested later but you really need to know, in order to have a sensible conversation with someone, whether they have sufficient memory to keep track of what you are saying and what they themselves have said. Simple assessment, using information supplied to the patient (e.g. your name, reason for the assessment), or by using a simple memory test such as the registration and recall items from the Mini Mental State Examination can be helpful: the latter involve asking the patient to name three objects in the room and asking that they be remembered; and after an intervening task, the patient is asked to recall the items.

7. Emotional State. This applies to both the mood (patient's prevailing emotional tone) and affect (the range and the appropriateness of the patient's responses on this background). In neuropsychological mental state examination, particular consideration must be given to the issues of emotional lability and control.

8. Special Pre-occupations and Experiences. A substantial proportion of severely head-injured persons develop post-traumatic epilepsy. Some forms of epilepsy (e.g. *grand mal* seizures) are unequivocally recognisable. Temporal lobe epilepsy (TLE) on the other hand is characterised by more subtle changes in consciousness. A comprehensive mental state examination should elicit such phenomena as changes in the experience of temporal sequence, *deja vu* experiences, visual and aural distortions, etc.

9. Insight. Some neuropsychological presentations are characterised by frank denial of disability. While extreme denial is fairly rare after head injury, it can occur. Much more common is a relative understating of deficit and denial of its consequences.

Formal Neuropsychological Examination

The characteristic picture is that abilities which are overlearned and well-practised, and which, presumably, involve a considerable element of redundancy, such as familiar verbal tasks, the use of language, capacity to define words, capacity to retrieve general knowledge, etc., are all relatively intact.

This means that crystallised intelligence (represented for example by some WAIS-R verbal subtests) is *relatively* intact and, therefore, not a sensitive measure for the kinds of damage which result from head injury. For example, in the studies by Brooks and his colleagues in which IQ was assessed at various times after head injury, a consistent picture emerged (see Brooks, 1984). Comparisons between severely head injured (SHI) individuals and controls showed only small, though statistically significant, differences on IQ measures. On verbal IQ measures the SHI-control differences were generally about 5 points. Given the error of measurement of IQ and the margin of error in estimating premorbid IQ, a difference of the average size − of 5 points − will be hard to detect in individual cases. As regards non-verbal IQ, the average SHI-control difference was about 9 points where the (untimed) Raven's Matrices were used − still a fairly modest difference.

On the other hand, tests such as four choice reaction time − which requires speedy response − or PASAT or Trails B − which require sustained speed of processing − cause particular difficulty for the head-injured (see Van Zomeren & Brouwer's chapter, also Gronwall & Wrightson, 1974). Perhaps most widely recognised of all, the severely head-injured have major difficulty with the learning of new information and do very badly on memory tests in general (e.g. Brooks 1984), although the choice of test must be appropriate. Formal testing should be aimed at those functions which are commonly disrupted in head injury, which are known to affect patients' daily functioning and which are indicated by mental status examination.

Initially, it is important to establish the level of premorbid ability as a basis for the interpretation of the rest of the examination. A professional person whose post-injury abilities remain above-average may be very handicapped, whereas a less able person with the same scores may have made a complete recovery. There are various methods of assessing premorbid ability. In the English language, the National Adult Reading Test (NART) (Nelson, 1982) has become established as an extremely useful element in this assessment, measuring an ability highly correlated with IQ, but which is, at the same time, fairly robust to the effects of many kinds of brain injury. The clinician may well use demographic information and other information about the patient's history alongside the score on the NART, but the severe limitations of simple demographic data need to be borne in mind. There is, however, evidence that predictive accuracy can be improved by adding a simple demographic index to the NART (Crawford et al., 1989; see also Chapter 3) although this work is still in progress. One instance when the NART may not be of value is where there is marked dysphasia or dysarthria and in this case the investigator will have to consider some other means of establishing an approximate premorbid level, for example, by using a best score approach (see Lezak, 1983).

Particularly where there are signs of focal brain damage, it will be useful to assess handedness as a clue to cerebral dominance (see Lezak, 1983).

The examiner will now move on to assess the present level of functioning and it may be useful to consider this under a number of headings.

1. Intelligence

Studies of intelligence test scores following head injury show, firstly, that scores are depressed following injury and on average show a recovery curve, although this masks great individual variability. The evidence that these effects are due to head injury comes from a number of sources: comparisons with appropriate controls with a similar demographic mix; sequential studies of head-injured patients which show recovery curves; and the fact that the severity of deficit is related to the severity of injury as assessed by duration of PTA (Brooks, 1984).

The general picture is that verbal IQ is less affected than performance IQ and that it recovers more rapidly to a plateau which is nearer to that obtained by controls and, presumably, nearer to the premorbid level. It is, therefore, quite possible that current verbal IQ is not very different from the premorbid estimate, even in a severely injured individual; it is more likely that the performance IQ will be impaired. There is often great variability in the subtest scores in brain-injured patients. It is important to remember that some subtests are fairly robust to the effects of diffuse brain injury, and indeed have been used by some to help estimate premorbid level. These include vocabulary-based tests and Information from the WAIS-R. It follows, therefore, that to calculate an overall verbal IQ score where the individual has high scores on the "robust" tests (sometimes called "hold" tests), and low scores on the "vulnerable" or "don't hold" tests will be misleading, averaging together impaired and relatively intact abilities. It is much more revealing to calculate Age Scaled Scores (which have a mean of 10 and a standard deviation of 3), thereby allowing a comparison of the patient, subtest by subtest, with the patient's peers (see Chapter 3).

The following is a hypothetical but characteristic example of verbal abilities following head injury, with age scaled scores quoted.

WAIS-R Subtest Scores		IQ Equivalent
Information	14	120
Comprehension	12	110
Arithmetic	9	95
Similarities	7	85
Vocabulary	15	125

To describe this person's abilities in terms of overall verbal IQ would be unhelpful. Verbal IQ may average out at 107, but it is likely that we have a previously very intelligent individual (whose high scores on "robust" subtests − Information and Vocabulary − gives a clue to previous high ability), who is impaired on the more "vulnerable" subtests. Assuming that the NART is used to estimate premorbid level, the most economical use of time is to concentrate on the more "vulnerable" subtests. Where the WAIS-R is used, these subtests would be Comprehension, Similarities, Arithmetic, Block Design and perhaps Digit Symbol or Object Assembly. Of course Digit Symbol may be excluded by motor problems.

2. Memory

Memory deficits are a hallmark of head injury. Remote memory is generally spared, so that some patients say their memory is good, they just can't remember what they did yesterday. Of memory tests in clinical use, probably only forward digit span is virtually intact, while story recall, paired associate learning, and visuospatial recall have all been shown to indicate impairments. The assessment of memory is discussed in detail elsewhere in this volume. However, it is worth remembering that the memory deficit is probably not homogeneous in head injury, sometimes involving registration and sometimes retrieval (see Levin et al., 1979) so that multiple-choice tests that assess recognition (and make retrieval easier) should not be used alone as they may miss deficits, e.g. the Recognition Memory Test (Warrington, 1984). It is, of course, the "real-life" outcome, the re-adjustment to home and family life, and the resumption of work and social activities, which really matter to the individual and deficits found in neuropsychological testing will not necessarily be of practical real-life significance. Checklists, filled in on a daily basis by patients and relatives are a useful supplement (Sunderland, Harris, & Baddeley, 1983).

3. Language

Frank aphasia may be rare after diffuse head injury, but it does occur where there is focal damage to the relevant areas of the dominant hemisphere. Therefore, when assessing the head injured one should be alert to the possibility of language dysfunction (the assessment of which is discussed elsewhere in this book). A screening assessment involving: consideration of spontaneous speech (convoluted?, hesitant?, etc.); confrontation naming (e.g. Boston Naming Test); repetition, obeying commands (e.g. Token Test); reading and writing (all elements suggested by Lezak, 1983), would generally suffice. If significant language dysfunction is present, fuller assessment will be indicated.

4. Attention/Concentration

In general, clinical tests in widespread use do not address these areas adequately and the methods that have proved to be valuable are relatively new and have been drawn from a more experimental psychology perspective than from a traditional psychometric approach. As with memory and language, attention is also discussed in more detail elsewhere in this book.

Attention and concentration should be tested at low levels using digit span and backwards digit span. Some information can be obtained from the Arithmetic subtest of the WAIS-R and from other arithmetic-type tests. The PASAT is the preferred way of checking for more subtle but important deficits in attention/concentration. Frontal lobe functioning may be tested by the Wisconsin Card Sort and this set of functions also heavily influences the Word Fluency Test.

Interviews with Patient and Relatives

There are a number of matters about which it is useful to interview parents and relatives *separately*. These topics are treated together in this section for convenience, but in practice will form part of the patient interview, elements of which have already been described, as well as forming a separate interview with a relative.

The reasons for conducting separate interviews have been described in a number of studies including that by McKinlay and Brooks (1984). This study demonstrated what was in fact a fairly common clinical observation:

that there is a systematic difference between the reports given by relatives and severely injured patients concerning some aspects of outcome. There was good agreement as regards physical and sensory difficulties suffered by the patient. There was a modest disagreement over cognitive abilities, particularly memory and concentration, whereby relatives reported these as being present to a greater extent than patients themselves. There was, however, a major difference over emotional and behavioural changes where the relatives were very likely to report these as being present, whereas the patient reported them as being absent.

One cannot conclude from this, of course, that the relatives are invariably right and the patients invariably wrong, but there are some reasons for believing that relatives are usually likely to be nearer the truth. Firstly, a number of patients show marked and blatant lack of insight, for example being grossly amnesic, while at the same time stating that their memory is better than ever. Secondly, careful work by Sunderland, Harris, and Baddeley (1983) provided important findings on the lack of validity of the self-reports of memory failure made by severely head-injured patients, whereas there was evidence for the validity of the accounts given by relatives.

The main part of the interview with both patient and relative will concern psychosocial effects of injury. In considering what areas to cover in these interviews, it is worth examining firstly the range of deficits which have been reported following head injury, and secondly concentrating on those deficits which have been found to be most persistent and disruptive to family life and the patient's return to work. In the reported long-term follow-ups (Brooks et al., 1987; Oddy et al., 1985; Thomsen, 1984), the most common difficulties included emotional, behavioural and cognitive changes as well as items such as slowness and tiredness. On the other hand physical or sensory incapacity was much less common. The importance of these common changes is not only that they persist in the long run, but that they are also an important source of stress for relatives (e.g. McKinlay et al., 1981) and an important barrier to the patient's return to work (Brooks et al., 1987). One observation which is important to note, is that recovery does not follow a smooth pattern with a gradual reduction in difficulties. It has been reported by a number of authors (McKinlay et al., 1981; McKinlay & Brooks 1984; McLean et al., 1983), that there is some rise in certain kinds of item over time, possibly reflecting that allowances are made for the injured person at first and that it is only when difficulties persist that they are thought remarkable.

In view of these studies in particular, and the now voluminous literature on head injury in general, the following matters should receive particular attention. The topics of anger and aggression are important. Where there is any evidence of untoward anger or aggression, it is important to determine the pattern, that is, whether we are looking at episodic dyscontrol (unprovoked outbursts, which some believe have a basis in epileptic-type discharges), "short fuse", or accumulating frustration.

Other areas about which questions should be asked are "post concussional" symptoms including headache, dizziness, irritability, anxiety, insomnia, and fatigue. Slowness and tiredness are very common indeed, and increased need for sleep may arise. Other matters which should receive attention are apathy, including lack of interest in previous activities and lack of social interest; lack of concern for personal hygiene; depression, mood swings, and childish behaviour; and practical memory, concentration, and language difficulties. Questions should also be asked about participation in rehabilitation-relevant activities, as many head-injured patients end up at home without suitable activities and structure to their days.

The purpose of the individual interviews is not only to give a more complete cover by relying on two independent sources, but to allow these two sources to be contrasted. We know that injured persons tend to under-report problems, and, to the extent that we have a mismatch between the relatives' and the head-injured persons' accounts, we can perhaps estimate the degree of insight or lack of it in the head-injured person.

Assessing the head-injured requires observational, interviewing, and formal testing skills. Such assessment, increasingly, represents the starting point for neuropsychological treatment and rehabilitation.

REFERENCES

Adams, J.H., Graham, D.I., Scott, G., Parker, L.S., & Doyle, D. (1980). Brain damage in fatal non-missile head injury. *Journal of Clinical Pathology, 33*, 1132-1145.

Brooks, N. (1984). Cognitive deficits after head injury. In N. Brooks (Ed.), *Closed Head Injury: Psychological, social, and family consequences*. Oxford: Oxford University Press.

Brooks, N., Campsie, L., Symington, C., Beattie, A., McKinlay, W. (1987). The effects of severe head injury on patient and relative within seven years of injury. *Journal of Head Trauma Rehabilitation, 2*, 1-13.

Brooks, D.N., Deelman, B.G., van Zomeren, A.H., van Dongen, H., van Harskamp, F., Aughton, M.E. (1984). Problems in measuring cognitive recovery after acute brain injury. *Journal of Clinical Neuropsychology, 6*, 71-85.

Brooks, N., McKinlay, W., Symington, C., Beattie, A., Campsie, L. (1987). Return to work within the first seven years of severe head injury. *Brain Injury, 1*, 5-19.

Crawford, J.R., Stewart, L.E., Parker, D.M., Besson, J.A.O., & Cochrane, R.H.B. (1989). Estimation of premorbid intelligence: Combining psychometric and demographic approaches improves predictive accuracy. *Personality and Individual Differences, 10*, 793-796.

Field, J.H. (1976). *The epidemiology of head injury in England and Wales*. London: HMSO.

Folstein, M., Folstein, S., & McHugh, P. (1975). Mini-Mental State: A practical method of grading the cognitive state of patients for the clinician. *Journal of Psychiatric Research, 12*, 189-198.

Gennarelli, T.A., Spielman, G.M., Langfitt, T.W., Gildenberg, P.L., Harrington, T., Jane, J.A., Marshall, L.F., Miller, J.D., & Pitts, L.H. (1982). Influence of the type of intracranial lesion on outcome from severe head injury. A multicenter study using a new classification system. *Journal of Neurosurgery, 56*, 26-32.

Gronwall, D., & Wrightson, P. (1974). Delayed recovery of intellectual function after minor head injury. *Lancet, 2*, 605-609.

Jennett, B., & Teasdale, G. (1981). *Management of head injuries*. Philadelphia: F.A. Davis.

Jennett, B. (1983). Post-traumatic epilepsy. In M. Rosenthal, E.R. Griffith, M.R. Bond, J.D. Miller, (Eds.), *Rehabilitation of the head injured adult*. Philadelphia: F.A. Davis Company.

Lezak, M.D. (1983). *Neuropsychological assessment* (2nd ed.). New York: Oxford University Press.

Levin, H.S., Grossman, R.G., Rose, J.E., & Teasdale, G. (1979). Long-term neuropsychological outcome of closed head injury. *Journal of Neurosurgery, 50*, 412-422.

Levin, H.S., O'Donnell, V.M., & Grossman, R.G. (1979). The Galveston Orientation and Amnesia test. A practical scale to assess cognition after head injury. *Journal of Nervous and Mental Diseases, 167*, 675-684.

Levin, H.S., Amparo, E., Eisenberg, H., Williams, D.H., High, W.M., McArdle, C.B., & Weiner, R.L. (1987) Magnetic resonance imaging and computerized tomography in relation to the neurobehavioural sequelae of mild and moderate head injuries. *Journal of Neurosurgery, 66*, 706-713.

Miller, D., & Jones, P. (1985). The work of a regional head injury service. *Lancet, 1*, 1141-1144.

McKinlay, W.W., Brooks, D.N., Bond, M.R., Martinage, D.P., & Marshall, M.M. (1981). The short-term outcome of severe blunt head injury as reported by relatives of the injured persons. *Journal of Neurology, Neurosurgery, and Psychiatry, 44*, 527-533.

McKinlay, W.W., & Brooks, D.N. (1984). Methodological problems in assessing psychosocial recovery following severe head injury. *Journal of Clinical Neuropsychology, 6*, 87-99.

McLean, A., Temkin, N.R., Dikmen, S., & Wyler, A.R. (1983). The behavioral sequelae of head injury. *Journal of Clinical Neuropsychology, 5*, 361-376.

Nelson, H.E., (1982). *National Adult Reading Test*. Windsor: NFER-Nelson.

Oddy, M., Coughlan, T., Tyerman, A., & Jenkins, D. (1985). Social adjustment after closed head injury: A further follow-up seven years after injury. *Journal of Neurology, Neurosurgery, and Psychiatry, 48*, 564-568.

Russell, W.R. (1971). *The traumatic amnesias*. London: Oxford University Press.

Sunderland, A., Harris, J.E., & Baddeley, A. (1983). Assessing everyday memory after severe head injury. In J.E. Harris & P.E. Morris (Eds.), *Everyday memory, actions and absentmindedness*. London: Academic Press.

Teasdale, G., & Brooks, N. (1985). Traumatic amnesia. In P.J. Vinken, G.W. Bruyn, & H.L. Klawans (Eds.), *Handbook of clinical neurology*, (Vol 45).

Teasdale, G., & Jennett, B. (1974). Assessment of coma and impaired consciousness. A practical scale. *Lancet, 2*, 81-84.

Thomsen, I.V. (1984). Late outcome of very severe blunt head trauma: A 10-15 year second follow-up. *Journal of Neurology, Neurosurgery, and Psychiatry, 47*, 260-268.

Warrington, E.K. (1984). *Recognition Memory test*. Windsor: NFER-Nelson.

Wechsler, D. (1987). *The Wechsler Memory Scale – Revised*. San Antonio: Psychological Corporation.

Wilson, J.T.L., Wiedmann, K.D., Hadley, D.M., Condon, B., Teasdale, G., & Brooks, D.N. (1988). Early and late magnetic resonance imaging and neuropsychological outcome after head injury. *Journal of Neurology, Neurosurgery, and Psychiatry, 51*, 391-396.

van Zomeren, A.H., & Brouwer, W.H. (1990). Attentional deficits after closed head injury. In B.G. Deelman, R.J. Saan, & A.H. van Zomeren, (Eds.), *Traumatic brain injury: clinical, social and rehabilitation aspects*. Amsterdam: Swets & Zeitlinger.

SECTION D:
SPECIALISED ASSESSMENT
TECHNIQUES

18 Assessment of the Head-injured for Compensation

William W. McKinlay
Chartered Psychologist, Case Management Services Ltd, 17A Main Street, Balerno. Edinburgh EH14 7EQ; Consulting Neuropsychologist, Scotcare Brain Injury Rehabilitation Unit, Newmains, Lanarkshire.

INTRODUCTION

The neuropsychologist with experience of the assessment and management of head-injured patients has a unique and important role to play in the process of litigation over compensation awards. If the neuropsychologist plays this part properly, it can provide the injured persons (with genuine deficits) and their family with the funds needed to secure necessary rehabilitation and re-education; to ensure that they are free from the added burden of poverty; and that they are freed from the worry of who will care for the injured parties should the nearest and dearest predecease them. If, on the other hand, the psychologist plays this part badly, the patient and family may find the problems of poverty, and lack of care and rehabilitation, added to the already-difficult problems posed by coming to terms with a head injury. Neuropsychologists may, of course, also be called as defence witnesses as well as for plaintiff/pursuer; in either case their task is to provide a careful and impartial assessment, identifying genuine deficits but also exposing any exaggeration.

ADMISSIBILITY

In order to play a proper part, it is, of course, essential that the psychologist's evidence is admitted to the legal process. Neuropsychologists have, rightly, been playing an ever-increasing role in the process of arriving at a fair and balanced view of the individual's needs for the purposes of settling financial compensation. There are, however, many different professions which may (potentially), give evidence, and confusion may arise. Instances have been reported where neuropsychological evidence has been admitted on a restricted basis. The reader is referred to an interesting paper by Schwartz (1987) for a more detailed discussion of this matter.

Schwartz reports a case in Florida in which neuropsychological testimony was challenged and, on appeal, it was held that it had been an error to admit a neuropsychologist's testimony as to the "future condition of the brain as the result of an accident". Schwartz describes the sequence of events which led to the evidence being challenged. In brief, it seems that the psychologist had emphasised that the individual's brain was affected, and that as a result of the injury the brain would deteriorate more rapidly than normal and had elaborated on this by bringing diagrams of brains into court and using these to illustrate the mechanics of the blow. A simple solution might be to confine one's remarks to the *effects* of the injury on brain function but, as Schwartz notes, this would be to avoid a core issue.

Neuropsychology is about brain-behaviour relationships. Psychological tests reflect the existence of brain damage and, in some circumstances, may provide some of the most sensitive indications thereof. However, it is also true that they are first and foremost measures of mental function, and that any conclusion about brain injury is *inferred* – and inferred moreover on the basis of more than just test evidence alone. It follows that where statements about brain damage are made on the basis of neuropsychological data they need to be suitably qualified and acknowledged to be probabilistic.

Schwartz concludes, as do many who write in this area, that the real danger is in inexperienced psychologists who are less likely to be precise about the limits of testimony and, therefore, more prone to having their evidence restricted.

Keeping firmly in mind and stating clearly to the court just what are the topics to which one can contribute expertise and those to which one cannot is essential. For instance, how a blow impacts on brain structure is primarily a neuropathological matter. An over-emphasis on the nature of structural brain damage may well leave the psychologist involved open to difficulties over admissibility. The prime emphasis should be on the neuropsychologist's core skills of identifying mental, behavioural, and emotional deficits, while, at the same time, not shrinking from making properly qualified inferences about brain dysfunction where appropriate.

"HORSES FOR COURSES"

The aforementioned is part of a general lesson to be noted in relation to questions of admissibility which applies not only to psychologists but to all expert witnesses. There are "horses for courses", and members of each of the many professions which may be called upon to give evidence have a contribution to make. If they are wise, they will make their own distinctive contributions, and not stray into areas where they are not qualified.

In the process of cross-examination one of the "tricks of the trade" which may be used by the cross-examining lawyer is to test out the limits of what the witness is and is not prepared to address. Incautious or rash witnesses may be willing to pontificate on all manner of subjects, including those for which they are not trained. If they do so, they will lay themselves open to criticism and to the devaluation of their evidence in the court. Thus, psychologists would be well advised not to offer opinions on the risk of epilepsy or, for example, on whether the degree of pain complained of is consistent with the known physical injury. The present author has been strongly encouraged by cross-examining lawyers to venture into such fields with such words as "It may not be *strictly* your field, but no doubt you have a view: Please tell me, I'd like to know". It is essential not to succumb and stray into fields where one's training and experience do not equip one to offer a well-informed view. Likewise, certain physicians will offer a view as to the intelligence and mental intactness of patients following brain injury. This is not on the basis of a careful examination and formal assessment but simply on their impressions. In the author's experience such physicians have sometimes found that their evidence is seriously devalued by so doing, even to the point of their reports being withdrawn by the lawyers who had instructed them in the first place.

What the neuropsychologist *can* do, on the basis of careful interview and examination, is describe the intact abilities and deficits, and whether the nature and extent of the apparent deficits is consonant with the nature and severity of the injury. Further comments can be made on the extent to which these deficits may be remediable or have the potential to be reduced by a specialised programme of rehabilitation, or indeed by less specialised local services provided in a properly organised way. The neuropsychologist can also consider the implications for return to work and for the degree of stress which is likely to be experienced by family members, and offer suggestions as to how best these problems may be dealt with. Accurate identification of deficits, and reasonable recommendations for rehabilitation may carry considerable financial implications.

THE EXAMINATION

The precise method of examining the patient and relative is something that will, to some extent, reflect the individual clinician's own experience as regards the tests and procedures with which that particular person is familiar. However, there are certain ground rules which are likely to be accepted by all with experience of examining such patients in a medico-legal context.

Firstly, it is extremely important to have access to the contemporary hospital records relating to the period following admission and, to a lesser extent, to any other records of hospital consultations thereafter.

The neuropsychologist will, of course, want to find out about the nature and severity of the injury. As indicated in the previous chapter, there are two key indices of severity of concussional injury (by far the most common kind of injury in peacetime). These are the Glasgow Coma Scale (GCS) score (Teasdale & Jennett, 1974) and the duration of post-traumatic amnesia (PTA) (see Teasdale & Brooks, 1985). These are not alternatives and both results should be obtained (indeed Professor Bryan Jennett, one of the authors of the GCS, has been a strong advocate of the use of PTA as well).

The two indices are not to be regarded as interchangeable: they do not necessarily correspond closely and, indeed, in recent work by Lindsay Wilson and his colleagues it has been shown that a group of patients whose GCS scores were never greatly reduced, nevertheless had prolonged PTA (Wilson, 1990). The long PTA was associated with poor outcome in spite of the lack of evidence of severe injury from the GCS, and the main neuropathology in this group appeared to be frontal and temporal contusion rather than diffuse axonal injury.

The contemporary records can and should provide important evidence to help the clinician in assessing both GCS and PTA. There should be observation charts which record the patient's level of responsiveness; and if these are not present, it may well be that observations by various individuals who examined the patients (particularly speech therapists, psychologists and occupational therapists), will report systematic evaluation of the orientation of the patient. Information about GCS and level of orientation allows one to chart the recovery of responsiveness; and the regaining of orientation is relevant to the assessment of PTA duration. Although there is not complete agreement on the matter, it seems probable that the return of orientation and the ending of PTA occur at about the same time, although they may not necessarily represent exactly the same event (see Teasdale & Brooks, 1985). To the extent that there may be a discrepancy it seems likely that the ending of PTA may post-date, although probably not to a very great extent, the return of continuous orientation.

The second element in the examination is a case history taken from the patient. This will cover the patient's background, including upbringing, education and employment history as well as previous health. It will also cover the effects of the injury as viewed by the patient. In this regard it is important to differentiate between what the patient tells you, what you observe, and what you infer. These may not always point in the same direction. It is well-known that head-injured patients may lack insight: for example, patients who are obviously considerably amnesic may claim that their memory is better than it ever was, so that what they say may not be taken at face value. For this reason it is particularly important in such cases to include a third element in the examination, namely to interview a suitable informant, usually a spouse or parent. This is something on which many authors have commented as being particularly useful in a medico-legal setting.

Two kinds of evidence have emerged from a number of studies of discrepancies between patients' and relatives' accounts. This bolsters the case for interviewing a relative separately. Firstly, it has been noted that the accounts of patients and relatives tend to differ in respect of cognitive and behavioural changes, with relatives likely to report as being present changes which the patient denies (McKinlay & Brooks, 1984). The patients may therefore be inclined to underestimate the extent of potentially important deficits in cognition and behaviour − assuming, of course, that the relatives are more accurate witnesses. Clearly, this is not necessarily always a correct assumption. However, as regards the memory problems of the head-injured, Sunderland et al. (1983), have provided evidence which suggests that the retrospective accounts given by relatives are indeed more valid than those of patients themselves. There is a further, quite separate, reason for interviewing relatives separately. The present author and his colleagues (McKinlay et al., 1983) found that the accounts of relatives appeared uninfluenced by whether or not a compensation case was pending, whereas the accounts of patients seemed to be slightly coloured. This issue receives further attention later.

The areas to be covered when interviewing patient and relative are broadly similar and cover the range of changes which may arise following head injury as well as the background factors referred to already. The range will include physical changes such as paralysis, weakness and sensory loss, impairment of sight, hearing, taste or smell, and the presence of fits or blackouts, dizzy spells and headaches. Of course, these are not the prime concern of the psychologist who should always make it clear when commenting on such matters that they should receive fuller attention in the reports of others; nonetheless such things are relevant to the individual's psychological state and it is, therefore, relevant to touch on them in order to get a broad picture.

Other matters of interest are whether or not there are deficits in speech or language, and in memory and concentration. In all of these it is worth asking for examples in order to form an impression of whether the complaints are realistic and credible. Changes in temperament and in social adjustment, loss of friends, and so on, are also important matters to ask about as are the prospects for a return to work including, for example, whether employment is being held open and whether the employer is likely to be sympathetic.

The final element will be the formal neuropsychological examination. The precise measures used vary to a considerable extent depending on the experience of the neuropsychologist. This aspect of the examination allows the neuropsychologist to view the patient's approach to, and performance on, a variety of standard tasks. The observation of this process and the results obtained from it are both important. The author's view is that it is not profitable to debate in detail the merits and demerits of individual tests as there is a tendency for particular psychologists to have measures with which they are comfortable. However, provided the tests meet the basic requirements of reliability and validity, and have adequate normative data, it is not crucial that particular tests are included or excluded.

However, it would probably not be a source of controversy to suggest that the examination should contain an assessment of handedness and orientation, an estimate of premorbid level of ability, and current verbal and performance intelligences, an assessment of language and praxis (possibly only on a screening basis), verbal and visuospatial memory, and concentration/mental speed/attention. The latter is particularly important despite the difficulties and complexities in defining the concepts, and the multiplicity of possible measures that have been described in Van Zomeren and Brouwer's chapter. In some traditional neuropsychological approaches, for example the Halstead-Reitan Battery, little assessment of this area is included. Yet, on measures such as choice reaction time and the Paced Auditory Serial Addition Task (PASAT) some large and important deficits have been found. Measures of such abilities, notably PASAT, have emerged alongside memory measures as being particularly important in differentiating between those who successfully return to work and those who do not (Brooks et al., 1987). In other words, deficits in this area are particularly likely after head injury and have functional significance so that it is extremely important they are not missed.

It should go without saying that it would be hopelessly inadequate simply to rely on a standard measure of intelligence and a unitary measure of memory in preparing a "neuropsychological" report. However, in the author's experience there are psychologists who have done just this.

In one case, a middle-aged man had been involved in a serious road traffic accident, in which members of his family had been killed. He was seen by an experienced and senior clinical psychologist but one who was neuropsychologically naive. Intelligence was assessed using two measures, the Mill Hill Vocabulary Scale and Raven's Standard Progressive Matrices, and memory, using the Memory Quotient from the original Wechsler Memory Scale. The three scores were in the 80s and 90s − not differing widely. It was concluded that there was "..little or no evidence of impairment...". In fact the patient had been earning a very high salary indeed prior to injury, having been pursuing a high-flying and successful career. The duration of PTA, not touched on in the report outlined earlier, was four weeks, indicating very severe injury, and a more detailed assessment revealed a man who appeared to be of very high previous ability with his highest islands of ability well above average. In contrast to this there were clear and significant deficits in aspects of memory, learning, and concentration.

One of the reasons why inexperienced psychologists fail to infer deficit is obviously lack of knowledge of what data to gather and what tests to use. Another may be that they feel exposed if they try to argue for deficits and do not know how, with reasonable confidence, to exclude the possibility of faking.

FAKING

The possibility of simulated disability following severe head injury has not been extensively discussed in the literature although there has been considerable controversy over the mildly head-injured. It has been argued that "post-concussional" symptoms of tiredness, headache, dizziness and irritability are especially likely after mild head injury and are motivated by the desire for financial gain (e.g. Miller, 1966). In support of this view, it has been argued that the severely injured do not suffer these "post-concussional" symptoms, which cannot, therefore, be a direct result of brain damage.

However, the observation that these "post-concussional" symptoms are largely absent in the severely injured may be erroneous, because other more severe symptoms and handicaps may be highly in evidence in the severely injured and mask the "post-concussional" symptoms. There is some relevant evidence (McKinlay et al., 1983): on careful examination a high level of post-concussional symptoms was found in severely injured patients and it was present whether or not they were claiming compensation. Moreover, other researchers have failed to find evidence that post-concussional symptoms and claims for compensation are linked. For example, Kelly (1975) has shown that many claimants make good recoveries before settlement while many non-claimants develop post-concussional symptoms. The evidence is now resolving the issue in favour of the view that compensation is not so important as was previously thought and that even mild injury results in a degree of injury to the brain. For example, in his widely quoted study, Oppenheimer (1968) found evidence of changes in the brains of mildly injured patients who subsequently died from other causes; neuro-otological and psychological examinations have revealed a high incidence of abnormalities in mildly injured patients (see Jennett & Teasdale, 1981 for a discussion); and studies of evoked potentials (the electrical response of the brain to simple sensory events), also suggest dysfunction in the mildly injured (e.g. Noseworthy et al., 1981).

As regards the severely injured, there has been more agreement in the literature. Even Henry Miller, who had argued strongly that the mildly injured make the most of their troubles, points out that the severely injured do not do so and indeed that they may fail to realise and admit the extent of their difficulties (Miller & Stern, 1965): "...their insistence that all is well is a potential source of injustice" unless expert assessment uncovers the full extent and nature of the disability. Rosenthal (1983, p.204) gives an example of such denial of disability: "Peter sustained a severe closed head injury .. at age 21. At the time he was a senior in college, achieving high grades .. " Injury resulted

in mild to moderate impairments in intelligence, memory and other higher
mental abilities.

Despite advice to the contrary, he persisted in pursuing law school entrance
immediately. His performance on the Law School Admission Test was marginal.
Nevertheless he did not acknowledge the possible persistence of mental deficits
and proceeded to enter a law school programme. Within four weeks after
entry, he dropped out, claiming that his professors were unfairly grading
him. He searched for another law school which would accept him, but failed
in this effort ...

In this case, the patient was unwilling to accept that any intellectual loss
had been suffered. Other authors have noted that the severely injured may also
fail to admit personality changes and emotional disturbances that are reported
by relatives or are apparent on careful examination (McKinlay & Brooks, 1984;
Thomsen, 1974). It is, therefore, necessary to obtain assessments from medical
practitioners and clinical psychologists experienced in assessing neurological
impairments if handicaps are not to be overlooked.

In one study there was no evidence that a group of compensation claimants
had faked low psychological test scores as their performance was equal to that of
non-claimants. Moreover, relatives of claimants and non-claimants gave virtually
identical reports of patients' symptoms. The only difference between the groups
was a slight tendency for claimants to report on average more symptoms than
non-claimants. This was a general effect, not specific to any particular kind
of symptom, and because it was small and not accompanied by poor test
performance or exaggerated reports of symptoms by relatives, it seemed
unlikely to represent deliberate simulation of disability. Finally, it was noted that
psychological testing and separate interviews with relatives were unaffected − at
least in the sample studied − by whether or not compensation was claimed, and
should, therefore, be important elements of the overall assessment (McKinlay
et al., 1983).

Of course, the contention that faking is seldom a problem does not mean
that it *never* arises. Many neuropsychologists have come across fairly clear
instances of faking, and the question of how it may be detected merits
consideration. A thorough examination including a review of the records
will generally reveal a consistent picture, and it is in those cases where
the deficits seem out of proportion to the documented severity of injury
that real worries about the possibility of faking arise. One tactic is to
repeat the examination, where possible using parallel test forms: few people
can convincingly fake bad scores over two quite lengthy examinations. Another
tactic arises from studies of faking. Heaton et al. (1978) mixed a group
of students who were to pretend to be head-injured with a group of real
head-injured patients. Both were assessed by psychologists who were unaware

of which were the confederates. The psychologists were poor at making the distinction, but they were doing so in very unrealistic conditions: they had only limited information (mainly a selection of test scores) to go on, with key information about nature and severity of injury not available to them. Of more interest was another finding from the study, that the test profiles of fakers and real patients differed significantly, with fakers tending to do poorly on *all* tests while real patients had no real difficulty with some tests (e.g. digit span, finger tapping) but great difficulty with others (e.g. Trails B, Category test). A further study by Gudjonssen and Shackleton (1986) produced results which were, in principle, very similar. They used a test of intelligence (Raven's Standard Progressive Matrices) involving five subtests of increasing difficulty and compared subjects asked to fake with real impaired subjects. The fakers did poorly across the board, on easy as well as difficult subtests, while impaired patients showed a gradient, coping with the easier items relatively well. On the basis of their data, these authors provided an index to distinguish fakers from non-fakers.

REPORTS

There are several areas which require consideration in the report:

1. It is important to consider the extent to which the individual has deficits. The inferring of deficits is not necessarily a particularly straightforward matter; there are various approaches which may be taken and which receive attention in Chapter 3 of this book. Nevertheless, the inconsistencies in levels of mental ability following head injury are often very striking. If an appropriate selection of tests has been used it is often not difficult to see that there is a clear-cut deficit in aspects of memory, for example, and particularly in attention/mental speed.

2. There is a considerable neuropsychological literature on recovery from head injury and a statement about the prognosis is of importance. In general, however, patients are only referred for medico-legal examinations a good number of months or even some years after injury so that often it will already be clear whether or not there are likely to be significant long-term deficits.

3. The extent to which deficits found are remediable is obviously a difficult matter, but there is a growing literature on the specialist neuro-rehabilitation after head injury which gives considerable grounds for optimism (see Brooks, 1991 for a discussion), the chief negative prognostic feature being poor premorbid adjustments (e.g. Prigatano, 1986).

4. There is a considerable literature on the degree of stress in relatives (e.g. Brooks, 1984) and this is relevant to consideration of whether respite care and other forms of help may be necessary.

5. Lastly, questions about return to work, or the possibility of sheltered work, are ones which should be addressed, taking into account the literature on return to work (e.g. Brooks et al., 1987).

REPORTS AND THE COURT

The presentation of all of this information is something which also requires consideration. It is widely accepted that a well-written report will make it less likely that the individual will need to go to the trouble of appearing in court and being cross-examined; and that a poorly written and inconsistent report is an invitation for a hostile and testing cross-examination to try to bring out the weaknesses which appear to be present.

As only a minority of cases will proceed to a full hearing in court, the report will very often be the only means by which expert witnesses communicate their view. In any event it will always be the first means. It is, therefore, important that the report be written in as clear and lucid a style as possible, avoiding unnecessary recourse to jargon terms and always keeping in mind that the role of the expert witness is to be "an educator" (Deutsch & Parker, 1985), making available to the court information drawn from their area of expertise that may be helpful in deciding the case under consideration. It is, therefore, imperative to communicate clearly and in a manner that can be understood by individuals not familiar with the relevant field.

The individual appearing in court should also be aware of the various techniques which may be used to test out the witness and to entice them to make unwise statements. A grasp of the basic mechanics of appearing in court and some of the "tricks of the trade" which may be used to test one in cross-examination is a valuable weapon to have. Being aware of the various possibilities and, therefore, prepared to encounter them, makes one able to give one's evidence in a more relaxed, clear, and straightforward fashion.

Cooke (1990), offers some practical advice on the actual giving of evidence. He notes that when you enter the witness box you will be asked to take the oath, thus providing a good chance to determine the acoustics of the courtroom. He also notes a courtroom convention which requires the witness to speak directly to the Judge (or Jury), whereas it is lawyers who are asking the questions. This can be turned to the witness's advantage simply by turning at the waist to receive the question and turning again to reply to the Judge or Jury, thereby allowing the witness to control the rate at which questions are asked. This avoids the aggressive lawyer pressuring the witness with quick-fire questions and puts the witness in more control of the situation. Cooke also outlines a number of "tricks of the trade" which may be used by lawyers to test out a witness. These include the asking of esoteric questions intended to fluster an expert: The wise expert will explain firmly that this is not the kind of information that one commits to memory but the kind of information for which a sensible expert uses reference books.

Lawyers may also try to unsettle you by asking questions in an unpredictable order or by interrupting. The remarks already made about controlling the rate at which evidence is given by directing answers to Judge or Jury are relevant here, as is the advisability of never starting an answer with "yes" or "no", but always giving any qualification first. The answer to the question: "Will the patient recover sufficiently to work?" might be given as: "Yes, if he receives a lengthy and intensive programme of rehabilitation". If cut off prematurely this would be a misleading answer; whereas the answer: "If he receives a prolonged intensive programme of rehabilitation, yes", is one that cannot be so cut off. Cooke also describes a number of further tricks amongst which is the so-called "slippery slope" whereby the witness is invited to agree to a series of statements which are made to sound as though they mean much the same thing but which, in fact, differ. For example, the witness might be asked on a number of occasions whilst giving evidence what are the possibilities that a particular patient will return to work. The witness's first response might have been that it was "extremely unlikely". In the course of further evidence, the witness would be invited to agree to the proposition that it was indeed "rather unlikely" and perhaps in the course of summing up very quickly the word "rather" would be dropped and the witness would simply be asked to agree to the proposition that it was unlikely, alongside many other propositions. The experienced witness will be pedantic and will always pick up the lawyer who tries to do this and insist that the same or an equivalent qualifying adjective, in this case "extremely", is invariably used. Otherwise the lawyer will be able to sum up by saying that the expert agreed to a whole series of statements ranging from "extremely unlikely", through "rather unlikely", to "unlikely", thereby implying that the expert is very lax in use of language.

CONCLUSION

In conclusion there is perhaps no better way of summing up the role of the neuropsychologist than to quote some key points advocated by Deutsch and Parker (1985) on the expert's role in litigation: (1) maintain intellectual honesty; (2) maintain consistency from case to case (in other words, do not take a "robust view" when acting for the defenders and a "sympathetic" one when acting for the plaintiff or pursuer); (3) avoid dogmatism; (4) avoid statements which cannot be substantiated by clear fact or observation; (5) if you do not know the answer to a question do not be afraid to say so; (6) avoid being pulled out of areas of expertise; (7) do not become flustered or angry on the stand; (8) do not become bogged down in minutiae; (9) be an educator not an advocate (Deutsch & Parker, 1985).

REFERENCES

Brooks, N. (1984). Head injury and the family. In Brooks, N. (Ed.) *Closed head injury: Psychological, social, and family consequences.* Oxford: Oxford University Press.

Brooks, N., McKinlay, W., Symington, C., Beattie, A., & Campsie, L. (1987). Return to work within the first seven years of severe head injury. *Brain Injury, 1,* 5-19.

Brooks, N. (1991). The effectiveness of post-acute rehabilitation. *Brain Injury, 5,* 103-109.

Cooke, D.J. (in press). Do I feel lucky? Survival in the witness box. *Neuropsychology.*

Deutsch, T.M., & Parker, E.C. (1985) *Rehabilitation testimony: Maintaining a professional perspective.* Albany, NY: Matthew Bender.

Gudjonssen, G.H., Shackleton, H. (1986). The pattern of scores on Raven's Matrices during "faking bad" and "non-faking" performance. *British Journal of Clinical Psychology, 25,* 35-41.

Heaton, R.K., Smith, H.H., Lehman, R.A.W., Vogt, A.T. (1978). Prospects for faking believable deficits on neuropsychological testing. *Journal of Consulting and Clinical Psychology, 46,* 892-900.

Jennett & Teasdale (1981). *Management of head injuries.* Philadelphia: F.A. Davis & Co.

Kelly, R. (1975). The post-traumatic syndrome: An iatrogenic disease. *Forensic Science, 6,* 17-24.

McKinlay, W.W., Brooks, D.N., Bond, M.R. (1983). Post-concussional symptoms, financial compensation and outcome of severe blunt head injury. *Journal of Neurology, Neurosurgery, and Psychiatry, 46,* 1084-1091.

McKinlay, W.W., Brooks, N. (1984). Methodological problems in assessing psychosocial recovery following severe head injury. *Journal of Clinical Neuropsychology, 6,* 87-99.

Miller, H. (1966). Mental after effects of head injury. *Proceedings of the Royal Society of Medicine, 59,* 257-261.

Miller, H., & Stern, G. (1965). The long term prognosis of severe head injury. *Lancet, 1,* 225-229.

Noseworthy, J.H., Miller, J., Murray, T.J., & Regan, D. (1981). Auditory brainstem responses in post concussion syndrome. *Archives of Neurology, 38,* 275-278.

Oppenheimer, D.R. (1968). Microscopic lesions in the brain following head injury. *Journal of Neurology, Neurosurgery, and Psychiatry, 31,* 199-206.

Prigatano, G.P. (1986). *Neuropsychological rehabilitation after brain injury.* Baltimore: John Hopkins University Press.

Rosenthal, M. (1983). Behavioural sequelae. In M. Rosenthal, E.R. Griffith, M.R. Bond, J.D. Miller, (Eds.), *Rehabilitation of the head injured adult.* Philadelphia: F.A. Davis Company.

Schwartz, M.L. (1987). Limitations on neuropsychological testimony by the Florida Appellate decisions: Action, reaction, and counteraction. *The Clinical Neuropsychologist, 1,* 51-60.

Sunderland, A., Harris, J.E., Baddeley, A.D. (1983). Assessing everyday memory after severe head injury. In J.E. Harris, & P.E. Morris (Eds.), *Everyday memory, actions and absentmindedness.* London: Academic Press.

Teasdale, G., & Brooks, N. (1985). Traumatic amnesia. In P.J. Vinken, G.W. Bruyn, & H.L. Klawans (Eds.), *Handbook of clinical neurology (Vol 45).*

Teasdale, G., & Jennett, B. (1974). Assessment of coma and impaired consciousness. *Lancet, 2,* 81-84.

Thomsen, I.V. The patient with severe head injury and his family. *Scandinavian Journal of Rehabilitation Medicine, 6,* 180-183.

Wilson, J.T.L. (1990). The significance of MRI in clarifying whether neuropsychological deficits after head injury are organically based. *Neuropsychology, 4,* 261-269.

19 Event-related Potentials in Clinical Neuropsychology

Michael D. Rugg
Wellcome Brain Research Group, Department of Psychology, University of St. Andrews

INTRODUCTION

Event-related potentials (ERPs)[1] are small perturbations of the spontaneous electrical activity of the brain (the electroencephalogram or EEG) time-locked to a defineable event such as the onset of a stimulus or the initiation of a movement. Because of their small size relative to the spontaneous EEG, ERPs are usually derived by averaging a number of EEG samples (typically 25 or more).

ERPs are commonly depicted as waveforms representing voltage against time. When displayed in this manner, they consist of a series of positive- and negative-going voltage deflections (see Fig. 19.1). The peaks of these deflections are conventionally labelled by their polarity and either their ordinal position in the waveform, or their approximate peak latency. Thus, N2 would be the second negative-going peak in a waveform, P200 would be a positive-going peak with a latency of approximately 200 msec, and so on. ERP peaks are often referred to as "components", reflecting the idea that a peak has a special significance in that it reflects the time of the maximum activity of an intracerebral ERP "generator". In fact, a voltage deflection on the scalp may result from the summation of activity of any number of generators, and the peak of the deflection need not coincide

---

[1] ERPs are also commonly referred to, especially in the fields of sensory physiology and clinical neurology, by the labels: "averaged evoked responses" (AERs); "averaged evoked potentials" (AEPs); or "evoked potentials" (EPs).

393

with the time of maximum activity of any one of these. It has been suggested, therefore, (e.g. Näätänen, 1982) that the term "component" be restricted to those features of a waveform which can be attributed to a single intracerebral source. Identifying such sources, and specifying the neurophysiological events which cause them to give rise to electrical fields on the scalp, is a formidable problem, an excellent introduction to which can be found in Wood (1987).

ERP components are commonly defined along an "exogenous/endogenous" dimension. This dimension correlates roughly with time, such that in each sensory modality, exogenous components tend to occur at earlier latencies than do endogenous components. At the exogenous extreme are components generated in an obligatory fashion following the presentation of a stimulus, and they are present in the ERP waveform largely irrespective of the subject's psychological state. A good example of exogenous components is given by the auditory brainstem potentials. These consist of a series of waves generated in the first 6 msec or so following an auditory transient such as a click, and are so insensitive to the psychological state of a subject that they can be recorded even in comatose patients (Chiappa, 1983). By contrast, endogenous components are not generated or modulated simply as a result of stimulus presentation, but as a consequence of the psychological processes associated with the processing of the stimulus. An endogenous component may modulate regions of a waveform containing one or more exogenous components, and may overlap with other endogenous components in time and distribution over the scalp. The paradigmatic example of such a component is the P3 (or P300; see p.395), the amplitude of which is modulated by such factors as stimulus probability and task relevance, and which can even be evoked by the omission of an expected stimulus (Sutton et al., 1967).

To date, the main clinical applications of ERPs have come about through the exploitation of the sensitivity of relatively short-latency exogenous components to pathology in sensory pathways. These applications will not be discussed further in the present chapter, which will concentrate instead on a discussion of the role of ERPs in the investigation of cognitive dysfunction in neurological patients. Readers wishing for further information about the use of ERPs in sensory testing should consult one of several recent texts on the subject (e.g. Chiappa, 1983; Halliday, 1982).

ENDOGENOUS ERPS

Although they have yet to find widespread clinical application, endogenous ERP components[2] have been the subject of a large body of research over the past 20 years or so (see Hillyard & Kutas, 1983, for a review).

---

[2] Note that although for the sake of historical consistency these phenomena are termed "components" in the following sections of this chapter, this does not imply that each reflects the activity of a single intracerebral source.

Major Endogenous Components

This section gives a brief outline of the most heavily researched endogenous components (see Fig. 19.1 for illustrative waveforms).

Processing negativity. This refers to an ERP component which is sensitive to the direction of selective attention. The phenomenon was first reported by Hillyard et al. (1973) in a task in which subjects were required to attend to auditory stimuli presented to one ear, while ignoring stimuli in the other ear. Hillyard et al. (1973) reported that the N1 component (peaking around 100 msec) of the ERPs elicited by attended stimuli was larger than that to unattended stimuli, and interpreted this as a sign of early (stimulus set) attentional selection. Subsequent work (e.g. Näätänen et al., 1978) has shown that this attention effect can be obtained in a variety of tasks, and is caused not by the enhancement of N1, as originally thought, but by the modulation of a negative-going wave (processing negativity) which often overlaps in time with the N1 component. Similar effects have been reported in the visual (e.g. Hillyard & Munte, 1984) and somatosensory (e.g. Desmedt & Robertson, 1977) modalities, and much of the relevant literature has been reviewed by Näätänen (1982; 1990).

N2. A number of separate phenomena are confusingly aggregated under the label "N2". Two of the most important of these are each evoked by rare stimuli (so called "oddballs") interspersed in a sequence of more frequent stimuli. When subjects are required to detect oddball stimuli, ERPs to these stimuli contain a negative-going deflection with a latency of approximately 200 msec (N2 or N2b), sometimes followed by a sharp, frontally-maximum positive peak (known as P3a). The amplitude of N2b is determined both by the probability of the evoking stimuli, in that it is larger for less probable items, and by the degree of "effort" required to identify a stimulus as a target, while its peak latency appears to co-vary with the time taken to identify the stimulus (Fitzgerald & Picton, 1983). Näätänen and colleagues (e.g. Näätänen & Gaillard, 1983) have documented the existence of a second negative component in the same latency range as N2b. This has been labelled "mismatch negativity" or "N2a", and is elicited by very rare auditory stimuli irrespective of whether the stimuli are identified, or even noticed, by the subject. This has been interpreted as a manifestation of the brain processes underlying the pre-attentive detection of environmental change. A useful classification and review of N2 components can be found in Näätänen and Picton (1986).

P3. Also known as P3b (to distinguish it from P3a mentioned earlier), P300, or the Late Positive Component, this is the most heavily researched endogenous ERP component to date. It takes the form of a positive wave, of variable latency,[3] which is usually largest over the parietal midline irrespective of the modality of the evoking stimulus. Originally described by Sutton et al. (1965) in a task in which subjects had to guess the identity of upcoming stimuli, P3 can be recorded in a wide variety of paradigms (for reviews see Pritchard, 1981; Verleger, 1988). One of the most common means of evoking a sizeable P3 is the "oddball" task, in which relatively rare stimuli, which must be actively processed by the subject in some way, are presented in a sequence of more frequent stimuli. The amplitude of P3 in oddball tasks is inversely proportional to the probability of the target stimulus, but other factors determining its amplitude, particularly in more complex tasks, are incompletely understood, and its psychological significance is the subject of considerable debate. However, because of its relatively large amplitude and robustness, and the fact that its peak latency appears to correlate well with the time required to categorise the evoking stimuli (McCarthy & Donchin, 1981), clinical studies have investigated P3 more than any other endogenous component.

N400. This refers to a negative wave, peaking around 400 msec, which is evoked by unexpected or "unprimed" words. N400 was originally described by Kutas and Hillyard (1981) in a paradigm in which subjects viewed sequentially presented words constituting a sentence. Compared to sentences with highly predictable endings, e.g. (he took a sip from the *tap*), unexpected endings, e.g. (he took a sip from the *waterfall*), or frankly anomalous endings (he took a sip from the *transmitter*) elicited large N400 components. Kutas and Hillyard (1984) subsequently demonstrated that N400 amplitude was inversely proportional to the expectedness of the sentence ending, and proposed that the amplitude of this component was inversely correlated with the degree to which a word had been semantically primed by its preceding context. Consistent with this, N400 has been found to be modulated by semantic associations between pairs of words (Rugg, 1985).

CNV. The Contingent Negative Variation (CNV) was first described by Walter et al. (1964). They found that when a warning stimulus (S1) preceded an imperative stimulus (S2) by a short period of time, the S1-S2 interval contained a negative-going wave (the CNV) which reached its maximum amplitude at the time of S2. This was originally thought to be a unitary phenomenon reflecting build-up of anticipation or expectation. Subsequent research has demonstrated that the CNV consists of at least two dissociable negative-going components: a relatively early, frontally-distributed wave that appears to be evoked specifically by the first stimulus, and a later, centrally distributed wave which seems to be associated with preparation to respond. Both of these components can be

---

[3] The label "P300" is misleading in that, depending on variables such as task difficulty and subject population, the peak latency of this component can vary from around 300 msec to as much as 800 msec.

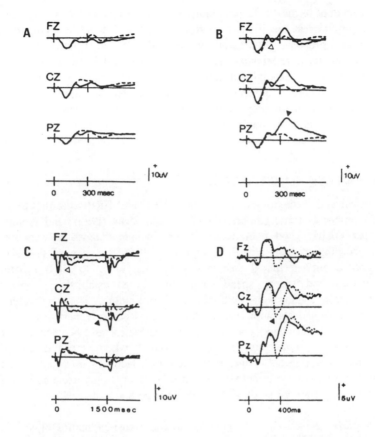

FIG. 19.1. Examples of four endogenous ERP components. In each case, the waveforms have been averaged over a group of normal subjects, and are from three midline electrodes situated over frontal (Fz), central (Cz) and parietal (Pz) regions of the scalp. A. Processing negativity—waveforms recorded during a task involving discrimination between high- and low-pitch tones of short and long duration. The stimulus parameters were chosen so that it was easier to discriminate pitch than duration, and subjects were required to respond to the longer-duration tones of a designated pitch. The waveforms shown here were evoked by the short-duration tones of the relevant (solid lines) and irrelevant (dashed lines) pitch. Waveforms evoked by stimuli of the relevant pitch are more negative-going than those evoked by irrelevant stimuli; this difference is processing negativity. B. N2 and P3—waveforms evoked in an auditory "oddball" task by rare 500 Hz tones (P = 0.25; solid lines) interspersed among frequent 250 Hz tones (P = 0.75; dashed lines). N2 and P3 components are indicated by open and filled triangles respectively. C. CNV—the frequency of an initial tone signalled whether a response was required to another tone 1500 msec later. Compared to the no-response condition (dashed lines), tones signalling the need to respond to the second stimulus list evoke an early frontally-distributed negativity (the "early" CNV; open triangle), and then a centrally-maximum negative wave (the "late" CNV; closed triangle). D. N400—ERPs evoked by words which were preceded either by a semantically associated (solid line) or unassociated word (dotted line). N400 is indicated by the triangle.

obtained outside the S1-S2 paradigm, implying that the CNV may not in fact reflect any process specific to a contingent relationship between pairs of stimuli. It has been proposed (Rohrbaugh & Gaillard, 1983) that the earlier of the two CNV components reflects an orienting response evoked by S1, while the later component is an example of the "readiness potential" – a negative wave which also precedes spontaneous voluntary movements and is thought to be associated with motor preparation. Whether any other component of the CNV exists, reflecting some non-motoric anticipatory process, is currently a matter of some controversy.

Methodological Considerations

Technical and methodological aspects of EEG and ERP recording are covered in a number of texts. Cooper, Osselton, and Shaw (1980), and Picton (1981), are particularly good references, as they include detailed information about the recording of long-latency, endogenous ERPs. In spite of the availability of good-quality technical information, a newcomer to ERP recording is, nonetheless, advised to spend some time in an established laboratory, so as to obtain a thorough methodological grounding. The remainder of the present section deals with issues which are particularly pertinent to work on endogenous ERP components in neuropsychological and neurological settings. Some of these issues are of less importance when recording short-latency exogenous components. Thus, ERP recording facilities provided by a clinical neurophysiology department which routinely records only exogenous ERPs may not be appropriate for studies of endogenous components.

Amplifier Bandwidth. In contrast to the transient nature of short-latency ERPs, endogenous ERPs often persist for relatively substantial periods (the reason why the term "slow potentials" is sometimes used for phenomena such as the CNV). For example, activity attributable to the P3 component in figure 19.1B lasts for some hundreds of milliseconds. To resolve such low frequency electrical activity it is necessary to use amplifiers with long time-constants. The time-constants should be at least 1 sec (meaning that a signal of 0.16 Hz would be attenuated by the amplifier to 70% of its true value), and ideally a time constant of at least 5 sec (30% attenuation of a 0.03 Hz signal) is desirable. The consequences of passing ERP components through amplifiers with time-constants that are too short are twofold: the components are attenuated in amplitude and, equally seriously, are artefactually displaced forward in time. It is important to note that EEG machines and commercial ERP averaging systems often do not possess the low-frequency characteristics necessary for long-latency ERP recording.

Eye-movement Artefact. Because of their frequency characteristics, and the fact that they are often formed by averaging relatively few trials, endogenous

ERP components are extremely susceptible to electro-oculographic (EOG) artefact from eye movements. The simplest way of dealing with eye-movement artefact is to record the EOG and use this to identify and reject any trial containing eye movements greater than some pre-set criterion. This procedure, although almost universal at present, is far from ideal. It is wasteful, and in subjects who have difficulty complying with instructions to suppress eye movements, it may prove impossible to collect sufficient artefact-free trials to form averages with adequate signal-to-noise ratios. In addition, the requirement to suppress eye movements presents subjects with a task additional to the one they are instructed to perform on the experimental stimuli. This can result in a further deterioration in performance in individuals who would in any case have difficulty coping with the experimental task. Because of these problems, a number of techniques for the statistical estimation and removal of EOG artefact from ERPs have been developed (O'Toole & Iacono, 1987). With modern laboratory computers these techniques can now be implemented quite easily, and are likely to become the norm in the near future.

Scalp Topography. Most endogenous ERP components are defined in part by their amplitude distribution over the scalp, especially along the midline. Moreover, differences between clinical and control subjects in the scalp distribution of an ERP component may occur in the absence of gross differences in amplitude or latency. At the minimum therefore, an anterior-posterior chain of three recording channels (situated over mid-frontal, mid-central and mid-parietal scalp regions) is required, and ideally these electrodes should be supplemented with others over lateral sites. Electrode positions are almost always chosen and described with reference to the "International ten-twenty system" (Jasper, 1958), which provides a means of placing electrodes in equivalent scalp locations irrespective of head size.

Conventionally, ERP recordings are carried out by referring all scalp electrodes to a single distant reference electrode, so that the relative amplitude of ERPs at different scalp sites can be assessed as unambiguously as possible. The most frequently employed reference for recording endogenous ERPs is linked mastoids (obtained by shorting two electrodes situated on the left- and right-mastoid processes respectively). However, the proximity of the mastoids to temporal regions of the scalp means that this reference is not ideal when temporal electrodes are employed. Alternatives include the tip of the nose or, possibly most suitable of all, a non-cephalic reference such as that suggested by Stephenson and Gibbs (1951).

It is important to note that considerable caution is required in using the scalp distribution of an ERP effect to infer the intracerebral location of its source(s). A unique solution for the location and orientation of the generator(s) of an electrical field on the surface of a three-dimensional object such as a head cannot be calculated using the distributional information alone (the so-called "inverse problem"). This problem can be made more tractable in a number of ways (e.g. constraining solutions by requiring anatomical and physiological plausibility, and allowing only a small number of sources to be active at any time; see Wood, 1982), but the fact remains that by themselves, scalp distribution data can be no more than suggestive. In particular, when an ERP effect is widely distributed over the scalp, it can be very difficult to know whether this should be ascribed to an anatomically circumscribed source deep in the brain, or to a source which is anatomically diffuse but near the scalp. Furthermore, much cortical tissue is situated in sulci oriented at right angles to the directly overlying scalp, and an ERP generator in such tissue can give rise to a voltage distribution apparently at variance with the generator's anatomical location. For example, slow potentials preceding hand movements are maximal over central scalp regions contralateral to the hand moved, consistent with the decussation of the cortico-spinal pathways, but analogous potentials preceding foot movements are largest over the hemisphere *ipsilateral* to the limb moved. This apparent paradox occurs because motor cortex controlling the foot is situated medially, in the central fissure, and is therefore oriented so as to produce a voltage field with a maximum over the contralateral hemisphere (Brunia & Vingerhoets, 1981). Because of such complexities, scalp distributional data are often of limited value for identifying the intracerebral locus of an ERP effect, and need to be supplemented by more direct evidence (see pp.404−408).

When comparing scalp distributions of an ERP component across groups, it is important to take account of the fact that ERP amplitudes at different scalp sites are related in a non-linear fashion, in that as the mean amplitude (averaged across electrodes) of a region of the waveform changes, the relative amplitudes at different scalp sites vary in a multiplicative rather than an additive fashion. This can cause problems when ANOVA is employed to analyse ERP data, in that if two groups differ significantly on a measure of ERP amplitude, the significance level of the group by electrode site interaction term cannot be used to decide whether the groups also differ with respect to the scalp distribution of the measure. Before a group by electrode site interaction term can be used to compare scalp distributions, it is necessary to re-scale the data so that the mean amplitude of the measure of interest is equivalent in the two groups (McCarthy & Wood, 1985).

Finally, it should be noted that skull defects, such as burr holes and plates, can seriously distort ERP scalp distributions. It is important to bear this in mind when considering whether any functional significance should be attached to abnormal distributions in neurosurgical patients.

Quantification of ERP data

There is as yet no agreed general method for the quantification of ERP waveforms. A comprehensive, though technical, introduction to many of the available techniques can be found in Glaser and Ruchkin (1976). The most difficult aspect of ERP measurement concerns how to separate, and thereby independently quantify, components that overlap both in time and scalp distribution. The most common approach to this problem at present is to try to separate components by such criteria as latency, scalp distribution and sensitivity to experimental manipulations. For instance, informed that relatively rare stimuli elicited a positive-going, parietally-maximum peak with a latency around 400 msec, few investigators would have any reservations about identifying the peak as the P3 component. Things are often not so simple however, and there are as yet no agreed rules about how to apply the three criteria noted earlier to determine the component structure of a waveform.

One quantitative approach to the problem of component overlap has been to subject ERP waveforms to principal components analysis (PCA), followed by rotation of the extracted factors (Donchin & Heffley, 1978). This is relatively easy to do, as most major statistical packages include the necessary programmes, which are variants of those used with many factor analytic techniques. The aim is to reduce a set of ERP waveforms to a small number of factors (components), and to estimate the relative contributions of these factors to each waveform in the data set. Although objective, and apparently tackling the problem of component overlap head-on, the application of PCA to ERP data suffers from two major problems. First, it is necessary to assume that each component in the waveform set has a constant latency across experimental treatments. Second, a simulation study (Wood & McCarthy, 1984) has shown that PCA can "misallocate" variance between components. That is, some of the variance due to one ERP component in the original data set becomes associated with a derived factor supposedly representing a different component. For these reasons, the use of PCA has declined markedly in recent years. Unfortunately, no more appropriate means of dealing with the complexities of ERP data has yet emerged.

Ultimately, the method employed to quantify ERP data depends on the use to which the data are to be put. In many circumstances, experimental questions do not necessitate the recovery of the fine-grained component structure of a waveform, but instead address the issue of whether an experimental manipulation gives rise to a reliable waveform modulation with particular topographical and temporal characteristics. In these circumstances it is often sufficient to quantify ERPs by measuring, with respect to a suitable baseline, the mean amplitude of selected latency regions of the waveforms. This form of amplitude measurement is often preferable to the more "traditional" method of measuring the amplitude of the peaks of a waveform. Peaks can be difficult to identify consistently across subjects and, because they comprise (by definition) only one sampling point, they can be unduly affected by unresolved noise in the waveform. When it is necessary to measure peak amplitude and latency, it is advisable, if possible, to choose experimental parameters known to maximise the amplitude, and "sharpen" the scalp distribution, of the peak in question, so as to make it as easy to identify as possible.

Neuropsychological applications often necessitate the statistical assessment of ERPs from individual subjects. This can be achieved by determining whether the measure(s) of interest fall within a confidence interval derived from the data of a suitable control group. This group should ideally consist of subjects who, in addition to being matched on conventional indices, yield ERPs with similar signal-to-noise characteristics to those of the patient(s). Because of the imperfect signal-from-noise separation of ERP waveforms, it is important to assess the reliability of the data from single-case studies by obtaining repeat recordings whenever possible.

Assumptions Underlying the Use of Averaging

The employment of averaging to enhance the signal/noise ratio of ERPs is based on two assumptions, namely that the signal (i.e. the ERP) remains constant over trials, and that "noise" (i.e. the background EEG plus any extracerebral artefact such as muscle activity) is uncorrelated with the signal. If these assumptions are met, the signal-to-noise ratio of an ERP will improve as a function of the square root of the number of trials used to form the average. For practical purposes, the first of these assumptions is the most important. It is difficult to assess whether ERPs embedded in single trials are homogeneous, yet if this is not so an average is obviously not representative of the single trials from which it is formed. This is particularly problematic when interpreting differences in the amplitude of an ERP component. Amplitude differences can be caused by differences in the size of the component on all trials, differences on only some of the trials, or by differences in across-trial variance in the latency of a component of unchanged amplitude (known as "latency jitter"). The standard deviation of averaged waveforms may sometimes be helpful in determining which of these situations prevails, in that a negative correlation between amplitude and inter-trial variability would suggest that variability may be an important factor in accounting for differences in amplitude.

A second problem brought about by the need to average ERPs is that psychological processes which change rapidly over a few trials (such as those underlying habituation) can be studied only with difficulty.

Neuropsychological Applications of ERPs

ERPs can play a number of roles in clinical neuropsychology. This section discusses these roles and some of their accompanying conceptual and interpretational problems.

Diagnosis

Very little work has attempted to develop endogenous ERPs as diagnostic tools in a neuropsychological context, with the exception of studies investigating P3 latency in dementia. The origins of this interest in P3 were contained in two reports (Goodin et al., 1978a; b) claiming, firstly, that the peak latency of P3 increases with age, and, secondly, that the P3s from demented patients are abnormally long. Subsequent work has amply confirmed that the latency of P3 increases with age, although there is a disagreement about the exact form of the age/P3 latency function (cf. Brown et al., 1982, and Picton et al., 1984). It has also been confirmed that, as a group, demented individuals exhibit longer P3 latencies than non-demented controls (e.g. Gordon et al., 1986), but it is not clear whether P3 latency gives an increase in diagnostic efficiency over what can be obtained using psychometric procedures (Kraiuhin et al., 1986; Pfefferbaum et al., 1990; for a different view, see Goodin, 1990). It may be, therefore, that the value of the association between prolonged P3 latency and dementia lies less in its diagnostic potential than in the clues it may provide about the nature of the diseases causing dementia. It should be noted that prolonged P3 latency has been reported in other conditions in which "cognitive slowing" is a significant feature, such as closed head injury (Campbell et al., 1986), and alcoholism (Pfefferbaum et al., 1979), and is, therefore, not specific to dementing illnesses. However, Goodin and Aminoff (1987) have reported that when combined with the latencies of the preceding N1 and P2 components, P3 latency allows the differentiation of patients suffering from Alzheimer's disease, Parkinson's disease with dementia, and Parkinson's disease without dementia.

Investigating Cognitive Dysfunction

Specifying a cognitive impairment in terms of a dysfunction in one or more components of an information-processing model is an important aspect of neuropsychological investigations, as exemplified by much recent work on disorders of language (e.g. Coltheart et al., 1987). In this respect ERPs can provide a valuable complement to conventional behavioural indices of cognitive functioning for the following reasons:

1. Because they provide a real-time record of neural events, ERPs allow an upper-bound estimate to be made of the time required for discrimination between two classes of stimuli. Such estimates require no assumptions about the relationship of different ERP components to specific cognitive processes, nor any knowledge about the neural generators of ERPs. The relatively direct nature of such inferences avoids many of the problems inherent in attempts to infer the same kind of information solely from reaction-times.

2. If it is assumed that the latency of a particular ERP component correlates with the time-course of a specific cognitive process, then measurement of such latencies can allow the partitioning of the time taken to make a behavioural response into various sub-processes. For example, Rugg et al. (1988) reported that the peak latency of the N2 component (peaking around 220 msec) elicited by rare auditory stimuli was prolonged in patients who had sustained a moderate or severe closed head injury. On the basis of previous work (Fitzgerald & Picton,

1983), Rugg et al. (1988) postulated that the peak latency of N2 correlates with the time taken to categorise the evoking stimulus, and proposed, therefore, that an impairment in perceptual categorisation contributes to the slow responding typical of head-injured patients.

3. Because ERPs can provide a measure of cognitive activity in the absence of overt behaviour, they are useful when the requirement to produce a response would alter the process of interest. For example, Rugg et al. (1989) investigated ERPs from head-injured and control subjects in a forewarned GO/NOGO reaction-time task, in which the warning stimulus signalled whether or not a response would be required to a second stimulus occurring 1.5 sec later. In the controls, ERPs to the stimulus signalling the need to respond contained a large frontally-distributed negative wave, which was much smaller in the ERPs elicited by the stimulus signalling that no response was required on that trial. By contrast, the patients' ERPs contained equally large frontal negativities to both classes of stimuli. In view of the evidence associating frontal negative waves in forewarned RT tasks with orienting (Rohrbaugh & Gaillard, 1983), Rugg et al. (1989) concluded that the head-injured patients, unlike the controls, did not attribute different levels of salience to the GO as opposed to the NOGO stimuli.

4. ERPs may also play a role when it is suspected that a subject's overt behaviour on some discrimination task results from a dissociation of "conscious processing" from brain processes still capable of performing the discrimination (see Milner & Rugg, 1991 and Schacter et al., 1988, for reviews of such phenomena). An early example of this approach, using an autonomic measure, is given by Bauer (1984), who demonstrated that skin conductance responses in a prosopagnosic patient differentiated individuals' names when these were correctly or incorrectly paired with faces that the patient could neither name nor identify by other means. Although skin conductance is, of course, a quite different physiological variable from scalp-recorded ERPs, Bauer's study elegantly demonstrates the benefits of employing "indirect" as well as "direct" measures of discrimination. More recently, Renault et al. (1989) have shown that ERPs too can reveal differential processing of familiar and unfamiliar faces in prosopagnosia, opening the way for more direct studies of the processes underlying this remarkable phenomenon.

Investigating the Neurological Basis of Cognitive Impairment

Because of the development of high resolution anatomic and metabolic imaging techniques, there is now rarely a clinical need to localise gross brain pathology by indirect methods such as ERPs. However, it is usually desirable to assess the integrity of a brain system at the functional as well as the anatomic level. Although metabolic techniques such as PET scanning provide functional information with a reasonably high level of anatomic resolution, the temporal resolution of these techniques is presently three or more orders of magnitude coarser than electrophysiological data. ERPs, therefore, still have a role to play in a neurological as well as a cognitive context.

In using ERPs to yield information about neural integrity it is important to distinguish between ERP components that are *generated* by a particular brain area or system, and those that are merely *modulated*. That is, a distinction must be made between ERP effects arising directly from the activity of some brain structure, and effects which, although generated by unknown mechanisms, are nonetheless known to depend on the integrity of an identified brain region. In the first case, changes in the scalp distribution of the ERP effect in question might be attributable to some abnormality of the generator. In the second case, the scalp distribution of the ERP effect will have no relation to the anatomical location of the brain region of interest, and only the size and latency of the effect will be informative with respect to an assessment of functional integrity. In either case, an ERP abnormality in a patient or patient sample can, of course, only be interpreted as indicating dysfunction in a given brain area if it can be ascertained that no functionally relevant pathology exists "upstream" of the brain structure in question. To take an extreme example, the absence of a P3 component to auditory stimuli is of little interest if the patient is deaf!

At present, because so little is known about the generators of scalp-recorded ERPs, very limited progress has been made in employing ERPs to assess the integrity of central brain systems. Considerable interest was generated by work employing intracerebral recordings which suggested that the P3 component might be generated in the hippocampus and/or adjacent structures (Halgren et al., 1980). Unfortunately, comparisons of scalp and intracerebral waveforms (Altafullah et al., 1986), recordings from patients with unilateral temporal lobe pathology (e.g. Johnson & Fedio, 1986; Rugg et al., 1991), and the effects of medial temporal lobe lesions on a monkey analogue of P3 (Paller et al., 1988), all suggest that the integrity of the hippocampus is not necessary for the generation of the scalp P3. At present, the inferior parietal cortex appears to be the most promising alternative (Knight et al., 1989; Smith et al., 1990).

Although not recordable from the scalp, P3-like activity evoked within the medial temporal lobes seems likely to prove a useful indicator of the functional state of these structures (Meador et al., 1987; Puce et al., 1989). Unfortunately, this application of ERPs is, of course, limited to the very few patients in whom intracerebral electrodes are implanted.

A more promising approach to the assessment of medial temporal function with scalp-recorded ERPs comes from work investigating recognition memory for visually presented words. Compared to ERPs elicited by words on their initial presentation, ERPs to the same words, when these are repeated within a minute or so, are more positive-going in the latency range approximately 250-700 msec post-stimulus (e.g. Halgren & Smith, 1987). This old-word/new-word ERP difference has been reported to be absent in patients who have undergone left, but not right, temporal lobectomy (Smith & Halgren, 1989). It is possible, therefore, that this ERP effect depends on the integrity of structures in the left temporal lobe, in which case it may have some value in the assessment of patients suspected of having pathology in these regions (see also Rugg et al., 1991).

Investigating the Functional Significance and Neural Origins of ERPs

The venerable tradition of employing neurological patients to elucidate the functional and neural basis of normal behaviour can also be applied to the elucidation of ERPs. In view of the present state of knowledge about endogenous ERP components, it is arguable that this is presently the most valuable and urgent application of ERPs in neuropsychology. As this enterprise begins to bear fruit, clinical applications of the type described in the foregoing sections will then become more numerous and based on an increasingly secure rationale.

There are two principal questions about ERPs that can be addressed by employing neurological populations. First, by using populations in which a cognitive impairment is reasonably well-specified, one can test hypotheses about the relationship of a particular ERP component to the putatively impaired process. For example, given the hypothesis that the "old-word/new-word" ERP effect described earlier depends on "explicit" rather than "implicit" memory for words, the effect should be attenuated or abolished in amnesic patients, in whom explicit memory is selectively impaired (Schacter, 1987). It is important to note that although this hypothesis could confidently be rejected if the old-word/new-word effect was normal in amnesics, the converse does not necessarily apply. An abnormal ERP effect could arise because of disruption to a system which depends on the *outcome* of the one that has been impaired, that is, a system "downstream" of the locus of impairment. Thus, if amnesic patients failed to show the old-word/new-word ERP difference, it could not be concluded that this difference must, in normal subjects, reflect explicit memory function. It could instead reflect a process which operated subsequent to the successful retrieval of an item from memory. Therefore, although it would be possible to conclude that explicit memory for words was necessary for the old-word/new-word effect to arise, further work would be needed to demonstrate that it was sufficient.

A second way of using neurological populations to elucidate ERPs is to record from patients with relatively circumscribed brain lesions, so as to investigate the role of different brain regions in the generation of an ERP component. Once again, the logic of lesion studies dictates a certain asymmetry in the conclusions that can be drawn. If the ERP component of interest is unaffected by a particular lesion, it can be concluded that the affected brain region(s) do not participate in the component's generation. However, if a lesion is associated with an abnormality in the ERP component, it cannot be concluded that the locus of the component's generator has been found; merely that the lesioned area is necessary for the component's appearance. It is only in the light of converging evidence, for example, from scalp distribution studies in normal subjects, that a stronger statement may be possible.

Relationship of ERPs to Behavioural Data

Most of the paradigms employed to obtain endogenous ERPs are tied to some form of task, and it is important to take advantage of this by recording and analysing subjects' overt performance whenever possible. ERPs and task performance can deviate from the normal pattern in three basic ways, as discussed in the following:

First, a dissociation between ERPs and behaviour can occur such that behaviour is normal but the ERP data are not. In this case it can be concluded that the neural structures damaged by the lesion, and the psychological processes mediated by these structures, are necessary for the ERP effect but not for task performance. Assuming that a suitable task has been employed, the refinement of relevant information-processing and/or neuropsychological models of ERP modulation can be accomplished knowing that the failure to find normal ERPs was not caused by a "low-level" deficit such as impaired sensory processing, because such a deficit would have also disrupted behavioural performance. Obviously, an important aspect of model refinement will be the generation of hypothesis about the behavioural relevance of those processes thought to be reflected by the ERP effect in question. This, in turn, will lead to the employment of tasks on which the abnormal ERP effect should be accompanied by impaired performance.

Second, the situation can arise in which performance is impaired, but task-related ERP effects are normal. In this case, it can be concluded that the brain structures and psychological processes impaired by the lesion are not necessary for the generation of the ERP effect. In an analogous fashion to the converse dissociation, it can also be concluded that the behavioural impairment is unlikely to be caused by a "low-level" deficit, as this would also be expected to disrupt ERPs.

Third, ERPs and behaviour can both be abnormal. This state of affairs is extremely hard to interpret, although a clue can sometimes be obtained by comparing the ERPs evoked by stimuli associated with correct and incorrect responses (this will only be possible, of course, if the error rate is high enough to yield sufficient "incorrect" trials to form an ERP with an acceptable signal-to-noise ratio). If ERPs on correct and incorrect trials do not differ, it is likely that the processes reflected by the ERPs are not tied closely to those required for task performance. By contrast, if the ERPs elicited on correct trials are more similar to control waveforms than those on incorrect trials, this may suggest that the processes they reflect are related in some way to those required for performance of the task. The nature of this relationship is still uncertain, however, as it cannot easily be determined whether the ERPs reflect processes necessary for, or merely correlated with, accurate task performance.

In the light of the foregoing discussion, it should be clear that the selection of appropriate tasks and performance measures is essential to the interpretation of endogenous ERPs in clinical populations. An important practical and conceptual problem is presented by the fact that the interpretation of abnormal ERPs is most difficult when they are associated with impaired task performance. The circumvention of this problem can require considerable experimental ingenuity.

CONCLUDING REMARKS

The employment of ERPs in neuropsychological populations, whether as an aid to understanding the reasons for a particular cognitive impairment, or as a means of increasing knowledge about the cognitive and neuropsychological basis of ERP components, is in its infancy. It should be apparent that numerous technical and conceptual difficulties must be overcome before ERPs can make a substantial contribution to clinical neuropsychology. Although at the present time there may be some situations in which ERPs might be helpful, most of their possible applications to clinical neuropsychology await a considerably greater understanding of the cognitive and neurophysiological determinants of ERP waveforms.

REFERENCES

Altafullah, I., Halgren, E., Stapleton, J., & Crandall, P.H. (1986). Interictal spike-wave complexes in the human medial temporal lobe: Typical topography and comparisons with cognitive potentials. *Electroencephalography and Clinical Neurophysiology, 63*, 503-516.

Bauer, R.M. (1984). Autonomic recognition of names and faces in prosopagnosia: A neuropsychological application of the guilty knowledge test. *Neuropsychologia, 22*, 457-469.

Brown, W.S., Marsh, J.T., & La Rue, A. (1982). Exponential electrophysiological aging: P3 latency. *Electroencephalography and Clinical Neurophysiology, 55*, 277-285.

Brunia, C.H., & Vingerhoets, A.J. (1981). Opposite hemisphere differences in movement-related potentials preceding foot and finger flexions. *Biological Psychology, 13*, 261-269.

Campbell, K., Houle, S., Lorrain, D., Deacon-Elliot, D., & Proulx, G. (1986). Event-related potentials as an index of functioning in head-injured outpatients. In W.C. McCallum, R. Zappoli, & F. Denoth (Eds.), *Cerebral psychophysiology: Studies in event-related potentials.* Amsterdam: Elsevier.

Chiappa, K.H. (1983). *Evoked potentials in clinical medicine.* New York: Raven Press.

Coltheart, M., Sartori, G., & Job, R., (Eds.), (1987). *The cognitive neuropsychology of language.* London: Lawrence Erlbaum Associates Ltd.

Cooper, R., Osselton, J.W., & Shaw, J.C. (1980). *EEG technology* (3rd ed.). London: Butterworths.

Desmedt, J.E., & Robertson, D. (1977). Differential enhancement of early and late components of the cerebral somatosensory evoked potentials during forced-pace cognitive tasks in man. *Journal of Physiology (London), 271*, 761-782.

Donchin, E., & Heffley, E. (1978). Multivariate analysis of event-related potential data: A tutorial review. In D.A. Otto (Ed), *Multidisciplinary perspectives in event-related potential research*. Washington, DC: Environmental Protection Agency.

Fitzgerald, P.G., & Picton, T.W. (1983). Event-related potentials recorded during the discrimination of improbable stimuli. *Biological psychology, 17*, 241-276.

Glaser, E.M., & Ruchkin, D.S. (1976). *Principles of neurobiological signal analysis*. London: Academic Press.

Goodin, D.S. (1990). Clinical utility of long latency "cognitive" event-related potentials (P3): The pros. *Electroencephalography and Clinical Neurophysiology, 76*, 2-5.

Goodin, D.S., & Aminoff, M.J. (1987). Electrophysiological differences between demented and non-demented patients with Parkinson's Disease. *Annals of Neurology, 21*, 90-94.

Goodin, D.S., Squires, K.C., Henderson, B., & Starr, A. (1978a). Age-related variations in evoked potentials to auditory stimuli in normal human subjects. *Electroencephalography and Clinical Neurophysiology, 44*, 447-458.

Goodin, D.S., Squires, K.C., & Starr, A. (1978b). Long-latency event-related components of the auditory evoked potential in dementia. *Brain, 101*, 635-648.

Gordon, E., Kraiuhin, C., Stanfield, P., Meares, R., & Howson, A. (1986). The prediction of normal P3 latency and the diagnosis of dementia. *Neuropsychologia, 24*, 823-830.

Halgren, E., & Smith, M.E. (1987). Cognitive evoked potentials as modulatory processes in human memory formation and retrieval. *Human Neurobiology, 6*, 129-139.

Halgren, E., Squires, N.K., Wilson, C.L., Rohrbaugh, J.W., Babb, T.L., & Crandall, P.H. (1980). Endogenous potentials generated in the human hippocampal formation and amygdala by infrequent events. *Science, 210*, 803-805.

Halliday, A.M. (Ed.). (1982). *Evoked potentials in clinical testing*. London: Churchill-Livingstone.

Hillyard, S.A., & Kutas, M. (1983). Electrophysiology of cognitive processing. *Annual Review of Psychology, 34*, 33-61.

Hillyard, S.A., Hink, R.F., Schwent, V.L., & Picton, T.W. (1973). Electrical signs of selective attention in the human brain. *Science, 182*, 177-180.

Hillyard, S.A., & Munte, T.F. (1984). Selective attention to color and location: An analysis with event-related brain potentials. *Perception and Psychophysics, 36*, 185-198.

Jasper, H.H. (1958). The ten twenty electrode system of the International Federation. *Electroencephalography and Clinical Neurophysiology, 10*, 371-375.

Johnson, R., & Fedio, P. (1986). P300 activity in patients following unilateral temporal lobectomy: A preliminary report. In W.C. McCallum, R. Zappoli, & F. Denoth (Eds.), *Cerebral psychophysiology: Studies in event-related potentials*. Amsterdam: Elsevier.

Knight, R.T., Scabini, D., Woods, D.L., & Clayworth, C. (1989). Contributions of the temporal-parietal junction to the human auditory P3. *Brain Research, 13*, 109-116.

Kraiuhin, C., Gordon, E., Meares, R., & Howson, A. (1986). Psychometrics and event-related potentials in the diagnosis of dementia. *Journal of Gerontology, 41*, 154-162.

Kutas, M., & Hillyard, S.A. (1981). Reading senseless sentences: Brain potentials reflect semantic incongruity. *Science, 207*, 203-205.

Kutas, M., & Hillyard, S.A. (1984). Brain potentials during reading reflect word expectancy and semantic association. *Nature, 307*, 161-163.

McCarthy, G., & Donchin, E. (1981). A metric for thought: A comparison of P300 latency and reaction time. *Science, 211*, 77-80.

McCarthy, G., & Wood, C.C. (1985). Scalp distributions of event-related potentials: An ambiguity associated with analysis of variance models. *Electroencephalography and Clinical Neurophysiology, 62*, 203-208.

Meador, K.J., Loring, D.W., King, D.W., Gallagher, B.B., Gould, M.J., Flanigan, H.F., & Smith, J.R. (1987). Limbic evoked potentials predict site of epileptic focus. *Neurology, 37*, 494-497.

Milner, A.D., and Rugg, M.D. (1991). *The neuropsychology of consciousness.* London: Academic Press.

Näätänen, R., (1990). The role of attention in auditory information processing as revealed by event-related potentials and other brain measures of cognitive function. *Behavioral and Brain Sciences, 13,* 201-288.

Näätänen, R. (1982). Processing negativity: An evoked-potential reflection of selective attention. *Psychological Bulletin, 92,* 605-640.

Näätänen, R., & Gaillard, A.W.K. (1983). The orienting reflex and the N2 deflection of the ERP. In A.W.K. Gaillard & W. Ritter (Eds.), *Tutorials in event-related potential research: Endogenous components.* Amsterdam: North-Holland.

Näätänen, R., & Picton, T.W. (1986). N2 and automatic versus controlled processes. In W.C. McCallum, R. Zappoli, & F. Denoth (Eds.), *Cerebral psychophysiology: Studies in event-related potentials.* Amsterdam: Elsevier.

Näätänen, R., Gaillard, A.W.K., & Mäntysalo, S. (1978). Early selective-attention effect on evoked potential reinterpreted. *Acta Psychologica, 42,* 313-329.

O'Toole, D.M., & Iacono, W.G. (1987). An evaluation of different techniques for removing eye-blink artifact from visual evoked response recordings. *Psychophysiology, 24,* 487-497.

Paller, K.A., Zola-Morgan, S., Squire, L.R., & Hillyard, S.A. (1988). P3-like brain waves in normal monkeys and monkeys with medial temporal lesions. *Behavioral Neuroscience, 102,* 714-725.

Pfefferbaum, A., Ford, J.M., & Kraemer, H.C. (1990). Clinical utility of long latency "cognitive" event-related potentials (P3): The cons. *Electroencephalography and Clinical Neurophysiology, 76,* 6-12.

Pfefferbaum, A., Horvath, T.B., Roth, W.T., & Kopell, B.S. (1979). Event-related potential changes in chronic alcoholics. *Electroencephalography and Clinical Neurophysiology, 47,* 637-647.

Picton, T.W. (1981). The use of human event-related potentials in psychology. In I. Martin & P.H. Venables (Eds.), *Techniques in psychophysiology.* Chichester: Wiley.

Picton, T.W., Stuss, D.T., Champagne, S.C., & Nelson, R.F. (1984). The effects of age on human event-related potentials. *Psychophysiology, 21,* 312-325.

Pritchard, W.S. (1981). Psychophysiology of P300. *Psychological Bulletin, 89,* 506-540.

Puce, A., Kalnins, R.M., Berkovic, S.F., Donnan, G.A., & Bladin, P.F. (1989). Limbic P3 potentials, seizure localisation and surgical pathology in temporal lobe epilepsy. *Annals of Neurology, 26,* 377-385.

Renault, B., Signoret, J.L., Debruille, B., Breton, F., & Bolgert, F. (1989). Brain potentials reveal covert facial recognition in prosopagnosia. *Neuropsychologia, 27,* 905-912.

Rohrbaugh, J.W., & Gaillard, A.W.K. (1983). Sensory and motor aspects of the contingent negative variation. In A.W.K. Gaillard & W. Ritter (Eds.), *Tutorials in event-related potential research: Endogenous components.* Amsterdam: North-Holland.

Rugg, M.D. (1985). The effects of semantic priming and word repetition on event-related potentials. *Psychophysiology, 22,* 642-647.

Rugg, M.D., Pickles, C.D., Potter, D.D., & Roberts, R.C. (1991). Normal P300 in a case of extensive unilateral medial temporal lobe damage. *Journal of Neurology, Neurosurgery, and Psychiatry, 54,* 217-222.

Rugg, M.D., Cowan, C.P., Nagy, M.E., Milner, A.D., Jacobson, I., & Brooks, D.N. (1988). Event-related potentials from closed head injury patients in an auditory "Oddball" task: Evidence of dysfunction in stimulus categorisation. *Journal of Neurology, Neurosurgery and Psychiatry, 51,* 691-698.

Rugg, M.D., Cowan, C.P., Nagy, M.E., Milner, A.D., Jacobson, I., & Brooks, D.N. (1989). CNV abnormalities in closed head injury. *Brain, 112,* 489-506.

Rugg, M.D., Roberts, R.C., Potter, D.D., Pickles, C.D., Nagy, M.E. (1991). Event-related potentials related to recognition memory: effects of unilateral temporal lobectomy and temporal lobe epilepsy. *Brain, 114*, 2313–2332.

Schacter, D.L. (1987). Implicit memory: History and current status. *Journal of Experimental Psychology: Learning Memory and Cognition, 13*, 501-518.

Schacter, D.L., McAndrews, M.P., & Moscovitch, M. (1988). Dissociations between implicit and explicit knowledge in neuropsychological syndromes. In L. Weiskrantz (Ed.), *Thought without language*. Oxford: Oxford University Press.

Smith, M.E., Halgren, E., Sokolik, M., Baudena, P., Musolino, A., Liegeois-Chauvel, C., & Chauvel, P. (1990). The intracranial topography of the P3 event-related potential elicited during auditory oddball. *Electroencephalography and Clinical Neurophysiology, 76*, 235-248.

Smith, M.E., & Halgren, E. (1989). Dissociation of recognition memory components following temporal lobe lesions. *Journal of Experimental Psychology: Learning Memory and Cognition, 15*, 50-60.

Stephenson, W.A., & Gibbs, F.A. (1951). A balanced non-cephalic reference electrode. *Electroencephalography and Clinical Neurophysiology, 3*, 237-240.

Sutton, S., Tueting, P., Zubin, J., & John, E.R. (1967). Information delivery and the sensory evoked potential. *Science, 155*, 1436-1439.

Sutton, S., Braren, M., Zubin, J., & John, E.R. (1965). Evoked potential correlates of stimulus uncertainty. *Science, 150*, 1187-1188.

Verleger, R. (1988). A critique of the context updating hypothesis and an alternative interpretation of P3. *Behavioral and Brain Sciences, 11*, 343-427.

Walter, W.G., Cooper, R., Aldridge, V., McCallum, W.C., & Winter, A.L. (1964). Contingent negative variation: An electrical sign of sensorimotor association and expectancy in the human brain. *Nature, 203*, 380-384.

Wood, C.C. (1987). Generators of event-related potentials. In A.M. Halliday, S.R. Butler, & R. Paul (Eds.), (1987). *A Textbook of clinical neurophysiology*. Chichester: Wiley.

Wood, C.C. (1982). Application of dipole localization methods to source identification of human evoked potentials. *Annals of the New York Academy of Sciences, 388*, 139-155.

Wood, C.C., & McCarthy, G. (1984). Principal component analysis of event-related potentials: Simulation studies demonstrate misallocation of variance across components. *Electroencephalography and Clinical Neurophysiology, 59*, 249-260.

20

Computer-Based Assessment in Neuropsychology

Sarah L. Wilson
Research Fellow (Psychology), Research Department, Royal Hospital and Home, Putney, London SW15 3SW

T.M. McMillan
Top Grade Clinical Psychologist, Department of Clinical Psychology, Wolfson Medical Rehabilitation Centre, Atkinson Morley's Hospital, Wimbledon, London SW20 0NE

INTRODUCTION

Microcomputers have become widespread in the working environment of the psychologist. Their use for functions such as word processing and the management and analysis of data is familiar; however they can, of course, also be used as a medium for the presentation of psychological tests. This application has a number of merits and disadvantages for the psychologist and careful consideration is required before deciding whether or not to embark on computer-based assessment.

Interest in computer-based psychological assessment began in the 1960s and the field has continued to develop. The initial work was carried out with machines that were larger and more cumbersome than contemporary microcomputers, and were relatively expensive. Such factors had a limiting effect on early work, and it was only with the arrival of the comparatively inexpensive, easy to operate and also portable microcomputer, that developments in computer-based assessment began to proliferate. There have been a number of general reviews of the advantages, problems and likely developments in the use of computers in psychological assessment (Bartram & Bayliss, 1984; French, 1986; Miller, 1968; Sampson, 1983; Thompson & Wilson, 1982).

THE ADVANTAGES OF COMPUTER-BASED ASSESSMENT

One of the major advantages of computerised over conventional forms of testing is that a machine can be relied upon to present material in a standardised manner; test stimuli will always be presented consistently. If comments from the tester are required, such as: "well done" or "are you happy with your answer?", delivery can be included in the test program and presentation will be standardised from subject to subject. One problem for the human examiner is the potential for conscious or inadvertent prompting of the patient by changes in gesture and posture. This is, of course, not a problem with computers, nor do they forget to administer individual items. Responses can be accurately recorded, timings such as response latencies can be made, analyses of response patterns can be carried out, and complex scoring schemes can be employed, all with greater accuracy and with no effort on the part of the psychologist. The results of tests can be made available immediately after the testing session. Data from tests can be automatically saved to computer files, either for use in further analyses such as in the collection of normative data, or for use in report writing. In short, computer-based tests can be more reliable than those in conventional form and their use can relieve the psychologist of the mechanical aspects of testing, and free them to concentrate on other aspects of the work that cannot be carried out by a machine.

It is possible to set up the testing system and allow the patient or client to proceed by following instructions on the computer screen or to leave less-skilled personnel to supervise the session, thus reducing the cost of testing. Furthermore, the use of computer-based tests can actually reduce the time needed for testing; Beaumont and French (1987), in a study of the use of computer-based cognitive tests in adult psychiatric patients, obtained estimates of savings of up to 60% of total assessment time. Tailored or adaptive testing techniques can speed the subject through areas of the test that they find easy, and concentrate the testing where errors are made, and they can produce further time-saving (Watts, Baddeley, & Williams, 1982, Wiess & Vale, 1987).

Concern has been expressed as to whether testing by computer-based methods would be acceptable to client groups such as the elderly with little past experience of this medium. French and Beaumont (1987) reported that computerised assessment seemed to be entirely acceptable to psychiatric patients, and of eight psychometric tests used, none were found to be more enjoyable in their standard form. Others have also used computer-based assessment systems successfully with the elderly, e.g. Carr et al. (1982); Morris et al. (1988); Simpson and Linney (1984). Working with computers seems to carry a certain cachet, and not just for many elderly people but also for such patients as those with acquired brain injury. By use of colour, animation or sound, tests can be made more interesting; imbuing tests with a games-like quality is perceived as helpful in enhancing motivation and maintaining attention.

In addition to assessment, computers have also been used for interviewing a number of different patient groups, e.g. general psychiatric, suicide risk, drug and alcohol abuse, sexual dysfuntion and emotionally disturbed children along with their parents; Erdman, Klein, and Greist (1985), and Stein (1987) indicated that the majority of respondents had positive attitudes.

A major advantage of computer-based testing is that it can enable assessment to take place in circumstances where it is normally not possible; that is, in the case of individuals whose physical disability is so severe that conventional techniques are difficult, if not impossible, to use (Wilson & McMillan, 1986). It can be surprisingly easy to provide alternative interfaces between a physically disabled person and a machine to substitute for the use of the machine's own keyboard (Wilson, Thompson, & Wylie, 1982; Wilson, 1990; Wylie, Wilson, & Wedgwood, 1984). There are also a number of commercially available keyboard substitutes suitable for use by physically disabled people. Experience has shown that computer-based assessment is acceptable to physically disabled adults. The ease with which communication between even the most severely physically disabled person and machine can be facilitated, has meant that computers have many applications for them; apart from communication they have uses in environmental control, recreation, and the provision of occupation. Unlike many aids for disabled people, computers do not have stigma attached to them: the contrary, in fact.

Some advantages of the computer over a human interviewer have been summarised by Colby (1980), and quoted by Erdman et al. (1985, p.114):

> It does not get tired, angry, or bored. It is always willing to listen and to give evidence to having heard. It can work at any time of the day or night, every day of the week, every month of the year. It does not have family problems of its own. It is never sick or hung over. Its performance does not vary from hour to hour or from day to day. It has no facial expression. It does not raise an eyebrow. It is very polite. It has a perfect memory. It need not be morally judgmental. It has no superior social status. It does not seek money. It can provide the patient with a copy of the interview to study. It does what it is supposed to and no more and no less.

THE DISADVANTAGES OF COMPUTER-BASED ASSESSMENT

Nevertheless, there are disadvantages, the most major being perhaps the limitation on the type of material that can be presented. If a questionnaire is to be administered with the sole purpose of obtaining descriptive information and no scoring is required but merely the storage of the individual's responses, this should be straightforward as long as the client or patient is competent enough to use a standard (QWERTY) keyboard. On the other hand, questions with open answers that have to be scored, such as those in the Comprehension section of the WAIS-R, are problematic. One possible approach is the use of "expert" systems with a "natural language interface" i.e. where the computer can interpret idiomatic language. However, for all but a limited number of applications, at the time of writing this is not a realistic proposition, particularly in English where there are synonymous ways of expressing ideas and where colloquial expressions vary widely. For example the expression: "Going like a bomb", has opposite meanings on opposite sides of the Atlantic! At present, approaches normally use a multiple choice format, or answers that can be precisely defined, e.g. a number or the spelling of a word. Such limitations make the items, such as those found in the Comprehension and Information subtests of the WAIS-R, impossible to automate without affecting their validity.

The representation of graphic material is also problematic. The quality of graphics depends in part on the resolution of the computer's visual display unit. If the screen resolution is insufficient for the complexity of the graphics required, then the validity of test material becomes questionable. Bartram et al. (1987) recommended that for simple graphics which require only vertical and horizontal lines a resolution of about 256 x 256 should be sufficient. For graphics requiring well-defined oblique lines, a minimum of 512 x 512 is likely to be needed, and for complex graphics involving fine detail and curved lines, a resolution of 1024 x 1024 may be the minimum requirement to obtain a quality of presentation equivalent to "pen and paper" tests. Items presented on the computer screen are also only two-dimensional and the third dimension needs to be represented graphically.

Travelling with the testing system can cause problems; in addition to the weight of items such as monitors, systems can be affected by temperature and connections can be loosened by vibration. Recent developments such as lap-top and notebook computers, however, may have a significant impact on this problem.

SETTING UP THE SYSTEM

i   Using Available Software

The allure of using off-the-shelf software is obvious. Finding suitable software for local computer systems or deciding upon the most appropriate software is not necessarily straightforward. If a system is chosen because it can run specific software, it is advisable to investigate what other software is available.

Software transfer directly from one type of micro to another is a possibility. Having transferred it however, there may still be problems in the use of the software, for example, appearance of the test material may vary from one system to another.

In choosing test software there are a number of issues to be considered. Factors such as user-friendliness (i.e. whether the level of expertise required to operate the software is matched by the expertise of those who will be using it), quantity and quality of normative and other supporting data, and also cost-effectiveness, should be examined.

Some computer-based tests are automated forms of standard tests which are already well-supported by normative data. If correlations between automated and standard tests for the relevant population are acceptable, then scores obtained from the automated version can be interpreted using the data from the standard form of the test with confidence. It may be required that test scores are automatically transferred to a database and therefore examination of the ease with which this may be accomplished could be appropriate. Lastly the issue of cost; some software can be bought with unlimited access, other software may only allow a set number of applications of the test before another payment is required.

ii Developing Your Own Software

It is advisable if the operator is not also the programmer, that they have some proficiency in the relevant software language to enable them to make minor modifications. If it is an existing test, then it will be necessary to seek the permission of the copyright holder in order to use it in automated form. The copyright holder may demand a fee which could depend on the purpose and frequency of test usage. The copyright holder may also make stipulations about presentation of test material. Development of an original test may require more work in terms of design and evaluation, but this approach bypasses these copyright issues.

Clearly, original software requires evaluation against existing measures to validate its use, and the development of normative data to allow interpretation. The costs of test development can be kept low by collaboration with colleagues, for example, through allowing free use of new software in return for data from test administration. If the testing system is set up to collect all the necessary data on disk, that data can be returned to the test developer either on the disk or via a modem. Thus, the accumulation of normative data can be rapid and relatively inexpensive. If a group of workers in computer-based assessment can agree to use the same hardware and adopt the same design for both assessment and database management systems, then the potential for fast and economic collection of data on individual tests and for continuously updating normative data, is enormous, e.g. see Bartram et al. (1987).

INPUT DEVICES

i Using the Computer Keyboard

The method of responding to questions must be appropriate for use by the target population.

The most common response medium is normally the standard QWERTY keyboard and/or numeric keypad; these have the advantages of being immediately available and impose no extra cost, but also have a number of disadvantages. First, unless irrelevant keys are disabled, the accidental or purposeful disruption of the program can be caused by use of keys such as "escape" or "break" and, should the testee have programming experience, potential invasion of the software. Beaumont (1982) described the use of a "software lock" to disable unused areas of the standard keyboard, with the use of a tone as feedback to the patient when the barred keys were operated. Physical masking of unused areas of the keyboard is an alternative approach.

Some neurological disorders cause sensory, motor or visuospatial problems including poor co-ordination and tremor which may preclude the use of a standard keyboard. Furthermore, the keyboard itself can be at risk of damage from use by those with poor motor or behavioural control. For most assessment applications the QWERTY keyboard has many more keys than are actually needed; the patient is confronted by a great deal of redundant information which may have a detrimental effect on performance, for example, in an individual with an attention deficit.

Bartram et al. (1987) listed disadvantages of the QWERTY keyboard which are relevant for many subject groups. In tests requiring visuo-motor speed the layout of keys can affect performance; for example, having to locate specific letters at speed in the QWERTY layout, as might happen in a multiple-choice test, while concentrating on the screen, may significantly increase the chance of errors. The positioning and labelling of the non-alphanumeric keys varies considerably between machines and this may have a detrimental effect on the performance of experienced computer users. Bartram et al. (1987) suggested that the client/patient should use a special interface for response in tests.

ii Other Standard Interfaces

There are a number of commercially available alternatives to the QWERTY keyboard. Devices such as light pens and touch sensitive screens can allow the patient to point directly to the answer of their choice and eliminates the need to identify the correct button. This can be of considerable advantage when dealing with patient groups such as the dementing elderly (Carr et al., 1982). The positioning of the screen when using these devices is important as prolonged periods of "reaching up" to it may be fatiguing.

Other alternatives include tracker balls, joysticks, and mice; these tend to be used when association between motor (hand) movements and movements on the screen is necessary. There are also touch pads, bit pads, and non-QWERTY keyboards. Touch pads include devices such as the Concept Keyboard, where areas of the board to be used for specific functions are demarcated by overlays, a variety of which may be used. Bit pads are similar in nature except that operation of the board is by a stylus rather than by hand. Non-QWERTY keyboards are usually designed for a specific purpose, and keys can be dedicated for specific functions such as "yes/no", while their layout can be matched by the arrangement of answers on screen (e.g. see Acker, 1982). Petheram (1988) compared the performance of stroke victims using a microcomputer with a mouse, joystick, trackerball, touchpad, and touch screen and also looked at subjective preference by the users. With these patients, the tracker ball proved the most successful in terms of performance, as well as being the most-liked device.

Carr, Woods, and Moore (1986a) evaluated the usefulness of the touch sensitive screen against a board with illuminated response buttons in testing cognitively impaired elderly patients. The touch sensitive screen produced lower response latencies and larger scores from the patients, who tended to prefer this device.

Apart from alternatives to standard keyboards, special keyboards for the physically disabled are commercially available. These include expanded keyboards with sunken keys, designed for those who have a full range of gross movement but insufficient co-ordination to enable them to pick out individual keys on a standard keyboard (e.g. athetoid spastics). Another keyboard substitute is used for those who are capable of operating one or two switches only. Here the "keys" are displayed in a matrix and selection can be made when the appropriate element is illuminated; one switch operation is used to indicate the column or row containing the required element, the second operation selects the element.

If more than one input device is to be used in testing, then the method of interface between device and machine must be considered as this may require modification to the software. For example, response media may be connected to the British Broadcasting Corporation (BBC) computer via the analogue input as well as the games I/O connector, but these require different software commands to access them. Although it is possible to have both in one programme, it may prove much more convenient not to do so.

If more than one response device is used for a particular test then it is important to consider whether there may be an interaction with the test which would convey an advantage to the users of a particular response device. An unpublished study using adult physically disabled subjects compared results from an automated version of the Mill Hill Vocabulary Scale, which collected responses either by way of a six-keyed response board, or a single switch operated in conjunction with a software-based cursor moving around the answer options. It showed that the response device made no difference to results. This test, however, is highly reliable whether in automated or standard form (Beaumont & French, 1987) and appears to produce consistent results with different methods of presentation and response. Other tests may not be as robust and the response medium may well influence performance. For example, Beaumont (1985) examined the effects of response media on a microcomputer-presented Digit Span test. He compared results from a QWERTY keyboard, numeric keypad and light pen used on undergraduates and found that the best performance was associated with the QWERTY keyboard and the worst with the light pen. However, in some cases such as those with severe physical disabilities, specially designed response media may be unavoidable.

iii   Non-standard Interfaces

If expertise in electronics is available it is possible to construct tailor-made response devices. Where patients have a range of disabilities, some of which are severe, it should be possible to provide each individual with a response device that is ergonomically appropriate for them. The response device used to operate a computer during testing may also be used to control a communication device; conversely the control medium already used by an individual to operate a wheelchair for example, may be adapted for use as a response medium in computerised testing e.g. the linguo-buccal switch developed by Parker (1981) of which test use has been described (Wilson & McMillan, 1986). The objective is to find a means of response that the individual can use as comfortably, quickly and reliably as possible to allow the patient to perform on the test, with any confounding difficulties caused by response media minimised.

Having identified the most ideal response medium for a particular patient, its manufacture need not be expensive. Everyday items have been adapted for use at the Royal Hospital and Home, Putney:

An eye make-up display case with two microswitches inserted proved to be a serviceable response device for individuals able to exert a light pressure in a downward direction (Wylie, unpublished); a sphygmomanometer bulb for those who can grip and squeeze, as in the case of a patient with severe choreioform movements, had the additional advantage of being able to be dropped without harming the patient or the switch (Sayegh, unpublished).

Even if switches tailored to individual needs are not required, purpose-built response media may prove advantageous by ensuring that all required design features are incorporated and can be less expensive than some commercially available devices. Response media constructed for use in computer-based neuropsychological assessment are further described elsewhere (see Acker, 1982; Wilson, 1990; Wylie, Wilson, & Wedgwood, 1984).

It is important to note that no matter how severe the disability of an individual, if they have a movement over which there is reliable voluntary control then it should be possible for them to develop some control over a computer. In more extreme cases, help may be needed from colleagues of other professions (e.g. physiotherapists) to identify reliable movements and the best placement of response media for optimum performance. In the most severe cases body position can determine whether or not an individual can be tested (Pope, Booth, & Gosling, 1988).

ETHICAL ISSUES/PRACTICALITIES OF TESTING

Computer-based tests cannot substitute for a trained psychologist in a clinical setting. They are merely a tool which can relieve the professional of some routine or mechanical aspects of their work, and can be of benefit in research.

The clinician is needed to ensure that the patient/client is physically, emotionally and cognitively in a state where it is appropriate to assess them. They must determine whether the patient is willing to attempt the tasks and to use a computer to do so. The patient should be able to perceive the test material, be able to use the response media, and understand instructions. As with any assessment situation it is important to establish any factors that may affect patient performance.

The issue of whether the clinician is present during testing has to be decided according to the individual situation. Some patients may need to be reminded of instructions or encouraged to maintain attention on the task in hand and it may not be appropriate to have such reminders as a feature of the assessment software. Clinicians may gain important information from observing aspects of performance which are not or cannot be recorded by the software. On the other hand, the presence of another individual may distract the patient and in certain situations such as an interview, the presence of the clinician may embarrass or be threatening to the patient. It is always possible to give the patient a call button in case of problems or to use remote viewing.

The clinician should also consider the issue of feedback of results to the client. This again should be judged in the individual situation. In some cases feedback on performance is automatically given after every item. If the patient makes many errors this can, however, have a demoralising effect. Others give neutral but encouraging messages regardless of the level of performance. In certain circumstances this may boost the patient's confidence and help maintain interest in the task; if the patient is aware of the poor quality of their performance, the continued use of praise may have the opposite effect. The use of feedback and reinforcement in the testing situation is a matter for the clinical judgement of the practitioner.

Although there is test software available which can provide an interpretation of performance in terms of available norms and patient factors, in most cases this must be based on the clinician's judgement using their experience and observations and, of course, their knowledge of the test and of the patient's past and present circumstances and conditions (Lezak, 1983). The psychologist should also be able to judge the usefulness of a piece of test software. There are no safeguards for the public at present against the sale of spurious tests and questionnaires in the form of software. Furthermore, as copying software is easy, *bona fide* tests may be made available to those without the skills to use or interpret them properly.

Matarazzo (1983, p.323) expressed concern about the use of computer-based tests (in the USA):

> There is a danger that wholesale use of automated tests by people without knowledge of their limitations will be a disservice to the public. Compounding this danger, the tests have a spurious objectivity and infallibility as a halo effect from the computer, and their ease of use may cause them to be more widely employed than are current tests.

Matarazzo continues to make the point that until research establishes that the validity of a computerised test is not dependent on the practitioner's experience and on training in psychometric science, automated test use should be restricted to qualified user groups. Similar concern has been expressed by the British Psychological Society (1984).

APPLICATIONS OF COMPUTER-BASED ASSESSMENT IN NEUROPSYCHOLOGY

The aim here is not to provide an exhaustive review, but rather to indicate what is possible at the present state of technology. Some workers have developed tests or test batteries aimed at particular target populations where specific deficits may be expected. Others have produced broader-based collections of tests. The philosophical background to the development of these tests is either in the applied clinical tradition or from models based on experimental work with animals.

1. Alcohol Abuse

One of the earliest published microcomputer-based test batteries in the UK was the Bexley-Maudsley Automated Psychological Screening (BMAPS), and the Bexley-Maudsley Category Sorting Test (BMCST), (Acker & Acker, 1982a; b). Acker (1982) described the six tests as a screening battery for non-specific dementia. Normative data are provided from 103 alcoholic patients and their matched non-alcoholic controls. The BMCST is a task analogous to the Wisconsin Card Sorting Test (Grant & Berg, 1948), or the Modified Card Sorting Test (Nelson, 1976). BMAPS consists of: the "Little Man" test in which subjects are asked to make left/right discriminations about a figure which is rotated about two axes; a symbol-digit coding test which is presented as a multiple-choice timed task; and a visual-perceptual analysis task, where subjects are required to indicate the non-identical design from three abstract patterns. Similar designs are used in the visuo-spatial recognition memory test. There is also a recognition memory test for verbal material. Acker, in his description of the BMCST, ascribes an advantage to the computerised test over standard analogues such as the Wisconsin Card Sorting Test; patients who are intellectually unable to deal with the test may become irritated by it and abandon it or modify their performance according to perceived non-verbal cues from the examiner rather than the "correct/incorrect" feedback. He suggests that the computer is not as threatening and gives no unintended emotional feedback. The battery was originally developed to run on a Commodore Pet computer and was later converted to run on an Apple. The patients respond using a "patient keyboard" which has nine keys that fit on to the computer as an overlay.

Tarter (1980) reviewed findings on intellectual competence in alcoholics, and suggested that although there was no global impairment on psychometric testing, there were specific deficits in: shifting cognitive set; utilisation of error responses; impersistence of cognitive set; spatial perseveration; spatial scanning in maze tests; and visual searching ability. Draper and his colleagues were also interested in identifying brain damage in alcoholics by use of computerised assessment (Draper, 1984; Draper et al., 1983; Draper & Larraghy, 1986; 1987). They concluded that no available test examined all functions described as impaired by Tartar, and developed a new test of cognitive function: "Cogfun". In this test a maze in the form of a matrix of squares is presented on screen and the rows and columns are labelled with letters of the alphabet. A pattern, formed according to simple, logical rules, is traced halfway across the maze by replacing some of the squares with other symbols. The test subject has to grasp the logic behind the pattern, and key in the co-ordinates that continue the track until two consecutive entries are correct; feedback is given on accuracy. If the subject responds correctly, there are four more patterns of increasing difficulty. If the subject fails then the pattern is repeated with up to five more trials, but each starting from a different point.

The test was originally developed on a Tandy microcomputer but has subsequently been produced for Apple II and IBM-compatible machines. No special response medium is used. Normative data are being collected from both alcoholic and control subjects in centres in Ireland, Scotland and England, including retest data.

2. Solvent Exposure

The assessment of the effects on performance as a result of exposure to industrial solvents has been investigated by Iregren (1986), and Iregren et al. (1986) who included computer-based tests in their study. These were: memory reproduction, colour-word vigilance, simple reaction time and choice reaction time. The simple reaction-time task required the subject to press a button when a light came on. In the choice reaction-time test, a cross was displayed on screen and the subject had to indicate which arm was shorter than the others. The task had three levels of difficulty according to the extent by which the arm had been shortened. The memory reproduction measurement was carried out by presenting a string of letters and numbers on the screen for 4 seconds, subjects being allowed 17 seconds to key in the series they had just seen. The test commenced with strings four-characters long. The colour-word vigilance test is similar to the Stroop test. The Swedish words for red, yellow, white and blue were used as they all have three letters. The words were presented on screen one at a time in any of these colours and the subject had to respond when a word and its colour were the same. The microcomputer used was an ABC800 made by Luxor AB and the response media were: a reaction-time panel and a modified numerical keyboard. Data were collected from spray painters who had been exposed to a mixture of solvents, printers exposed solely to toluene, and controls.

The battery has now been extended (Iregen, 1988) to include the following tests: colour word stress, digit span, Baddeley's Reasoning Test, search and memory, Sternberg Memory Scanning, numerical ability, finger-tapping, synonyms, digit classification and digit addition. The software is now presented on an IBM-compatible machine.

3. Elderly/Dementing Patients

A battery of tests for the cognitively impaired elderly has been developed by Carr, Woods, and Moore (1986a; b). The five tests are designed to cover a range of cognitive abilities, both verbal and non-verbal, and have been constructed to ensure that most people with dementia who can be tested score above chance levels. The tests included in the battery are: a lexical decision task, which requires subjects to identify non-words among four-letter strings; a matching-to-sample test, which requires the subject to match a target pattern with one of four sample patterns presented simultaneously; verbal and non-verbal memory tests using a recognition paradigm; and also a tracking task. The battery was developed on a Commodore 64 computer and uses a touch sensitive screen for response. The battery was standardised on people with dementing conditions. Data have also been collected on elderly people without cognitive impairment, and on elderly depressed patients, and comparison is also made with performance on established tests such as the National Adult Reading Test, Kendrick's Digit Copying Test and Object Learning Test and Warrington's Forced-Choice Faces Recognition Test.

Carr, Woods, and Moore (1986b) describe their test as being designed with features to maintain the test subject's motivation and interest. These are:

1. Use of different colours and colour combinations.

2. Written instructions on screen are brief throughout to reduce demands on memory.

3. Instructions and prompts written word-by-word teletype style, accompanied by auditory prompts to stimulate attention.

4. Large character set and large TV monitor used to reduce visual problems.

5. Immediate auditory feedback for each response from patient (although they do not say whether the feedback is just a sound to signify that the response has been recognised or whether correct and wrong are being indicated).

6. Familiar tunes are played by the computer between items.

7. The subject's name is incorporated in the instructions on screen.

8. In practice trials, animation is used to demonstrate the principle involved and to draw attention to correct response.

9. Each outline shape resembles a familiar object.

Others have developed a computerised test battery, based on animal work, in their studies of the Alzheimer-type dementia and of Parkinson's disease (Morris et al., 1987; 1988; Sahakian et al., 1988). The Cambridge Neuropsychological Test Automated Battery (CANTAB) includes tests of visuo-spatial memory, learning, attention, and planning. It was developed on the BBC microcomputer using a touch sensitive screen as the response medium. CANTAB commences with a motor screening test, which trains the patient to use the touch sensitive screen and also gives a measure of tremor and response speed. The delayed matching-to-sample test is similar to that used by Carr et al. (1986b) in that the test commences with presentation of the target with four sample stimuli. Unlike the Carr et al. (1986b) test it continues with the target and samples being shown separately with an increasing delay between the two events; the stimuli are random patterns rather than recognisable objects.

There is a visual recognition memory test which uses abstract patterns and a forced choice paradigm; also a spatial memory test using the same paradigm, which has squares presented in different locations on the screen as stimuli. The delayed response test requires both pattern and spatial recognition memory as the subjects are required to locate individual target abstract patterns that are "hidden" on the computer screen, having first been shown the locations of all of them at once. There is a working memory test which requires the subject to locate counters hidden in boxes on the computer screen with the objective of remembering not to search a box, once a counter has already been found in it. Both the delayed response and the matching-to-sample test are cited by the authors as paradigms that have been used to elucidate characteristics of memory in animals. The battery also includes a Corsi Block Span test, (a spatial analogue of the auditory verbal digit span), and a Tower of London (also known as Tower of Hanoi) task which has been associated with the detection of planning deficits in patients with frontal lobe damage. Normative data on the battery are in the form of comparisons between the two diagnostic groups and matched controls.

Morris et al. (1987) describe the main features of their battery as including:

1. The ability to provide performance profiles of different patient groups by testing different aspects of mental functioning.
2. If appropriate the tests are graded in difficulty to aid subject comprehension of test principles and to permit assessment of a broad range of cognitive ability.
3. The tests are designed to be largely self-explanatory to the patient, employing non-verbal stimuli and requiring non-verbal responses.
4. The tests are designed to be visually attractive and interesting, using positive feedback with the aim of maintaining motivation.

4. Hydrocephalus

The problem of obtaining early warning of shunt blockage in hydrocephalic children has led to the development of AMVIHS (Automated Monitoring for Variations in Hydrocephalic Status) by Grant (1986). The objective is to monitor functions associated with the right posterior areas of the brain and also fine motor control, as these have been found to be particularly vulnerable to increases in CSF pressure. The battery is presented using a BBC microcomputer with a light pen as response medium. There are three tests: a hand-eye co-ordination task, a visual matching task, and a test of spatial imagery. In the latter test, the child has to "take a cat on a journey". A path is shown through a maze on the screen, and when it disappears the child must trace it through the maze from memory. There are two conditions: "day" in which the reference markers of the maze are visible, and "night" where they are not. As the test proceeds the paths become more complex. The battery is designed for self-administration and for repeated serial use. Validation data are being collected (Grant, 1988).

5. Head Injury

Wilson, Brooks, and Phillips (1982) describe two tests developed for assessing cognitive deficits after head injury. The first of these is described as a reaction-time task in which processing load can be varied. In the study presented, subjects were given either a simple reaction-time task, in which they had to attend to a single light or a four-choice task (using four lights). In the second task, a measure of visual memory, a pattern of seven squares was shown on the screen for four seconds. After a short blank interval the pattern returned with one square missing and the subject had to indicate from where the square had been removed by pointing. The testing system did not utilise a touch sensitive screen, so the tester had to enter the response via the keyboard. A long-term memory test showed three patterns in sequence and then tested in reverse order. The testing system was based on an Apple II microcomputer with a response box for reaction time. Data are presented from nine head-injured subjects, two alcoholics, and a comparison group of university staff and students.

The Otago Computer-assisted Neuropsychological Assessment Battery is described by Davidson et al. (1987) as a series of semi-animated tests. They describe an evaluation study of 51 traumatic head-injured patients and 51 controls. Some standard tests were also used in the study for comparison. Six automated tests were used in the study and all gave feedback about the accuracy of performance of individual trials within tests. There was an animated tracking task, in which the subjects had to keep a "car" within road boundaries by use of a joystick. The speed of movement of the images was in accordance with the success of the subject. The Colour Match Reversal test was based on a paradigm from animal operant research, and was included to assess rule acquisition and speed of discrimination. A coloured bar was presented at the top of the screen and underneath two further bars, one the same colour and one not. The subject was instructed to press the right- or left-hand button according to the side that matched the target bar, and the rule for matching was reversed after every ten trials. Measures of speed and accuracy were recorded. The non-verbal memory task, using nonsense figures, had three sections: (1) a matching-to-sample test; (2) a multiple-choice recognition test with samples presented simultaneously after a two-second interval; (3) the same test as the second except that the samples were presented consecutively. There was a reaction-time test based on a proprietary gunfight game. Another proprietary game used was "Applesimon"; this was used to test short-term and serial memory. In this game a coloured number between one and four is flashed on screen, each number having its own position and audible note. Starting with one number, sequences of increasing length are presented and the subject has to respond by keying each sequence back to the computer. Sequences are increased in length until the subject fails to recall one correctly. Lastly there was a version of the Wisconsin Card Sorting Test. The system was based on an Apple II microcomputer with a two-button response box and joystick (the computer keyboard was used for response in some tests).

6. Physical Disability

The testing systems described so far have been developed for use with patient populations that are diagnostically homogeneous and are also relatively physically able, at least as far as upper limb function is concerned. Wilson and colleagues have had a different problem to deal with. They have had to develop a testing system for use with adults who are severely physically disabled — and from a variety of neurological disorders, including: multiple sclerosis, cerebrovascular accident, cereral palsy, head injury, anoxia, Parkinson's disease, and Huntington's disease. (Wilson, 1987; 1990; Wilson, Thompson, & Wylie, 1982; Wylie, Wilson, & Wedgwood, 1984). Most of the patients were extremely physically disabled and the potential for use of conventional tests was limited or zero. The requirement was for a system with a battery of tests which would assess a broad range of cognitive functions. As many of these patients had a severely restricted range of movements, it was also important that, where possible, responding should only require the operation of a single switch. The development of a range of response media suitable for use by severely physically disabled people with the testing system was an integral part of the project. Initially, the battery was developed on an Apple microcomputer, and later on a BBC machine.

The battery includes vocabulary scales, digit span (Wilson et al., 1982; Wilson, 1987), a visual vigilance task, a card sorting test, a line bisection task, a pattern copying test, an assessment of judgements of spatial orientation, Cattell's 16PF personality test and a programme for training the most severely disabled to operate their response medium reliably. The switch-user training programme simply "rewards" the patient every time they correctly operate the response device. The "rewards" are a variety of animated displays and tunes, all performed by the computer and each lasting less than one minute. In the visual vigilance task, two rows of three squares are shown on the screen, the squares being shown in two contrasting colours. During the test, the colours of the squares in the top row change randomly. The subject has to operate the response device when the top row looks the same as the bottom row; and every time the switch is operated, regardless of whether the match is correct, the bottom row pattern changes. The speed of the changes is adjusted according to the reaction time of the subject which is measured at the start of the test; this is in order to avoid confounding attentional and motor problems.

The Putney Automated Digit Span presents numbers on screen one at a time, and response is via a 9-keyed response board. This test utilises a scoring scheme which gives credit for partially correct responses, thereby making use of every response. The line bisection task presents lines of different lengths, one at a time, either left-, right- or middle-centred on screen. The subject has to operate the response device when they perceive that the moving marker has reached the centre of the line. A random pattern is given as reward regardless of accuracy. Each line is presented twice, on one occasion the marker moves from right to left and on the other, the opposite way; the marker continues tracking until a response is made. Evaluation data, for comparison of computerised with standard forms, have been collected on all these tests using physically disabled adults. A software program for assessing function in people with very severe impairments of both physical and mental ability is currently being evaluated.

7. Psychiatric Patients

The computer-based battery developed for the Leicester/DHS project was evaluated on a psychiatric rather than a neurologically impaired population, however, the tests used could also have a neuropsychological application. The battery consists of automated versions of conventional tests, namely: the Mill Hill Vocabulary Scale; the Eysenck Personality Questionnaire; Differential Aptitude Test — Language Usage and Spelling; Raven's Standard Progressive Matrices; a Digit Span test; Wisconsin Card Sorting test; and the Money Road Map Test. The testing system was based on an Apple II microcomputer and used both computer keyboard and a touch screen as response media (Beaumont & French, 1987; French & Beaumont, 1987). In this extensive study, the evaluation of the automated tests against their standard forms was carried out using 367 subjects. They found good reliabilities between automated and standard forms for the Mill Hill Vocabulary Scale, Raven's Progressive Matrices and all the scales of the Eysenck Personality Questionnaire except for the P scale, and acceptable reliability on the Money Road Map Test. The measures from the Digit Span test produced quite low reliabilities and those from the Differential Aptitude tests were described as ''disappointing''. Beaumont and French (1987) concluded that although it was possible to produce psychometrically parallel computerised versions of existing tests, some tests were not so amenable to automation, although the reasons for this were not clear.

CONCLUSION

Computer-based tests can be a useful, and in some cases a necessary tool in neuropsychological assessment, both in clinical practice and in research. At the very least it can free the practitioner from some of the more mechanical elements of the work; but, more excitingly, it can be used as a medium for innovation.

REFERENCES

Acker, W. (1982). A computerized approach to psychological screening — the Bexley-Maudsley automated psychological screening and the Bexley-Maudsley category sorting test. *International Journal of Man-Machine Studies, 17 (3)*, 361-369.

Acker, W., & Acker, C.F. (1982a). *Bexley-Maudsley automated psychological screening.* London: NFER-Nelson.

Acker, W., & Acker, C.F. (1982b). Bexley-Maudsley category sorting test. London: NFER-Nelson.

Bartram, D., & Bayliss, D. (1984). Automated testing: Past, present and future. *Journal of Occupational Psychology, 57*, 221-237.

Bartram, D., Beaumont, J.G., Cornford, T., Dann, P.L., & Wilson, S.L. (1987). Recommendations for the design of software for computer-based assessment (CBA). *Bulletin of the British Psychological Society, 40*, 86-87.

Beaumont, J.G. (1982). System requirements for interactive testing. *International Journal of Man-Machine Studies, 17 (3)*, 311-320.

Beaumont, J.G. (1985). The effect of microcomputer presentation and response medium on digit span performance. *International Journal of Man-Machine Studies, 22*, 11-18.

Beaumont, J.G., & French, C.C. (1987). A clinical field study of eight automated psychometric procedures: The Leicester/DHS Project. *International Journal of Man-Machine Studies, 26*, 661-682.

British Psychological Society. (1984). Notes on the computerization of printed psychological tests and questionnaires. *Bulletin of the British Psychological Society, 37,* 416-417.

Carr, A.C., Wilson, S.L., Ancill, R.J., Ghosh, A., & Woods, R.T. (1982). Automated testing of geriatric patients using a microcomputer-based system. *International Journal of Man-Machine Studies, 17 (3),* 297-300.

Carr, A.C., Woods, R.T., & Moore, B.J. (1986a). Automated cognitive assessment of elderly patients: A comparison of two types of response device. *British Journal of Clinical Psychology, 25,* 305-306.

Carr, A.C., Woods, R.T., & Moore, B.J. (1986b). Developing a microcomputer-based automated testing system for use with psychogeriatric patients. *Bulletin of the Royal College of Psychiatrists, 10,* 309-312.

Colby, K.M. (1980). Computer psychotherapists. In J.B. Sidowski, J.H. Johnson, & T.A. Williams (Eds.), *Technology in mental health care delivery systems.* Norwood, Ablex.

Davidson, O.R., Stevens, D.E., Goddard, G.V., Bilkey, D.K., & Bishara, S.N. (1987). The performance of a sample of traumatic head-injured patients on some novel computer-assisted neuropsychological tests. *Applied Psychology: An International Review, 36,* 329-342.

Draper, R. (1984, 23 May). *Cogfun – development and application.* Presented at Symposium on Automated Psychological Testing, Royal Hospital & Home, Putney.

Draper, R., & Larraghy, J. (1986, September). *Specificity in the measurement of cognitive impairment in man using a novel automated procedure.* Paper presented at the 36th Annual Meeting of the Canadian Psychiatric Association, Vancouver, BC.

Draper, R., & Larraghy, M. (1987, March). *Automated identification of covert alcohol induced intellectual impairment.* Paper presented at CATCH '87, Toronto.

Draper, R., Manning, A., Daly, M., & Larraghy, J. (1983). A novel cognitive function test for the detection of alcoholic brain damage. *Neuropharmacology, 22,* 567-569.

Erdman, H., Klein, M., & Greist, J. (1985). Direct patient computer interviewing. *Journal of Consulting and Clinical Psychology, 53 (6),* 760-773

French, C.C. (1986). Microcomputers and psychometric assessment. *British Journal of Guidance and Counselling, 14 (1),* 33-45.

French, C.C., & Beaumont, J.G. (1987). The reaction of psychiatric patients to computerised assessment. *British Journal of Clinical Psychology, 26,* 267-278.

Grant, D.A., & Berg, E.A. (1948). A behavioural analysis of the degree of reinforcement and ease of shifting to new responses in a Wiegl-type card sorting problem. *Journal of Experimental Psychology, 38,* 401-411.

Grant, D.W. (1986, May). *Cats and fishes: An automated neurological, self-administered program for hydrocephalic children.* Paper presented at Innovations in the Application of Microcomputers to Psychological Assessment and Therapy, Royal Hospital & Home, Putney.

Grant, D.W. (1988). In S.L. Wilson (Ed.), *Directory of research into automated testing.* London: Royal Hospital & Home.

Iregren, A. (1986). Effects of industrial solvent interactions. Studies of behavioural effects in man. Arbete och Halsa 1986: 11, *Monographs of the National Board of Occupational Safety & Health, Sweden.*

Iregren, A. (1988). In S.L. Wilson (Ed.). *Directory of research into automated testing.* London: Royal Hospital & Home.

Iregren, A., Akerstedt, T., Anshelm Olson, B., & Gamberale, F. (1986). Experimental exposure to toluene in combination with ethanol intake. *Scandinavian Journal of Work and Environmental Health, 12,* 469-475.

Lezak, M.D. (1983). *Neuropsychological assessment.* New York: Oxford University Press.

Matarazzo, J.D. (1983). Computerised psychological testing. *Science, 221,* 323.

Miller, E. (1968). A case for automated clinical testing. *Bulletin of the British Psychological Society, 21,* 75-78.

Morris, R.G., Downes, J.J., Sahakian, B.J., Evenden, J.L., Heald, A., & Robbins, T.W. (1988). Planning and spatial working memory in Parkinson's disease. *Journal of Neurology, Neurosurgery & Psychiatry, 51,* 757-766.

Morris, R.G., Evenden, J.L., Sahakian, B.J., & Robbins, T.W. (1987). Computer-aided assessment of dementia: Comparative studies of neuropsychological deficits in Alzheimer-type dementia and Parkinson's disease. In S. Stahl, S. Iversen, & E. Goodman (Eds.), *Cognitive neurochemistry.* Oxford: Oxford University Press.

Nelson, H.E. (1976). A modified card sorting test sensitive to frontal lobe deficits. *Cortex, 12,* 313-324.

Parker, C.B. (1981). A linguo-buccal aid to control an electric wheelchair. *British Dental Journal, 151,* 263.

Petheram, B. (1988). Enabling stroke victims to interact with a microcomputer – a comparison of input devices. *International Disability Studies, 10,* 73-80.

Pope, P.M., Booth, E., & Gosling, G. (1988). The development of alternative seating and mobility systems. *Physiotherapy Practice, 4,* 78-93.

Sahakian, B.J., Morris, R.G., Evenden, J.L., Heald, A., Levy, R., Philpot, M., & Robbins, T.W. (1988). A comparative study of visuospatial memory and learning in Alzheimer-type dementia and Parkinson's disease. *Brain, 111,* 695-718.

Sampson, J.P. (1983). Computer-assisted testing and assessment: Current status and implications for the future. *Measurement and Evaluation in Guidance, 15 (3),* 293-299.

Simpson, J., & Linney, A. (1984). Use of computer-automated psychological tests to assess mentally impaired old people. In F.C. Rose (Ed.), *Modern approaches to dementia, Pt 2: Clinical and therapeutic aspects. Interdisciplinary topics in gerontology, vol. 20,* pp. 43-51. Basel: Kager.

Stein, S.J. (1987): Computer assisted diagnosis in children's mental health. *Applied Psychology: An International Review, 36,* 343-356.

Tartar, R.E. (1980). Brain damage in chronic alcoholics. A review of the psychological evidence. In D. Richter (Ed.), *Addiction and brain damage* (pp. 267-297). London: Croom Helm.

Thompson, J.A., & Wilson, S.L. (1982). Automated psychological testing. *International Journal of Man-Machine Studies, 17 (3),* 279-290.

Watts, K., Baddeley, A., & Williams, M. (1982). Automated tailored testing using Raven's matrices and the Mill Hill vocabulary tests: A comparison with manual administration. *International Journal of Man-Machine Studies, 17 (3),* 331-344.

Weiss, D.J., & Vale, C.D. (1987). Adaptive testing. *Applied Psychology: An International Review, 36,* 249-262.

Wilson, J.T.L., Brooks, D.N., & Phillips, W.A. (1982, June). *Using a microcomputer to study perception, memory and attention after head injury.* Paper presented at the 5th INS European Conference, Deauville, France.

Wilson, S.L. (1987). The development of an automated test of immediate memory and its evaluation on severely physically disabled adults. *Applied Psychology: An International Review, 36,* 311-328.

Wilson, S.L. (1990). Psychological assessment and severe physical disability. In R. West, M. Christie, & J. Weinman (Eds.), *Microcomputers, psychology and medicine.* Chichester: Wiley.

Wilson, S.L., & McMillan, T.M. (1986). Finding able minds in disabled bodies. *Lancet, 8521/22,* 1444-1446.

Wilson, S.L., Thompson, J.A., & Wylie, G. (1982). Automated psychological testing for the severely physically handicapped. *International Journal of Man-Machine Studies, 17 (3),* 291-296.

Wylie, G.A., Wilson, S.L., & Wedgwood, J. (1984). The use of microcomputers for the psychological assessment of physically disabled adults. *Journal of Medical Engineering & Technology, 8,* 224-229.

Author Index

Subject Index